64495

P9-DEV-846

Genetic Disorders Sourcebook,
   1st Edition
Genetic Disorders Sourcebook,
   2nd Edition
Head Trauma Sourcebook
Headache Sourcebook
Health Insurance Sourcebook
Health Reference Series Cumulative
   Index 1999
Healthy Aging
Healthy Children
Healthy Heart Sourcebook for Women
Heart Disease & Disorders
   Sourcebook, 2nd Edition
Household Safety Sourcebook
Immune System Disorders Sourcebook
Infant & Toddler Health Sourcebook
Injury & Trauma Sourcebook
Kidney & Urinary Tract Diseases &
   Disorders Sourcebook
Learning Disabilities Sourcebook,
   1st Edition
Learning Disabilities Sourcebook,
   2nd Edition
Liver Disorders Sourcebook
Lung Disorders Sourcebook
Medical Tests Sourcebook
Men's Health Concerns Sourcebook
Mental Health Disorders Sourcebook,
   1st Edition
Mental Health Disorders Sourcebook,
   2nd Edition
Mental Retardation Sourcebook
Movement Disorders Sourcebook
Obesity Sourcebook
Ophthalmic Disorders Sourcebook
Oral Health Sourcebook
Osteoporosis Sourcebook
Pain Sourcebook, 1st Edition
Pain Sourcebook, 2nd Edition
Pediatric Cancer Sourcebook
Physical & Mental Issues in Aging
   Sourcebook

Podiatry Sourcebook
Pregnancy & Birth Sourcebook
Prostate Cancer
Public Health Sourcebook
Reconstructive & Cosmetic Surgery
   Sourcebook
Rehabilitation Sourcebook
Respiratory Diseases & Disorders
   Sourcebook
Sexually Transmitted Diseases
   Sourcebook, 1st Edition
Sexually Transmitted Diseases
   Sourcebook, 2nd Edition
Skin Disorders Sourcebook
Sleep Disorders Sourcebook
Sports Injuries Sourcebook, 1st Edition
Sports Injuries Sourcebook, 2nd Edition
Stress-Related Disorders Sourcebook
Substance Abuse Sourcebook
Surgery Sourcebook
Transplantation Sourcebook
Traveler's Health Sourcebook
Vegetarian Sourcebook
Women's Health Concerns Sourcebook
Workplace Health & Safety Sourcebook
Worldwide Health Sourcebook

DATE DUE

SEP 18 ....
NOV 03 2005
JAN 0 5 2011
FEB 1 3 2019
DISCARDED

GAYLORD No. 2333   PRINTED IN U.S.A.

Teen Health Series

Diet Information for Teens
Drug Information for Teens
Mental Health Information
   for Teens
Sexual Health Information
   for Teens

Stress-Related Disorders
SOURCEBOOK

Table of Contents

Preface ix

Part I: Identifying Stress

Chapter 1—The Origin of "Stress" 3
Chapter 2—Understanding Stress: Characteristics and
               Caveats 13
Chapter 3—Stress Signals 33
Chapter 4—Different Kinds of Stress 37
Chapter 5—Health Risk Assessment 41

Part II: Environmental Stress

Chapter 6—Family Stress 57
Chapter 7—Resilience in Children 69
Chapter 8—The Role of Stress in Alcohol Use,
               Alcoholism Treatment, and Relapse 77
Chapter 9—Does Cigarette Smoking Cause Stress? 93
Chapter 10—Drug Addiction and Stress 103
Chapter 11—Today's Workplace 109

        Section 11.1—Stress at Work 110
        Section 11.2—Workplace Stress and
                    Women's Health 127
        Section 11.3—Work Stress and Alcohol
                    Use 130

Chapter 12—Evaluating Caregiver Stress 149
Chapter 13—Social Inequality Harms Health 157

Part III: Mental and Emotional Effects of Stress

Chapter 14—Emotions and Disease... 161
Chapter 15—Stress and Personality 167
Chapter 16—Stress Intensifies Depression 171

    Section 16.1—The Invisible Disease 172
    Section 16.2—Co-Occurrence of Depression
        with Medical, Psychiatric,
        and Substance Abuse
        Disorders 195
    Section 16.3—Women Are at Greater Risk
        for Depression Than Men 209
    Section 16.4—Suicide and Depression 214
    Section 16.5—Dealing with the Depths of
        Depression 230

Chapter 17—Panic Disorder Diagnosis and Treatment 241
Chapter 18—Trauma—Extreme or Life-Threatening
    Events 251

    Section 18.1—Traumatic Stress 252
    Section 18.2—Post-Traumatic Stress
        Disorder (PTSD) 272
    Section 18.3—Helping Children and
        Adolescents Cope with
        Violence and Disasters 288

Chapter 19—Stress-Related Substance Abuse........................ 307

Part IV: Physical Effects of Stress

Chapter 20—The Biology of Stress 319
Chapter 21—The Brain and Stress 337
Chapter 22—Stress and Heart Disease 347
Chapter 23—Morning Coffee Boosts Blood Pressure
    and Stress Hormones All Day 357
Chapter 24—Stress Affects the Immune System..................... 359
Chapter 25—The Physiological and Psychological
    Effects of Compassion and Anger 365

Chapter 26—Psychological Stress and Cancer 373
Chapter 27—Stress and Ulcers—Just a Myth? 375
Chapter 28—Stress Is a Factor in Women's Health 381
Chapter 29—Stress and Multiple Sclerosis 395
Chapter 30—Stress Affects Skin Conditions 399
Chapter 31—The Role of Acute and Chronic Stress in
              Asthma Attacks in Children 425
Chapter 32—Alcohol, Aging, and the Stress Response 431

Part V: Stress Management

Chapter 33—Coping with Everyday Problems 457
Chapter 34—Physical Activity, Weight Control, and
              Nutrition 465
Chapter 35—Managing Your Stress with Arthritis or
              Related Diseases 483
Chapter 36—Does Drinking Reduce Stress? 489
Chapter 37—Coping with Grief 503
Chapter 38—Spirituality and Stress Reduction 513
Chapter 39—EEG Biofeedback Training 525
Chapter 40—Music's Effects and Enhancements of the
              Emotional State 535
Chapter 41—Massage Therapy: Key Questions and
              Answers 541

Part VI: Additional Help and Information

Chapter 42—Glossary 551
Chapter 43—Resource Directory 559

Index 569

Preface

About This Book

At some point, virtually everyone will experience stressful events or situations that overwhelm the body's natural coping mechanisms. Chronic stress produces a particular set of danger signs and symptoms that affect the most vulnerable parts of the body, including the brain, heart, and immune system. Unrelieved, these symptoms lead to emotional, cognitive, and physical consequences.

This *Sourcebook* provides health information about stress and stress-related disorders. Readers will learn about acute and chronic stress, the causes of stress, and the effects of stress on the physical, mental, and emotional body systems. Guidelines for stress management through exercise, nutrition, massage, spirituality, biofeedback, and counseling are included, along with a glossary and a listing of additional resources.

How to Use This Book

This book is divided into parts and chapters. Parts focus on broad areas of interest. Chapters are devoted to single topics within a part.

Part I: Identifying Stress provides an overview of the history of stress, types of stress, stress characteristics and signals, and identification of stress through a health risk assessment.

Part II: Environmental Stress presents information on the increase of chronic stress from family and caregiving relationships, substance abuse, the workplace, and social inequalties.

Part III: Mental and Emotional Effects of Stress explains stress effects on emotions and personality and how stress intensifies depression, panic disorder, and post-traumatic stress disorder.

Part IV: Physical Effects of Stress identifies the body's possible responses to stress by the brain, cardiovascular system, immune system, gastrointestinal system, and respiratory system. It also includes specific stress effects for women and information about how alcohol changes the stress response as people age.

Part V: Stress Management gives practical advice for reducing stress, including how to manage stress for people with arthritis and related diseases; tips for coping with everyday problems; using physical activity, weight control, nutrition, spirituality, biofeedback, massage, and music to reduce stress; coping with grief; and alcohol's influence on stress reduction.

Part VI: Additional Help and Information includes a glossary of important terms, and directories of on-line resources and organizations that provide additional information.

Bibliographic Note

This volume contains documents and excerpts from publications issued by the following U.S. government agencies: Centers for Disease Control and Prevention (CDC); National Cancer Institute (NCI); National Institute of Diabetes and Digestive and Kidney Diseases (NIDDK); National Institute on Alcohol Abuse and Alcoholism (NIAAA); National Institute on Drug Abuse (NIDA); National Institutes of Health (NIH); National Institute of Mental Health (NIMH); National Institute for Occupational Safety and Health (NIOSH); Office of Behavioral and Social Sciences Research (OBSSR); U.S. Food and Drug Administration (FDA); and U.S. National Library of Medicine (NLM).

In addition, this volume contains copyrighted documents from the following organizations and individuals: American Academy of Experts in Traumatic Stress (AAETS); American College of Physicians (ACP); American Heart Association (AHA); American Massage

Therapy Association (AMTA); American Psychological Association (APA); Arthritis Foundation; Center for Social Epidemiology; The Cleveland Clinic; Duke University Medical Center; EEG Spectrum International; *The Lancet* Ltd.; Leo Galland, MD; Greenstone Internet & Health Assessment of YOU*First*.com; HeartMath LLC; International Center for the Integration of Health and Spirituality; Lyle H. Miller, PhD; Mid-Columbia Medical Center; National Mental Health Association (NMHA); National Women's Health Information Center; North Carolina Division of Aging Department of Health and Human Services; Andy C. Parrott; Barbara Reade M.S., L.C.P.C., N.C.C.; Reuters Health Information; Alma Dell Smith, PhD; University of Florida Institute of Food and Agriculture Sciences; Vibrant Life Online; and Yale Law School (Connecticut Voices for Children).

Full citation information is provided on the first page of each chapter. Every effort has been made to secure all necessary rights to reprint the copyrighted material. If any omissions have been made, please contact Omnigraphics to make corrections for future editions.

Acknowledgements

Special thanks to the many organizations, agencies, and individuals who have contributed materials for this *Sourcebook* and to the managing editor Karen Bellenir, medical consultant Dr. David Cooke, permissions specialists Liz Barbour and Carol Munson, verification assistant Dawn Matthews, indexer Edward J. Prucha, and document engineer Bruce Bellenir.

Note from the Editor

This book is part of Omnigraphics' *Health Reference Series*. The *Series* provides basic information about a broad range of medical concerns. It is not intended to serve as a tool for diagnosing illness, in prescribing treatments, or as a substitute for the physician/patient relationship. All persons concerned about medical symptoms or the possibility of disease are encouraged to seek professional care from an appropriate health care provider.

Our Advisory Board

The *Health Reference Series* is reviewed by an Advisory Board comprised of librarians from public, academic, and medical libraries. We would like to thank the following board members for providing guidance to the development of this series:

Dr. Lynda Baker, Associate Professor of Library and Information Science, Wayne State University, Detroit, MI

Nancy Bulgarelli, William Beaumont Hospital Library, Royal Oak, MI

Karen Imarisio, Bloomfield Township Public Library, Bloomfield Township, MI

Karen Morgan, Mardigian Library, University of Michigan-Dearborn, Dearborn, MI

Rosemary Orlando, St. Clair Shores Public Library, St. Clair Shores, MI

Medical Consultant

Medical consultation services are provided to the *Health Reference Series* editors by David A. Cooke, M.D. Dr. Cooke is a graduate of Brandeis University, and he received his M.D. degree from the University of Michigan. He completed residency training at the University of Wisconsin Hospital and Clinics. He is board-certified in Internal Medicine. Dr. Cooke currently works as part of the University of Michigan Health System and practices in Brighton, MI. In his free time, he enjoys writing, science fiction, and spending time with his family.

Health Reference Series *Update Policy*

The inaugural book in the *Health Reference Series* was the first edition of *Cancer Sourcebook* published in 1992. Since then, the *Series* has been enthusiastically received by librarians and in the medical community. In order to maintain the standard of providing high-quality health information for the layperson the editorial staff at Omnigraphics felt it was necessary to implement a policy of updating volumes when warranted.

Medical researchers have been making tremendous strides, and it is the purpose of the *Health Reference Series* to stay current with the most recent advances. Each decision to update a volume will be made on an individual basis. Some of the considerations will include how much new information is available and the feedback we receive from people who use the books. If there is a topic you would like to see added to the update list, or an area of medical concern you feel has not been adequately addressed, please write to:

Editor
Health Reference Series
Omnigraphics, Inc.
615 Griswold Street
Detroit, MI 48226

The commitment to providing on-going coverage of important medical developments has also led to some format changes in the *Health Reference Series*. Each new volume on a topic is individually titled and called a "First Edition." Subsequent updates will carry sequential edition numbers. To help avoid confusion and to provide maximum flexibility in our ability to respond to informational needs, the practice of consecutively numbering each volume has been discontinued.

Part One

Identifying Stress

Chapter 1

The Origin of "Stress"

Stress and Deprivation

During the same few decades which saw great advances in the understanding of placebos, psychosomatic medicine also underwent significant changes, both in the research and clinical field and in the wider area of popular interest. The most important changes centered on the virtual abandonment of ideas about the role of unconscious emotions, early childhood experiences, and personality peculiarities— all derived from psychoanalysis. These ideas were replaced by a focus on manifest emotions, current life situations, and the socio-environmental circumstances in which disease occurred.[1] Scientists often stated the newer formulations in terms of maladaptation and loss or, more commonly, "stress" and "deprivation." Researchers drew from physiological theory and experiment and extended their concepts to all diseases, not just the classic "psychosomatic seven" (which included peptic ulcer, asthma, hypertension, and depending on the psychosomatic texts, colitis, cardiac arrhythmia, neurodermatitis, and hyperthyroidism). Yet at the same time scientists broadened the range of emotion-disease connections, the once almost unquestioned presumption of psychogenic etiology for the "psychosomatic" diseases gave way to an increasingly somatic orientation. In the realm of therapy and disease management, individual psychotherapy was replaced by stress reduction, structured mobilization

"Stress and Deprivation," U.S. National Library of Medicine, updated December 18, 2000.

against feelings of loss and loneliness, and increased reliance on the therapeutic options of biomedicine.

The decline in the medical popularity of psychoanalysis, evident in the late 1950s and continuing in the 1960s and 1970s, set many of these changes in motion.[2] Leading researchers submitted analytically-based theories of peptic ulcer, asthma, and ulcerative colitis to searching criticism and substantial revision. Therapeutic approaches relied more and more on new drugs and medical interventions and less and less on psychodynamic psychotherapy.[3] In the most dramatic case, scientists recently attributed the cause of peptic ulcer to a spiral bacterium, best managed clinically with antibiotics. This new movement even attacked conversion hysteria—one of the major contributions of Freud and a mainstay of psychosomatic theory. Several important critics started picking at the loose and unreflective consensus that had come to surround symbolically interpreted hysteria. One of the most influential critics, the respected neurologist Eliot Slater, in a widely noted paper published in 1965, called the diagnosis of conversion hysteria "a disguise for ignorance and a fertile source of clinical error." [4]

> Taught to deal with concrete and demonstrable bodily changes, we are likely to minimize or neglect the influence of an emotional upset, or to call the patient who complains of it "neurotic," perhaps tell him to "go home and forget it," and then be indifferent to the consequences. But emotional upsets have concrete and demonstrable effects in the organism.—Walter Bradford Cannon (1871–1945) *Bodily Changes in Pain, Hunger, Fear and Rage: An Account of Recent Researches into the Functions of Emotional Excitement*, New York, 1915.

This discrediting of psychoanalysis created a widening gap in psychosomatic thought that was steadily filled by a variety of theoretical alternatives. These concepts rested on more directly observable and less arcane linkages between emotions and the onset of disease. However much these theoretical alternatives differed, they had in common a psychobiological orientation, in the sense that they were clearly based on notions of holistic body and mind response of the total human organism to various stimuli, threats, and assaults from its environment. A common origin explained the similar orientation of these new theoretical approaches, for they all derived in some sense from the fundamental work of early twentieth century Harvard physiologist Walter B. Cannon. Cannon's general program was to show how the biological organism automatically mobilized its physiological and biochemical resources by a built-in "wisdom of the body," to defend itself against real or threatened assault. As an example of defensive mobilization, he explained in *Bodily Changes in Pain, Hunger, Fear and Rage* (1915), the organism responds to fear and rage as though preparing for fight or flight, by shutting down energy-storing functions and activating energy-releasing ones. In the 1940s, psychosomatic investigator Harold G. Wolff and his associates at Cornell Medical School incorporated many of Cannon's ideas.[5] Wolff then moved from a model of organismic self-defense directly borrowed from Cannon to a generalized notion of "stress and disease," according to which disease was the "inept" version of a normally "apt protective reaction pattern" that allowed the human organism to mobilize against stressful situations or events.[6]

Stress became a leading new idea in psychosomatic theory in the 1950s and Hans Selye emerged as its best known and most effective proponent. Selye was a Vienna-born, Prague-trained physician and biochemist who settled in Montreal in the 1930s and wrote the leading endocrinology textbook in 1947. In 1950 he published a 1,025 page monograph entitled *The Physiology and Pathology of Exposure to Stress*, in which he elaborated ideas he had been developing since 1936 on what he called the "General Adaptation Syndrome."[7] Selye's theory was that various "stressors" (cold, heat, solar radiation, burns, and "nervous stimuli") produce a generalized, stereotyped response in the biological organism as it works to "perform certain adaptive functions and then to reestablish normalcy." As the organism automatically mobilizes its defense mechanisms, the hypothalamus (a nerve center at the base of the brain) is excited first. Later, after a chain of effects, the adrenal glands produce "corticoid" hormones. Corticoid hormones cause a characteristic set of somatic reactions including the development of gastrointestinal ulcers.

Due largely to their synthetic scope, Selye's ideas swept the field and exerted an enormous influence. As F.L. Engel noted in 1956, "(Selye's theory of stress and the diseases of adaptation) has permeated medical thinking and influenced medical research in every land, probably more rapidly and more intensely than any other theory of disease ever proposed."[8] The "stress syndrome" became even more popular and widely known in the sixties, partly because of its appeal as a replacement for older, increasingly discredited psychoanalytically-based psychosomatic theories and partly due to Selye's charisma and prodigious output. He published forty books and over 1,700 scientific papers in the course of his career.[9] Selye was frequently quoted throughout medicine, nursing, and other health fields, and his fame spread to the wider culture, a reputation he deliberately cultivated by publishing such books for the general reader as *The Story of the Adaptive Syndrome* (1952), *The Stress of Life* (1956 and 1976), and *Stress Without Distress* (1974). Yet by the 1970s there was discord in the field of stress research as Selye conceived it. Growing confusion and controversy riddled theory and experiment. Some critics blamed Selye for having caused a great deal of it with his conceptual inconsistencies and his shifting and sometimes contradictory formulations.[10]

One major alternative challenged the stress model during the height of its initial popularity. George Engel and his colleagues at the University of Rochester Medical Center developed a theory they ultimately called "conservation-withdrawal." Like Selye, Engel and his associates focused on psychobiological threats to an individual's well-being. But instead of considering threats as "stressors" that elicited defensive and protective behaviors from the hyperaroused organism, the Rochester group conceptualized the most important of these behaviors in terms of "losses" and "deprivations" that caused the organism to become withdrawn, depressed, and shut-down.[11] The Rochester group was generally attuned to psychoanalytic theory and remained committed to preserving a place for it even in psychosomatic medicine. They thus developed a complex scheme framed in terms of disrupted relationships between individuals, affects of "helplessness" and "hopelessness," and a state of "conservation-withdrawal" in which physiological function was depressed to the point of creating a "final common pathway" to illness and death.

The Rochester group's work grew at the juncture between clinical studies on such diseases as leukemia and ulcerative colitis[12] and a naturalistic experiment on an infant, "Monica," who was fortuitously admitted to Rochester's Strong Memorial Hospital during the course of their work.[13] Monica had been born with a blockage in her esophagus, which required that two surgical openings be made, one in her neck to drain anything she took by mouth and one in her stomach through which she could be fed. Monica did not do well and was admitted to the hospital at fifteen months in a dangerous condition. While she was being nursed back to health, Engel and his associates designed a study in which they measured her gastric secretion continuously and correlated their observations with Monica's moods. They found that Monica's physiological activity increased when she was engaged with the members of the group, whether joyfully or angrily, and especially on reunion after separation. By contrast, her gastric secretion ceased entirely, and even became unresponsive to histamine (which normally stimulates gastric secretion), when she withdrew physically and emotionally from a stranger who replaced the familiar members of the group. Monica's behavior made sense as a psychological and physiological shutdown that served to conserve her organismic resources. It also helped put into perspective the separately collected clinical data on patients who articulated feelings of "giving up" or being "given up" shortly before the onset or exacerbation of a variety of somatic diseases.[14]

New Concepts

By the 1970s the psychosomatic field thus had a pair of new concepts, one emphasizing stress-induced hyperarousal and the other deprivation-caused hypoarousal. A major achievement of the next decade was the merger of this pair of ideas into one model of socio-environmental challenge and response and the connection of that model with other streams of work focused on "life change events" (divorce, bereavement, and job loss) and "social stressors" (high intensity living and work situations and major social dislocations from normal support networks).[15] The seventies were also notable for the application of progressively more sophisticated biostatistical techniques and more rigorous epidemiological study designs.[16] Striking landmarks were Sidney Cobb and Robert M. Rose's study of "Hypertension, Peptic Ulcer, and Diabetes in Air Traffic Controllers," the 1973 conference in New York City on "Stressful Life Events," John Cassel's Wade Hampton Frost Lecture of 1976 at the American Public Health Association on "The Contribution of the Social Environment to Host Resistance," and David Jenkins's report in the *New England Journal of Medicine* the same year of substantial evidence confirming the significance of the "Type A" behavior pattern as a risk factor for coronary artery disease.[17] Although there were critics of some of this new work in psychosomatic medicine, the strong consensus in the 1970s—both within the psychosomatic field and more broadly in science and medicine—was that studies on the relationship between social support, life stress, and disease onset were significant and very promising for the future.[18] It was well established in the popular imagination that the stress of modern life, work-related tension and anxiety, and devastating tragedy accompanied by the loss of community could lead to very severe health consequences.

> The chief and primary cause of....[the] very rapid increase of nervousness is modern civilization, which is distinguished from

the ancient by these five characteristics: steampower, the periodical press, the telegraph, the sciences, and the mental activity of women.—George M. Beard, *American Nervousness, Its Causes and Consequences*, 1881

Also notable in the seventies was the translation of new theoretical insights into practical intervention strategies, sometimes actively promoted by the researchers themselves. Thus, Meyer Friedman and Ray Rosenman, the physicians who initially defined the Type A concept, published a popular book which included practical chapters on how to "reengineer" one's daily life and develop "drills" to replace old and harmful habits.[19] Similarly, Harvard's Herbert Benson promoted a simple, "noncultic" technique to elicit the "relaxation response" as a counter to the stress-induced "emergency response." He showed that physicians could teach the relaxation response to patients as either a preventive or therapeutic strategy.[20] Several other investigators introduced "biofeedback" techniques (in which various physiological variables such as heart rate and muscle tension were displayed to the patient) as practical clinical methods for managing hypertension and a variety of other conditions.[21]

Volvo Assembly Line, Sweden

In 1987 the Volvo Truck Corporation initiated a significant effort to improve the environment of its factories and alter the assembly process. Scientists documented blood pressure, stress hormones, and attitudes of workers before and after restructuring the way car and truck engines were put together and found that after the changes, perceived stress, blood pressure, and epinephrine levels of the employees decreased and morale increased.

In work settings, employers introduced timeouts for stress-reducing exercise sessions and even redesigned the production process itself. Of course, the time-honored "vacation in the country" or "stay at the spa" remained popular outlets for people's accumulated tension. But in a period sensitive to the importance of loss as well as overload, health practitioners introduced newer interventions to affiliate isolated and vulnerable people with one another through support groups, to provide them with beloved objects of affection, and to encourage shared group solidarity of great symbolic and emotional significance. If stress and deprivation could cause disease, relaxation and reconnection may be able to cure it, or at least mitigate its effects.

Notes

1. Chase P. Kimball, "Conceptual Developments in Psychosomatic Medicine: 1939-1969," *Annals of Internal Medicine,* 73 (1970): 307-316; Z.J. Lipowski, "Psychosomatic Medicine in a Changing Society: Some Current Trends in Theory and Research," *Comprehensive Psychiatry,* 14 (1973): 203-215; Z.J. Lipowski, "Psychosomatic Medicine in the Seventies: An Overview," *American Journal of Psychiatry,* 134 (1977): 233-244.

2. Nathan G. Hale, *The Rise and Crisis of Psychoanalysis in the United States* (New York: Oxford University Press, 1995), p. 322.

3. Ibid., pp. 312; 323-324; 326-327; 449, n. 43; 451-453, n. 3-8; 13-16. See also Robert Aronowitz and Howard M. Spiro, "The Rise and Fall of the Psychosomatic Hypothesis in Ulcerative Colitis," *Journal of Clinical Gastroenterology,* 10 (1988): 298-305.

4. Eliot Slater, "Diagnosis of 'Hysteria'," *British Medical Journal,* 1 (1965): 1399.

5. Bela Mittelmann and Harold G. Wolff, "Emotions and Gastroduodenal Function," *Psychosomatic Medicine,* 4 (1942): 5B61 and Harold G. Wolff, "Protective Reaction Patterns and Disease," *Annals of Internal Medicine,* 27 (1947): 944B969.

6. Harold G. Wolff, *Stress and Disease* (Springfield IL: Charles C. Thomas, 1953).

7. Montreal: Acta, Inc., Medical Publishers, 1950. See also Hans Selye, "The Evolution of the Stress Concept," *American Scientist,* 61 (1973): 692-699.

8. Quoted in John W. Mason, "A Historical View of the Stress Field," Part I, *Journal of Human Stress,* 1 (March, 1975): 10.

9. S. Szabo, "The Creative and Productive Life of Hans Selye: A Review of His Major Scientific Discoveries," *Experientia,* 41 (1985): 564B567 and Y. Tache, "A Tribute to the Pioneering Contributions of Hans Selye: An Appraisal Through His Books," *Experientia,* 41 (1985): 567-568.

10. John W. Mason, "A Historical View of the Stress Field," Part II, *Journal of Human Stress* 1 (June, 1975): 22B36.

11. Arthur H. Schmale, "Relationship of Separation and Depression to Disease," *Psychosomatic Medicine*, ns., 20 (1958): 259-277; George L. Engel, "A Life Setting Conducive to Illness," *Annals of Internal Medicine*, 69 (1968): 293-300; George L. Engel and Arthur H. Schmale, "Conservation-Withdrawal: A Primary Regulatory Process for Organismic Homeostasis," in *Physiology, Emotion & Psychosomatic Illness*, Ciba Foundation Symposium 8, ns (Amsterdam: Elsevier-Excerpta Medica, 1972), pp. 57-85.

12. William A. Greene, Jr., "Psychological Factors and Reticuloendothelial Disease," *Psychosomatic Medicine*, 16 (1954): 220-230 and George L. Engel, "Biologic and Psychologic Features of the Ulcerative Colitis Patient," *Gastroenterology*, 40 (1961): 313-317.

13. George L. Engel, Franz Reichsman, and Harry L. Segal, "A Study of an Infant With a Gastric Fistula," *Psychosomatic Medicine*, 18 (1956): 374-398 and George L. Engel and Franz Reichsman, "Spontaneous and Experimentally Induced Depressions in an Infant With a Gastric Fistula," *Journal of the American Psychoanalytic Association*, 4 (1956): 428-452.

14. A.H. Schmale, "Giving Up as a Final Common Pathway to Changes in Health," in Z. J. Lipowski, ed., *Psychosocial Aspects of Physical Illness* (Basel: Karger, 1972), pp. 20-40.

15. George L. Engel, "The Need for a New Medical Model: A Challenge for Biomedicine," Science, 196 (1977): 129-135 and George L. Engel, "The Clinical Application of the Biopsychosocial Model," *American Journal of Psychiatry*, 137 (1980): 535-543.

16. Z.J. Lipowski, "Psychosomatic Medicine: An Overview," *Modern Trends in Psychosomatic Medicine*, 3 (1976): 1-20.

17. Cobb and Rose, JAMA, 224 (1973): 489-492; Barbara Snell Dohrenwend and Bruce P. Dohrenwend, eds., *Stressful Life Events: Their Nature and Effects* (New York: John Wiley & Sons, 1974); John Cassel, "The Contribution of the Social Environment to Host Resistance," *American Journal of Epidemiology*, 104 (1976): 107-123; C. David Jenkins, "Recent Evidence Supporting Psychologic and Social Risk Factors for

Coronary Disease," *New England Journal of Medicine*, 294 (1976): 1033-1038.

18. Evelyn L. Goldberg and George W. Comstock, "Life Events and Subsequent Illness," *American Journal of Epidemiology*, 104 (1976): 146-158; Sidney Cobb, "Social Support as a Moderator of Life Stress," *Psychosomatic Medicine*, 38 (1976): 300-314; Judith G. Rabkin and Elmer L. Struening, "Life Events, Stress, and Illness," *Science*, 194 (1976): 1013-1020.

19. Meyer Friedman and Ray Rosenman, *Type A Behavior and Your Heart* (New York: Alfred A. Knopf, 1974), Chapters 16 & 17.

20. Herbert Benson, *The Relaxation Response* (New York: Morrow, 1975).

21. See, for example, Lee Birk, ed., *Biofeedback: Behavioral Medicine* (New York: Grune and Stratton, 1973).

Chapter 2

Understanding Stress: Characteristics and Caveats

Exposure to stressful situations is among the most common human experiences. These types of situations can range from unexpected calamities (e.g., bereavement, natural disaster, or illness) to routine daily annoyances. Regardless of their degree of severity, however, stressors may promote physiological and behavioral disturbances, ranging from psychiatric disorders (Brown 1993) to immune system dysfunction (Herbert and Cohen 1993). Stressful events also may profoundly influence the use of alcohol or other drugs (AODs). For example, the resumption of AOD use after a lengthy period of abstinence may reflect a person's attempt to self-medicate to attenuate the adverse psychological consequences of stressors (e.g., anxiety). Alternatively, stress may increase the reinforcing effects of AODs.

This chapter provides a working definition of stress and describes research on the physiological and psychological responses to different types of stressful stimuli, focusing particularly on processes that may be relevant to the development of alcohol use disorders.

Stress: A Working Definition

As commonly used, the term "stressor" indicates a situation or event appraised as being aversive in that it elicits a stress response

"Understanding Stress: Characteristics and Caveats," by Hymie Anisman, Ph.D. and Zul Merali, Ph.D., *Alcohol Research & Health*, Vol. 23, No. 4, 1999, National Institute on Alcohol Abuse and Alcoholism (NIAAA), NIH Publication No. 00-3466.

which taxes a person's physiological or psychological resources as well as possibly provokes a subjective state of physical or mental tension. As relevant scientific data have accumulated, however, a simple, universally accepted definition of stress has become increasingly elusive.

This chapter focuses on some of the factors that may influence the mechanisms by which a person responds to stressful situations (i.e., stressors). Much of the information presented here is based on animal research, which can provide essential information not obtainable from human studies. However, the human stress response is influenced by a host of personality characteristics and life experiences that cannot be duplicated in animal studies.

Many researchers view the stress response as an adaptive mechanism designed to maintain the relative stability of the body's overall physiological functioning (i.e., homeostasis) in response to a challenge. However, not all stress responses are clearly adaptive. Some physiological reactions to stress that appear to confer short-term benefits are followed by adverse long-term repercussions. In other instances, changes that appear to have adverse consequences may, on closer examination, turn out to be beneficial. Finally, some changes that may have little positive value and no adaptive significance may yet comprise part of the overall stress response.

The ambiguity of the stress response can be illustrated by examining the functions of cortisol, a hormone released by the adrenal glands in response to stressful stimuli. Among other functions, cortisol helps promote the release of energy stores essential for coping with stress. Yet, cortisol may suppress the normal functioning of the immune system, a response that could theoretically render the body more susceptible to infectious diseases. However, cortisol-induced immune suppression also may serve a protective function (Munck et al. 1984), preventing the development of illnesses characterized by immune attack on the body's own tissues (e.g., rheumatoid arthritis). Even when cortisol release has adaptive consequences, the elevated cortisol levels persist for an extended period, then the adaptive nature of the response may be lost and adverse effects may ensue. Thus, what we consider to be an adaptive short-term response may subsequently provoke long-term pathophysiological consequences (Sapolsky et al., 1986).

Because stressful stimuli often elicit cortisol secretion, some researchers have proposed the use of cortisol levels as an index of the stress response. However, not all events perceived as stressful lead to the release of hormones specifically associated with stress. Indeed, several other hormones and similar chemical messengers are extremely

14

responsive to stressful stimuli and may influence the cascade of events activated by stress. Furthermore, positive stimuli may elicit physiological responses comparable in many respects to those provoked by adverse events, and increased cortisol release is not uniquely provoked by events perceived as stressful. For example, rats that were offered food in the laboratory exhibited activation of the hypothalamic-pituitary adrenal axis (HPA) identical to that elicited by stressful stimuli, such as physical restraint (Merali et al. 1998). HPA activation could arguably represent an anticipatory response to any strong stimulus, preparing the animal to respond appropriately. Alternatively, the presentation of food, at least in animals, may actually threaten to disrupt homeostasis. In that case, the stress response may help mobilize the body's physiological response to the potential onslaught of nutrients, which require digestion and absorption. In addition, food may naturally contain or be contaminated by any number of toxic compounds that must be eliminated or destroyed (e.g., by immune system activity or enzymatic degradation in the liver). Furthermore, in the wild, an animal approaching a food source may experience some risk from either predators or competitors. The evaluation of these hypotheses is complicated by individual differences in the perception and appraisal of a stimulus as stressful.

Characteristics of the Stressor

Several factors serve a fundamental role in determining the nature and consequences of the stress response. These factors include inherent features of a given type of stressor as well as the conditions under which the stressor is encountered (i.e., the stressor regimen).

Evaluating the Stress Response

In general, stressors may be psychogenic and/or neurogenic. Psychogenic stressors are purely of psychological origin (e.g., anticipating an adverse event, experiencing the death of a loved one, or caring for a chronically ill person). Neurogenic stressors involve a physical stimulus (e.g., a headache, bodily injury, or recovery from surgery).

In addition, environmental stressors can be classified as either processive or systemic. Processive stressors are those that require appraisal of a situation or involve high-level cognitive processing of incoming sensory information. Examples of processive stressors among animals include exposure to new environments, predators, or situations that trigger fear because of previous association with unpleasant stimuli (i.e., fear cues). In contrast, systemic stressors are of physiological origin (e.g., disturbances of normal bodily metabolism resulting from bacterial or viral infection).

Herman and Cullinan (1997) have suggested that both processive and systemic stressors might activate the HPA axis through distinct but converging neurological circuits. Specifically, processive stressors may primarily activate the limbic system, a region of the brain comprising interconnected structures that are associated with arousal, emotion, and goal-directed behavior. Conversely, systemic stressors may more directly influence the hypothalamus, a brain structure with multiple regulatory functions that interacts extensively with the limbic system. In the absence of experimental evidence, it seems reasonable to speculate that processive stressors might be more closely associated with increased alcohol consumption than would systemic stressors.

When evaluating the impact of adverse events on an individual, a researcher or health professional must consider the specific nature of the stressor involved. Although most stressors elicit some common neurochemical and behavioral effects, their responses are not always identical.

In animal studies, researchers have employed a wide range of stressors to assess behavioral and biological outcomes. Some of these stressors are ethologically sound (i.e., they represent situations that the animal would ordinarily encounter in its natural environment and for which it may have developed natural, evolutionary defenses). Ethological stressors may include the sight or odor of predators, confrontation with unfamiliar members of the same species, or fear cues.

Other commonly employed experimental stressors include exposure to cold air, immersion in cold water, and mild electric shocks administered to the animal's foot or tail. In various studies, investigators have administered footshock and tailshock at varying intensities, thereby obtaining information on the effects of controllable (i.e., escapable) versus uncontrollable (i.e., inescapable) stressors. However, the ability to generalize experimental results involving some stressors is limited. For example, the effects of exposure to cold air or cold water may reflect physiological processes specific to the generation of body heat rather than the psychological consequences of stress.

The nature of the stress response varies depending on the nature of the stressor and the stressor regimen. This fact is illustrated by the phenomenon of adaptation (i.e., a diminished response after prolonged or repeated exposure to a stressor). For example, within a single experimental session, the brain's chemical response exhibits

16

adaptation to some stressors (e.g., restraint) but is less likely to occur in response to others (e.g., footshock or tailshock). Although the reason for this finding is unknown, one possibility is that restraint is continuous, whereas footshock is intermittent. Thus, drawing firm conclusions about the adverse effects of a stressor based on a specific stressor regimen can sometimes be difficult. The variability of the stress response may provide important clues to the identification of the psychological and physical processes that govern voluntary alcohol consumption.

> The human stress response is influenced by a host of personality characteristics and life experiences that cannot be duplicated in animal studies.

Stressor effects in humans are more complex than in animals. Some investigations of the human stress response have been conducted under contrived conditions in the laboratory, and the meaningfulness of such studies may be limited. Studies that attempt to simulate natural conditions are more likely to produce realistic outcomes. Some of the latter studies rely on a person's recollection of past events (i.e., retrospective studies). The disadvantage of retrospective studies, however, includes the potential distortion of recall resulting from subsequent experience or the subject's current mental state. Prospective studies, which are less commonly employed, involve an initial baseline examination of the subject with subsequent follow-up evaluations (Sklar and Anisman 1981).

Irrespective of the experimental approach, research clearly indicates that stressors, which are usually multidimensional, produce not only immediate actions but also protracted effects secondary to the primary stressor. For instance, stressful experiences are often followed by persistent brooding (i.e., rumination) that may in itself be stressful, and some events (e.g., bereavement) may have secondary effects (e.g., financial burden and loss of social support). Whereas some stressor effects may diminish over time (e.g., sadness, remorse, or guilt), the effects of other stressors may increase (e.g., financial burden and loss of social support). In addition, the stress response itself may function as a stressor. For example, symptoms of depression induced by stress may lead to interpersonal conflict or, conversely, social withdrawal, further exacerbating depression (Hammen 1991).

With respect to behavioral outcomes, some stressors (e.g., loss of social support) are more likely than others to provoke depressive symptoms (Monroe and Simons 1991), whereas other stressors (e.g., threats or impending stress) are more closely associated with anxiety symptoms (Finlay, Jones, and Brown 1981). Surprisingly, stress induced psychiatric pathology is often elicited not by a major adverse life event but by a series of relatively mild stressors (i.e., day-to-day hassles). Furthermore, the effects of the minor stressors may be especially profound if they occur following a major stressful event (Lazarus 1990; Ravindran et al. 1997).

The severity of stress-induced effects may be related to characteristics of the individual coupled with the nature of the stressor. Relevant stressor characteristics include the following:

1. the degree to which stress can be mitigated or eliminated by an appropriate response (i.e., controllability),

2. the predictability of onset of the stressor,

3. the duration or chronic nature of exposure (i.e., either acute or over a relatively protracted period), and

4. the timing and frequency of exposure (e.g., intermittent).

Nerve Cell Communication and the Stress Response

Nerve cells communicate with one another through chemical messengers called neurotransmitters. The neurotransmitters discussed in this article interact extensively to perform a variety of regulatory activities. Serotonin affects a wide range of physiological functions, including appetite, sleep, and body temperature. Serotonin also influences emotional states, and its dysfunction has been implicated in both psychiatric and addictive disorders. Dopamine helps regulate goal-directed behaviors (including the reinforcing effects of alcohol and other drugs) as well as certain motor functions. Within the brain, norepinephrine (NE) plays a role in arousal and in the modulation of other neurotransmitter systems. When released into the bloodstream by the adrenal glands, norepinephrine functions as a stress-related hormone, preparing the body for "fight or flight" in response to threatening situations.

The Ability to Control and Cope

Perceived ability to control clearly influences some (but not all) stress responses. For example, uncontrollable stressors provoke behavioral disturbances in animals that are not induced by controllable stressors of comparable severity. Some investigators interpret these differences as the consequences of "learned helplessness" (Seligman 1975). Other researchers interpret these findings in terms of the strain that such events place on the neurotransmitter systems in the brain (Anisman et al. 1991; Weiss and Simson 1985).

The excessive strain on, or the resulting variations of, neurotransmitters may increase an individual's vulnerability to pathological states. Indeed, studies in rodents have indicated that in some brain regions (e.g., the hypothalamus), the response of the neurotransmitter norepinephrine (NE) to uncontrollable stressors is more profound than that provoked by controllable stressors. Likewise, the controllability of stressors may differentially influence the functions of the neurotransmitters serotonin (5-HT) and dopamine (DA) in specific brain regions. In addition, some behavioral disturbances evoked by uncontrollable stressors can be mimicked by drugs that disrupt the functioning of these neurotransmitters. Conversely, treatments that attenuate the neurochemical alterations elicited by stressors limit such behavioral disturbances (Anisman et al. 1991). In effect, an individual's response to a stressor may be dictated by the availability of appropriate coping strategies, and certain behavioral disturbances may be most pronounced under conditions where stressor controllability is not possible or where coping responses are ineffective.

Although researchers may be tempted to conclude that the ability to neutralize a stressor is the fundamental feature in predicting neurochemical and behavioral change, this conclusion may be premature. For instance, when stressed animals are permitted to fight with a member of their species, the effects ordinarily elicited by uncontrollable stressors may be mitigated, a phenomenon known as displacement (Anisman et al. 1991). Nevertheless, displacement aggression may not eliminate the stressor and may in fact create additional stress. An important aspect of displacement behaviors, such as aggression, is that by offsetting the impact of stressors, the displacement behaviors may become reinforced. AOD use may serve, in part, as such a displacement behavior. Whether or not the displacement behaviors related to stressful events actually support both the initiation and maintenance of AOD abuse remains to be determined.

Not all neurochemical or physiological processes are differentially influenced by stressor controllability. The ability to respond rapidly to a stressful challenge may have greater adaptive value than the ability to assess controllability. Moreover, determining whether a given stressor is controllable may require sustained or repeated exposure, a luxury that may not be affordable. Thus, systems designed for immediate response (e.g., activation of the HPA axis or the immune system) ought to react comparably to both controllable and uncontrollable stressors. Conversely, systems that are uniquely involved in the appraisal of processive stressors might react differently to controllable than to uncontrollable stressors.

Studies in humans support the view that stressor controllability may be fundamental in determining the stress response, despite the fact that in a great number of instances, control is actually illusory. Rather than assessing stressor controllability, researchers may find it more profitable to consider the specific coping mechanisms that are available to the individual (Lazarus 1993). Broadly speaking, coping can be subdivided into several subtypes, including emotion-focused coping (e.g., emotional expression, emotional containment, blame, avoidance, denial, and passivity); problem-focused coping; social support; cognitive restructuring; and problem-solving.

Researchers often assume that emotion-focused coping is a relatively ineffective strategy, whereas social buffering, problem-solving, and cognitive restructuring may be more efficacious. To some extent, this conclusion is based on findings that depressed patients, relative to control subjects, tend to favor emotion-focused coping and revert to a more problem-focused strategy with successful treatment (Ravindran et al. 1997). Although emotion-focused coping can be ineffective and even counterproductive, the effectiveness of a strategy may depend on the specific stressor regimen. A given strategy may be ineffective under one set of conditions but be highly effective under another. Ultimately, the abilities to maintain flexibility and be prepared to use different strategies may be the hallmark of effective coping.

Chronicity and Predictability

Intuitively, one would suspect that the behavioral and neurochemical impact of an acute stressor would be exacerbated by repeated exposure to the stressor. However, some stressor-induced behavioral, neurochemical, and immunological disturbances in rats and mice may be mitigated by prolonged stressor exposure. For example, the decline of brain NE concentrations associated with acute stressor exposure may reverse following protracted or repeated exposure (Weiss and Simson 1985). Such adaptation appears to represent an active process, because NE levels in chronically stressed animals do not simply return to pre-stress levels, but instead exceed basal values. Chronic stressors appear to promote a compensatory increase in the production of NE (or, in the case of DA, moderation of excessive utilization), leading to increased neurotransmitter concentrations.

Factors that prevent or limit neurochemical adaptation may be associated with behavioral or physiological disorders. For example, some of the behavioral and neurochemical changes associated with chronic predictable stressors are less apt to appear following chronic unpredictable stressors (Anisman et al. 1991). Interestingly, a regimen of chronic mild stressors may result in an inability to experience pleasure (i.e., anhedonia) similar to that elicited by relatively intense stressors. Thus, even stressors that have modest effects when applied acutely may have pronounced behavioral repercussions when experienced on a chronic, unpredictable basis (Willner 1997).

In humans, stressors are typically of a varied nature, are encountered on an intermittent and unpredictable basis, and may be experienced over protracted periods. As indicated earlier, many stressors have secondary effects (e.g., rumination, financial loss, or loss of social support), which are themselves stressful or limit coping abilities. A chronic, intermittent stressor regimen is less likely to lead to neurochemical adaptation and hence favor the development of pathology. When the chronic stressor regimen is not only unpredictable, but is also uncontrollable and associated with secondary stressors, the occurrence of behavioral disturbances might, perhaps, increase (Anisman et al. 1991).

Two important caveats must be stressed with respect to the impact of chronic stressors.

- First, the compensatory neurotransmitter changes associated with repeated stressor exposure vary widely and occur in several brain regions. Not all of these variations necessarily progress at comparable rates or in all species of laboratory animals. Thus, the nature of the pathology associated with a chronic stressor regimen may depend on the specific neurochemical disturbances incurred.

- Second, the process of coping with chronic stressor exposure creates prolonged and intense demands on neurochemical systems, a condition termed "allostatic load." Sustained and excessive allostatic load may culminate in pathological outcomes (Schulkin et al. 1998).

Evaluating the contribution of stressors to behavioral disturbances (e.g., alcoholism) in humans requires large scale prospective studies assessing the impact of acute and chronic insults, the contribution of coping factors, and allostatic load associated with certain stressor regimens.

PROPERTY OF
AUBURN RIVERSIDE HIGH SCHOOL
LIBRARY

Effects of Genetics, Gender, Age, and Previous Stressor Exposure

Genetic Differences

Both the psychological and physiological responses to a given stressor may vary greatly between individuals, thereby influencing the type of pathology to which a person is vulnerable. Such vulnerability may be influenced by genetic factors.

In mice and rats, behavioral, hormonal, immunological, and neurochemical effects of a given environmental stressor may differ significantly between different genetic strains. For example, some rodent strains exposed to a stressor may display marked HPA alterations or variations of brain neurotransmitter levels, whereas other strains may display fewer or less profound effects. Similarly, the same stressful event may induce opposite effects on certain aspects of immune functioning in different rodent strains. Rather than regarding such inter-individual or inter-strain variations as a "noise factor," the experimenter can use them to help identify both the factors that predict the response to a stressor and the occurrence of a pathological state related to the stressor (Anisman et al. 1991, 1998).

Individual or genetic differences in the stress response may indicate either an overall increase of reactivity or a highly specific increase in the reactivity of a particular biological system. Similarly, alterations of transmitter function in one brain region, or alterations of one aspect of immune functioning, do not suggest similar alterations in other brain regions or in other aspects of immunity. Inter-individual differences in the fragility of different biological systems may determine why a stressor increases the vulnerability to a particular pathology in one individual but a different pathology in another individual. In addition, if the organism is endowed with increased vulnerability to stressor effects on neurochemical processes as well as increased genetic vulnerability to a particular pathology, then the stressor would be expected to increase the risk for this particular pathology. In the case of alcoholism, genetic factors favoring increased alcohol intake, coupled with an inherited disposition toward excessive stressor reactivity or inappropriate coping styles, could potentially contribute to alcohol abuse.

Gender

Data concerning gender-dependent effects of stressors are relatively limited, although researchers have found that the HPA response to stressors is greater in female rats than in male rats. This effect appears to occur at almost every level of HPA functioning, and the responses, to some extent, are regulated by interaction among the hypothalamus, pituitary gland, and gonadal organs (Ferrini et al. 1997; Viau and Meaney 1991). Such factors may contribute to the gender differences often seen with respect to some behavioral disturbances (e.g., mood disorders), but the contribution of these factors to AOD consumption is not yet clear.

Age

In humans, the age-dependent effects of stressors intertwine with numerous psychosocial factors (e.g., reduced physical abilities; financial constraints; and loss of coping resources, social support, and psychological flexibility). Animal studies further suggest that certain neurochemical systems that are sensitive to stressors react differently in aged compared with young individuals. In aged rats, stressor-provoked neurochemical alterations are induced more readily than in young rats, and the return to basal levels of neuronal functioning requires a relatively sustained period of time. Theoretically, stressors should generate rapid neurochemical responses that readily normalize upon stressor termination. Thus, the sustained neuronal activation of aged animals may reflect a lack of adaptability of functioning. Aged animals might therefore be more vulnerable to stressor-provoked pathology (Anisman et al. 1991; Sapolsky et al. 1986). In humans, where aging is frequently associated with reduced coping abilities or opportunities (owing, for example, to diminished social supports following loss of friends and loved ones, reduced physical abilities, and possibly financial concerns), the effects of stressors on pathological processes may be particularly marked. Given that developmental, social, and cultural factors influence not only stressor perception but also individual coping styles (Aldwin 1994). Ultimately, such variables probably contribute to pathological states and should be considered in relating stress to alcoholism.

Similar to an aged animal, however, a very young organism may lack or may not have developed the behavioral and neurochemical repertoire to cope with stressors effectively and thus may be at increased risk for pathology. As discussed shortly, stressors in young animals may act to program (or reprogram) neuronal functioning to increase vulnerability to neurochemical disturbances encountered later in life.

Effects of Prior Life Events or Stressor Exposure

Sensitization. Stressful events not only have marked immediate effects but also may influence one's response to later stressor experiences. Such a sensitization effect may be responsible for the high rates of relapse associated with psychiatric disorders, such as depression (Post 1992). Studies in animals have indicated that exposure to stressors typically induces physiological changes that persist for a relatively brief duration. However, if animals are re-exposed to the same stressor at a later time, then the neurochemical changes in the brain occur more readily. Such effects have been noted with respect to several neurotransmitters, but particular attention has been devoted to the analysis of norepinephrine and dopamine (see reviews in Kalivas and Stewart 1991). Interestingly, these effects have not only been observed when the re-exposure session involves the same stressor, but also when it involves an entirely different stressor (Nisenbaum et al. 1991). Furthermore, such cross-sensitization effects have been witnessed between processive stressors and drug treatments. Thus, treatment with amphetamine or cocaine may enhance the response introduced by subsequent exposure to a stressor (Kalivas and Stewart 1991).

The sensitization appears to depend on the characteristics of the stressors to which the animal had previously been exposed. As indicated earlier, young animals that have been exposed to an acute stressor demonstrate increased activity of NE and DA when they are later exposed to a stressor. As a result, re-exposure may result in declining neurotransmitter levels. However, in animals that have been exposed to a chronic stressor regimen, subsequent re-exposure to the stressor induces a sensitization with respect to both synthesis and utilization of NE and DA. As a result, the level of the neurotransmitter does not decline readily. In effect, the nature of the previous stressor experiences (and the neurochemical changes engendered) determine an animal's response to stressor re-exposure and thus might also influence behavioral responses engendered by subsequent challenges (Anisman et al. 1991).

When animals are repeatedly exposed to a particular stressor, adaptation may occur and, consequently, neurotransmitter alterations may become progressively less pronounced. However, when animals are subsequently introduced to a stressor not previously encountered, then the adaptation is not evident, and a marked neurochemical change is again elicited. Thus, the adaptation that occurs with sustained exposure to a stressor may be unique to that particular stressful stimulus, and diminished responsivity may not occur in response to a new stimulus. Conversely, a chronic stressor regimen may result in an increased response following exposure to a different type of stressor. In effect, it seems that although repeated exposure to a particular stressor may promote either adaptation with respect to stressor appraisal or some aspects of neuronal functioning (e.g., the stressor is appraised as being less aversive, or variations occur with respect to either the receptor sensitivity and/or number present at presynaptic or postsynaptic sites, or with respect to transmitter release), these processes may be affected in a different fashion when a novel stressor is introduced, culminating in augmented neuronal functioning.

Studies by Tilders and colleagues (Tilders and Schmidt 1998; Tilders et al. 1993) have revealed important processes concerning the sensitization of neuroendocrine functioning that occur in response to both processive and systemic stressors. These investigators have found that stressors may induce prolonged changes of neuroendocrine functioning within certain neurons of the hypothalamus that communicate with the pituitary gland. Both corticotropin-releasing hormone (CRH) and arginine vasopressin (AVP) can stimulate the release of adrenocorticotropic hormone (ACTH) and, hence, corticosterone release from the adrenal glands. Furthermore, AVP may potentiate the effects ordinarily elicited by CRH. With the passage of time following stressor exposure, the CRH neurons may co-produce AVP, thus rendering the HPA axis more sensitive to stressors. Essential features of these findings include the following:

- changes of AVP and CRH co-production may be long-lasting and thus account for some of the protracted effects of stressors that have been reported, and

- the long-term effects of stressors also could be provoked by the administration of cytokines (i.e., substances that act as signaling molecules within the immune system), suggesting that immune activation also may proactively influence the response to subsequently encountered adverse experiences.

Early Life Stimulation. The stimulation or handling of laboratory animals during their first few weeks after birth (which also entailed a brief separation from their mothers) was found to decrease age-related learning disturbances and increased resistance to the effects of later stressors (Meaney et al. 1996). Animals that had experienced stimulation during the first 21 days of life showed basal

25

concentrations of ACTH and corticosterone comparable to that of non-stimulated animals. However, as adults, when exposed to a stressor, the stimulated animals displayed blunted ACTH and corticosterone responses and a faster return to basal hormone levels. These long-lasting variations may have involved a cascade of neuronal changes, culminating not only in altered regulatory processes associated with HPA functioning (Meaney et al. 1996), but also in variations with respect to the propensity to consume alcohol during later adulthood (Lancaster 1998; Jones et al. 1985).

Liu and colleagues (1997) conducted studies to determine why brief handling involving separation from the mother (i.e., for as little as 15 minutes per day) had such pronounced and persistent effects. After reuniting with their young following the brief separation, mothers exhibited increased licking, grooming, and nursing of their offspring. Moreover, because the high levels of these maternal responses were correlated with altered hormonal responses to stressors, the researchers suggested that maternal behavioral style acted to "program" HPA responses to later environmental stressors. Whether such factors also contribute to alcohol intake remains to be established.

Anisman and colleagues (1998) studied two mouse strains that exhibit very different behavioral and neurochemical profiles in response to stressors. The more stress-reactive strain displayed relatively poor maternal behavior, spent less time within the nest, and took longer to retrieve young offspring, which had been placed in different portions of the cage, compared with the less stress-reactive strain (Anisman et al. 1998). Thus, the exaggerated response to stressors in the more reactive mice may be related in part to maternal factors. When young mice of the stress-reactive strain were raised by mothers from the less reactive strain (cross-fostered on the day of birth), some behavioral disturbances and the exaggerated HPA alterations of the more reactive mice were decreased. However, maternal behavior alone is not sufficient for this outcome to emerge. In particular, being raised by a mother from the more reactive strain did not engender behavioral or hormonal disturbances in young mice of the more resilient strain. This finding implies that heightened stress reactivity in these mice results from a combination of genetic factors and inadequate maternal care (Zaharia et al. 1996).

Early Life Deprivation. In contrast to early life stimulation, early life stressors (e.g., separation from the mother for relatively long periods, such as 3 hours per day) may increase the potential for later stressor-promoted HPA activation. Indeed, protracted separation provokes an increase of plasma ACTH and corticosterone and increased behavioral and neuroendocrine reactivity to stressors encountered during adulthood (Meaney et al. 1996). Paralleling the effects of early life deprivation in which young animals were made ill by the administration of a bacterial toxin several aspects of the HPA response to stressors during adulthood were increased (Shanks et al. 1995). Of course, bacterial toxins may induce fever, possibly altering the mother's behavior toward the young (e.g., elevations of body temperature may serve as a cue for termination of nursing), which, in turn, precipitates the altered response to subsequently encountered stressors. It remains to be determined whether metabolic stressors that do not elevate body temperature also induce such long-term effects. In any case, early life trauma, which includes not only separation from the mother but also bacterial infection, appears to have potentially far reaching implications. Thus, various early life experiences in newborn humans might significantly affect reactivity to stressors encountered during adulthood.

Regulating the Stress Response

The maintenance of a relatively stable balance of physiological functions (i.e., homeostasis) is constantly challenged by illness; injury; hostile environmental conditions; unpleasant emotional states; and even certain normal functions, such as sexual activity and exposure to new environments. The body's response to such stressors is regulated largely by interactions among the hypothalamus, pituitary gland, and adrenal glands, together termed the HPA axis. In response to potentially harmful stimuli, the hypothalamus, which is located near the base of the brain, secretes two hormones that travel directly to the adjacent pituitary gland. These two hormones, corticotropin-releasing hormone (CRH) and arginine vasopressin (AVP)—AVP also serves a key function in maintaining the body's water balance—promote the secretion of adrenocorticotropic hormone (ACTH) from the pituitary gland. Traveling through the bloodstream, ACTH reaches the adrenal glands, which are located on top of the kidneys. In humans, the adrenal glands respond to ACTH by releasing the steroid hormone cortisol into the bloodstream—the corresponding hormone in rodents is corticosterone. Cortisol exerts widespread physiological effects throughout the body, acting in concert with other chemical messengers to help direct oxygen and nutrients to the stressed body site and suppress the immune response, while influencing certain functions, such as appetite and satiety; arousal, vigilance, and attention; and mood.

Under normal circumstances, the presence of cortisol in the bloodstream signals the hypothalamus to terminate CRH secretion, thereby preventing overactivity of the stress response. The regulation of a physiological response through inhibition mediated by the end product of the response is called negative feedback. When negative feedback control of the HPA axis does not operate adequately, as may occur following chronic stress or as a consequence of certain psychiatric disorders (possibly including severe depression), persistent activation of the HPA axis may occur. Damage resulting from HPA overactivity may include suppression of growth, immune system dysfunction, and localized brain cell damage that might result in impairment of learning and memory.

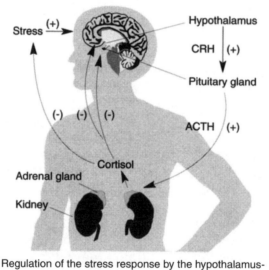

Regulation of the stress response by the hypothalamus-pituitary-adrenal (HPA) axis.

ACTH = adrenocorticotropic hormone; CRH = corticotropin-releasing hormone; + = stimulates; - = inhibits.

Figure 2.1. Regulation of the Stress Response

Summary

In response to stressors, a series of behavioral, neurochemical, and immunological changes occur that ought to serve in an adaptive capacity. However, if these systems become overly taxed, the organism may become vulnerable to pathology. Likewise, the biological changes, if sufficiently sustained, may themselves adversely affect the organism's wellbeing. Several factors may dictate an individual's response to environmental stressors, including characteristics of the stressor (i.e., type of stressor and its controllability, predictability, and chronicity); biological factors (i.e., age, gender, and genetics); and the subject's previous stressor history and early life experiences. Ultimately, these factors interact to determine the organism's biological responses to environmental stressors; thus, not surprisingly, much inter-individual variability exists with respect to the impact of stressors. Of course, the retinue of biological changes and the broad range of variables that influence these outcomes often make it difficult to identify the mechanisms associated with stressor-provoked pathology.

References

Aldwin, C.M. *Stress, Coping, and Development: An Integrated Perspective*. New York: Guilford Press, 1994.

Anisman, H.; Zalcman, S.; Shanks, N.; and Zacharko, R.M. Multisystem regulation of performance deficits induced by stressors: An animal model of depression. In: Boulton, A.; Baker, G.; and MartinIverson, M., eds. *Neuromethods*. Volume 19: *Animal Models of Psychiatry*, II. Totowa, NJ: Humana Press, 1991. pp. 159.

Anisman, H.; Zaharia, M.D.; Meaney, M.J.; and Merali, Z. Proactive hormonal, neurochemical and behavioral effects of early life stimulation: Genetic differences. *International Journal of Developmental Neuroscience* 16:149-164, 1998.

Brown, G.W. Life events and affective disorder: Replications and limitations. *Psychosomatic Medicine* 55:248-259, 1993.

Ferrini, M.G.; Grillo, C.A.; Piroli, G.; De Kloet, E.R.; and De Nicola, A.F. Sex difference in glucocorticoid regulation of vasopressin mRNA in the paraventricular hypothalamic nucleus. *Cellular and Molecular Neurobiology* 17:671-686, 1997.

Finlayjones, R., and Brown, G.W. Types of stressful life events and the onset of anxiety and depressive disorders. *Psychological Medicine* 11:803-816, 1981.

Hammen, C. Generation of stress in the course of unipolar depression. *Journal of Abnormal Psychology* 100:555-561, 1991.

Herbert, T.B., and Cohen, S. Stress and immunity in humans: A metaanalytic review. *Psychosomatic Medicine* 55:364-379, 1993.

Herman, J.P., and Cullinan, W.E. Neurocircuitry of stress: Central control of hypothalamo-pituitary-adrenocortical axis. *Trends in Neuroscience* 20:78-84, 1997.

Jones, B.; Golstine, R.; Gurley, M.; and Reyes, E. Appetite for alcohol: Influence of genetics and early experience. *Neurobehavioral Toxicology and Teratology* 2:125-127, 1985.

Kalivas, P.W., and Stewart, J. Dopamine transmission in the initiation and expression of drug and stress-induced sensitization of motor activity. *Brain Research Reviews* 16:223-244, 1991.

Lancaster, F.E. Sex differences in voluntary drinking by Long Evans rats following early stress. *Alcoholism: Clinical and Experimental Research* 4:830-836, 1998.

Lazarus, R.S. Theory-based stress measurement and commentaries. *Psychological Inquiry* 1:351, 1990.

Lazarus, R.S. Coping theory and research: Past, present, and future. *Psychosomatic Medicine* 55:234-247, 1993.

Liu, D.; Diorio, J.; Tannenbaum, B.; Caldji, C.; Francis, D.; Freedman, A.; Sharma, S.; Pearson, D.; Plotsky, P.; and Meaney, M.J. Maternal care during infancy: Hippocampal glucocorticoid receptor gene expression and hypothalamic-pituitary-adrenal responses to stress. *Science* 277:1659-1662, 1997.

Meaney, M.J.; Diorio, J.; Francis, D.; Widdownson, J.; Laplante, P.; Caldji, C.; Sharma, S.; Seckl, J.R; and Plotsky, P.M. Early environmental regulation of forebrain glucocorticoid receptor gene expression:

Implications for adrenocortical responses to stress. _Developmental Neuroscience_ 18:49-72, 1996.

Merali, Z.; Mcintosh, J.; Kent, P.; Michaud, D.; and Anisman, H. Aversive as well as appetitive events evoke the release of corticotropin releasing hormone and bombesinlike peptides at the central nucleus of the amygdala. _Journal of Neuroscience_ 18:4758-4766, 1998. 248

Monroe, S.M., and Simons, A.D. Diathesis stress theories in the context of life stress research: Implications for the depressive disorders. _Psychological Bulletin_ 110:406-425, 1991.

Munck, A.; Guyre, P.M.; and Holbrook, N.J. Physiological functions of glucocorticoids in stress and their relation to pharmacological actions. _Endocrine Review_ 5:25-44, 1984.

Nisenbaum, L.K.; Zigmond, M.J.; Sved, A.F.; and Abercrombie, E.D. Prior exposure to chronic stress results in enhanced synthesis and release of hippocampal norepinephrine in response to a novel stressor. _Journal of Neuroscience_ 11:1478-1484, 1991. POST, R.M. Transduction of psychosocial stress into the neurobiology of recurrent affective disorder. _American Journal of Psychiatry_ 149:999-1010, 1992.

Ravinddran, A.V.; Merali, Z.; and Anisman, H. Dysthymia: A biological perspective. In: Licinio, J.; Bolis, C.L.; and Gold, P., eds. _Dysthymia: From Clinical Neuroscience to Treatment_. Washington, DC: World Health Organization, 1997. pp. 21-44.

Sapolsky, R.M.; Krey, L.C.; and McEwen, B.S. The neuroendocrinology of stress and aging: The glucocorticoid cascade hypothesis. _Endocrinology Review_ 7:284-301, 1986.

Schulkin, J.; Gold, P.W.; and McEwen, B.S. Induction of corticotrop in releasing hormone gene expression by glucocorticoids: Implication for understanding the states of fear and anxiety and allostatic load. _Psychoneuroendocrinology_ 23:219-243, 1998.

Seligman, M.E.P. _Helplessness: On Depression, Development and Death_. San Francisco: Freeman Press, 1975.

Shanks, N.; Larocque, S.; and Meaney, N. Neonatal endotoxin exposure alters the development of the hypothalamic-pituitary-adrenal axis: Early illness and later responsivity to stress. *Journal of Neuroscience* 15:376-384, 1995.

Sklar, L.S., and Anisman, H. Stress and cancer. *Psychological Bulletin* 89:369-406, 1981.

Tilders, F.J.H, and Schmidt, E.D. Interleukin1 induced plasticity of hypothalamic CRH neurons and long-term stress hyper-responsiveness. *Annals of the New York Academy of Sciences* 840:65-73, 1998.

Tilders, F.J.H.; Schmidt, E.D.; and De Goeij, D.C.E. Phenotypic plasticity of CRF neurons during stress. *Annals of the New York Academy of Sciences* 697:39-52, 1993.

Viau, V., and Meaney, M.J. Variations in the hypothalamic-pituitary-adrenal response to stress during the estrous cycle in the rat. *Endocrinology* 129:2503-2511, 1991.

Weiss, J.M., and Simson, P.G. Neurochemical mechanisms underlying stressinduced depression. In: Field, T.; McCabe, P.; and Schneiderman, N., eds. *Stress and Coping*. Hillsdale, NJ: Lawrence Erlbaum, 1985. pp. 93-116.

Willner, P. Validity, reliability and utility of the chronic mild stress model of depression: A 10year review and evaluation. *Psychopharmacology* 134: 319-329, 1997.

Zaharia, M.; Kulczycki, J.; Shanks, N.; Meaney, M.J.; and Anisman, H. The effects of early postnatal stimulation on Morris watermaze acquisition in adult mice: Genetic and maternal factors. *Psychopharmacology* 128:227-239, 1996.

Chapter 3

Stress Signals

When the body is under stress, it responds with a particular set of danger signs and symptoms that are caused by malfunctioning of the most vulnerable parts of the body. Many of us don't recognize the warning signs when they occur. Physical and emotional symptoms or certain kinds of behavior can be signs of stress.

These are some but not all the symptoms and signs of stress. How many are you experiencing? Are they interfering with your ability to function at your normal or preferred level? If they are then stress therapy can help relieve these symptoms.

Automatic Nervous System Responses to Stress (The "Fight or Flight" Response)

- Increased heart rate
- Elevation of blood-pressure
- Secretion of adrenaline and other hormones
- Increased muscle tone
- Pupils dilate
- Perspiration increases
- Increase in oxygen uptake
- Mobilization of glucose and fatty acids
- Release of blood coagulants

"Stress," © Barbara Reade, M.S., L.C.P.C., N.C.C. Licensed Clinical Professional Counselor & National Board of Certified Counselor and www.heart-healing.com, reprinted with permission.

Physical Signs of Stress

- Headaches
- Backaches
- Muscle fatigue
- Appetite changes
- Insomnia
- Oversleeping
- Accident proneness
- Exacerbation of present illnesses
- Dryness of mouth
- Stiff neck/shoulders
- Pounding heart
- Hyperventilation
- Fluttering eyelids
- Cold or sweaty hands
- "Butterflies"
- Eye strain
- Teeth grinding
- Indigestion
- Fatigue
- Rashes
- Constipation/diarrhea
- Nervous tics
- Trembling hands
- Frequent urination
- Premenstrual tension or missed menstrual cycles
- Stuttering

Most Common Emotional Problems and/or Disorders Related to Stress

- Alcoholism
- Drug abuse
- Depression
- Suicide
- Marriage/family problems
- Sexual dysfunction
- Neurotic behavior
- Psychosis
- Compulsive behaviors

Physical Disorders Related to Stress

- Coronary heart disease
- Heart attack
- High blood pressure
- Ulcers
- Diabetes
- Allergies
- Eczema
- Asthma
- Chronic Bronchitis
- Colitis
- Arthritis
- Kidney disease
- Sinusitis

Emotional Signs of Stress

- Excessive preoccupation with ideas or people
- Increased absences
- Increased tardiness
- Marked and prolonged indifference in productivity
- Crying episodes
- Sudden angry outbursts
- Mood swings
- Withdrawal
- Isolation from relationships in the work setting
- Inability to concentrate
- Nightmares
- Irritability
- Hyperexcitation
- Impulsive behavior
- Weakness/dizziness
- Disorientation
- Overpowering tendency to run and hide
- Easily startled
- "Floating anxiety" (afraid, but not sure of what)

Chapter 4

The Different Kinds of Stress

Stress management can be complicated and confusing because there are different types of stress—acute stress, episodic acute stress, and chronic stress—each with its own characteristics, symptoms, duration, and treatment approaches. Let's look at each one.

Acute Stress

Acute stress is the most common form of stress. It comes from demands and pressures of the recent past and anticipated demands and pressures of the near future. Acute stress is thrilling and exciting in small doses, but too much is exhausting. A fast run down a challenging ski slope, for example, is exhilarating early in the day. That same ski run late in the day is taxing and wearing. Skiing beyond your limits can lead to falls and broken bones. By the same token, overdoing on short-term stress can lead to psychological distress, tension headaches, upset stomach, and other symptoms.

Fortunately, acute stress symptoms are recognized by most people. It's a laundry list of what has gone awry in their lives: the auto accident that crumpled the car fender, the loss of an important contract, a deadline they're rushing to meet, their child's occasional problems at school, and so on.

Reprinted with permission, "Psychology at Work: The Different Kinds of Stress," Adapted from *The Stress Solution: An Action Plan to Manage the Stress in Your Life* by Lyle H. Miller, Ph.D., and Alma Dell Smith, Ph.D. (Pocket Books, 1993) © 1993.

Because it is short term, acute stress doesn't have enough time to do the extensive damage associated with long-term stress. The most common symptoms are:

- emotional distress—some combination of anger or irritability, anxiety, and depression, the three stress emotions;

- muscular problems including tension headache, back pain, jaw pain, and the muscular tensions that lead to pulled muscles and tendon and ligament problems;

- stomach, gut and bowel problems such as heartburn, acid stomach, flatulence, diarrhea, constipation, and irritable bowel syndrome;

- transient over arousal leads to elevation in blood pressure, rapid heartbeat, sweaty palms, heart palpitations, dizziness, migraine headaches, cold hands or feet, shortness of breath, and chest pain.

Acute stress can crop up in anyone's life, and it is highly treatable and manageable.

Episodic Acute Stress

There are those, however, who suffer acute stress frequently, whose lives are so disordered that they are studies in chaos and crisis. They're always in a rush, but always late. If something can go wrong, it does. They take on too much, have too many irons in the fire, and can't organize the slew of self-inflicted demands and pressures clamoring for their attention. They seem perpetually in the clutches of acute stress.

It is common for people with acute stress reactions to be over aroused, short-tempered, irritable, anxious, and tense. Often, they describe themselves as having "a lot of nervous energy." Always in a hurry, they tend to be abrupt, and sometimes their irritability comes across as hostility. Interpersonal relationships deteriorate rapidly when others respond with real hostility. The work becomes a very stressful place for them.

The cardiac prone, "Type A" personality described by cardiologists, Meyer Friedman and Ray Rosenman, is similar to an extreme case of episodic acute stress. Type A's have an "excessive competitive drive, aggressiveness, impatience, and a harrying sense of time urgency." In addition there is a "free-floating, but well-rationalized form of hostility, and almost always a deep-seated insecurity." Such personality characteristics would seem to create frequent episodes of acute stress for the Type A individual. Friedman and Rosenman found Type A's to be much more likely to develop coronary heart disease than Type B's, who show an opposite pattern of behavior.

Another form of episodic acute stress comes from ceaseless worry. "Worry warts" see disaster around every corner and pessimistically forecast catastrophe in every situation. The world is a dangerous, unrewarding, punitive place where something awful is always about to happen. These "awfulizers" also tend to be over aroused and tense, but are more anxious and depressed than angry and hostile.

The symptoms of episodic acute stress are the symptoms of extended over arousal: persistent tension headaches, migraines, hypertension, chest pain, and heart disease. Treating episodic acute stress requires intervention on a number of levels, generally requiring professional help, which may take many months.

Often, lifestyle and personality issues are so ingrained and habitual with these individuals that they see nothing wrong with the way they conduct their lives. They blame their woes on other people and external events. Frequently, they see their lifestyle, their patterns of interacting with others, and their ways of perceiving the world as part and parcel of who and what they are.

Sufferers can be fiercely resistant to change. Only the promise of relief from pain and discomfort of their symptoms can keep them in treatment and on track in their recovery program.

Chronic Stress

While acute stress can be thrilling and exciting, chronic stress is not. This is the grinding stress that wears people away day after day, year after year. Chronic stress destroys bodies, minds and lives. It wreaks havoc through long-term attrition. It's the stress of poverty, of dysfunctional families, of being trapped in an unhappy marriage or in a despised job or career. It's the stress that the never-ending "troubles" have brought to the people of Northern Ireland, the tensions of the Middle East have brought to the Arab and Jew, and the endless ethnic rivalries that have been brought to the people of Eastern Europe and the former Soviet Union.

Chronic stress comes when a person never sees a way out of a miserable situation. It's the stress of unrelenting demands and pressures for seemingly interminable periods of time. With no hope, the individual gives up searching for solutions.

Some chronic stresses stem from traumatic, early childhood experiences that become internalized and remain forever painful and present. Some experiences profoundly affect personality. A view of the world, or a belief system, is created that causes unending stress for the individual (e.g., the world is a threatening place, people will find out you are a pretender, you must be perfect at all times). When personality or deep-seated convictions and beliefs must be reformulated, recovery requires active self-examination, often with professional help.

The worst aspect of chronic stress is that people get used to it. They forget it's there. People are immediately aware of acute stress because it is new; they ignore chronic stress because it is old, familiar, and sometimes, almost comfortable.

Chronic stress kills through suicide, violence, heart attack, stroke, and, perhaps, even cancer. People wear down to a final, fatal breakdown. Because physical and mental resources are depleted through long-term attrition, the symptoms of chronic stress are difficult to treat and may require extended medical as well as behavioral treatment and stress management.

Chapter 5

Health Risk Assessment

The Purpose of HRAs

Every day, many people mortgage their long-term health with the lifestyle they lead today. Behaviors such as smoking, poor diet, lack of exercise, and not wearing seat belts are among the factors that increase a person's risk of getting sick or dying prematurely. However, general knowledge of these risks does not always change behavior, and people don't necessarily know which of their risks needs the most attention. Health risk assessments (HRAs) provide a scientific way of turning intuitive knowledge into measurable odds.

HRA Components

HRAs have three standard elements:

- A questionnaire
- A computation of risk
- Educational messages and individual risk reports

The questionnaire asks about family history, general health parameters (weight, blood pressure, cholesterol levels, etc.), and lifestyle behaviors (diet, tobacco and alcohol use, safety precautions, etc.).

This chapter includes "About HRAs," "Health Risks," "Introduction," and "Frequently Asked Questions," reprinted with permission from YOU*First*™ Health Risk Assessment, located at www.youfirst.com. © 1997-2000 Greenstone Internet & Health.

An HRA risk computation compares answers to the questionnaire to data gathered from a large general population. Individual risk factors are matched with disease "precursors" such as high-fat diet and sedentary lifestyle which have been measurably associated with disease in the larger population. Every precursor has a numerical "relative risk" for every associated disease which indicates how much that precursor contributes to the disease. A number of diseases have multiple precursors. For example, heart disease can be affected by diet, exercise, and smoking.

Put simply, individual risk reports are based on statistics for the population group that matches the individual's surveyed characteristics. The HRA report generally includes the individual's chronological age; his or her calculated risk age (meaning how old the general population is that matches the individual's health status); a target or achievable age (meaning the age of the general population that has the characteristics the individual could achieve with improvements); and a summary of the person's various health risks and lifestyle behaviors with suggestions on how to reduce risk for disease.

Limitations of HRAs

HRAs are extremely useful for assessing individual and group health risks. However, they are not substitutes for complete medical histories or medical exams. HRAs are also not appropriate for all people. People with chronic illnesses such as cancer or heart disease, for instance, will not obtain accurate risk projections in those areas. Also, some reference population databases exclude information on the very young or elderly, on socio-economically challenged populations, and on some minorities. In these cases, HRAs may not accurately project risks for these groups.

The Role of HRAs in Health Care

HRAs were introduced more than 20 years ago by Lewis C. Robbins, M.D. to help doctors communicate health risks to their patients. Dr. Robbins and Jack Hall, MD published a book for physicians entitled *How to Practice Prospective Medicine* which explained how to create a health risk questionnaire and how to calculate and interpret the results. However, with advancing sophistication of health risk estimation methods, HRA use has become more widespread. A recent U.S. study reported HRA use in as many as 30 percent of workplaces. In the past decade, the number of HRAs has risen from 12 to over 50.

The questions asked by today's HRAs are not noticeably different from those asked 20 years ago, but how the answers are used is different. Today, prospective (preventive) medicine and HRAs play a big role in disease management. In fact, in recent years, large employers, insurance companies, and managed care networks have used HRAs and national health statistics to project and prioritize group risks and plan health intervention programs.

For example, results of an employer's HRAs might indicate that a large number of employees are not physically active and could benefit from an exercise program at lunch. Or, a managed care network might discover that a large percentage of its members have high blood pressure and therefore might decide to develop and promote education information about diet, exercise, and medication options for hypertension. One of the key benefits of HRAs is the identification of high-risk individuals whose health status can be closely monitored.

Individual HRA Use

The last decade has seen increasing use of HRAs in group settings usually for the purpose of assessing group health needs. However, individual use of HRAs, such as the YOU*First*™ Health Assessment, offers truly personalized health education, and possibly the greatest potential for personal health improvement. The individual is in control throughout the entire process. Not only does the individual input his or her own data, he or she receives prompt feedback on their personal health risk. This gives the individual control over the educational aspects of the instrument and provides them with prompt and detailed information about how health risks can be modified with changes in behavior.

Source: KW Peterson and SB Hilles, (Editors): Society of Prospective Medicine. *Handbook of Health Risk Appraisals*, 3rd Edition. 1996, pages 5-29.

Health Risks

Risk factors associated with the leading causes of death include:

- Alcohol use
- Diet
- High blood pressure

- Pap smear
- Protected sexual activity
- Seat belts
- Stress
- Breast/testicular self-examination
- Exercise
- Mammogram
- Prostate screening
- Radon exposure
- Smoke detectors
- Tobacco use—tobacco use is linked to as many as one out of every six deaths in the U.S.

Cigarette smoking is estimated to contribute to 21 percent of all deaths from coronary heart disease and as many as 30 percent of all cancer deaths. Lack of exercise can be tied to coronary heart disease, hypertension, diabetes, osteoporosis, and depression. Colon cancer and stroke incidence also appear to be affected.

Being overweight affects more than a quarter of the U.S. population.

Alcohol is a factor in as many as 50 percent of all homicides, suicides, and deaths by motor vehicle accident.

Sources: *National Center for Health Statistics. Monthly Vital Statistics Report.* 1997:45(11S2); 23, 40-43. U.S. Department of Health and Human Services. *Healthy People 2000.* Conference Edition, pages 57-60.

Personal Health Risk Assessment

Want to add years to your life? A personal health assessment report will help you:

- Learn about current health conditions or habits that may lead to future health problems
- List actions you can take to avoid health problems
- Improve and protect your health
- Strengthen your positive attitude

This Health Risk Assessment is free on the internet at www.youfirst.com.

About the Assessment Results

This individualized health report is comprised of the latest available national statistics about how risk is increased or reduced by personal behavior and preventive care. This Health Risk Assessment includes major factors relating health risk, health promotions, wellness, exercise, nutrition, smoking, alcohol use, weight, cholesterol, blood pressure, back pain, vehicle safety, stress, depression, and cancer.

The report has a reader-friendly format with simple graphs and charts. The information you receive is tailored for you as a function of your stated risks.

About Privacy and Confidentiality

The Health Risk Assessment is offered to you by Greenstone Healthcare Solutions. Your risk information is strictly confidential. Data collected will not be shared except to be combined to produce aggregate or general trend data.

In general, health risk assessments are used by major employers, insurance companies, and managed care organizations to survey certain populations and determine areas of high risk. Companies use the aggregate or combined information from assessments to create beneficial, wellness, promoting programs such as exercise or smoking counseling programs. The idea behind this is that preventive measures may improve health status and lower health care costs.

About the Questionnaire

A survey with approximately 50 questions for men and women will appear on the computer monitor. It takes only 5-10 minutes to complete. Depending on your answers, you may be asked a few follow-up questions. Once you've answered all appropriate questions, click on the "Submit" button to receive your personalized health report. Your health assessment will be calculated and a customized web page containing your results will be built. After reviewing your report, press the "Submit" button. You will then be asked for information that will be used to generate a second report. Review your health assessment, and take note of how you can make each day count toward building a healthier life.

Frequently Asked Questions

1. What is the Health Risk Assessment?

The YOU*First*™com Health Risk Assessment is the Internet's first health risk assessment, created in mid-1996 through collaboration between Greenstone Healthcare Solutions and Occupational Health Strategies. The HRA asks a specific set of questions in order to "map" attitudes and health behaviors that predictively influence health and survival. Once completed, a personal report of HRA results is returned to you in just a few seconds.

2. So, this is more than just a video game?

As it turns out, many people like to know the relationship between their lifestyle decisions (health habits) and the effects that these types of living decisions have upon their quality and quantity of life. This HRA employs a carefully designed set of questions that will allow you to learn the impact that lifestyle habits have upon your survival. Once you have completed the HRA, you'll also receive a "Personal Action Plan" which guides you toward the development of a healthier lifestyle suited to your interests. In most cases, improved health opportunities are a personal choice. No one can decide a "life course of wellness" for you, but the HRA can serve as a mirror and a coach, influencing your next steps toward improved health.

3. Is there anyone that the HRA is not appropriate for?

The internet version HRA is developed for Americans between the ages of 15 years and 74 years of age who do not have life-threatening diseases or conditions. While the HRA is built upon American-based culture and social science, it is being successfully used in other countries as well. The fundamental epidemiology and predictive algorithm of the HRA is rooted in American studies and culture. However, it is being used in several international sites with success.

4. Can people of other nationalities and countries use this HRA?

Within the software are tables of the most common causes of death and equations indicating how various health habits and medical information affects the risk of dying. Individuals from other countries should feel free to try the HRA. In general, the feedback received will still be appropriate.

5. Can youngsters (under age 15) use this HRA?

The "probabilities of death algorithms" do work for younger ages, but the health education messages of the HRA are targeted at adults. The risk of dying for pre-teen individuals is extremely small. If you are a youth, you may want to adjust your birth date to see what will be reported (like if you are smoking now and you want to test how it will shorten your life if you are, say, 25 years old and still smoking). Remember, the purpose of the HRA is to influence the behavior of someone who is older.

6. Can this HRA be used by people age 75 or older?

The "chances of death algorithms" do work for these ages, but the risk of dying in the next 10 years (of anything if you are 75 years old) is much higher than the normal. Still, the messages from the HRA to the "senior web wizards" out there are still powerful in helping you influence your quality, and, to some degree, your quantity of life. We encourage you to try the HRA because there is great learning for you once you've experienced it. Remember though—the best match of the HRA is with persons a little younger than you. Why not recommend it to your 50 and 60-year-old children?

7. How do life-threatening conditions affect my answers?

The equations and health education messages are based on individuals without serious medical diseases and conditions. For example, the risk of dying from heart disease is based on individuals who have not already had a heart attack or stroke. The HRA will underestimate the risk of death for individuals who have life-threatening conditions. It is okay to answer the questionnaire, but you should print and take the report to your medical professional to see how your particular pre-existing condition(s) impacts your risk.

8. Who developed this HRA and what are their credentials?

The YOU*First*™.com HRA is a product from Greenstone Healthcare Solutions, Bridgewater, NJ, a Division of Greenstone Limited, a wholly-owned subsidiary of Pharmacia & Upjohn. Greenstone has secured the services of Occupational Health Strategies, Charlottesville, VA, to assist in the development of this application.

9. What, or who, is Greenstone Healthcare Solutions?

Greenstone is a disease management, analytic, and outcomes company. It had its origins in 1995. Greenstone, like many analytic companies, is a small team made up of medical/professional people who want to understand more about illnesses and the health of individuals. This is why the YOU*First*™.com HRA is so important. It provides a communication channel between Greenstone's professionals and people who are seeking answers to some very important personal questions. As Greenstone's researchers analyze the data available from users, new discoveries about health and wellness become available. These discoveries have found their way into new educational messages for the public, improvements in subsequent HRA products, further research in community and employee health, and accelerated development of new medical education aimed at promoting and preserving the public health well being.

10. Why is the HRA being offered for free?

After many years on the Internet, the HRA has made a difference in the lives of people. This is evident from the e-mails received each week from users of the HRA. The Internet has many rules that guide its products and their use. One of those rules is that tools, software, applications, or health risk assessments must be widely used in order to be useful, valuable to the web community.

11. I am a little anxious about a pharmaceutical company getting access to a piece of my personal medical information. How can I be sure that my participation will not be exploited?

Greenstone keeps your data in a special, protected place, available to only a few Greenstone team members. Your answers are scrambled, making them into complex coded bits. This protects them from being readable. In addition, your name and any other personal identifiable information you send is encrypted. Your privacy and security is important. Greenstone voluntarily adheres to the Federal Guidelines regulating data transfer, storage, and analysis and has secured the best technology available for encryption and secure data transmission. Security processes are audited regularly by an outside agency to assure that we are aware of opportunities to improve our security procedures and technologies. You are in charge of the information you pass over to us. To summarize the key security points:

- YOU*First*™.com & Greenstone respect your privacy and value your trust.

- Providing a private and secure environment is our top priority.

- All data that you submit is held entirely in confidence.

- Your personal information and identity will never be released to anyone without your explicit permission.

- We do not sell, rent, or barter mailing lists of our users.

- We utilize industry standard methods for encryption and security to ensure that no unauthorized person can access your data. Remember, the HRA can serve as a regular "wellness coach," assisting you with your lifestyle. Once you have completed the HRA, information will be stored and available at your next visit. By storing your information, you can compare your scores between visits and realize the difference your lifestyle decisions and actions are having upon your health and survival.

12. How often can I complete the HRA?

There are two answers to this question. The quick answer is "Come back and take the HRA anytime you like." The longer answer is "In light of the fact that it takes several months for new lifestyle changes to affect the mind and body (as such relate to living longer), we recommend taking the HRA about every three months." Many people use the HRA as a "self-report card." The best answer is "Use the HRA as often as you have a need for it."

13. Once I "submit" my completed HRA to Greenstone, where does it go?

Once you send your completed questionnaire, it moves at great speed over secure lines to computers that quickly calculate your personalized report. A copy of your report is kept in a secure file with Greenstone and another is sent back to you within seconds. You can save this report to a disk, print it to paper copy, or read it and erase it. An increasing number of users are e-mailing or sending a copy to their physicians and other members of their health support team, asking that the report become part of their health record.

14. Some questions are very personal. Do all these areas relate to my health, longevity, and survival?

In developing the HRA, a holistic approach was taken, tying the mind, body, and spirit together. Emotions and moods affect health, so we would be less than honest with you if we asked questions about high blood pressure and neglected the questions about stress, as an example. The added advantage of the HRA is that it is private and you do not need to rush through the process. This tool was designed to enable you to make well-informed decisions. You can choose to chart a course of action and promote a better lifestyle for yourself.

15. The HRA does not seem to take into account some really important areas such as my ethnic group, my geographic location, my work site exposures, and my economic status.

There is a trade-off between increasing the number of questions that are asked and the willingness of individuals to complete a questionnaire. This HRA contains the minimal number of questions that can accurately predict a person's health risk. In order to have a short questionnaire that could be completed in minutes, questions were picked that focused on the health behaviors under the individual's control that contributed the most to the leading causes of disease and death.

16. With whom can I discuss this information?

The HRA is a questionnaire designed to provide you with personal awareness of your current health status. The best people to talk with about your results are your health care provider and your significant other, family, and circle of friends. Your health care provider can assist you in developing a wellness plan that will help you reduce your level of risk for a particular health problem. When you are ready to take action and change your health behaviors, it will affect everyone in your social environment. For most people, this would include your immediate family members, your friends, and coworkers. People engaging in change need social support to cope with the stresses of behavior change.

17. Where can I get additional health information?

There are several links to health information on the Internet. Healthcare professionals have carefully assessed the Internet sites for their accuracy of information and quality of presentation. Your local public health department, community health agencies, such as the American Heart Association, your area hospital, and your local library can provide you with additional information. The materials are often free. Searching local web addresses, your Chamber of Commerce's web site, the web white and yellow pages are also options for you. Remember though, the information gathered from the web, like any source of information, must be studied closely and validated by you. The content provided you from any web site might not be perfectly suited to your situation. If in doubt about the quality of what you receive at health sites on the web, check with your health professional. Physicians, nurses, and allied health professionals are becoming increasingly active in evaluating web content for your use. Your health professional may already have a list of recommended web sites for you to visit.

18. What assistance is available to help me change my lifestyle's health behavior?

To make a successful personal health behavior change you will need to draw on your own inner strength. Identify individuals in your social environment that can provide the motivation and encouragement you need to successfully meet these challenges. The change process also includes gaining new knowledge. Pay special attention to the "Readiness to Change" questions which follow the initial questionnaire. Your answers to this part of the HRA will guide your lifestyle-change plans significantly.

19. Do you have recommendations about nutritional requirements for the elderly, or information about other specific programs?

The respondents to the HRA are people who, like you, are seeking ways to be healthier. We are often asked for information on specific weight-management, smoking cessation, and stress reduction programs. As healthcare professionals, we are excited that people are looking for answers, but it is not possible for us to have recommendations for the large variety of programs available. Nutritional requirements for anyone at any age or activity level are very individualized. We caution you to be very careful in self-administering so called "natural remedies." There is little scientific evidence for these "therapies" in many cases. As a healthcare consumer, it is important to gather as much information as possible to assess what is best for you. Once you have gathered information, it is important to discuss your health concerns with your healthcare provider. Together you can decide which program is best for you.

20. What theories or models are the foundations for facilitating lifestyle change in the "YOUFirst™ Health Risk Assessment?

The theories or models that establish the foundations for facilitating behavior change in the Health Risk Assessment include the "Behavior Change Theory" as developed and researched by James Prochaska, PhD and Carlo DiClemente, PhD. This model identifies the different stages of readiness to change: precontemplation, contemplation, preparation, action, and maintenance. For this Health Risk Assessment, tailored behavior-change messages are provided for people in the precontemplation, contemplation, and preparation stages. Another theory incorporated into the Health Risk Assessment is the "Health Belief Model." The "Health Belief Model" is based on motivational theory to include an individual's perceptions, modifying factors, and variables likely to affect the behavior change. Individual's perceptions include: perceived susceptibility (i.e., risk factors, family history); perceived seriousness (How much will I be damaged if I don't pay attention?); and, perceived threat—a combination of susceptibility and seriousness. The other theory used in the Health Risk Assessment is the "Adult Learning Theory." Behavior change always involves learning something new—new knowledge; new understanding; new attitudes; new skills; and new values.

21. Where can I find a specific learning aid to help me in my behavior change process?

If you are in the pre-contemplation or contemplation stage, there are specific techniques that can help you move to the next stage of readiness in successfully changing your behaviors. Consciousness-raising enables a person to gain more information about the health problem. Reading a book, searching the web, reading a health magazine, or viewing a video will reveal new knowledge about the health problem. Self re-evaluation is a technique important to the contemplation and preparation stages of readiness to change. This includes your thoughts and emotions that you associate with the "old" health problem or behavior. Feeling bad about not exercising and continuing to gain weight is an example. An important aspect of re-evaluation is establishing your goals for what will happen after you change the behavior. This is an important stage where getting the new sneakers, sports outfit, or exercise equipment may enhance your self-image and provide motivation to move to the action stage of readiness to change. Self-liberation involves thoughts you have that promote your inner belief that you have the ability to make the behavior change. Telling yourself that you do not need a morning cigarette with your coffee is an example of self-liberation. Self-liberation is most valued during the preparation and action stages of readiness to change. It is related to your self-concept and self-esteem. It is believing that you can make the change and successfully overcome barriers in your environment. A dedicated notebook for your action plan would be valuable at this stage. Attractive paper to print and post your affirmations may also be helpful. An air purifier might encourage you in your efforts toward quitting smoking. A health scale that records your weight and proportionate body fat would be a declaration of your commitment to losing weight. Some relaxing music on a CD or cassette tape might be just the thing if you're focusing on reducing stress in your life.

22. Is it also important to provide yourself with rewards after obtaining your short-term goals?

Remember that contract you set-up for yourself? If I do this, then I'll award myself with that! This could be a new CD, new cosmetics, some bubble bath or fragrant soap, a night off watching Monday Night Football—something that would make you feel good. Remember to also show your appreciation for those supportive people around you.

23. I am an employer. Can this HRA improve the health of my employees and thereby, my company's productivity?

The HRA brings to the surface behaviors that can be linked to important utilization, absenteeism, safety, productivity, and workplace morale issues. It can be used as part of an employee benefit, workplace fitness package, or corporate health education curriculum. Greenstone Healthcare Solutions will fashion executive reports for the employer and provide detailed analyses of the data at the employee aggregate level. Greenstone will not provide personally identifiable healthcare data as supplied by participating employees. In many cases, the HRA has provided direction for prioritizing employer benefit programs, health benefit strategies, and overall corporate wellness.

24. Is there a conversion scale for international data (e.g., millimoles, stones)?

There is a conversion scale for many different international data types. We will research and post conversions in response to questions from our users.

25. A Cholesterol Example: I have the results of my Cholesterol, but it is in Canadian numbers that the questionnaire will not accept, so I have to answer "I don't know." I am sure a lot of us Canadians would like to answer that question properly. Is there somewhere we can find a table of equivalence for cholesterol?

Cholesterol is measured by various techniques throughout the world. In Canada they use mmol (millimoles) as a unit of measurement. If your results are between 4 and 6 then this is the method that we need to convert to. Multiply your result by 38.76—this translates to U.S. units of mg/dl. If your units are not mmol or if your results are vastly different from 4 to 6 (Cholesterol) then there is another approach. Most people may not remember their actual cholesterol results, but they do remember generally how their results compare to others. Here are reference numbers for you.

Cholesterol United States range of results:

- Good Less than 180
- Borderline 180 - 219
- Slightly high 220 - 239
- High 240 - 259
- Very High 260 or higher

For HDL:

- Low Less than 35
- Average 35 - 49
- Good 50 - 59
- Very good 60 or higher

Part Two

Environmental Stress

Chapter 6

Family Stress

What Is Family Stress?

Stress has become a common word as people learn to recognize and control the pressures in their lives. Men and women work long hours to support their families, meet work demands and career goals, and to gain a sense of personal satisfaction. When parents work, there is often little time for personal and family leisure.

Even though we usually think of stress as affecting only individuals, it is possible for an entire family to be affected by stress. How can you tell if your family is under stress? Some signs are family members becoming withdrawn or irritable and relationships between them may be unpleasant or argumentative. Family stress is the tension that arises from demands or pressures (stressors) on the family to change. These demands include a move to a new home, a job change, a child starting school, as well as other reasons. These periods are marked by feelings of uncertainty, loss, and anxiety as family members learn to cope with the changes.

One reason entire families experience stress is because the lives of family members are intertwined and a problem in one person's life affects the others. For example, a person who works long hours and has many work deadlines may carry home his or her tension. Unresolved,

"Stress Management: Strategies for Families," by Suzanna Smith and Joe Pergola, © 1999 University of Florida, Institute of Food and Agricultural Sciences (UF/IFAS), Fact Sheet FCS 2078, reprinted with permission.

this tension may spread to other family members, possibly creating misunderstandings and arguments.

At the same time, many couples are rethinking traditional ways men and women care for the home and children, which may be stressful itself.

Family stress also occurs when an entire family is affected by a transition, such as marriage, parenthood, a child going off to college, and middle age. For example, a new baby is a normal family stressor that often results in sleepless nights, less time together for the couple, and a new role for an older brother or sister. Everyone in this family is forced to change to adjust to the new child. Other transitions require more dramatic changes. A divorce changes the entire family's financial resources, parental roles, emotional and communication patterns.

People are often surprised when they experience stress from expected or positive events. They usually don't expect and plan for the changes all family members will have to make. Yet, like negative events, positive events create stress because they require the family to change.

In this chapter, we focus on the stress families face at different stages in their development. We then turn to how families can best cope with the many changes they experience throughout their lives.

Stress and Family Development

The needs of individuals and families change over the course of the life cycle as persons grow up, establish families, rear and launch their children, experience an empty nest period, and reach the ends of their lives.

Family Life-Cycle Stages

Family life-cycle stages are often defined by the age of the oldest child, because this child usually introduces the family to a new series of developmental changes.

1. Couples—Couples are usually concerned with developing and negotiating individual and family goals and lifestyles. These families do not have children.

2. Preschool—In these families children have not yet entered school. The family is oriented toward the child's growth and development.

3. School Age—The oldest child is between 6 and 12 years of age and has entered school. The family becomes more focused on socialization and education.

4. Adolescent—The family now has a teenager, and much attention goes toward dealing with his or her, as well as the family's changes. At the same time, the family is preparing the adolescent to leave home.

5. Launching—Young adults begin to leave home to establish identities and roles outside the family unit. Parental roles and rules change and the family is occupied with successfully launching its children.

6. Empty Nest—Families are defined by the absence of children in the home. Parents still hold former roles as employees, volunteers, and homemakers, but the family is oriented toward the couple's needs and establishing different relationships with children and grandchildren.

7. Retirement and Aging—Working family members have retired. Residential changes may be made necessary by illness, frailty, or the death of a spouse. Parenting and grandparenting roles continue.

Family Stressors

Many life events are expected such as the birth of a child or retirement. Other events are unexpected and sudden, such as divorce or the death of a child. These events, called stressors, have the potential to change your family.

The following common demands may cause family stress at all stages of the life cycle.

- Emotional problems
- Sexual difficulties
- Economic strains
- Job changes
- Physical losses
- Things that just don't get done

Some stressors and strains have a noticeably greater impact on families at certain points in the family life cycle. For instance, some research has found that financial strains are most problematic for families with young children and adolescents, and for people entering retirement.

Strains and struggles between family members are most common when children are in elementary and high school, perhaps because of new or increased demands such as children's outside activities, chores that don't get done, and difficulty communicating with adolescents. These struggles often occur at a time when parents, particularly fathers, are developing careers and are frequently away from home. This may place additional strains on working mothers who must manage many responsibilities without another adult's assistance. In fact, work-family strains are most common during the school-age years, when adults experience the pressures of job changes and promotions while trying to keep up with their children's many activities.

When Stressors Pile Up

These families may be experiencing a type of stressor some researchers call pile up. This can refer to the accumulation of unfinished tasks, such as needed auto repairs, unfinished spring cleaning and household repairs, and unpaid bills. These incomplete tasks seem to hang over families and create strain and tension.

When demands pile up, it may be difficult to pinpoint the source of stress, making stress hard to resolve. This leads to more tension and frustration that may result in family arguments, but without anyone understanding why.

Pile-Up Case Scenario

Doug and Cheryl found themselves arguing on Wednesday and Thursday about things that happened days earlier. After some thought they realized that during the week a number of chores didn't get done because of work, school, and family schedules. Laundry piled up, the lawn didn't get mowed, and needed household supplies weren't purchased. During the weekend Doug, Cheryl, and their children made a frantic effort to catch up on cleaning and other tasks. This left little time to do the things they enjoyed together as a family, or for personal recreation. Tension mounted, and by midweek, resulted in conflict.

Some studies have found that the pile-up of strains is most common during the years a family has an adolescent at home and then launches him or her into a life apart from the family. These couples may also be coping with the loss of a parent, or questioning the meaning or importance of their jobs. Many studies have found that couples experience lower levels of marital satisfaction during the periods of the life cycle when they are rearing and launching children, but that following an adjustment to children leaving home, couples find renewed satisfaction with marriage.

How Families Cope with Stress

Some families are able to recover from stress and even grow stronger, while others seem to have a great deal of trouble healing. How do families cope successfully with stress? Experts believe that a family's ability to adjust to stressful situations depends a great deal on family resources and strengths, and family outlook on the world and on their situation.

Family Resources

The word resources usually brings to mind money and material goods, such as a car, house, tools, clothes, and other belongings. Money and material possessions are, of course, important and may help people solve some of their problems or ease their burdens. For example, having a car for transportation when a child is sick or the money to provide nursing care for an ailing relative are valuable resources. There are other, non-economic resources that enable families to cope. These personal, family, and community resources are powerful tools in preventing or managing stress.

Physical and Psychological Health

The physical and psychological resources of each family member affect the entire family. Physically fit and healthy people find it easier to manage stress than those who are unhealthy. Research indicates that personal health practices such as weight control and exercise also contribute to a family member's ability to cope with stress.

People who are confident, optimistic, and have high self-esteem handle stress better than those who are unsure and have low self-esteem. People who feel they can take charge of difficult situations and are assertive handle many types of stress better than those who believe they are powerless to change things.

Similarly, families that feel confident and in control seem to respond effectively to stress. This does not mean they are rigid or suppress individual members' feelings or ideas. Instead, these families are flexible and adaptable to change. Family members are respected as individuals and are encouraged to develop many different intellectual and physical abilities as well as practical skills. These help them prevent or reduce their own stress before it becomes a problem for other family members, and to use their resources for problem solving in difficult or crisis times.

Some studies have found that psychological health-promoting behaviors are used most often by families in the empty nest period of the life cycle. This may be because couples without children at home have more time for shared leisure activities, have reached a comfortable level of financial stability, and are confident about their accomplishments. Families with preschoolers also seem to score high on psychological health-promotion, while childless couples score high on physical exercise. School-age and launching families spend less time on physical exercise and score lower on psychological health-promotion, although these families in particular might benefit from the stress-reducing effects of exercise, optimism, and lifestyle balance.

Communication

Families who are able to cope effectively with stress seem to have a problem-solving style based on affirming communication. These families talk things through calmly until they reach a solution. They respect other family members' feelings, taking care not to hurt each other and taking time to hear what each person has to say. These families end conflict on a positive note.

The opposite type of communication style is discouraging communication, which tends to inflame the situation. Not talking things through, yelling and screaming, fighting and bringing up old problems, and walking away from conflicts make problems worse, especially if this communication continues.

Some studies have found that the discouraging communication style may be more prevalent during the school-age and adolescent years of the life cycle, and may increase during crises. This may be a result of the many pressures and changes during these periods and difficulty making time for family communication. Affirming communication seems to be prevalent among preschool families. Throughout the life cycle, there are opportunities to learn and practice affirming communication, which is a vital family resource for coping with stress and maintaining family strength.

This is not to say that families with good communication skills don't have conflict, they do. But they practice effective ways of handling conflict.

Basic Steps to Effective Conflict Management

- Be calm. This makes it easier to discuss a problem.

- Define your feelings, needs, and what you would like to change.

- Communicate your needs by saying how you feel and what your needs are. Avoid blame.

- Listen carefully and attentively to the other person's point of view, respect their feelings. Be open-minded—don't argue mentally.

- Brainstorm. When you are ready to look at alternatives, come up with as many solutions as possible.

- Evaluate alternatives. Go over suggestions. Come up with a plan everyone involved can accept.

- Try out a plan. Practice the solution. Keep up your end of the agreement. Be positive and optimistic.

- Reevaluate. After a week or two, assess how the plan worked. Make any needed adjustments. Try out the new plan.

Social and Spiritual Support

Another resource that influences how families respond to stress is the social support they receive from friends, neighbors, and relatives. One of the most important types of social support is psychological support, which provides a person with feelings of being cared about, valued, and admired as an individual, and of belonging to a network of people who are committed to one another. Members of a support network help solve problems before they become difficult to handle, and provide emotional support to deal with events that create stress.

In difficult times, being cared about may actually protect us from the negative impact of stress on physical health. Families experiencing stress associated with life-cycle changes might especially benefit from the positive effects of social support. While families at the preschool and empty nest stages of the life cycle report high levels of social support, families in the school-age and launching years report lower levels of support, even though these years are stressful in many ways.

In addition to friends, neighbors, and family, there are community resources that provide support. These include religious organizations, volunteer groups, parent groups and classes, and social services. These groups provide informational support, knowledge and skills that help people manage their lives, and practical support with food, shelter, and financial aid. They may provide referral support to physicians, counselors, and community agencies. Spiritual support is an important resource for many families. Religious beliefs help a person maintain individual self-esteem and guide these families through stressful situations.

Family Outlook

Another factor that determines the degree of stress is family outlook. While one family sees a situation as a problem, another family may see the same situation as a challenge. There are no right or wrong ways of looking at events, but the way you look at a situation influences how you react and handle stress. In fact, your outlook may be more important than the events themselves in determining how able you are to handle stress effectively and how much stress you experience. The following example illustrates the importance of how families define a stressor event.

Defining a Stressful Event

Tom learns that he is going to be laid off from his job. Tom and his family may define the situation as an opportunity for him to go back to school and retrain for a new job in computer science. Tom has always been intrigued by computers but never had the time to pursue his interest. His family realizes that the long-term employment prospects are far better for Tom in computer science than in his old field. If this is the case, the present hardships associated with being laid off will have a considerably different effect on Tom and his family than if the family blames him personally for losing his job and holds him responsible for the resulting hardships.

One of the most important ways families can adjust positively to stress is to take a long-term view of stressful events and problems. Believing that in the long run problems will work out seems to help families endure daily hassles and major events. Long-term family rewards are seen as outweighing the short-term problems.

Another effective way of adjusting is to reframe the situation. Reframing redefines the meaning of a stressful event in a way that makes it more rational and manageable. Reframing is seeing the good in the bad, or optimistically creating challenges from obstacles. Another approach is to sit back and wait out a crisis or a problem. This usually is used when family members see themselves as only able to tolerate but not to master a difficult situation. Although this strategy is frequently used at later stages of the life cycle, it is not as effective at reducing or managing stress as reframing or seeking support.

Managing the Effects of Stress

In most situations, learning to cope with daily stressors and pile-up or demands will help families adjust. The experience of responding successfully to demands may even help some families grow closer. In some cases, however, it may be better for families to make a radical change rather than to adjust. It may be better for a woman who is abused by her husband to leave home with her children and enter a spouse abuse shelter than to learn to tolerate the abuse. It may be best for a family with a failing business to sell the business rather than to sink further into debt. Even though these changes would be disruptive at first, a complete change may be better in the long run.

There are ways you and your family can increase your abilities to prevent and respond to stress. Following are some of the most effective ways to build resistance to stress and to develop effective coping skills.

- Prevent and recognize your own stress before it has a negative impact on you or your family. Your personal experience of stress affects family stress. Healthy lifestyle behaviors have a major impact on your ability to withstand stress. These include getting regular exercise; eating nutritious foods; limiting your drinking of alcoholic beverages, if you do drink; taking precautions in use of prescription and over-the-counter drugs; practicing stress reduction techniques; and taking safety precautions.

- Practice new skills and stay flexible. One way you can increase your ability to cope with stress is to take stock of your organizational skills and abilities and make a conscious effort to learn new skills. Other ways to increase family flexibility are planning new experiences, rotating responsibilities for chores, and inviting new people to dinner. These new experiences will increase your ability to adapt whenever stressors require changes in your family.

- Recognize life events and transitions that may have caused stress. What events or transitions have you experienced in the last year? What are the daily strains your family experiences? Are strains and tasks piling up? What symptoms of stress have you noticed? Remember, although your answers to these questions may provide useful clues in identifying possible sources of stress, your family's or individual reaction to events depends to a great extent on your resources.

- Support other family members and find sources of support for yourself. Think about the people you confide in most and depend on first for emotional support. Think about the people who are not as close but still might be helpful to you. Do you feel satisfied with your support network? Do you feel you have people you can count on for help? Do you need or want to strengthen some friendships? If you want to strengthen your support network extend your friendship and support. Call a lonely neighbor or have coffee with a friend. Accept others' offers of help.

- Develop family communication skills that will improve your understanding of each other and your ability to work together to solve problems.

- Practice looking at difficulties and problems in a positive light. Turn the tables on stress and find positive, effective ways to cope with challenges.

References

Glick, P.C. (1989). The family life cycle and social change. *Family Relations*, 38, 123-129.

Grimes, S., Cockrel, J., and Quick, S. (1989). *Dealing Creatively with Conflict*. Lexington, KY: College of Agriculture, Cooperative Extension Service (H.E. 1-320).

Hansen, G. (1987). *Understanding Family Stress*. Lexington, KY: College of Agriculture, Cooperative Extension Service (H.E. 7-131).

Family Stress

Hansen, G. (1987). *Coping with Family Stress*. Lexington, KY: College of Agriculture, Cooperative Extension Service (H.E. 7-132).

Hughes, R. (1986). *Parenting on Your Own*. University of Illinois at Urbana-Champaign, College of Agriculture, Cooperative Extension Service (Circular 1248).

McCubbin, H.I., and Thompson, A.I. (1989). *Balancing Work and Family Life on Wall Street*. Edina, MN: Burgess International Group.

Olson, D.H., and McCubbin, H.I. (1983). *Families: What Makes Them Work?* Beverly Hills: Sage Publications.

Smith, C. (1986). *Friends Indeed: A Course in Helping*. Manhattan, KS: Cooperative Extension Service (MF-806).

67

Chapter 7

Resilience in Children

In the face of serious life stresses, such as exposure to violence and crime, living in extreme poverty, or parents' divorce, illness, or death, many children develop behavioral, psychological, and physical difficulties. Other children, referred to as "resilient," defy expectation by developing into well-adapted individuals despite these serious stresses.[1] In a society where children increasingly are exposed to many of these extreme stresses it is vital to promote the factors that build resilience in all children.

What Is Resilience?

Resilience is an ability to overcome adversity, survive stress, and recover from disadvantage.[2] Even when faced with profound disadvantages, such as the ones listed above, resilient children "beat the odds" by achieving school success and developing social and cognitive competence, a positive self-concept, an optimistic outlook, and a responsible, achievement-oriented attitude.[3] In the most disadvantaged environments, it can require resilience to avoid severe delinquency and mental illness.[4] Thus, defining resilience depends somewhat upon individual circumstances. However, the factors that

"Strong Under Stress, Factors in the Development of Resilience in Children," by Lisa M. Powell, © 1999 Yale Law School, Connecticut Voices for Children, reprinted with permission; and "Childhood Losses Affect Adult Health," by Karen Hines © 1998 *Inside DUMC* December 21, 1998, Vol 7 Number 25, Duke University Medical Center Office of Publications, reprinted with permission.

promote resilience across a variety of situations can be delineated more clearly.

Researchers have identified three important categories of factors that protect children against stress. The first are children's dispositional attributes, such as intelligence, temperament, self-esteem, and social adeptness.[5] All of these qualities buffer children from the effects of life stresses. Interventions that enhance these natural qualities (such as Head Start programs), which may strengthen children's self-esteem and intellectual and social skills, can promote resilience in children at-risk.[6]

The other two factors—the child's relationships with parents and other family members and the social support available to the child and family—emphasize the importance of the presence of caring adults in the lives of the children.[7] The stable presence of at least one caring adult throughout childhood appears to be necessary for the development of resilience in all children, even those exposed to the more routine stresses associated with growing up. Public policy can be used to promote the presence of caring adults in children's lives.

The Importance of the Family

Studies have consistently emphasized the central role of the family in promoting psychological well-being, reducing problem behavior, and in buffering the effects of stress on children.[8] A positive home environment is associated with numerous positive outcomes, including lower levels of juvenile crime, mental illness, and substance abuse, as well as greater school achievement, social competence, and better health outcomes.[9]

Many factors contribute to a positive home environment. The most important factors relate to family relationships. Children are influenced by the quality of their relationships with their parents, much more than their parents' status in terms of occupation, income, and other socio-demographic variables.[10] Family characteristics that foster resilience include:

- A strong bond between the child and primary caretaker during infancy

- Respect for the child's individuality and autonomy

- A consistent relationship, throughout childhood, between the child and at least one primary caregiver that is characterized by high levels of warmth, affection, and emotional support, and the absence of severe criticism

- Identifying and reinforcing children's strengths by communication of realistic appreciation and encouragement

- Good parental supervision, with clear rules and balanced discipline.[11]

Parental Employment

In general, employment of both parents outside the home has no significant negative effects on the development of resilience in children. Maternal employment can be linked to better educational achievement and social adjustment in children, as well as competence and independence in female children.[12] However, excessive time in day care and placement in childcare of low quality is associated with poorer parent-child attachment, more problem behaviors, weaker language skills, and lower school readiness scores in children. The most important factors to the development of resilience when both parents are employed are the availability and affordability of high-quality childcare and parents' attitudes towards working while raising young children.[13]

Parental Absence

The absence of a parent from the family often has negative effects on the development of resilience in children. Children raised with a single parent are likely to be poorer, receive less parental supervision, and move more frequently (limiting their connections to external social supports) than children raised by both parents. Research shows that children from single-parent households suffer negative effects across a variety of outcomes. Children from single parent families are more likely to become pregnant as teenagers, develop serious mental health problems in adolescence, have behavioral problems in school including fighting and hyperactivity, drop out of school, and abuse illegal substances as teenagers. These effects persist even when controlling for family income.[14] When a parent is absent from the home, the presence of other caring adults in the child's life becomes more critical; these adults must receive support to properly fulfill their roles.

The Importance of External Support

For children, external support means access to caring adults whom they trust and in whom they can confide. Contact and connections with supportive persons and networks beyond the family can foster resilience. These persons and networks often include grandparents or other relatives, childcare workers, older friends, coaches, religious leaders, mentors, teachers, neighbors, and others.[15] External support networks may foster resilience in children by offering consistent and unconditional acceptance, advice, encouragement, and even financial support.[16] Children who rely on well-developed and accessible social support systems fare better when faced with stressful life situations. Where there is family discord, an external network of caring adults is especially important to buffer the effects of family problems.

Conclusion

Taken together, a child's dispositional attributes, family atmosphere, and network of external support can result in positive adaptation to common or severe life stresses. Ensuring that all children have access to the stable presence of caring adults in their lives is vital for healthy development. Caring adults, most notably a child's parents, need support from communities, corporations, and government to fulfill their roles in children's lives.

Notations

1. Luthar & Zigler, 1991.
2. Hauser et al., 1989.
3. Luthar & Zigler, 1991.
4. Werner & Smith, 1989.
5. Luthar & Zigler, 1991; Herrenkohl, Herrenkohl, & Egolf, 1994; Brooks, 1994.
6. Luthar & Zigler, 1991.
7. Garmezy, 1985; Gruendel & Anderson, 1995.
8. For example: Gore & Aseltine, 1995; Wills & Cleary, 1996; and Luthar & Zigler, 1991.
9. Wills & Cleary, 1996; Rolf et al., 1990; Hauser et al., 1989.
10. Luthar & Zigler, 1991.
11. Gruendel & Anderson, 1995; Brooks, 1994; Schwartz et al., 1989.
12. For example: Werner & Smith, 1989.
13. NICHD Study of Early Child Care, 1998.
14. McLanahan, 1997.

15. Luthar & Zigler, 1991; Gruendel & Anderson, 1995.
16. Gruendel & Anderson, 1995.

References

Brooks RB. (1994). Children at risk: Fostering resilience and hope, *American Journal of Orthopsychiatry*, 64, 545-53.

Garmezy N. (1985). Stress-resistant children: The search for protective factors. In JE Stevenson (Ed.), *Recent Research in Developmental Psychopathology*, Oxford: Pergamon Press.

Gore S and Aseltine RH. (1995). Protective processes in adolescence: matching stressors with social resources, *American Journal of Community Psychology*, 23, 301-27.

Gruendel JM and Anderson, GR. (1995). Building child- and family-responsive support systems. Chapter 10 in S Geballe, JM Gruendel, and W Andiman (Eds.), *Forgotten Children of the AIDS Epidemic*, New Haven: Yale University Press.

Hauser ST, Vieyra MA, Jacobson AM, & Wertlieb D. (1989). Family aspects of vulnerability and resilience in adolescence: A theoretical perspective. Chapter 6 in TF Dugan and R Coles (Eds.), *The Child in our Times: Studies in the Development of Resilience*, New York: Brunner/Mazel, Inc.

Herrenkohl EC, Herrenkohl RC, and Egolf B. (1994). Resilient early school-age children from maltreating homes: Outcomes in late adolescence, *American Journal of Orthopsychiatry*, 64, 301-09.

Luthar SS and Zigler E. (1991). Vulnerability and competence: A review of research on resilience in childhood, *American Journal of Orthopsychiatry*, 61, 6-22.

McLanahan SS. (1997). Parent absence or poverty: Which matters more? Chapter 3 in GJ Duncan and J Brooks-Gunn (Eds.), *The Consequences of Growing Up Poor*, New York: Russell Sage Foundation.

The NICHD Study of Early Child Care. National Institute of Child Health and Human Development. U.S. Department of Health and Human Services, Public Health Service, National Institutes of Health. NIH Pub. No. 98-4318.

Rolf JE, Masten AS, Cicchetti D, Nuechterlein KH, and Weintraub S, Eds. (1990). *Risk and Protective Factors in the Development of Psychopathology*. New York: Cambridge University Press.

Schwartz JM, Jacobson AM, Hauser ST, and Dornbush BB. (1989). Explorations of vulnerability and resilience: Case studies of diabetic adolescents and their families. Chapter 7 in TF Dugan and R Coles (Eds.), *The Child in our Times: Studies in the Development of Resilience*, New York: Brunner/Mazel, Inc.

Werner EE and Smith RS. (1989). *Vulnerable but Invincible: A Longitudinal Study of Resilient Children and Youth*. New York: Adams, Bannister, Cox.

Wills TA and Cleary SD. (1996). How are social support effects mediated? A test with parental support and adolescent substance use, *Journal of Personality and Social Psychology*, 71, 937-52.

Childhood Losses Affect Adult Health

Children who lose a parent or grow up with poor quality family relationships face a greater risk as adults for health problems such as heart disease, according to a Duke University Medical Center study.

A study of young adults' reaction to stressful situations showed that those who had a parent die when they were a youngster and those who reported poor relationships with family members had higher blood pressure and disrupted stress hormone response, said Linda Luecken, PhD, primary investigator for the study done through Duke's behavioral medicine program. The study appears in the Nov. 23, 1998 issue of *Psychosomatic Medicine*. Chronic high blood pressures and elevated stress hormone levels have been linked to heart disease and other illnesses.

"This provides evidence that the parent-child relationship can have important impact on mental and physical health, and that poor relationships within the family can have serious long-term effects on health," said Luecken, who conducted the study at Duke but is now at the University of Vermont.

In the study of 61 college students, the participants' blood pressure and cortisol levels were monitored during two tasks intended to induce stress. Thirty of the students had lost a parent before reaching age 16, and 31 students had not experienced a parent's death. All participants were surveyed to determine the perceived quality of their family relationships while growing up. The blood pressure of all the students jumped while performing the first task, giving a three-minute speech with only 30 seconds for preparation. However, those who had lost a parent and those who had poor family relationships had significantly higher blood pressure at all time periods during the study.

Poor family relationships, Luecken said, were characterized as those involving a lot of conflict or arguing, not getting along well with family members, the lack of encouragement to express feelings, and feelings of a lack of support. The incidence of reported poor family relationship (poor FR) was about the same in both groups of study participants, indicating that losing a parent doesn't imply a poor family environment, Luecken said. In the second task, the students were asked to watch a portion of a movie, "Terms of Endearment," that depicts children experiencing the death of a parent. Again, the blood pressure of loss subjects and those with poor FR was consistently higher than the blood pressure of subjects without loss who had good family relationships.

But researchers found a different type of response in cortisol, or stress hormone, levels. They initially expected to find high cortisol levels in the loss and poor FR groups, and low levels in the non-loss group. But instead, they found that cortisol levels were initially lower and increased during the tasks for loss subjects and those with poor FR, while others showed initially higher levels that decreased during the study.

"Increased levels of cortisol can be an adaptive response to stress, and in this case, it is appropriate to experience stress at the onset of such a task," Luecken explained. "The decreasing cortisol level of the non-loss group would be considered normal response—they adapted better to stress. But the lower initial cortisol level of the loss group (and poor FR group) that increases when the stress should be diminishing may represent a disrupted response to stress." Some studies have shown that high or chronic stress in childhood can result in unusually low cortisol levels, she said. Disrupted responses to stress could stem from lower cortisol levels, leaving the long-term result of not being able to adapt as well to stress.

"What we see then is that parent-child relationships can impact health, and that those who as children had poor relationships or had a parent die may be at higher risk for a number of different illnesses, high among them cardiac disease because of long-term higher blood pressure," Luecken said. "Further, there are specific characteristics of a parent-child relationship that are key to good health in adulthood— togetherness in the family, avoiding conflict, nurturing, closeness, and supportive behavior.

"Children depend on their parents for more than just food and protection," she added. "They depend on parents in learning how to regulate their moods, and not only through learned behaviors, but adaptive physiology that may last throughout the child's life."

Chapter 8

The Role of Stress in Alcohol Use, Alcoholism Treatment, and Relapse

Clinicians and researchers consider the addiction to alcohol or other drugs (AODs) a complex problem determined by multiple factors, including psychological and physiological components. Many theories involving numerous variables (e.g., personality and access to AODs) have sought to explain the initiation and maintenance of AOD abuse and dependence. Most of those theoretical models consider stress a major contributor to the initiation and continuation of AOD use as well as to relapse. Accordingly, the relationship between stress and alcohol use has received much attention.

The notion that exposure to stress-inducing factors in everyday life (i.e., life stressors) can cause susceptible people to initiate or relapse to alcohol use has intuitive appeal. Whereas the relationship between stress and AOD use can be studied fairly easily in laboratory animals, a definitive exploration of this connection in humans has been more difficult. Animal studies generally have supported the positive relationship between stress and alcohol use and abuse. Researchers also have begun to focus on an organism's response to stress and the consequences of AOD use and how it affects biological processes in the brain. These studies have identified several neurobiological connections between the changes produced by stress and the changes produced by both short-term (i.e., acute) and long-term (i.e., chronic) AOD use (Piazza and Le Moal 1998).

"The Role of Stress in Alcohol Use, Alcoholism Treatment, and Relapse," by Kathleen T. Brady, M.D., Ph.D., and Susan C. Sonne, Pharm.D., *Alcohol Research & Health*, Vol. 23, No. 4, 1999, NIH Publication No. 00-3466.

In the clinical arena, however, the relationship between stress and alcohol use has been more difficult to characterize. For example, human laboratory studies have not uniformly supported a prominent theory called the tension reduction hypothesis of alcohol use, which posits that people use alcohol to reduce stress. Furthermore, studies of the relationship between stress and alcohol use are difficult to conduct in alcoholic patients and, as a result, have numerous inherent limitations. Study participants may recall only selective events that have contributed to alcohol use, may be inconsistent about which events to include as stressors, and may have difficulties distinguishing between events that precipitate alcohol use and those that result from alcohol use and relapse.

Because of these difficulties, many studies that have demonstrated an association between AOD use and stress have been unable to establish a causal relationship between the two. For example, heavy

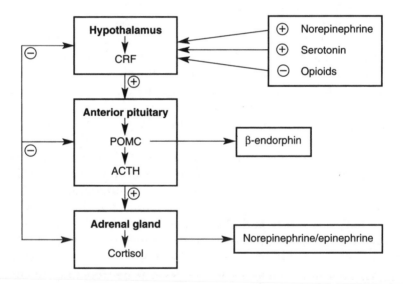

Figure 8.1. *The Hormone Activity of the Hypothalamic-Pituitary-Adrenal (HPA) Axis. (For clarity, the brain and body regions that produce the hormones appear in bold.)*

Note: ACTH = adrenocorticotropic hormone; CRF = corticotropin-releasing factor; POMC = proopiomelanocortin.

alcohol users frequently experience stress related to occupational, social, legal, and financial problems. When interpreting such observations, some investigators have chosen to classify stressful events as illness dependent or illness independent, depending on whether they are caused by the AOD use. This classification has not been consistently adopted, however, and many studies fail to determine the degree to which such stressors occur independent of alcohol use, cause alcohol use, or are a consequence of alcohol use.

The type of stressor studied also influences analyses of the relationship between stress and alcohol use. For example, many studies investigating the role of stress in relapse after treatment have limited their focus to stressors that occurred after treatment completion. Some stressful life events that affect the lives of alcoholics after treatment, however, may have occurred before treatment (e.g., a divorce or job loss). Moreover, stressors can range from dramatic and severe events (e.g., a divorce or death of a loved one) to chronic irritants of daily life (e.g., job hassles or financial worries). Both the temporal relationship between stress and alcohol use and the type of stressor studied, however, can profoundly affect study results. This chapter explores the relationship between stress and alcohol use, alcoholism treatment, and relapse. The chapter also considers the results of clinical and naturalistic studies[1] that explore the connection between stress and AOD use in humans. Finally, the role of stress management and stress reduction techniques in alcoholism treatment is reviewed.

Stress and the Body's Response

The term "stress" generally refers to the reactions of the body to certain events or stimuli that the organism perceives as potentially harmful or distressful. Such stress-inducing events or stimuli, which are referred to as stressors, can be either physical (e.g., unusual environmental conditions or a physical attack) or psychological (e.g., occupational or familial difficulties) in nature. Individual people respond differently to different stressors. An event that is perceived as extremely stressful by one person may be perceived as harmless by another.

Whenever an organism perceives a situation as stressful, it initiates a stress response that is, a complex spectrum of behavioral reactions, such as escape or avoidance behaviors; biological reactions, such as increases in heart rate, blood pressure, or sweating; and (in humans) emotional reactions, such as feelings of anxiety.

The stress response is coordinated through two mechanisms:

1. changes in the activities of various brain regions and brain chemicals (i.e., neurotransmitters) and

2. changes in the activity of a hormonal system called the hypothalamic-pituitary-adrenal (HPA) axis.

Neurotransmitters involved in controlling the stress response include serotonin, dopamine, and opioid peptides. These neurotransmitter systems act through a variety of mechanisms. Thus, opioid peptides directly lead to pain relief, and dopamine release results in increases in blood pressure and heart rate. Furthermore, various neurotransmitters can affect the body more indirectly by inhibiting or enhancing the activity of the HPA axis.

The HPA axis consists of three hormones:

1. Corticotropin-releasing hormone (CRH), which is produced in a brain region called the hypothalamus;

2. Adrenocorticotropic hormone (ACTH), which is released from the pituitary gland located below the hypothalamus; and

3. Glucocorticoid hormones, which are secreted from the adrenal glands located on top of the kidneys.

The three types of hormones form a tightly regulated hormone cascade. Activation of various nerve cells (i.e., neurons) in the brain in response to stress results in the production and release of CRH from certain cells in the hypothalamus. Through specific blood vessels in the brain, CRH is transported from the hypothalamus to the pituitary gland, where it induces the production and secretion of ACTH into the body's general circulation. Through the blood, ACTH reaches the adrenal glands and initiates the production and release of glucocorticoid hormones. (The major glucocorticoid in humans is cortisol, whereas the major glucocorticoid in rodents is corticosterone.) These glucocorticoids induce and regulate the body's diverse physiological responses to stress, such as changes in cardiovascular function and sweat gland activity.

The activity of the HPA axis is regulated by a negative feedback mechanism in which glucocorticoids released into circulation act back on the hypothalamus and/or pituitary gland to suppress further release of CRH and/or ACTH.

The body's neurochemical and hormonal responses to stress do not act independently of each other, but are tightly interconnected. Thus, CRH release in the hypothalamus is regulated by neurons releasing serotonin or endogenous opioids. Furthermore, CRH release not only results in ACTH release, but also in the release of certain endogenous opioids from specific neurons in the brain, which may contribute to various behavioral and emotional consequences of stress.

Neurobiological Connections between Stress and Addiction

Animal studies have suggested that exposure to stress facilitates both the initiation and the reinstatement of AOD use after a period of abstinence (Kreek and Koob 1998). To better understand the biological basis of the effects of stress on AOD self-administration in animals, researchers have focused primarily on two neurobiological systems. The first system involves the organism's hormonal and subsequent biological responses to stress and the influence of those responses on the reinforcing effects of AODs. Those studies, which aim mainly to identify specific, stress-induced hormonal changes that mediate the effects of stress on AOD self-administration, primarily have examined the activity of a hormone system called the hypothalamic-pituitary-adrenal (HPA) axis.

Glucocortocoid secretion by the adrenal gland is considered one of the central biological responses to stressful events (Piazza and Le Moal 1998). Studies have shown that both acute stress and alcohol or cocaine administration can activate the HPA axis, probably by acting on CRH. Consistent with this hypothesis, agents that interfere with CRH function also decrease sensitivity to environmental stress in animal models and prevent some of the reinforcing effects of cocaine (Kreek and Koob 1998).

The second neurobiological system investigated in animal studies of stress and AOD use involves the stress-induced changes in the activity of certain brain regions and brain molecules (i.e., neurotransmitters) assumed to play a role in mediating the reinforcing effects of AODs. This approach is based on the hypothesis that stress facilitates AOD self-administration in laboratory animals and humans by enhancing the activity of those neurobiological systems. This research has focused mostly on nerve cells (i.e., neurons) that are located in the midbrain (i.e., mesencephalon) and which use the neurotransmitter dopamine. Some of these neurons extend to the nucleus accumbens, which is considered one of the primary brain areas involved in mediating the reinforcing effects of various AODs.

One likely explanation for the connection between stress and AOD use is that stress modifies the motivational and/or reinforcing effects[2] of AODs at the neurobiological level. For example, stress increases the activity of the dopaminergic brain systems that are involved in motivation and reward and which also mediate AOD-induced rewarding effects. Accordingly, stress-induced changes in those systems could enhance the organism's responsiveness to the effects of AODs. Furthermore, when an organism is in a stressful situation, numerous biological systems are activated to help the organism cope with the stress. For example, the adrenal glands release epinephrine to prepare the organism for a "fight or flight" response, and various brain regions secrete pain-relieving chemicals. Similarly, stress possibly results in increased activity in the dopaminergic system in an attempt to counteract the negative emotional state associated with stress (Piazza and Le Moal 1998).

Animal studies have suggested that another neurotransmitter, serotonin, also may play a role in the relationship between stress and AOD use. For example, alcohol administration increases brain serotonin metabolism in animals (LeMarquand et al. 1994). Furthermore, increases in serotonin levels and metabolism have been shown to decrease alcohol consumption in experimental animals (LeMarquand et al. 1994). Studies in nonhuman primates found that animals with low brain serotonin activity are high consumers of alcohol (Higley et al. 1998). When these high alcohol-consuming animals were treated with an agent that prevents serotonin breakdown and thus prolongs serotonin's activity in the brain (i.e., a selective serotonin reuptake inhibitor [SSRI]), their alcohol consumption declined substantially. Clinical trials investigating the use of SSRIs in humans, however, have generated mixed results regarding the ability of those agents to decrease alcohol consumption.

In addition, animal studies have indicated that the brain's serotonin systems also affect the brain regions that mediate another stress-related reaction, the fear response (Maier and Watkins 1998). Consistent with this observation, many SSRIs have demonstrated powerful activity in the treatment of anxiety disorders in humans in addition to their antidepressant activity. This association of the serotonin system with both consummatory behaviors and anxiety states further supports the notion that a neurobiological connection exists between stress and AOD use and abuse.

The Relationship between Stress and Alcohol Use in Humans

Consistent with the animal studies described, clinical studies indicate that both acute and chronic stress may play a role in the development of AOD use disorders, the initiation of AOD abuse treatment, and the precipitation of relapse in recovering alcoholics.

Stress and the Development of Alcoholism

Clinical and naturalistic studies have assessed the influence of both acute and chronic stress on drinking behavior and the development of alcoholism. Many of those investigations have focused on occupational stress as an example of chronic stress. For example, Seeman and Seeman (1992) found in a survey of more than 500 men that drinking problems were closely related to stressful experiences whether they resulted from acute and severe stressors (e.g., illness or death of a loved one) or from chronic occupational stressors that were combined with a strong sense of powerlessness. With respect to occupational stress, men in positions combining little freedom in choosing how to fulfill their job obligations (i.e., low job latitude) and high job demands reported the highest drinking levels and most alcohol-related problems.

The extent to which job stress influences drinking behavior also depends on the type of stress experienced. Thus, Crum and colleagues (1995) found that men employed in high-strain jobs (i.e., jobs with high demands and low control) generally had a higher risk of developing alcohol use disorders when compared with men in low-strain occupations (i.e., jobs with low demands and high control). However, this increase was greater for men in positions with high physical demands (three to four times higher risk) than for men in positions with high psychological demands (two to three times higher risk). Other studies noted that chronic, low-level, work-related stressors (e.g., uncooperative coworkers or daily parking problems) also were associated with higher drinking levels (Takeshita et al. 1998).

Several studies have focused specifically on the relationship between stress and alcohol consumption in women. Such analyses are of particular interest, because women may be more susceptible than men are to some of alcohol's harmful health effects (Lex 1991). Furthermore, women have been reported to be more likely than men to consider stressful events as being associated with the initiation of problem drinking (Lex 1991). The latter association was not confirmed, however, in a critical review of stressful life events and drinking behavior in women. In that review, Allan and Cooke (1985) found no evidence of a gender specific relationship between stress and alcohol abuse in women, although the researchers noted a high prevalence of stressful life events (e.g., divorce or death of a loved one), particularly among middle-aged women who developed alcohol dependence later in life. Most studies reviewed, however, failed to address the possibility that heavy drinking may be the cause rather than the consequence of life stressors.

Although the general association between stress and drinking behavior in women has remained controversial, some studies have found an important relationship between women's coping styles and stress-related alcohol consumption. In those studies, women who used problem-focused coping strategies (i.e., who took specific measures to eliminate or address the source of the stress) consumed less alcohol during stressful periods in their lives than did women who used coping strategies that focused on emotions or which merely served to relieve the immediate negative emotions (i.e., were palliative) rather than address the problem (Breslin et al. 1995). Accordingly, treatment modules teaching problem-focused coping skills may be an important component of effective therapy for some AOD-abusing clients.

Another approach to investigating the role of stress in the development of alcoholism has been to analyze alcohol's stress-response dampening (SRD) effects in different populations. SRD effects are those consequences of alcohol consumption that result in a reduction of both the body's emotional responses (e.g., anxiety, tension, and nervousness) and physiological responses (e.g., changes in heart rate or sweating) to stress. Sher and Levenson (1982) found that alcohol's SRD effects were more pronounced in nonalcoholic people who demonstrated personality traits that have been associated with a risk for the development of alcoholism (e.g., aggressiveness, impulsiveness, and outgoing) than in people without those characteristics. The researchers suggested that because of their enhanced SRD experience, people with those personality traits were likely to find alcohol consumption particularly reinforcing, increasing their risk for alcoholism. More recently, Sinha and colleagues (1998) determined that women with a family history of alcoholism or anxiety disorders, who are at increased risk for alcoholism, exhibit a greater SRD effect of alcohol than do women without such a family history. Again, it is an intriguing notion that this population has an increased risk of alcoholism, because alcohol may be particularly reinforcing as the result of its potent SRD effect. Thus, these studies suggest that an enhanced sensitivity to alcohol's SRD effect may contribute to an increased vulnerability of people with anxiety disorders for initiating and escalating alcohol use.

Stress and Treatment Initiation

Discrete stressful events often provide impetus to an alcoholic person to seek treatment, especially when other resources and responses have failed to alleviate the stressful situation. This correlation between stress and treatment initiation was highlighted in several studies comparing alcoholics who had initiated treatment with alcoholics who received no treatment. In those comparisons, alcoholics entering treatment were more likely to perceive their drinking problems as severe, had more symptoms of alcohol dependence, and experienced more stressors and negative events in various life domains (Finney and Moos 1995). Of prime importance, these stressors included both chronic hardships (e.g., strains in employment or marriage) and acute stressful events (e.g., accidents, criminal charges, or divorce) that often are associated with drinking.

Alcoholics with greater resources in multiple domains (e.g., those who are employed and have an intact marriage) are likely to seek treatment for alcohol-related problems more quickly than are alcoholics with fewer resources. For example, social resources, such as an extended network of family members and friends, may increase the probability that a drinker's alcohol-related problems are pointed out to him or her by other people, thereby leading to early treatment seeking. This hypothesis contradicts the notion that an alcoholic must lose all his or her resources (i.e., "hit bottom") before seeking treatment; rather, it suggests that resources should be increased ("the bottom should be raised") so that the person seeks treatment before experiencing multiple devastating consequences of alcoholism.

In summary, stress in many cases may play a causal role in the initiation of treatment. This role, however, probably is moderated and mediated by numerous factors, including a drinker's resources, social pressure, problem-solving skills, and coping strategies (Finney and Moos 1995).

Stress and Relapse

Both discrete, stressful life events and chronic stressors may play a role not only in the development of alcoholism and AOD treatment initiation, but also in the relapse of people recovering from AOD abuse.

To explain the association between stress and relapse, as well as the fact that not all AOD abusers relapse when encountering stress, Brown and colleagues (1990) have proposed the stress-vulnerability hypothesis. This hypothesis posits that AOD use in the face of severe stressors is mediated by the presence or absence of both protective factors (e.g., good social support) and risk factors (e.g., homelessness and unemployment). The hypothesis is supported by findings that severe stress (defined as life adversity posing either a high personal threat or chronic coping demands) which occurred prior to and independent of alcohol use was related to relapse after treatment (Brown et al. 1990). Thus, during a 3 month follow-up period after treatment, patients who relapsed had experienced twice as much severe stress before entering treatment compared with patients who remained abstinent. The study also calculated a composite "psychosocial vulnerability score" based on the patient's coping skills, social resources, confidence that he or she would be able to resist an urge to drink, and level of depression. According to that analysis, people whose scores in these areas improved during treatment had better outcomes (i.e., a lower risk of relapse). These findings emphasize the connection between stress and relapse and suggest that resilience to stress-induced relapse can be improved during treatment.

Another study followed a large group of alcoholics, opiate users, and cigarette smokers in early abstinence to investigate the effects of acute stress and commitment to abstinence on relapse (Hall et al. 1990). The commitment to abstinence was measured using a scale that allowed the participants to choose between six different treatment goals, ranging from abstinence to no change in use. The researchers found that commitment to abstinence was the strongest predictor of abstinence during the follow-up period. Furthermore, an association between elevated stress levels and relapse existed only when the subjects were interviewed after their relapse (i.e., retrospectively) about the factors contributing to their relapse, but not when stress levels were assessed before a relapse occurred (i.e., prospectively). This observation suggests that stress may not actually lead to relapse; instead, the relapse may have resulted in increased stress and the subjects may have used the attribution of stress as causing the relapse as a way to make sense of the relapse. The actual relationship between stress and relapse in this study is difficult to assess, however, because the follow-up period was rather brief (i.e., 12 weeks) and the study did not assess the effects of chronic stress. Nevertheless, the study results emphasize the need for more careful, prospective studies of the relationship between stress and relapse.

Stress Management in AOD Abuse Treatment

Stress may play a crucial role in the relapse to AOD abuse after treatment. Accordingly, the incorporation of treatment strategies to help patients cope with stressful events could reduce relapse risk. Such strategies may include pharmacotherapeutic as well as psychosocial approaches.

Pharmacotherapy

Besides contributing to relapse to alcohol, stress also may play a role in relapse to other psychiatric disorders, such as depression and anxiety. As with the treatment of such disorders, it therefore makes sense that pharmacological management for recovering AOD users should be maximized during times of stress to help reduce risk of relapse. Accordingly, treatment of anxiety may be a useful component of alcoholism treatment.

As mentioned earlier in this chapter, at a neurochemical level the connection between stress (and/or anxiety) and resumption of alcohol use appears to involve several neurotransmitter systems in the brain, including serotonin pathways and reward pathways, which use dopamine and opioid peptides. Accordingly, medications affecting those systems (e.g., SSRIs and opioid antagonists) may play a significant role in minimizing the risk of relapse after stressful events. Other anxiety-reducing therapeutic agents that act on the same systems, such as benzodiazepines, have abuse potential themselves, making their use in people with AOD use disorders risky.

SSRIs may have particular appeal for use in AOD users, because these agents are easy to take (e.g., require only one daily dose), have no abuse potential, and are relatively safe when used in excessive doses or combined with AODs. Higley and colleagues (1998) examined the efficacy of the SSRI sertraline in mitigating the effects of stress on alcohol consumption in non-human primates. In that study, sertraline reduced alcohol consumption and aggressiveness in animals that had been exposed to stress before being returned to their home cages, presumably by increasing serotonin activity in the central nervous system. Under conditions of extreme stress, however, sertraline became ineffective and the animals resumed high drinking levels.

Based on those observations, the investigators suggested that relapse to drinking may be most likely to occur during periods of stress and that SSRIs may not be able to prevent such a relapse. Under non-stress conditions, including following a stressful situation, however,

SSRIs, such as sertraline, may be effective in reducing alcohol consumption. Thus, pharmacological treatment with SSRIs may be most effective in conjunction with other nonpharmacological therapies, such as cognitive-behavioral therapy, for improving or preventing stress. Interestingly, in a study among patients with posttraumatic stress disorder (PTSD), patients treated with the SSRI fluoxetine (Prozac ®) showed improvement on a scale designed to measure stress resilience (Connor et al. 1999).

The opioid antagonist naltrexone also has been shown to be effective in preventing relapse in detoxified alcoholics (O'Malley et al. 1992; Volpicelli et al. 1992). These effects result at least in part from the agent's effect on reward pathways. In animal models opioid antagonists also have been shown to prevent increased drinking in animals that had experienced a stressful situation, suggesting that these medications also may influence the stress-drinking correlation (Volpicelli et al. 1986). However, researchers have not yet studied systematically this potential role of naltrexone.

Psychosocial Therapy

If stress, the vulnerability to stress, and the presence or absence of protective factors are important mediators in the initiation of and relapse to AOD use, then specific treatment approaches targeting these areas might play a central role in the prevention and treatment of AOD use. Indeed, most AOD treatment approaches currently used contain social skills training and problem-solving components. This treatment philosophy is based on the classic relapse prevention model proposed by Marlatt and Gordon (1985), which features such important stress management components as cognitive restructuring, coping skills, and problem-solving skills. For example, cognitive restructuring teaches people to interpret events, attitudes, and feelings in a rational way and to respond constructively to a crisis or stressful situation. Similarly, problem-solving skills training teaches patients to analyze problem situations and act constructively rather than impulsively. Finally, most treatment programs recognize the importance of social support systems in managing stress and therefore encourage patients to attend such self-help groups as Alcoholics Anonymous and Narcotics Anonymous and/or to recruit support from friends and family.

Although such a stress management approach has intuitive appeal, researchers have not thoroughly explored and evaluated this approach experimentally. For example, whereas numerous studies have demonstrated the usefulness of relapse prevention protocols using these and other strategies in the treatment of AOD abuse, weight loss, and smoking cessation, many of those studies could not assess the specific contributions of the stress reduction techniques to recovery.

A few studies, however, have attempted to identify the effective components of therapy. For example, in one study of 130 AOD abusers, patients who received supplemental skills training and social network development after treatment showed greater improvement in several areas (e.g., avoidance of AOD use; problem-solving; and coping with stress, relapse, and social interaction) compared with a control group (Hawkins et al. 1986). In a study of coping responses and relapse in adolescents, lower stress management abilities (e.g., fewer problem-solving and/or coping strategies and less self-assurance) were associated with a higher risk of relapse (Myers and Brown 1990). In another study of relapse among adolescent AOD users, self-esteem, high quality of support, and social support satisfaction all of which are likely to improve stress vulnerability were crucial determinants of a subject's outcome at 6 months (Richter et al. 1991).

In summary, stress management techniques are an integral part of most AOD abuse treatment programs, although it is difficult to specifically ascertain the value of these techniques. Studies that have attempted to examine this issue, however, have demonstrated that measures both to enhance healthy coping strategies and problem-solving techniques and to maximize social support systems are important components of successful treatment.

Summary

The relationship between stress and AOD use is complex. Most likely, however, stress and the body's response to it do play a role in the vulnerability to initial AOD use, initiation of AOD abuse treatment, and relapse in recovering AOD users. This relationship probably is mediated, at least in part, by common neurochemical systems, such as the serotonin, dopamine, and opiate peptide systems, as well as the HPA axis. Further exploration of these connections should lead to important pharmacological developments in the prevention and treatment of AOD abuse, including alcohol use disorders.

Effective psychosocial approaches to AOD abuse treatment all contain elements aimed at reducing and managing stress. It is difficult, however, to separate the effects of such specific stress-reduction techniques from the effects of other effective treatment components. Nevertheless, studies indicate that treatment techniques that foster coping skills, problem-solving skills, and social support play a pivotal role in successful treatment. In the future, individualized treatment approaches that emphasize stress management strategies in those patients in whom a clear connection between stress and relapse exists will become particularly important.

References

Allan, C.A., and Cooke, D.J. Stressful life events and alcohol misuse in women: A critical review. *Journal of Studies on Alcohol* 46:147–152, 1985.

Breslin, F.C.; O'Keefe, M.K.; Burrell, L.; Ratliffcrain, J.; and Baum, A. The effects of stress and coping on daily alcohol use in women. *Addictive Behaviors* 20:141–147, 1995.

Brown, S.A.; Vik, P.W.; Mcquaid, J.R.; Patterson, T.L.; Irwin, M.R.; and Grant, I. Severity of psychosocial stress and outcome of alcoholism treatment. *Journal of Abnormal Psychology* 99:344–348, 1990.

Connor, K.M.; Sutherland, S.M.; Tupler, L.A.; Malik, M.L.; and Davidson, J.R. Fluoxetine in posttraumatic stress disorder. Randomised double-blind study. *British Journal of Psychiatry* 175:17–22, 1999.

Crum, R.M.; Muntaner, C.; Eaton, W.W.; and Anthony, J.C. Occupational stress and the risk of alcohol abuse and dependence. *Alcoholism: Clinical and Experimental Research* 19:647–655, 1995.

Erb, S.; Shaham, Y.; and Stewart, J. Stress reinstates cocaine-seeking behavior after prolonged extinction and a drug-free period. *Psychopharmacology* 128: 408–412, 1996.

Finney, J.W., and Moos, R.H. Entering treatment for alcohol abuse: A stress and coping model. *Addiction* 90:1223–1240, 1995.

Haleem, D.J. Adaptation to repeated restraint stress in rats: Failure of ethanol-treated rats to adapt in the stress schedule. *Alcohol & Alcoholism* 31:471–477, 1996.

Hall, S.M.; Havassy, B.E.; and Wasserman, D.A. Commitment to abstinence and acute stress in relapse to alcohol, opiates, and nicotine. *Journal of Consulting and Clinical Psychology* 58:175–181, 1990.

Hawkins, D.J.; Catalano, R.F.; and Wells, E.A. Measuring effects of a skills training intervention for drug abusers. *Journal of Consulting and Clinical Psychology* 54:661–664, 1986.

Heyser, C.J.; Schulteis, G.; Durbin, P.; and Koob, G.F. Chronic acamprosate decreases deprivation induced ethanol self-administration in rats. *Alcoholism: Clinical and Experimental Research* 20:15A, 1996.

Higley, J.; Hasert, M.S.; Suomi, S.; and Linnoila, M. The serotonin reuptake inhibitor sertraline reduces excessive alcohol consumption in nonhuman primates: Effect of stress. *Neuropsychopharmacology* 18:431–443, 1998.

Kreek, M.J., and Koob, G.F. Drug dependence: Stress and dysregulation of brain reward pathways. *Drug and Alcohol Dependence* 51:23–47, 1998.

Lemarquand, D.; Pihl, R.O.; and Benkelfat, C. Serotonin and alcohol intake, abuse and dependence: Findings of animal studies. *Biological Psychiatry* 36(6):395–421, 1994.

Lex, B.W. Some gender differences in alcohol and polysubstance users. *Health Psychology* 10:121–132, 1991.

Maier, S.F., and Watkins, L.R. Stressor controllability, anxiety, and serotonin. *Cognitive Therapy and Research* 22:595–613, 1998.

Marlatt, G.A., and Gordon, J.R. Relapse Prevention: *A Self-Control Strategy for the Maintenance of Behavior Change*. New York: Guilford Press, 1985.

Myers, M.G., and Grown, S.A. Coping responses and relapse among adolescent substance abusers. *Journal of Substance Abuse* 2:177–189, 1990.

O'Malley, S.S.; Jaffe, A.J.; Chang, G.; Schottenfeld, R.S.; Meyer, R.E.; and Rounsaville, B. Naltrexone and coping skills therapy for alcohol dependence: A controlled study. *Archives of General Psychiatry* 49:881–887, 1992.

Piazza, P.V.; and LeMoal, M. Stress as a factor in addiction. In: Graham, A.W., and Schultz, T.K., eds. *Principles of Addiction Medicine*. Chevy Chase, MD: American Society of Addiction Medicine, Inc., 1998. pp. 83–93.

Ramsey, N.F., and VanRee, J.M. Emotional but not physical stress enhances intravenous cocaine self-administration in drug-naïve rats. *Brain Research* 608:216–222, 1993.

Richter, S.S.; Brown, S.A.; and Mott, M.A. The impact of social support and self-esteem on adolescent substance abuse treatment outcome. *Journal of Substance Abuse* 3:371–385, 1991.

Schuckit, M.A. Recent developments in the pharmacotherapy of alcohol dependence. *Journal of Consulting & Clinical Psychology* 64(4)669–676, 1996.

Seeman, M., and Seeman, A.Z. Life strains, alienation, and drinking behavior. *Alcoholism: Clinical and Experimental Research* 16:199–205, 1992.

Shaham, Y. Immobilization stress-induced oral opioid self-administration and withdrawal in rats: Role of conditioning factors and the effect of stress on "relapse" to opioid drugs. *Psychopharmacology* 111:477–485, 1993.

Shaham, Y., and Stewart, J. Effects of opioid and dopamine receptor antagonists on relapse induced by stress and reexposure to heroin in rats. *Psychopharmacology* 125:385–391, 1996.

Sher, K.J., and Levenson, R.W. Risk for alcoholism and individual differences in the stress-response-dampening effect of alcohol. *Journal of Abnormal Psychology* 91:350–367, 1982.

Sinha, R.; Robinson, J.; and O'Malley, S. Stress response dampening: Effects of gender and family history of alcoholism and anxiety disorders. *Psychopharmacology* 137:311–320, 1998.

Takeshita, T.; Maruyama, S.; and Morimoto, K. Relevance of both daily hassles and the ALDH2 genotype to problem drinking among Japanese male workers. *Alcoholism: Clinical and Experimental Research* 22:115–120, 1998.

Volpicelli, J.R.; Dowis, M.A.; and Olgin, J.E. Naltrexone blocks the postshock increase of ethanol consumption. *Life Science* 38:841–847, 1986.

Volpicelli, J.R.; Alterman, A.; Hyashida, M.; and O'Brien, C.P. Naltrexone in the treatment of alcohol dependence. *Archives of General Psychiatry* 49:876–880, 1992. Vol. 23, No. 4, 1999 271

Footnotes

1. Naturalistic studies are investigations that are not conducted in a clinical setting.

2. The motivational, reinforcing, or rewarding effects of a drug (e.g., euphoria) are those effects that motivate the drug user to seek the "reward" and therefore consume more of the drug.

Chapter 9

Does Cigarette Smoking Cause Stress?

Smokers often report that cigarettes help relieve feelings of stress. However, the stress levels of adult smokers are slightly higher than those of nonsmokers, adolescent smokers report increasing levels of stress as they develop regular patterns of smoking, and smoking cessation leads to reduced stress. Far from acting as an aid for mood control, nicotine dependency seems to exacerbate stress. This is confirmed in the daily mood patterns described by smokers, with normal moods during smoking and worsening moods between cigarettes. Thus, the apparent relaxant effect of smoking only reflects the reversal of the tension and irritability that develop during nicotine depletion. Dependent smokers need nicotine to remain feeling normal. The message that tobacco use does not alleviate stress but actually increases it needs to be far more widely known. It could help those adult smokers who wish to quit and might prevent some schoolchildren from starting.

The relationship between tobacco smoking and stress has long been an area for controversy. The basic conundrum is that although adult smokers state that cigarettes help them feel relaxed, in a paradoxical fashion they also report feeling slightly more stressed than nonsmokers. This positive association between smoking and stress is also evident in adolescent smokers, who report increasing levels of stress as they develop regular patterns of smoking. Furthermore, when

"Does Cigarette Smoking Cause Stress?" by Andy C. Parrott, *American Psychologist*, Vol. 54, No. 10, 817-820 (October 1999) © 1999 The American Psychological Association (APA), reprinted with permission.

smokers manage to quit smoking, they gradually become less stressed over time. Why do smokers believe that cigarettes help relieve stress, when the empirical evidence shows that tobacco dependency is associated with heightened stress? The aim of this chapter is to review the empirical evidence on the smoking—stress relationship, first in adult smokers, then in novice adolescent smokers, and last during smoking cessation. Finally, an explanatory model for the smoking—stress relationship is proposed, based on the concept of nicotine dependency as a direct cause of stress.

Smoking and Stress in Adult Regular Smokers

The majority of smokers report feeling more relaxed when they smoke a cigarette and state that mood control is an important reason for smoking cigarettes. Ikard, Green, and Horn (1969) found that 80% of smokers agreed with statements indicating that cigarette smoking was "relaxing" or "pleasurable." In questionnaire surveys, most smokers respond positively to statements such as "Smoking relaxes me when I am upset or nervous," "Smoking calms me down," and "I am not contented for long unless I am smoking a cigarette" (Ikard et al., 1969; Russell, Peto, & Pavel, 1974; Speilberger, 1986; Tomkins, 1968). These findings suggest that smoking aids mood control: "Cigarette smoking is a mood modifier for smokers, calming and reducing the smokers' feelings of anxiety and anger" (Warburton, 1992, p. 57). However, regular smokers also report adverse moods when they have not smoked recently, with feelings of stress and irritability building up during periods of nicotine abstinence (Hughes, Higgins, & Hatsukami, 1990; Parrott, Garnham, Wesnes, & Pincock, 1996; Office of the U.S. Surgeon General, 1988). The positive mood changes experienced during smoking may therefore reflect instead the simple reversal of these unpleasant abstinence effects: "Smoking doesn't make the smoker less irritable or vulnerable to annoyance, not smoking or insufficient nicotine makes him more vulnerable" (Schachter, 1978, p. 210).

When smokers are asked about their moods over the day, they typically report a pattern of repetitive mood fluctuations, with normal moods during smoke inhalation followed by periods of increasing stress between cigarettes (O'Neill & Parrott, 1992; Parrott, 1994a, 1994b). These mood fluctuations also tend to be strongest in the most dependent smokers, who also report mood control is a core reason for their smoking (Parrott, 1994b). However, smokers' stress levels tend to be similar to nonsmokers' only when they have just smoked and become worse during periods of nicotine abstinence (Parrott & Garnham, 1998). Moreover, when nicotine-deprived and nondeprived smokers were allowed to smoke a single cigarette, mood improvements occurred only in the deprived smokers, who were already suffering from poor moods. When nondeprived smokers had a cigarette, their self-rated stress levels were hardly affected by smoking; rather, they remained at normal or average levels very similar to those of nonsmokers (Parrott & Garnham, 1998). This shows that the apparent mood benefits of smoking only reflect a process of mood normalization: the simple reversal of the tension and irritability that build up during nicotine abstinence (Schachter, 1978).

Regular smokers, therefore, experience periods of heightened stress between cigarettes, and smoking briefly restores their stress levels to normal. However, soon they need another cigarette to forestall abstinence symptoms from developing again. The repeated occurrence of negative moods between cigarettes means that smokers tend to experience slightly above-average levels of daily stress. Thus, nicotine dependency seems to be a direct cause of stress. Various surveys have shown that smokers report slightly higher levels of daily stress than do nonsmokers. In the U.K. Health and Lifestyle Survey of 9,003 participants, significantly more smokers than nonsmokers reported feeling constantly under stress and strain (Warburton, Revell, & Thompson, 1991). In a survey of male shift workers, the cigarette smokers reported significantly higher levels of self-rated stress than did the nonsmokers during both day and night shifts (Jones & Parrott, 1997). West (1992, p.166) has similarly noted, "Against the anxiety reduction theory, is the finding that smokers do not present as less anxious than non-smokers. Indeed, in surveys they emerge as significantly more anxious overall."

Smoking Initiation and Stress during Adolescence

If nicotine dependency leads to heightened stress, then novice smokers should report increasing stress as they develop regular patterns of smoking. The empirical evidence is consistent with this model. In a cross-sectional survey of 1,684 Canadian schoolchildren, the regular and heavy smokers reported significantly higher stress (nervousness, anxiety, worry) than did similarly aged nonsmokers (Mitic, McGuire, & Neumann, 1985). When adolescents in British schools were surveyed, the lowest levels of self-rated stress were found with the nonsmokers, comparatively greater stress was noted by occasional smokers, and the highest levels of self-rated stress emerged from the regular smokers (Lloyd & Lucas, 1997). When American adolescents were asked to retrospectively describe their changes in smoking behavior and feeling states over the previous two years, an increase in affective distress accompanied the move from experimental to more regular smoking (Hirschman, Leventhal, & Glynn, 1984). In a two-year prospective study, stress levels increased in schoolchildren who became more frequent smokers (Wills, 1986). When female schoolchildren were asked about their moods during smoking, the regular smokers reported that they felt calmer when actually smoking but suffered abstinence symptoms without their cigarettes. The authors concluded that the apparent mood benefits of smoking only reflected the relief of withdrawal symptoms. Moreover, nicotine dependency was evident even among the youngest smokers: "The relationship between feeling calmer when smoking and reports of aversive symptoms when attempting to give up was evident even among those in their first year of smoking" (McNeill, 1991, p. 591).

Smoking Cessation and Stress

If smoking does lead to increased stress, then quitting should reduce stress. Again, this has been empirically confirmed in a number of studies. In a review of cross-sectional studies in this area, the U.S. Surgeon General concluded that former smokers were found to be less stressed than current smokers in some studies, whereas in other studies the two groups did not differ significantly; however, not a single study found former smokers to be more stressed than continuing smokers (Davis, 1990, pp. 533-541). Longitudinal or prospective research designs are more powerful than cross-sectional studies; they generally demonstrate a pattern of poor moods for the first few weeks after cessation, followed by mood improvements in the longer term. Hughes (1992) found increased anger, anxiety, and restlessness in the first few days after quitting. By the 14-day session, the group average mood scores had returned to baseline; at subsequent sessions, these moods gradually improved over those found at baseline. Cohen and Lichtenstein (1990) monitored smokers who were attempting to quit unaided. Over the six-month period, each volunteer regularly completed the Perceived Stress Scale, at which time their current smoking status was also noted. Those smokers who failed to quit reported unchanging levels of high stress at every session. In contrast, those former smokers who completely abstained for the six-month period reported a steady decrease in stress over time. Crucially, the successful and unsuccessful quitters reported similar stress levels at baseline; thus, it was not just the less stressed smokers who managed to quit. Other longitudinal studies have confirmed that quitting leads to a significant reduction in self-reported stress. Parrott (1995) found a slight reduction in stress levels three months post-cessation, followed by a further lowering of stress six months after quitting. Carey, Kalra, Carey, Halperin, and Richards (1993) noted a significant reduction in self-rated stress in Australians who successfully quit smoking. West and Hajek (1997, p.1589) similarly found that quitting resulted in significantly lower state anxiety scores: "Giving up smoking is quite rapidly followed by a reduction in anxiety that may reflect removal of an anxiolytic agent, nicotine." However, one prospective study (Gilbert et al., 1998) failed to find mood improvements after quitting; instead, their "former" smokers reported mood decrements during the month after quitting. However, abstinence was not biochemically confirmed, and their volunteers were allowed to smoke a few cigarettes and still be counted as quitters. Overall, therefore, Gilbert et al. (1998) cannot be seen as a true cessation study. It is crucial that abstinence is total, because any smoking relapse will probably reestablish nicotine dependency as a problem (Parrott, 1995; West & Hajek, 1997); merely cutting down will probably lead to increased stress.

Traditional Explanations for the Smoking-Stress Relationship

The traditional explanation for the smoking-stress relationship is that smoking relieves stress. The smoker feels relaxed when smoking and tense without nicotine; thus, their tobacco and cigarettes are seen as helping them cope with the stresses and strains of everyday life (Warburton, 1992). Certainly the positive association between smoke inhalation and stress relief is so strong that few smokers question it. Schoolchildren in the mid-1990s gave stress control as a reason for smoking (Lloyd & Lucas, 1997), just as their parents did in earlier surveys (Ikard et al., 1969). However, this raises the crucial question: Why does the smoker feel stressed without nicotine? There seem to be two possible answers to this. Smokers may be constitutionally neurotic. Alternatively, their stress may be caused by nicotine dependency.

In support of the first explanation, in a number of studies researchers have found above-average neuroticism scores in adult smokers compared with nonsmokers, although some studies have failed to confirm this (see Gilbert, 1995, p. 152). Thus, it may be suggested that nicotine helps constitutionally anxious (i.e., neurotic) individuals cope with stress. However, there are several problems with this notion. Most importantly, there is no empirical evidence to support it. When tobacco-naive adults are first administered nicotine, they report feelings of anxiety and tension rather than relaxation (Newhouse et al., 1990). Similarly, when adolescents take up occasional smoking, they become more rather than less stressed, and their stress levels increase as they become regular smokers. Thus, there is no empirical evidence that nicotine does alleviate stress. Furthermore, when adults quit smoking, they become less stressed rather than more stressed. Thus, there is no evidence that smokers suffer without tobacco or nicotine (other than during the initial brief period after quitting; Hughes, 1992; Parrott, 1998). There is also no neurochemical rationale for predicting that nicotine should alleviate stress, because it is a cholinergic agonist with sympathomimetic rather than sedative properties (Davis, 1990; Office of the U.S. Surgeon General, 1988; Parrott, 1998). Given that nicotine does not alleviate stress, explanations for the (slight) positive association between neuroticism and smoking need to be sought. One possible explanation is that neurotic individuals develop nicotine dependency more readily. Another is that if nicotine dependency causes stress, then some smokers may become slightly more neurotic as they develop regular patterns of smoking (note that these explanations are not alternatives and may be linked).

Nicotine Dependency: A Cause of Stress?

The model proposed here is that nicotine dependency can cause stress. The regular smoker needs nicotine to maintain normal moods and suffers from unpleasant feelings of irritability and tension between cigarettes, when his or her plasma nicotine levels are falling. Abstinence symptoms are therefore central to any understanding of nicotine dependency, just as they are with many other addictive drugs (e.g., heroin, cocaine). The main difference between nicotine and these other drugs is that nicotine users feel normal on the drug. Thus, there are few differences between smokers replete with nicotine and nonsmokers. This means that regular smokers need to maintain their nicotine intake in every type of situation: at work, rest, and play. This model also explains why smoking is most pleasurable after an extended period of abstinence (e.g., the first cigarette of the day). Indeed, the degree of satisfaction provided by a cigarette has been shown to be a direct monotonic function of the duration of prior abstinence (Fant, Schuh, & Stizer, 1995).

Smokers also learn that regular smoking prevents abstinence symptoms from developing. Thus, the link between regular smoke intake and keeping moods within normal bounds becomes strongly conditioned over time. With around 60,000 inhalations each year, a regular smoker soon finds smoking is a highly overlearned behavior, which is why quitting can be so difficult. Many smokers also use cigarettes to cope with adverse moods in stressful situations (Office of the U.S. Surgeon General, 1988; Schachter, 1978). The indirect coping strategy of "lighting up" under stress is reported by both adult and adolescent smokers (Lloyd & Lucas, 1997; Office of the U.S. Surgeon General, 1988). However, this drug-based strategy may be counterproductive, because although the smoker may feel somewhat relieved, it can leave the real problem unresolved (Lloyd & Lucas, 1997). The frequent failure of smokers to tackle problems directly may provide a further reason why they suffer from more stress than do nonsmokers.

This model raises a number of practical and theoretical issues, which need to be empirically investigated. If stress levels are increased by smoking, what exactly is the nature of this link—is it direct and causal or more subtle and indirect? What neurochemical changes occur in the novice child smoker, which lead the child to feel irritable when without nicotine? How crucial are the ineffectual coping strategies cigarette use provides (e.g., lighting up instead of tackling the problem); do they make the smoker less effective at handling negative life events? Are there individual differences (e.g., in neuroticism) that influence the development of adverse moods during abstinence, and how crucial are these withdrawal symptoms for explaining nicotine dependency? Shiffman (1989, p.545) noted, "While dependent smokers showed signs of acute withdrawal that were relieved by smoking, chippers (light occasional smokers) showed no signs of withdrawal prior to smoking, and little subjective reaction to smoking." Does the absence of withdrawal symptoms in light or occasional smokers explain how they manage to avoid becoming nicotine dependent? Patterns of cigarette uptake also differ across socioeconomic group, race, gender, and psychiatric status; is there a common factor of susceptibility to stress in at-risk groups? Finally, what are the effects of no-smoking policies? They may exacerbate stress in highly dependent smokers. However, because drug use, craving, and expectancy are strongly context dependent, the widespread adoption of no-smoking policies could help prevent some occasional smokers from becoming more habitual smokers.

Implications for Health Education

The message that smoking can increase stress needs to be more widely known. The majority of smokers recognize that smoking is physically unhealthy but mistakenly believe it has positive psychological functions. In particular, most smokers state that cigarettes help relieve the feelings of stress that they seem to experience so frequently (Lloyd & Lucas, 1997; Office of the U.S. Surgeon General, 1988). Smokers need to become aware of why these beliefs are incorrect. Health education packages should contain information on how smoking can exacerbate stress, and how quitting can lead to reduced stress. This may help many adults to stop smoking. Former smokers who have recently quit are also in danger of relapse (Davis, 1990); one way to help maintain abstinence would be to inform them that their stress levels will probably increase again if they do relapse (Cohen & Lichtenstein, 1990). Pre-teenage and adolescent schoolchildren also need to be taught that not only is nicotine highly addictive but it can also increase stress. Hopefully, this might help more youngsters withstand the social pressures to initially try cigarettes.

References

Carey, M. P., Kalra, D. L., Carey, K. B., Halperin, S. & Richards, C. S. (1993). Stress and unaided smoking cessation: A prospective investigation. *Journal of Consulting and Clinical Psychology*, 61, 831–838.

Cohen, S. & Lichtenstein, E. (1990). Perceived stress, quitting smoking, and smoking relapse. *Health Psychology*, 9, 466–478.

Davis, R. M. (1990). The health benefits of smoking cessation: A report of the Surgeon General, 1990. (Washington, DC: U.S. Government Printing Office.)

Fant, R. V., Schuh, K. J. & Stizer, M. L. (1995). Response to smoking as a function of prior smoking amounts. *Psychopharmacology*, 119, 385–390.

Gilbert, D. G. (1995). Smoking: Individual differences, psychopathology, and emotion. (London: Taylor & Francis.)

Gilbert, D. G., McClernon, F. J., Rabinovich, N. E., Plath, L. C., Jensen, R. A. & Meliska, C. J. (1998). Effects of smoking abstinence on mood and craving in men: Influence of negative-affect-related personality traits, habitual nicotine intake and repeated measurements. *Personality and Individual Differences*, 25, 399–423.

Hirschman, R. S., Leventhal, H. & Glynn, K. (1984). The development of smoking behavior: Conceptualization and supportive cross-sectional survey data. *Journal of Applied and Social Psychology*, 14, 184–206.

Chapter 10

Drug Addiction and Stress

Drug-addicted patients who are trying to remain off drugs can often resist the cravings brought on by seeing reminders of their former drug life, NIDA-funded researcher Dr. Mary Jeanne Kreek of Rockefeller University in New York City has noted. "For 6 months or so, they can walk past the street corner where they used to buy drugs and not succumb to their urges. But then all of a sudden they relapse," she says. "When we ask them why they relapse, almost always they tell us something like, 'Well, things weren't going well at my job,' or 'My wife left me.' Sometimes, the problem is as small as 'My public assistance check was delayed,' or 'The traffic was too heavy.'"

Anecdotes such as these are common in the drug abuse treatment community. These anecdotes plus animal studies on this subject point toward an important role for stress in drug abuse relapse. In addition, the fact that addicts often relapse apparently in response to what most people would consider mild stressors suggests that addicts may be more sensitive than non-addicts to stress.

This hypersensitivity may exist before drug abusers start taking drugs and may contribute to their initial drug use, or it could result from the effects of chronic drug abuse on the brain, or its existence could be due to a combination of both, Dr. Kreek has proposed. She has demonstrated that the nervous system of an addict is hypersensitive

---

"Studies Link Stress and Drug Addiction," by Steven Stocker, *NIDA Research Findings* Volume 14, Number 1, National Institute on Drug Abuse (NIDA), April 1999.

to chemically induced stress, which suggests that the nervous system also may be hypersensitive to emotional stress.

How the Body Copes with Stress

The body reacts to stress by secreting two types of chemical messengers—hormones in the blood and neurotransmitters in the brain. Scientists think that some of the neurotransmitters may be the same or similar chemicals as the hormones but acting in a different capacity.

Some of the hormones travel throughout the body, altering the metabolism of food so that the brain and muscles have sufficient stores of metabolic fuel for activities, such as fighting or fleeing, that help the person cope with the source of the stress. In the brain, the neurotransmitters trigger emotions, such as aggression or anxiety, that prompt the person to undertake those activities.

Normally, stress hormones are released in small amounts throughout the day, but when the body is under stress the level of these hormones increases dramatically. The release of stress hormones begins in the brain. First, a hormone called corticotropin-releasing factor (CRF) is released from the brain into the blood, which carries the CRF to the pituitary gland, located directly underneath the brain. There, CRF stimulates the release of another hormone, adrenocorticotropin (ACTH), which, in turn, triggers the release of other hormones—principally cortisol—from the adrenal glands. Cortisol travels throughout the body, helping it to cope with stress. If the stressor is mild, when the cortisol reaches the brain and pituitary gland it inhibits the further release of CRF and ACTH, which return to their normal levels. But if the stressor is intense, signals in the brain for more CRF release outweigh the inhibitory signal from cortisol, and the stress hormone cycle continues.

Researchers speculate that CRF and ACTH may be among the chemicals that serve dual purposes as hormones and neurotransmitters. The researchers posit that if, indeed, these chemicals also act as neurotransmitters, they may be involved in producing the emotional responses to stress.

The stress hormone cycle is controlled by a number of stimulatory chemicals in addition to CRF and ACTH and inhibitory chemicals in addition to cortisol both in the brain and in the blood. Among the chemicals that inhibit the cycle are neurotransmitters called opioid peptides, which are chemically similar to opiate drugs such as heroin and morphine. Dr. Kreek has found evidence that opioid peptides also may inhibit the release of CRF and other stress-related neurotransmitters in the brain, thereby inhibiting stressful emotions.

How Addiction Changes the Body's Response to Stress

Heroin and morphine inhibit the stress hormone cycle and presumably the release of stress-related neurotransmitters just as the natural opioid peptides do. Thus, when people take heroin or morphine, the drugs add to the inhibition already being provided by the opioid peptides. This may be a major reason that some people start taking heroin or morphine in the first place, suggests Dr. Kreek. "Every one of us has things in life that really bother us," she says. "Most people are able to cope with these hassles, but some people find it very difficult to do so. In trying opiate drugs for the first time, some people who have difficulty coping with stressful emotions might find that these drugs blunt those emotions, an effect that they might find rewarding. This could be a major factor in their continued use of these drugs."

When the effects of opiate drugs wear off, the addict goes into withdrawal. Research has shown that, during withdrawal, the level of stress hormones rises in the blood and stress-related neurotransmitters are released in the brain. These chemicals trigger emotions that the addict perceives as highly unpleasant, which drive the addict to take more opiate drugs. Because the effects of heroin or morphine last only 4 to 6 hours, opiate addicts often experience withdrawal three or four times a day. This constant switching on and off of the stress systems of the body heightens whatever hypersensitivity these systems may have had before the person started taking drugs, Dr. Kreek says. "The result is that these stress chemicals are on a sort of hair-trigger release. They surge at the slightest provocation," she says.

Studies have suggested that cocaine similarly heightens the body's sensitivity to stress, although in a different way. When a cocaine addict takes cocaine, the stress systems are activated, much like when an opiate addict goes into withdrawal, but the person perceives this as part of the cocaine rush because cocaine is also stimulating the parts of the brain that are involved in feeling pleasure. When cocaine's effects wear off and the addict goes into withdrawal, the stress systems are again activated—again, much like when an opiate addict goes into withdrawal. This time, the cocaine addict perceives the activation as unpleasant because the cocaine is no longer stimulating the pleasure circuits in the brain. Because cocaine switches on the stress systems both when it is active and during withdrawal, these systems rapidly become hypersensitive, Dr. Kreek theorizes.

Evidence for the Link between Stress and Addiction

This theory about stress and drug addiction is derived in part from studies conducted by Dr. Kreek's group in which addicts were given a test agent called metyrapone. This chemical blocks the production of cortisol in the adrenal glands, which lowers the level of cortisol in the blood. As a result, cortisol is no longer inhibiting the release of CRF from the brain and ACTH from the pituitary. The brain and pituitary then start producing more of these chemicals.

Physicians use metyrapone to test whether a person's stress system is operating normally. When metyrapone is given to non-addicted people, the ACTH level in the blood increases. However, when Dr. Kreek and her colleagues administered metyrapone to active heroin addicts, the ACTH level hardly rose at all. When the scientists gave metyrapone to heroin addicts who were abstaining from heroin use and who were not taking methadone, the synthetic opioid medication that suppresses cravings for opiate drugs, the ACTH level in the majority of the addicts increased about twice as high as in non-addicts. Finally, when the scientists gave metyrapone to heroin addicts maintained for at least 3 months on methadone, the ACTH level rose the same as in nonaddicts.

Addicts on heroin under-react because all the excess opioid molecules in the brain greatly inhibit the brain's stress system, Dr. Kreek explains. Addicts who are heroin-free and methadone-free overreact because the constant on-off of daily heroin use has made the stress system hypersensitive, she says, and heroin addicts who are on methadone react normally because methadone stabilizes this stress system. Methadone acts at the same sites in the brain as heroin, but methadone stays active for about 24 hours while the effects of heroin are felt for only 4 to 6 hours. Because methadone is long-acting, the heroin addict is no longer going into withdrawal three or four times a day. Without the constant activation involved in these withdrawals, the brain's stress system normalizes.

Dr. Kreek's group reported that a majority of cocaine addicts who are abstaining from cocaine use overreact in the metyrapone test, just like the heroin addicts who are abstaining from heroin and not taking methadone. As with heroin addicts, this overreaction in cocaine addicts reflects hypersensitivity of the stress system caused by chronic cocaine abuse.

"We think that addicts may react to emotional stress in the same way that their stress hormone system reacts to the metyrapone test," says Dr. Kreek. At the slightest provocation, CRF and other stress-related neurotransmitters pour out into the brain, producing unpleasant emotions that make the addict want to take drugs again, she suggests. Since life is filled with little provocations, addicts in withdrawal are constantly having their stress system activated, she concludes.

Sources

Kreek, M.J., and Koob, G.F. Drug dependence: Stress and dys-regulation of brain reward pathways. *Drug and Alcohol Dependence* 51:23-47, 1998.

Kreek, M.J., et al. ACTH, cortisol, and b-endorphin response to metyrapone testing during chronic methadone maintenance treatment in humans. *Neuropeptides* 5:277-278, 1984.

Schluger, J.H., et al. Abnormal metyrapone tests during cocaine abstinence. In: L.S. Harris, ed. Problems of Drug Dependence, 1997: Proceedings of the 59th Annual Scientific Meeting, College on Problems of Drug Dependence, Inc. *NIDA Research Monograph Series, Number 178*. NIH Publication No. 98-4305. Pittsburgh, PA: Superintendent of Documents, U.S. Government Printing Office, p. 105, 1998.

Schluger, J.H., et al. Nalmefene causes greater hypothalamic-pituitary-adrenal axis activation than naloxone in normal volunteers: Implications for the treatment of alcoholism. *Alcoholism: Clinical and Experimental Research* 22(7):1430-1436, 1998.

Chapter 11

Today's Workplace

Chapter Contents

Section 11.1—Stress at Work 110
Section 11.2—Workplace Stress and Women's Health 127
Section 11.3—Work Stress and Alcohol Use 130

Section 11.1

Stress at Work

"Stress at Work," National Institute for Occupational Safety and Health (NIOSH), DHHS (NIOSH) Publication No. 99-101, 1999. Prepared by Steven Sauter, Lawrence Murphy, Michael Colligan, Naomi Swanson, Joseph Hurrell, Jr., Frederick Scharf, Jr., Raymond Sinclair, Paula Grubb, Linda Goldenhar, Toni Alterman, Janet Johnston, Anne Hamilton, Julie Tisdale.

The nature of work is changing at whirlwind speed. Perhaps now more than ever before, job stress poses a threat to the health of workers and, in turn, to the health organizations. Through its research program in job stress and through educational materials, NIOSH is committed to providing organizations with knowledge to reduce this threat. This section highlights knowledge about the causes of stress at work and outlines steps that can be taken to prevent job stress.

Stress in Today's Workplace

The longer he waited, the more David worried. For weeks he had been plagued by aching muscles, loss of appetite, restless sleep, and a complete sense of exhaustion. At first he tried to ignore these problems, but eventually he became so short-tempered and irritable that his wife insisted he get a checkup. Now, sitting in the doctor's office and wondering what the verdict would be, he didn't even notice when Theresa took the seat beside him. They had been good friends when she worked in the front office at the plant, but he hadn't seen her since she left three years ago to take a job as a customer service representative. Her gentle poke in the ribs brought him around, and within minutes they were talking and gossiping as if she had never left.

"You got out just in time," he told her. "Since the reorganization, nobody feels safe. It used to be that as long as you did your work, you had a job. That's not for sure anymore. They expect the same production rates even though two guys are now doing the work of three. We're so backed up I'm working twelve-hour shifts six days a week. I swear I hear those machines humming in my sleep. Guys are calling in sick just to get a break. Morale is so bad they're talking about bringing in some consultants to figure out a better way to get the job done."

"Well, I really miss you guys," she said. "I'm afraid I jumped from the frying pan into the fire. In my new job, the computer routes the calls and they never stop. I even have to schedule my bathroom breaks. All I hear the whole day are complaints from unhappy customers. I try to be helpful and sympathetic, but I can't promise anything without getting my boss's approval. Most of the time I'm caught between what the customer wants and company policy. I'm not sure who I'm supposed to keep happy. The other reps are so uptight and tense they don't even talk to one another. We all go to our own little cubicles and stay there until quitting time. To make matters worse, my mother's health is deteriorating. If only I could use some of my sick time to look after her. No wonder I'm in here with migraine headaches and high blood pressure. A lot of the reps are seeing the employee assistance counselor and taking stress management classes, which seems to help. But sooner or later, someone will have to make some changes in the way the place is run."

What Workers Say about Stress on the Job

- Forty percent of workers report their job is "very or extremely stressful." (Source: Northwestern National Life Survey)

- Twenty-six percent of workers report they are "often or very often burned out or stressed by their work." (Source: Families and Work Institute Survey)

- Twenty-nine percent of workers report they feel "quite a bit or extremely stressed at work." (Source: Yale University Survey)

Scope of Stress in the American Workplace

David's and Theresa's stories are unfortunate but not unusual. Job stress has become a common and costly problem in the American workplace, leaving few workers untouched. For example, studies report the following:

- One-fourth of employees view their jobs as the number one stressor in their lives. (Northwestern National Life)

- Three-fourths of employees believe the worker has more on-the-job stress than a generation ago. (Princeton Survey Research Associates)

- Problems at work are more strongly associated with health complaints than are any other life stressor—more so than even financial problems or family problems. (St. Paul Fire and Marine Insurance Co.)

Fortunately, research on job stress has greatly expanded in recent years. But in spite of this attention, confusion remains about the causes, effects, and prevention of job stress. This section summarizes what is known about job stress and what can be done about it.

What Is Job Stress?

Job stress can be defined as the harmful physical and emotional responses that occur when the requirements of the job do not match the capabilities, resources, or needs of the worker. Job stress can lead to poor health and even injury.

The concept of job stress is often confused with challenge, but these concepts are not the same. Challenge energizes us psychologically and physically, and it motivates us to learn new skills and master our jobs. When a challenge is met, we feel relaxed and satisfied. Thus, challenge is an important ingredient for healthy and productive work. The importance of challenge in our work lives is probably what people are referring to when they say "a little bit of stress is good for you."

But for David and Theresa, the situation is different—the challenge has turned into job demands that cannot be met, relaxation has turned to exhaustion, and a sense of satisfaction has turned into feelings of stress. In short, the stage is set for illness, injury, and job failure.

What Are the Causes of Job Stress?

Nearly everyone agrees that job stress results from the interaction of the worker and the conditions of work. Views differ, however, on the importance of worker characteristics versus working conditions as the primary cause of job stress. These differing viewpoints are important because they suggest different ways to prevent stress at work.

According to one school of thought, differences in individual characteristics such as personality and coping style are most important in predicting whether certain job conditions will result in stress—in other words, what is stressful for one person may not be a problem for someone else. This viewpoint leads to prevention strategies that focus on workers and ways to help them cope with demanding job conditions.

Although the importance of individual differences cannot be ignored, scientific evidence suggests that certain working conditions are stressful to most people. The excessive workload demands and conflicting expectations described in David's and Theresa's stories are good examples. Such evidence argues for a greater emphasis on working conditions as the key source of job stress, and for job redesign as a primary prevention strategy.

1995 Workers Compensation Yearbook

In 1960, a Michigan court upheld a compensation claim by an automotive assembly line worker who had difficulty keeping up with the pressures of the production line. To avoid falling behind, he tried to work on several assemblies at the same time and often got parts mixed up. As a result, he was subjected to repeated criticism from the foreman. Eventually he suffered a psychological breakdown.

By 1995, nearly one-half of the States allowed worker compensation claims for emotional disorders and disability due to stress on the job [note, however, that courts are reluctant to uphold claims for what can be considered ordinary working conditions or just hard work].

NIOSH Approach to Job Stress

On the basis of experience and research, NIOSH favors the view that working conditions play a primary role in causing job stress. However, the role of individual factors is not ignored. According to the NIOSH view, exposure to stressful working conditions (called job stressors) can have a direct influence on worker safety and health. Individual and other situational factors can intervene to strengthen or weaken this influence. Theresa's need to care for her ill mother is an increasingly common example of an individual or situational factor that may intensify the effects of stressful working conditions. Examples of individual and situational factors that can help to reduce the effects of stressful working conditions include the following:

• Balance between work and family or personal life
• A support network of friends and coworkers
• A relaxed and positive outlook

Job Conditions That May Lead to Stress

The Design of Tasks. Heavy workload, infrequent rest breaks, long work hours and shiftwork; hectic and routine tasks that have little inherent meaning, do not utilize workers' skills, and provide little sense of control.

Example: David works to the point of exhaustion. Theresa is tied to the computer, allowing little room for flexibility, self-initiative, or rest.

Management Style. Lack of participation by workers in decision-making, poor communication in the organization, lack of family-friendly policies.

Example: Theresa needs to get the boss's approval for everything, and the company is insensitive to her family needs.

Interpersonal Relationships. Poor social environment and lack of support or help from coworkers and supervisors.

Example: Theresa's physical isolation reduces her opportunities to interact with other workers or receive help from them.

Work Roles. Conflicting or uncertain job expectations, too much responsibility, too many "hats to wear."

Example: Theresa is often caught in a difficult situation trying to satisfy both the customer's needs and the company's expectations.

Career Concerns. Job insecurity and lack of opportunity for growth, advancement, or promotion; rapid changes for which workers are unprepared.

Example: Since the reorganization at David's plant, everyone is worried about their future with the company and what will happen next.

Environmental Conditions. Unpleasant or dangerous physical conditions such as crowding, noise, air pollution, or ergonomic problems.

Example: David is exposed to constant noise at work.

Job Stress and Health

Stress sets off an alarm in the brain, which responds by preparing the body for defensive action. The nervous system is aroused and hormones are released to sharpen the senses, quicken the pulse, deepen respiration, and tense the muscles. This response (sometimes called the fight or flight response) is important because it helps us defend against threatening situations. The response is preprogrammed biologically. Everyone responds in much the same way, regardless of whether the stressful situation is at work or home.

Short-lived or infrequent episodes of stress pose little risk. But when stressful situations go unresolved, the body is kept in a constant state of activation, which increases the rate of wear and tear to biological systems. Ultimately, fatigue or damage results, and the ability of the body to repair and defend itself can become seriously compromised. As a result, the risk of injury or disease escalates.

In the past 20 years, many studies have looked at the relationship between job stress and a variety of ailments. Mood and sleep disturbances, upset stomach, headache, and disturbed relationships with family and friends are examples of stress-related problems that are quick to develop and are commonly seen in these studies. These early signs of job stress are usually easy to recognize. But the effects of job stress on chronic diseases are more difficult to see because chronic diseases take a long time to develop and can be influenced by many factors other than stress. Nonetheless, evidence is rapidly accumulating to suggest that stress plays an important role in several types of chronic health problems—especially cardiovascular disease, musculoskeletal disorders, and psychological disorders.

- Health care expenditures are nearly 50% greater for workers who report high levels of stress. (*Journal of Occupational and Environmental Medicine*)

Early Warning Signs of Job Stress

- Headache
- Difficulty in concentrating
- Upset stomach
- Low morale
- Sleep disturbances
- Short temper
- Job dissatisfaction

Job Stress and Health: What the Research Tells Us

Cardiovascular Disease

Many studies suggest that psychologically demanding jobs that allow employees little control over the work process increase the risk of cardiovascular disease.

Musculoskeletal Disorders

On the basis of research by NIOSH and many other organizations, it is widely believed that job stress increases the risk for development of back and upper extremity musculoskeletal disorders.

Psychological Disorders

Several studies suggest that differences in rates of mental health problems (such as depression and burnout) for various occupations are due partly to differences in job stress levels. (Economic and lifestyle differences between occupations may also contribute to some of these problems.)

Workplace Injury

Although more study is needed, there is a growing concern that stressful working conditions interfere with safe work practices and set the stage for injuries at work.

Suicide, Cancer, Ulcers, and Impaired Immune Function

Some studies suggest a relationship between stressful working conditions and these health problems. However, more research is needed before firm conclusions can be drawn. (Source: *Encyclopaedia of Occupational Safety and Health*)

Stress, Health, and Productivity

Some employers assume that stressful working conditions are a necessary evil—that companies must turn up the pressure on workers and set aside health concerns to remain productive and profitable in today's economy. But research findings challenge this belief. Studies show that stressful working conditions are actually associated with increased absenteeism, tardiness, and intentions by workers to quit their jobs—all of which have a negative effect on the bottom line.

Recent studies of so-called healthy organizations suggest that policies benefiting worker health also benefit the bottom line. A healthy organization is defined as one that has low rates of illness, injury, and disability in its workforce and is also competitive in the marketplace. NIOSH research has identified organizational characteristics associated with both healthy, low-stress work and high levels of productivity. Examples of these characteristics include the following:

- Recognition of employees for good work performance
- Opportunities for career development
- An organizational culture that values the individual worker
- Management actions that are consistent with organizational values

Stress Prevention and Job Performance

St. Paul Fire and Marine Insurance Company conducted several studies on the effects of stress prevention programs in hospital settings. Program activities included

1. employee and management education on job stress,
2. changes in hospital policies and procedures to reduce organizational sources of stress, and
3. establishment of employee assistance programs.

In one study, the frequency of medication errors declined by 50% after prevention activities were implemented in a 700-bed hospital. In a second study, there was a 70% reduction in malpractice claims in 22 hospitals that implemented stress prevention activities. In contrast, there was no reduction in claims in a matched group of 22 hospitals that did not implement stress prevention activities. (Source: *Journal of Applied Psychology*)

- According to data from the Bureau of Labor Statistics, workers who must take time off work because of stress, anxiety, or a related disorder will be off the job for about 20 days.

What Can Be Done about Job Stress?

The examples of Theresa and David illustrate two different approaches for dealing with stress at work.

Stress Management. Theresa's company is providing stress management training and an employee assistance program (EAP) to improve the ability of workers to cope with difficult work situations. Nearly one-half of large companies in the United States provide some type of stress management training for their workforces. Stress management programs teach workers about the nature and sources of stress, the effects of stress on health, and personal skills to reduce stress—for example, time management or relaxation exercises. (EAPs provide individual counseling for employees with both work and personal problems.) Stress management training may rapidly reduce stress symptoms such as anxiety and sleep disturbances; it also has the advantage of being inexpensive and easy to implement. However, stress management programs have two major disadvantages:

- The beneficial effects on stress symptoms are often short-lived.

- They often ignore important root causes of stress because they focus on the worker and not the environment.

Organizational Change. In contrast to stress management training and EAP programs, David's company is trying to reduce job stress by bringing in a consultant to recommend ways to improve working conditions. This approach is the most direct way to reduce stress at work. It involves the identification of stressful aspects of work (e.g., excessive workload, conflicting expectations) and the design of strategies to reduce or eliminate the identified stressors. The advantage of this approach is that it deals directly with the root causes of stress at work. However, managers are sometimes uncomfortable with this approach because it can involve changes in work routines or production schedules, or changes in the organizational structure.

As a general rule, actions to reduce job stress should give top priority to organizational change to improve working conditions. But even the most conscientious efforts to improve working conditions are unlikely to eliminate stress completely for all workers. For this reason, a combination of organizational change and stress management is often the most useful approach for preventing stress at work.

How to Change the Organization to Prevent Job Stress

- Ensure that the workload is in line with workers' capabilities and resources.

- Design jobs to provide meaning, stimulation, and opportunities for workers to use their skills.

- Clearly define workers' roles and responsibilities.

- Give workers opportunities to participate in decisions and actions affecting their jobs.

- Improve communications—reduce uncertainty about career development and future employment prospects.

- Provide opportunities for social interaction among workers.

- Establish work schedules that are compatible with demands and responsibilities outside the job.

Source: *American Psychologist*

Preventing Job Stress—Getting Started

No standardized approaches or simple "how to" manuals exist for developing a stress prevention program. Program design and appropriate solutions will be influenced by several factors—the size and complexity of the organization, available resources, and especially the unique types of stress problems faced by the organization. In David's company, for example, the main problem is work overload. Theresa, on the other hand, is bothered by difficult interactions with the public and an inflexible work schedule.

Although it is not possible to give a universal prescription for preventing stress at work, it is possible to offer guidelines on the process of stress prevention in organizations. In all situations, the process for stress prevention programs involves three distinct steps: problem identification, intervention, and evaluation. For this process to succeed, organizations need to be adequately prepared. At a minimum, preparation for a stress prevention program should include the following:

- Building general awareness about job stress (causes, costs, and control)

- Securing top management commitment and support for the program

- Incorporating employee input and involvement in all phases of the program

- Establishing the technical capacity to conduct the program (e.g., specialized training for in-house staff or use of job stress consultants)

Bringing workers or workers and managers together in a committee or problem-solving group may be an especially useful approach for developing a stress prevention program. Research has shown these participatory efforts to be effective in dealing with ergonomic problems in the workplace, partly because they capitalize on workers' first-hand knowledge of hazards encountered in their jobs. However, when forming such working groups, care must be taken to be sure that they are in compliance with current labor laws. The National Labor Relations Act may limit the form and structure of employee involvement in worker-management teams or groups. Employers should seek legal assistance if they are unsure of their responsibilities or obligations under the National Labor Relations Act.

Steps Toward Prevention

Low morale, health and job complaints, and employee turnover often provide the first signs of job stress. But sometimes there are no clues, especially if employees are fearful of losing their jobs. Lack of obvious or widespread signs is not a good reason to dismiss concerns about job stress or minimize the importance of a prevention program.

Step 1—Identify the Problem

The best method to explore the scope and source of a suspected stress problem in an organization depends partly on the size of the organization and the available resources. Group discussions among managers, labor representatives, and employees can provide rich sources of information. Such discussions may be all that is needed to track down and remedy stress problems in a small company. In a larger organization, such discussions can be used to help design formal surveys for gathering input about stressful job conditions from large numbers of employees.

Regardless of the method used to collect data, information should be obtained about employee perceptions of their job conditions and perceived levels of stress, health, and satisfaction. The list of job conditions that may lead to stress and the warning signs and effects of stress provide good starting points for deciding what information to collect.

- Hold group discussions with employees.

- Design an employee survey.

- Measure employee perceptions of job conditions, stress, health, and satisfaction.

- Collect objective data.

- Analyze data to identify problem locations and stressful job conditions.

Objective measures such as absenteeism, illness, turnover rates, or performance problems can also be examined to gauge the presence and scope of job stress. However, at best these measures are only rough indicators of job stress.

Data from discussions, surveys, and other sources should be summarized and analyzed to answer questions about the location of a stress problem and job conditions that may be responsible—for example, are problems present throughout the organization or confined to single departments or specific jobs?

Survey design, data analysis, and other aspects of a stress prevention program may require the help of experts from a local university or consulting firm. However, overall authority for the prevention program should remain in the organization.

Step 2—Design and Implement Interventions

Once the sources of stress at work have been identified and the scope of the problem is understood, the stage is set for design and implementation of an intervention strategy.

In small organizations, the informal discussions that helped identify stress problems may also produce fruitful ideas for prevention. In large organizations, a more formal process may be needed. Frequently, a team is asked to develop recommendations based on analysis of data from Step 1 and consultation with outside experts.

Certain problems, such as a hostile work environment, may be pervasive in the organization and require company-wide interventions. Other problems such as excessive workload may exist only in some departments and thus require more narrow solutions such as redesign of the way a job is performed. Still other problems may be specific to certain employees and resistant to any kind of organizational change, calling instead for stress management or employee assistance interventions. Some interventions might be implemented rapidly (e.g., improved communication, stress management training), but others may require additional time to put into place (e.g., redesign of a manufacturing process).

- Target source of stress for change.

- Propose and prioritize intervention strategies.

- Communicate planned interventions to employees.

- Implement interventions.

Before any intervention occurs, employees should be informed about actions that will be taken and when they will occur. A kick-off event, such as an all-hands meeting, is often useful for this purpose.

Step 3—Evaluate the Interventions

Evaluation is an essential step in the intervention process. Evaluation is necessary to determine whether the intervention is producing desired effects and whether changes in direction are needed.

Time frames for evaluating interventions should be established. Interventions involving organizational change should receive both short- and long-term scrutiny. Short-term evaluations might be done quarterly to provide an early indication of program effectiveness or possible need for redirection. Many interventions produce initial effects that do not persist. Long-term evaluations are often conducted annually and are necessary to determine whether interventions produce lasting effects.

- Conduct both short- and long-term evaluations.

- Measure employee perceptions of job conditions, stress, health, and satisfaction.

- Include objective measures.

- Refine the intervention strategy and return to Step 1.

Evaluations should focus on the same types of information collected during the problem identification phase of the intervention, including information from employees about working conditions, levels of perceived stress, health problems, and satisfaction. Employee perceptions are usually the most sensitive measure of stressful working conditions and often provide the first indication of intervention effectiveness. Adding objective measures such as absenteeism and health care costs may also be useful. However, the effects of job stress interventions on such measures tend to be less clear-cut and can take a long time to appear.

The job stress prevention process does not end with evaluation. Rather, job stress prevention should be seen as a continuous process that uses evaluation data to refine or redirect the intervention strategy.

Stress Prevention Programs: What Some Organizations Have Done

A Small Service Organization. A department head in a small public service organization sensed an escalating level of tension and deteriorating morale among her staff. Job dissatisfaction and health symptoms such as headaches also seemed to be on the rise. Suspecting that stress was a developing problem in the department, she decided to hold a series of all-hands meetings with employees in the different work units of the department to explore this concern further. These meetings could be best described as brainstorming sessions where individual employees freely expressed their views about the scope and sources of stress in their units and the measures that might be implemented to bring the problem under control.

Using the information collected in these meetings and in meetings with middle managers, she concluded that a serious problem probably existed and that quick action was needed. Because she was relatively unfamiliar with the job stress field, she decided to seek help from a faculty member at a local university who taught courses on job stress and organizational behavior.

After reviewing the information collected at the brainstorming sessions, they decided it would be useful for the faculty member to conduct informal classes to raise awareness about job stress—its causes, effects, and prevention—for all workers and managers in the department. It was also decided that a survey would be useful to obtain a more reliable picture of problematic job conditions and stress-related health complaints in the department. The faculty member used information from the meetings with workers and managers to design the survey. The faculty member was also involved in the distribution and collection of the anonymous survey to ensure that workers felt free to respond honestly and openly about what was bothering them. He then helped the department head analyze and interpret the data.

Analysis of the survey data suggested that three types of job conditions were linked to stress complaints among workers:

- Unrealistic deadlines

- Low levels of support from supervisors

- Lack of worker involvement in decision-making

Having pinpointed these problems, the department head developed and prioritized a list of corrective measures for implementation. Examples of these actions included (1) greater participation of employees in work scheduling to reduce unrealistic deadlines and (2) more frequent meetings between workers and managers to keep supervisors and workers updated on developing problems.

A Large Manufacturing Company. Although no widespread signs of stress were evident at work, the corporate medical director of a large manufacturing company thought it would be useful to establish a stress prevention program as a proactive measure. As a first step he discussed this concept with senior management and with union leaders. Together, they decided to organize a labor-management team to develop the program. The team comprised representatives from labor, the medical/employee assistance department, the human resources department, and an outside human resources consulting firm. The consulting firm provided technical advice about program design, implementation, and evaluation. Financial resources for the team and program came from senior management, who made it clear that they supported this activity. The team designed a two-part program. One part focused on management practices and working conditions that could lead to stress. The second part focused on individual health and well-being.

To begin the part of the program dealing with management practices and job conditions, the team worked with the consulting firm to add new questions about job stress to the company's existing employee opinion survey. The survey data were used by the team to identify stressful working conditions and to suggest changes at the work group and/or organizational level. The employee health and well-being part of the program consisted of 12 weekly training sessions. During these sessions, workers and managers learned about common sources and effects of stress at work, and about self-protection strategies such as relaxation methods and improved health behaviors. The training sessions were offered during both work and non-work hours.

The team followed up with quarterly surveys of working conditions and stress symptoms to closely monitor the effectiveness of this two-part program.

Additional Information

National Institute for Occupational Safety and Health (NIOSH)
4676 Columbia Parkway
Cincinnati, Ohio 45226-1998
Toll-Free: 800-356-4674
Telephone Outside the U.S.: 513-533-8328
Fax: 513-533-8573
Website: www.cdc.gov/niosh

ILO Publications Center
P.O. Box 753
Waldorf, MD 20604
Tel: 301-638-3152
Fax: 301-638-3152
Website: http://us.ilo.org/resources/ilopubs.html
E-mail: ILOPubs@Tasco1.com

The Encyclopaedia of Occupational Health and Safety, 4th Edition (ISBN 92-2-109203-8) contains a comprehensive summary of the latest scientific information about the causes and effects of job stress (see Vol. 1, Chapter 5, *Mental Health*; Vol. 2, Chapter 34, Psychosocial and Organizational Factors).

For other examples of job stress interventions, see the *Conditions of Work Digest*, Vol. 11/2, pp. 139-275. This publication may be obtained by contacting the ILO Publications Center.

American Psychological Association (APA)
750 First St., NE
Washington, DC 20002-4242
Toll-Free: 800-964-2000
Fax: 202-336-5723
Website: http://helping.apa.org/find.html.

State psychological associations maintain a listing of licensed psychologists who may be able to help with stress-related issues. Call the APA or your State psychological association for more information, or refer to the APA internet site.

Sources Used in Preparing This Document

Elisburg D [1995]. Workplace stress: legal developments, economic pressures, and violence. In: Burton JF, ed. *1995 Workers' Compensation Year Book*. Horsham, PA: LRP Publications, pp. I-217–I-222.

Sauter SL, Murphy LR, Hurrell JJ, Jr. [1990]. Prevention of work-related psychological disorders. *American Psychologist* 45(10):1146–1158.

Bureau of Labor Statistics [1996]. Bureau of Labor Statistics Homepage [http://stats.bls.gov/]. Tabular data, 1992-96: Number and percentage distribution of nonfatal occupational injuries and illnesses involving days away from work, by nature of injury or illness and number of days away from work. Date accessed: 1998.

Sauter S, Hurrell J, Murphy L, Levi L [1997]. Psychosocial and organizational factors. In: Stellman J, ed. *Encyclopaedia of Occupational Health and Safety*. Vol. 1. Geneva, Switzerland: International Labour Office, pp. 34.1–34.77.

Bond JT, Galinsky E, Swanberg JE [1998]. *The 1997 national study of the changing workforce*. New York, NY: Families and Work Institute.

Jones JW, Barge BN, Steffy BD, Fay LM, Kuntz LK, Wuebker LJ [1988]. Stress and medical malpractice: organizational risk assessment and intervention. *Journal of Applied Psychology* 73(4):727–735.

Goetzel RZ, Anderson DR, Whitmer RW, Ozminkowski RJ, Dunn RL, Wasserman J, Health Enhancement Research Organization (HERO) Research Committee [1998]. The relationship between modifiable health risks and health care expenditures: an analysis of the multi-employer HERO health risk and cost database. *Journal of Occupational and Environmental Medicine* 40(10).

Northwestern National Life Insurance Company [1991]. *Employee burnout: America's newest epidemic*. Minneapolis, MN: Northwestern National Life Insurance Company (now ReliaStar Financial Corporation).

Northwestern National Life Insurance Company [1992]. *Employee burnout: causes and cures*. Minneapolis, MN: Northwestern National Life Insurance Company (now ReliaStar Financial Corporation).

Princeton Survey Research Associates [1997]. *Labor day survey: state of workers*. Princeton, NJ: Princeton Survey Research Associates.

St. Paul Fire and Marine Insurance Company [1992]. *American workers under pressure technical report*. St. Paul, MN: St. Paul Fire and Marine Insurance Company.

Barsade S, Wiesenfeld B, The Marlin Company [1997]. *Attitudes in the American workplace III*. New Haven, CT: Yale University School of Management.

Section 11.2

Workplace Stress and Women's Health

Reprinted with permission, "Workplace Stress Can Lead to Declines in Overall Health of Working Women," by Steven Reinberg, May 26, 2000 © Reuters Limited, 2000; and "Is the Stress of Mothering a Health Risk?" © *Inside DUMC*, August 4, 1997, Vol. 6 Number 16, Duke University Medical Center, reprinted with permission.

Workplace Stress Can Lead to Declines in Overall Health of Working Women

Working women who have little control over their job, combined with high job demands and low work-related social support, have declining health status over time, according to researchers from Harvard University.

Dr. Ichiro Kawachi and colleagues from Boston, Massachusetts, studied 21,290 female nurses over 4 years using a novel way of characterizing work stress. Bad stress was defined as high levels of workload with little ability to control that workload and low work-related social support. Good stress was defined as high workload but also a high degree of control over that workload. Low stress was defined as low workload with lots of control.

"What's new about this," Dr Kawachi told Reuters Health, "is that we typically tend to ask people about stress in a very simplistic way. When you ask most people, 'Are you stressed on the job?' you are likely to have the CEO of a company saying yes, as well as a secretary and other people in the firm. Whereas if you ask about stress the way we did, you get a big difference in the way people respond."

Using the Karasek's job content questionnaire and a modified version of the short form 36 questionnaire, the team measured "physical functioning, role limitations due to physical health problems, bodily pain, vitality, social functioning, role limitations due to emotional problems and mental health," according to their report in the *British Medical Journal* for May 26, 2000.

Dr. Kawachi said, "We found that women in the bad stress category deteriorated much faster in terms of mental health and activities of daily living compared to women who reported low stress or good stress categories. The model has been linked in the past to increased risk of heart attack, hypertension, and pregnancy complications."

He noted that rather than looking at these somewhat rare events, he and his group looked at the way that job stress affects people's daily lives. "People got more symptoms of anxiety and depression. They reported more physical problems, such as difficulty climbing stairs, getting about, and less energy, all of which has a close link to sickness absences."

In the same population, he said, "women who were smoking throughout the 4-year period had their health decline as well, and the amount of decline was almost comparable to the effect of job strain or vice versa. To the extent that we as doctors counsel patients to stop smoking to improve their health, we might say the same about trying to avoid a stressful work environment."

According to Dr. Kawachi, there are two responses to findings like his: focus on the workers and send them off to stress management courses, or focus on the workplace itself. "There are a number of things that employers can do to increase the amount of control in the workplace and thereby improve their employees' health," he said. In nursing, for example, that might include things like more flexible hours, less forced overtime, and less interference by managed care.

"And," Dr. Kawachi said, "I would argue that a less stressful workplace environment means lower sickness and absenteeism rates, which is good for the bottom line as well as for the workers."

Is the Stress of Mothering a Health Risk for Working Women?

Stress hormone levels in working mothers rise each morning and stay high until bedtime, putting them at higher risk than other working women for health problems such as heart attacks, according to a study by Duke researchers. The number of children at home made no difference in stress levels—stress hormone levels were as high with one child as with several.

"The good news would be that working mothers' stress levels don't go up with the number of children in the home," said Dr. Redford Williams, chief of behavioral medicine at Duke and primary investigator for the study, published in the July 23, 1997 issue of *Psychosomatic Medicine*. "The bad news is it only takes one to boost that stress level."

Linda Luecken, lead author of the study, cautioned that since the study did not include stay-at-home mothers, the researchers can't compare stress levels of working mothers and mothers not employed outside the home. "It is tempting to consider this as evidence that mothers should not work outside the home, but until we compare stress levels of the two groups of mothers, we cannot draw any such conclusions," she said.

The research, funded by the National Heart, Lung, and Blood Institute, studied 109 women working in clerical and customer service positions. The level of hormones associated with stress that are excreted in urine was measured over a two-day period. Study participants collected urine samples in three time periods—during the workday, in the evening after work, and from bedtime through waking. Urine samples were later measured for hormones related to stress, including cortisol, norepinephrine, and epinephrine.

The women also completed a series of questionnaires, including demographic information, evaluation of stress at home and at work, and measures of social support. Researchers correlated hormone excretion levels with other factors such as whether the women were single or married, whether they had children at home, and the number of children in the household.

Regardless of marital status, women with children living at home excreted higher levels of the stress hormone cortisol throughout a 24-hour period than did working women without children, the researchers reported. Mothers with one child at home had stress hormone levels as high as working mothers with more than one child. While the level of cortisol peaked during working hours for all women, the levels were consistently higher throughout the day for working mothers.

All participants showed a significant increase in levels of epinephrine and norepinephrine, known as catecholamines, during the workday and there was little, if any, change from workday to evening levels. In contrast, other studies have shown men experience a drop in catecholamines when they come home from work.

Catecholamines are associated with "effort" or activity, Williams said, while cortisol has been shown to relate to "distress" and a lack of personal control. Chronic elevations of cortisol in working mothers could lead to health problems, he said, by suppressing the immune system and also heightening the impact of the catecholamines.

"We believe the increased stress levels seen in the employed mothers is related to increased strain at home, rather than work strain, but that the increased strain exerts its physiological effects over the entire day," Luecken said.

Williams said job strain was about the same in all the women, but the working mothers reported significantly higher levels of home strain than women without children at home. The level of home strain was independent of marital status. The working mothers reported both higher demand on them in the home and lower control of the situation.

In other studies, increasing social support reduced stress levels, but the Duke researchers found social support did not buffer the effect of having a child. Instead, Williams and the other Duke researchers said quality of work and family experiences may be key factors in the women's stress levels.

"The level of satisfaction at work and home may be what makes a difference," Williams said. "Maybe the only way to reduce the burden on these working mothers is to share it, to more equally divide home responsibility."

Section 11.3

Work Stress and Alcohol Use

"Work Stress and Alcohol Use," by Michael R. Frone, Ph.D., *Alcohol Research & Health*, Vol. 23, No. 4, 1999, pp.284-291, National Institute on Alcohol Abuse and Alcoholism (NIAAA), NIH Publication No. 00-3466.

Employee alcohol use[1]—whether or not it occurs on the job—is an important social policy issue, because it can undermine employee health as well as productivity. From a managerial perspective, the specific problems created by alcohol or other drug (AOD) use may include impaired performance of job-related tasks, accidents or injuries, poor attendance, high employee turnover, and increased health care costs (e.g., Ames et al. 1997; Dawson 1994; Frone 1998; Martin et al. 1994; Normand et al. 1994; Roman and Blum 1995).

These outcomes may reduce productivity, increase the costs of doing business, and more generally impede employers' ability to compete effectively in an increasingly competitive economic environment. It is therefore not surprising that alcohol researchers, as well as researchers in the management and economics fields, take considerable interest in the factors that cause or explain employee alcohol use.

The literature on the causes of employee alcohol use generally takes one of two perspectives. The first perspective views the causes of employee alcohol use as external to the workplace. In other words, an employee may have a family history of alcohol abuse that leaves him or her vulnerable to developing drinking problems, have personality traits reflecting low behavioral self-control that make it difficult to avoid alcohol, or experience social norms and social networks outside work—such as friends who drink heavily—that affect drinking behavior (e.g., Ames and Janes 1992; Normand et al. 1994; Trice and Sonnenstuhl 1990).

Although external factors clearly influence employee drinking habits, a second perspective views the causes of employee alcohol use as arising, at least in part, from the work environment itself. This perspective can be further disaggregated into several narrower paradigms. Although researchers differ somewhat in how they label and categorize those narrower paradigms (for reviews, see Ames and Janes [1992] and Trice and Sonnenstuhl [1990]), three versions appear consistently in the literature:

- **The social control** paradigm suggests that alcohol use may be higher among employees who are not integrated into or regulated by the work organization. Thus, two important risk factors in the social control paradigm are low levels of supervision and low visibility of work behavior (Trice and Sonnenstuhl 1990).

- **The culture/availability** paradigm suggests that work settings where alcohol is physically or socially available may promote alcohol use among employees (Ames and Grube 1999; Ames and Janes 1992; Trice and Sonnenstuhl 1990).

- **Physical availability of alcohol at work** is defined as the ease with which alcohol can be obtained for consumption on the job, during breaks, and at work-related events (Ames and Grube 1999). Social availability of alcohol at work is defined as the degree to which fellow workers support drinking either off or on the job (Ames and Grube 1999; Ames and Janes 1992; Trice and Sonnenstuhl 1990).

- **The alienation/stress** paradigm suggests that employee alcohol use may be a response to the physical and psychosocial qualities of the work environment (Ames and Janes 1992; Trice and Sonnenstuhl 1990), such as work demands on an employee, an employee's level of boredom, lack of participation in decision-making, and interpersonal conflict with supervisors and co-workers.

Work-Stress Paradigm

In the alcohol literature, work alienation and work stress typically have been treated as separate paradigms (e.g., Trice and Sonnenstuhl 1990). The work-alienation paradigm focuses on work characteristics that lead to unenriched jobs, such as those in which workers use only minimal skills, have little job control (e.g., lack control over the pace of work or its content), and have little or no input into decision-making. In contrast, the work-stress paradigm emphasizes other potentially aversive work conditions, which are labeled "work stressors." Common work stressors include dangerous work conditions; noxious physical work environments (e.g., conditions that are too hot or cold, noisy, or dirty); interpersonal conflict with supervisors or coworkers; heavy workloads; unfair treatment regarding pay, benefits, and promotions; and job insecurity (e.g., threat of layoffs). Trice and Sonnenstuhl (1990) argued that the stress and alienation paradigms are conceptually distinct, because the alienation paradigm assumes that work is universally important in people's lives, whereas the stress paradigm does not make this assumption. In other words, the alienation paradigm proposes that factors leading to unenriched jobs will be aversive to all employees, whereas the stress paradigm suggests that work stressors may not be aversive to all employees, because work is not universally important. Although Martin (1990) pointed out many similarities between the alienation and stress paradigms, he maintained a distinction between them in his review of the literature.

Four compelling reasons, however, support subsuming the work-alienation paradigm under a general work-stress paradigm:

1. The literature on work stress includes workplace alienation factors in taxonomies of work stressors and in major models of work stress (for a review, see Hurrell et al. 1998).

2. Both paradigms are based on the assumption that alcohol use represents a means of regulating negative emotions (e.g., depression, anxiety, or anger) or thoughts that result from aversive work environments.

3. Despite a basic assumption of the work-alienation paradigm, evidence shows that work does not have a high level of importance

in every person's life. Variability in the psychological importance of work exists from person to person (Frone et al. 1997a).

4. Both theoretical and empirical research suggest that individual differences in the psychological importance of work may be important in explaining when work stressors will be related to alcohol use (e.g., Frone et al. 1997a).

Based on these considerations, this document simply treats work-alienation factors as work stressors.

Even if one subsumes the alienation paradigm into a broad work-stress paradigm, the focus of past work-stress research has been restrictive in that attention has generally focused on stressors that occur within the work role (e.g., work demands and conflict with coworkers). Another type of work-related stressor, however, occurs when the demands of work begin to interfere with other social roles. For example, work-family conflict represents the extent to which work and family life interfere with one another (Frone et al. 1997c). This type of stressor should be incorporated into the work-stress paradigm, because only employed people can experience it. This article, however, separately examines past research on work stressors (within-role stressors) and work-family conflict (between-role stressors) because they represent qualitatively different aspects of a person's work life.

Evidence from Research

A comprehensive review of the entire body of literature on work stressors and alcohol use is beyond the scope of this article,[2] it does, however, offer a taxonomy consisting of four work-stress models that provides a useful way of organizing recent research. The following sections define each model and summarize representative studies. Although a few studies explicitly tested more than one model, the primary goal of most studies was to test one of the four models (see Figure 11.1).

Among the studies reviewed in this article, two basic research designs are used. The most common research design is the cross-sectional study, in which work stressors and alcohol outcomes are measured at the same time. Although the underlying hypothesis tested in these studies is that work stressors cause alcohol use, cross-sectional studies cannot support conclusions regarding cause and effect. Those studies can only document that work stressors are related to alcohol use. A cross-sectional relation may be attributable to the fact that work stressors cause alcohol use. However, equally plausible is the concept that alcohol use may cause increased levels of work stress or that the relation is spurious, because some other unmeasured variables, such as personality traits, cause some people to choose stressful jobs and to drink heavily. The second research design is the longitudinal study, in which work stressors and alcohol outcomes are measured at two or more different points in time. In the typical longitudinal study, work stressors assessed at baseline (e.g., 1996) are used to predict alcohol use at a later point in time (e.g., 1997) after controlling for initial

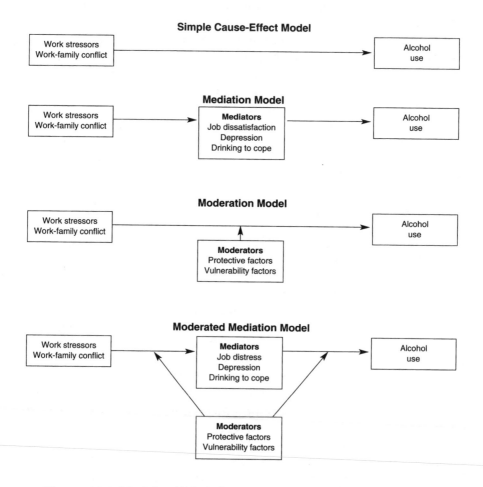

Figure 11.1. *Models of Work Stress and Alcohol Use.*

differences in alcohol use at baseline. Although less common, longitudinal studies offer more convincing evidence that exposure to work stressors causes increases in alcohol use. Unless a study is explicitly labeled as longitudinal, the reader should assume that the studies reviewed below are cross-sectional.

Simple Cause-Effect Model

The first model presented in the figure is the simple cause-effect model of work stress and alcohol use. Research based on this model simply attempts to document an overall relation between various work stressors and different dimensions of alcohol use, usually controlling for basic demographic variables, such as age, gender, income, and occupation. Support for the simple cause-effect model is mixed.

For example, Parker and Farmer (1990) and Roxburgh (1998) reported that low levels of job complexity (i.e., jobs that require little thought and independent judgment) are related to impaired control over drinking and elevated daily consumption. Ragland and colleagues (1995) found that a measure of work problems was positively related to heavy drinking[3] and average weekly consumption; job demands, and job control, however, were not related to alcohol use. Using longitudinal data, Crum and colleagues (1995) reported that men holding jobs that were high in demands and low in job control were more likely to develop either an alcohol abuse or alcohol dependence disorder than were men in jobs that lacked one or both of these two job stressors.

The researchers, however, found no such relation among women. Hemmingsson and Lundberg (1998) found that low job control, but not high job demands, was associated with a diagnosis of alcohol abuse or dependence among men. These researchers did not include women in their study.

The studies summarized so far suggest that jobs low in complexity and control and high in demands are related to increased employee alcohol use. Some evidence indicates that these work stressors may be more strongly related to alcohol use among men. Nonetheless, a number of studies assessing similar work stressors have failed to support the simple cause-effect model (Frone et al. 1997a; Greenberg and Grunberg 1995). Furthermore, even when gender differences are found in the strength of the relation between work stressors and alcohol use, no clear pattern exists across studies (Romelsjo et al. 1992; Roxburgh 1998).

The inconsistent findings from studies testing the simple cause-effect model are not surprising, because the model has two inherent limitations. First, the model is based on the premise that work stressors are causal antecedents of alcohol use for all, or at least many, employees. Although most adults consume alcohol, it is unlikely that most adults use alcohol to cope with unpleasant work conditions. Many coping behaviors, such as talking to friends or relatives, exercise, leisure activities, and addressing work problems at their source, relieve the resulting negative emotions from work stressors more effectively and have fewer negative side effects than alcohol consumption. It may be more reasonable to assume that only employees who lack certain resources or who have certain vulnerabilities (e.g., holding the belief that alcohol use relieves negative emotions or having heavily drinking peers) will use alcohol to cope with work stressors. If this assumption is true, then researchers who do not identify subgroups at risk for stress-induced drinking may have inconsistent and nonsignificant findings.

The second limitation is that even if the simple cause-effect model supports a relation between work stressors and alcohol use, no information is provided about why work stressors cause increased alcohol use. That is, the model makes no attempt to account for intervening variables, such as negative emotions, that would explain how work stressors are related to alcohol use. The underlying assumption of the simple cause-effect model of work stress and alcohol use is that work stressors cause negative emotions, which, in turn, cause alcohol use to relieve those emotions. Nonetheless, this assumption needs to be tested; failing to model intervening variables may render a study less likely to find a work stressor-alcohol relation. These observations have motivated many researchers to move beyond simple models of work stress and alcohol use (Wilsnack and Wilsnack 1992).

Mediation Model

The mediation model explicitly incorporates the variables thought to link work stressors to alcohol use, such as sadness or anger (i.e., negative affect), inability to relax, and the drinker's reason for drinking (i.e., drinking motives), such as to "let off steam." By including these mediating (i.e., intervening) variables, the mediation model goes beyond the simple cause-effect model by trying to explain why or by what mechanism work stressors are related to alcohol use.

Although two studies (Cooper et al. 1990; Kawakami et al. 1993) failed to support the mediating role of negative affect, a number of studies support mediated models of work stress. For example, Vasse and colleagues (1998) reported that high work demands and poor interpersonal relations with supervisors and coworkers were positively related to anxiety, which was positively related to average weekly alcohol consumption. Martin and colleagues (1996) found that job demands and low job control were related to higher levels of drinking to cope with negative affect, which was positively related to both average monthly alcohol consumption and problem drinking. In addition, one study examined the mediating role of both job dissatisfaction and drinking to cope. Greenberg and Grunberg (1995) reported that workers who felt their skills were underused, had low job control, and had little participation in decision-making were more likely to be dissatisfied with their jobs. This dissatisfaction was, in turn, positively related to drinking to cope, which was positively related to both heavy drinking and problem drinking.

Moderation Model

The moderation model explicitly includes variables that moderate the relation between work stressors and alcohol use. This model is an interactional one, in which work stressors interact with certain variables that either place a worker at increased risk for or protect the worker from developing problems with alcohol. The basic premise is that the strength of the relation between work stressors and alcohol use differs as a function of the level of the risk and protective variables. The moderation model, therefore, goes beyond the simple cause-effect model by trying to explain when or under what conditions work stressors are related to alcohol use. In other words, work stressors are not assumed to be related to alcohol use among all employees.

Several studies have tested this model. For example, building from identity theory,[4] Frone and colleagues (1997a) showed that both job demands and the lack of a clearly defined role at the workplace (i.e., role ambiguity) were positively related to heavy drinking only among employees who reported that their work role was psychologically important for self-definition. Among participants who reported low psychological importance of work, the work stressors were unrelated to heavy drinking. Grunberg and colleagues (1999) reported that work pressure predicted higher average daily alcohol consumption and problem drinking among people who reported that they typically drank to relax and forget about problems than among people who did not drink for those reasons. Among people in the latter group, work pressure was unrelated to the alcohol outcomes. Finally, Parker and Harford (1992) examined the moderating influence of gender-role attitudes on the relation of job competition to alcohol use. Traditional gender-role attitudes represent the belief that men should be bread-winners and women should take care of home and family. Egalitar-ian gender-role attitudes represent the belief that men and women should share bread-winning and domestic responsibilities. For women, job competition was more strongly related to drinks per drinking oc-casion, whereas loss of control over drinking was more strongly re-lated among those with more traditional gender-role attitudes. In contrast, for men, job competition was more strongly related to drinks per drinking occasion and loss of control over drinking among those individuals with more egalitarian gender-role attitudes.

Moderated Mediation Model

This model combines the features of the mediation and the mod-eration models. By explicitly including both mediating and moderat-ing variables, the moderated mediation model goes beyond each of the other three models by simultaneously trying to explain how as well as when work stressors are related to alcohol use. Several variations of this model can be devised, depending on the moderator variables. For example, one could have a model in which a given vulnerability or protective factor only moderates one of the paths connecting work stressors to alcohol use. One also might hypothesize moderating ef-fects on both paths, but with different vulnerability or protective fac-tors moderating each path.

Only two studies have proposed and tested a moderated mediation model of work stress and alcohol use. Building from several different theoretical frame-works, Cooper and colleagues (1990) and Grunberg and colleagues (1998) hypothesized that (1) work stressors are posi-tively related to job dissatisfaction and (2) job dissatisfaction is posi-tively related to alcohol use among vulnerable people. Supporting the first hypothesis, Cooper and colleagues (1990) found that work de-mands and lack of job control were positively related to job dissatis-faction. Likewise, Grunberg and colleagues (1998) reported that high levels of job demands, interpersonal criticism from supervisors and coworkers, and feeling stuck in one's job were positively related to job dissatisfaction. With regard to the second hypothesis, Cooper and colleagues (1990) found some support that positive alcohol expectan-cies,[5] the general belief that one is competent, and coping with diffi-cult situations by avoiding them (i.e., avoidance coping) had a moderating influence. For example, job dissatisfaction was more strongly related to problem drinking among people who reported high levels of avoidance coping. Likewise, Grunberg and colleagues (1998) reported that job dissatisfaction was related to problem drinking among those who reported that they drank to reduce negative emotions. Among people who did not drink for this reason, job dissatisfaction was unrelated to problem drinking.

Work-Family Conflict

Work-family conflict represents the extent to which demands and responsibilities in one role (work or home) interfere with meeting the demands and responsibilities in the other role (home or work) (Frone et al. 1997c). Because work-family conflict involves difficulties with integrating work and family life, it is a between-role stressor that may cause increased alcohol consumption. In a review of workplace predictors of women's drinking, Shore (1992) concluded that conflict between work and other social roles is not predictive of alcohol use. This conclusion was based on the finding that women who had a large number of social roles (e.g., employee, spouse, parent, and church member) did not report higher levels of alcohol consumption or problem drinking than did women who had only a few social roles. This research, however, suffers from an important conceptual limitation. The number of social roles a person holds is not a good indicator of the amount of conflict among those roles. Having several social roles is a necessary but not sufficient condition for inter-role conflict. Depending on a variety of circumstances, some people with work and family roles experience no conflict between the roles, whereas other people experience a high degree of conflict between them (Frone et al. 1997c). Alcohol researchers in this area, therefore, need to measure work-family conflict directly. Several recent studies have done so and have provided tests of the first three models shown in Figure 11.1.

Simple Cause-Effect Model

One study, which used a small sample of 71 workers, failed to find a relation between work-family conflict and the amount of alcohol consumed over the preceding 7 days (Steptoe et al. 1998). In contrast, Bromet and colleagues (1990) reported that work-family conflict was positively related to daily alcohol consumption in a sample of blue-collar working women. Frone and colleagues (1996) found that work-family conflict was positively related to heavy drinking among men and women in two community samples of employed parents. In a longitudinal follow-up study, Frone and colleagues (1997b) reported that work-family conflict assessed in 1989 predicted heavy drinking in 1993 among men and women. Using a representative national sample, Frone reported that work-family conflict was positively related to a diagnosis of AOD dependence, but not AOD abuse, among men and women. In summary, past research based on the simple cause-effect model provides consistent evidence that work-family conflict is related to elevated alcohol use among men and women. Nonetheless, this model does not explain why work-family conflict is related to alcohol use or whether certain people are more prone to alcohol use when exposed to work-family conflict.

Mediation Model

Two studies tested the process that explains why work-family conflict is related to alcohol use. Both studies tested the general hypothesis that work-family conflict causes negative emotions, which in turn cause increased alcohol use. Vasse and colleagues (1998) found that work-family conflict was positively related to overall emotional distress, which in turn was positively related to average weekly alcohol consumption. Frone and colleagues (1994) tested the mediating role of both role-related and general negative emotions. They reported that work-family conflict was positively related to both job and family dissatisfaction, which were positively related to general psychological distress (i.e., combined symptoms of depression and anxiety) that was in turn positively related to heavy drinking.

Moderation Model

Only one study tested the moderation model. Frone and colleagues (1993) tested the moderating role of tension-reduction expectancies, which are the belief that alcohol promotes relaxation and alleviates negative emotions. They reported that work-family conflict was positively related to drinking to cope and problem drinking only among people with strong tension-reduction expectancies.

Conclusions

Research on work stress (work stressors and work-family conflict) and alcohol use is growing—the number of studies published on the subject grew from 17 in the 1980s (Cooper et al. 1990) to 39 in the 1990s (at the time this article was written). Several conclusions can be drawn from the recent research on work stress and alcohol use.

First, research has expanded to include sources of stress within the work role (i.e., work stressors) as well as sources of stress representing the integration of work and family roles (i.e., work-family conflict). Second, evidence is growing that work stressors and work-family conflict are related to alcohol use. Finally, despite a continuing over-reliance on the simple cause-effect model, a clear trend exists toward the development and testing of more sophisticated models of work stress and alcohol use. Few studies published during the 1980s moved beyond the simple cause-effect model; however, increasingly sophisticated models have provided insight on how work stressors and work-family conflict are related to alcohol use. These models have also offered a richer picture of the people most at risk for engaging in work stress-induced drinking.

Future Research

Although research on work stress and alcohol use is increasingly sophisticated, future research could benefit from several refinements. More attention needs to be devoted to the assessment of work stressors. In the 31 studies reviewed for this article, the most common work stressors studied were job demands, job control, and job complexity. The research evidence suggests that these stressors are related to alcohol use, but we do not know whether they are the most important work stressors. Thus, future research should be more systematic and inclusive in its assessment of work stressors. In addition, researchers often develop their own measures of work stressors, even though validated measures exist in the organizational behavior and occupational health literatures. Consequently, the comparability of studies is limited. This problem is partly remedied by Hurrell and colleagues' (1998) review describing work-stressor measures that could be helpful for future research. Because most research on work stress and alcohol use has used self-report measures of perceived stressors, more attention should be paid to developing and using objective measures of work stressors (Greiner et al. 1997). For example, rather than relying on employee self-reports of whether the work environment is too noisy or the air quality is low, physical measurements of noise and air quality could be used. Likewise, trained observers might rate specific variables, such as workload or conflicts with customers. Examination of general models of work stress, including models of work-family conflict, developed outside the alcohol literature may provide additional insights for alcohol researchers (Frone et al. 1997c; Hurrell et al. 1998).

Studies vary widely in the types of alcohol outcomes they assess. One issue is whether the type of alcohol outcome used affects the strength of the relation of work stressors and work-family conflict to alcohol use. Perhaps work stressors are more strongly related to increases in episodes of heavy drinking than they are to increases in average daily consumption. Such differences may explain some of the inconsistencies across studies. Another issue is that little attention has been paid to the context of alcohol use. Most studies use measures of over-all alcohol use and have given almost no attention to on-the-job alcohol use. An interesting question is whether different relations exist between work stressors and measures of general versus on-the-job alcohol use.

The results summarized in this article demonstrate that the relation between work stress and alcohol consumption is more complex than implied by the simple cause-effect model. Therefore, more attention should be devoted to identifying and testing plausible mediating and moderating variables. Of the four models presented, the moderated mediation model may have the most potential for helping researchers understand the relation between work stress and alcohol use, because it simultaneously addresses the two fundamental issues of why and when work stressors are related to alcohol use.

In addition, future research should focus on how different developmental stages might play a role in the connection between work stressors and alcohol consumption. For example, the relation between work stressors and alcohol use may be more pronounced among adolescents and young adults because they are just entering the work force and are the most likely to engage in heavy alcohol use. Extensive literature documents that the number of hours worked per week is cross-sectionally and longitudinally related to higher levels of alcohol use among employed adolescents (for a review, see Frone 1999). This finding suggests that employment has a causal influence on adolescent drinking. Because of the narrow focus on work hours, however, we do not know what it is about the work environment that promotes increases in adolescents' alcohol use. It could be exposure to work stressors, low social control, or the social and physical availability of alcohol. Frone and Windle (1997) provided initial evidence of the possible role of work stress. They found that job dissatisfaction was positively related to the frequency of drinking and the quantity consumed per drinking occasion in a sample of employed high school students.

142

The final issue for future research is the need for longitudinal studies of work stress and alcohol use. Crum and colleagues (1995) found that workload and job control predicted new cases of alcohol abuse and alcohol dependence over a 12-month period, and Frone and colleagues (1997b) found that work-family conflict predicted increases in heavy drinking over a 4-year period. Nonetheless, scant longitudinal data exist in the literature. Although we can conclude that work stressors and work-family conflict are related to alcohol use, the causal direction of this relation is still unclear because of the heavy reliance on cross-sectional research designs. In future longitudinal research, daily or weekly diary studies (in which participants record their drinking behaviors and stressors each day) would be especially useful. Because variations in exposure to stressors and drinking behaviors may follow a short-term (daily or weekly) cycle, diary methods are likely to be more sensitive than traditional panel designs, which follow a group of study participants over time but collect data at time points that are separated by several months to several years.

Issues for Future Research on Work Stress and Alcohol Use

Future research on work stress and alcohol use should include the following:

- More attention to types of job stressors examined and their measurement

- More attention to types of alcohol use outcomes, including
    - Level of involvement (i.e., drinking motives, usual consumption, heavy consumption, and alcohol problems or dependence)
    - Context of use (i.e., overall consumption and on-the-job consumption)

- Broader focus on mediators and moderators of the relation between work-related stressors and alcohol use

- Examination of developmental stages, especially the study of employed adolescents and young adults

- Longitudinal designs with closely spaced waves of measurement, such as daily diary studies

Footnotes

1. Most studies of work stress have used a broad array of alcohol consumption measures (e.g., drinks per day, frequency of drinking, drinks per drinking occasion, and frequency of heavy drinking) or non-diagnostic measures of problematic alcohol use (e.g., a count of the number of alcohol-related problems experienced). For general discussion, the term "alcohol use" is used to refer collectively to all possible alcohol outcomes. When reviewing a specific study, alcohol consumption is described as it was assessed (e.g., average monthly consumption). If a study used an outcome variable that reflected general and non-diagnostic alcohol-related problems, it is referred to as problem drinking. The terms "alcohol abuse" and "alcohol dependence" are only used when the study being reviewed used criteria defined in the American Psychiatric Association's *Diagnostic and Statistical Manual of Mental Disorders* (DSM-III, DSM-III-R, and DSM-IV).

2. For this article, the author located a total of 31 studies published during the 1990s that examined the relation between work stressors and alcohol use. A complete list of those studies can be obtained from the author. All studies that specifically examined the relation of work-family conflict to alcohol use are cited in this article.

3. The definition of the term "heavy drinking" can vary from study to study. However, researchers usually measure "heavy drinking" based on the frequency in which a subject consumes five or more drinks per day or per sitting or the frequency of drinking to intoxication. A standard drink is defined as one 12-ounce beer, one 5-ounce glass of wine, or 1.5 ounces of distilled spirits.

4. Identity theory suggests that people define who they are in terms of social roles (e.g., employee, spouse, and parent). However, a given social role (e.g., employee) may not be equally important for self-definition for all people. In other words, the psychological importance of social roles may vary across people. Therefore, problems that occur in a given social role (e.g., conflict with one's supervisor) may or may not be experienced as stressful. For example, work stressors should only have a negative effect on people who define themselves in

144

terms of their work, whereas job stressors should not affect people who do not define themselves in terms of their work.

5. Alcohol expectancies are a drinker's expectations of how alcohol will affect him or her. For example, people with positive alcohol expectancies may believe that alcohol relaxes them and makes them more socially competent.

References

Ames, G.M., and Grube, J.W. Alcohol availability and workplace drinking: Mixed method analyses. *Journal of Studies on Alcohol* 60:383-393, 1999.

Ames, B.M., and Janes, C. A cultural approach to conceptualizing alcohol and the workplace. *Alcohol Health & Research World* 16:112-119, 1992.

Ames, G.M.; Grube, J.W.; and Moore, R.S. The relationship of drinking and hangovers to workplace problems: An empirical study. *Journal of Studies on Alcohol* 58:37-47, 1997.

Bromet, E.J.; Dew, M.A.; and Parkinson, D.K. Spillover between work and family: A study of blue-collar working women. In: Eckenrode, J., and Gore, S., eds. *Stress Between Work and Family*. New York: Plenum Press, 1990. pp. 133-151.

Cooper, M.L.; Russell, M.; and Frone, M.R. Work stress and alcohol effects: A test of stress-induced drinking. *Journal of Health and Social Behavior* 31:260-276, 1990.

Crum, R.M.; Muntaner, C.; Eaton, W.W.; and Anthony, J.C. Occupational stress and the risk of alcohol abuse and dependence. *Alcoholism: Clinical and Experimental Research* 19:647-655, 1995.

Dawson, D.A. Heavy drinking and the risk of occupational injury. *Accident Analysis and Prevention* 26:655-665, 1994.

Frone, M.R. Predictors of work injuries among employed adolescents. *Journal of Applied Psychology* 83:565-576, 1998.

Frone, M.R. Developmental consequences of youth employment. In: Barling, J., and E.K. Kelloway, eds. *Young Workers: Varieties of Experience*. Washington, DC: American Psychological Association, 1999.pp. 89-128.

Frone, M.R. Work-family conflict and employee psychiatric disorders: The national comorbidity survey. *Journal of Applied Psychology*, in press.

Frone, M.R., and Windle, M. Job dissatisfaction and substance use among employed high school students: The moderating influence of active and avoidant coping styles. *Substance Use and Misuse* 32:571-585, 1997.

Frone, M.R.; Russell, M; and Cooper, M.L. Relationship of work-family conflict, gender, and alcohol expectancies to alcohol use/abuse. *Journal of Organizational Behavior* 14:545-558, 1993.

Frone, M.R.; Barnes, G.M.; and Farrell, M.P. Relationship of work-family conflict to substance use among employed mothers: The role of negative affect. *Journal of Marriage and the Family* 56:1019-1030, 1994.

Frone, M.R.; Russell, M.; and Barnes, G.M. Work-family conflict, gender, and health-related outcomes: A study of employed parents in two community samples. *Journal of Occupational Health Psychology* 1:57-69, 1996.

Frone, M.R.; Russell, M.R.; and Cooper, M.L. Job stressors, job involvement, and employee health: A test of identity theory. *Journal of Occupational and Organizational Psychology* 68:1-11, 1997a.

Frone, M.R.; Russell, M.; and Cooper, M.L. Relation of work-family conflict to health outcomes: A four-year longitudinal study of employed parents. *Journal of Occupational and Organizational Psychology* 70:325-336, 1997b.

Frone, M.R.; Yardley, J.K.; and Markel, K. Developing and testing an integrative model of the work-family interface. *Journal of Vocational Behavior* 50:145-167, 1997c.

Greenberg, E.S., and Grunberg, L. Work alienation and problem alcohol behavior. *Journal of Health and Social Behavior* 36:83-102, 1995.

Greiner, B.A.; Ragland, D.R.; Kruase, N.; Syme, S.L; and Fisher, J.M. Objective measurement of occupational stress factors: An example with San Francisco urban transit operators. *Journal of Occupational Health Psychology* 4:325-342, 1997.

Grunberg, L.; Moore,S.; and Greenberg, E.S. Work stress and problem alcohol behavior: A test of the spill-over model. *Journal of Organizational Behavior* 19:487-502, 1998.

Grunberg, L.; Moore, S.; Anderson-Connolly, R; and Greenberg, E.S. Work stress and self-reported alcohol use: The moderating role of escapist reasons for drinking. *Journal of Occupational Health Psychology* 4:29-36, 1999.

Hemmingsson, T., and Lundberg, I. Work control, work demands, and work social support in relation to alcoholism among young men. *Alcoholism: Clinical and Experimental Research* 22:921-927, 1998.

Hurrell, J.J., Jr.; Nelson, D.L.; and Simmons, B.L. Measuring job stressors and strains: Where we have been, where we are, and where we need to go. *Journal of Occupational Health Psychology* 3:368- 389, 1998.

Kawakami, N.; Araki, S.; Haratani, T.; and Hemmi, T. Relations of work stress to alcohol use and drinking problems in male and female employees of a computer factory. *Environmental Research* 62:314-324, 1993.

Martin, J.D. Jobs, occupations, and patterns of alcohol consumption: A review of literature. In: Roman, P.M., ed. *Alcohol Problem Intervention in the Workplace*. New York: Quorum Books, 1990. pp. 45-65.

Martin, J.K.; Kraft, J.M.; and Roman, P.M. Extent and impact of alcohol and drug use problems in the workplace: A review of empirical evidence. In: Macdonald, S., and Roman, P.M., eds. *Research Advances in Alcohol and Drug Problems. Volume II: Drug Testing in the Workplace*. New York: Plenum Press, 1994. pp. 3-31.

Martin, J.K.; Roman, P.M.; and Blum, T.C. Job stress, drinking networks, and social support at work: A comprehensive model of employees' problem drinking. *Sociological Quarterly* 37:579-599, 1996.

Normand, J.; Lempert, R.O.; and O'Brien, C.P. *Under the Influence? Drugs and the American Workforce*. Washington, DC: National Academy Press, 1994.

Parker, D.A., and Farmer, G.C. Employed adults at risk for diminished self-control over alcohol use: The alienated, the burned out, and the unchallenged. In: Roman, P.M., ed. *Alcohol Problem Intervention in the Workplace*. New York: Quorum Books, 1990. pp. 27-43.

Parker, D.A., and Harford, T.C. Gender-role attitudes, job competition and alcohol consumption among women and men. *Alcoholism: Clinical and Experimental Research* 16:159-165, 1992.

147

Ragland, D.R.; Greiner, B.A., Krause, N.; Holman, B.L.; and Fisher, J.M. Occupational and nonoccupational correlates of alcohol consumption in urban transit drivers. *Preventive Medicine* 24:634- 645, 1995.

Roman, P.M., and Blum, T.C. Systems-oriented prevention strategies and programs: Employers. In: Coombs, R.H., and Ziedonis, D.M., eds. *Handbook on Drug Abuse Prevention: A Comprehensive Strategy to Prevent the Abuse of Alcohol and Other Drugs*, Boston, MA: Allyn and Bacon, 1995. pp. 139-158.

Romelsjo, A.; Hasin, D.; Hilton, M.; Bostrom, G.; Diderichsen, F.; Haglund, B.; Hallqvist, J.; Karlsson, G.; and Svanstrom, L. The relationship between stressful working conditions and high alcohol consumption and severe alcohol problems in an urban general population. *British Journal of Addiction* 87:1173-1183, 1992.

Roxburgh, S. Gender differences in the effect of job stressors on alcohol consumption. *Addictive Behaviors* 23:101-107, 1998.

Shore, E.R. Drinking patterns and problems among women in paid employment. *Alcohol Health & Research World* 16:160-164, 1992.

Steptoe, A.; Wardle, J.; Lipsey, Z.; Mills, R.; Oliver, G.; Jarvis, M.; and Kirschbaum, C. A longitudinal study of workload and variations in psychological well-being, cortisol, smoking, and alcohol consumption. *Annals of Behavioral Medicine* 20:84-91, 1998.

Trice, H.M., and Sonnenstuhl, W.J. On the construction of drinking norms in work organizations. *Journal of Studies on Alcohol* 51:201-220, 1990.

Vasse, R.M.; Nijhuis, F.J.N.; and Kok, G. Associations between work stress, alcohol consumption, and sickness absence. *Addiction* 93:231-241, 1998.

Wilsnack, R.W., and Wilsnack, S.C. Women, work, and alcohol: Failures of simple theories. *Alcoholism: Clinical and Experimental Research* 16:172-179, 1992.

Chapter 12

Evaluating Caregiver Stress

While caregiving can be very satisfying, especially when it is an expression of love and care for someone important to you, it can also be psychologically and physically draining. When demands become overwhelming, your energy, good humor, and coping capacity are taxed.

This can make you feel very stressed out. The stresses you face probably vary from day to day because your caregiving responsibilities shift according to your family member's health and your own energy level.

Maybe you aren't even aware of how much you are doing. To figure out your caregiving tasks, take a minute to complete this list of activities.

Check which of the following kinds of caregiving you currently provide:

__ Household management (cooking, shopping, cleaning, housekeeping)
__ Transportation
__ Personal care (bathing, grooming, toileting)

"Why Is Caregiving Often Stressful?" *North Carolina Caregiver's Handbook* pp. 7-12, © North Carolina Department of Health and Human Services, Division of Aging, 1997-1998, reprinted with permission; and "Caregiver Stress," The National Women's Health Information Center, 1998.

__ Medical care (help with taking medications, applying dressings)
__ Emotional support and companionship
__ Supervision for safety
__ Financial management and decision-making assistance
__ Coordination and management of care provided by others
__ Other (list) _____

Did the number of items you checked surprise you?

Managing stress requires balancing the demands in your life with the resources that can help you cope. Learn to recognize, anticipate, and offset the demands and stresses in your life with positive self-esteem, coping skills, and adequate social support. This means taking care of yourself as well as spending time and energy with the person(s) for whom you are caring.

Taking care of her father helped Nan Harris learn more about her own strengths and limitations. "From the time I was in grammar school I've taken care of people—my brothers and sisters, nieces and nephews. It's very easy for me to give and give and with Dad I've had to learn to say no," she said. Part of that process happened when she was hospitalized twice for exhaustion last year.

Table 12.1. Stress Questionnaire

Statement	"Describes me"	"Does not describe me"
I find I can't get enough rest.	_____	_____
I don't have time for myself.	_____	_____
I feel frustrated or angry.	_____	_____
I feel guilty about my situation.	_____	_____
I don't get out much anymore.	_____	_____
I argue with the person I am caring for.	_____	_____
I argue with other family members.	_____	_____
I don't feel I know enough to be an effective caregiver.	_____	_____

If the response to one or more of these statements is "describes me," it may be time to begin looking for help with caring for your older relative and help in taking care of yourself.

Now that you have sketched out how you spend your time, you can determine how much time you have for yourself and how much time you have with friends or other family members.

Nan Harris felt guilty about asking someone to stay with her father while she did errands but she couldn't find time to go food shopping or keep her own doctors' appointments. Even more troubling, she realized that the only person she was regularly talking to was her sister. Somehow, the challenges of arranging care for dad had taken a priority over keeping up with friends and her own interests.

Second Step of Stress Management

Arrange for a substitute caregiver for short periods of time so that you can get some time away from your caregiving responsibilities.

Nan called her Area Agency on Aging for information about eldercare services in her county. She was fortunate because there was a respite program near her that provides trained volunteers to act as substitute caregivers for short (2-4 hours) periods of time once a week. Nan later related that the "time I spent alone revitalized and recharged me."

Listening to music, reading, taking walks, and other forms of exercise, can help you to better handle the stresses you may experience during the day. Taking care of personal business also can help you feel more in control of daily pressures. While most caregivers feel that they can, should, or must provide all the care to their family member, carrying the total burden is not helpful and probably impossible in the long run.

Third Step of Stress Management

Ask for other assistance from family, friends, churches, in-home aide services, and community agencies. Before you dismiss the idea of seeking help consider these three points:

1. Additional help allows you to be a more effective caregiver by giving you time away from the person you are caring for.

2. Your spouse or older relative benefits by seeing and being with someone other than you.

3. Community-based services often allow the older family member to postpone using a nursing home by providing the more difficult and/or skilled care that is needed and can be provided in the home.

The help provided by you, other family members, friends, and neighbors may still not be enough to enable an older person to remain independent. In this case you will need to look for other avenues of support. One of the first places you should contact is your Area Agency on Aging. If your family member has a limited income, he or she may be elgible for services provided through the AOA including homemaker home health aide services, transportation, home-delivered meals, chore, and home repair as well as legal assistance.

Area Agencies on Aging can direct you to other sources of help for older persons with limited incomes such as subsidized housing, food stamps, Supplemental Security Income, Medicaid or the Qualified Medicare Beneficiary program which covers the cost of the Part A and B insurance premiums for low-income elderly.

Home Health Care Help

If you decide to hire a home care worker, you will need to determine how much help your older relative needs. You also need to decide what type of home care worker your relative needs. Following are descriptions of the types of home care personnel available:

- A Housekeeper or Chore Worker is supervised by the person hiring them and performs basic household tasks and light cleaning.

- A Homemaker or Personal Care Worker is supervised by an agency or you and provides personal care, meal planning and household management, and medication reminders.

- A Companion or Live-in is supervised by an agency or you and provides personal care, light housework, exercise, companionship, and medication reminders.

- A Home Health Aide, Certified Nurse Assistant, or Nurses Aide is supervised by an agency's registered nurse and provides personal care, help with transfers, walking, and exercise; household services that are essential to health care; assistance with medications, and reports changes in the patient's condition to the RN or Therapist; and completes appropriate records.

Nonprofit and for profit home care agencies recruit, train, and pay the worker. You pay the agency. Social Service agencies, in addition to home care services, may provide an assessment of the client's needs by a nurse or social worker, and help with the adjustment or coordination of the care plan. Other avenues for finding aides who charge lower fees include churches, senior employment services, and agencies that assist displaced homemakers and others entering the employment market.

Home Health Care Agencies focus on the medical aspects of care and provide trained health care personnel, such as nurses and physical therapists. Their services may be paid for by Medicare, if they are ordered by a physician.

Additional Information

Children of Aging Parents
1609 Woodbourne Road, Suite 302A
Levittown, PA 19057-1511
Toll-Free: 800-227-7294
Tel: 215-945-6900
Fax: 215-945-8720
Website: www.caps4caregivers.org

Family Caregiver Alliance
690 Market Street, Suite 600
San Francisco, CA 94104
Tel: 415-434 3388
Fax: 415-434 3508
Website: www.caregiver.org
E-mail: info@caregiver.org

National Alliance for Caregiving
4720 Montgomery Lane, Suite 642
Bethesda, MD 20814
Toll-Free: 800-677-1116
Tel: 301-718-8444
Website: www.caregiving.org

The National Council on Aging, Inc.
409 Third St., SW, Suite 200
Washington, DC 20024
Tel: 202 479-1200
Fax 202 479-0735
TDD: 202-479-6674
Website: www.ncoa.org
E-mail: info@ncoa.org

National Family Caregivers Association
10400 Connecticut Avenue, #500
Kensington, MD 20895-3944
Toll-Free: 800-896-3650
Tel: 301-942-2302
Website: www.nfcacares.org
E-mail: info@nfcacares.org

Administration on Aging
330 Independence Avenue, SW
Washington, DC 20201
Toll-Free: 800-677-1116 (Eldercare Locator—to find services for an older person in his or her locality)
TTY: 800-877-8339
Website: www.aoa.dhhs.gov
E-mail: www.aoa.dhhs.gov

Chapter 13

Social Inequality Harms Health

When the rich get richer and the poor get poorer, consequences to public health are grave. "Socioeconomic differentials are arguably the most important public health problem facing our nation," reported Dr. James S. House, the featured speaker at a recent NIH Office of Behavioral and Social Sciences Research seminar and scientist at the Institute for Social Research in Ann Arbor, Michigan.

Although advances in medical science and practice have been important to human health and wellbeing, a mounting body of evidence indicates that behavioral, psychosocial, and environmental factors are the major determinants of health and the way health changes with age, according to House. "It has been widely assumed in the pages of *Science* and elsewhere that advances in medical science and practice were the principal causes of the rapid increase in human life expectancy of the past several centuries," he said, "but studies now show that improved nutrition and better living conditions are the critical factors that have improved health in human populations."

Consistent with this conclusion, House continued, is evidence that the United States spends more money than any other nation in the world on medical care and research, yet levels of population health in terms of life expectancy—at all but the oldest ages—lag increasingly behind the most developed countries of Europe and Asia, and even some less developed ones. Greece, Spain, the United Kingdom,

"Social Inequality Harms Health, Sociologist Says," A Summary of a Presentation by James S. House, Ph.D., University of Michigan, by Susan M. Persons, *NIH Record*, August 12, 1997, National Institutes of Health.

and Denmark, he said, spend one-half to one-third as much on health, and yet all have the same or better population life expectancy both for males and females at age 60 and at birth.

While improving the inequalities of access to medical care in the U.S. would help make a significant difference, social inequalities in health are not due primarily to a lack of health care. "People of lower socioeconomic status by education and income have a multitude of psychosocial risk factors that health care alone will not be able to overcome including smoking, lack of exercise, immoderate eating and drinking, and high fat/low fiber diets," House said.

These individuals also experience more chronic and acute stress, higher rates of ill health and death among family and friends, lower levels of social support and personal efficacy, and higher levels of depression and hostility, and typically live and work in environments that are hazardous to health.

Why persons of low socioeconomic status (SES) are vulnerable to virtually all psychosocial and environmental risk factors is not fully understood, although science has discovered much about how socioeconomic factors can get "under the skin." Further, improving risk factors is not enough. "We need to improve the socioeconomic context which generates and sustains these risk factors," House recommended.

While investing in science and improving access to health care are important and would improve the health of lower SES populations, research findings suggest that doing so would likely have only a limited impact on population health unless these gains are accompanied by policies and conditions that mitigate current levels of deprivation and inequality.

"To have a substantial impact on public health," House said, "there would need to be a decrease both in absolute and relative deprivation and inequality of the lower 30 to 50 percent of the socioeconomic distribution."

Investments in biomedical research should continue at the current levels and higher, in House's opinion, but "a broader psychosocial perspective must be considered very seriously as we plan our science, practice, and policy for health and aging in the 21st century. Greater emphasis," he said, "has to be placed on the role that social factors and social policy play in the development of future health science and health policy, and should be seen not as an alternative, but as a necessary complement."

Part Three

Mental and Emotional Effects of Stress

Chapter 14

Emotions and Disease

How tightly are emotions and diseases linked to each other? Can someone actually die from loneliness? Is it really possible to become sick with fear?

When the great French Impressionist painter Renoir suffered from both severe arthritis and bouts of depression, his contemporaries gave only passing thought to the possibility that his two problems might in some way be connected. But today there are so many examples of tie-ins between the workings of the brain and the reactions of the body—stressed executives who die of heart attacks during fiery board meetings, survivors of wars, earthquakes, and floods who subsequently experience severe physical disabilities, and widows and widowers who become ill themselves soon after their spouses have died—that the question has changed from "are emotions and diseases related?" to "how are the two related?"

These issues and questions are the subjects of "Emotions and Disease," a museum exhibit[1] that examines the evolution of scientific, medical, and public understanding of the links between health and strong emotions like anger, love, stress, and fear. Two powerful and changing variables—the tools of the day and the philosophies of the times—shape and influence understanding of these relations.

In the 18th and 19th centuries, when it became possible to listen to the sounds of the heart with a stethoscope and look at cells and tissues with microscopes, doctors found they could account for most of

"Emotions and Disease," *Research in the News* by Ruth Levy Guyer, Ph.D., Science-Education, National Institute of Health (NIH), 1997.

the diseases of their patients with concrete examples of changes in anatomy or physiology—the numbers of white cells in the bloodstream would definitely increase in response to infections, the heart would beat much too rapidly when a patient experienced episodes of lightheadedness or breathlessness, and so on. Because they could point to such "evidence," most doctors were skeptical that emotions "could have much to do with disease."

But there was always the rare patient who had a serious illness for which no "organic" cause could be found or measured. These patients were said to have "functional neuroses," problems that in some vague way had to do with their nervous systems.

At the end of the 19th century, the French neurologist Jean-Martin Charcot set his large boxy accordion-sized camera to the study of hysterical patients. Charcot's photographs captured the "fits" of his patients and thereby demonstrated that hysteria was no different from the organic diseases: it too was associated with distinguishing symptoms. "The camera did not lie." Although Charcot's pictures showed what was happening, they did not come close to explaining why.

Enter Sigmund Freud and his colleague Josef Breuer. Their approach—"less in looking and more in listening"—was known as psychoanalysis. It involved intensive probing over many months, years, or even decades into past events in patients' lives that may have led to the patients' current problems. Their slant was that physical symptoms could have "emotional causes and biographical meanings."

A landmark book called *Emotions and Bodily Changes* was published in 1935. The author, Helen Flanders Dunbar, was both a doctor and a theologian, and her book and her ideas—that spiritual, emotional, and physical suffering were inextricably linked—inaugurated a new field, psychosomatic medicine. It applied the Freud-Breuer psychoanalytic approach to medical problems in general and not just to the puzzling neuroses.

Psychosomatic medicine was highly controversial from the start. Some doctors argued that, if seriously ill patients relied too heavily on curing their diseases with positive thoughts, they might jeopardize their chances of benefiting from established therapies that worked best if started early in the course of a disease. Others worried that patients might blame themselves if they could not get well. Still, many patients found that "the power of positive thinking" was strong and that they were helped by relaxation, meditation. and similar self-help techniques.

By 1950, psychosomatic illness and medicine were so deeply embedded in popular culture that they had found their way to Broadway.

In the musical Guys and Dolls, which premiered that year, Adelaide sings, "just from worrying whether the wedding is on or off, a person can develop a cough."

Adelaide was suffering from what Hans Selye, a physician in Montreal, had labeled a "stress syndrome." And she was not alone. Stress seemed to be an increasing fact of life. Selye said that, under certain circumstances, it was right for people and other animals to respond with stress responses to dangerous and frightening stimuli. He identified three stages to the response. The first was the "alarm reaction" during which bodily defenses are mobilized to the stressful situation; the second was the "stage of resistance" in which the person adapts to the situation that is causing stress, and the third was the "stage of exhaustion" in which the stress response dies out.[2] When a person sees a tiger, for example, there is initial shock but then flight. And when tiger and person no longer share the same turf, the stress response appropriately ends.

Selye speculated that, in western cultures, people are bombarded with constant noise, constant danger, relentless feelings of powerlessness and hopelessness, and unremitting pressures at home and at work—what cartoonist Scott Adams has been capturing in his popular character Dilbert. Simply stated, stress never ends, and the stress response remains stuck in the "on" position for days, months, even years, tipping the balance away from health toward stress syndromes that can have both physical and emotional components.

Selye's insights and hypotheses came unintentionally from his laboratory experiments with rats. He had not been studying stress at all. He was not adept at handling the rats and often bungled an experiment by dropping an animal while he was trying to give it an injection. Over the course of the experimental period, many of Selye's rats developed ulcers, shrunken immune tissues, enlarged glands, and other physical signs and symptoms that were in no way associated with the substances he was injecting. He concluded that the animals' physiologic problems must be "due to the strains of life in his laboratory."

If the pace of everyday life could cause stress responses in animals and people, then it came as no surprise that crises—wars and other traumatic situations—could produce even more dramatic stress responses and stress-associated diseases. In fact, roughly 20% of the disabled soldiers from World War II were classified as "shell shocked" or suffered from "combat neuroses."

In a fascinating documentary film made after World War II by Hollywood director John Huston, a soldier with paralyzed legs is

163

helped onto a hospital bed by two attendants. The doctor in the film hypnotizes the soldier, taking "a shortcut to his unconscious mind" by injecting him with the drug sodium amytal. Doctor and patient discuss the soldier's inability to walk, the nature of his "neuropsychiatric problem," why and how the paralysis began two days earlier, and what sorts of stresses he has encountered at home since he returned from the battleground. The film ends with the hypnotized soldier moving his legs, getting up off the table, and then rapidly regaining his ability to walk as a result of the doctor's "suggestion" and verbal encouragement. Days later, the soldier is playing a vigorous game of baseball, hitting a home run, and sprinting around the bases.

Few psychiatric symptoms and illnesses are "solved" as easily as were the problems of the film's soldier. (Few strictly medical ones are either.) But, the movie graphically illustrates the point that health is "a state of the whole brain and body."

Today "a critical mass of solid sophisticated scientific research" documents the mind-body connection, notes exhibit co-director[3] Dr. Esther Sternberg and these data are being accepted by "researchers in the hard-core biological disciplines." Sternberg commented that at a recent meeting of brain-immune interactions[4] that included researchers in numerous fields—psychiatry, neurobiology, neurology, endocrinology, immunology, neuroimaging, rheumatology, psychology—"scientists all along the spectrum were learning the language of other disciplines and finding ways to interact."

Among the most valuable new tools for studying emotions and disease are "imaging" devices, like PET and MRI scanners, which record brain activities as they are taking place. These cutting-edge technologies were, says exhibition manager Patricia Tuohy, the most challenging parts of the exhibit to develop and present. "Everyone can relate to feeling withdrawn, to feeling anxiety. But making science accessible to the public was the hardest part. We had a big chunk of science to deal with, but we still had to talk about 'me' and what happens to my body. This most sophisticated science is all brand new." Commented one guest at the opening of the exhibit: "Scientists have instincts; technology is letting them prove them."

New model systems—knockout and transgenic mice—have also boosted understanding and given insights into the roles of individual genes in various diseases. Says Sternberg: "Part of how stress affects disease severity depends on you and your genes. Genes affect susceptibility and resistance to inflammatory and infectious diseases. You have to look at it as a package. But with strong enough stresses, even the most tuned-down system will respond." She comments that it may be most accurate to say that "stress is not what happens to you but how you respond to it."

Ancient physicians understood disease as an imbalance of four fluid "humors" in the body—phlegm, blood, black bile, and yellow bile; a person could become healthy only when the balance was restored. Scientists today also talk about achieving a balance. This time around, the balance is understood in molecular terms, involving circulating molecules called interleukins, neurotransmitters, and hormones that send signals to each other and make people sick or well.

Strong, painful emotions trigger these chemical messengers in ways that tip the balance toward disease. Good health represents a different molecular balance. Laughter may thus actually be, as the saying goes, "the best medicine."

References

1. Emotions and Disease was on display at the National Library of Medicine on the campus of the National Institutes of Health in Bethesda, Maryland through April 1997. The exhibit was made possible by support from the Charles A. Dana Foundation, the John D. and Catherine T. MacArthur Foundation, the Fetzer Institute, and the National Institute of Mental Health.

2. From *American Journal of Nursing* 1965, 65(3): page 98.

3. The exhibit was developed by Sternberg, a neuroendocrinimmunologist and Dr. Elizabeth Fee, a historian of medicine.

4. Third International Congress of the International Society for Neuroimmunomodulation, Bethesda, MD, November, 1996.

Chapter 15

Stress and Personality

Study Finds Control Has Role in Health Effects of Hard-Driving Personality

Contrary to popular belief, people with hard-driving, control-oriented personalities are not necessarily at greater risk for high blood pressure, heart attacks, and other stress-related ailments unless they are unable to exert that control over their life circumstances, according to Duke University Medical Center researchers.

In fact, many people with this personality trait can accomplish a great deal in their careers without damaging their health, as long they approach work without hostility and their jobs allow them a fair amount of control and advancement, the researchers found.

Conversely, men with hard-charging personalities who lack job control can experience dangerous health effects, said Gary Bennett Jr., co-author of a study prepared for presentation at the Society of Behavioral Medicine meeting in Nashville. The study was funded by the National Institutes of Mental Health.

"Study Finds Control Has Role in Health Effects of Hard-Driving Personality," *Duke News* April 5, 2000, © Duke University Medical Center, reprinted with permission; and "Personality Influences Psychological Adjustment and Recovery from Stroke," by co-authors Marjan Ghahramanlou, M.A.; Jodi Aronoff, M.A.; Marcella A. Wozniak, M.D., Ph.D.; Stephen J. Kittner, M.D.; and Thomas R. Price, M.D., reproduced with permission from the American Stroke Association Web site, http://216.185.112.7/presenter.jhtml?identifier=2609, © 2001, American Heart Association Inc.

In the study of 74 healthy African-American men between the ages of 18 and 47, Bennett found that men with this personality trait, who also had little ability to influence their workload or advancement potential, responded to a stressful situation by significantly increasing levels of a stress hormone called cortisol. Cortisol helps the body maintain its energy levels when under stress. But when produced in excess, cortisol can increase blood pressure and weaken the immune system.

"Approaching each work day as a 'must-win' competition can be a highly effective approach for some," Bennett said. "But significant health ramifications may accompany this type of behavior among those with jobs that are characterized by little control over workload, promotion, or earning potential."

Unlike the "Type A" personality—fraught with anger, hostility, and cynicism, and therefore considered a dangerous trait—the hard-driven, super-charged behavior type can, in some people, be a successful strategy for dealing with stress, said Bennett. Although such people tended to produce more cortisol when under stress than did people with a mellow approach, their cortisol still did not reach dangerous levels, the study found. But in men with little ability to control decisions that affected their jobs and their futures, the hard-driving approach at work raised cortisol to levels known to be harmful to health.

"Vigorously responding to work stressors can be a positive coping strategy, if you have influence over the stressors you are handling," Bennett said. "But when you continually encounter stress in your job that cannot be alleviated, your body reacts to that by overproducing stress hormones."

In Bennett's study, subjects first completed a written questionnaire assessing their personality type, coping strategies, and their perceived level of job control. Then, the researchers presented subjects with a stressful scenario and asked them to prepare a response to it. They measured cortisol levels in the subjects' saliva before and after they prepared a response to the stressful situation.

Results of the study showed that men who responded vigorously to stress in the experimental scenario, but who had low control over alleviating that stress (as measured by the questionnaire), experienced significant increases in cortisol while preparing to respond to the stressful event. Other subjects experienced much smaller and insignificant increases in cortisol while preparing their responses.

"The magnitude of their response to the stressful scenario was indicative of the accumulation of stress they experienced in their jobs,"

Bennett said. "Hard-charging people feel good about themselves and their jobs if they have a good income, good work environment, and good social support. But when you don't have these, the experience of dealing head-on with stress can be a negative one."

While researchers have known for years that people with low job control tend to be at greater risk for adverse health effects, Bennett said the new study highlights an important reason as to why: a worker's behavior traits and coping strategies can influence how he deals with a frustrating, dead-end job.

Bennett's future studies will study this same phenomenon in women, whose social support systems and coping strategies may cause them to react differently from men. Marcellus Merritt and Dr. Redford Williams, director of Duke's Behavioral Medicine Research Center were co-authors of the study.

Personality Influences Psychological Adjustment and Recovery from Stroke

Pre-stroke personality has a greater influence on stroke recovery than the brain injury itself, according to research presented at the American Stroke Association's 26th International Stroke Conference. The American Stroke Association is a division of the American Heart Association. Some stroke survivors are highly susceptible to emotional changes from the brain injury and psychological reactions to that injury. How they cope with the changes—and how well they recover—is based on the individual's unique pre-stroke persona, according to new research.

"In some cases, two people with the exact same stroke-related deficits can have very different results," says Lynn M. Grattan, Ph.D., lead author and associate professor of neurology at the University of Maryland School of Medicine in Baltimore. "One person might return to work and social and leisure activities, while the other may end up on permanent disability. Our research is the first to demonstrate that in many cases, personality has a greater influence than the brain injury itself."

Grattan says healthcare providers should act promptly to identify an individual's pre-existing personality features including previous methods of coping, problem-solving, and emotional styles and sensitivities. "By harnessing and mobilizing their strengths early on, you can help reduce the disappointment, confusion, and pain brought on by the stroke and engage them immediately in the rehabilitation process," says Grattan. She suggests that this can easily be done with a brief neuropsychological examination of the patient within the first few days of a stroke.

The psychological reaction to having a stroke can cause feelings of frustration, anxiety, apathy, anger, or depression. Depression can seriously hinder an individual's willingness and ability to participate in rehabilitation, as well as their ability to avoid another stroke.

In this study, researchers hoped to identify which elements of an individual's baseline personality changed and determine which personality types are vulnerable to depression after a stroke. Investigators studied the personalities of 35 stroke survivors—20 female, 15 male with an average age of 57. They administered standard psychological tests to the close relatives (spouse, child, or sibling) of the individuals who had a stroke. They were asked questions about the patients' interpersonal style, degree of extroversion or introversion, openness to new experiences, and how they coped with stress. The test was given a few days after the stroke and again one year later.

Researchers found that people whose families described them as highly self-conscious or as "deep thinkers" were most vulnerable to post-stroke depression. "After the stroke, these people became more self-conscious, moody, withdrawn, and socially isolated," says Grattan. "Their subsequent depression made it very difficult for them to participate in and benefit from rehabilitation as they lacked the energy or interest to succeed."

In contrast, people described as more energetic, outgoing, flexible, and self-confident before a stroke can often successfully dedicate themselves to a rigorous post-stroke rehabilitation routine and get themselves back to a higher level of recovery, she says.

Much of stroke care has focused on medically stabilizing patients and sending them home, she says. "While this is clearly crucial for recovery, more attention should be placed on working with patients and their families soon after hospital admission to understand the changes a stroke can cause so that they can all better deal with the stroke-related deficits and subsequent disability. "Pre-existing personality is exceedingly important to how an individual faces the painful aspects of stroke recovery, how they approach the challenge of rehabilitation and maximize recovery," she says. Ultimately, the researchers hope to develop counseling and medical regimes that will optimize psychosocial outcomes following stroke.

Grattan's research was supported by a grant from the National Institutes of Health/National Institute of Neurological Disorders and Stroke.

Chapter 16

Stress Intensifies Depression

Chapter Contents

Section 16.1—The Invisible Disease 172
Section 16.2—Co-Occurrence of Depression with
            Medical, Psychiatric, and Substance
            Abuse Disorders 195
Section 16.3—Women Are at Greater Risk for
            Depression Than Men 209
Section 16.4—Suicide and Depression 214
Section 16.5—Dealing with the Depths of Depression 230

Section 16.1

The Invisible Disease

This section includes "The Invisible Disease: Depression," National
Institute of Mental Health (NIMH), updated January 2001; excerpts from
"What Do These Students Have in Common," National Institute of Mental
Health (NIMH), NIH Publication No. 97-4266 , updated 6/1/99; and
"Depression Research," Fact Sheet, National Institute of Mental Health
(NIMH), NIH Publication No. 00-4501, 2000.

Depression Overview

Depression is a serious medical condition. In contrast to the normal emotional experiences of sadness, loss, or passing mood states,
clinical depression is persistent and can interfere significantly with
an individual's ability to function. There are three main types of depressive disorders: major depressive disorder, dysthymic disorder, and
bipolar disorder (manic-depressive illness).

Symptoms and Types of Depression

Symptoms of depression include sad mood, loss of interest or pleasure in activities that were once enjoyed, change in appetite or weight,
difficulty sleeping or oversleeping, physical slowing or agitation, energy loss, feelings of worthlessness or inappropriate guilt, difficulty
thinking or concentrating, and recurrent thoughts of death or suicide.
A diagnosis of major depressive disorder is made if a person has 5 or
more of these symptoms and impairment in usual functioning nearly
every day during the same two-week period. Major depression often
begins between ages 15 to 30 but also can appear in children.[1] Episodes typically recur.

Some people have a chronic but less severe form of depression,
called dysthymic disorder, which is diagnosed when depressed mood
persists for at least 2 years (1 year in children) and is accompanied
by at least 2 other symptoms of depression. Many people with dysthymia develop major depressive episodes.

Episodes of depression also occur in people with bipolar disorder. In
this disorder, depression alternates with mania, which is characterized

172

by abnormally and persistently elevated mood or irritability and symptoms including overly-inflated self-esteem, decreased need for sleep, increased talkativeness, racing thoughts, distractibility, physical agitation, and excessive risk taking. Because bipolar disorder requires different treatment than major depressive disorder or dysthymia, obtaining an accurate diagnosis is extremely important.

Facts about Depression

- Major depression is the leading cause of disability in the U.S. and worldwide.[2]

- Depressive disorders affect an estimated 9.5 percent of adult Americans ages 18 and over in a given year,[3] or about 18.8 million people in 1998.[4]

- Nearly twice as many women (12 percent) as men (7 percent) are affected by a depressive disorder each year.[3]

Depression can be devastating to family relationships, friendships, and the ability to work or go to school. Many people still believe that the emotional symptoms caused by depression are "not real," and that a person should be able to shake off the symptoms. Because of these inaccurate beliefs, people with depression either may not recognize that they have a treatable disorder or may be discouraged from seeking or staying on treatment due to feelings of shame and stigma. Too often, untreated or inadequately treated depression is associated with suicide.[5]

Treatments

Antidepressant medications are widely used, effective treatments for depression.[6] Existing antidepressants influence the functioning of certain chemicals in the brain called neurotransmitters. The newer medications, such as the selective serotonin reuptake inhibitors (SSRIs), tend to have fewer side effects than the older drugs, which include tricyclic antidepressants (TCAs) and monoamine oxidase inhibitors (MAOIs). Although both generations of medications are effective in relieving depression, some people will respond to one type of drug, but not another. Other types of antidepressants are now in development.

Certain types of psychotherapy, specifically cognitive-behavioral therapy (CBT) and interpersonal therapy (IPT), have been found helpful for depression. Research indicates that mild to moderate depression often can be treated successfully with either therapy alone; however, severe depression appears more likely to respond to a combination of psychotherapy and medication.[7] More than 80 percent of people with depressive disorders improve when they receive appropriate treatment.[8]

In situations where medication, psychotherapy, and the combination of these interventions prove ineffective, or work too slowly to relieve severe symptoms such as psychosis (e.g., hallucinations, delusional thinking) or suicidality, electroconvulsive therapy (ECT) may be considered. ECT is a highly effective treatment for severe depressive episodes. The possibility of long-lasting memory problems, although a concern in the past, has been significantly reduced with modern ECT techniques. However, the potential benefits and risks of ECT, and of available alternative interventions, should be carefully reviewed and discussed with individuals considering this treatment and, where appropriate, with family or friends.[9]

One herbal supplement, hypericum or St. John's wort, has been promoted as having antidepressant properties. There is evidence that St. John's wort can reduce the effectiveness of certain medications. Use of any herbal or natural supplements should always be discussed with your doctor before they are tried.

Research Findings

- Brain imaging research is revealing that in depression, neural circuits responsible for moods, thinking, sleep, appetite, and behavior fail to function properly, and that the regulation of critical neurotransmitters is impaired.[10]

- Genetics research, including studies of twins, indicates that genes play a role in depression. Vulnerability to depression appears to result from the influence of multiple genes acting together with environmental factors.[11]

- Other research has shown that stressful life events, particularly in the form of loss such as the death of a close family member, may trigger major depression in susceptible individuals.[12]

- The hypothalamic-pituitary-adrenal (HPA) axis, the hormonal system that regulates the body's response to stress, is overactive in many people with depression. Research findings suggest that persistent overactivation of this system may lay the groundwork for depression.[13]

- Studies of brain chemistry, mechanisms of action of antidepressant medications, and the cognitive distortions and disturbed interpersonal relationships commonly associated with depression, continue to inform the development of new and better treatments.

References

1. Birmaher B, Ryan ND, Williamson DE, et al. Childhood and adolescent depression: a review of the past 10 years. Part I. *Journal of the American Academy of Child and Adolescent Psychiatry*, 1996; 35(11): 1427-39.

2. Murray CJL, Lopez AD, eds. *Summary: The global burden of disease: a comprehensive assessment of mortality and disability from diseases, injuries, and risk factors in 1990 and projected to 2020.* Cambridge, MA: Published by the Harvard School of Public Health on behalf of the World Health Organization and the World Bank, Harvard University Press, 1996.

3. Regier DA, Narrow WE, Rae DS, et al. The de facto mental and addictive disorders service system. Epidemiologic Catchment Area prospective 1-year prevalence rates of disorders and services. *Archives of General Psychiatry*, 1993; 50(2): 85-94.

4. Narrow WE. One-year prevalence of depressive disorders among adults 18 and over in the U.S.: NIMH ECA prospective data. Population estimates based on U.S. Census estimated residential population age 18 and over on July 1, 1998. Unpublished.

5. Conwell Y, Brent D. Suicide and aging I: patterns of psychiatric diagnosis. *International Psychogeriatrics,* 1995; 7(2): 149-64.

6. Mulrow CD, Williams JW Jr., Trivedi M, et al. Evidence report on treatment of depression-newer pharmacotherapies. *Psychopharmacology Bulletin*, 1998; 34(4): 409-795.

7. Hyman SE, Rudorfer MV. Depressive and bipolar mood disorders. In: Dale DC, Federman DD, eds. *Scientific American®️ Medicine.* Volume 3. New York: Healtheon/WebMD Corp., 2000, Sect. 13, Subsect. II, p. 1.

8.   National Advisory Mental Health Council. Health care reform for Americans with severe mental illnesses. *American Journal of Psychiatry*, 1993; 150(10): 1447-65.

9.   U.S. Department of Health and Human Services. *Mental health: a report of the Surgeon General.* Rockville, MD: U.S. Department of Health and Human Services, Substance Abuse and Mental Health Services Administration, Center for Mental Health Services, National Institutes of Health, National Institute of Mental Health, 1999.

10.   Soares JC, Mann JJ. The functional neuroanatomy of mood disorders. *Journal of Psychiatric Research*, 1997; 31(4): 393-432.

11.   NIMH Genetics Workgroup. *Genetics and mental disorders*. NIH Publication No. 98-4268. Rockville, MD: National Institute of Mental Health, 1998.

12.   Mazure CM, Bruce ML, Maciejewski PW, et al. Adverse life events and cognitive-personality characteristics in the prediction of major depression and antidepressant response. *American Journal of Psychiatry*, 2000; 157(6): 896-903.

13.   Arborelius L, Owens MJ, Plotsky PM, et al. The role of corticotropin-releasing factor in depression and anxiety disorders. *Journal of Endocrinology*, 1999; 160(1): 1-12.

Clinical Depression

When "the blues" last for weeks, or interfere with academic or social functioning, it may be clinical depression. Clinical depression is a common, frequently unrecognized illness that can be effectively treated.

Clinical depression can affect your body, mood, thoughts, and behavior. It can change your eating habits, how you feel and think about things, your ability to work and study, and how you interact with people.

Clinical depression is not a passing mood, a sign of personal weakness, or a condition that can be willed away. Clinically depressed people cannot "pull themselves together" and get better.

Depression can be successfully treated by a mental health professional or certain health care providers. With the right treatment, 80 percent of those who seek help get better. And many people begin to feel better in just a few weeks.

Types of Depressive Illness

Depressive illnesses come in different forms. The following are general descriptions of the three most prevalent, though for an individual, the number, severity, and duration of symptoms will vary.

Major depression is manifested by a combination of symptoms that interfere with your ability to work, sleep, eat, and enjoy once pleasurable activities. These impairing episodes of depression can occur once, twice, or several times in a lifetime.

Symptoms of Major Depression

- Sadness, anxiety, or "empty" feelings
- Decreased energy, fatigue, being "slowed down"
- Loss of interest or pleasure in usual activities
- Sleep disturbances (insomnia, oversleeping, or waking much earlier than usual)
- Appetite and weight changes (either loss or gain)
- Feelings of hopelessness, guilt, and worthlessness
- Thoughts of death or suicide, or suicide attempts
- Difficulty concentrating, making decisions, or remembering
- Irritability or excessive crying
- Chronic aches and pains not explained by another physical condition

A less intense type of depression, dysthymia, involves long-term, chronic symptoms that are less severe, but keep you from functioning at your full ability and from feeling well.

In bipolar illness (also known as manic-depressive illness), cycles of depression alternate with cycles of elation and increased activity, known as mania.

How to Recognize Depression

The first step in defeating depression is recognizing it. It's normal to have some signs of depression some of the time. But five or more symptoms for two weeks or longer, or noticeable changes in usual functioning, are all factors that should be evaluated by a health or mental health professional. And remember, people who are depressed may not be thinking clearly and may need help to get help.

What Causes Depression?

The causes of depression are complex. Very often a combination of genetic, psychological, and environmental factors is involved in the onset of clinical depression. At times, however, depression occurs for no apparent reason. Regardless of the cause, depression is almost always treatable.

Family History—Depression often runs in families, which usually means that some, but not all, family members have a tendency to develop the illness. On the other hand, sometimes people who have no family history also develop depression.

Stress—Psychological and environmental stressors can contribute to a depressive episode, though individuals react differently to life events and experiences. In coping with stress, some people find writing in a journal, exercising, or talking with friends helpful. But in clinical depression you need some form of treatment (usually medication and short-term psychotherapy) to start feeling better soon.

College and Stress

Common stressors in college life include:

- Greater academic demands
- Being on your own in a new environment
- Changes in family relations
- Financial responsibilities
- Changes in your social life
- Exposure to new people, ideas, and temptations
- Awareness of your sexual identity and orientation
- Preparing for life after graduation

Psychological make-up can also play a role in vulnerability to depression. People who have low self-esteem, who consistently view themselves and the world with pessimism, or are readily overwhelmed by stress may be especially prone to depression.

Bipolar Disorder (Manic Depression)

As mentioned earlier, bipolar disorder is a type of depressive illness that involves mood swings that go from periods of depression to periods of being overly "up" and irritable. Sometimes the mood swings are dramatic or rapid, but most often they occur gradually, over several weeks. The "up" or manic phase can include increased energy and activity, insomnia, grandiose notions and impulsive or reckless behavior, including sexual promiscuity.

Medication usually is effective in controlling manic symptoms and preventing the recurrence of both manic and depressive episodes.

Suicide

Thoughts of death or suicide are usually signs of severe depression. "If you're feeling like you can't cope anymore, or that life isn't worth living, get help," advised Darrel, a student who tried to kill himself during his freshman year. "Talking to a professional can get you past those intense feelings and save your life."

Suicidal feelings, thoughts, impulses, or behaviors always should be taken seriously. If you are thinking about hurting or killing yourself, *seek help immediately*. Contact someone you trust to help you: a good friend, academic or resident advisor, or:

- Staff at the student health or counseling center

- A professor, coach, or advisor

- A local suicide or emergency hotline (get the phone number from the information operator or directory)

- A hospital emergency room

- Call 911

If someone you know has thoughts about suicide, the best thing to do is help him or her get professional help.

Depression and Alcohol and Other Drugs

A lot of depressed people, especially teenagers, also have problems with alcohol or other drugs. (Alcohol is a drug, too.) Sometimes the depression comes first and people try drugs as a way to escape it. (In the long run, drugs or alcohol just make things worse!) Other times, the alcohol or other drug use comes first, and depression is caused by:

- the drug itself, or
- withdrawal from it, or
- the problems that substance use causes.

179

And sometimes you can't tell which came first—the important point is that when you have both of these problems, the sooner you get treatment, the better.

Getting Help—Treatment Works

If you think you might be depressed, discuss this with a qualified health care or mental health professional who can evaluate your concerns. Bring along an understanding friend for support if you are hesitant or anxious about the appointment.

Several effective treatments for depression are available and can provide relief from symptoms in just a few weeks. The most commonly used treatments are psychotherapy, antidepressant medication, or a combination of the two. Which is the best treatment for an individual depends on the nature and severity of the depression.

Sharing your preferences and concerns with your treatment provider helps determine the course of treatment. Certain types of psychotherapy, particularly cognitive behavioral therapy, can help resolve the psychological or interpersonal problems that contribute to, or result from, the illness. Antidepressant medications relieve the physical and mood symptoms of depression and are not habit-forming. In severe depression, medication is usually required.

Individuals respond differently to treatment. If you don't start feeling better after several weeks, talk to the professional you are seeing about trying other treatments or getting a second opinion.

Making a Decision

Don't let fear of what others might say or think stop you from doing what's best for you. Parents and friends may understand more than you think they might, and they certainly want you to feel better.

Help Yourself: Be an Informed Consumer

Don't give in to negative thinking. Depression can make you feel exhausted, worthless, helpless, and hopeless, making some people want to give up. Remember, these negative views are part of the depression, and will fade as treatment takes effect.

Take an active role in getting better. Make the most of the help available by being actively involved in your treatment and by working with a qualified therapist or doctor. Once in treatment, don't hesitate to ask questions in order to understand your illness and the way treatment works. And, if you don't start feeling better in a few weeks, speak with the professional you are seeing about new approaches.

Be good to yourself while you're getting well. Along with professional help, there are some other simple things you can do to help yourself get better, for example: participating in a support group, spending time with other people, or taking part in activities, exercise, or hobbies. Just don't overdo it and don't set big goals for yourself. The health care professional you are seeing may suggest useful books to read and other self-help strategies.

Helping a Depressed Friend

The best thing you can do for a depressed friend is to help him or her get treatment. This may involve encouraging the person to seek professional help or to stay in treatment once it is begun. The next best thing is to offer emotional support. This involves understanding, patience, affection, and encouragement. Engage the depressed person in conversation or activities and be gently insistent if you meet with resistance. Remind that person that with time and help, he or she will feel better.

Helpful Resources

The professionals at a student health center or counseling service, the Resident Advisor in your dorm, your family health care provider, and your clergy can be helpful resources for getting treatment. You also might contact any of the following organizations in your area for mental health services or referrals:

- A community mental health agency
- A hospital psychiatric outpatient department or clinic
- A private or nonprofit counseling center
- Your local Mental Health Association

The telephone directory or information operator at your school or in your community, or a local hotline, should have telephone numbers for these and other mental health services.

Finding Affordable Treatment

People are sometimes reluctant to seek help because they are concerned about the cost of treatment. Services at college counseling centers are often low-cost or free. Also city or county mental health services are often offered on a "sliding scale" (the fee is based on your financial resources). Check out any health insurance you may have and see if it pays for private mental health services.

Depression Research

Depressive disorders affect approximately 19 million American adults. The suffering endured by people with depression and the lives lost to suicide attest to the great burden of this disorder on individuals, families, and society. Improved recognition, treatment, and prevention of depression are critical public health priorities. The National Institute of Mental Health (NIMH), the world's leading mental health biomedical organization, conducts and supports research on the causes, diagnosis, prevention, and treatment of depression.

Evidence from neuroscience, genetics, and clinical investigation demonstrate that depression is a disorder of the brain. Modern brain imaging technologies are revealing that in depression, neural circuits responsible for the regulation of moods, thinking, sleep, appetite, and behavior fail to function properly, and that critical neurotransmitters—chemicals used by nerve cells to communicate—are out of balance. Genetics research indicates that vulnerability to depression results from the influence of multiple genes acting together with environmental factors. Studies of brain chemistry and of mechanisms of action of antidepressant medications continue to inform the development of new and better treatments.

In the past decade, there have been significant advances in our ability to investigate brain function at multiple levels. NIMH is collaborating with various scientific disciplines to effectively utilize the tools of molecular and cellular biology, genetics, epidemiology, and cognitive and behavioral science to gain a more thorough and comprehensive understanding of the factors that influence brain function and behavior, including mental illness. This collaboration reflects the Institute's increasing focus on "translational research," whereby basic and clinical scientists are involved in joint efforts to translate discoveries and knowledge into clinically relevant questions and targets of research opportunity. Translational research holds great promise for disentangling the complex causes of depression and other mental disorders and for advancing the development of more effective treatments.

Symptoms and Types of Depression

Symptoms of depression include a persistent sad mood; loss of interest or pleasure in activities that were once enjoyed; significant change in appetite or body weight; difficulty sleeping or oversleeping; physical slowing or agitation; loss of energy; feelings of worthlessness or inappropriate guilt; difficulty thinking or concentrating; and recurrent thoughts of death or suicide. A diagnosis of **major depressive disorder (or unipolar major depression)** is made if an individual has five or more of these symptoms during the same two-week period. Unipolar major depression typically presents in discrete episodes that recur during a person's lifetime.

Bipolar disorder (or manic-depressive illness) is characterized by episodes of major depression as well as episodes of mania—periods of abnormally and persistently elevated mood or irritability accompanied by at least three of the following symptoms: overly-inflated self-esteem; decreased need for sleep; increased talkativeness; racing thoughts; distractibility; increased goal-directed activity or physical agitation; and excessive involvement in pleasurable activities that have a high potential for painful consequences. While sharing some of the features of major depression, bipolar disorder is a different illness.

Dysthymic disorder (or dysthymia), a less severe yet typically more chronic form of depression, is diagnosed when depressed mood persists for at least two years in adults (one year in children or adolescents) and is accompanied by at least two other depressive symptoms. Many people with dysthymic disorder also experience major depressive episodes. While unipolar major depression and dysthymia are the primary forms of depression, a variety of other subtypes exist.

In contrast to the normal emotional experiences of sadness, loss, or passing mood states, depression is extreme and persistent and can interfere significantly with an individual's ability to function. In fact, a recent study sponsored by the World Health Organization and the World Bank found unipolar major depression to be the leading cause of disability in the United States and worldwide.

There is a high degree of variation among people with depression in terms of symptoms, course of illness, and response to treatment, indicating that depression may have a number of complex and interacting causes. This variability poses a major challenge to researchers attempting to understand and treat the disorder. However, recent advances in research technology are bringing NIMH scientists closer

183

than ever before to characterizing the biology and physiology of depression in its different forms and to the possibility of identifying effective treatments for individuals based on symptom presentation.

One of the most challenging problems in depression research and clinical practice is refractory—hard to treat—depression. While approximately 80 percent of people with depression respond very positively to treatment, a significant number of individuals remain treatment refractory. Even among treatment responders, many do not have complete or lasting improvement, and adverse side effects are common. Thus, an important goal of NIMH research is to advance the development of more effective treatments for depression—especially treatment-refractory depression—that also have fewer side effects than currently available treatments.

Research on Treatments for Depression

Medication

Studies on the mechanisms of action of antidepressant medication comprise an important area of NIMH depression research. Existing antidepressant drugs are known to influence the functioning of certain neurotransmitters in the brain, primarily serotonin and norepinephrine, known as monoamines. Older medications—tricyclic antidepressants (TCAs) and monoamine oxidase inhibitors (MAOIs)—affect the activity of both of these neurotransmitters simultaneously. Their disadvantage is that they can be difficult to tolerate due to side effects or, in the case of MAOIs, dietary restrictions. Newer medications, such as the selective serotonin reuptake inhibitors (SSRIs), have fewer side effects than the older drugs, making it easier for patients to adhere to treatment. Both generations of medications are effective in relieving depression, although some people will respond to one type of drug, but not another.

Antidepressant medications take several weeks to be clinically effective even though they begin to alter brain chemistry with the very first dose. Research now indicates that antidepressant effects result from slow-onset adaptive changes within the brain cells, or neurons. Further, it appears that activation of chemical messenger pathways within neurons, and changes in the way that genes in brain cells are expressed, are the critical events underlying long-term adaptations in neuronal function relevant to antidepressant drug action. A current challenge is to understand the mechanisms that mediate, within cells, the long-term changes in neuronal function produced by antidepressants and other psychotropic drugs and to understand how these mechanisms are altered in the presence of illness.

Knowing how and where in the brain antidepressants work can aid the development of more targeted and potent medications that may help reduce the time between first dose and clinical response. Further, clarifying the mechanisms of action can reveal how different drugs produce side effects and can guide the design of new, more tolerable, treatments.

As one route toward learning about the distinct biological processes that go awry in different forms of depression, NIMH researchers are investigating the differential effectiveness of various antidepressant medications in people with particular subtypes of depression. For example, this research has revealed that people with atypical depression, a subtype characterized by reactivity of mood (mood brightens in response to positive events) and at least two other symptoms (weight gain or increased appetite, oversleeping, intense fatigue, or rejection sensitivity), respond better to treatment with MAOIs, and perhaps with SSRIs than with TCAs.

Many patients and clinicians find that combinations of different drugs work most effectively for treating depression, either by enhancing the therapeutic action or reducing side effects. Although combination strategies are used often in clinical practice, there is little research evidence available to guide psychiatrists in prescribing appropriate combination treatment. NIMH is in the process of revitalizing and expanding its program of clinical research, and combination therapy will be but one of numerous treatment interventions to be explored and developed.

Untreated depression often has an accelerating course, in which episodes become more frequent and severe over time. Researchers are now considering whether early intervention with medications and maintenance treatment during well periods will prevent recurrence of episodes. To date, there is no evidence of any adverse effects of long-term antidepressant use.

Psychotherapy

Like the process of learning, which involves the formation of new connections between nerve cells in the brain, psychotherapy works by changing the way the brain functions. NIMH research has shown that certain types of psychotherapy, particularly cognitive-behavioral therapy (CBT) and interpersonal therapy (IPT), can help relieve depression. CBT helps patients change the negative styles of thinking and behaving often associated with depression. IPT focuses on working through disturbed personal relationships that may contribute to depression.

Research on children and adolescents with depression supports CBT as a useful initial treatment, but antidepressant medication is indicated for those with severe, recurrent, or psychotic depression. Studies of adults have shown that while psychotherapy alone is rarely sufficient to treat moderate to severe depression, it may provide additional relief in combination with antidepressant medication. In one recent NIMH-funded study, older adults with recurrent major depression who received IPT in combination with an antidepressant medication during a three-year period were much less likely to experience a recurrence of illness than those who received medication only or therapy only. For mild depression, however, a recent analysis of multiple studies indicated that combination treatment is not significantly more effective than CBT or IPT alone. Preliminary evidence from an ongoing NIMH-supported study indicates that IPT may hold promise in the treatment of dysthymia.

Electroconvulsive Therapy (ECT)

Electroconvulsive therapy (ECT) remains one of the most effective yet most stigmatized treatments for depression. Eighty to ninety percent of people with severe depression improve dramatically with ECT. ECT involves producing a seizure in the brain of a patient under general anesthesia by applying electrical stimulation to the brain through electrodes placed on the scalp. Repeated treatments are necessary to achieve the most complete antidepressant response. Memory loss and other cognitive problems are common, yet typically short-lived side effects of ECT. Although some people report lasting difficulties, modern advances in ECT technique have greatly reduced the side effects of this treatment compared to earlier decades. NIMH research on ECT has found that the dose of electricity applied and the placement of electrodes (unilateral or bilateral) can influence the degree of depression relief and the severity of side effects.

A current research question is how best to maintain the benefits of ECT over time. Although ECT can be very effective for relieving acute depression, there is a high rate of relapse when the treatments are discontinued. NIMH is currently sponsoring two multi-center studies on ECT follow-up treatment strategies. One study is comparing different medication treatments, and the other study is comparing maintenance medication to maintenance ECT. Results from these studies will help guide and improve follow-up treatment plans for patients who respond well to ECT.

186

Genetics Research

Research on the genetics of depression and other mental illnesses is a priority of NIMH and constitutes a critical component of the Institute's multi-level research effort. Researchers are increasingly certain that genes play an important role in vulnerability to depression and other severe mental disorders.

In recent years, the search for a single, defective gene responsible for each mental illness has given way to the understanding that multiple gene variants, acting together with yet unknown environmental risk factors or developmental events, account for the expression of psychiatric disorders. Identification of these genes, each of which contributes only a small effect, has proven extremely difficult.

However, new technologies, which continue to be developed and refined, are beginning to allow researchers to associate genetic variations with disease. In the next decade, two large-scale projects that involve identifying and sequencing all human genes and gene variants will be completed and are expected to yield valuable insights into the causes of mental disorders and the development of better treatments. In addition, NIMH is currently soliciting researchers to contribute to the development of a large-scale database of genetic information that will facilitate efforts to identify susceptibility genes for depression and other mental disorders.

Stress and Depression

Psychosocial and environmental stressors are known risk factors for depression. NIMH research has shown that stress in the form of loss, especially death of close family members or friends, can trigger depression in vulnerable individuals. Genetics research indicates that environmental stressors interact with depression vulnerability genes to increase the risk of developing depressive illness. Stressful life events may contribute to recurrent episodes of depression in some individuals, while in others depression recurrences may develop without identifiable triggers. Other NIMH research indicates that stressors in the form of social isolation or early-life deprivation may lead to permanent changes in brain function that increase susceptibility to depressive symptoms.

Brain Imaging

Advances in brain imaging technologies are allowing scientists to examine the brain in living people with more clarity than ever before. Functional magnetic resonance imaging (fMRI), a safe, noninvasive method for viewing brain structure and function simultaneously, is one new technique that NIMH researchers are using to study the brains of individuals with and without mental disorders. This technique will enable scientists to evaluate the effects of a variety of treatments on the brain and to associate these effects with clinical outcome.

Brain imaging findings may help direct the search for microscopic abnormalities in brain structure and function responsible for mental disorders. Ultimately, imaging technologies may serve as tools for early diagnosis and subtyping of depression and other mental disorders, thus advancing the development of new treatments and evaluation of their effects.

Hormonal Abnormalities

The hormonal system that regulates the body's response to stress, the hypothalamic-pituitary-adrenal (HPA) axis, is overactive in many patients with depression, and NIMH researchers are investigating whether this phenomenon contributes to the development of the illness.

The hypothalamus, the brain region responsible for managing hormone release from glands throughout the body, increases production of a substance called corticotropin releasing factor (CRF) when a threat to physical or psychological well-being is detected. Elevated levels and effects of CRF lead to increased hormone secretion by the pituitary and adrenal glands which prepares the body for defensive action. The body's responses include reduced appetite, decreased sex drive, and heightened alertness. NIMH research suggests that persistent overactivation of this hormonal system may lay the groundwork for depression. The elevated CRF levels detectable in depressed patients are reduced by treatment with antidepressant drugs or ECT, and this reduction corresponds to improvement in depressive symptoms. NIMH scientists are investigating how and whether the hormonal research findings fit together with the discoveries from genetics research and monoamine studies.

Co-Occurrence of Depression and Anxiety Disorders

NIMH research has revealed that depression often co-exists with anxiety disorders (panic disorder, obsessive-compulsive disorder, post-traumatic stress disorder, social phobia, or generalized anxiety disorder). In such cases, it is important that depression and each co-occurring illness be diagnosed and treated.

Several studies have shown an increased risk of suicide attempts in people with co-occurring depression and panic disorder—the anxiety disorder characterized by unexpected and repeated episodes of intense fear and physical symptoms, including chest pain, dizziness, and shortness of breath.

Rates of depression are especially high in people with post-traumatic stress disorder (PTSD), a debilitating condition that can occur after exposure to a terrifying event or ordeal in which grave physical harm occurred or was threatened. In one study supported by NIMH, more than 40 percent of patients with PTSD had depression when evaluated both at one month and four months following the traumatic event.

Co-Occurrence of Depression and Other Illnesses

Depression frequently co-occurs with a variety of other physical illnesses, including heart disease, stroke, cancer, and diabetes, and also can increase the risk for subsequent physical illness, disability, and premature death. Depression in the context of physical illness, however, is often unrecognized and untreated. Furthermore, depression can impair the ability to seek and stay on treatment for other medical illnesses. NIMH research suggests that early diagnosis and treatment of depression in patients with other physical illnesses may help improve overall health outcome.

The results of a NIMH-supported study provide the strongest evidence to date that depression increases the risk of having a future heart attack. Analysis of data from a large-scale survey revealed that individuals with a history of major depression were more than four times as likely to suffer a heart attack over a 12-13 year follow-up period, compared to people without such a history. Even people with a history of two or more weeks of mild depression were more than twice as likely to have a heart attack, compared to those who had had no such episodes. Although associations were found between certain psychotropic medications and heart attack risk, the researchers determined that the associations were simply a reflection of the primary relationship between depression and heart trouble. The question of whether treatment for depression reduces the excess risk of heart attack in depressed patients must be addressed with further research.

Women and Depression

Nearly twice as many women (12 percent) as men (7 percent) are affected by a depressive illness each year. At some point during their lives, as many as 20 percent of women have at least one episode of depression that should be treated. Although conventional wisdom holds that depression is most closely associated with menopause, in fact, the childbearing years are marked by the highest rates of depression, followed by the years prior to menopause.

NIMH researchers are investigating the causes and treatment of depressive disorders in women. One area of research focuses on life stress and depression. Data from a recent NIMH-supported study suggests that stressful life experiences may play a larger role in provoking recurrent episodes of depression in women than in men.

The influence of hormones on depression in women has been an active area of NIMH research. One recent study was the first to demonstrate that the troublesome depressive mood swings and physical symptoms of premenstrual syndrome (PMS), a disorder affecting three to seven percent of menstruating women, result from an abnormal response to normal hormone changes during the menstrual cycle. Among women with normal menstrual cycles, those with a history of PMS experienced relief from mood and physical symptoms when their sex hormones, estrogen and progesterone, were temporarily "turned off" by administering a drug that suppresses the function of the ovaries. PMS symptoms developed within a week or two after the hormones were reintroduced. In contrast, women without a history of PMS reported no effects of the hormonal manipulation. The study showed that female sex hormones do not cause PMS—rather, they trigger PMS symptoms in women with a preexisting vulnerability to the disorder. The researchers currently are attempting to determine what makes some women but not others susceptible to PMS. Possibilities include genetic differences in hormone sensitivity at the cellular level, differences in history of other mood disorders, and individual differences in serotonin function.

NIMH researchers also are currently investigating the mechanisms that contribute to depression after childbirth (postpartum depression), another serious disorder where abrupt hormonal shifts in the context of intense psychosocial stress disable some women with an apparent underlying vulnerability. In addition, an ongoing NIMH clinical trial is evaluating the use of antidepressant medication following delivery to prevent postpartum depression in women with a history of this disorder after a previous childbirth.

Child and Adolescent Depression

Large-scale research studies have reported that up to 2.5 percent of children and up to 8.3 percent of adolescents in the United States suffer from depression. In addition, research has discovered that depression onset is occurring earlier in individuals born in more recent decades. There is evidence that depression emerging early in life often persists, recurs, and continues into adulthood, and that early onset depression may predict more severe illness in adult life. Diagnosing and treating children and adolescents with depression is critical to prevent impairment in academic, social, emotional, and behavioral functioning and to allow children to live up to their full potential.

Research on the diagnosis and treatment of mental disorders in children and adolescents, however, has lagged behind that in adults. Diagnosing depression in these age groups is often difficult because early symptoms can be hard to detect or may be attributed to other causes. In addition, treating depression in children and adolescents remains a challenge, because few studies have established the safety and efficacy of treatments for depression in youth. Children and adolescents are going through rapid, age-related changes in their physiological states, and there remains much to be learned about brain development during the early years of life before treatments for depression in young people will be as successful as they are in older people. NIMH is pursuing brain-imaging research in children and adolescents to gather information about normal brain development and what goes wrong in mental illness.

Depression in children and adolescents is associated with an increased risk of suicidal behaviors. Over the last several decades, the suicide rate in young people has increased dramatically. In 1996, the most recent year for which statistics are available, suicide was the third leading cause of death in 15-24 year olds and the fourth leading cause among 10-14 year olds. NIMH researchers are developing and testing various interventions to prevent suicide in children and adolescents. However, early diagnosis and treatment of depression and other mental disorders, and accurate evaluation of suicidal thinking, possibly hold the greatest suicide prevention value.

Until recently, there were limited data on the safety and efficacy of antidepressant medications in children and adolescents. The use of antidepressants in this age group was based on adult standards of treatment. A recent NIMH-funded study supported fluoxetine, an SSRI, as a safe and efficacious medication for child and adolescent depression. The response rate was not as high as in adults, however, emphasizing the need for continued research on existing treatments and for development of more effective treatments, including psychotherapies designed specifically for children. Other complementary studies in the field are beginning to report similar positive findings in depressed young people treated with any of several newer antidepressants. In a number of studies, TCAs were found to be ineffective for treating depression in children and adolescents, but limitations of the study designs preclude strong conclusions.

NIMH is committed to developing an infrastructure of skilled researchers in the areas of child and adolescent mental health. In 1995, NIMH co-sponsored a conference that brought together more than 100 research experts, family and patient advocates, and representatives of mental health professional organizations to discuss and reach consensus on various recommendations for psychiatric medication research in children and adolescents. Outcomes of this conference included awarding additional funds to existing research grants to study psychotropic medications in children and adolescents and establishing a network of Research Units of Pediatric Psychopharmacology (RUPPs). Recently, a large, multi-site, NIMH-funded study was initiated to investigate both medication and psychotherapeutic treatments for adolescent depression. Continuing to address and resolve the ethical challenges involved with clinical research on children and adolescents is an NIMH priority.

Older Adults and Depression

In a given year, between one and two percent of people over age 65 living in the community, i.e., not living in nursing homes or other institutions, suffer from major depression and about two percent have dysthymia. Depression, however, is not a normal part of aging. Research has clearly demonstrated the importance of diagnosing and treating depression in older persons. Because major depression is typically a recurrent disorder, relapse prevention is a high priority for treatment research. As noted previously, a recent NIMH-supported study established the efficacy of combined antidepressant medication and interpersonal psychotherapy in reducing depressive relapses in older adults who had recovered from an episode of depression.

Additionally, recent NIMH studies show that 13 to 27 percent of older adults have subclinical depressions that do not meet the diagnostic criteria for major depression or dysthymia but are associated with increased risk of major depression, physical disability, medical illness, and high use of health services. Subclinical depressions cause considerable suffering, and some clinicians are now beginning to recognize and treat them.

Suicide is more common among the elderly than in any other age group. NIMH research has shown that nearly all people who commit suicide have a diagnosable mental or substance abuse disorder. In studies of older adults who committed suicide, nearly all had major depression, typically a first episode, though very few had a substance abuse disorder. Suicide among white males aged 85 and older was nearly six times the national U.S. rate (65 per 100,000 compared with 11 per 100,000) in 1996, the most recent year for which statistics are available. Prevention of suicide in older adults is a high priority area in the NIMH prevention research portfolio.

Alternative Treatments

There is high public interest in herbal remedies for various medical conditions including depression. Among the herbals is hypericum or St. John's wort, promoted as having antidepressant effects. Adverse drug interactions have been reported between St. John's wort and drugs used to treat HIV infections as well as those used to reduce the risk of organ transplant rejection. In general, preparations of St. John's wort vary significantly. No adequate studies have been done to determine the antidepressant efficacy of the herbal, consequently, the NIMH is conducting the first large-scale, multi-site, controlled study of St. John's wort as a potential treatment for depression.

The Future of NIMH Depression Research

Research on the causes, treatment, and prevention of all forms of depression will remain a high NIMH priority for the foreseeable future. Areas of interest and opportunity include the following:

- NIMH researchers will seek to identify distinct subtypes of depression characterized by various features including genetic risk, course of illness, and clinical symptoms. The aims of this research will be to enhance clinical prediction of onset, recurrence, and co-occurring illness; to identify the influence of environmental stressors in people with genetic vulnerability for major depression; and to prevent the development of co-occurring physical illnesses and substance use disorders in people with primary recurrent depression.

- Because many adult mental disorders originate in childhood, studies of development over time that uncover the complex interactions among psychological, social, and biological events are needed to track the persistence, chronicity, and pathways into and out of disorders in childhood and adolescence. Information about behavioral continuities that may exist between specific dimensions of child temperament and child mental disorder, including depression, may make it possible to ward off adult psychiatric disorders.

- Research on thought processes that has provided insights into the nature and causes of mental illness creates opportunities for improving prevention and treatment. Among the important findings of this research is evidence that points to the role of negative attentional and memory biases—selective attention to and memory of negative information—in producing and sustaining depression and anxiety. Future studies are needed to obtain a more precise account of the content and life course development of these biases, including their interaction with social and emotional processes, and their neural influences and effects.

- Advances in neurobiology and brain imaging technology now make it possible to see clearer linkages between research findings from different domains of emotion and mood. Such "maps" of depression will inform understanding of brain development, effective treatments, and the basis for depression in children and adults. In adult populations, charting physiological changes involved in emotion during aging will shed light on mood disorders in the elderly, as well as the psychological and physiological effects of bereavement.

- An important long-term goal of NIMH depression research is to identify simple biological markers of depression that, for example, could be detected in blood or with brain imaging. In theory, biological markers would reveal the specific depression profile of each patient and would allow psychiatrists to select treatments known to be most effective for each profile. Although such data-driven interventions can only be imagined today, NIMH already is investing in multiple research strategies to lay the groundwork for tomorrow's discoveries.

Additional Information

National Institute of Mental Health (NIMH)
Office of Communications and Public Liaison
6001 Executive Boulevard, Rm. 8184, MSC 9663
Bethesda, MD 20892-9663 U.S.A.
Tel: 301-443-4513; Fax: 301-443-4279; TTY: 301-443-8431
Website: www.nimh.nih.gov
E-mail: nimhinfo@nih.gov

Section 16.2.

The Co-Occurrence of Depression with Medical, Psychiatric, and Substance Abuse Disorders

This section includes "Depression: Co-Occurrence of Depression with Medical, Psychiatric, and Substance Abuse Disorders," Fact Sheet © National Mental Health Association (NMHA), reprinted with permission; "Depression Can Break Your Heart," National Institute of Mental Health (NIMH), NIH Publication No. 01-4592, 2001; excerpts from "Co-Occurrence of Depression with Cancer," Fact Sheet, National Institute of Mental Health (NIMH), updated November 29, 1999; excerpts from "Co-Occurrence of Depression with Stroke," National Institute of Mental Health, Updated June 1, 1999; and "Depression, Bone Mass, and Osteoporosis," National Institute of Mental Health (NIMH), June 29, 2001, updated October 18, 2001.

Clinical Depression and Serious Medical Illness

Clinical depression is a common and serious medical illness that can be effectively treated. The risk of clinical depression is often higher in individuals with serious medical illnesses, such as heart disease, stroke, cancer, and diabetes. However, the warning signs are frequently discounted by patients and family members, who mistakenly assume feeling depressed is normal for people struggling with serious health conditions. In addition, the symptoms of depression are frequently masked by these other medical illnesses, resulting in treatment that addresses the symptoms but not the underlying depression. It is a myth that depression is a "normal" emotional response to another illness; it's extremely important to simultaneously treat both medical illnesses.

Impact of Depression in Primary Care Settings

- Nearly 74 percent of Americans who seek help for depression or symptoms of depression will go to a primary care physician rather than a mental health professional.[1]

195

- The rate of depression among those with medical illnesses in primary care settings is estimated at five to 10 percent. Among those hospitalized, the rate is estimated at 10 to 14 percent.[2]

- The more severe the medical condition, the more likely that patient will experience clinical depression.[2]

- People with depression experience greater distress, an increase in impaired functioning, and less ability to follow medical regimens, thus hindering the treatment of any other medical conditions.[2]

- Unfortunately, the diagnosis of depression is missed 50 percent of the time in primary care settings.[1]

Why Depression and Medical Illnesses Often Occur Together

- Medical disorders may contribute biologically to depression.[3]

- Medically ill people may become clinically depressed as a psychological reaction to the prognosis, the pain and/or incapacity caused by the illness or its treatment.[3]

- Though occurring together, depression and a general medical disorder may be unrelated.[3]

Prevalence of Depression Co-Occurring with Other Medical Illnesses

Heart Disease and Depression

- Depression occurs in 40 to 65 percent of patients who have experienced a heart attack, and in 18 to 20 percent of people who have coronary heart disease, but who have not had a heart attack.[4]

- After a heart attack, patients with clinical depression have a three to four times greater chance of death within the next six months.[4]

- Men and women with depression are at increased risk for coronary artery disease but only men are at greater risk for dying.[5]

Depression Can Break Your Heart

Research over the past two decades has shown that depression and heart disease are common companions and, what is worse, each can lead to the other. It appears now that depression is an important risk factor for heart disease along with high blood cholesterol and high blood pressure. A study conducted in Baltimore, MD found that of 1,551 people who were free of heart disease, those who had a history of depression were 4 times more likely than those who did not to suffer a heart attack in the next 14 years.[A] In addition, researchers in Montreal, Canada found that heart patients who were depressed were 4 times as likely to die in the next 6 months as those who were not depressed.[B]

Depression may make it harder to take the medications needed and to carry out the treatment for heart disease.[C] Depression also may result in chronically elevated levels of stress hormones, such as cortisol and adrenaline, and the activation of the sympathetic nervous system (part of the "fight or flight" response), which can have deleterious effects on the heart.[D] The first studies of heart disease and depression found that people with heart disease were more likely to suffer from depression than otherwise healthy people.[D] While about 1 in 20 American adults experience major depression in a given year, the number goes to about 1 in 3 for people who have survived a heart attack.[E,F] Furthermore, other researchers have found that most heart patients with depression do not receive appropriate treatment. Cardiologists and primary care physicians tend to miss the diagnosis of depression;[D] and even when they do recognize it, they often do not treat it adequately.[G]

The public health impact of depression and heart disease, both separately and together, is enormous. Depression is the estimated leading cause of disability worldwide,[H] and heart disease is by far the leading cause of death in the United States.[I] Approximately 1 in 3 Americans will die of some form of heart disease.

Studies indicate that depression can appear after heart disease and/or heart disease surgery. In one investigation, nearly half of the patients studied one week after cardiopulmonary bypass surgery experienced serious cognitive problems, which may contribute to clinical depression in some individuals.[J]

There are also multiple studies indicating that heart disease can follow depression.[D] Psychological distress may cause rapid heartbeat, high blood pressure, and faster blood clotting. It can also lead to elevated insulin and cholesterol levels. These risk factors, with obesity, form a constellation of symptoms and often serve as a predictor of and a response to heart disease. People with depression may feel slowed down and still have high levels of stress hormones. This can increase the work of the heart. As high levels of stress hormones are signaling a "fight or flight" reaction, the body's metabolism is diverted away from the type of tissue repair needed in heart disease.

Regardless of cause, the combination of depression and heart disease is associated with increased sickness and death, making effective treatment of depression imperative. Pharmacological and cognitive-behavioral therapy treatments for depression are relatively well developed and play an important role in reducing the adverse impact of depression.[D] With the advent of the selective serotonin reuptake inhibitors to treat depression, more medically ill patients can be treated without the complicating cardiovascular side effects of the previous drugs available. Ongoing research is investigating whether these treatments also reduce the associated risk of a second heart attack. Furthermore, preventive interventions based on cognitive-behavior theories of depression also merit attention as approaches for avoiding adverse outcomes associated with both disorders. These interventions may help promote adherence and behavior change that may increase the impact of available pharmacological and behavioral approaches to both diseases. Exercise is another potential pathway to reducing both depression and risk of heart disease. A recent study found that participation in an exercise training program was comparable to treatment with an antidepressant medication (a selective serotonin reuptake inhibitor) for improving depressive symptoms in older adults diagnosed with major depression.[K] Exercise, of course, is a major protective factor against heart disease as well.[L]

The NIMH and the National Heart, Lung, and Blood Institute are invested in uncovering the complicated relationship between depression and heart disease. They support research on the basic mechanisms and processes linking co-occurring mental and medical disorders to identify potent, modifiable risk factors and protective processes amenable to medical and behavioral interventions that will reduce the adverse outcomes associated with both types of disorders.

References

A.   Pratt LA, Ford DE, Crum RM, et al. Depression, psychotropic medication, and risk of myocardial infarction. Prospective data from the Baltimore ECA follow-up. *Circulation*, 1996; 94(12): 3123-9.

B.   Frasure-Smith N, Lesperance F, Talajic M. Depression and 18-month prognosis after myocardial infarction. *Circulation*, 1995; 91(4): 999-1005.

C. Ziegelstein RC, Fauerbach JA, Stevens SS, et al. Patients with depression are less likely to follow recommendations to reduce cardiac risk during recovery from a myocardial infarction. *Archives of Internal Medicine*, 2000; 160(12): 1818-23.

D. Nemeroff CB, Musselman DL, Evans DL. Depression and cardiac disease. *Depression and Anxiety*, 1998; 8(Suppl 1): 71-9.

E. Regier DA, Narrow WE, Rae DS, et al. The de facto mental and addictive disorders service system. Epidemiologic Catchment Area prospective 1-year prevalence rates of disorders and services. *Archives of General Psychiatry*, 1993; 50(2): 85-94.

F. Lesperance F, Frasure-Smith N, Talajic M. Major depression before and after myocardial infarction: its nature and consequences. *Psychosomatic Medicine*, 1996; 58(2): 99-110.

G. Hirschfeld RM, Keller MB, Panico S, et al. The National Depressive and Manic-Depressive Association consensus statement on the undertreatment of depression. *Journal of the American Medical Association*, 1997; 277(4): 333-40.

H. Murray CJL, Lopez AD, eds. Summary: The global burden of disease: a comprehensive assessment of mortality and disability from diseases, injuries, and risk factors in 1990 and projected to 2020. Cambridge, MA: Published by the Harvard School of Public Health on behalf of the World Health Organization and the World Bank, Harvard University Press, 1996. http://www.who.int/msa/mnh/ems/dalys/intro.htm

I. Murphy SL. Deaths: final data for 1998. *National Vital Statistics Report*, 48(11). DHHS Publication No. 2000-1120. Hyattsville, MD: National Center for Health Statistics, 2000. http://www.cdc.gov/nchs/data/nvs48_11.pdf

J. Chabot RJ, Gugino LD, Aglio LS, et al. QEEG and neuropsychological profiles of patients after undergoing cardiopulmonary bypass surgical procedures. *Clinical Electroencephalography*, 1997; 28(2): 98-105.

K. Blumenthal JA, Babyak MA, Moore KA, et al. Effects of exercise training on older patients with major depression. *Archives of Internal Medicine*, 1999; 159(19): 2349-56.

L. Fletcher GF, Balady G, Blair SN, et al. Statement on exercise: benefits and recommendations for physical activity programs for all Americans. A statement for health professionals by the Committee on Exercise and Cardiac Rehabilitation of the Council on Clinical Cardiology, American Heart Association. *Circulation,* 1996; 94(4): 857-62.

Stroke and Depression

The association between depression and stroke has long been recognized for its negative impact on an individual's rehabilitation, family relationships, and quality of life. Appropriate diagnosis and treatment of depression can shorten the rehabilitation process and lead to more rapid recovery and resumption of routine. It can also save health care costs (e.g., eliminate nursing home expenses).

• Depression occurs in 10 to 27 percent of stroke survivors and usually lasts about one year.[6]

• An additional 15-40 percent of stroke survivors experience some symptoms of depression within two months after the stroke.[6]

• Individuals reporting five or more depressive symptoms have more than a 50 percent risk of mortality due to stroke in the subsequent 29 years.[7]

• Of particular significance, depression often co-occurs with stroke. When this happens, the presence of the additional illness, depression, is frequently unrecognized, leading to serious and unnecessary consequences for patients and families.

• Though depressed feelings can be a common reaction to a stroke, clinical depression is not the expected reaction. For this reason, when present, specific treatment should be considered for clinical depression even in the presence of a stroke.

• Appropriate diagnosis and treatment of depression may bring substantial benefits to the patient through improved medical status, enhanced quality of life, a reduction in the degree of pain and disability, and improved treatment compliance and co-operation.

• The mean duration of major depression in stroke patients has been shown to be just under a year.

- Among the factors that effect the likelihood and severity of depression following a stroke are the location of the brain lesion, previous or family history of depression, and pre-stroke social functioning

- Post-stroke patients who are also depressed, particularly those with major depressive disorder, are less compliant with rehabilitation, more irritable and demanding, and may experience personality change.

Action Steps

Don't Ignore Symptoms! Health care professionals should always be aware of the possibility of depression co-occurring with stroke. Patients or family members with concerns about this possibility should discuss these issues with the individuals' physicians. A consultation with a psychiatrist or other mental health clinician may be recommended to clarify the diagnosis.

Get the Word Out! Emphasize the importance of professional and public awareness of the co-occurrence of depression with stroke and proper diagnosis and treatment of depression.

Community, Professional, Advocacy Organizations, and the Media can help spread important messages about depression co-occurring with stroke.

Cancer and Depression

- One in four people with cancer also suffer from clinical depression.[8]

- Depression is sometimes mistaken as a side effect of corticosteroids or chemotherapy, both treatments for cancer.[8]

- Depressive symptoms can be mistakenly attributed to the cancer itself, which can also cause appetite and weight loss, insomnia, and loss of energy.[8]

Facts on Depression and Cancer

Each year, an estimated 1.2 million Americans will be diagnosed with cancer. Receiving such a diagnosis is often traumatic, causing emotional upset, sadness, anxiety, poor concentration, and with-drawal. Often, this turmoil begins to abate within two weeks, with a return to usual functioning in about a month. When that doesn't happen, the patient must be evaluated for clinical depression, which occurs in about 10% of the general population and in about 25% of persons with cancer. Early diagnosis and treatment are important because depression adds to a patient's suffering and interferes with his or her motivation to engage in cancer treatment.

Treating Depression Has Many Benefits for Cancer Patients

Research shows that, compared to patients without depression, depressed cancer patients experience greater distress, more impaired functioning, and less ability to follow medical regimens. Studies also show that treating depression in these patents not only improves the psychological condition but also reduces suffering and enhances quality of life. Therefore, professionals, patients, and families must be alert for depressive symptoms in cancer patients, and seek evaluation for depression when indicated.

Risk Factors

Studies also indicate that the more severe the medical condition, the more likely it is that a person will experience clinical depression. Other factors which increase the risk of depression in persons with cancer are: history of depressive illness each year, alcohol or other substance abuse, poorly controlled pain, advanced disease, disability or disfigurement, medications such as steroids and chemotherapy agents, the presence of other physical illness, social isolation, and socio-economic pressures.

Effective Treatment for Depression

With treatment, up to 80% of all depressed people can improve, usually within weeks. Treatment includes medication, psychotherapy, or a combination of both. The severity of the depression, the other conditions present, and the medical treatments being used must be considered to determine the appropriate treatment. Altering the cancer treatment may also help diminish depressive symptoms.

Antidepressant Medications. Several types of antidepressant medication are effective, none of them habit-forming. Most side-effects can be eliminated or minimized by adjustment in dosage or type of medication, so it is important for patients to discuss all effects with the doctor. Also, because responses differ, several trials of medicine may be needed before an effective treatment is found. In severe depression, medication is usually required and is often enhanced by psychotherapy.

In special circumstances, low doses of psychostimulant can be used to treat depression in cancer patients. These may be used when standard antidepressants produce side effects that, due to the patient's physical condition are either intolerable or medically dangerous. Also psychostimulants may help alleviate post-surgical pain and their rapid effect (1-2 days) can aid medical recovery.

Psychotherapy. Interpersonal Therapy and Cognitive/Behavioral Therapy have also been shown to be effective in treating depression. These short-term (10-20 weeks) treatments involve talking with a therapist to recognize and change behaviors, thoughts, or relationships that cause or maintain depression and to develop more healthful and rewarding habits.

Psychological treatment of patients with cancer, even those without depression, has been shown to be beneficial in a number of ways. These include: improving self-concept and sense of control, and reducing distress, anxiety, pain, fatigue, nausea, and sexual problems. In addition, there is some indication that psychological intervention may increase survival time in some cancer patients.

Electroconvulsive Therapy. Electroconvulsive therapy (ECT) is a safe and often effective treatment for severe depression. Because it is fast-acting, it may be of particular use for depression in cancer patients who experience severe weight loss or debilitation, or who cannot take or do not respond to antidepressant medications.

Medical Management. The benefits from the standard treatments described above are maximized by the effective management of pain and other medical conditions in depressed cancer patients.

Diabetes and Depression

* People with adult onset diabetes have a 25 percent chance of having depression.[9]

* Depression also affects as many as 70 percent of patients with diabetic complications.[9]

Eating Disorders and Depression

- Research shows a strong relationship between depression and eating disorders (anorexia and bulimia nervosa) in women.[10]

Alcohol/Drugs and Depression

- Research shows that one in three depressed people also suffer from some form of substance abuse or dependence.[1]

- Substance abuse disorders are present in 32 percent of individuals with depressive disorders. They co-occur in 27 percent of those with major depression and 56 percent of those with bipolar disorder.

Substance use must be discontinued in order to clarify the diagnosis and maximize the effectiveness of psychiatric interventions. Treatment for depression as a separate condition is necessary if the depression remains after the substance use problem is ended.

Depression Co-Occurs with Psychiatric Disorders

A higher than average co-occurrence of depression with other psychiatric disorders, such as anxiety and eating disorders, has been documented.

- Concurrent depression is present in 13 percent of patients with panic disorder. In about 24 percent of these patients, the panic disorder preceded the depressive disorder.

- Between 50 and 75 percent of eating disorder patients (anorexia nervosa and bulimia) have a lifetime history of major depressive disorder.

In such cases, detection of depression can help clarify the initial diagnosis and may result in more effective treatment and better outcome for the patient.

Common Symptoms of Depression and Other Medical Disorders

- Weight loss, sleep disturbances, and low energy may occur in people with diabetes, thyroid disorders, some neurological disorders, heart disease, cancer, and stroke—and also are common symptoms of depression.

• Apathy, poor concentration, and memory loss can occur in individuals with Parkinson's disease and Alzheimer's disease—and also are common symptoms of depression.

• Medications for high blood pressure, Parkinson's disease, and other medical problems can produce side effects similar to the symptoms of depression.

Depression, Bone Mass, and Osteoporosis

In a review of published research, NIMH-funded scientists report a strong association between depression and osteoporosis. The literature suggests that depression may be a significant risk factor for osteoporosis, a progressive decrease in bone density that makes bones fragile and more likely to break. Low bone mineral density (BMD), a major risk factor for fracture, is more common in depressed people than in the general population.

"Using different data, all of the studies point to the same conclusion," said NIMH researcher and first author Giovanni Cizza, M.D., Ph.D. "Depression is not only a disease of the brain, but it also has long-term consequences for other medical conditions, such as osteoporosis." Dr. Cizza and Philip Gold, M.D., NIMH, George Chrousos, M.D., National Institute of Child Health and Human Development, and Pernille Ravn, M.D, Center for Clinical and Basic Research, Ballerup, Denmark, present a summary of the findings in the July 2001 issue of *Trends in Endocrinology & Metabolism.*

Both the clinical trial and research review underscore the seriousness of depression, a treatable illness that affects 5 to 9 percent of women and 1 to 2 percent of men. Depression symptoms include loss of interest or pleasure in activities that were once enjoyed, including sex; fatigue, decreased energy; difficulty concentrating, remembering, making decisions; insomnia, early-morning awakening, or oversleeping; appetite and weight loss or overeating and weight gain; thoughts of death or suicide; suicide attempts; restlessness, irritability; and persistent symptoms that do not respond to treatment, such as headaches, digestive disorders, and chronic pain.

Although its causes are unclear, major depression is associated with hormonal abnormalities that can lead to changes in tissue, such as bone. Research suggests that higher cortisol levels, often found in depressed patients, may contribute to bone loss and changes in body composition. Fragile bones and increased risk of fracture are signs of osteoporosis. When one or more risk factors occur, such as low BMD, family history, previous fracture, thinness, or smoking, a clinical evaluation for osteoporosis is recommended. Identifying depression as a risk factor would improve patient diagnosis and treatment.

In one study, evidence revealed that bone density at the lumbar spine was 15% lower in 80 men and women older than 40 with major depression compared to 57 men and women who were not depressed. Factors such as smoking, a history of excessive or inadequate exercise, or estrogen treatment did not affect the study, implying that depression per se had an effect on bone mass.

Another study measured bone mineral density at the spine, hip, and radius in 22 pre- and 2 postmenopausal women with previous or current major depression. The 24 controls were matched by age, menopausal status, race, and body mass index. BMD was 6% lower at the spine and 14% lower at the hip in the depressed women. No premenopausal women in the control group had such a deficit.

The association between depression, BMD, falls, and risk of fracture was examined in a study of 7,414 elderly women. Depression prevalence was 6%. Depressed women were more likely to fall (70% versus 59%) and had more vertebral (11% versus 5%) and non-vertebral (28% versus 21%) fractures compared with controls. This research underlines depression as a risk factor for osteoporotic fractures.

The relationship between osteoporosis and mental health was evaluated in a sample of 102 middle-aged Portuguese women. Osteoporosis had a 47% prevalence, and depression was significantly more common in women with osteoporosis than in women without it (77% versus 54%). Women with the disorder had depressive scores 25%-35% higher than those with normal bone mass. This study did not find a link between depressive symptoms and low BMD, suggesting that only fully developed depression is a risk factor for osteoporosis.

In their summary, the researchers show a consistent association between depression and osteoporosis, suggesting that depression is a substantial risk factor. Some bone-loss studies combined actively depressed subjects with those who had a previous diagnosis, so it is unknown whether current depression and past diagnoses affect bone loss equally. With major depression as the threshold, most studies revealed a clear association between depression and osteoporosis.

Cizza and colleagues concluded that a clinical evaluation of subjects with unexplained bone loss, especially premenopausal women and young or middle-aged men, should include an assessment of depression. Conversely, non-traumatic fractures in a depressed patient should alert the physician to the possibility of osteoporosis.

Importance of Treatment

- People who get treatment for co-occurring depression often experience an improvement in their overall medical condition, better compliance with general medical care, and a better quality of life.[9]

- More than 80 percent of people with depression can be treated successfully with medication, psychotherapy, or a combination of both.[2]

- Early diagnosis and treatment can reduce patient discomfort and morbidity, and can also reduce the costs associated with misdiagnosis, and the risks and costs associated with suicide.[1]

References

1. Montano B: "Recognition and Treatment of Depression in a Primary Care Setting," *Journal of Clinical Psychiatry* 1994; 55(12):18-33.

2. National Institute of Mental Health, "Co-occurrence of Depression with Medical, Psychiatric and Substance Abuse Disorders," Accessed July 1999. http://www.nimh.nih.gov/depression/co_occur/abuse.htm.

3. National Institute of Mental Health, "Depression Co-occurring with General Medical Disorders," Accessed July 1999. http://www.nimh.nih.gov/depression/co_occur/co_oc.htm.

4. National Institute of Mental Health, "Co-occurrence of Depression with Heart Disease," Accessed July 1999. http://www.nimh.nih.gov/depression/co_occur/heart.htm.

5. Ferketich, A, Schwartzbaum, J, Frid, D, Moeschberger, M. Depression as an Antecedent to Heart Disease Among Women and Men in the NHANES I Study. *Archives of Internal Medicine* 2000; 160:1261-1268

6. National Institute of Mental Health, "Co-occurrence of Depression with Stroke," Accessed July 1999. http://www.nimh.nih.gov/depression/co_occur/stroke.htm.

7. Everson SA, Roberts RE, Goldberg DE, Kaplan GA: "Depressive Symptoms and Increased Risk of Stroke Mortality Over a 29-Year Period," *Archives of Internal Medicine* 1998; 158:1133-1138.

8. National Institute of Mental Health, "Co-occurrence of Depression with Cancer," Accessed July 1999. http://www.nimh.nih.gov/depression/co_occur/cancer.htm.

9. Lamberg L: "Treating Depression in Medical Conditions May Improve Quality of Life." *JAMA* 1996; 276(Dec. 18):857-858.

10. Willcox M, Sattler DN: "The Relationship Between Eating Disorders and Depression," *Journal of Social Psychology* 1996; 136:269-271.

Additional Information

National Mental Health Association
1021 Prince Street
Alexandria, VA 22314
Toll-Free: 800-969-6642
Toll-Free TTY: 800-433-5959
Fax: 703-684-5968
Website: www.nmha.org

Section 16.3

Women Are at Greater Risk for Depression Than Men

Excerpts from "Depression: What Every Woman Should Know,"
National Institute of Mental Health (NIMH), NIH Publication No. 00-4779,
August 2000.

Major depression and dysthymia affect twice as many women as men. This two-to-one ratio exists regardless of racial and ethnic background or economic status. The same ratio has been reported in ten other countries all over the world.[6] Men and women have about the same rate of bipolar disorder (manic-depression), though its course in women typically has more depressive and fewer manic episodes. Also, a greater number of women have the rapid cycling form of bipolar disorder, which may be more resistant to standard treatments.[3]

A variety of factors unique to women's lives are suspected to play a role in developing depression. Research is focused on understanding these, including: reproductive, hormonal, genetic, or other biological factors; abuse and oppression; interpersonal factors; and certain psychological and personality characteristics. And yet, the specific causes of depression in women remain unclear; many women exposed to these factors do not develop depression. What is clear is that regardless of the contributing factors, depression is a highly treatable illness.

The Many Dimensions of Depression in Women

The Issues of Adolescence

Before adolescence, there is little difference in the rate of depression in boys and girls. But between the ages of 11 and 13 there is a precipitous rise in depression rates for girls. By the age of 15, females are twice as likely to have experienced a major depressive episode as males.[1] This comes at a time in adolescence when roles and expectations change dramatically. The stresses of adolescence include forming an identity, emerging sexuality, separating from parents, and making decisions for the first time, along with other physical, intellectual,

209

and hormonal changes. These stresses are generally different for boys and girls, and may be associated more often with depression in females. Studies show that female high school students have significantly higher rates of depression, anxiety disorders, eating disorders, and adjustment disorders than male students, who have higher rates of disruptive behavior disorders.[4]

Adulthood: Relationships and Work Roles

Stress in general can contribute to depression in persons biologically vulnerable to the illness. Some have theorized that higher incidence of depression in women is not due to greater vulnerability, but to the particular stresses that many women face. These stresses include major responsibilities at home and work, single parenthood, and caring for children and aging parents. How these factors may uniquely affect women is not yet fully understood.

For both women and men, rates of major depression are highest among the separated and divorced, and lowest among the married, while remaining always higher for women than for men. The quality of a marriage, however, may contribute significantly to depression. Lack of an intimate, confiding relationship, as well as overt marital disputes, have been shown to be related to depression in women. In fact, rates of depression were shown to be highest among unhappily married women.

Reproductive Events

Women's reproductive events include the menstrual cycle, pregnancy, the post-pregnancy period, infertility, menopause, and sometimes, the decision not to have children. These events bring fluctuations in mood that for some women include depression. Researchers have confirmed that hormones have an effect on the brain chemistry that controls emotions and mood; a specific biological mechanism explaining hormonal involvement is not known, however.

Many women experience certain behavioral and physical changes associated with phases of their menstrual cycles. In some women, these changes are severe, occur regularly, and include depressed feelings, irritability, and other emotional and physical changes. Called premenstrual syndrome (PMS) or premenstrual dysphoric disorder (PMDD), the changes typically begin after ovulation and become gradually worse until menstruation starts. Scientists are exploring how the cyclical rise and fall of estrogen and other hormones may affect the brain chemistry that is associated with depressive illness.

Postpartum mood changes can range from transient "blues" immediately following childbirth to an episode of major depression to severe, incapacitating, psychotic depression. Studies suggest that women who experience major depression after childbirth very often have had prior depressive episodes even though they may not have been diagnosed and treated.

Pregnancy (if it is desired) seldom contributes to depression, and having an abortion does not appear to lead to a higher incidence of depression. Women with infertility problems may be subject to extreme anxiety or sadness, though it is unclear if this contributes to a higher rate of depressive illness. In addition, motherhood may be a time of heightened risk for depression because of the stress and demands it imposes.

Menopause, in general, is not associated with an increased risk of depression. In fact, while once considered a unique disorder, research has shown that depressive illness at menopause is no different than at other ages. The women more vulnerable to change-of-life depression are those with a history of past depressive episodes.

Specific Cultural Considerations

As for depression in general, the prevalence rate of depression in African American and Hispanic women remains about twice that of men. There is some indication, however, that major depression and dysthymia may be diagnosed less frequently in African American and slightly more frequently in Hispanic than in Caucasian women. Prevalence information for other racial and ethnic groups is not definitive. Possible differences in symptom presentation may affect the way depression is recognized and diagnosed among minorities. For example, African Americans are more likely to report somatic symptoms, such as appetite change and body aches and pains. In addition, people from various cultural backgrounds may view depressive symptoms in different ways. Such factors should be considered when working with women from special populations.

Victimization

Studies show that women molested as children are more likely to have clinical depression at some time in their lives than those with no such history. In addition, several studies show a higher incidence of depression among women who have been raped as adolescents or adults. Since far more women than men were sexually abused as children, these findings are relevant. Women who experience other commonly occurring forms of abuse, such as physical abuse and sexual harassment on the job, also may experience higher rates of depression. Abuse may lead to depression by fostering low self-esteem, a sense of helplessness, self-blame, and social isolation. There may be biological and environmental risk factors for depression resulting from growing up in a dysfunctional family. At present, more research is needed to understand whether victimization is connected specifically to depression.

Poverty

Women and children represent seventy-five percent of the U.S. population considered poor. Low economic status brings with it many stresses, including isolation, uncertainty, frequent negative events, and poor access to helpful resources. Sadness and low morale are more common among persons with low incomes and those lacking social supports. But research has not yet established whether depressive illnesses are more prevalent among those facing environmental stressors such as these.

Depression in Later Adulthood

At one time, it was commonly thought that women were particularly vulnerable to depression when their children left home and they were confronted with "empty nest syndrome" and experienced a profound loss of purpose and identity. However, studies show no increase in depressive illness among women at this stage of life.

As with younger age groups, more elderly women than men suffer from depressive illness. Similarly, for all age groups, being unmarried (which includes widowhood) is also a risk factor for depression. Most important, depression should not be dismissed as a normal consequence of the physical, social, and economic problems of later life. In fact, studies show that most older people feel satisfied with their lives.

About 800,000 persons are widowed each year. Most of them are older, female, and experience varying degrees of depressive symptomatology. Most do not need formal treatment, but those who are moderately or severely sad appear to benefit from self-help groups or various psychosocial treatments. However, a third of widows/widowers do meet criteria for major depressive episode in the first month after the death, and half of these remain clinically depressed one year later. These depressions respond to standard antidepressant treatments, although research on when to start treatment or how medications should be combined with psychosocial treatments is still in its early stages.[2,5]

References

1. Cyranowski JM, Frank E, Young E, Shear MK. Adolescent onset of the gender difference in lifetime rates of major depression. *Archives of General Psychiatry*, 2000; 57:21-27.

2. Lebowitz BD, Pearson JL, Schneider LS, Reynolds CF, Alexopoulos GS, Bruce ML, Conwell Y, Katz IR, Meyers BS, Morrison MF, Mossey J, Niederehe G, and Parmelee P. Diagnosis and treatment of depression in late life: Consensus statement update. *Journal of the American Medical Association*, 1997;278:1186-90.

3. Leibenluft E. Issues in the treatment of women with bipolar illness. *Journal of Clinical Psychiatry* (supplement 15), 1997;58:5-11.

4. Lewisohn PM, Hyman H, Roberts RE, Seeley JR, and Andrews JA. Adolescent psychopathology: 1. Prevalence and incidence of depression and other DSM-III-R disorders in high school students. *Journal of Abnormal Psychology*, 1993;102:133-44.

5. Reynolds CF, Miller MD, Pasternak RE, Frank E, Perel JM, Cornes C, Houck PR, Mazumdar S, Dew MA, and Kupfer DJ. Treatment of bereavement-related major depressive episodes in later life: A controlled study of acute and continuation treatment with nortriptyline and interpersonal psychotherapy. *American Journal of Psychiatry*, 1999;156:202-8.

6. Weissman MM, Bland RC, Canino GJ, Faravelli C, Greenwald S, Hwu HG, Joyce PR, Karam EG, Lee CK, Lellouch J, Lepine JP, Newman SC, Rubin-Stiper M, Wells JE, Wickramaratne PJ, Wittchen H, and Yeh EK. Cross-national epidemiology of major depression and bipolar disorder. *Journal of the American Medical Association*, 1996;276:293-9.

Section 16.4

Suicide and Depression

This section includes the following documents from the National Institute of Mental Health: "In Harm's Way: Suicide in America," NIH Publication No. 01-4594, 2001; "Frequently Asked Questions about Suicide," December 1999; and "Older Adults: Depression and Suicide Facts," NIH Publication No. 01-4593, 2001.

In Harm's Way: Suicide in America

Suicide is a tragic and potentially preventable public health problem. In 1997, suicide was the 8th leading cause of death in the U.S.[1] Specifically, 10.6 out of every 100,000 persons died by suicide. The total number of suicides was approximately 31,000, or 1.3 percent of all deaths. Approximately 500,000 people received emergency room treatment as a result of attempted suicide in 1996.[2] Taken together, the numbers of suicide deaths and attempts show the need for carefully designed prevention efforts.

Suicidal behavior is complex. Some risk factors vary with age, gender, and ethnic group and may even change over time. The risk factors for suicide frequently occur in combination. Research has shown that more than 90 percent of people who kill themselves have depression or another diagnosable mental or substance abuse disorder.[3] In addition, research indicates that alterations in neurotransmitters such as serotonin are associated with the risk for suicide.[4] Diminished levels of this brain chemical have been found in patients with depression, impulsive disorders, a history of violent suicide attempts, and also in postmortem brains of suicide victims.

Adverse life events in combination with other risk factors such as depression may lead to suicide. However, suicide and suicidal behavior are not normal responses to stress. Many people have one or more risk factors and are not suicidal. Other risk factors include: prior suicide attempt; family history of mental disorder or substance abuse; family history of suicide; family violence, including physical or sexual abuse; firearms in the home; incarceration; and exposure to the suicidal behavior of others, including family members, peers, and even in the media.[5]

Gender Differences

More than 4 times as many men than women die by suicide;[1] however, women report attempting suicide about 2 to 3 times as often as men.[6] Suicide by firearm is the most common method for both men and women, accounting for 58 percent of all suicides in 1997. Seventy-two percent of all suicides were committed by white men, and 79 percent of all firearm suicides were committed by white men. The highest suicide rate was for white men over 85 years of age—65 per 100,000 persons.

Children, Adolescents, and Young Adults

Over the last several decades, the suicide rate in young people has increased dramatically.[7] In 1997, suicide was the 3rd leading cause of death in 15 to 24 year olds—11.4 of every 100,000 persons—following unintentional injuries and homicide.[1] Suicide also was the 3rd leading cause in 10 to 14 year olds, with 303 deaths among 19,097,000 children in this age group. For adolescents aged 15 to 19, there were 1,802 suicide deaths among 19,146,000 adolescents. The gender ratio in this age group was about 4:1 (males: females). Among young people 20 to 24 years of age, there were 2,384 suicide deaths among 17,488,000 people in this age group. The gender ratio in this age range was about 6:1 (males: females).[8]

Attempted Suicides

There may be as many as 8 attempted suicides to 1 completion;[9] the ratio is higher in women and youth and lower in men and the elderly. Risk factors for attempted suicide in adults include depression, alcohol abuse, cocaine use, and separation or divorce.[10,11] Risk factors for attempted suicide in youth include depression, alcohol or other drug use disorder, physical or sexual abuse, and aggressive or disruptive behaviors.[12-14] The majority of suicide attempts are expressions of extreme distress and not just harmless bids for attention. A suicidal person should not be left alone and needs immediate mental health treatment.

Prevention

All suicide prevention programs need to be scientifically evaluated to demonstrate whether or not they work. Preventive interventions for suicide must also be complex and intensive if they are to have lasting effects. Most school-based, information-only, prevention programs focused solely on suicide have not been evaluated to see if they are effective, and research suggests that such programs may actually increase distress in the young people who are most vulnerable.[15] School and community prevention programs designed to address suicide and suicidal behavior as part of a broader focus on mental health, coping skills in response to stress, substance abuse, aggressive behaviors, etc., are more likely to be successful in the long run. Recognition and appropriate treatment of mental and substance abuse disorders also hold great suicide prevention value. For example, because most elderly suicide victims—70 percent—have visited their primary care physician in the month prior to their suicides,[16] improving the recognition and treatment of depression in medical settings is a promising way to prevent suicide in older adults. Toward this goal, NIMH-funded researchers are currently investigating the effectiveness of a depression education intervention delivered to primary care physicians and their elderly patients. If someone is suicidal, he or she must not be left alone. You may need to take emergency steps to get help, such as calling 911. It is also important to limit the person's access to firearms, large amounts of medication, or other lethal means of committing suicide.

References

1. Hoyert DL, Kochanek KD, Murphy SL. *Deaths: final data for 1997. National Vital Statistics Report*, 47(19). DHHS Publication No. 99-1120. Hyattsville, MD: National Center for Health Statistics, 1999. http://www.cdc.gov/nchs/data/nvs47_19.pdf

2. McCraig LF, Stussman BJ. National Hospital Ambulatory Care Survey: 1996. Emergency department summary. Advance Data from Vital and Health Statistics, no. 293. Hyattsville, MD: National Center for Health Statistics, 1997. http://www.cdc.gov/nchs/data/ad293.pdf

3. Conwell Y, Brent D. Suicide and aging I: patterns of psychiatric diagnosis. *International Psychogeriatrics*, 1995; 7(2): 149-64.

4. Mann JJ, Oquendo M, Underwood MD, et al. The neurobiology of suicide risk: a review for the clinician. *Journal of Clinical Psychiatry*, 1999; 60(Suppl 2): 7-11; discussion 18-20, 113-6.

5. Blumenthal SJ. *Suicide: a guide to risk factors, assessment, and treatment of suicidal patients*. Medical Clinics of North America, 1988; 72(4): 937-71.

6. Weissman MM, Bland RC, Canino GJ, et al. Prevalence of suicide ideation and suicide attempts in nine countries. *Psychological Medicine*, 1999; 29(1): 9-17.

7. National Center for Injury Prevention and Control. Fact book for the year 2000: suicide and suicide behavior. http://www.cdc.gov/ncipc/pub-res/FactBook/suicide.htm

8. National Center for Injury Prevention and Control. Suicide deaths and rates per 100,000: United States 1994-1997. http://www.cdc.gov/ncipc/data/us9794/Suic.htm

9. Moscicki EK. Epidemiology of suicide. In: Jacobs D, ed. *The Harvard Medical School guide to suicide assessment and intervention*. San Francisco, CA: Jossey-Bass, 1999, 40-71.

10. Kessler RC, Borges G, Walters EE. Prevalence of and risk factors for lifetime suicide attempts in the National Comorbidity Survey. *Archives of General Psychiatry*, 1999; 56(7): 617-26.

11. Petronis KR, Samuels JF, Moscicki EK, et al. An epidemiologic investigation of potential risk factors for suicide attempts. *Social Psychiatry and Psychiatric Epidemiology*, 1990; 25(4): 193-9.

12. Gould MS, King R, Greenwald S, et al. Psychopathology associated with suicidal ideation and attempts among children and adolescents. *Journal of the American Academy of Child and Adolescent Psychiatry*, 1998; 37(9): 915-23.

13. Fergusson DM, Horwood LJ, Lynskey MT. Childhood sexual abuse and psychiatric disorder in young adulthood, II: psychiatric outcomes of childhood sexual abuse. *Journal of the American Academy of Child and Adolescent Psychiatry*, 1996; 35(10): 1365-74.

14. Kaplan SJ, Pelcovitz D, Salzinger S, et al. Adolescent physical abuse and suicide attempts. *Journal of the American Academy of Child and Adolescent Psychiatry*, 1997; 36(6): 799-808.

15. Vieland V, Whittle B, Garland A, et al. The impact of curriculum-based suicide prevention programs for teenagers: an 18-month follow-up. *Journal of the American Academy of Child and Adolescent Psychiatry*, 1991; 30(5): 811-5.

16. Conwell, Y. Suicide in elderly patients. In: Schneider LS, Reynolds CF III, Lebowitz, BD, Friedhoff AJ, eds. *Diagnosis and treatment of depression in late life*. Washington, DC: American Psychiatric Press, 1994; 397-418.

Older Adults: Depression and Suicide Facts

Major depression, a significant predictor of suicide in older adults,[1] is a widely under-recognized and under-treated medical illness. In fact, several studies have found that many older adults who commit suicide have visited a primary care physician very close to the time of the suicide: 20 percent on the same day, 40 percent within one week, and 70 percent within one month of the suicide.[2] These findings point to the urgency of enhancing both the detection and the adequate treatment of depression as a means of reducing the risk of suicide among the elderly.

Older Americans are disproportionately likely to commit suicide. Comprising only 13 percent of the U.S. population, individuals ages 65 and older accounted for 19 percent of all suicide deaths in 1997. The highest rate is for white men ages 85 and older: 64.9 deaths per 100,000 persons in 1997, about 6 times the national U.S. rate of 10.6 per 100,000.[3]

An estimated 6 percent of Americans ages 65 and older in a given year, or approximately 2 million of the 34 million adults in this age group in 1998, have a diagnosable depressive illness (major depressive disorder, bipolar disorder, or dysthymic disorder).[4] In contrast to the normal emotional experiences of sadness, grief, loss, or passing mood states, depressive disorders can be extreme and persistent and can interfere significantly with an individual's ability to function. Dysthymic disorder as well as depressive symptoms that do not meet full diagnostic criteria for a disorder are common among the elderly and are associated with an increased risk of developing major depression.[5] In any of its forms, however, depression is not a normal part of aging.

Depression often co-occurs with other medical illnesses such as cardiovascular disease, stroke, diabetes, and cancer.[6] Because many older adults face such physical illnesses as well as various social and economic difficulties, individual health care professionals often mistakenly conclude that depression is a normal consequence of these problems—an attitude often shared by patients themselves.[7] These factors conspire to make the illness under-diagnosed and under-treated.

Both doctors and patients may have difficulty identifying the signs of depression. NIMH-funded researchers are currently investigating the effectiveness of a depression education intervention delivered in primary care clinics for improving recognition and treatment of depression and suicidal symptoms in elderly patients. In addition, NIMH has developed a cue card for older adults.

Research and Treatment

Modern brain imaging technologies are revealing that in depression, neural circuits responsible for the regulation of moods, thinking, sleep, appetite, and behavior fail to function properly, and that critical neurotransmitters—chemicals used by nerve cells to communicate—are out of balance.[8] Genetics research indicates that vulnerability to depression results from the influence of multiple genes acting together with environmental factors.[9] Studies of brain chemistry and of mechanisms of action of antidepressant medications continue to inform the development of new and better treatments.

Antidepressant medications are widely used effective treatments for depression.[10] Existing antidepressant drugs are known to influence the functioning of certain neurotransmitters in the brain, primarily serotonin and norepinephrine, known as monoamines. Older medications—tricyclic antidepressants (TCAs) and monoamine oxidase inhibitors (MAOIs)—affect the activity of both of these neurotransmitters simultaneously. Their disadvantage is that they can be difficult to tolerate due to side effects or, in the case of MAOIs, dietary and medication restrictions. Newer medications, such as the selective serotonin reuptake inhibitors (SSRIs), have fewer side effects than the older drugs, making it easier for patients including older adults to adhere to treatment. Both generations of medications are effective in relieving depression, although some people will respond to one type of drug, but not another.

Certain types of psychotherapy also are effective treatments for depression. Cognitive-behavioral therapy (CBT) and interpersonal therapy (IPT) are particularly useful. Approximately 80 percent of older adults with depression improve when they receive appropriate treatment with medication, psychotherapy, or the combination.[11]

In fact, recent research has shown that a combination of psychotherapy and antidepressant medication is extremely effective for reducing recurrence of depression among older adults. Those who received both interpersonal therapy and the antidepressant drug nortriptyline (a TCA) were much less likely to experience recurrence over a three-year period than those who received medication only or therapy only.[12]

Studies are in progress on the efficacy of SSRIs and short-term specific psychotherapies for depression in older persons. Findings from these studies will provide important data regarding the clinical course and treatment of late-life depression. Further research will be needed to determine the role of hormonal factors in the development of depression, and to find out whether hormone replacement therapy with estrogens or androgens is of benefit in the treatment of depression in the elderly.

References

1. Conwell Y, Brent D. Suicide and aging I: patterns of psychiatric diagnosis. *International Psychogeriatrics*, 1995; 7(2): 149-64.

2. Conwell, Y. Suicide in elderly patients. In: Schneider, LS, Reynolds CF III, Lebowitz, BD, Friedhoff AJ, eds. *Diagnosis and treatment of depression in late life*. Washington, DC: American Psychiatric Press, 1994; 397-418.

3. Hoyert DL, Kochanek KD, Murphy SL. *Deaths: final data for 1997. National Vital Statistics Report*, 47(19). DHHS Publication No. 99-1120. Hyattsville, MD: National Center for Health Statistics, 1999. http://www.cdc.gov/nchs/data/nvs47_19.pdf

4. Narrow WE. One-year prevalence of depressive disorders among adults 18 and over in the U.S.: NIMH ECA prospective data. Population estimates based on U.S. Census estimated residential population age 18 and over on July 1, 1998. Unpublished.

5. Horwath E, Johnson J, Klerman GL, et al. Depressive symptoms as relative and attributable risk factors for first-onset major depression. *Archives of General Psychiatry*, 1992; 49(10): 817-23.

6. Depression Guideline Panel. Depression in primary care: volume 1. Detection and diagnosis. Clinical practice guideline,

number 5. AHCPR Publication No. 93-0550. Rockville, MD: Agency for Health Care Policy and Research, 1993.

7. Lebowitz BD, Pearson JL, Schneider LS, et al. Diagnosis and treatment of depression in late life. Consensus statement update. *Journal of the American Medical Association*, 1997; 278(14): 1186-90.

8. Soares JC, Mann JJ. The functional neuroanatomy of mood disorders. *Journal of Psychiatric Research*, 1997; 31(4): 393-432.

9. NIMH Genetics Workgroup. *Genetics and mental disorders.* NIH Publication No. 98-4268. Rockville, MD: National Institute of Mental Health, 1998.

10. Mulrow CD, Williams JW Jr., Trivedi M, et al. Evidence report on treatment of depression-newer pharmacotherapies. *Psychopharmacology Bulletin*, 1998; 34(4): 409-795.

11. Little JT, Reynolds CF III, Dew MA, et al. How common is resistance to treatment in recurrent, nonpsychotic geriatric depression? *American Journal of Psychiatry*, 1998; 155(8): 1035-8.

12. Reynolds CF III, Frank E, Perel JM, et al. Nortriptyline and interpersonal psychotherapy as maintenance therapies for recurrent major depression: a randomized controlled trial in patients older than 59 years. *Journal of the American Medical Association*, 1999; 281(1): 39-45.

Frequently Asked Questions about Suicide

What Should You Do if Someone Tells You They Are Thinking about Suicide?

If someone tells you they are thinking about suicide, you should take their distress seriously, listen nonjudgmentally, and help them get to a professional for evaluation and treatment. People consider suicide when they are hopeless and unable to see alternative solutions to problems. Suicidal behavior is most often related to a mental disorder (depression) or to alcohol or other substance abuse. Suicidal behavior is also more likely to occur when people experience stressful events (major losses, incarceration). If someone is in imminent danger of harming himself or herself, do not leave the person alone. You may need to take emergency steps to get help, such as calling 911. When someone is in a suicidal crisis, it is important to limit access to firearms or other lethal means of committing suicide.

What Are the Most Common Methods of Suicide?

Firearms are the most commonly used method of suicide for men and women, accounting for 60 percent of all suicides. Nearly 80 percent of all firearm suicides are committed by white males. The second most common method for men is hanging; for women, the second most common method is self-poisoning including drug overdose. The presence of a firearm in the home has been found to be an independent, additional risk factor for suicide. Thus, when a family member or health care provider is faced with an individual at risk for suicide, they should make sure that firearms are removed from the home.

Why Do Men Commit Suicide More Often Than Women Do?

More than four times as many men as women die by suicide; but women attempt suicide more often during their lives than do men, and women report higher rates of depression. Several explanations have been offered: a) Completed suicide is associated with aggressive behavior that is more common in men, and which may in turn be related to some of the biological differences identified in suicidality. b) Men and women use different suicide methods. Women in all countries are more likely to ingest poisons than men. In countries where the poisons are highly lethal and/or where treatment resources scarce, rescue is rare and hence female suicides outnumber males. More research is needed on the social-cultural factors that may protect women from completing suicide, and how to encourage men to recognize and seek treatment for their distress, instead of resorting to suicide.

Who Is at Highest Risk for Suicide in the U.S.?

There is a common perception that suicide rates are highest among the young. However, it is the elderly, particularly older white males that have the highest rates. And among white males 65 and older, risk goes up with age. White men 85 and older have a suicide rate that is six times that of the overall national rate. Why are rates so high for this group? White males are more deliberate in their suicide intentions; they use more lethal methods (firearms), and are less likely to talk about their plans. It may also be that older persons are less likely to survive attempts because they are less likely to recuperate. Over 70 percent of older suicide victims have been to their primary care physician within the month of their death, many with a depressive illness that was not detected. This has led to research efforts to determine how to best improve physicians' abilities to detect and treat depression in older adults.

Do School-Based Suicide Awareness Programs Prevent Youth Suicide?

Despite good intentions and extensive efforts to develop suicide awareness and prevention programs for youth in schools, few programs have been evaluated to see if they work. Many of these programs are designed to reduce the stigma of talking about suicide and encourage distressed youth to seek help. Of the programs that were evaluated, none has proven to be effective. In fact, some programs have had unintended negative effects by making at-risk youth more distressed and less likely to seek help. By describing suicide and its risk factors, some curricula may have the unintended effect of suggesting that suicide is an option for many young people who have some of the risk factors and in that sense "normalize" it—just the opposite message intended. Prevention efforts must be carefully planned, implemented, and scientifically tested. Because of the tremendous effort and cost involved in starting and maintaining programs, we should be certain that they are safe and effective before they are further used or promoted.

There are number of prevention approaches that are less likely to have negative effects, and have broader positive outcomes in addition to reducing suicide. One approach is to promote overall mental health among school-aged children by reducing early risk factors for depression, substance abuse, and aggressive behaviors. In addition to the potential for saving lives, many more youth benefit from overall enhancement of academic performance and reduction in peer and family conflict. A second approach is to detect youth most likely to be suicidal by confidentially screening for depression, substance abuse, and suicidal ideation. If a youth reports any of these, further evaluation of the youth takes place by professionals, followed by referral for treatment as needed. Adequate treatment of mental disorder among youth, whether they are suicidal or not, has important academic, peer, and family relationship benefits.

Are Gay and Lesbian Youth at High Risk for Suicide?

With regard to completed suicide, there are no national statistics for suicide rates among gay, lesbian, or bisexual (GLB) persons. Sexual orientation is not a question on the death certificate, and to determine whether rates are higher for GLB persons, we would need to know the proportion of the U.S. population that considers themselves gay, lesbian, or bisexual. Sexual orientation is a personal characteristic that people can, and often do choose to hide, so that in psychological autopsy studies of suicide victims where risk factors are examined, it is difficult to know for certain the victim's sexual orientation. This is particularly a problem when considering GLB youth who may be less certain of their sexual orientation and less open. In the few studies examining risk factors for suicide where sexual orientation was assessed, the risk for gay or lesbian persons did not appear any greater than among heterosexuals, once mental and substance abuse disorders were taken into account.

With regard to suicide attempts, several state and national studies have reported that high school students who report to be homosexually and bisexually active have higher rates of suicide thoughts and attempts in the past year compared to youth with heterosexual experience. Experts have not been in complete agreement about the best way to measure reports of adolescent suicide attempts, or sexual orientation, so the data are subject to question. But they do agree that efforts should focus on how to help GLB youth grow up to be healthy and successful despite the obstacles that they face. Because school based suicide awareness programs have not proven effective for youth in general, and in some cases have caused increased distress in vulnerable youth, they are not likely to be helpful for GLB youth either. Because young people should not be exposed to programs that do not work, and certainly not to programs that increase risk, more research is needed to develop safe and effective programs.

Are African American Youth at Great Risk for Suicide?

Historically, African Americans have had much lower rates of suicides compared to white Americans. However, beginning in the 1980s, the rates for African American male youth began to rise at a much faster rate than their white counterparts. The most recent trends suggest a decrease in suicide across all gender and racial groups, but health policy experts remain concerned about the increase in suicide by firearms for all young males. Whether African American male youth are more likely to engage in "victim-precipitated homicide" by deliberately getting in the line of fire of either gang or law enforcement activity, remains an important research question, as such deaths are not typically classified as suicides.

Is Suicide Related to Impulsiveness?

Impulsiveness is the tendency to act without thinking through a plan or its consequences. It is a symptom of a number of mental disorders, and therefore, it has been linked to suicidal behavior usually through its association with mental disorders and/or substance abuse. The mental disorders with impulsiveness most linked to suicide include borderline personality disorder among young females, conduct disorder among young males, antisocial behavior in adult males, and alcohol and substance abuse among young and middle-aged males. Impulsiveness appears to have a lesser role in older adult suicides. Attention deficit hyperactivity disorder that has impulsiveness as a characteristic is not a strong risk factor for suicide by itself. Impulsiveness has been linked with aggressive and violent behaviors including homicide and suicide. However, impulsiveness without aggression or violence present has also been found to contribute to risk for suicide.

Is There Such a Thing as "Rational" Suicide?

Some right-to-die advocacy groups promote the idea that suicide, including assisted suicide, can be a rational decision. Others have argued that suicide is never a rational decision and that it is the result of depression, anxiety, and fear of being dependent or a burden. Surveys of terminally ill persons indicate that very few consider taking their own life, and when they do, it is in the context of depression. Attitude surveys suggest that assisted suicide is more acceptable by the public and health providers for the old who are ill or disabled, compared to the young who are ill or disabled. At this time, there is limited research on the frequency with which persons with terminal illness have depression and suicidal ideation, whether they would consider assisted suicide, the characteristics of such persons, and the context of their depression and suicidal thoughts, such as family stress, or availability of palliative care. Neither is it yet clear what effect other factors such as the availability of social support, access to care, and pain relief may have on end-of-life preferences. This public debate will be better informed after such research is conducted.

What Biological Factors Increase Risk for Suicide?

Researchers believe that both depression and suicidal behavior can be linked to decreased serotonin in the brain. Low levels of a serotonin metabolite, 5-HIAA, have been detected in cerebral spinal fluid in persons who have attempted suicide, as well as by postmortem studies examining certain brain regions of suicide victims. One of the goals of understanding the biology of suicidal behavior is to improve treatments. Scientists have learned that serotonin receptors in the brain increase their activity in persons with major depression and suicidality, which explains why medications that desensitize or downregulate these receptors (such as the serotonin reuptake inhibitors, or SSRIs) have been found effective in treating depression. Currently, studies are underway to examine to what extent medications like SSRIs can reduce suicidal behavior.

Can the Risk for Suicide Be Inherited?

There is growing evidence that familial and genetic factors contribute to the risk for suicidal behavior. Major psychiatric illnesses, including bipolar disorder, major depression, schizophrenia, alcoholism and substance abuse, and certain personality disorders, which run in families, increase the risk for suicidal behavior. This does not mean that suicidal behavior is inevitable for individuals with this family history; it simply means that such persons may be more vulnerable and should take steps to reduce their risk, such as getting evaluation and treatment at the first sign of mental illness.

Does Depression Increase the Risk for Suicide?

Although the majority of people who have depression do not die by suicide, having major depression does increase suicide risk compared to people without depression. The risk of death by suicide may, in part, be related to the severity of the depression. New data on depression that has followed people over long periods of time suggests that about 2% of those people ever treated for depression in an outpatient setting will die by suicide. Among those ever treated for depression in an inpatient hospital setting, the rate of death by suicide is twice as high (4%). Those treated for depression as inpatients following suicide ideation or suicide attempts are about three times as likely to die by suicide (6%) as those who were only treated as outpatients. There are also dramatic gender differences in lifetime risk of suicide in depression. Whereas about 7% of men with a lifetime history of depression will die by suicide, only 1% of women with a lifetime history of depression will die by suicide.

Another way about thinking of suicide risk and depression is to examine the lives of people who have died by suicide and see what proportion of them were depressed. From that perspective, it is estimated that about 60% of people who commit suicide have had a mood disorder (e.g., major depression, bipolar disorder, dysthymia). Younger persons who kill themselves often have a substance abuse disorder in addition to being depressed.

Does Alcohol and Other Drug Abuse Increase the Risk for Suicide?

A number of recent national surveys have helped shed light on the relationship between alcohol and other drug use and suicidal behavior. A review of minimum-age drinking laws and suicides among youths age 18 to 20 found that lower minimum-age drinking laws were associated with higher youth suicide rates. In a large study following adults who drink alcohol, suicide ideation was reported among persons with depression. In another survey, persons who reported that they had made a suicide attempt during their lifetime were more likely to have had a depressive disorder, and many also had an alcohol and/or substance abuse disorder. In a study of all non-traffic injury deaths associated with alcohol intoxication, over 20 percent were suicides.

In studies that examine risk factors among people who have completed suicide, substance use and abuse occurs more frequently among youth and adults, compared to older persons. For particular groups at risk, such as American Indians and Alaskan Natives, depression and alcohol use and abuse are the most common risk factors for completed suicide. Alcohol and substance abuse problems contribute to suicidal behavior in several ways. Persons who are dependent on substances often have a number of other risk factors for suicide. In addition to being depressed, they are also likely to have social and financial problems. Substance use and abuse can be common among persons prone to be impulsive, and among persons who engage in many types of high risk behaviors that result in self-harm. Fortunately, there are a number of effective prevention efforts that reduce risk for substance abuse in youth, and there are effective treatments for alcohol and substance use problems. Researchers are currently testing treatments specifically for persons with substance abuse problems who are also suicidal, or have attempted suicide in the past.

What Does "Suicide Contagion" Mean, and What Can Be Done to Prevent It?

Suicide contagion is the exposure to suicide or suicidal behaviors within one's family, one's peer group, or through media reports of suicide and can result in an increase in suicide and suicidal behaviors. Direct and indirect exposure to suicidal behavior has been shown to precede an increase in suicidal behavior in persons at risk for suicide, especially in adolescents and young adults.

The risk for suicide contagion as a result of media reporting can be minimized by factual and concise media reports of suicide. Reports of suicide should not be repetitive, as prolonged exposure can increase the likelihood of suicide contagion. Suicide is the result of many complex factors; therefore media coverage should not report oversimplified explanations such as recent negative life events or acute stressors. Reports should not divulge detailed descriptions of the method used to avoid possible duplication. Reports should not glorify the victim and should not imply that suicide was effective in achieving a personal goal such as gaining media attention. In addition, information such as hotlines or emergency contacts should be provided for those at risk for suicide.

Following exposure to suicide or suicidal behaviors within one's family or peer group, suicide risk can be minimized by having family members, friends, peers, and colleagues of the victim evaluated by a mental health professional. Persons deemed at risk for suicide should then be referred for additional mental health services.

Is It Possible to Predict Suicide?

At the current time there is no definitive measure to predict suicide or suicidal behavior. Researchers have identified factors that place individuals at higher risk for suicide, but very few persons with these risk factors will actually commit suicide. Risk factors include mental illness, substance abuse, previous suicide attempts, family history of suicide, history of being sexually abused, and impulsive or aggressive tendencies. Suicide is a relatively rare event and it is therefore difficult to predict which persons with these risk factors will ultimately commit suicide.

Additional Information

American Association of Suicidology
4201 Connecticut Ave. NW
Suite 408
Washington, DC 20008
Tel: 202-237-2280
Fax: 202-237-2282
Website: www.suicidology.org
E-mail: ajkulp@suicidology.org

American Foundation for Suicide Prevention
120 Wall Street, 22nd Floor
New York, NY 10005
Toll-Free: 888-333-AFSP
Tel: 212-363-3500
Fax: 212-363-6237
Website: www.afsp.org
E-mail: inquiry@afsp.org

Suicide Prevention Advocacy Network
5034 Odins Way
Marietta, GA 30096
Toll-Free: 888-649-1366
Fax: 770-642-1419
Website: www.spanusa.org
E-mail: act@spanusa.org

Section 16.5

Dealing with the Depths of Depression

"Dealing with the Depths of Depression," by Liora Nordenberg, *FDA Consumer* (July-August 1998); "Holiday Depression & Stress," Fact Sheet, © 1998 National Mental Health Association (NMHA), reprinted with permission; and "Alternative Medicine: Information about St. John's Wort," National Institute of Mental Health (NIMH), updated May 29, 2001.

Dealing with the Depths of Depression

"I am now the most miserable man living. If what I feel were equally distributed to the whole human family, there would be not one cheerful face on earth. Whether I shall ever be better, I cannot tell. I awfully forebode I shall not. To remain as I am is impossible. I must die or be better it appears to me."—Abraham Lincoln

Imagine attending a party with these prominent guests: Abraham Lincoln, Theodore Roosevelt, Robert Schumann, Ludwig von Beethoven, Edgar Allen Poe, Mark Twain, Vincent van Gogh, and Georgia O'Keefe. Maybe Schumann and Beethoven are at the dinner table intently discussing the crescendos in their most recent scores, while Twain sits on a couch telling Poe about the plot of his latest novel. O'Keefe and Van Gogh may be talking about their art, while Roosevelt and Lincoln discuss political endeavors.

But in fact, these historical figures also had a much more personal common experience: Each of them battled the debilitating illness of depression.

It is common for people to speak of how "depressed" they are. However, the occasional sadness everyone feels due to life's disappointments is very different from the serious illness caused by a brain disorder. Depression profoundly impairs the ability to function in everyday situations by affecting moods, thoughts, behaviors, and physical well-being.

Twenty-seven-year-old Anne (not her real name) has suffered from depression for more than 10 years. "For me it's feelings of worthlessness," she explains. "Feeling like I haven't accomplished the things that I want to or feel I should have and yet I don't have the energy to do them. It's feeling disconnected from people in my life, even friends and family who care about me. It's not wanting to get out of bed some mornings and losing hope that life will ever get better."

Depression strikes about 17 million American adults each year—more than cancer, AIDS, or coronary heart disease—according to the National Institute of Mental Health (NIMH). An estimated 15 percent of chronic depression cases end in suicide. Women are twice as likely as men to be affected.

Many people simply don't know what depression is. "A lot of people still believe that depression is a character flaw or caused by bad parenting," says Mary Rappaport, a spokeswoman for the National Alliance for the Mentally Ill. She explains that depression cannot be overcome by willpower, but requires medical attention.

Fortunately, depression is treatable, says Thomas Laughren, M.D., team leader for psychiatric drug products in FDA's division of neuropharmacological drug products.

In the past 13 years, the Food and Drug Administration has approved several new antidepressants, including Wellbutrin (bupropion), Prozac (fluoxetine), Zoloft (sertraline), Paxil (paroxetine), Effexor (venlafaxine), Serzone (nefazodone), and Remeron (mirtazapine).

According to the American Psychiatric Association (APA), 80 to 90 percent of all cases can be treated effectively. However, two-thirds of the people suffering from depression don't get the help they need, according to NIMH. Many fail to identify their symptoms or attribute them to lack of sleep or a poor diet, the APA says, while others are just too fatigued or ashamed to seek help.

Left untreated, depression can result in years of needless pain for both the depressed person and his or her family. And depression costs the United States an estimated $43 billion a year, due in large part to absenteeism from work, lost productivity, and medical costs, according to the National Depressive and Manic Depressive Association.

Three Types

The three main categories of depression are major depression, dysthymia, and bipolar depression (sometimes referred to as manic depression).

Major depression affects 15 percent of Americans at one point during their lives, according to the U.S. Department of Health and

Human Services. Its effects can be so intense that things like eating, sleeping, or just getting out of bed become almost impossible.

Major depression "tends to be a chronic, recurring illness," Laughren explains. Although an individual episode may be treatable, "the majority of people who meet criteria for major depression end up having additional episodes in their lifetime."

Unlike major depression, dysthymia doesn't strike in episodes, but is instead characterized by milder, persistent symptoms that may last for years. Although it usually doesn't interfere with everyday tasks, victims rarely feel like they are functioning at their full capacity. According to the National Alliance for the Mentally Ill, almost 10 million Americans may experience dysthymia each year.

Finally, bipolar disorder cycles between episodes of major depression and highs known as mania. Bipolar disorder is much less common than the other types, afflicting about 1 percent of the U.S. population. Symptoms of mania include irritability, an abnormally elevated mood with a decreased need for sleep, an exaggerated belief in one's own ability, excessive talking, and impulsive and often dangerous behavior.

Genes and Environment

Study after study suggests biochemical and genetic links to depression. A considerable amount of evidence supports the view that depressed people have imbalances in the brain's neurotransmitters, the chemicals that allow communication between nerve cells. Serotonin and norepinephrine are two neurotransmitters whose low levels are thought to play an especially important role. The fact that women have naturally lower serotonin levels than men may contribute to women's greater tendency to depression.

Family histories show a recurrence of depression from generation to generation. Studies of identical twins confirm that depression and genes are related, finding that if one twin of an identical pair suffers from depression, the other has a 70 percent chance of developing the disease. For fraternal twins or siblings, the rate is just 25 percent.

Environmental factors, however, may also play a role in depression. When combined with a biochemical or genetic predisposition, life stressors (such as relationship problems, financial difficulties, death of a loved one, or medical illness) may cause the disease to manifest itself.

John (not his real name), 25, was diagnosed with depression for the first time last year when he and his girlfriend ended their three-year relationship. "I couldn't do anything because I was totally absorbed with the whole break-up issue," he says. "It was impossible for me to sleep, and I would wake up at 3 or 4 in the morning and literally shake. And when it was time to wake up, I just couldn't get out of bed."

In addition, substance abuse and side effects from prescription medication may also lead to a depressive episode. And research shows that people battling serious medical conditions are especially prone to depression. According to the U.S. Department of Health and Human Services, those who have had a heart attack, for example, have a 40 percent chance of being depressed.

Seasonal affective disorder, often called "SAD," is a striking example of an environmental factor playing a major role in depression. SAD usually starts in late fall, with the decrease in daylight hours and ends in spring when the days get longer.

The symptoms of SAD, which include energy loss, increased anxiety, oversleeping, and overeating, may result from a change in the balance of brain chemicals associated with decreased sunlight. The exact reason for the association between light and mood is unknown, but research suggests a connection with the sleep cycle. Several studies have suggested that light therapy, which involves daily exposure to bright fluorescent light, may be an effective treatment for SAD.

Diagnosing the Disease

Medical professionals generally base a diagnosis of depressive disorder on the presence of certain symptoms listed in the American Psychiatric Association's *Diagnostic and Statistical Manual*. The DSM (presently in the fourth edition) lists the following symptoms for depression:

- depressed mood
- loss of interest or pleasure in almost all activities
- changes in appetite or weight
- disturbed sleep
- slowed or restless movements
- fatigue, loss of energy
- feelings of worthlessness or excessive guilt
- trouble in thinking, concentrating, or making decisions
- recurrent thoughts of death or suicide.

The diagnosis depends on the number, severity, and duration of these symptoms.

Even with this list of symptoms, diagnosing depression is not simple. According to the National Alliance for the Mentally Ill, it takes an average of eight years from the onset of depression to get a proper diagnosis.

In making a diagnosis, a health professional should also consider the patient's medical history, the findings of a complete physical exam, and laboratory tests to rule out the possibility of depressive symptoms resulting from another medical problem.

The symptoms of the depressive part of bipolar disorder are the same as those expressed in major (unipolar) depression. Because of the similarities in symptoms and the fact that manic episodes usually don't appear until the mid-20s, some people with bipolar disorder may mistakenly be diagnosed with unipolar depression. This may lead to improper treatment because antidepressants carry the risk of triggering a manic episode.

Antidepressant Drugs

One major approach for treating depression is the use of antidepressant medications. The older antidepressants include tricyclic antidepressants such as Tofranil (imipramine) and monoamine oxidase inhibitors such as Nardil (phenelzine). Antidepressants approved more recently include the selective serotonin reuptake inhibitors Prozac, Paxil, and Zoloft, and the other newer antidepressants Wellbutrin, Effexor, Serzone, and Remeron.

The effects of antidepressants on the brain are not fully understood, but there is substantial evidence that they somehow restore the brain's chemical balance. These medications usually can control depressive symptoms in four to eight weeks, but many patients remain on antidepressants for six months to a year following a major depressive episode to avoid relapse.

Different drugs work for different people, and it is difficult to predict which people will respond to which drug or who will experience side effects. So it may take more than one try to find the appropriate medication.

Since the mid-1950s, tricyclic antidepressants have been the standard against which other antidepressants have been measured. Monoamine oxidase inhibitors were discovered around the same time as tricyclic antidepressants, but were prescribed less because, if mixed with certain foods or medications, the drugs sometimes resulted in a fatal rise in blood pressure.

Laughren describes Prozac as the "first of a new type of more selective antidepressants." The older antidepressants had unpleasant and sometimes dangerous side effects, such as insomnia, weight gain, blurred vision, sexual impairment, heart palpitations, dry mouth, and constipation. Prozac, other selective serotonin reuptake inhibitors, and other recently approved antidepressants have had generally safer side effect profiles.

Other types of therapy, such as natural substances extracted from plants, are currently being studied. Although not approved by FDA, some people believe St. John's wort, for example, is extremely helpful in alleviating their depressive symptoms. The FDA has issued a public alert on St. John's wort stating that adverse interactions have been reported between St. John's wort (hypericum), a herbal product used to treat depression and two drugs: indinavir, a protease inhibitor used to treat HIV, and cyclosporine, a drug used to reduce the risk of organ transplant rejection. Potentially dangerous changes in drug effects can occur when medications such as cyclosporine (Neoral, Sandimmune), digoxin (Lanoxin, Lanoxicaps), and warfarin (Coumadin) are taken with hypericum extracts. Hypericum extracts can decrease the blood levels of antiretroviral medications that are used in the treatment of HIV infection, thus making these drugs less effective. Data show that the plasma levels of the portease inhibitor indinavir (Crixivan) were reduced by more than 50% by hypericum (St. John's wort) products.

When people are unresponsive to antidepressant medications or can't take them because of their age or health problems, electroconvulsive therapy (ECT), or "shock therapy," can offer a lifesaving alternative. Like antidepressants, ECT is believed to affect the chemical balance of the brain's neurotransmitters.

Before ECT, the patient is given anesthesia and a muscle relaxant to prevent injury or pain. Then electrodes are placed on the person's head, and a small amount of electricity is applied. This procedure is usually done three times a week until the patient improves. Some patients may experience a temporary loss of short-term memory.

Talking It Out

For severe depressive episodes, medications are often the first step because of the relatively quick relief they can bring to physical symptoms. For the long term, however, psychotherapy may be needed to address certain aspects of the illness that drugs cannot. "Although the biological features of depression may respond better to drugs,"

Laughren says, "people may need to relearn how to interact with their environment after the biological part of the depression is controlled."

"I wanted to talk things out and get better in that way," John says. "And even after the first couple of times I saw my therapist, I could do a little bit more. Talking with her gave me some reality that how I was feeling wasn't so abnormal, so unusual, or so terrible."

Anne explains, "It's just comforting sometimes to share the little day-to-day happenings in my life with someone who doesn't get to see them first-hand."

Some find support groups to be invaluable in helping them cope with their depression. "It's through talking with others with similar experiences," says Mary Rappaport, "that you can better understand what you're going through."

Changes in lifestyle are also important in the management of depression. Exercise, even in moderate doses, seems to enhance energy and reduce tension. Some research suggests that a rush of the hormone norepinephrine following exercise helps the brain deal with stress that often leads to depression and anxiety. A similar effect may be obtained through meditation, yoga, and certain diets.

A Bright Future

Like many others who have not had to face depression themselves, John's friends lacked knowledge about the disease. "I think the whole thing really affected my relationships with people," he says. "I was pretty much a jerk all of the time. I didn't want to talk to anybody. I just wanted them to leave me alone."

With the growing awareness of the seriousness of the disorder and the biological causes, the understanding and support of family and friends may be easier to come by. "The future looks very bright for individuals who in the past have often had to suffer alone," says Rappaport. "More and more people are coming out, which encourages people to talk about it." Among those who have "come out" recently to publicly discuss their personal bouts with depression are comedian Drew Carey and "60 Minutes" correspondent Mike Wallace.

Experts say that no one, young or old, has to accept feelings of depression as a necessary part of life. The National Depressive and Manic Depressive Association and other organizations offer medical information and referrals. By trying different options for facing their personal challenges, Anne and others have learned what treatments help them most. "All in all," Anne says, "I think my ability to weather the ups and downs of life has gotten better."

Researchers continue to make great strides in understanding and treating depression. For example, scientists are beginning to learn more about the chromosomes where affective disorder genes appear to be located. "While there is a long way to go in coming up with even more effective drugs," Laughren says, "there's much ongoing research and reason for optimism."

If Someone You Know Is Depressed

According to the National Institute of Mental Health, to help someone recover from depression:

- Encourage the person to make an appointment with a doctor, or make the appointment yourself. You may want to go along for support.

- Encourage the person to stick with the treatment plan, including taking prescribed medicine. Improvement may take several weeks. If no improvement occurs, encourage the person to seek a different treatment rather than giving up.

- Give emotional support by listening carefully and offering hope.

- Invite the person to join you in activities that you know he or she used to enjoy, but keep in mind that expecting too much too soon can lead to feelings of failure.

- Do not accuse the person of faking illness or expect them to "snap out of it."

- Take comments about suicide seriously, and seek professional advice.

What Causes Holiday Blues?

Many factors can cause the "holiday blues": stress, fatigue, unrealistic expectations, over-commercialization, financial constraints, and the inability to be with one's family and friends. The demands of shopping, parties, family reunions, and houseguests also contribute to feelings of tension. People who do not become depressed may develop other stress responses, such as: headaches, excessive drinking, over-eating, and difficulty sleeping. Even more people experience post-holiday let down after January 1. This can result from disappointments during the preceding months compounded with the excess fatigue and stress.

Coping with Stress and Depression during the Holidays

- Keep expectations for the holiday season manageable. Try to set realistic goals for yourself. Pace yourself. Organize your time. Make a list and prioritize the important activities. Be realistic about what you can and cannot do. Do not put entire focus on just one day (i.e., Thanksgiving Day) remember it is a season of holiday sentiment and activities can be spread out (time-wise) to lessen stress and increase enjoyment.

- Remember the holiday season does not banish reasons for feeling sad or lonely; there is room for these feelings to be present, even if the person chooses not to express them.

- Leave "yesteryear" in the past and look toward the future. Life brings changes. Each season is different and can be enjoyed in its own way. Don't set yourself up in comparing today with the "good ol' days."

- Do something for someone else. Try volunteering some time to help others.

- Enjoy activities that are free, such as driving around to look at holiday decorations; going window shopping without buying; making a snowman with children.

- Be aware that excessive drinking will only increase your feelings of depression.

- Try something new. Celebrate the holidays in a new way.

- Spend time with supportive and caring people. Reach out and make new friends or contact someone you have not heard from for awhile.

- Save time for yourself! Recharge your batteries! Let others share responsibility of activities.

Can Environment be a Factor?

Recent studies show that some people suffer from seasonal affective disorder (SAD) which results from fewer hours of sunlight as the days grow shorter during the winter months. Phototherapy, a treatment involving a few hours of exposure to intense light, is effective in relieving depressive symptoms in patients with SAD.

Other studies on the benefits of phototherapy found that exposure to early morning sunlight was effective in relieving seasonal depression. Recent findings, however, suggest that patients respond equally well to phototherapy whether it is scheduled in the early afternoon or morning. This has practical applications for antidepressant treatment since it allows the use of phototherapy in the workplace as well as the home.

Additional Information

Depression Awareness, Recognition, and Treatment (D/ART) Program
National Institute of Mental Health
6001 Executive Boulevard
Rm. 8184, MSC 9663
Bethesda, MD 20892-9663
Tel: 301-443-4513
Fax: 301-443-4279
Website: www.nimh.nih.gov
E-mail: nimhinfo@nih.gov

National Depressive and Manic Depressive Association
730 N. Franklin St., Suite 501
Chicago, IL 60610-7204
Toll-Free: 800-826-3632
Tel: 312-642-0049
Fax: 312-642-7243
Website: www.ndmda.org

National Alliance for the Mentally Ill
Colonial Place Three
2107 Wilson Blvd., Suite 300
Arlington, VA 22201
Toll-Free Helpline: 800-950-6264
Tel: 703-524-7600
Website: www.nami.org

Chapter 17

Panic Disorder Diagnosis and Treatment

Facts about Panic Disorder

Panic disorder is characterized by unexpected and repeated episodes of intense fear accompanied by physical symptoms that may include chest pain, heart palpitations, shortness of breath, dizziness or abdominal distress. These sensations often mimic symptoms of a heart attack or other life-threatening medical conditions. As a result, the diagnosis of panic disorder is frequently not made until extensive and costly medical procedures fail to provide a correct diagnosis or relief.

Many people with panic disorder develop intense anxiety between episodes. It is not unusual for a person with panic disorder to develop phobias about places or situations where panic attacks have occurred, such as in supermarkets or other everyday situations. As the frequency of panic attacks increases, the person often begins to avoid situations where they fear another attack may occur or where help would not be immediately available. This avoidance may eventually develop into agoraphobia, an inability to go beyond known and safe surroundings because of intense fear and anxiety. Fortunately, through research supported by the National Institute of Mental

This chapter includes "Facts about Panic Disorder," National Institute of Mental Health (NIMH) Publication No. OM-99 4155 (Revised), printed September 1999, updated: December 8, 2000; "Young People Are Most Susceptible to Panic Disorder," National Institute of Mental Health (NIMH), updated: October 8, 1999; and "Getting Treatment for Panic Disorder," NIH Publication No. 93-3509, printed 1994, updated: September 13, 2001.

Health (NIMH) and by industry, effective treatments have been developed to help people with panic disorder.

How Common Is Panic Disorder?

About 1.7% of the adult U.S. population ages 18 to 54—approximately 2.4 million Americans—has panic disorder in a given year. Women are twice as likely as men to develop panic disorder. Panic disorder typically strikes in young adulthood. Roughly half of all people who have panic disorder develop the condition before age 24.

What Causes Panic Disorder?

Heredity, other biological factors, stressful life events, and thinking in a way that exaggerates relatively normal bodily reactions are all believed to play a role in the onset of panic disorder. The exact cause or causes of panic disorder are unknown and are the subject of intense scientific investigation.

Studies in animals and humans have focused on pinpointing the specific brain areas and circuits involved in anxiety and fear, which underlie anxiety disorders such as panic disorder. Fear, an emotion that evolved to deal with danger, causes an automatic, rapid protective response that occurs without the need for conscious thought. It has been found that the body's fear response is coordinated by a small structure deep inside the brain, called the amygdala.

The amygdala, although relatively small, is a very complicated structure, and recent research suggests that anxiety disorders may be associated with abnormal activitation in the amygdala. One aim of research is to use such basic scientific knowledge to develop new therapies.

What Treatments Are Available for Panic Disorder?

Treatment for panic disorder includes medications and a type of psychotherapy known as cognitive-behavioral therapy, which teaches people how to view panic attacks differently and demonstrates ways to reduce anxiety. NIMH is conducting a large-scale study to evaluate the effectiveness of combining these treatments. Appropriate treatment by an experienced professional can reduce or prevent panic attacks in 70% to 90% of people with panic disorder. Most patients show significant progress after a few weeks of therapy. Relapses may occur, but they can often be effectively treated just like the initial episode.

Can People with Panic Disorder Also Have Other Illnesses?

Research shows that panic disorder can coexist with other disorders, most often depression and substance abuse. About 30% of people with panic disorder abuse alcohol and 17% abuse drugs, such as cocaine and marijuana, in unsuccessful attempts to alleviate the anguish and distress caused by their condition. Appropriate diagnosis and treatment of other disorders such as substance abuse or depression are important to successfully treat panic disorder.

Young People are Most Susceptible to Panic Disorder

People with panic disorder experience unexpected and repeated episodes of intense fear accompanied by physical symptoms that may include chest pain, heart palpitations, shortness of breath, dizziness, or abdominal distress. A panic attack often mimics the symptoms of a heart attack or other life-threatening medical condition, necessitating the immediate use of extensive and costly medical procedures to rule out these conditions before the panic disorder is diagnosed correctly and treated properly. Often, people with panic disorder develop other anxiety disorders such as phobias, which further restrict and impair their lives.

In the early 1980s, a large survey—the ECA (Epidemiologic Catchment Area) survey—estimated that about 1.7 percent of U.S. adults, approximately 2.4 million people—have panic disorder in any given year, with women twice as likely as men to develop the disorder. This measurement zeroed in on the magnitude of this mental disorder across the nation, but left many unanswered questions, such as how many of the people experiencing panic disorder each year represent new, and how many repeat, cases or what the natural progression of the disorder is likely to be in these individuals.

In 1981, the original ECA survey interviewed approximately 3500 people living in Baltimore—one of 5 different cities in the study. About 12 years later, almost 2000 of these same people, or 73 percent of the survivors, were interviewed again. The interviews at both time points required each participant to undergo a standard diagnostic test to detect any current or previous mental disorders. In the intervening years, new cases of panic disorder occurred at a rate of 1.43 cases per 1000 people per year. The incidence was greater in females than males; in fact, 31 of the 35 new cases were in women. The incidence rate also declined with age: it was 3.43 cases (per 1000 people per year) for ages 18-29 years, 2.32 for ages 30-44, 0.61 for ages 45-64,

243

and 0 for people over 65 in this group. Over half the people with new cases of panic disorder had a pre-existing anxiety of some sort for many years before the onset of the panic disorder.

Implications: This study tells us that panic disorder is most apt to begin when a person is young and suggests that it may often, but not always, be an outgrowth of a pre-existing anxiety the person has. Panic disorder only rarely begins after mid-life. Recovery is usually rapid after a full-blown episode of panic disorder, although, after the initial episode, a significant number of people continue to have frequent panic attacks for many years before undergoing a rapid recovery. It is important that people with panic disorder seek professional help so they can receive appropriate treatment, which can reduce or prevent panic attacks in 70 to 90 percent of people with the disorder. (Source: Eaton WW et al.: Onset and recovery from panic disorder in the Baltimore Epidemiologic Catchment Area follow-up. *British Journal of Psychiatry* 173: 501-507, 1998.)

Could You Have Panic Disorder?

Do you experience sudden episodes of intense and overwhelming fear that seem to come on for no apparent reason?

During these episodes, do you also experience several of the following:

- Racing, pounding, or skipping heartbeat
- Chest pain, pressure, or discomfort
- Difficulty catching your breath
- Choking sensation or lump in your throat
- Excessive sweating
- Lightheadedness or dizziness
- Nausea or stomach problems
- Tingling or numbness in parts of your body
- Chills or hot flashes
- Shaking or trembling
- Feelings of unreality, or being detached from your body

During these episodes:

- Do you have the urge to flee, or the feeling that you need to escape?

- Do you think something terrible might happen—that you might die, have a heart attack, suffocate, lose control, or embarrass yourself?

- Do you worry a lot about these episodes or fear that they will happen again? And does this fear cause you to avoid places or situations that you think might have triggered the attack?

If you answered yes to most of these questions, chances are you are suffering from panic disorder. If so, you are not alone.

Panic disorder is very different from everyday anxiety. More than 3 million American adults have, or will have, panic disorder at some time in their lives. Most frequently, it starts in young adulthood. Usually, it does not go away by itself. But with proper treatment, people with panic disorder can be helped.

Why Seeking Treatment Is Critical

Repeated episodes of fear—commonly called panic attacks—that are typical of panic disorder can be devastating. The panic attacks, or avoidance of them, can completely take control of your life.

- Without treatment, you may continue to have panic attacks for years. The disorder can seriously interfere with your relationships with family, friends, and co-workers.

- Without treatment, your life may become severely restricted. For example, you may start to avoid certain situations where you fear you will experience a panic attack—even normal, everyday activities, such as grocery shopping or driving. In extreme cases, people with untreated panic disorder grow afraid to leave the house, a condition known as agoraphobia.

- Without treatment, you may find it difficult to be productive at work. Your symptoms may keep you from getting to your job or staying there once you arrive. You may turn down promotions or job assignments that you believe will make you more likely to have panic attacks. Some people with panic disorder even quit their jobs. Many can keep working but otherwise rarely leave home.

- Without treatment, you may become severely depressed. You may try unsuccessfully to numb the symptoms of panic disorder or depression with alcohol or other drugs. You may even begin to have thoughts about suicide.

You do not have to live this way. You need to know that panic disorder is treatable. In fact, proper treatment reduces or completely prevents panic attacks in 70 to 90 percent of people. Many people feel substantial relief in just weeks or months.

Unfortunately, some people are reluctant to pursue treatment. Perhaps they think their condition is not serious. Perhaps they feel embarrassed. They may blame themselves or have trouble asking for help. Perhaps they dislike the idea of medication or therapy. Or, maybe they have sought help but are frustrated because their condition was not diagnosed or treated effectively.

Do not let these or any other reasons stop you from getting proper treatment. If you have panic disorder, you should get whatever help is necessary to overcome it, just as you would for any serious medical illness. Do not be discouraged if some people say, "It's nothing to worry about," "It's just stress," "It's all in your head," or "Snap out of it." While they often mean well, the fact is that most people who do not have panic disorder do not understand that it is real and, therefore, tend to doubt its seriousness.

Most importantly, do not try to numb the effects of panic attacks with alcohol or other drugs. This will only make the problem worse.

Getting a Diagnosis

Since panic disorder can mimic a variety of medical conditions, such as heart problems and digestive complaints, the first thing you should do is have a full medical evaluation. Although it is important for you and your doctor to concentrate on your physical symptoms, you should not overlook other aspects of your attacks. You may want to re-read the questions at the beginning of this section and tell your doctor anything you notice about how your attacks make you feel and when they usually occur.

Information on both the physical and emotional aspects of the attacks can be very useful to the doctor in making a diagnosis. For example, the doctor will want to know if your attacks, or fear of having attacks, keep you from carrying out any of your normal activities.

Many people with panic disorder also suffer from depression—feelings of intense sadness, even hopelessness. Depression is accompanied by an impaired ability to think, concentrate, and enjoy the normal pleasures of life. Be sure to make your doctor aware of these symptoms as well. If you have been drinking or using drugs to try to control your symptoms, let your doctor know about that too. Once you have been properly diagnosed, your doctor—perhaps in consultation with a mental health specialist—can help you determine which treatment is best for you.

Effective Treatments for Panic Disorder

Treatment for panic disorder can consist of taking a medication to adjust the chemicals in your body—just as you might take medicine to correct a thyroid imbalance. Or treatment might involve working with a psychotherapist to gain more control over your anxieties—just as some people work with specialists to learn techniques to control migraine headaches or lower their blood pressure.

Research shows that both kinds of treatment can be very effective. For many patients, the combination of medication and psychotherapy appears to be more effective than either treatment alone. Early treatment can help keep panic disorder from progressing.

Cognitive-Behavioral Therapy

Cognitive-behavioral therapy (CBT) teaches you to anticipate and prepare yourself for the situations and bodily sensations that may trigger panic attacks. CBT usually includes the following elements:

- A therapist helps you identify the thinking patterns that lead you to misinterpret sensations and assume "the worst" is happening. These patterns of thinking are deeply ingrained, and it will take practice to notice them and then to change them.

- A therapist can teach you breathing exercises that calm you and that can prevent the over breathing, or hyperventilation, that often occurs during a panic attack.

- A therapist can help you gradually become less sensitive to the frightening bodily sensations and feelings of terror. This is done by helping you, step-by-step, to safely test yourself in the places and situations you've been avoiding.

CBT generally requires at least 8 to 12 weeks. Some people may need a longer time in treatment to learn the skills and put them into practice. Most panic disorder patients are successful in controlling or preventing their panic attacks after completing treatment with CBT.

CBT requires a motivated patient and a specially trained therapist. Make sure any therapist you work with has proper training and experience in this method of panic disorder treatment. Indeed, in some parts of the country, you may find limited access to professionals trained and experienced in CBT.

Medication

Several types of medication that alter the ways chemicals interact in the brain can reduce or prevent panic attacks and decrease anxiety. Two major categories of medication that have been shown to be safe and effective in the treatment of panic disorder are antidepressants and benzodiazepines.

Each medication works differently. Some work quickly and others more gradually. All of them have to be taken on a regular basis. Usually, treatment with medication lasts at least 6 months to a year. But within 8 weeks, you and your doctor should be able to assess whether it's effectively blocking the panic attacks.

Clinical experience suggests that for many patients with panic disorder, a combination of CBT and medication may be the best treatment.

How to Choose the Right Treatment for You

Various types of health professionals may have the training and experience needed to treat panic disorder. Sometimes panic disorder patients are treated by two health care professionals—one who prescribes and monitors medication and another who provides CBT.

Each professional will use the treatments with which he or she is most familiar and successful. It is vital to choose a professional who is trained and experienced in the treatment methods described earlier; it is equally important to choose someone with whom you feel comfortable.

Many people begin looking for treatment by visiting their family doctor or a local clinic or health maintenance organization. Other places to seek help include your local health department or community mental health clinic. If there is a university near you, you may wish to ask about participating in a panic disorder study. Many universities have ongoing treatment research programs in their psychology or psychiatry departments that may provide care at less expense.

To help you locate mental health professionals in your area, NIMH has available a Referral List, which gives the names and telephone numbers of organizations that can provide you with a referral. You can get one by calling 1-800-64-PANIC.

When seeking a health care professional to treat your panic disorder, you may want to ask the following questions:

- How many patients with panic disorder have you treated?

- Do you have any special training in panic disorder treatment?

- What is your basic approach to treatment—cognitive-behavioral therapy, medication, or both? If you provide only one type of treatment, how do I get the other if I need it?

- How long is a typical course of treatment?

- How frequent are treatment sessions? How long does each session last?

- What are your fees?

- Can you help me determine whether my health insurance will cover this?

How to Make Your Treatment Successful

From the beginning, it is important to be a full participant in your treatment. Be active and assertive. Ask questions. Maintain open communication with your treatment professional and let him or her know your concerns.

Every patient responds differently, but it is important to know that none of the treatments for panic disorder works instantly. So, you must stick with a particular treatment for at least 8 weeks to see if it works. If you do not see significant improvement within that time, you and your treatment professional can adjust your treatment plan. It may take a bit of trial and error before you find what works best for you. Be patient and be sure to communicate with your treatment professional. Of course, if at any time you feel uncomfortable with the professional you have chosen or don't think your treatment is going well, you should feel free to consider seeking a second opinion or even changing providers.

If your treatment involves medication, talk with your doctor about how often and in what manner your dosage will be monitored. No matter what medication you are taking, your doctor is likely to start you on a low dose and gradually increase it to the full dose. You should know that every medication has side effects, but they usually become tolerated or diminish with time. If side effects become a problem, the doctor may advise you to stop taking the medication and to wait a week or so before trying another medication. When your treatment is near an end, your doctor will taper the dosage gradually.

Support Groups and Self-Help Tools

Patient-run support groups can be a rich source of information for people with panic disorder. These groups typically involve 5 to 10 people who meet weekly to talk about their experiences, encourage each other, and share tips on coping strategies and local treatment resources. Sometimes, family members are invited to attend.

The NIMH Referral List can help you find a support group in your area. If there are no groups near you, you may want to form your own. Some of the sources listed can aid you in doing this. NIMH also has a Resource List that provides some self-help information about panic disorder, including books, articles, and videotapes.

Another way to get help is to enlist the support of friends and family members. You may want to share this chapter and other materials with them so they can better understand panic disorder and its treatment.

Take The Next Step Today

Panic disorder is far too serious—and far too treatable—to delay getting help. Recognizing the situation is the first step to recovery.

Now take the next step. If you think you may have panic disorder, act now. See your health professional for a diagnosis and then follow the suggestions in this chapter for making your treatment successful. Educate yourself about your condition. The more you know about panic attacks and panic disorder, the better you will understand your role in treatment.

Remember, panic disorder is very treatable. You can get better.

Additional Information

The Anxiety Disorders Education Program
National Institute of Mental Health
6001 Executive Blvd., Room 8184, MSC 9663
Bethesda, MD 20892-9663
Toll-Free: 888-826-9438; Tel: 301-443-4513; TTY: 301-443-8431
Fax: 301-443-4279
Website: www.nimh.nih.gov; E-mail: nimhinfo@nih.gov

Anxiety Disorders Association of America (ADAA)
11900 Parklawn Drive, Suite 100
Rockville, MD 20852
Tel: 301-231-9350
Website: www.adaa.org

Chapter 18

Trauma—
Extreme or Life-Threatening
Events

Chapter Contents

Section 18.1—Traumatic Stress 252
Section 18.2—Post-Traumatic Stress Disorder
        (PTSD) 272
Section 18.3—Helping Children and Adolescents
        Cope with Violence and Disasters 288

Section 18.1

Traumatic Stress

This section includes "Trauma Facts," © Barbara Reade, M.S., L.C.P.C., N.C.C., Website: http://www.heart-healing.com, reprinted with permission; and "Traumatic Stress: An Overview," by Joseph S. Volpe, Ph.D., B.C.E.T.S., F.A.A.E.T.S. © 1996 American Academy of Experts in Traumatic Stress (AAETS) and "An Overview of Acute Traumatic Stress Management: Keeping People Functioning & Mitigating Long-Term Suffering During Today's Traumatic Events," by Mark D. Lerner, Ph.D., President of the American Academy of Experts in Traumatic Stress, © 2002 American Academy of Experts in Traumatic Stress (AAETS). This article originally appeared in the Fall/Winter 2002 issue of *Trauma Response*, a publication of AAETS. Both articles are reprinted with permission of Dr. Lerner and AAETS, 368 Veterans Memorial Highway, Commack, NY 11725, Phone: 631-543-6977, Fax: 631-543-6977. For more information about acute traumatic stress management, visit www.atsm.org.

Trauma Facts

All people experience crises in their lives. Trauma differs from crisis events because trauma involves great danger and complete powerlessness in a situation. Trauma situations involve possibility of death or injury. The magnitude of horror or intensity of this type of event would overtax any human being's ability to cope.

The loss of many family members, at one time, due to natural disaster or accident, would be considered a traumatic event, not a simple crisis situation. The loss of one person, under most circumstances, would not be considered traumatic in nature, though very painful.

Traumatic reactions can either appear directly after the event, or within 6 months of the event, or they can occur in a delayed manner. One year, or more than twenty years after the event, the reaction can surface for the first time.

Traumatic reaction is caused by a significant wound to the psyche. Thoughts, beliefs, and feelings change in major ways and the usual methods for handling stress no longer work. Often a sense of depersonalization (feeling de-humanized) occurs at the time of the event. This is especially true in crime situations and any kind of violent assault.

Traumatic Reactions

- You may have dreams that cause you to wake feeling terrified. You may or may not remember their content. Because of this sleep can become a major problem.

- Your sense of security and safety may have been severely effected by the trauma. The ability to trust may have been seriously damaged.

- You may experience flashbacks of the event, or thoughts or feelings that overwhelm you for no apparent reason. This means feelings that stop you from functioning because of their extreme strength.

- You may have severe anger or irritability that don't seem to be related to any specific event or person.

- Numbing of feelings is common. It may seem as if you can't find or have any feelings.

- Avoiding people, places, or things, that remind you of the event, because of overwhelming feelings, can also be caused by the trauma.

- You may find yourself fleeing from situations as you never had previous to the event. Or you may simply freeze.

- Or you may find yourself fighting, in reaction to fearing for your life, when the situation is not life-threatening.

- Sweating, nausea, fatigue, anxiety, an easy startle reflex, when exposed to a trigger like the event, indicates traumatic response.

Therapy with a well trained trauma specialist can help you relieve these significantly. Seeing a specialist in this area of therapy is essential for lasting recovery.

Acute Traumatic Stress Management

During time of crisis, we address physical and safety needs. We focus on the stabilization of injury and ultimately, the preservation of life. Today's traumatic events call for us to raise our level of care—to address emergent psychological needs.

Much has been written about post-crisis intervention—"psychological first-aid" introduced in the aftermath of a tragedy. In recent years,

253

effective interventions have been developed for "demobilizing," "defusing," and "debriefing" people after disengagement from a crisis—following a traumatic experience. Notwithstanding, there is little information offering practical strategies to help people during a traumatic event. This is a time when individuals are perhaps most suggestible and vulnerable to traumatic stress—a tremendous opportunity for intervention.

Traumatic stress refers to the emotional, cognitive, behavioral, and physiological experience of individuals who are exposed to, or who witness, events that overwhelm their coping and problem-solving abilities. These events, sometimes referred to as "critical incidents," are typically unexpected and uncontrollable. They compromise an individual's sense of safety and security, and leave people feeling insecure and vulnerable.

Traumatic stress disables people, causes disease, precipitates mental disorders, leads to substance abuse, and destroys relationships and families. In organizations, traumatic stress causes communication breakdowns, excessive absenteeism, an inability to retain effective personnel, and ultimately, a marked decrease in productivity.

During today's trying times, we must work to keep people functioning and to mitigate long-term emotional suffering.

Acute Traumatic Stress Management™

We have all been exposed to the "Imprint of Horror," the sights, sounds, and/or smells recorded in our minds during our nation's crisis September 11, 2001. These perceptions are the precipitators of acute traumatic stress reactions and chronic stress disorders. In the same way that these negative stimuli have been etched in our minds during traumatic exposure, a time of heightened suggestibility and vulnerability, so too can a positive, adaptive force.

Acute Traumatic Stress Management™ (ATSM) is a practical approach to address the emergent psychological needs of people during traumatic events. It offers a cognitive "road map" to guide people through times of crisis.

ATSM provides caregivers with "practical tools" for addressing the spectrum of traumatic experiences—from mild to the most severe. It is a goal-directed process delivered within the framework of a facilitative or helping attitudinal climate. ATSM aims to "jump-start" an individual's coping and problem-solving abilities. It seeks to stabilize acute symptoms of traumatic stress and stimulate healthy, adaptive functioning. Finally, ATSM may increase the likelihood of an individual pursuing mental health intervention, if need be, in the future.

ATSM is not a comprehensive crisis intervention or disaster response plan and does not require advanced training or a degree in mental health. Rather, ATSM may be viewed as a practical strategy to complement your repertoire of helping skills.

Today, we are seeing ATSM effectively implemented in diverse settings by:

- police and security personnel,
- firefighters and EMS technicians,
- governmental personnel,
- the military,
- corporate executives,
- business administrators and managers,
- EAP and human resource professionals,
- health care providers,
- hospitals and universities,
- educators,
- the clergy,
- the airline and railroad industry, and
- hotel and entertainment personnel.

The Stages of Acute Traumatic Stress Management™

ATSM is implemented through 10 practical stages that will empower you to address others' emergent psychological needs during traumatic exposure. These states offer a degree of structure during a typically unstructured period of time:

1. Assess for Danger/Safety for Self and Others
2. Consider the Mechanism of Injury
3. Evaluate the Level of Responsiveness
4. Address Medical Needs
5. Observe and Identify
6. Connect with the Individual
7. Ground the Individual
8. Provide Support
9. Normalize the Response
10. Prepare for the Future

Following is a discussion of the stages of ATSM. The first five stages are of primary importance to emergency, or first responders, and have to do with considerations surrounding situation management and emergency medical care. The latter five stages may be implemented by all caregivers. Recognize that the nature of the event, as well as the intensity of individuals' reactions, will vary during traumatic exposure. Consequently, appropriate intervention may not fall neatly into a linear progression of stages. Thus, you will need to be flexible given the presenting circumstances.

1. Assess for Danger/Safety for Self and Others

Upon arrival at the scene of a traumatic event, assess the situation in order to determine whether there are factors that can compromise your safety or the safety of others. You will be of little help to someone else if you are injured. Depending upon the nature of the event, it may be necessary to approach with police/security or other emergency personnel. It may be important to remove the individual(s) from a location, or from other individuals, rather than risk further traumatic exposure.

2. Consider the Mechanism of Injury

Form an initial impression of those impacted by the event. In order to understand the nature of an individual's exposure, it is important to assess how the event may have physically impacted the individual—that is, how environmental factors transferred to the person. It is also important to consider the perceptual experiences of victims. Particularly gruesome sights such as severe burns, dismemberment, open wounds, and viewing the dead will leave a powerful impact on those who are directly involved with, or those who witness, the event. Similarly, the sounds of people screaming, and the smell of fire will etch a lasting impression in the individual's psyche (i.e., the "Imprint of Horror").

3. Evaluate the Level of Responsiveness

It is important to determine if an individual is alert and responsive to verbal stimuli. Does he feel pain? Is he aware of what has occurred, or what is presently occurring? Is he under the influence of a substance? During a traumatic event it is quite possible that the individual is in "emotional shock." Therefore, symptomatology may mimic acute medical conditions (i.e., rapid changes in respiration, pulse, blood pressure, etc.). Recognize that a psychological state of shock may be adaptive in preventing the individual from experiencing the full impact of the event too quickly.

4. Address Medical Needs

Emergency responders are trained to assess the ABCs (i.e. airway, breathing, and circulation). If an individual is not breathing, there will be little else that can be done to help him. It is important to address significant symptomatology (e.g., severe chest pains), to be aware of existing medical conditions (e.g., diabetes), and to know the kinds of injuries that may present a threat to life (e.g., internal bleeding). Medical needs should be addressed only by individuals who have been trained to do so. Additionally, it is imperative that life-threatening illness and injury are always addressed prior to psychological needs.

5. Observe and Identify

Observe and identify those who have been exposed to the traumatic event. Very often, these individuals will not be the direct victims. They may be "secondary" or "hidden victims." Remember, witnessing or even being exposed to another individual who has faced traumatic exposure can cause traumatic stress. As you observe and identify who has been exposed to the event (i.e., directly and/or indirectly), begin to observe and identify who is evidencing signs of traumatic stress. An awareness of the emotional, cognitive, behavioral, and physiological reactions suggestive of traumatic stress is important. These will be outlined later in this section. Carefully look around you. Anyone, including yourself, may be a direct or hidden victim.

6. Connect with the Individual

Introduce yourself and state your title and position. If the individual has been medically evaluated, move him away from further traumatic stimuli. Begin to develop rapport by making an effort to understand and appreciate his situation. A simple question such as, "How are you doing?" may be used to engage the individual. Use appropriate non-verbal communication (e.g., eye contact, body turned toward him, a gentle touch, etc.).

During traumatic exposure, individual reactions may present on a continuum from a totally detached, withdrawn reaction to the most intense displays of emotion (e.g., uncontrollable crying, screaming, panic, anger, fear, etc.). These situations present a challenge to the caregiver. The ATSM model offers specific practical tools to break through these emotional states. See the publication, *Acute Traumatic Stress Management™* for discussion available at www.atsm.org.

7. Ground the Individual

When you have established a connection with an individual who has been exposed to a traumatic event (e.g., eye contact, body turned toward you, dialogue directed at you, etc.), you can initiate this grounding stage. Begin by acknowledging the traumatic event at a factual level. Here, you attempt to orient the individual by discussing the facts surrounding the event.

Address the circumstances of the event at a cognitive, or thinking level. While we do not discourage the expression of emotion, attempt to focus on the facts in the here-and-now, and help the individual to know the reality of the situation. Oftentimes, his "reality" may be seriously clouded due to the nature of the event. Remember, traumatic events overwhelm an individual's usual coping and problem-solving abilities. Assure the individual that he is now safe, if he is.

By reviewing facts, you may disrupt "negative cognitive rehearsal" and help the individual to begin to deal with the actual circumstances at hand. In other words, the individual may still be "playing the tape" of the accident over and over in his head. It is important to "place the individual in the situation." Encourage him to "tell his story" and describe where he was, what he saw, what it sounded like, what it smelled like, what he did, and how his body responded. Encourage the individual to discuss his behavioral and physiological response to the event—rather than "how it felt."

8. Provide Support

Factual discussion and the realization of a traumatic event, particularly when the event is still occurring, may likely stimulate thoughts and feelings. This is often the time when individuals who are exposed to trauma need the most support. However, in reality, it is also the time when many people look the other way. Many individuals feel terribly unprepared to handle others' painful thoughts and feelings. Oftentimes, they fear that they will "open a can of worms" or "say the wrong thing."

It is important to establish and maintain a facilitative or helping attitudinal climate. Here, you attempt to understand and respect the uniqueness of the individual—the thoughts and feelings that he is experiencing. You strive to "give back" a sense of control that has been "taken from" him by virtue of his exposure to the event. You support him, and you allow him to think and feel.

In the face of traumatic exposure, many people experience an overwhelming sense of aloneness and withdraw into their own world. You should make a respectful effort to "enter that world," and to help the individual to know that he is not alone and that his unique perception of his experience is important. Do not attempt to talk a person out of a feeling (e.g. "Don't be scared, you're fine."). Communicate an appreciation of the other person's experience. Attempt to understand the feelings that lie behind his words (or perhaps actions) and convey that understanding to him.

9. Normalize the Response

While you are attempting to support an individual by giving him the opportunity to express his thoughts and feelings, begin to normalize his reaction to the traumatic event. This is an important component when intervening with people who have been exposed to trauma and who may be feeling very alone. Experiencing a cascade of emotions or perhaps a lack of emotional expression, may cause him to feel as if he is "losing it" and perhaps, "going crazy."

Normalizing and validating an individual's experience will help him to know that he is a normal person trying to deal with an abnormal event. It is important that you do not become sympathetic and over-identify with the situation with statements such as, "I know what it feels like—a close friend of mine was killed in a car accident last year." Rather, you should attempt to normalize and validate the individual's experience with statements like, "I see this is overwhelming for you right now. This kind of experience would be hard for anyone to handle."

An important component of the normalization process is to begin to educate the individual by helping him to know how people typically respond to traumatic events. The following emotional, cognitive, behavioral, and physiological reactions are often experienced by people during traumatic exposure. It is important to recognize that these reactions do not necessarily represent an unhealthy or maladaptive response. Rather, they may be viewed as normal responses to an abnormal event. When these reactions are experienced in the future (i.e., weeks, months, or even years after the event), are joined by other symptoms (e.g., recurrent distressing dreams "flashbacks," avoidance behaviors, etc.), and interfere with social, occupational, or other important areas of functioning, a psychiatric disorder may be in evidence. These individuals should pursue help with a mental health professional.

Emotional Responses during a traumatic event may include shock, in which the individual may present a highly anxious, active response of perhaps a seemingly stunned, emotionally-numb response. He may describe feeling as though he is "in a fog." He may exhibit denial, in which there is an inability to acknowledge the impact of the situation or perhaps, that the situation has occurred. He may evidence dissociation, in which he may seem dazed and apathetic, and he may express feelings of unreality. Other frequently observed acute emotional responses may include panic, fear, intense feelings of aloneness, hopelessness, helplessness, emptiness, uncertainty, horror, terror, anger, hostility, irritability, depression, grief, and feelings of guilt.

Cognitive Responses to traumatic exposure are often reflected in impaired concentration, confusion, disorientation, difficulty in making a decision, a short attention span, suggestibility, vulnerability, forgetfulness, self-blame, blaming others, lowered self-efficacy, thoughts of losing control, hypervigilance, and perseverative thoughts of the traumatic event. For example, upon extrication of a survivor from an automobile accident, he may cognitively still "be in" the automobile "playing the tape" of the accident over and over in his mind.

Behavioral Responses in the face of a traumatic event may include withdrawal, "spacing-out," non-communication, changes in speech patterns, regressive behaviors, erratic movements, impulsivity, a reluctance to abandon property, seemingly aimless walking, pacing, an inability to sit still, an exaggerated startle response, and antisocial behaviors.

Physiological Responses may include rapid heart beat, elevated blood pressure, difficulty breathing*, shock symptoms*, chest pains*, cardiac palpitations*, muscle tension and pains, fatigue, fainting, flushed face, pale appearance, chills, cold clammy skin, increased sweating, thirst, dizziness, vertigo, hyperventilation, headaches, grinding of teeth, twitches, and gastrointestinal upset. *Require immediate medical evaluation.*

Overall, the primary purpose of the normalization stage is to help an individual who is experiencing traumatic stress to know that he is not alone, that he is a normal person trying to cope with an abnormal event—that his experience is perhaps his mind's attempt to "make sense of the senseless."

10. Prepare for the Future

The final phase of the ATSM process is aimed at preparing the individual for what lies on the road ahead. It is helpful to 1) review the nature of the traumatic event, 2) bring the person to the present, and 3) describe likely events in the future. The educational process initiated during the previous normalization stage should continue during this final stage of ATSM.

The following strategies for managing responses to traumatic events will help you, as a caregiver, to remain functional during a crisis. These strategies should additionally be incorporated in the final "Prepare for the Future" stage of ATSM. Depending upon the nature of the event, the individual's reaction to the event, and the amount of time you have available in working with the individual, the following strategies may prove quite helpful.

Specific Strategies for Managing Responses to Traumatic Events

Addressing the emergent psychological needs of others during a crisis can be a draining experience. Working with individuals who are in acute emotional distress requires an intensity that, for the caregiver, is both mental and physical. Realize that you may likely be exposed to the very event to which you are called upon to help others. It is imperative that you consider your own state of mind prior to engaging in the provision of ATSM. If you are overwhelmed by the situation, or if you are currently experiencing a time of emotional distress in your life, it would be wise to have another individual implement ATSM. Following is a list of strategies that you may utilize in managing your own responses during a crisis and in its immediate aftermath. As indicated previously, these strategies may also be shared with individuals with whom you are helping.

During the Event

- Become aware of and monitor your emotional, cognitive, behavioral, and physiological reactions. Consider the effect the event is having on you. Acknowledge to yourself that your involvement is creating these reactions.

- If you find that the discussion is causing you to react physically (i.e., rapid heart rate, breathing increase, sweating, etc.) take a slow deep breath and tell yourself to relax—take a second deep breath and relax.

- If you are finding the event overwhelming, and it is possible, separate and share you feelings with a peer. Realize that acute traumatic stress may compromise your ability to make good decisions and can therefore place you in danger.

- If you find that you are unable to concentrate, focus on the individual and the specific words they are saying—work to actively listen to what they are communicating. Slow down the conversation and try repeating what you have just heard.

- Acknowledge and speak of the impact the event is having on you as a human being. For example, you might say, "What we're seeing out here is really tough for all of us." However, make every effort to avoid self-disclosure of specific, personal information (e.g., "This reminds me of when my sister was involved in a car accident.").

Remember that it is okay not to be okay, and that displaying your emotions can reinforce for victims your genuine concern.

Following the Event

- Acknowledge that the event itself and the connections you have established with others can have a lasting impact on you. Words people have spoken and the emotions they displayed may become imprinted in your mind.

- Reflect upon what has just occurred. Maintain an awareness of your emotional, cognitive, behavioral, and physiological reactions. Find a trusted friend to talk to about your experience. Remember to keep in confidence what people shared with you. Talk about your reactions to the experience. Sharing the experience will help you to assimilate what has occurred.

- Realize that the repetitive thoughts and sleep difficulties are normal reactions. Do not fight the sleep difficulty, this will usually pass in a few days. Try the following. Eliminate caffeine for four hours prior to your bedtime, create the best sleep environment you can, consider taking a few moments before turning out the lights to write down your thoughts, thus emptying your mind. Try reading or listening to peaceful music.

- Avoid excessive media exposure, particularly during highly publicized tragedies. Take time to get away from the action. Give yourself permission to rest, relax, and engage in some non-threatening activity.

- Engage in physical exercise to dissipate the stress energy that has been generated.

- Spend time with your family and friends; stay connected with them. Resist the urge to retreat into your own world. You need their support following an emotionally charged event.

- Create a journal. Writing about traumatic experiences is helpful in exposing ourselves to painful thoughts and feelings, and in helping us to assimilate these experiences.

- If necessary, seek the assistance of a professional. If you find that the experience is powerful and is staying with you for an extended period of time, allow yourself the advantage of professional support and education. Remember that you are a normal person who has experienced an abnormal event.

- Have the strength to let go. It requires courage to face the powerful emotions within you.

Conclusion

Recent unprecedented events have, and continue to scar our nation. Early efforts must be made to keep people functioning and to mitigate long-term emotional suffering. The purpose of this information was to provide an overview of *Acute Traumatic Stress Management*™. It is not intended, in and of itself, to prepare a caregiver to implement the ATSM model. Rather, it aims to introduce the reader to a process that has helped many people during times of crisis.

By reaching people early, during traumatic events, we can keep individuals functioning and potentially prevent the acute traumatic stress reactions of today from becoming the posttraumatic stress disorders of tomorrow.

Traumatic Stress: An Overview

Traumatic stress encompasses exposure to events or the witnessing of events that are extreme and/or life-threatening. Traumatic exposure may be brief in duration (e.g., an automobile accident) or involve prolonged, repeated exposure (e.g., sexual abuse). The former type has been referred to as "Type I" trauma and the latter form, as "Type II" trauma (Terr, 1991). In North America, four out of ten people are exposed to at least one traumatic event in their lifetime (Meichenbaum, 1994). Approximately, 25% to 30% of individuals who witness a traumatic event may develop chronic posttraumatic stress disorder (PTSD) and other forms of mental disorders (e.g., depression) (Yehuda, Resnick, Kahana, & Giller, 1993). Approximately 50% of individuals who develop PTSD continue to suffer from its effects decades later without treatment (Meichenbaum, 1994). Knowledge about traumatic stress—how it develops, how it manifests, and how it affects the lives of those who suffer with it—is the first step in its assessment and, ultimately, its treatment.

History of Traumatic Stress

Traumatic exposure and its aftermath are not new phenomena. Humans have experienced tragedies and disaster throughout history. Evidence for post-traumatic reactions date back as far as the Sixth century B.C.; early documentation typically involved the reactions of soldiers in combat (Holmes, 1985). Beginning in the 17th century, anecdotal evidence of trauma exposure and subsequent responses were more frequently reported. In 1666, Samuel Pepys wrote about individual's responses to the Great Fire of London (Daly, 1983). It had been reported that the author Charles Dickens suffered from numerous traumatic symptoms after witnessing a tragic rail accident outside of London (Trimble, 1981).

Traumatic stress responses have been labeled in numerous ways over the years. Diagnostic terms applied to symptoms have included Soldier's Heart, Battle Fatigue, War Neurosis, Da Costa's Syndrome, Tunnel Disease, Railway Spine Disorder, Shell Shock, Gross Stress Reaction, Adjustment Reaction of Adult Life, Transient Situational Disturbance, Traumatic Neurosis, Post-Vietnam Syndrome, Rape Trauma Syndrome, Child Abuse Syndrome, and Battered Wife Syndrome (Everly, 1995; Meichenbaum, 1994). *The Diagnostic and Statistical Manual of Mental Disorders-Third Edition* (DSM-III) first recognized Posttraumatic Stress Disorder (PTSD) as a distinct diagnostic entity in

1980 (APA, 1980). It was categorized as an anxiety disorder because of the presence of persistent anxiety, hypervigilance, exaggerated startle response, and phobic-like avoidance behaviors (Meichenbaum, 1994). This recognition of stress-related reactions was a major step in the development of an empirical literature base investigating traumatic stress. In 1994, *The Diagnostic and Statistical Manual of Mental Disorders-Fourth Edition* (DSM-IV) was published and the current diagnostic criteria reflect the findings of numerous empirical studies and field trials (APA, 1994).

Types of Traumatic Events

Traumatic events are typically unexpected and uncontrollable. They may overwhelm an individual's sense of safety and security and leave a person feeling vulnerable and insecure in their environment. Events that are abrupt, often lasting a few minutes and as long as a few hours can be referred to as short-term or Type I traumatic events (Terr, 1991). Included within this category are natural and accidental disasters as well as deliberately caused human-made disasters. Natural disasters include events such as hurricanes, floods, tornadoes, earthquakes, volcanic eruptions, and avalanches. Accidental disasters may include motor vehicle accidents (MVA), boat, train, airplane accidents, fires, and explosions. Deliberately caused human-made disasters (i.e., intentional human design or IHD) involve bombings, rape, hostage situations, assault and battery, robbery, and industrial accidents.

Sustained and repeated traumatic events (or Type II traumatic events) typically involve chronic, repeated, and ongoing exposure. Examples include natural and technological disasters such as chronic illness, nuclear accidents, and toxic spills. Events resulting from intentional human design include combat, child sexual abuse, battered syndrome (i.e., spousal abuse), being taken as political prisoner or prisoner of war (POW), and Holocaust victimization. It is important to consider that research indicates that, despite the heterogeneity of traumatic events, individuals who directly or vicariously experience such events show similar profiles of psychopathology including chronic PTSD and commonly observed comorbid disorders such as depression, generalized anxiety disorder, and substance abuse (Solomon, Gerrity, & Muff, 1992).

Current Diagnostic Criteria and Other Considerations

The DSM-IV stipulates that in order for an individual to be diagnosed with posttraumatic stress disorder, he or she must have experienced or witnessed a life-threatening event and reacted with intense fear, help-lessness, or horror. The traumatic event is persistently re-experienced (e.g., distressing recollections), there is persistent avoidance of stimuli associated with the trauma, and the victim experiences some form of hyperarousal (e.g., exaggerated startle response). These symptoms persist for more than one month and cause clinically significant impairment in daily functioning. When the disturbance lasts a minimum of two days and as long as four weeks from the traumatic event, Acute Stress Disorder may be a more accurate diagnosis.

It has been suggested that responses to traumatic experience(s) can be divided into at least four categories (see Meichenbaum for a complete review, 1994). Emotional responses include shock, terror, guilt, horror, irritability, anxiety, hostility, and depression. Cognitive responses are reflected in significant concentration impairment, confusion, self-blame, intrusive thoughts about the traumatic experience(s) (also referred to as flashbacks), lowered self-efficacy, fears of losing control, and fear of reoccurrence of the trauma. Biologically-based responses involve sleep disturbance (i.e., insomnia), nightmares, an exaggerated startle response, and psychosomatic symptoms. Behavioral responses include avoidance, social withdrawal, interpersonal stress (decreased intimacy and lowered trust in others), and substance abuse. The process through which the individual has coped prior to the trauma is arrested; consequently, a sense of helplessness is often maintained (Foy, 1992).

Post-traumatic symptoms often co-occur with other psychiatric conditions; this is referred to as comorbidity. For instance, substance abuse (especially alcoholism), anxiety (e.g., panic disorder), depression, eating disorders, dissociative disorders, and personality disorders may all co-occur with PTSD. With regard to specific populations, Matsakis (1992) reported that between 40% to 60% of women in treatment for bulimia, anorexia, and obesity had described traumatic experiences at some point in their life. Kilpatrick et al. (1989) reported that, among crime victims with PTSD, 41% had sexual dysfunction, 82% had depression, 27% had obsessive-compulsive symptoms, and 18% had phobias. Sipprelle (1992) reported that personality disorders were especially widespread among Vietnam Veterans. Thus, it is important to assess for comorbid disorders when seeing a patient who presents with trauma-induced symptoms.

Assessment of Traumatic Stress

The clinician working with survivors of traumatic stress and post-traumatic stress disorder must consider the multifaceted nature of these disorders. A multimodal approach which involves the collection of information from a number of sources, using several different methods over multiple contacts is highly recommended (Meichenbaum, 1994). A comprehensive clinical interview is a primary assessment tool in the evaluation of traumatic stress. Careful questioning during an interview allows the survivor to tell his or her account of the event. Individuals need the opportunity to talk about their experience in a safe, non-judgmental setting. Survivors (and oftentimes, their significant others) need to feel understood and supported as they try to make sense of the traumatic event. Questioning also facilitates a working alliance with the person; the "connection" that the person feels with the treating clinician is often associated with continuation of treatment and psychotherapy treatment outcome (Safran & Segal, 1990; Wolfe, 1992). Questioning allows for the gathering of details about the trauma, assessment of current and past levels of functioning, and the development of a treatment plan. Interviews with family members and significant others may provide further insight into the nature of the trauma and presenting symptomatology. Commonly used structured interviews include the Clinician Administered PTSD scale (CAPS; Blake et al., 1990) and the Anxiety Disorders Interview Schedule-IV (ADIS-IV; DiNardo, Brown, & Barlow, 1994). A number of paper-and-pencil assessment measures of PTSD have evolved over the past few years as well. Some of the more popular measures include the PTSD subscale of the Minnesota Multiphasic Personality Inventory (MMPI; Keane, Malloy, & Fairbank, 1984; Schlenger & Kulka, 1987), the Penn Inventory for PTSD (Hammarberg, 1992). Some screening instruments for anxiety and depression that are also useful include the Beck Anxiety Inventory (BAI; Beck, 1993) and Beck Depression Inventory (BDI; see Beck, Rush, Shaw, & Emery, 1979). One performance-based measure that has been used successfully with combat, rape, and accident disaster patients is the Stroop Color Word Test (McNally, English, & Lipke, 1993). As indicated earlier, assessment for comorbid disorders must be part of the evaluative process (see Meichenbaum, 1994 for a complete review of assessment measures).

Treatment of Traumatic Stress

Many techniques have been used to treat survivors after exposure to traumatic events. Presently, no one form of intervention has been shown to be superior for the treatment of traumatic stress and PTSD. Ochberg (1995) divides treatment methods into four categories. Education is the first method. This includes educating the survivor (and their families) about trauma and its effects on daily functioning. Cognitive, behavioral, and physical aspects of the stress response are explored with the individual. The clinician and patient may share books and articles relevant to the treatment of the traumatic symptoms. This process helps give meaning to the symptoms that he or she experiences and may ultimately facilitate a sense of control over them.

The second category involves holistic health. This includes physical activity, nutrition, spirituality, and humor as they contribute to the healing of the individual. The clinician functions as both a teacher and a coach to his patient, offering support and encouragement as the individual attempts various ways to appropriately heal him or herself.

The third group of treatment techniques includes methods to enhance social support and social integration. Included within this category are family therapy and group psychotherapy. The former typically helps to improve communication and cohesion between family members. Group treatment allows individuals to reduce feelings of isolation, share difficult feelings and perceptions regarding the trauma, and learn more adaptive coping strategies.

Finally, there are clinical interventions best described as therapy. The goal of most forms of therapy is to help the individual work through their grief, extinguish fear responses, and improve the quality of the individual's life. For example, cognitive-behavior therapy typically relies on exposure strategies to reduce intrusive memories, flashbacks, and nightmares related to the traumatic experience. Exposure to fear-producing stimuli and cognitions in a safe and supportive environment, over time, often reduces the impact of these stimuli on the individual's reactivity (Foa & Kozak, 1986). Cognitive restructuring strategies are also utilized to address the meaning and, oftentimes, distortions in thought processes that accompany traumatic exposure (e.g., "Life is awful," "All people are cruel"). Problem-solving training (D'Zurilla, 1986) may help the individual combat indecisiveness and perceptions of helplessness. Other techniques include relaxation training, and guided imagery-based interventions.

Pharmacological treatment of traumatic stress and PTSD indicates that different medications may affect the multi-faceted symptoms of PTSD. For example, Clonidine has been shown to reduce hyperarousal symptoms. Propranolol, Clonazepam, and Alprazolam appear to regulate anxiety and panic symptoms. Fluoxetine may reduce avoidance and explosiveness whereas re-experiencing of traumatic symptoms and depression may be treated with tricyclic antidepressants and selective serotonin reuptake inhibitors. It is important to note that pharmacotherapy as a sole source of intervention is rarely sufficient to provide complete remission of PTSD (Vargas & Davidson, 1993).

As indicated earlier, traumatic stress and particularly, PTSD, are complex and multi-faceted and consequently, a multimodal assessment is recommended. It is suggested that effective treatment will involve a number of the aforementioned techniques. Future research needs to address the outcomes of combining various treatment approaches and maintaining treatment gains over time.

Conclusions

It has been stated that post-traumatic stress may represent "one of the most severe and incapacitating forms of human stress known" (Everly, 1995, p. 7). Fortunately, traumatic stress and its consequences continue to gain recognition and investigation in the helping professions although, clearly, more research needs to be done. For example, motor-vehicle accidents (MVAs) are quite common and often precipitate traumatic stress and PTSD, yet there is a dearth of literature examining their impact as well as the treatment of survivors of motor vehicle accidents.

Recognition of trauma-related stress is the first step in an individual's road to a healthier life. Medical and mental health professionals are in an ideal position to offer information, support, and/or the appropriate referrals to victims of traumatic stress. Treatment with a clinician knowledgeable and experienced in working with anxiety and trauma-related difficulties can be a crucial factor in helping victims learn to cope and live life more fully.

References

American Psychiatric Association (1980). *Diagnostic and statistical manual of mental disorders* (3rd ed.). Washington, DC: Author.

American Psychiatric Association (1994). *Diagnostic and statistical manual of mental disorders* (4th ed.). Washington, DC: Author.

Beck, A.T., Rush, A.J., Shaw, B.F., Emery, G. (1979). *Cognitive therapy of depression*. New York: Guilford.

Beck, A. T. (1993). *Beck Anxiety Inventory*. The Psychological Corporation.

Blake, D., Weathers, F., Nagy, L., Kaloupek, D., Klauminzer, G., Charney, D., & Keane, T. (1990). *Clinician Administered PTSD Scale* (CAPS). Boston: National Center for Post-Traumatic Stress Disorder, Behavioral Science Division, Boston VA.

Cummings, N., & Vanden Bos, G.R. (1981). The twenty year Kaiser-Permanente experience with psychotherapy and medical utilization. *Health Policy Quarterly*, 1, 159-175.

Daly, R.J. (1983). Samuel Pepys and posttraumatic stress disorder. *British Journal of Psychiatry*, 143, 64-68.

DiNardo, P.A., Brown, T.A., & Barlow, D.H. (1994). Anxiety Disorders Interview Schedule for DSM-IV: *Clinician's Manual*. New York: Graywind.

D'Zurilla, T.J. (1986). Problem solving therapy: A social competence approach to clinical intervention. New York: Springer.

Everly, G.S. (1995). Psychotraumatology. In G.S. Everly & J.M. Lating (Eds.), *Psychotraumatology: Key papers and core concepts in post-traumatic stress* (pp. 9-26). New York: Plenum.

Foa, E.B., & Kozak, M.J. (1986). Emotional processing of fear: Exposure to corrective information. *Psychological Bulletin*, 99, 20-35.

Foy, D.W. (1992). Introduction and description of the disorder. In D. W. Foy (Ed.), *Treating PTSD: Cognitive-Behavioral strategies* (pp 1-12). New York: Guilford.

Hammarberg, M. (1992). Penn Inventory for posttraumatic stress disorder: Psychometric properties. *Psychological Assessment*, 4, 67-76.

Holmes, R. (1985). *Acts of war*. New York: Free Press.

Keane, T.M., Malloy, P.F., & Fairbank, J.A. (1984). Empirical development of an MMPI subscale for the assessment of combat-related post-traumatic stress disorder. *Journal of Consulting and Clinical Psychology*, 52, 888-891.

Kilpatrick, D. G., Saunders, B.E., Amick-McMullen, A., Best, C.L., Veronen, L.J., & Resnick, H.S. (1989). Victim and crime factors associated with the development of crime-related posttraumatic stress disorder. *Behavior Therapy*, 20, 199-214.

Matsakis, A. (1992). *I can't get over it: A handbook for trauma survivors*. Oakland, CA: New Harbinger Publications.

McNally, R.J., English, G.E., Lipke, H.J. (1993). Assessment of intrusive cognition in PTSD: Use of the modified Stroop paradigm. *Journal of Traumatic Stress*, 6, 33-42.

Meichenbaum, D. (1994). *A clinical handbook / practical therapist manual for assessing and treating adults with post-traumatic stress disorder*. Ontario, Canada: Institute Press.

Ochberg, F.M. (1995). Post-traumatic therapy. In G.S. Everly & J.M. Lating (Eds.), *Psychotraumatology: Key papers and core concepts in post-traumatic stress* (pp. 245-264). New York: Plenum.

Safran, J.D., & Segal, Z.V. (1990). *Interpersonal process in cognitive therapy*. New York: Basic Books.

Schlenger, W.E., & Kulka, R.A. (1987). *Performance of the Keane-Fairbank MMPI scale and other self-report measures in identifying post-traumatic stress disorder*. Paper presented at the 95th annual meeting of the American Psychological Association, New York.

Sipprelle, R.C. (1992). A vet center experience: Multievent trauma, delayed treatment type. In D.W. Foy (Ed.), *Treating PTSD: Cognitive-Behavioral strategies* (pp 13-38). New York: Guilford.

Solomon, S., Gerrity, E.T., & Muff, A.M. (1992). Efficacy of treatments for posttraumatic stress disorder: An empirical review. *Journal of the American Medical Association*, 268, 633-638.

Terr, L. (1991). Childhood trauma: An outline and overview. *American Journal of Psychiatry*, 148, 10-20.

Trimble, M.R. (1981). *Post-traumatic neurosis*. Chicester: Wiley.

Vargas, M.A., & Davidson, J. (1993). Post-traumatic stress disorder. *Psychopharmacology*, 16, 737-748.

Wolfe, B.E. (1992). Integrative psychotherapy of the anxiety disorders. In J.C. Norcross & M.R. Goldfried (Eds.), *Handbook of Psychotherapy Integration*. (pp 373-401). New York: Basic Books.

Yehuda, R., Resnick, H., Kahana, J., & Giller, E. (1993). Long-lasting hormonal alterations to extreme stress in humans: Normative or maladaptive? *Psychosomatic Medicine*, 55, 287-297.

Additional Information

American Academy of Experts in Traumatic Stress
368 Veterans Memorial Highway
Commack, NY 11725
Tel: 631-543-2217
Fax: 631-543-6977
Website:www.aaets.org *and* www.atsm.org
E-mail: aaets@traumatic-stress.org

The American Academy of Experts in Traumatic Stress published *Acute Traumatic Stress Management™* and has established a standard for professionals who have extensive knowledge of ATSM, *Certification in Acute Traumatic Stress Management™*. Additional information as well as downloadable documents, are available as a public service at their website.

Section 18.2

Post-Traumatic Stress Disorder (PTSD)

"Reliving Trauma: Post-Traumatic Stress Disorder," National Institute of Mental Health (NIMH), updated January 2001; "Research Brings Hope for Veterans and Millions of Other Americans Who Suffer from Post-Traumatic Stress Disorder," National Institute of Mental Health (NIMH), November 10, 1999; and "Escaping the Prison of a Past Trauma: New Treatment for Post-Traumatic Stress Disorder," by Tamar Nordenberg, *FDA Consumer*, May-June 2000.

Reliving Trauma: Facts about Post-Traumatic Stress Disorder

Post-traumatic stress disorder (PTSD) is an anxiety disorder that can develop after exposure to a terrifying event or ordeal in which grave physical harm occurred or was threatened. Traumatic events that may trigger PTSD include violent personal assaults, natural or human-caused disasters, accidents, or military combat.

Among those who may experience PTSD are military troops who served in Vietnam and the Gulf Wars; rescue workers involved in the aftermath of disasters like the Oklahoma City bombing; survivors of accidents, rape, physical and sexual abuse, and other crimes; immigrants fleeing violence in their countries; survivors of the 1994 California earthquake, the 1997 South Dakota floods, and hurricanes Hugo and Andrew; and people who witness traumatic events. Family members of victims also can develop the disorder. PTSD can occur in people of any age, including children and adolescents.

Many people with PTSD repeatedly re-experience the ordeal in the form of flashback episodes, memories, nightmares, or frightening thoughts, especially when they are exposed to events or objects reminiscent of the trauma. Anniversaries of the event can also trigger symptoms. People with PTSD also experience emotional numbness and sleep disturbances, depression, anxiety, and irritability or outbursts of anger. Feelings of intense guilt are also common. Most people with PTSD try to avoid any reminders or thoughts of the ordeal. PTSD is diagnosed when symptoms last more than 1 month.

Physical symptoms such as headaches, gastrointestinal distress, immune system problems, dizziness, chest pain, or discomfort in other parts of the body are common in people with PTSD. Often, doctors treat these symptoms without being aware that they stem from an anxiety disorder.

Facts about PTSD

- An estimated 5.2 million American adults ages 18 to 54, or approximately 3.6 percent of people in this age group in a given year, have PTSD.[1]

- About 30 percent of Vietnam veterans developed PTSD at some point after the war.[2] The disorder also has been detected among veterans of the Persian Gulf War, with some estimates running as high as 8 percent.[3]

- More than twice as many women as men experience PTSD following exposure to trauma.[4]

- Depression, alcohol or other substance abuse, or other anxiety disorders frequently co-occur with PTSD.[5] The likelihood of treatment success is increased when these other conditions are appropriately diagnosed and treated as well.

Treatments for PTSD

PTSD can be extremely debilitating. Fortunately, research—including studies supported by NIMH and the Department of Veterans Affairs (VA)—has led to the development of treatments to help people with PTSD.

Studies have demonstrated the efficacy of cognitive-behavioral therapy, group therapy, and exposure therapy, in which the person repeatedly relives the frightening experience under controlled conditions to help him or her work through the trauma.[6,7] Studies also have found that several types of medication, particularly the selective serotonin reuptake inhibitors and other antidepressants, can help relieve the symptoms of PTSD.[8]

Other research shows that debriefing people very soon after a catastrophic event may reduce some of the symptoms of PTSD. A study of 12,000 schoolchildren who lived through a hurricane in Hawaii found that those who got counseling early on were doing much better 2 years later than those who did not.[9]

Research Findings

Research is continuing to reveal factors that may lead to PTSD. People who have been abused as children or who have had other previous traumatic experiences are more likely to develop the disorder.[10] In addition, it used to be believed that people who tend to be emotionally numb after a trauma were showing a healthy response, but now some researchers suspect that people who experience this emotional distancing may be more prone to PTSD.[11]

Studies in animals and humans have focused on pinpointing the specific brain areas and circuits involved in anxiety and fear, which underlie anxiety disorders such as PTSD.[12] Fear, an emotion that evolved to deal with danger, causes an automatic, rapid protective response that occurs without the need for conscious thought. It has been found that the body's fear response is coordinated by a small structure deep inside the brain, called the amygdala.

The amygdala, although relatively small, is a very complicated structure, and recent research suggests that different anxiety disorders may be associated with abnormal activation of the amygdala. One aim of research is to use such basic knowledge to develop new therapies.

People with PTSD tend to have abnormal levels of key hormones involved in response to stress.[13] Some studies have shown that cortisol levels are lower than normal and epinephrine and norepinephrine are higher than normal.

When people are in danger, they produce high levels of natural opiates, which can temporarily mask pain. Scientists have found that people with PTSD continue to produce those higher levels even after the danger has passed; this may lead to the blunted emotions associated with the condition.

Research to understand the neurotransmitter system involved in memories of emotionally charged events may lead to discovery of drugs that, if given early, could block the development of PTSD symptoms.

References

1. Narrow WE, Rae DS, Regier DA. NIMH epidemiology note: prevalence of anxiety disorders. One-year prevalence best estimates calculated from ECA and NCS data. Population estimates based on U.S. Census estimated residential population age 18 to 54 on July 1, 1998. Unpublished.

2. Kulka RA, Schlenger WE, Fairbank JA, et al. Contractual report of findings from the *National Vietnam veterans readjustment study*. Research Triangle Park, NC: Research Triangle Institute, 1988.

3. Wolfe J, Erickson DJ, Sharkansky EJ, et al. Course and predictors of posttraumatic stress disorder among Gulf War veterans: a prospective analysis. *Journal of Consulting and Clinical Psychology*, 1999; 67(4): 520-8.

4. Davidson JR. Trauma: the impact of post-traumatic stress disorder. *Journal of Psychopharmacology*, 2000; 14(2 Suppl 1): S5-S12.

5. Breslau N, Davis GC, Andreski P, et al. Traumatic events and postraumatic stress disorder in an urban population of young adults. *Archives of General Psychiatry*, 1991; 48(3): 216-22.

6. Marks I, Lovell K, Noshirvani H, et al. Treatment of posttraumatic stress disorder by exposure and/or cognitive restructuring: a controlled study. *Archives of General Psychiatry*, 1998; 55(4): 317-25.

7. Lubin H, Loris M, Burt J, et al. Efficacy of psychoeducational group therapy in reducing symptoms of posttraumatic stress

disorder among multiply traumatized women. *American Journal of Psychiatry*, 1998; 155(9): 1172-7.

8.   Kent JM, Coplan JD, Gorman JM. Clinical utility of the selective serotonin reuptake inhibitors in the spectrum of anxiety. *Biological Psychiatry*, 1998; 44(9): 812-24.

9.   Chemtob CM, Tomas S, Law W, et al. Postdisaster psychosocial intervention: a field study of the impact of debriefing on psychological distress. *American Journal of Psychiatry*, 1997; 154(3): 415-7.

10. Widom CS. Posttraumatic stress disorder in abused and neglected children grown up. *American Journal of Psychiatry*, 1999; 156(8): 1223-9.

11. Feeny NC, Zoellner LA, Fitzgibbons LA, et al. Exploring the roles of emotional numbing, depression, and dissociation in PTSD. *Journal of Traumatic Stress*, 2000; 13(3): 489-98.

12. LeDoux J. Fear and the brain: where have we been, and where are we going? *Biological Psychiatry*, 1998; 44(12): 1229-38.

13. Yehuda R. Psychoneuroendocrinology of post-traumatic stress disorder. *Psychiatric Clinics of North America*, 1998; 21(2): 359-79.

Research Brings Hope for Veterans and Millions of Other Americans Who Suffer from Post Traumatic Stress Disorder

For many of the military personnel being honored this Veteran's Day, the terror of war didn't end when they came back home. Some 30 percent of the men and women who have spent time in war zones experience symptoms of a debilitating condition called post-traumatic stress disorder (PTSD).

"War veterans first brought PTSD to public attention," said Farris Tuma, Sc.D., Chief of the Traumatic Stress Program at the National Institute of Mental Health (NIMH). "Now, through research and clinical experience, we know that PTSD can result from many kinds of traumatic incidents."

Dr. Tuma said that "trauma" has historically been defined in medical terms and is often associated with trauma medicine practiced in emergency rooms. However, in psychiatry, trauma has assumed a different meaning and refers to a painful emotional experience or shock, often producing a lasting psychic effect.

Each year, millions of people experience traumatic events. Among those who may develop PTSD are: survivors and rescue workers involved in disasters like the Oklahoma City bombing; survivors of accidents, rape, physical and sexual abuse, and other crimes; immigrants fleeing violence in their countries; survivors of natural disasters such as the 1994 California earthquake or the 1999 North Carolina floods; and people who witness traumatic events such as shootings in schools. Families of victims and survivors can also develop the disorder. A conservative estimate is that about 3.6 percent of U.S. adults ages 18 to 54 (5.2 million people in 1998) have PTSD during the course of a given year.

People with PTSD often feel emotionally numb and detached from others. They may be easily startled, subject to unexpected emotional outbursts, and depressed. Many have nightmares or trouble sleeping, difficulty concentrating, and some suffer from panic attacks or chronic anxiety. At any time, the trauma may come flooding back in the form of flashbacks. Often, PTSD symptoms can hamper the ability to hold down a job or feel pleasure from normal relationships with family and friends.

PTSD is commonly understood as a psychological disorder that results from exposure to life-threatening situations. In recent years, however, it has become increasingly clear that PTSD also can be understood from a biological perspective. Research sponsored by NIMH and the Department of Veterans Affairs (VA) shows that PTSD affects several body systems including the central nervous system; it causes changes in brain chemicals and possibly in brain structures.

"The development of PTSD may be linked to the way in which the brain ties the emotions generated during the traumatic event to the memory of the event," said Matthew Friedman, M.D., Ph.D., executive director of the VA National Center for PTSD. "For most people, memories of fearful traumatic events diminish over time. But for people with PTSD, the events they experience are so overwhelming that they continue to suffer from high levels of fear and anxiety, even though the original stimuli are no longer present."

Flashbacks, which can happen many times each day and are one of the major symptoms of PTSD, are not a "remembering" of the traumatic experience, but a "reliving" of it, said Friedman. The mind of the person experiencing a flashback is essentially transported in time and place to the traumatic event. Scientists at both the VA and NIMH are working to understand what brain changes are associated with flashbacks and other symptoms of the disorder such as emotional numbing and being easily startled.

NIMH and the VA are supporting animal and preliminary human brain imaging investigations to pinpoint the specific brain areas and circuits involved in anxiety and fear, which underlie anxiety disorders such as PTSD. This type of research has shown that the hippocampus—a part of the brain critical to memory and emotion—appears to be different in cases of PTSD.

Researchers do not know why some people who suffer traumatic events go on to develop PTSD and others do not, but recent NIMH- and VA-funded research may help doctors better identify people who may be more prone to developing the disorder. People with PTSD tend to have abnormal levels of key hormones involved in response to stress. Cortisol levels are lower than normal and epinephrine and norepinephrine are higher than normal. Scientists have also found that people with this condition have alterations in the function of the thyroid and in neurotransmitter activity involving serotonin and opiates.

"Findings from these and other investigations have important potential implications for both behavioral and biological treatment of traumatized persons and are helping to guide the development of improved treatment approaches," said Tuma.

Treatments developed through research help many people with PTSD deal effectively with their symptoms. Studies show that people can improve with cognitive-behavioral therapy, group therapy, psychoeducation, or exposure therapy. Support from family and friends can also be an important part of recovery. For example, a large study of Vietnam veterans found that soldiers who had good social support after they returned home were less likely to develop PTSD.

"There is also a great deal of current research on medications for PTSD with some very promising preliminary results," said Terence Keane, Ph.D., director of behavioral science at the National Center for PTSD. Studies have shown that medications help ease associated symptoms of depression and anxiety and help promote sleep.

Escaping from the Prison of a Past Trauma

January 18 marks the anniversary of a mighty adrenaline rush for Kellie Greene. She went sky diving on that day, in search of a high-flying thrill to overwhelm her traumatic anniversary memories of the rape she had endured exactly five years earlier.

"Sky-diving, you're screaming," says 34-year-old Greene, founder of the Orlando-based rape education group SOAR (Speaking Out

About Rape), "but you're screaming because you're excited. 'Oh my God, I'm doing this!' The whole world is underneath you, and it's so amazing. It just looks like the Earth's standing still, not like you're falling toward it." "Sky-diving, I controlled the adrenaline rush," Greene continues. "I had gotten tired of getting so anxious every year around that day. Now, it's no longer the date that I was raped, but the day I went sky diving."

It was on Jan. 18 in 1994 that a knife-wielding stranger raped Greene inside her own apartment as she returned there from the laundry room in her complex. The intruder smashed Greene on the head with a teakettle as she opened the apartment door, paying no mind to her pleas, "Take my money. I have money!"

Since the day she was raped, Greene has battled mental demons previously unknown to her. "For someone who had been pretty normal her whole life and had never needed counseling, it was frightening to be so out of control with my feelings and not know why," Greene recalls. "I would cry uncontrollably at any time. It was just a sadness that was so heavy, some days I wouldn't even want to get out of bed. Not being able to organize my daily routine—deciding what to wear or what to eat—because those might be the wrong choices to make. I would lock myself in the house an hour before it got dark, and not answer the phone and not answer the door. I was afraid to drive places or to be alone. I wasn't able to sleep at night, then was so tired during the day it's all I did. There were bad flashbacks, too, but they were strange flashbacks because they were dark. It was just darkness."

The flashbacks, troublesome sleep, and other symptoms Greene experienced are not uncommon for someone who has lived through the stressful ordeal of rape. Her types of symptoms are among the tell-tale signs of post-traumatic stress disorder, or PTSD, a debilitating condition that can beset anyone who has felt fear, helplessness, or horror during a traumatic event that caused or threatened to cause that person or someone else to die or be seriously injured. "All of us have had experiences that are sufficiently upsetting that we go over and over them in our minds," says Thomas Laughren, M.D., head of the Food and Drug Administration's psychiatric drug products group. "But with PTSD, it's worse. It can be a very severe kind of illness that limits people to an extent that is completely foreign to most of us."

About "Shell Shock"

In a given year, more than 10 million Americans (about 4 percent) will experience the life-disrupting symptoms of PTSD, which was first widely recognized during World War I and known as "shell shock" or "battle fatigue." Like combat horrors, other "man-made" tragedies such as criminal assaults or sexual attacks can provoke PTSD symptoms, as can a fire, earthquake, or other natural disaster. Accidents—car and airplane crashes, for example—are also common precipitators of PTSD.

By definition, the disorder can only develop in response to a traumatic event, says Edna Foa, Ph.D., director of the University of Pennsylvania's Center for the Treatment and Study of Anxiety. It can't arise from other seriously stressful occurrences that are less extreme—losing a job, say, or going through a divorce.

And, while not all life stressors are traumatic enough to lead to a PTSD diagnosis (but instead might cause "generalized anxiety"), not everyone who experiences a trauma will develop post-traumatic stress disorder, either.

As many as 70 percent of American adults have been through at least one major trauma, according to the "Expert Consensus Treatment Guidelines for Post-Traumatic Stress Disorder: A Guide For Patients and Families," a guide written by Foa and others based on a survey of 100 PTSD experts. But, Foa explains, "Most people who go through a traumatic event may be more frightened and act more cautiously than they used to, but don't develop the disorder. That is, they don't get symptoms that would disrupt their daily life in a significant way and render them dysfunctional on some level."

Experts divide symptoms that rise to the level of PTSD into these main types:

- **Re-experiencing the traumatic event**. Re-experiencing can refer to having intrusive memories of the ordeal, flashbacks when awake, recurring nightmares, and exaggerated emotional and physical responses to triggers that remind the person of the event. "Sometimes I've thought I was back in Vietnam. When you start dreaming, you can smell the flesh of your buddies burning," says veteran John Palmer Sr., who recalls being among 19 wounded survivors of a 1968 ambush by the North Vietnamese that killed the rest of his 59-strong battalion.

- **Avoidance.** After a trauma, people may lose interest in and avoid certain activities, places, and thoughts and feelings related to the trauma. July 4th is "really hard" for 51-year-old veteran Palmer because the loud noises remind him of wartime. And Palmer avoided seeing the critically acclaimed "Saving

Private Ryan." "I chose not to go," he explains, "even though some people thought it was pretty good—if there could be anything good about it. Watching movies about the war bothers me, and I start having nightmares."

- **Emotional detachment.** Foa's patients have told her, "I'm not the person I used to be. I don't trust people. I can't feel loving anymore." One of her patients, who had been injured in an explosion at his factory that killed many others, was "like a zombie emotionally," Foa says. The man's daughter complained, "He's not there for us. All he cares about is himself, and indulging in his own misery."

- **Increased arousal.** This symptom can show itself in difficulty sleeping, irritability or angry outbursts, difficulty concentrating, and unusually startled reactions in certain situations. Palmer says, "When I first came back [from Vietnam], people were afraid to be around me. I got in a lot of trouble, drinking and fighting, and I didn't really care."

People can have wide-ranging reactions to a certain stressor. Some people will have no long-lasting effects, while on the other end of the spectrum, people can have problems that last for months or years. The symptoms must last for at least a month, however, to be classified as post-traumatic stress disorder.

While symptoms usually begin immediately after a trauma or within the following few weeks, sometimes they can show up months or years later. Many of the World War II prisoners of war that Veterans Administration counselor James Boehnlein, M.D., talks with have had stable lives—were married long-term, raised children, and worked steadily—and developed delayed PTSD symptoms after they retired and when people their age began to die of natural causes. "Their losses brought back memories of their wartime sadness and loss," Boehnlein explains, "and they would start having nightmares of combat experience and being prisoners of war."

So far, science can't predict precisely how a certain individual will react to a traumatic event. But certain factors can provide clues about the likelihood and severity of PTSD:

- How severe and long-lasting was the trauma? The more intense and long-lasting the traumatic experience, the more likely it is that the victim will develop PTSD.

- How close was the person to the trauma, and how dangerous did it seem? Foa's patient who was injured in the factory explosion was more vulnerable to PTSD than if he had been across the street, merely heard the bang, and only later found out about the explosion's tragic consequences. Foa cites one recent study that found that women who perceived their lives were in danger during a rape had 2.5 times the incidence of PTSD than did others who didn't fear for their lives during the rape.

- Has the person been traumatized in the past, and if so, how many times? One of Foa's patients didn't develop PTSD until the third sudden death in her circle of friends and acquaintances. The third time, "that was it," says the therapist. "Now she's thinking, 'What's next? Next it will be me.'"

- Was the trauma inflicted by other people? PTSD is more likely after a rape or other man-made trauma than after an earthquake, hurricane, flood, or other naturally occurring disaster. Psychologically, it seems to matter whether the trauma is intentionally aimed at the victim or is random and suffered by many people together.

- What is the person's coping style—does he or she tend to stay enraged? And, does the person get support from friends and family, or negative reactions? People are less likely to have PTSD, elaborates Foa, if they think about the trauma, talk to other people about it, and let go of their anger over the incident. Foa encourages people to face the trauma: "Talk to someone you trust, write about it, do anything but push it away." And, she says, if the symptoms still cause suffering after several months, professional help should be sought.

But many people don't seek professional help for their condition, according to mental health experts. Possible reasons cited in the PTSD expert consensus guidelines: Sufferers may feel withdrawn, guilty, and mistrustful and naturally want to avoid dealing with unpleasant feelings, and they may not even realize they have a problem or that it can be treated. But PTSD is treatable—with medication, psychotherapy, or both.

Like many trauma victims, at first Greene was reluctant to seek professional treatment. "I was afraid if I told anyone how out of control I was really feeling, they would commit me to a mental institution." When Greene did finally confide in a therapist, he explained that her symptoms were a common reaction to a traumatic event and she wasn't going insane. Greene learned to manage her anxiety by breathing deeply and counting until she felt calm. And her doctor prescribed Zoloft (sertraline hydrochloride), the first FDA-approved drug for PTSD.

First PTSD Drug

Before its approval in December 1999 for post-traumatic stress disorder, Zoloft was already approved by FDA for depression, panic disorder, and obsessive-compulsive disorder. Its effectiveness for PTSD is in line with its benefit for depression and the other disorders, says FDA's Laughren. Studies show that about two-thirds of PTSD patients improve with Zoloft, while one-third improve when taking a placebo.

Zoloft's approval for PTSD was based on two 12-week studies of the drug that demonstrated its effectiveness. While Zoloft's benefit over placebo was clear in women patients, little effect was seen in the male group. Scientists aren't certain why the gender difference exists, but some have theorized that PTSD in veterans, a mostly male population, might differ somehow from the disorder in the mostly female population of sexual assault victims.

After her rape, Greene says, Zoloft played a big part in helping her heal. "It really took the edge off. I had been playing the attack over and over in my mind, like a broken record, and Zoloft helped me get out of that groove. It didn't make me a zombie or make me ecstatically happy, either. But all of a sudden I woke up and said, 'I can handle the day.'"

Greene took Zoloft for about a year, which was within the typical range of six to 24 months. She didn't notice any bothersome side effects, though some people do experience dry mouth, nausea, sleepiness, or other negative reactions.

While Zoloft is the only drug approved by FDA to treat PTSD, doctors sometimes prescribe other drugs that they believe may improve a patient's condition. For PTSD, doctors sometimes prescribe drugs in the same class as Zoloft. These selective serotonin reuptake inhibitors, or SSRI's, include Paxil (paroxetine), Prozac (fluoxetine), Luvox (fluvoxamine), and Celexa (citalopram). Based on an individual patient's medical circumstances, a doctor may in some cases choose to prescribe other types of antidepressants or anti-anxiety medications.

Facing Fears

As an alternative to medication or coupled with it, some patients opt to rely on group or individual psychotherapy to manage their

PTSD symptoms. Three types are considered especially effective, according to the expert consensus guidelines:

- **Exposure therapy.** To help patients confront the everyday reminders of their trauma, therapists sometimes use "exposure in the imagination" or "exposure in reality." In the first type, patients imagine the trauma and recount the memories in detail, over and over again, with a therapist they trust and at home between sessions. The goal of therapy: to give people an opportunity to reprocess what happened until the thoughts lose their distressful impact. Lyn Rezer, 35, re-examined a traumatic gang rape that had occurred when she was 12 years old and had haunted her for more than 20 years. Using this approach, Rezer says she conquered her feelings of worthlessness and despair. "I walked around for 23 years feeling extremely suicidal, wanting to flee, wanting to cry. I thought I was bad, I was filthy, I was nothing. I detached myself emotionally from a lot, and today I'm not detached. I feel everything, like a normal 35-year-old woman with normal impulses and instincts. I haven't had a suicidal thought since midway through treatment." With exposure in reality, therapists ask patients to gradually expose themselves to situations or places they had been avoiding because they are reminders of the trauma.

- **Cognitive behavioral therapy.** With CBT, therapists work on changing victims' irrational beliefs, such as self-blame for a rape, criminal assault, or accident.

- **Anxiety management.** This classification refers to techniques such as slow abdominal breathing to relax and avoid hyperventilation, and positive thinking and self-talk to replace negative thoughts.

Therapist Foa, who at her University of Pennsylvania clinic uses exposure therapy, sometimes combined with other types, estimates that 80 percent of patients accomplish significant improvement in their lives over the 12 weeks or so of therapy.

Foa acknowledges that it's difficult to directly face a traumatic memory that one has been avoiding, sometimes for years. But getting help is critical, she says, if the stifling symptoms of PTSD do not resolve themselves pretty quickly after a trauma. Immediately after the trauma, it's normal to experience emotional swings, Foa says, so "you needn't rush to treatment." But if your symptoms begin to appear chronic, at four to six months, she says, they're not likely to improve on their own.

In light of the healing effects of PTSD treatment in her own life, rape survivor and rookie sky diver Greene has committed herself to encouraging others to take brave steps to deal with their traumatic memories. Greene says she has been inspired by popular singer Tori Amos, a rape victim herself and co-founder of the trauma support organization RAINN (the Rape, Abuse, and Incest National Network). Amos, who says she wrote her song "Me and a Gun" as a healing step for herself, wrote a public letter to others who have faced similar traumas. The message: "Healing takes courage, and we all have courage, even if we have to dig a little to find it!"

It's worth digging up the courage, Rezer confirms. "It's a lot of hard work, but your life doesn't have to be dictated by your past. I never believed you could go back in time and change things, but I know now that you can change them—not the events, just the feelings and thoughts surrounding them that have taken over your life."

Making the Diagnosis: Simple Stress or Post-Traumatic Stress Disorder?

Answering these questions may help your health-care provider determine if you have PTSD:

Have you experienced or witnessed a life-threatening event that caused you to feel intense fear, helplessness, or horror?

Do you re-experience the event in at least one of the following ways?

- Repeated, distressing memories and/or dreams
- Flashbacks, or a sense of reliving the event
- Intense physical and/or emotional distress when exposed to things that remind you of the event

Do you avoid reminders of the event and feel numb, compared with the way you felt before, in three or more of the following ways?

- Avoiding thoughts, feelings, or conversation about it
- Avoiding activities, places, or people who remind you of it
- Being unable to remember important parts of it
- Losing interest in significant activities in your life

- Feeling detached from other people
- Feeling that your range of emotions is restricted
- Feeling as if your future has shrunk (for example, you don't expect to have a career, marriage, children, or a normal lifespan)

Are you troubled by two or more of the following?

- Problems sleeping
- Irritability or outbursts of anger
- Problems concentrating
- Feeling "on guard"
- An exaggerated startle response

Do your symptoms interfere with your daily life?

Have your symptoms lasted at least a month?

(Source: Anxiety Disorders Association of America, based on the *Diagnostic and Statistical Manual of Mental Disorders*, Fourth Edition.)

Resources for Trauma Survivors

Anxiety Disorders Association of America
11900 Parklawn Drive, Suite 100
Rockville, MD 20852
Tel: 301-231-9350
Website: www.adaa.org

International Society for Traumatic Stress Studies
60 Revere Drive, Suite 500
Northbrook, IL 60062
Tel: 847-480-9028
Fax: 847-480-9282
Website: www.istss.org
E-mail: istss@istss.org

National Center for Victims of Crime
2111 Wilson Blvd., Suite 300
Arlington, VA 22201
Toll-Free: 800-394-2255
Website: www.nvc.org

National Center for Post-Traumatic Stress Disorder
215 North Main St.
White River Junction, VT 05009
Tel: 802-296-5132
Website: www.ncptsd.org

Rape, Abuse, and Incest National Network (RAINN)
635 Pennsylvania Ave., SE
Washington, DC 20002
Toll-Free: 800-656-HOPE (1-800-656-4673) (24-hour confidential hot line)
Fax: 202-544-3556
Website: www.rainn.org
E-mail: rainnmail@aol.com

National Institute of Mental Health (NIMH)
Office of Communications and Public Liaison
6001 Executive Boulevard, Rm. 8184, MSC 9663
Bethesda, MD 20892-9663
Tel: 301-443-4513
Fax: 301-443-4279
Website: www.nimh.nih.gov
E-mail: nimhinfo@nih.gov

Section 18.3

Helping Children and Adolescents Cope with Violence and Disasters

This section includes "Helping Children and Adolescents Cope with Violence and Disasters," National Institute of Mental Health (NIMH), NIH Publication No. 99-3518, updated January 13, 2000; and "Effects of Domestic Violence on Children and Adolescents: An Overview," by Joseph S. Volpe, Ph.D., B.C.E.T.S., F.A.A.E.T.S. © 1996. Reprinted with permission of Dr. Volpe and the American Academy of Experts in Traumatic Stress, 368 Veterans Memorial Highway, Commack, NY 11725, Phone: 631-543-2217, Fax: 631-543-6977, www.aaets.org.

Helping Children and Adolescents Cope with Violence and Disasters

The National Institute of Mental Health has joined with other Federal agencies to address the issue of reducing school violence and assisting children who have been victims of or witnesses to violent events. Nationally reported school shootings such as those that occurred in Bethel, Alaska; Pearl, Mississippi; West Paducah, Kentucky; Jonesboro, Arkansas; Edinboro, Pennsylvania; Springfield, Oregon; and Littleton, Colorado have shocked the country. Many questions are being asked about how these tragedies could have been prevented, how those directly involved can be helped, and how we can avoid such events in the future.

Research has shown that both adults and children who experience catastrophic events show a wide range of reactions. Some suffer only worries and bad memories that fade with emotional support and the passage of time. Others are more deeply affected and experience long-term problems. Research on post-traumatic stress disorder (PTSD) shows that some soldiers, survivors of criminal victimization, torture and other violence, and survivors of natural and man-made catastrophes suffer long-term effects from their experiences. Children who have witnessed violence in their families, schools, or communities are also vulnerable to serious long-term problems. Their emotional reactions, including fear, depression, withdrawal, or anger can occur immediately or some time after the tragic event. Youngsters who have experienced a catastrophic event often need support from parents and

288

teachers to avoid long-term emotional harm. Most will recover in a short time, but the minority who develop PTSD or other persistent problems need treatment.

The school shootings caught the Nation's attention, but these events are only a small fraction of the many tragic episodes that affect children's lives. Each year many children and adolescents sustain injuries from violence, lose friends or family members, or are adversely affected by witnessing a violent or catastrophic event. Each situation is unique, whether it centers upon a plane crash where many people are killed, automobile accidents involving friends or family members, or natural disasters such as Hurricane Andrew where deaths occur and homes are lost—but these events have similarities as well, and cause similar reactions in children. Helping young people avoid or overcome emotional problems in the wake of violence or disaster is one of the most important challenges a parent, teacher, or mental health professional can face. The purpose of this section is to tell what is known about the impact of violence and disasters on children and suggest steps to minimize long-term emotional harm.

Trauma—What Is It?

Trauma includes emotional as well as physical experiences and injuries. Emotional injury is essentially a normal response to an extreme event. It involves the creation of emotional memories, which arise through a long-lasting effect on structures deep within the brain. The more direct the exposure to the traumatic event, the higher the risk for emotional harm. Thus in a school shooting, the student who is injured probably will be most severely affected emotionally. And the student who sees a classmate shot, even killed, probably will be more emotionally affected than the student who was in another part of the school when the violence occurred. But even second-hand exposure to violence can be traumatic. For this reason, all children and adolescents exposed to violence or a disaster, even if only through graphic media reports, should be watched for signs of emotional distress. In addition to this psychiatric definition, trauma also has a medical definition, which refers to a serious or critical bodily injury, wound, or shock, often treated with trauma medicine practiced in emergency rooms.

How Children and Adolescents React to Trauma

Reactions to trauma may appear immediately after the traumatic event or days and even weeks later. Loss of trust in adults and fear of the event occurring again are responses seen in many children and adolescents who have been exposed to traumatic events. Other reactions vary according to age:

For children 5 years of age and younger, typical reactions can include a fear of being separated from the parent, crying, whimpering, screaming, immobility and/or aimless motion, trembling, frightened facial expressions, and excessive clinging. Parents may also notice children returning to behaviors exhibited at earlier ages (these are called regressive behaviors), such as thumb-sucking, bedwetting, and fear of darkness. Children in this age bracket tend to be strongly affected by the parents' reactions to the traumatic event.

Children 6 to 11 years old may show extreme withdrawal, disruptive behavior, and/or inability to pay attention. Regressive behaviors, nightmares, sleep problems, irrational fears, irritability, refusal to attend school, outbursts of anger and fighting are also common in traumatized children of this age. Also the child may complain of stomach aches or other bodily symptoms that have no medical basis. Schoolwork often suffers. Depression, anxiety, feelings of guilt, and emotional numbing or "flatness" are often present as well.

Adolescents 12 to 17 years old may exhibit responses similar to those of adults, including flashbacks, nightmares, emotional numbing, avoidance of any reminders of the traumatic event, depression, substance abuse, problems with peers, and anti-social behavior. Also common are withdrawal and isolation, physical complaints, suicidal thoughts, school avoidance, academic decline, sleep disturbances, and confusion. The adolescent may feel extreme guilt over his or her failure to prevent injury or loss of life, and may harbor revenge fantasies that interfere with recovery from the trauma.

Some youngsters are more vulnerable to trauma than others, for reasons scientists don't fully understand. It has been shown that the impact of a traumatic event is likely to be greatest in the child or adolescent who previously has been the victim of child abuse or some other form of trauma, or who already had a mental health problem. And the youngster who lacks family support is more at risk for a poor recovery.

Helping the Child or Adolescent Trauma Victim

Early intervention to help children and adolescents who have suffered trauma from violence or a disaster is critical. Parents, teachers and mental health professionals can do a great deal to help these youngsters recover. Help should begin at the scene of the traumatic event. According to the National Center for Post-Traumatic Stress Disorder of the Department of Veterans Affairs, workers in charge of a disaster scene should:

- Find ways to protect children from further harm and from further exposure to traumatic stimuli. If possible, create a safe haven for them. Protect children from onlookers and the media covering the story.

- When possible, direct children who are able to walk away from the site of violence or destruction, away from severely injured survivors, and away from continuing danger. Kind but firm direction is needed.

- Identify children in acute distress and stay with them until initial stabilization occurs. Acute distress includes panic (marked by trembling, agitation, rambling speech, becoming mute, or erratic behavior) and intense grief (signs include loud crying, rage, or immobility).

- Use a supportive and compassionate verbal or non-verbal exchange (such as a hug, if appropriate) with the child to help him or her feel safe. However brief the exchange, or however temporary, such reassurances are important to children.

After violence or a disaster occurs, the family is the first-line resource for helping. Among the things that parents and other caring adults can do are:

- Explain the episode of violence or disaster as well as you are able.

- Encourage the children to express their feelings and listen without passing judgment. Help younger children learn to use words that express their feelings. However, do not force discussion of the traumatic event.

- Let children and adolescents know that it is normal to feel upset after something bad happens.

- Allow time for the youngsters to experience and talk about their feelings. At home, however, a gradual return to routine can be reassuring to the child.

- If your children are fearful, reassure them that you love them and will take care of them. Stay together as a family as much as possible.

- If behavior at bedtime is a problem, give the child extra time and reassurance. Let him or her sleep with a light on or in your room for a limited time if necessary.

- Reassure children and adolescents that the traumatic event was not their fault.

- Do not criticize regressive behavior or shame the child with words like "babyish."

- Allow children to cry or be sad. Don't expect them to be brave or tough.

- Encourage children and adolescents to feel in control. Let them make some decisions about meals, what to wear, etc.

- Take care of yourself so you can take care of the children.

When violence or disaster affects a whole school or community, teachers and school administrators can play a major role in the healing process. Some of the things educators can do are:

- If possible, give yourself a bit of time to come to terms with the event before you attempt to reassure the children. This may not be possible in the case of a violent episode that occurs at school, but sometimes in a natural disaster there will be several days before schools reopen and teachers can take the time to prepare themselves emotionally.

- Don't try to rush back to ordinary school routines too soon. Give the children or adolescents time to talk over the traumatic event and express their feelings about it.

- Respect the preferences of children who do not want to participate in class discussions about the traumatic event. Do not force discussion or repeatedly bring up the catastrophic event; doing so may re-traumatize children.

- Hold in-school sessions with entire classes, with smaller groups of students, or with individual students. These sessions can be very useful in letting students know that their fears and concerns are normal reactions. Many counties and school districts have teams that will go into schools to hold such sessions after a disaster or episode of violence. Involve mental health professionals in these activities if possible.

- Offer art and play therapy for children in primary school.

- Be sensitive to cultural differences among the children. In some cultures, for example, it is not acceptable to express negative emotions. Also, the child who is reluctant to make eye contact with a teacher may not be depressed, but may simply be exhibiting behavior appropriate to his or her culture.

- Encourage children to develop coping and problem-solving skills and age-appropriate methods for managing anxiety.

- Hold meetings for parents to discuss the traumatic event, their children's response to it, and how they and you can help. Involve mental health professionals in these meetings if possible.

Most children and adolescents, if given support such as that described, will recover almost completely from the fear and anxiety caused by a traumatic experience within a few weeks. However, some children and adolescents will need more help over a longer period of time in order to heal. Grief over the loss of a loved one, teacher, friend, or pet may take months to resolve, and may be reawakened by reminders such as media reports or the anniversary of the death.

In the immediate aftermath of a traumatic event, and in the weeks following, it is important to identify the youngsters who are in need of more intensive support and therapy because of profound grief or some other extreme emotion. Children who show avoidance and emotional numbing may need the help of a mental health professional, while more common reactions such as re-experiencing the event and hyperarousal (including sleep disturbances and a tendency to be easily startled) may respond to help from parents and teachers.

Post-Traumatic Stress Disorder

As stated earlier, some children and adolescents will have prolonged problems after a traumatic event. These potentially chronic conditions include depression and prolonged grief. Another serious and potentially long-lasting problem is post-traumatic stress disorder

(PTSD). This condition is diagnosed when the following symptoms have been present for longer than one month:

- Re-experiencing the event through play or in trauma-specific nightmares or flashbacks, or distress over events that resemble or symbolize the trauma.

- Routine avoidance of reminders of the event or a general lack of responsiveness (e.g., diminished interests or a sense of having a foreshortened future).

- Increased sleep disturbances, irritability, poor concentration, startle reaction, and regressive behavior.

Rates of PTSD identified in child and adult survivors of violence and disasters vary widely. For example, estimates range from 2% after a natural disaster (tornado), 28% after an episode of terrorism (mass shooting), and 29% after a plane crash. The disorder may arise weeks or months after the traumatic event. PTSD may resolve without treatment, but some form of therapy by a mental health professional is often required in order for healing to occur. Fortunately, it is more common for a traumatized child or adolescent to have some of the symptoms of PTSD than to develop the full-blown disorder. People differ in their vulnerability to PTSD, and the source of this difference is not known in its entirety.

Research has shown that PTSD clearly alters a number of fundamental brain mechanisms. Because of this, abnormalities have been detected in brain chemicals that affect coping behavior, learning, and memory among people with the disorder. Recent brain imaging studies have detected altered metabolism and blood flow as well as anatomical changes in people with PTSD.

Treatment of PTSD

People with PTSD are treated with specialized forms of psychotherapy and sometimes with medications or a combination of the two. One of the forms of psychotherapy shown to be effective is cognitive/behavioral therapy, or CBT. In CBT, the patient is taught methods of overcoming anxiety or depression and modifying undesirable behaviors such as avoidance. The therapist helps the patient examine and re-evaluate beliefs that are interfering with healing, such as the belief that the traumatic event will happen again. Children who undergo CBT are taught to avoid "catastrophizing." For example, they are reassured that dark clouds do not necessarily mean another hurricane, that the fact that someone is angry doesn't necessarily mean that another shooting is imminent, etc. Play therapy and art therapy also can help younger children to remember the traumatic event safely and express their feelings about it. Other forms of psychotherapy that have been found to help persons with PTSD include group and exposure therapy. A reasonable period of time for treatment of PTSD is 6 to 12 weeks with occasional follow-up sessions, but treatment may be longer depending on a patient's particular circumstances. Research has shown that support from family and friends can be an important part of recovery and that involving people in group discussion very soon after a catastrophic event may reduce some of the symptoms of PTSD.

There has been a good deal of research on the use of medications for adults with PTSD, including research on the formation of emotionally charged memories and medications that may help to block the development of symptoms. Medications appear to be useful in reducing overwhelming symptoms of arousal (such as sleep disturbances and an exaggerated startle reflex), intrusive thoughts, and avoidance; reducing accompanying conditions such as depression and panic; and improving impulse control and related behavioral problems. Research is just beginning on the use of medications to treat PTSD in children and adolescents. There is preliminary evidence that psychotherapy focused on trauma and grief, in combination with selected medications, can be effective in alleviating PTSD symptoms and accompanying depression. More medication treatment research is needed to increase our knowledge of how best to treat children who have PTSD.

A mental health professional with special expertise in the area of child and adolescent trauma is the best person to help a youngster with PTSD. Organizations on the accompanying resource list may help you to find such a specialist in your geographical area.

What Are Scientists Learning about Trauma in Children and Adolescents?

The National Institute of Mental Health (NIMH), a part of the Federal Government's National Institutes of Health, supports research on the brain and a wide range of mental disorders, including PTSD and related conditions. The Department of Veterans Affairs also conducts research in this area with adults and their family members.

Recent research findings include:

- Some studies show that counseling children very soon after a catastrophic event may reduce some of the symptoms of PTSD. A study of 12,000 schoolchildren who lived through a hurricane in Hawaii found that those who got counseling early on were doing much better two years later than those who did not.

- Parents' responses to a violent event or disaster strongly influence their children's ability to recover. This is particularly true for mothers of young children. If the mother is depressed or highly anxious, she may need to get emotional support or counseling in order to be able to help her child.

- Community violence can have a profound effect on teachers as well as students. One study of Head Start teachers who lived through the 1992 Los Angeles riots showed that 7% had severe post-traumatic stress symptoms, and 29% had moderate symptoms. Children also were acutely affected by the violence and anxiety around them. They were more aggressive and noisy and less likely to be obedient or get along with each other.

- PTSD is often accompanied by depression. In a group of teenage students who survived a terrorist shooting in Brooklyn, New York, 4 of the 11 survivors interviewed had both PTSD and depression. In another study, this one involving adults, depression occurred in 44.5% of PTSD patients at 1 month after the traumatic event and in 43.2% at 4 months. Depression must be treated along with PTSD in these instances, and early treatment is best.

- Either being exposed to violence within the home for an extended period of time or exposure to a one-time event like an attack by a dog can cause PTSD in a child. Some scientists believe that younger children are more likely to develop the disorder than older ones.

- Inner-city children experience the greatest exposure to violence. A study of young adolescent boys from inner-city Chicago showed that 68% had seen someone beaten up and 22.5% had seen someone shot or killed. Youngsters who had been exposed to community violence were more likely to exhibit aggressive behavior or depression within the following year.

What Is Domestic Violence?

In the past two decades, there has been growing recognition of the prevalence of domestic violence in our society. Moreover, it has become apparent that some individuals are at greater risk for victimization than others. Domestic violence has adverse effects on individuals, families, and society in general.

Domestic violence includes physical abuse, sexual abuse, psychological abuse, and abuse to property and pets (Ganley, 1989). Exposure to this form of violence has considerable potential to be perceived as life-threatening by those victimized and can leave them with a sense of vulnerability, helplessness, and in extreme cases, horror. Physical abuse refers to any behavior that involves the intentional use of force against the body of another person that risks physical injury, harm, and/or pain (Dutton, 1992). Physical abuse includes pushing, hitting, slapping, choking, using an object to hit, twisting of a body part, forcing the ingestion of an unwanted substance, and use of a weapon. Sexual abuse is defined as any unwanted sexual intimacy forced on one individual by another. It may include oral, anal, or vaginal stimulation or penetration, forced nudity, forced exposure to sexually explicit material or activity, or any other unwanted sexual activity (Dutton, 1994). Compliance may be obtained through actual or threatened physical force or through some other form of coercion. Psychological abuse may include derogatory statements or threats of further abuse (e.g., threats of being killed by another individual). It may also involve isolation, economic threats, and emotional abuse.

Prevalence of Domestic Violence

Domestic violence is widespread and occurs among all socioeconomic groups. In a national survey of over 6,000 American families, it was estimated that between 53% and 70% of male batterers (i.e., they assaulted their wives) also frequently abused their children (Straus & Gelles, 1990). Other research suggests that women who have been hit by their husbands were twice as likely as other women to abuse a child (CWP, 1995).

Over 3 million children are at risk of exposure to parental violence each year (Carlson, 1984). Children from homes where domestic violence occurs are physically or sexually abused and/or seriously neglected at a rate 15 times the national average (McKay, 1994). Approximately, 45% to 70% of battered women in shelters have reported the presence of child abuse in their home (Meichenbaum, 1994).

297

About two-thirds of abused children are being parented by battered women (McKay, 1994). Of the abused children, they are three times more likely to have been abused by their fathers.

Studies of the incidence of physical and sexual violence in the lives of children suggest that this form of violence can be viewed as a serious public health problem. State agencies reported approximately 211,000 confirmed cases of child physical abuse and 128,000 cases of child sexual abuse in 1992. At least 1,200 children died as a result of maltreatment. It has been estimated that about 1 in 5 female children and 1 in 10 male children may experience sexual molestation (Regier & Cowdry, 1995).

Domestic Violence as a Cause of Traumatic Stress

As the incidence of interpersonal violence grows in our society, so does the need for investigation of the cognitive, emotional, and behavioral consequences produced by exposure to domestic violence, especially in children. Traumatic stress is produced by exposure to events that are so extreme or severe and threatening, that they demand extraordinary coping efforts. Such events are often unpredicted and uncontrollable. They overwhelm a person's sense of safety and security.

Terr (1991) has described "Type I" and "Type II" traumatic events. Traumatic exposure may take the form of single, short-term event (e.g., rape, assault, severe beating) and can be referred to as "Type I" trauma. Traumatic events can also involve repeated or prolonged exposure (e.g., chronic victimization such as child sexual abuse, battering); this is referred to as "Type II" trauma. Research suggests that this latter form of exposure tends to have greater impact on the individual's functioning. Domestic violence is typically ongoing and therefore, may fit the criteria for a Type II traumatic event.

With repeated exposure to traumatic events, a proportion of individuals may develop Posttraumatic Stress Disorder (PTSD). PTSD involves specific patterns of avoidance and hyperarousal. Individuals with PTSD may begin to organize their lives around their trauma. Although most people who suffer from PTSD (especially, in severe cases) have considerable interpersonal and academic/occupational problems, the degree to which symptoms of PTSD interfere with overall functioning varies a great deal from person to person.

The *Diagnostic and Statistical Manual of Mental Disorders - Fourth Edition* (DSM-IV; APA, 1994) stipulates that in order for an individual to be diagnosed with posttraumatic stress disorder, he or she must have experienced or witnessed a life-threatening event and reacted with intense fear, helplessness, or horror. The traumatic event is persistently re-experienced (e.g., distressing recollections), there is persistent avoidance of stimuli associated with the trauma, and the victim experiences some form of hyperarousal (e.g., exaggerated startle response). These symptoms persist for more than one month and cause clinically significant impairment in daily functioning. When the disturbance lasts a minimum of two days and as long as four weeks from the traumatic event, Acute Stress Disorder may be a more accurate diagnosis.

It has been suggested that responses to traumatic experience(s) can be divided into at least four categories (for a complete review, see Meichenbaum, 1994). Emotional responses include shock, terror, guilt, horror, irritability, anxiety, hostility, and depression. Cognitive responses are reflected in significant concentration impairment, confusion, self-blame, intrusive thoughts about the traumatic experience(s) (also referred to as flashbacks), lowered self-efficacy, fears of losing control, and fear of reoccurrence of the trauma. Biologically-based responses involve sleep disturbance (i.e., insomnia), nightmares, an exaggerated startle response, and psychosomatic symptoms. Behavioral responses include avoidance, social withdrawal, interpersonal stress (decreased intimacy and lowered trust in others), and substance abuse. The process through which the individual has coped prior to the trauma is arrested; consequently, a sense of helplessness is often maintained (Foy, 1992).

Possible Signs and Symptoms of Domestic Violence in Children and Adolescents

More than half of the school-age children in domestic violence shelters show clinical levels of anxiety or posttraumatic stress disorder (Graham-Bermann, 1994). Without treatment, these children are at significant risk for delinquency, substance abuse, school drop-out, and difficulties in their own relationships.

Children may exhibit a wide range of reactions to exposure to violence in their home. Younger children (e.g., preschool and kindergarten) oftentimes, do not understand the meaning of the abuse they observe and tend to believe that they "must have done something wrong." Self-blame can precipitate feelings of guilt, worry, and anxiety. It is important to consider that children, especially younger children, typically do not have the ability to adequately express their feelings verbally. Consequently, the manifestation of these emotions are often behavioral. Children may become withdrawn, non-verbal, and exhibit regressed behaviors such as clinging and whining. Eating and sleeping difficulty, concentration problems, generalized anxiety, and physical complaints (e.g., headaches) are all common.

Unlike younger children, the pre-adolescent child typically has greater ability to externalize negative emotions (i.e., to verbalize). In addition to symptoms commonly seen with childhood anxiety (e.g., sleep problems, eating disturbance, nightmares), victims within this age group may show a loss of interest in social activities, low self-concept, withdrawal or avoidance of peer relations, rebelliousness and oppositional-defiant behavior in the school setting. It is also common to observe temper tantrums, irritability, frequent fighting at school or between siblings, lashing out at objects, treating pets cruelly or abusively, threatening of peers or siblings with violence (e.g., "give me a pen or I will smack you"), and attempts to gain attention through hitting, kicking, or choking peers and/or family members. Incidentally, girls are more likely to exhibit withdrawal and unfortunately, run the risk of being "missed" as a child in need of support.

Adolescents are at risk of academic failure, school drop-out, delinquency, and substance abuse. Some investigators have suggested that a history of family violence or abuse is the most significant difference between delinquent and non-delinquent youth. An estimated 1/5 to 1/3 of all teenagers who are involved in dating relationships are regularly abusing or being abused by their partners verbally, mentally, emotionally, sexually, and/or physically (SASS, 1996). Between 30% and 50% of dating relationships can exhibit the same cycle of escalating violence as marital relationships (SASS, 1996).

Helping Children and Adolescents Exposed to Domestic Violence

For some children and adolescents, questions about home life may be difficult to answer, especially if the individual has been "warned" or threatened by a family member to refrain from "talking to strangers" about events that have taken place in the family. Referrals to the appropriate school personnel could be the first step in assisting the child or teen in need of support. When there is suggestion of domestic violence with a student, consider involving the school psychologist, social worker, guidance counselor, and/or a school administrator (when indicated). Although the circumstances surrounding each case may vary, suspicion of child abuse is required to be reported to the local child protection agency by teachers and other school personnel. In some cases, a contact with the local police department may also be necessary. When in doubt, consult with school team members.

If the child expresses a desire to talk, provide them with an opportunity to express their thoughts and feelings. In addition to talking, they may be also encouraged to write in a journal, draw, or paint; these are all viable means for facilitating expression in younger children. Adolescents are typically more abstract in their thinking and generally have better developed verbal abilities than younger children. It could be helpful for adults who work with teenagers to encourage them to talk about their concerns without insisting on this expression. Listening in a warm, non-judgmental, and genuine manner is often comforting for victims and may be an important first step in their seeking further support. When appropriate, individual and/or group counseling should be considered at school if the individual is amenable. Referrals for counseling (e.g., family counseling) outside of the school should be made to the family as well. Providing a list of names and phone numbers to contact in case of a serious crisis can be helpful.

References

American Psychiatric Association (1994). *Diagnostic and statistical manual of mental disorders* (4th ed.). Washington, DC: Author.

Carlson, B. E. (1984). Children's observations of interpersonal violence. In A. R. Edwards (Ed.), *Battered women and their families* (pp. 147-167). New York: Springer.

Child Welfare Partnership (1995). *Domestic violence summary: The intersection of child abuse and domestic violence*. Published by Portland State University.

Dutton, M.A. (1994). Post-traumatic therapy with domestic violence survivors. In M.B. Williams & J.F. Sommer (Eds.), *Handbook of posttraumatic therapy* (pp. 146-161). Westport, CT: Greenwood Press.

Dutton, M.A. (1992). *Women's response to battering: Assessment and intervention*. New York: Springer.

Foy, D.W. (1992). Introduction and description of the disorder. In D. W. Foy (Ed.), *Treating PTSD: Cognitive-Behavioral strategies* (pp 1-12). New York: Guilford.

Ganley, A. (1989). Integrating feminist and social learning analyses of aggression: Creating multiple models for intervention with men who battered. In P. Caesar & L. Hamberger (Eds.), *Treating men who batter* (pp. 196-235). New York: Springer.

Graham-Bermann, S. (1994). *Preventing domestic violence.* University of Michigan research information index. UM-Research-WEB@umich.edu.

McKay, M. (1994). *The link between domestic violence and child abuse: Assessment and treatment considerations.* Child Welfare League of America, 73, 29-39.

Meichenbaum, D. (1994). *A clinical handbook / practical therapist manual for assessing and treating adults with post-traumatic stress disorder.* Ontario, Canada: Institute Press.

Regier, D.A., & Cowdry, R.W. (1995). Research on violence and traumatic stress (program announcement, PA 95-068). National Institute of Mental Health.

Sexual Assault Survivor Services (1996). *Facts about domestic violence.*

Straus, M.A., & Gelles, R.J. (1990). *Physical violence in American families.* New Brunswick, NJ: Transaction Publishers.

Terr, L. (1991). Childhood trauma: An outline and overview. *American Journal of Psychiatry*, 148, 10-20.

Additional Information

National Institute of Mental Health (NIMH)
Information Resources and Inquiries Branch
6001 Executive Boulevard
Rm. 8184
MSC 9663
Bethesda, MD 20892-9663
Tel: 301-443-4513
Fax: 301-443-4279
Website: www.nimh.nih.gov
E-mail: nimhinfo@nih.gov

Center for Mental Health Services (CMHS)
Emergency Services and Disaster Relief Branch
5600 Fishers Lane
Room 16C-26
Rockville, MD 20857
Tel: 301-443-4735
Fax: 301-443-8040
Website: www.samhsa.gov/cmhs/cmhs.htm

U.S. Department of Education
400 Maryland Avenue, SW
Washington, DC 20202-0498
Toll-Free: 800-USA-LEARN (872-5327)
Fax: 202-401-0689
Website: www.ed.gov
E-mail: customerservice@inet.ed.gov

U.S. Department of Justice
950 Pennsylvania Avenue, NW
Washington, DC 20530-0001
Website: www.usdoj.gov
E-mail: askdoj@usdoj.gov

Federal Emergency Management Agency
500 C Street, SW
Washington, DC 20472
Toll-Free: 800-480-2520
Tel: 202-566-1600
Website: www.fema.gov/kids (Information for children and
adolescents)
E-mail: opa@fema.gov

International Society for Traumatic Stress Studies (ISTSS)
60 Revere Drive, Suite 500
Northbrook, IL 60062
Tel: 847-480-9028
Fax: 847-480-9282
Website:www.istss.org
E-mail: istss@istss.org

National Center for PTSD
215 N. Main Street
White River Junction, VT 05009
Tel: 802-296-5132
Website: www.ncptsd.org

National Organization for Victim Assistance (NOVA)
1730 Park Rd., NW
Washington, DC 20010
Toll-Free: 800-879-6682
Tel: 202-232-6682
Fax: 202-462-2255
Website: www.try-nova.org

National Victim Center
2111 Wilson Blvd., Suite 300
Arlington, VA 22201
Tel: 730-276-2880
Website: www.nvc.org

Office for Victims of Crime Resource Center
National Criminal Justice Reference Service
P.O. Box 6000
Rockville, MD 20850
Toll-Free: 800-627-6872
Website: www.ncjrs.org
E-mail: askovc@ojp.usdoj.gov

American Psychiatric Association
1400 K Street, NW
Washington, DC 20005
Toll-Free: 888-357-7924
Fax: 202-682-6850
Answer Center: 202-682-6000
Website: www.psych.org
E-mail: apa@psych.org

American Psychological Association
750 First Street, NE
Washington, DC 20002
Toll-Free: 800-374-2721
Tel: 202-336-5500
Website: www.apa.org

American Academy of Child and Adolescent Psychiatry
3615 Wisconsin Avenue, NW
Washington, DC 20016-3007
Tel: 202-966-7300
Fax: 202-966-2891
Website: www.aacap.org

Anxiety Disorders Association of America (ADAA)
11900 Parklawn Drive
Suite 100
Rockville, MD 20852
Tel: 301-231-9350
Website: www.adaa.org

Chapter 19

Stress-Related Substance Abuse

In the aftermath of the terrorist attacks on New York City and Washington, DC, people across the country and abroad are struggling with the emotional impact of large-scale damage and loss of life, as well as the uncertainty of what will happen next. These are stressful times for all and may be particularly difficult times for people who are more vulnerable to substance abuse or may be recovering from an addiction. For example, we know that stress is one of the most powerful triggers for relapse in addicted individuals, even after long periods of abstinence. NIDA-supported ethnographers are already reporting increases in street sales of various drugs. Given that individuals may turn to drugs to cope with life's stressors, it is more important than ever that NIDA supports a comprehensive research portfolio that better informs how we prevent and treat drug abuse and addiction.

Stress and Relapse to Drug Abuse

Many clinicians and addiction medicine specialists suggest that stress is the number one cause of relapse to drug abuse, including smoking. Now, research is elucidating a scientific basis for these clinical observations. In both people and animals, stress leads to an increase in the brain levels of a peptide known as corticotropin releasing factor (CRF). The increased CRF levels in turn triggers a cascade of

"Stress and Substance Abuse: A Special Report," National Institute on Drug Abuse (NIDA), November 5, 2001.

biological responses. Animal and human research has implicated this cascade in the pathophysiology of both substance use disorders and Posttraumatic Stress Disorder (PTSD) (Jacobsen, et al. *Am J Psychiatry* 2001). Research also has shown that administering CRF or a chemical that mimics the action of CRF in animals produces increases in stress-related behaviors (Koob, Heinrichs. *Brain Research* 1999; Jones, et al. *Psychopharmacology* 1998). And, mice that lack a receptor for CRF (CRF1) have impaired stress responses and express less anxiety-related behavior (Smith, et al. Neuron 1998; Timpl, et al. *Nature Genetics* 1998). Furthermore, people subjected to chronic stress or those who show symptoms of PTSD often have hormonal responses that are not properly regulated and do not return to normal when the stress is over. This may make these individuals more prone to stress-related illnesses and may prompt patients to relapse to drug use.

Selected Research Findings on Stress and Drug Abuse; Stress and Relapse to Drug Abuse

- Studies have reported that individuals exposed to stress are more likely to abuse alcohol and other drugs or undergo relapse.

   Kosten TR, Rounsaville BJ, Kleber HD: A 2.5 year follow-up of depressions, life crises, and treatment effects on abstinence among opioid addicts. *Arch Gen Psychiatry* 1986; 43:733-739.

   Dawes MA, Antelman SM, Vanyukov MM, Giancola P, Tarter RE, Susman EJ, Mezzich A, Clark DB: Developmental sources of variation in liability to adolescent substance use disorders. *Drug and Alcohol Dependence* 2000; 61(1): 3-14.

   Sinha R, Fuse T, Aubin LR, O'Malley SS: Psychological stress, drug-related cues, and cocaine craving. *Psychopharmacology* 2000; 152:140-148.

- In an analysis of studies regarding factors that can lead to continued drug use among opiate addicts, high stress was found to predict continued drug use.

   Brewer DD, Catalano RF, Haggerty K, Gainey RR, Fleming CB: A meta-analysis of predictors of continued drug use during and after treatment for opiate addiction. *Addiction* 1998; 93:73-92.

- Research has shown that in animals not previously exposed to illicit substances, stressors increase vulnerability for drug self-administration.

  Piazza PV, Deminiere JM, Le Moal M, Simon H: Stress- and pharmacologically-induced behavioral sensitization increases vulnerability to acquisition of amphetamine self-administration. *Brain Research* 1990; 514:22-26.

- Acute stress can improve memory, whereas chronic stress can impair memory and may impair cognitive function.

  McEwan BS, Sapolsky RM: Stress and Cognitive Function. *Current Opinion in Neurobiology* 1995; 5:205-216.

- Research has shown that there is overlap between neurocircuits that respond to drugs and those that respond to stress.

  Piazza PV, Le Moal M: Pathophysiological basis of vulnerability to drug abuse: role of an interaction between stress, glucocorticoids, and dopaminergic neurons. *Annu Rev Pharmacol Toxicol* 1996; 36:359-378.

  Kreek MJ, Koob G: Drug dependence: Stress and dysregulation of brain reward pathways. *Drug Alcohol Depend* 1998; 51:23-47.

  Piazza PV, Le Moal M: The role of stress in drug self-administration. *Trends Pharmacol Sci* 1998; 19(2):67-74.

- Researchers have shown that, among drug-free cocaine abusers in treatment, exposure to personal stress situations led to consistent and significant increases in cocaine craving, along with activation of emotional stress and a physiological stress response. In another study of cocaine abusers in treatment, significant increases in cocaine and alcohol craving were observed with stress and drug cues imagery but not with neutral-relaxing imagery.

  Sinha R, Catapano D, O'Malley S: Stress-induced craving and stress response in cocaine dependent individuals. *Psychopharmacology* 1999; 142:343-351.

  Sinha R, Fuse T, Aubin LR, O'Malley SS: Psychological stress, drug-related cues, and cocaine craving. *Psychopharmacology* 2000; 152:140-148.

- A follow-up study of smokers who had completed a national smoking cessation program showed that there is a strong relationship between stress coping resources and the ability to sustain abstinence.

    Matheny KB, Weatherman KE: Predictors of Smoking Cessation and Maintenance. *Journal of Clinical Psychology* 1998; 54(2):223-235.

- Animal studies have shown that stress induces relapse to heroin, cocaine, alcohol, and nicotine self-administration.

    Shaham Y, Stewart J: Stress reinstates heroin-seeking in drug-free animals: an effect mimicking heroin, not withdrawal. *Psychopharmacology* 1995; 119:334-341.

    Erb S, Shaham Y, Stewart J: Stress reinstates cocaine-seeking behavior after prolonged extinction and a drug-free period. *Psychopharmacology* 1996; 128:408-412.

    Stewart J: Pathways to relapse: the neurobiology of drug- and stress-induced relapse to drug-taking. *Journal of Psychiatry & Neuroscience* 2000; 25:125-136

    Ahmed SH, Koob GF: Cocaine—but not food-seeking behavior is reinstated by stress after extinction. *Psychopharmacology* 1997; 132:289-295.

    Lê AD, Quan B, Juzytch W, Fletcher PJ, Joharchi N, Shaham Y: Reinstatement of alcohol-seeking by priming injections of alcohol and exposure to stress in rats. *Psychopharmacology* 1998; 135:169-174.

    Y. Buczek, Lê AD, Wang A, Stewart J, Shaham Y: Stress reinstates nicotine seeking but not sucrose solution seeking in rats. *Psychopharmacology* 1999; 144:183-188.

Posttraumatic Stress Disorder (PTSD) and Substance Abuse

Research shows that Posttraumatic Stress Disorder (PTSD), a psychiatric disorder, may develop in people after they experience or witness life-threatening events such as terrorist incidents, military combat, natural disasters, serious accidents, or violent personal assaults like rape. Research also shows that PTSD is a risk factor for substance abuse and addiction. Because the events that occurred on September 11, 2001, were experienced by thousands of people, as well as rescue workers in and around the vicinity of the attacks, and were televised to millions across the world, it is likely that some individuals may develop behavioral and emotional re-adjustment problems. Symptoms of PTSD can include re-experiencing the trauma; avoidance of people, places, and thoughts connected to the event; and arousal, which may include trouble sleeping, exaggerated startle response, and hypervigilance. People who develop such symptoms may be more prone to escape from the realities of the day by self-medicating with drugs (Khantzian. *Am J Psychiatry* 1985). In fact, clinical observations suggest that PTSD patients may use psychoactive substances without a physician's directions to relieve traumatic memories and other symptoms associated with PTSD (Brown. *Drug Alcohol Dependence* 1994).

Selected Research Findings on PTSD and Substance Use Disorders

* High rates of comorbidity of PTSD and substance use disorders were first reported in war-related studies, in which as many as 75% of combat veterans with lifetime PTSD also met criteria for alcohol abuse or dependence.

   Kulka RA, Schlenger WE, Fairbank JA, Hough RL, Jordan BK, Marmar CR, Weiss DS: *Trauma and the Vietnam War Generation: Report of Findings From the National Vietnam Veterans Readjustment Study*. New York, Brunner/Mazel, 1990.

* In a general population study, the overall lifetime rate of PTSD was 7.8%. Among men with a lifetime history of PTSD, 34.5% reported drug abuse or dependence at some point in their lives versus 15.1% of men without PTSD. For women, 26.9% with a lifetime history of PTSD reported drug abuse or dependence during their lives versus 7.6% of women without PTSD.

   Kessler RC, Sonnega A, Bromet E, Hughes M, Nelson CB: Posttraumatic stress disorder in the National Comorbidity Survey. *Arch Gen Psychiatry* 1995; 52:1048-1060.

* Among adolescents lifetime rates of PTSD have been found ranging from 6.3%, in a community sample of older adolescents, to 29.6%, in substance-dependent adolescents aged 15 to 19

receiving treatment. And, among the substance-dependent adolescents, 19.2% currently had PTSD.

Giaconia RM, Reinherz HZ, Silverman AB, Pakiz B, Frost AK, Cohen E: Traumas and posttraumatic stress disorder in a community population of older adolescents. *J Am Acad Child Adolesc Psychiatry* 1995; 34:1369-1379.

Deykin EY, Buka SL: Prevalence and risk factors for posttraumatic stress disorder among chemically dependent adolescents. *Am J Psychiatry* 1997; 154:752-757

- Persons with a lifetime history of PTSD have elevated rates of co-occurring disorders. Among men with PTSD during their lives, rates of co-occuring alcohol abuse or dependence are the highest, followed by depression, conduct disorder, and drug abuse or dependence. Among women with PTSD during their lives, rates of comorbid depression are highest, followed by some anxiety disorders, alcohol abuse or dependence, and drug abuse or dependence.

Kessler RC, Sonnega A, Bromet E, Hughes M, Nelson CB: Posttraumatic stress disorder in the National Comorbidity Survey. *Arch Gen Psychiatry* 1995; 52:1048-1060.

- Patients with PTSD commonly have substance use disorders, particularly abuse of and dependence on central nervous system depressants. This frequent co-occurrence of PTSD and substance use, suggests that the two are related.

Jacobsen LK, Southwick SM, Kosten TR: Substance Use Disorders in Patients with Posttraumatic Stress Disorder: A Review of the Literature. *Am J Psychiatry* 2001; 158(8):1184-1190.

- The most recent thinking about the association between PTSD and substance use disorders suggests that for combat veterans (Bremner. *Am J Psychiatry* 1996) and civilians (Chilcoat. *Arch Gen Psych* 1998), the onset of PTSD typically precedes the onset of substance use disorders.

Saxon AJ, Davis TM, Sloan KL, McKnight KM, McFall ME, Kivlahan DR: Trauma, Symptoms of Posttraumatic Stress Disorder, and Associated Problems Among Incarcerated Veterans. *Psychiatric Services* 2001; 52(7):959-964.

- In a study of 1007 young adults designed to look for a causal relationship between PTSD and substance use disorders, researchers found that when they reevaluated the participants at 3 and 5 years after an initial assessment, PTSD was associated with a more than 4-fold increased risk of drug abuse and dependence. The risk for abuse or dependence was highest for prescribed psychoactive drugs. The results suggest that drug abuse or dependence in persons with PTSD might be caused by efforts to self-medicate.

  Chilcoat HD, Breslau N: Postraumatic Stress Disorder and Drug Disorders. *Archives of General Psychiatry*, 1998; 55:913-917.

NIDA's Research Portfolio: Current and Future Directions

NIDA has a robust research portfolio that encompasses the overall role that stress can play in initiation of drug use and relapse to drug use, as well as the intensification of symptoms as a result of stress. For example, NIDA is pursuing research to develop better ways to teach drug addicts how to cope with stress, craving, and drug-associated stimuli. Also, NIDA supports research to help determine what makes some individuals more or less vulnerable to abuse and addiction, particularly after experiencing a traumatic event. More specifically, NIDA is supporting several projects studying PTSD and substance abuse. For example, NIDA-funded researchers are investigating the role of anxiety and anger in self-medication with benzodiazepines among people with PTSD; mapping the occurrence of PTSD and substance use symptoms and their impact across the life-span of Vietnam veterans; and determining the role of stress in relapse to drug use among cocaine dependent individuals with and without PTSD. NIDA's broad research portfolio regarding stress and PTSD will be particularly useful as we attempt to develop interventions to help people better cope with stress and trauma.

To respond to the demands of these changed times, NIDA is assigning very high priority to research on all aspects of the relationships between stress and substance abuse. We are seeking research proposals that can extend our knowledge of the impact of stress on vulnerability to drug use initiation, the transition from episodic to chronic drug abuse and addiction, and the complex phenomenon of relapse. In immediate response to the events of September 11, 2001, NIDA has awarded several grant supplements to researchers in the New York City region so that they can provide a rapid assessment of the impact on drug abuse and addiction prevalence rates and evaluate service delivery needs and opportunities. Grants awarded supplements include:

Hepatitis C in New York: Implications for HIV Prevention

This study will evaluate the impact of the World Trade Center Disaster on drug use patterns among injection and non-injection drug users in New York City over the short and long-term. Ethnographic interviews, focus groups, and participant observation with drug users and dealers will help researchers determine changes in drug use patterns and service availability in response to this public health disaster. This research will help us identify the extent to which persons using drugs and seeking treatment are in fact receiving treatment, and the response of the drug treatment community to this acute and then ongoing set of events.

Self-Report/Biological Measures Database of Drug Use

This funding will be used to build a large meta-analytic database comparing self-reports of drug, alcohol, and tobacco use with biological and other indicators of drug use.

HIV Risk and Club Drugs Among Men—A Two City Comparison

Researchers will rapidly assess the aftermath of the World Trade Center attack among men who have sex with men who use club drugs, and two contrasting and vulnerable populations, injection drug users and rescue workers. This supplemental study will use ethnographic methods developed in the parent study to assess acute and short-term changes in drug use patterns, coping strategies of individuals vulnerable to higher drug use, and changes in HIV-related risk behaviors.

Expanded Syringe Access Program—NY Evaluation

This study will determine the prevalence and correlates of smoking, alcohol, and marijuana use among residents of New York City following the September 11, attacks on that city. The researchers will attempt to determine the association, if any, between drug use patterns and disaster-event-experiences (proximity to event, involvement of friends/relatives) one and six months after the disaster. Researchers will include demographics about the populations studied and identify the prevalence of psychological distress and early PTSD among New York City residents.

Additional Research

- NIDA will pursue further research to determine whether chronic drug abuse alters the individual's ability to cope with stress or makes individuals more vulnerable to stress-induced relapse.

- NIDA will use neuroimaging technologies to clarify the neurochemical links between stress, addiction, and relapse. Identifying these neural circuits can be advantageous as we develop new targets for treatment.

- NIDA will further investigate the role of CRF and CRF receptors in stress and initiation of and relapse to drug use, and will explore the use of CRF antagonists, chemicals that block the action of CRF, as potential compounds to treat addiction.

Part Four

Physical Effects of Stress

Chapter 20

The Biology of Stress

The dashboard clock reads 7:55 a.m. and you're trapped in traffic, miles from your office. Despite leaving earlier than usual, there is absolutely no chance you'll arrive on time for that important 8:00 a.m. meeting. In addition to coping with such routine, everyday annoyances of our busy lives, 9 out of 10 of us will experience a much more serious stressor—a life-threatening event such as a car accident, or an act of personal violence such as a rape or mugging. Fifty percent of us will encounter two such events.

In all these instances, our brain snaps to attention, preparing the rest of the body for the potential consequences of the insult at hand. Blood pressure climbs. The heart pumps more blood, chock full of surging levels of stress hormones. The so-called "fight-or-flight" response has commenced.

And while such compensatory mechanisms help us (or any organism) cope with an immediate crisis, scientists are discovering that longer-term perturbations also occur—in the brain and elsewhere throughout the body—following a stressful and/or traumatic event. What's more, individuals may be significantly and inherently differ-

This chapter includes "Stress—It Might Be Even Worse Than You Think," a summary of the conference "Biology of Stress" by Alison Davis co-sponsored by the Office of Behavioral and Social Sciences Research (OBSSR) and National Institute of General Medical Sciences (NIGMS), and "Social Support, Stress and the Common Cold," a summary of a presentation by Sheldon Cohen, Ph.D. Carnegie Mellon University by Susan M. Persons, *NIH Record*, December 2, 1997, Office of Behavioral and Social Sciences Research (OBSSR).

ent in the ways they deal with stress, and may even be differentially vulnerable to its effects.

"We don't walk into trauma the same way. . .and we don't walk out of trauma the same way," said Dr. Rachel Yehuda, a research psychologist at Mount Sinai School of Medicine in New York City, at a recent National Institutes of Health (NIH) symposium on the biology of stress. Furthermore, she emphasized, not all stress is the same.

Yehuda was one of a dozen leading scientists studying the biological impacts of stress on the body who presented talks at the all-day meeting, held on February 4, 1999 and co-sponsored by the National Institute of General Medical Sciences (NIGMS) and the NIH Office of Behavioral and Social Sciences Research (OBSSR). A prominent theme that emerged from the day's presentations was that reactions to stress vary widely, and that—as appears to be the case for much of biology—both behavioral and physiological outcomes of stressful events arise from a complex interplay between genes and the environment.

Stress, Hostility, Aggression Worsen Heart Disease: Stress and the Cardiovascular System

Researchers are discovering that the impact of stress, anger, and other of life's unpleasantries may have far-reaching effects on cardiovascular health.

Stress, Sex, and Atherosclerosis, Dr. Jay Kaplan, Wake Forest University

When fed a high-fat, "cheeseburger diet," macaque monkeys in an unstable social environment were twice as likely than their socially stable peers fed a leaner diet to develop atherosclerosis—so-called hardening of the arteries, which is a strong impetus for the occurrence of serious cardiovascular complications such as heart attack and stroke. Those are the conclusions of Dr. Jay Kaplan, who has found that while "monkeys spend most of their time in social groups doing nothing," dominant male monkeys exhibit large changes in heart rate in response to what might seem to be minor perturbations in their social setting, such as being touched or spending short periods alone. (Researchers who study monkeys classify them behaviorally into two groups: dominant and subordinate.) Kaplan found that pre-treating the dominant males fed the cheeseburger-equivalent diet "like [the diet] we eat," with the heart-protective drug propranolol decreased the number of fatty streaks in those animals' blood vessels. (Propranolol and other such "beta-blockers" blunt the body's response to the flight-or-flight hormones norepinephrine and epinephrine.)

Kaplan, curious as to the effects of sex hormones on heart disease, also studied female monkeys. Interestingly, Kaplan found that premenopausal dominant female monkeys were less likely to develop atherosclerosis. Through a series of experiments, Kaplan has found that, in dominant female monkeys estrogen performs a protective role against the development of coronary artery disease. Moreover, behaviorally subordinate females had significantly impaired ovarian function. What about women with menstrual problems? Kaplan said there is currently some preliminary data from a study in humans to suggest a link between ovarian dysfunction and the propensity for developing coronary heart disease.

Selected References

Kaplan J, Manuck. Monkeys, aggression, and the pathobiology of atherosclerosis. *Aggr. Behav.* 1998; 24:323-34.

Kaplan J et al. Psychosocial factors, sex differences, and atherosclerosis: Lessons from animal models. *Psychosom Med* 1996; 58:598-611.

Kaplan J et al. Cerebrospinal fluid monoaminergic metabolites differ in wild anubis and hybrid baboons: possible relationships to life history and behavior. *Neuropsychopharmacology* 1999.

Rozanskik, Blumenthal, Kaplan J. Impact of psychological factors on the pathogenesis of cardiovascular disease and implications for therapy. *Circulation* 1999.

Stress as an Acute Trigger of Cardiac Events, Dr. David Krantz, Uniformed Services University of the Health Sciences

Could it be that ordinary, run-of-the-mill activities—as innocuous as talking on the telephone or as strenuous as climbing the stairs—might spell trouble for the heart? Dr. David Krantz thinks so. Krantz discussed evidence for how everyday stressful events can "push" susceptible people over a certain threshold for developing symptomatic heart disease, thus precipitating a heart attack. Other factors, of course, such as diet, smoking, genes, and exercise, all play important roles in setting that threshold.

Myocardial infarctions (heart attacks) are caused by a sudden loss of blood flow to the heart. This can be provoked by a crimped blood-and-oxygen-supplying vessel or by a physical blockage, say from plaque buildup characteristic of atherosclerosis. Whatever the cause, such a lack of oxygen is called ischemia. Ischemia can be detected by telltale changes in an electrical recording of heart activity (an EKG) or by actually looking at the vessels feeding the heart. New technologies have made it ever easier to view blockages with modified x-ray techniques called angiograms. Using such techniques, Krantz and his colleagues performed a study in which they asked patients wearing heart rhythm monitors to record "what they're doing and feeling" every day, and then looked for signs of ischemia. They discovered that many incidents of ischemia are silent—that is, producing no outright symptoms. Most events also occur in the morning, they found, and there was a detectable association between ischemia and mental and emotional activities. Importantly, Krantz noted that many such silent ischemia events go unnoticed via standard hospital tests, such as EKG testing. Yet by knowing about patients' susceptibility to these events, Krantz said, their physicians might be better able to predict their patients' risk for trouble. Better yet, Krantz suggested, they might actually do something about it, such as try to keep a lid on the stress in their lives. To that end, he cited a recent study conducted at Duke University showing that practicing stress management techniques can lessen the occurrence of heart problems in cardiac patients with inadequate blood flow to the heart.

Selected References

Krantz DS, Kop WJ, Santiago HT, Gottdiener JS. Mental stress as a trigger for myocardial ischemia and infarction. *Cardiology Clinics* 1996, 14(2): 271-87.

Gabbay FH, Krantz DS, Hedges SM, Kop WJ, Klein J, Gottdiener JS, Rozanski A. Triggers of daily life myocardial ischemia in patients with coronary artery disease: Physical and mental activities, anger, and smoking. *Journal of the American College of Cardiology* 1996, 27:585-92.

Jiang W, Babyak M, Krantz DS, Waugh RA, Coleman E, Hanson MM, Frid DJ, McNulty S., Morris JJ, O'Connor CM, Blumenthal JA. Mental stress-induced myocardial ischemia and cardiac events. *Journal of the American Medical Association* 1996, 275: 1651-6.

Krantz DS, Kop WJ, Gabbay FH, Rozanski A, Barnard M, Klein J, Pardo Y, Gottdiener JS. Circadian variation of ambulatory myocardial ischemia: Triggering by daily activities and evidence for an endogenous circadian component. *Circulation* 1996, 93:1364-71.

Hostility and Increased Risk of Cardiovascular Disease and All-Cause Mortality: Biological Mechanisms and Neurobiological Substrates, Dr. Redford Williams, Duke University

Social instability, improper diet, mental stress—studies suggest that all can provoke an already unhealthy cardiovascular system to fail. Other dangerous spurs, research by Dr. Redford Williams has shown, are hostility and anger. Years ago, Williams began studying the now-infamous "type-A" behavior as a risk for coronary disease. In the years since, Williams and others have pinpointed hostility in particular as being the most "toxic component" of type-A behavior. Of course, not all type-A personalities are necessarily hostile. Nevertheless, hostility, especially in combination with other risk factors, such as depression, job strain, and low socioeconomic status, can precipitate heart disease, cancer, and even death.

Nearly a quarter century ago, Williams reported, a group of college freshman were administered a psychological test that identified those with "high hostility" personality profile. When tested years later, at age 42, the same individuals were more likely to consume more caffeine, alcohol, and tobacco; to weigh more; and to have higher cholesterol levels than their "low-hostility" peers. Williams and his colleagues have begun to try to pin down the molecular culprits whereby hostility provokes and/or causes heart disease. Among other things, another of the fight-or-flight hormones, epinephrine, is notably higher in "high-hostility" subjects early in the morning (which is also the time when other hormones are also naturally elevated due to the regularity of circadian biological rhythms). Most heart attacks occur between 6:00 a.m. and noon. Williams' work, and that of others, has also pointed an incriminating finger at the neurotransmitter serotonin, which appears, when low, to be involved in the establishment and maintenance of a variety of behavioral states and tendencies, such as substance abuse.

During the question-and-answer period, all three speakers emphasized the impact that psychosocial intervention—for instance, stress management and coping skills training—can have on biological functioning, especially protection against heart disease. "We need to distribute psychosocial interventions [as we do] drugs," Williams urged.

Selected References

Barefoot JC, Dahlstrom WG, Williams RB. Hostility, CHD incidence and total mortality: A 25-year follow-up study of 255 physicians. *Psychosom Med* 1983, 45:59-63.

Barefoot JC, Peterson BL, Dahlstrom WG, Siegler IC, Anderson NB, Williams Jr., RB. Hostility patterns and health implications: Correlates of Cook-Medley Hostility scale scores in a national survey. *Health Psychology* 1991, 10(1):18-24.

Williams RB. Lower socioeconomic status and increased mortality: Early childhood roots and the potential for successful interventions. *Journal of the American Medical Association* 1998, 279:1745-6.

Williams RB, Chesney MA. Psychosocial factors and prognosis in established coronary artery disease: The need for research on interventions. *Journal of the American Medical Association* 1993, 270:1860-1.

Williams RB et al. Type A behavior, hostility, and coronary atherosclerosis. *Psychosom Med* 1980, 42:539-49.

Not Just the Same Old Hormones: Stress and Endocrinology and Metabolism

The ebb and flow of hormones coursing through the blood impacts many of the body's organ systems.

Maternal Touch: A Prime Regulator for Growth-Related Gene Expression, Dr. Saul Schanberg, Duke University

Against the backdrop of a slide of a nursing mother, Dr. Saul Schanberg told the audience about the profound effects a mother has on her developing child. Schanberg's talk mostly focused on his research with rat pups, but Schanberg—a pediatrician by training—also buttressed the rodent data with results of human studies on the effect of physical contact on premature infants in neonatal wards. Separation from the mother, Schanberg said in jest, "is what some people consider a stress." So much so, Schanberg said in referring to the rat pup data, that when the pup realizes that "mother is not there," it enters into a survivalist state, conserving energy by shifting to a non-growing metabolic state. Through careful observation, Schanberg and his group narrowed down the particulars of that special "maternal touch" to mothers' licking the rat pups during a critical developmental window: the first 20 days of a rat's life. Interestingly, day 22 is when a mother usually leaves her rat pups to fend for themselves. Through a series of molecular analyses, Schanberg has begun to correlate specific changes in the expression of select genes, one of which controls the production of an enzyme (ornithine decarboxylase) that performs cellular housekeeping functions.

Similar studies with human babies are consistent with the rat data, showing that massaging "preemies" in neonatal hospital wards led to a 46 percent increase in growth rate, as well as a perceived decrease in stress-correlated behaviors (such as clenched fists and grimacing).

Selected References

Field TM., Schanberg SM, Scafidi F, Bauer CR, Vega-Lahr N, Garcia R, Nystrom J, Kuhn CM. Tactile/Kinesthetic Stimulation Effects on Pre-term Neonates. *Pediatrics* 1986, 77:654-8.

Kuhn CM., Schanberg SM, Field TM, Symanski R, Zimmermann E, Scafidi F, Roberts J. Tactile-kinetic Stimulation effects on Symapthetic and Adrenocortical Function in Pre-term Infants. *Journal of Pediatrics* 1991, 119:434-40.

Wang S, Bartolome JV, Schanberg SM. Neonatal Deprivation of Maternal Touch May Suppress Ornithine Decarboxylase Via Downregulation of the Protooncogenes C-Myc and Max. *Journal of Neuroscience.* 1996, 16(2):836-42.

Kuhn CM, Schanberg SM. Responses to Maternal Separation: Mechanisms and Mediators. Int. *J. Devl. Neuroscience* 1998, 16:261-9.

Glycemic Responsivity to Stress in Individuals Predisposed to Type 2 Diabetes, Dr. Richard Surwit, Duke University

Dr. Richard Surwit and his colleagues have investigated a diabetic study group, the Pima Indians of Arizona. Fifty percent of this population becomes obese and develops Type 2 (non-insulin-dependent) diabetes before their 30th birthday. Such a population can be analyzed to evaluate behavioral/pyschosocial effects on a particular health state (diabetes/obesity in this case), since such a high fraction of the population develops the disease and is very similar when compared otherwise (environment, diet, and genes, for example). Surwit and his colleagues found that stress—in the form of a challenging mathematics task—had an impact on elevating blood sugar in Pimas.

Just like people, mice who eat a high-fat, high-sugar diet can develop diet-induced (Type 2) diabetes. Reinforcing the notion that genes play an important role, certain breeds are much more prone to develop diabetes than others. Surwit has created such a strain of obese/diabetic mice, and he is using it to tease out the molecular causes and influences of diabetes. Already, he has identified two related genes whose protein products help control general metabolism that appear to be expressed in obese, diabetic mice and not in lean, healthy control mice.

Selected References

Surwit RS, Kuhn CM, Cochrane C, McCubbin JA, Feinglos MN. Diet-induced type II diabetes in C57BL/6J mice. *Diabetes*, 1988, 37:1163-7.

Mills E, Kuhn CM, Feinglos MN, Surwit RS. Hypertension in the C57BL/6J mouse model of non-insulin dependent diabetes mellitus. *American Journal of Physiology* 1993, 264 (Regulatory Integrative Comp. Physiol. 330: R73-R78.

Esposito-del Puente A, Lillioja S, Bogardus C, McCubbin JA, Feinglos MN, Kuhn CM, Surwit RS. Glycemic response to stress is altered in euglycemic Pima Indians. *International Journal of Obesity,* 1994, 18: 766-70.

Fleury C, Neverova M, Collins S, Raimbault S, Champign O, Levi-Meyrueis C, Bouillaud F, Seldin MF, Surwit RS, Ricquier D, and Warden CH. Uncoupling protein-2: A novel candidate thermogenic protein linked to obesity and insulin resistance. *Nature Genetics* 1997, 15:269-72.

Surwit RS, Wang S, Petro AE, Sanchis D, Raimbault S, Ricquier D, Collins S. Diet-induced changes in uncoupling proteins in obesity-prone and obesity-resistant strains of mice. *Proc. Nation. Acad. Sci.* 1998, 95:4061-5.

Stress Effects on Serum Lipoprotein Concentrations, Dr. Catherine Stoney, Ohio State University

Our bodies are hardly static collections of the proteins, fats, and sugars that we ingest. Rather, throughout the course of an ordinary day, levels of all of these substances fluctuate widely. A case in point is the level of circulating fat (blood lipids). Changes in the amount of cholesterol and another lipid type called triglycerides go up and down by 20 or so percent, reported Dr. Catherine Stoney, who noted that pervasive, long-term stressors increased blood levels of cholesterol, which can put people at risk for developing atherosclerosis and further heart disease. Stoney found that the bigger the perceived stress—caused, for example by a major earthquake—the greater the fluctuations in blood lipid levels, and the effects appeared to be completely independent of changes in other health behaviors. "It is not just poor dietary and exercise habits that accompany [such] profound stressors that [cause] the increases in cholesterol," Stoney emphasized. Stoney has also conducted studies in which she has examined the effects of much shorter and milder forms of stress—the inevitable kind we all experience in everyday life. Studying the consequences of so-called "short-term" stress (asking people to count backwards by increments of 13), Stoney detected increases in a host of molecules considered potentially dangerous to maintaining optimal heart health: cholesterol, especially low-density lipoproteins (LDLs, the "bad" form of cholesterol), triglycerides, and others. Contrary to the usual assumption that such levels rise due to enhanced concentration of the blood, Stoney proposed a different explanation: that stress (the shortterm variety, at least) leads to a delayed processing and clearance of fats: triglycerides in particular.

Selected References

Stoney CM, Bausserman L, Niaura R, Marcus B, Flynn M. Lipid reactivity to stress: I. Comparison of chronic and acute stress responses in middle-aged airline pilots. *Health Psychology* 1999.

Stoney CM, Bausserman L, Niaura R, Marcus B, Flynn M. Lipid reactivity to stress: II. Biological and behavioral influences. *Health Psychology* 1999.

The Hypothalamic-Pituitary-Adrenal Axis Paradox in PTSD, Dr. Rachel Yehuda, Mount Sinai School of Medicine

Counting backwards by 13 may qualify as a stressful exercise for many, but such mental gymnastics are merely an annoyance when compared to what researchers call "extreme" stress or trauma: being raped or assaulted, subjected to childhood sexual abuse, or involved in a motor vehicle crash. As a consequence of such a harrowing experience, 1 in 4 people will develop post-traumatic stress disorder (PTSD), according to Dr. Rachel Yehuda. Typified by the occurrence of flashbacks, nightmares and other sleep problems, emotional outbursts or numbness, and memory and concentration difficulties, PTSD is indeed a disabling condition. The problem, described Yehuda, is that "the stress doesn't go away."

Yehuda's research has shown that blood levels of certain stress hormones, especially one called cortisol, are markedly low in people with PTSD. And, she found, they are lowest in those people witnessing (or participating in) the most severely stressful events, such as being in combat during the Vietnam War. Yehuda has also studied

Holocaust survivors and found similarly low levels of cortisol. In probing the root causes of PTSD, Yehuda has unearthed some interesting biology. Her studies show that the body's master stress control circuit, called the hypothalamic-pituitary-adrenal (HPA) axis, appears to have been re-set in PTSD victims compared to healthy control subjects. In other words, her research suggests, the HPA axis, which connects the brain to the hormone-secreting adrenal glands, are ultra-sensitive in people with PTSD, with a higher-than-normal level of proteins called glucocorticoid receptors, ultimately leading to an inappropriately meager production of cortisol. A potentially utilitarian outcome of Yehuda's research is that measuring a person's immediate (up to 1 hour after the traumatic event) response level can be predictive of how likely that person is to develop PTSD. However useful that might be, Yehuda emphasized, such a strategy may be difficult to implement.

Selected References

Yehuda R, McFarlane. Conflict between current knowledge about posttraumatic stress disorder and its original conceptual basis. *Am J Psychiatry* 1995:1705-13.

Yehuda R. Sensitization of the hypothalamic-pituitary-adrenal axis in posttraumatic stress disorder: In: Yehuda R, McFarlane AC, editors. *Psychobiology of posttraumatic stress disorder*, New York: The New York Academy of Sciences, pp. 57-75.

Yehuda R, McFalane AC, Shalev AY. Predicting the Development of posttraumatic stress disorder from the acute response to a traumatic event. *Biological Psychiatry* 1998: 44:1305-13.

Yehuda R; and Sapolsky R. Stress and glucocorticoid. *Science* 1997, 275:1662-3.

Stress and the Endocrine Immune Interface, Dr. William Malarkey, Ohio State University

Despite the fact that the body has distinctly functioning systems—such as the nervous system, the cardiovascular system, and the immune system—in reality all such systems are intertwined. Indeed, a prevailing theme in research on the effects of stress on physiology is that the situation is complex. Dr. William Malarkey reinforced that very notion in his talk. Malarkey has found that lymphocytes (immune cells) produce the hormones prolactin (which, among other things, helps mothers produce breast milk) and growth hormone, two proteins not typically associated with either the immune system or physiological responses to stress. Moreover, he has discovered that the amount of lymphocyte-manufactured growth hormone declines with age and as a result of chronic stress (in his model, caregivers of people with Alzheimer's Disease). Since growth hormone levels are set in part by stress hormones such as norepinephrine and cortisol, stressful situations (in which levels of these hormones are typically elevated) may work to influence the immune system. To that end, Malarkey and his colleagues (including Dr. Ron Glaser, Ohio State University) have observed diminished immune responses (as reflected by the time it takes to produce antibodies after a flu shot) in chronically stressed populations.

Selected References

Varma S, Sabharwal P, Sheridan JF, Malarkey WB. Growth hormone secretion by human peripheral blood mononuclear cells detected by an enzyme linked immunoplaque assay. *J Clin Endocrinol Metab* 1993, 76:49-53.

Wu H, Devi R, Malarkey WB. Expression and localization of prolactin mRNA in the human immune system. *Endocrinology* 1996, 137:349-53.

Wu H, Wang J, Cacioppo JT, Glaser R, Kiecolt-Glaser JK, Malarkey WB. Chronic stress associated with spousal caregiving of patients with dementia is associated with downregulation of B-lymphocyte GH mRNA. *Journal of Gerontology: Medical Sciences* 1999.

This Is Your Brain on Stress: Stress and the Brain

A jalapeno pepper-sized region of the brain called the hippocampus houses both short- and long-term memories—remembrances of what you ate for breakfast just a few hours ago as well as what flavor of birthday cake you had at your 10th birthday party. The region may also be particularly vulnerable to stress.

Protective and Damaging Effects of Stress Mediators, Dr. Bruce McEwen, Rockefeller University

The hippocampal formation, a brain region that contains the hippocampus and an area called the dentate gyrus, is studded with proteins that receive and transmit the signals of stress hormones called glucocorticoids. Dr. Bruce McEwen framed his talk around that finding, which was made by his group years ago. The dentate gyrus is particularly susceptible to the effects of stress, which are mediated largely through glucocorticoid receptor signaling. Chronic stress, aging, and/or compromised blood flow, McEwen reported, can all lead to a diminution of hippocampal functioning, a primary example of which is spatial and declarative memory. McEwen described this type of memory by reciting a familiar Gary Larsen phrase, "All forest animals, to this very day, remember exactly where they were and what they were doing when they heard that Bambi's mother had been shot." McEwen discussed data showing that the ability of the dentate gyrus to "bounce back" (regenerate and re-sprout neuronal connections) is hampered as a consequence of chronic stress. McEwen also cited data revealing that the dentate gyrus and the hippocampus have begun to atrophy in depressed patients, and in people with PTSD, as well as during the normal aging process. In fact, a recent paper was published reporting that cortisol levels during aging are elevated in individuals with hippocampal atrophy and specific memory impairments associated with the brain region. The big question, McEwen said, is how much of this atrophy reflects irreversible damage and how much represents a reversible, and perhaps treatable, form of brain dysfunction.

Selected References

McEwen BS. Protective and damaging effects of stress mediators. *New England Journal of Medicine* 1998, 238:171-9.

McEwen BS. Possible mechanisms for atrophy of the human hippocampus. *Molecular Psychiatry* 1997, 2:255-62.

McEwen BS, Sapolsky RM. Stress and cognitive function. *Current Opinion in Neurobiology* 1995, 5:205-16.

Magarinos AM, McEwen BS, Flugge G, Fuchs E. Chronic Psychosocial Stress Causes Apical Dendritic Atrophy of Hippocampal CA3 Pyramidal Neurons in Subordinate Tree Shrews. *Journal of Neuroscience* 1996, 16: 3534-40.

Gould E, Tanapat P, McEwen BS, Flugge G, Fuchs E. Proliferation of granule cell precursors in the dentate gyrus of adult monkeys is diminished by stress. *Proc. Natl. Acad. Sci. USA* 1998, 95: 3168-71.

Lupien SJ, de Leon M, de Santi S, Convit A, Tarshish C, Nair NPV, Thakur M, McEwen BS, Hauger RL, Meaney MJ. Cortisol Levels during human aging predict hippocampal atrophy and memory deficits. *Nature Neuroscience* 1998, 1:69-73.

Early Life Events Influence Vulnerability to Stress-Induced Illness: Freud Goes Molecular, Dr. Michael Meaney, McGill University

Continuing with the hippocampal theme, Dr. Michael Meaney went on to illustrate the importance of the same brain region in his talk. Meaney's findings echo those presented by Dr. Saul Schanberg, dealing with the remarkable influence of maternal handling on the general health and well-being of rat pups as they age. Meaney's studies show that rat pups handled during a critical developmental window (the first 3 weeks of life, which also correlates with the sculpting of the dentate gyrus) have a permanent increase in the number of glucocorticoid receptors in the hippocampus. Meaney's group has begun to analyze the molecular determinants of the "handling effect" (mothers extensively lick and groom their young pups), and so far has pinpointed the chemical messenger serotonin as a key player. Perhaps most remarkable is the long-lasting nature of such handling effects. Meaney's results suggest that the primary means for cementing the handling effect is through the mothers themselves. His data show that mothers behave differently toward handled pups than they do toward their non-handled counterparts. In this way, the behavior is passed on to the next generation, Meaney said. What's more, he added, pups that received more licking and grooming during those critical early days were much more able to deal effectively with stress later in life.

Selected References

Liu D, Tannenbaum B, Caldji C, Francis D, Freedman A, Sharma S, Pearson D, Plotsky PM, Meaney MJ. Moms, Pups, Glucocorticoid Receptor Gene Expression and Responses to Stress. *Science* 1997, 277:1659-62.

Caldji C, Tannenbaum B, Sharma S, Francis D, Plotsky PM, Meaney MJ. *Maternal care during infancy regulates the development of neural systems mediating the expression of behavioral fearfulness in adulthood in the rat.* Proceedings of the National Academy of Sciences 1998, 95: 5335-40.

Stressed Out and Sick: Stress and the Immune System

Reducing stress may also protect people from a variety of ills, and could even prompt a speedier immune response.

Stress and Wound Healing, Dr. Janice Kiecolt-Glaser, Ohio State University

Time may heal all wounds, but stress doesn't. That is the conclusion of a set of studies performed by Dr. Janice Kiecolt-Glaser, in collaboration with Dr. Ron Glaser on the impact of stress on wound healing. Employing second-year medical and dental students as subjects, Kiecolt-Glaser and her colleagues inflicted minor ("not very painful") wounds before and after periods of stress.

What signifies stress to a student? Exams, of course. Kiecolt-Glaser reported that exam stress negatively impacted various immune-related processes, ranging from a delay in the ability to produce antibodies to a Hepatitis B shot to the time it took to heal a minor mouth or arm wound. While primarily discussing the student/healing model, Kiecolt-Glaser also described data in which chronic stress of another sort (caring for a person with a long-term illness) also delayed the wound healing response by approximately 25 percent.

Since wound healing is a primary factor determining hospital stay in post-surgery patients, Kiecolt-Glaser also mentioned studies conducted by others that suggest that a very moderate level of behavioral intervention aimed at reducing stress ("reading a pamphlet or watching a video about the procedure the night before surgery") has been shown to have a substantial impact on the outcome of surgery, leading in some cases to a shorter recovery period in the hospital.

Selected References

Kiecolt-Glaser JK, Marucha PT, Malarkey WB, Mercado AM, Glaser R. Slowing of wound healing by psychological stress. *Lancet* 1995, 346:1194-6.

Marucha PT, Kiecolt-Glaser JK, Favagehi M. Mucosal wound healing is impaired by examination stress. *Psychosom Med* 1998, 60:3625.

Kiecolt-Glaser JK, Page GG, Marucha PT, MacCallum RC, Glaser R. Psychological influences on surgical recovery: Perspectives from psychoneuroimmunology. *American Psychologist* 1998,53:1209-18.

Glaser R, Kiecolt-Glaser JK. Stress-associated immune modulation: relevance to viral infections and chronic fatigule syndrome. *American Journal of Medicine* 1998, 105: (3a) 35s-42s.

Kiecolt-Glaser JK, Glaser R, Gravenstein S, Malarkey WB, Sheridan J. Chronic stress alters the immune respnse to influenza virus vaccine in older adults. *Proc. Natl. Acad. Sci.* 1996, 93: 3043-7.

Glaser R, Kiecolt-Glaser JK, Bonneau R, Malarkey W, Hughes J. Stress-induced modulation of the immune response to recombinant hepatitis B vaccine. *Psychosom Med* 1992, 54:22-9.

Stress Responses and Management in HIV/AIDS, Dr. Neil Schneiderman, University of Miami

Being diagnosed with a disease, especially an incurable one, is no doubt a significant life stressor. Dr. Neil Schneiderman wrapped up the day's talks by describing his work with newly diagnosed HIV-positive men. In his talk, Schneiderman detailed his studies over the past decade probing the effects of stress management on this population, which is greatly at risk for developing both psychological and physical health problems. Schneiderman began his study in the mid-1980s, when the social stigma for being HIV-positive was already high. He offered confidential testing for the virus, followed by counseling. Denial, Schneiderman reported, was a common response to learning of HIV infection, and the denial itself exacerbated disease progression. He also investigated the impact of behavioral intervention on the health and well-being of the HIV-positive subjects. As a result of those studies, Schneiderman concludes that stress management can indeed lessen the impact of the disease by diminishing some HIV-related complications, such as the emergence and reoccurrence of other (opportunistic) viral infections in HIV-positive men.

Selected References

Schneiderman N. Behavioral medicine and the management of HIV/AIDS. International *Journal of Behavioral Medicine* 1999, 6:2-14.

Lutgendorf S, Antoni MH, Ironson G, Starr K, Costello N, Zuckerman M, Klimas N, Fletcher MA, Schneiderman N. Changes in cognitive coping skills and social support mediate distress outcomes in symptomatic HIV-seropositive gay men during a cognitive behavioral stress management intervention. *Psychosom Med* 1998, 60:204-14.

Lutgendorf S, Antoni M, Ironson G, Klimas N, Starr K, Schneiderman N, McCabe P, Cleven K, Fletcher MA. Cognitive behavioral stress management decreases dysphoric mood and Herpes Simplex Virus Type-2 antibody titers in symptomatic HIV seropositive gay men. *Journal of Consulting and Clinical Psychology* 1997, 65:31-43.

Ironson G, Friedman A, Klimas N, Antoni M, Fletcher MA, LaPerriere A, Simoneau J, Schneiderman N. Distress, denial, and low adherence to behavioral interventions predict faster disease progression in HIV-1 infected gay men. *International Journal of Behavioral Medicine* 1994, 1:90-105.

Social Support, Stress, and the Common Cold

Friends are good medicine, especially during cold season. A study presented by Dr. Sheldon Cohen at a recent NIH Office of Behavioral and Social Sciences Research (OBSSR) seminar has found that diverse ties to friends, family, work, and community help to reduce susceptibility to upper respiratory illness. Although chicken soup may provide soothing relief to cold symptoms, it is the friend who brings you the soup that is proving to be important in maintaining health.

"Psychological and social factors play an important role in determining our resistance to upper respiratory illness," reported Cohen. For the past 10 years, Cohen, professor of psychology at Carnegie Mellon University and adjunct professor of pathology and psychiatry at the University of Pittsburgh School of Medicine, has been studying the effects of psychological stress and social support on immunity and susceptibility to infectious disease. At the OBSSR seminar, Cohen described his study of 276 healthy volunteers ages 18 to 55, who were given nasal drops containing viruses that cause a common cold. "Only 40 percent of those exposed to a virus actually develop a clinical illness," Cohen said.

"Our work has shown that those having more types of social relationships including family but also neighbors, friends, work mates, and members of religious and social groups were less likely to develop a cold when exposed to a rhinovirus." Those who had 1-3 types of social relationships were over 4 times more likely to develop a cold than those with 6 or more types. "Not only were they less susceptible to developing colds, they produced less mucus, were more effective in mucocilliary clearance of the nasal passage, and shed less virus," Cohen stated. In addition, "network diversity was a more important determinant of susceptibility than the total number of people in one's social network," he said.

The association between social network diversity and colds occurred in both those who entered the study with and without antibody to the experimental viruses. Cohen also found that health practices including smoking, alcohol consumption, sleep quality, exercise, and dietary intake of vitamin C were also associated with susceptibility to illness. However, differences in health practices were not responsible for the relationship between diverse social networks and susceptibility.

Cohen also discussed his work on the relationship of psychological stress and susceptibility to upper respiratory infections. Again, study participants who completed questionnaires assessing psychological stress were subsequently given nasal drops containing respiratory viruses. "In all three studies, we found that those reporting higher levels of stress before exposure to the virus were more likely to develop respiratory illness," Cohen said. "We have found stress is associated with increased susceptibility to illness induced by 7 different viruses, including 6 cold viruses and an influenza virus."

However, not every stressful event increases the risk of illness. "The longer the duration of the stressful event the greater the risk," according to Cohen. For example, an argument with your spouse that is resolved in a few days has little effect. However, if the marital discord lasts a month or longer, there is a substantial increase in the risk of illness. "The type of stress also plays an important role in disease susceptibility. Job loss and divorce produced the most serious threat to the individual, whereas other less significant life challenges may not have the same impact," Cohen said.

The association between psychological stress and illness could not be explained by differences in stressed and non-stressed people in their demographics, allergic status, weight, or height. Nor did the season, viral specific antibody status before virus-exposure, nor their health behaviors provide an explanation. "The relation between stress and susceptibility is probably attributable to stress induced changes in the immune function," Cohen said. "Our most recent work is moving toward identifying the relevant components of immunity with stress-induced changes in the production of proinflammatory cytokines as the most likely culprit."

Chapter 21

The Brain and Stress

Stress and the Developing Brain

It is well known that the early months and years of life are critical for brain development. But the question remains: just how do early influences act on the brain to promote or challenge the developmental process? Research has suggested that many both positive and negative experiences, chronic stressors, and various other environmental factors may affect a young child's developing brain. And now, studies involving animals are revealing in greater detail how this may occur.

One important line of research has focused on brain systems that control stress hormones—cortisol, for example.[1,2] Cortisol and other stress hormones play an important role in emergencies: they help our bodies make energy available to enable effective responses, temporarily suppress the immune response, and sharpen attention. However, a number of studies conducted in people with depression indicate that excess cortisol released over a long time span may have many negative consequences for health.[3,4,5] Excess cortisol may cause shrinking of the

---

"Stress and the Developing Brain," National Institute of Mental Health (NIMH), NIH Publication No. 01-4603, updated: January 2001; "The Emotional Brain," from Lessons from Fear Conditioning by Mary Lynn Hendrix, National Institute on Mental Health (NIMH), updated: 11/10/1997; and "Some CFS Patients Benefit from Low-Dose Steroid, But Side Effects Too Risky," NIH Press Release Tuesday, September 22, 1998, National Institute of Allergy and Infectious Diseases (NIAID).

hippocampus, a brain structure required for the formation of certain types of memory.

In experiments with animals, scientists have shown that a well-defined period of early postnatal development may be an important determinant of the capacity to handle stress throughout life.[2] In one set of studies, rat pups were removed each day from their mothers for a period as brief as 15 minutes and then returned. The natural maternal response of intensively licking and grooming the returned pup was shown to alter the brain chemistry of the pup in a positive way, making the animal less reactive to stressful stimuli. While these pups are able to mount an appropriate stress response in the face of threat, their response does not become excessive or inappropriate. Rat mothers who spontaneously lick and groom their pups with the same intensity even without human handling of the pups also produce pups that have a similarly stable reaction, including an appropriate stress hormone response.[6]

Striking differences were seen in rat pups removed from their mothers for periods of 3 hours a day, a model of neglect compared to pups that were not separated. After 3 hours, the mother rats tended to ignore the pups, at least initially, upon their return. In sharp contrast to those pups that were greeted attentively by their mothers after a short absence, the "neglected" pups were shown to have a more profound and excessive stress response in subsequent tests. This response appeared to last into adulthood.[7,8]

The implications of these animal studies are worrisome. However, research is in progress to determine the extent to which the hypersensitive or deregulated stress response of "neglected" rat pups can be reversed if, for example, foster mothers are provided who will groom the pups more intensely, or if the animals are raised in an "enriched" environment following their separation. An enriched setting may include, for example, a diverse and varied diet, a running wheel, mazes, and changes of toys.

Animal investigators are well aware of another kind of long-term change, again rooted in the first days of life. Laboratory rats are often raised in shoebox cages with few sources of stimulation. Scientists have compared these animals to rats raised in an enriched environment and found that the "privileged" rats consistently have a thicker cerebral cortex and denser networks of nerve cells than the "deprived" rats.[9,10]

Another study recently reported that infant monkeys raised by mothers who experienced unpredictable conditions in obtaining food showed markedly high levels of cortiocotropin releasing factor (CRF) in their cerebrospinal fluid and, as adults, abnormally low levels of cerebrospinal fluid cortisol.[11] This is a pattern often seen in humans with post-traumatic stress disorder and depression.[5] The distressed monkey mothers, uncertain about finding food, behaved inconsistently and sometimes neglectfully toward their offspring. The affected young monkeys were abnormally anxious when confronted with separations or new environments. They were also less social and more subordinate as adult animals.

It is far too early to draw firm conclusions from these animal studies about the extent to which early life experience produces a long-lived or permanent set point for stress responses, or influences the development of the cerebral cortex in humans. However, animal models that show the interactive effect of stress and brain development deserve serious consideration and continued study.

References

1. McEwen BS. Allostasis and allostatic load: implications for neuropsychopharmacology. *Neuropsychopharmacology*, 2000; 22(2): 108-24.

2. Liu D, Diorio J, Tannenbaum B, Caldji C, Francis D, Freedman A, Sharma S, Pearson D, Plotsky PM, Meaney MJ. Maternal care, hippocampal glucocorticoid receptors, and hypothalamic-pituitary-adrenal responses to stress. *Science*, 1997; 277(5332): 1659-62.

3. Sheline YI, Sanghavi M, Mintun MA, Gado MH. Depression duration but not age predicts hippocampal volume loss in medically healthy women with recurrent major depression. *Journal of Neuroscience*, 1999; 19(12): 5034-43.

4. Brown ES, Rush AJ, McEwen BS. Hippocampal remodeling and damage by corticosteroids: implications for mood disorders. *Neuropsychopharmacology*, 1999; 21(4): 474-84.

5. Heim C, Newport DJ, Heit S, Graham YP, Wilcox M, Bonsall R, Miller AH, Nemeroff CB. Pituitary-adrenal and autonomic responses to stress in women after sexual and physical abuse in childhood. *Journal of the American Medical Association*, 2000; 284(5): 592-7.

6. Francis D, Diorio J, Liu D, Meaney MJ. Nongenomic transmission across generations of maternal behavior and stress responses in the rat. *Science*, 1999; 286(5442): 1155-8.

7. Plotsky PM, Meaney MJ. Early, postnatal experience alters hypothalamic corticotropin-releasing factor (CRF) mRNA, median eminence CRF content and stress-induced release in adult rats. Brain Research. *Molecular Brain Research*, 1993; 18(3): 195-200.

8. Ladd CO, Huot RL, Thrivikraman KV, Nemeroff CB, Meaney MJ, Plotsky PM. Long-term behavioral and neuroendocrine adaptations to adverse early experience. *Progress in Brain Research*, 2000; 122: 81-103.

9. Jones TA, Klintsova AY, Kilman VL, Sirevaag AM, Greenough WT. Induction of multiple synapses by experience in the visual cortex of adult rats. *Neurobiology of Learning and Memory*, 1997; 68(1): 13-20.

10. Green EJ, Greenough WT, Schlumpf BE. Effects of complex or isolated environments on cortical dendrites of middle-aged rats. *Brain Research*, 1983; 264(2): 233-40.

11. Coplan JD, Andrews MW, Rosenblum LA, Owens MJ, Friedman S, Gorman JM, Nemeroff CB. *Persistent elevations of cerebrospinal fluid concentrations of corticotropin-releasing factor in adult nonhuman primates exposed to early-life stressors: implications for the pathophysiology of mood and anxiety disorders*. Proceedings of the National Academy of Sciences USA, 1996; 93(4): 1619-23.

The Emotional Brain

You are walking through the woods, and you see a coiled shape lying across your path. Instantly—before you even think "a snake!"—your brain begins to respond fearfully. Fear is an ancient emotion that is involved in a number of mental disorders, says neuroscientist Joseph LeDoux, Ph.D., of New York University. His research and that of other scientists, reported at the 24th Mathilde Solowey Lecture in the Neurosciences at the National Institutes of Health on May 8, 1997, has shown that the fear response has been tightly conserved in evolution, and probably follows much the same pattern in humans and other vertebrates.

According to LeDoux, he and others are making progress in tracing the brain circuitry underlying the fear response. Research attention is now focused on the amygdala, a small almond-shaped structure deep inside the brain. A portion of the amygdala known as the lateral nucleus appears to play a key role in fear conditioning—an experimental procedure in which an animal (rats were used in most of these experiments)—is taught to fear a harmless stimulus such as a sound tone. The conditioning is accomplished by pairing the tone with a mild electrical shock to the animal's foot. After a few times, the animal comes to exhibit defensive responses whenever it hears the tone. These responses include freezing (remaining motionless) and elevation of blood pressure.

Use of cell-staining procedures to trace the connections between the neurons of the amygdala and other brain structures shows that frightening stimuli trigger neuronal responses along a dual pathway. One path, dubbed the "high road," carries nerve impulses from the ear to the thalamus (a brain structure near the amygdala that serves as a way station for incoming sensory signals). From the thalamus, the nerve impulses are sent to the auditory portion of the sensory cortex, a region of the brain that conducts sophisticated analysis of inputs and sends appropriate signals to the amygdala. Alternatively, nerve impulses may be sent much faster from the thalamus directly to the amygdala. This "low road" signal system does not convey detailed information about the stimulus, but it has the advantage of speed. And speed is of great importance to an organism facing a threat to its survival.

When the amygdala receives nerve signals indicating a threat, it sends out signals that trigger defensive behavior, autonomic arousal (usually including rapid heartbeat and raised blood pressure), hypoalgesia (a diminished capacity to feel pain), somatic reflex potentiation (such as an exaggerated startle reflex), and pituitary-adrenal axis stimulation (production of stress hormones). In animals that have consciousness, these physical changes are accompanied by the emotion of fear.

LeDoux pointed out that having a very rapid, if imprecise, method of detecting danger is of high survival value. "You're better off mistaking a stick for a snake than a snake for a stick," he said.

Cell-tracing and physiological studies show that the lateral nucleus of the amygdala has all the ingredients necessary for fear conditioning to take place: a rich supply of nerve cell extensions connecting it to the thalamus, other portions of the amygdala, and various parts of the cortex; rapid response to stimuli; high threshold for stimulation (so that unimportant stimuli are filtered out); and high frequency preference (which corresponds to the pitch of rat distress calls).

Another part of the amygdala, the central nucleus, is the portion responsible for sending out the signals to trigger the "fight or flight" response.

The various portions of the amygdala communicate with each other by way of internal nerve cell connections. Once fear conditioning has taken place, these interior circuits tend to perpetuate the response to the frightening stimulus. So a person with a phobia, such as a morbid fear of snakes or heights, may undergo behavioral treatment and seem to be cured, only to have the phobia return during an episode of high stress. What happened, LeDoux suggests, is that the signal pathways from the thalamus to the amygdala and sensory cortex have been normalized, but the internal circuits in the amygdala have not.

There are far more cell circuits leading from the amygdala to the prefrontal cortex (the area of the brain most responsible for planning and reasoning) than there are going the other direction. This may be one reason why it is so difficult to exert conscious control over fear, LeDoux said.

These findings have important implications for treating people who suffer from anxiety disorders, according to LeDoux. Recent functional magnetic resonance imaging (MRI) scans of brains in living human subjects are beginning to show that the amygdala is the central site of fear conditioning, just as in rats. And fear conditioning is believed to play a role in such anxiety disorders as phobias, post-traumatic stress disorder, and panic disorder. If, as research suggests, the memories stored in the amygdala are relatively indelible, the aim of therapy for anxiety disorders must be to increase cortical control over the amygdala and its outputs, LeDoux said.

LeDoux sees the need for more behavioral and neuroscientific research to increase understanding of how multiple memory systems work together in fear conditioning and other emotional responses. The brain is closer to yielding secrets of emotion now than ever before, he said, because more scientists are focusing on emotion. Soon we will have a very clear picture of fear and other ancient aids to survival that are products of the emotional brain.

Cortisol and Chronic Fatigue Syndrome

Some CFS Patients Benefit from Low-Dose Steroid, But Side Effects Too Risky

Low doses of the steroid hydrocortisone can cause slight improvement in some chronic fatigue syndrome (CFS) symptoms but at the risk of inducing adrenal suppression. This finding, researchers from the National Institute of Allergy and Infectious Diseases (NIAID) claim, precludes the use of hydrocortisone in people with the illness. Their report appeared in the September 23/30, 1998 issue of *The Journal of the American Medical Association.*

"The data show that about half the people on placebo and two-thirds of those taking hydrocortisone reported some improvement in well-being," comments Stephen E. Straus, M.D., chief of the Laboratory of Clinical Investigation at NIAID and senior author on the study. "The greater benefit seen in the hydrocortisone group, however, was modest, and there was clear evidence of adrenal suppression by the drug." Twelve of 33 patients on the therapy developed laboratory evidence of adrenal insufficiency. "It was manageable and completely reversible," says Dr. Straus, "but it's the kind of suppression that in the context of minimal improvement afforded by the drug cannot, in our minds, justify using this treatment for CFS.

"Any time that long-term steroid therapy is considered, even at a low dose," adds Dr. Straus, "one needs to be concerned that the treatment itself may suppress the adrenal gland's normal production of steroids, which can lead to serious complications. When suppressed, the adrenal gland can't respond well to sudden stressful events such as a heart attack or an accident."

Hydrocortisone Study Rationale

People with CFS can suffer for years from an array of symptoms, including prolonged, debilitating fatigue, unrefreshing sleep, muscle pains, and memory and concentration problems. Although painkillers, antidepressants, and other symptom-based therapies can provide some relief, specific treatments for CFS do not exist, the search for them frustrated by the unknown etiology of the illness.

Several years ago, Dr. Straus and his colleagues found that CFS patients had slightly lower levels of circulating cortisol, the major glucose-regulating stress hormone, than did healthy individuals. Doctors have long believed that even subtle deficiencies in cortisol can result in lethargy and fatigue. A subsequent study indicated that the low cortisol levels in the CFS patients might be due to deficiencies in corticotropin-releasing hormone (CRH), a brain chemical that helps regulate cortisol secretion. To determine if they could restore the hormonal balance and thereby improve certain CFS symptoms, Dr. Straus and his former NIAID colleague, Robin McKenzie, M.D., designed a clinical trial to treat CFS patients with hydrocortisone, a synthetic form of cortisol.

The Hydrocortisone Trial and Its Results

The trial opened in 1992 at the National Institutes of Health Clinical Center in Bethesda, Md. From 683 carefully screened individuals, the investigators enrolled 70 people with CFS, although only 66 were included in the final analysis. "The strict entry criteria were an important part of the study design," says Dr. Straus. The investigators rejected anyone for whom steroids would be contraindicated—people with a history of ulcer disease, glaucoma, hypertension, diabetes, untreatable tuberculosis, or extreme obesity—as well as those who required many other kinds of potent medications.

By random selection, half of the participants received low-dose oral hydrocortisone and the other half a placebo. The researchers tried to mimic the natural diurnal fluctuations in cortisol levels by giving two doses of treatment or placebo daily (a larger dose early in the morning and a smaller dose in mid-afternoon, equivalent to a total of about 25 to 35 milligrams of hydrocortisone per day). During the 12-week treatment period, all participants were carefully monitored for adrenal suppression. They completed multiple self-rating questionnaires describing their energy levels, activities, moods, and symptoms for two weeks before, during, and for six weeks after this treatment period.

Based on the primary self-rating instrument used, the Wellness scale, 54.3 percent of placebo recipients and 66.7 percent of those who received treatment judged their symptoms as improved. The hydrocortisone recipients experienced significantly greater average improvement (6.3 vs. 1.7 points on a 100-point scale), and more of them improved by at least 5, 10, or 15 points. Moreover, they improved more rapidly and had consistently higher average increases in Wellness scores than the placebo recipients.

Twelve of the patients, however—all from the 33 in the hydrocortisone group—experienced significant adrenal suppression. None of an equal number of placebo recipients did.

"Although the therapeutic outcome was disappointing," says Dr. Straus, "we hope the results dissuade CFS patients from using a drug that potentially could cause them harm.

"The fact that the treatment worked to some degree," he adds, "was encouraging, but we would expect to see a greater benefit if low cortisol levels were directly responsible for symptoms of CFS. The amount of CRH may be more important than the amount of circulating cortisol because CRH receptors are located in the brain, and it is an important substance for stimulating mood, attention, and activity. Unfortunately, we don't have convenient ways of supplementing CRH."

However, supplementing other adrenal steroids, as they are doing in another open trial, may yield a more beneficial treatment effect, Dr. Straus says, because the regulation of the hypothalamic-pituitary-adrenal axis is not as sensitive to changes in the circulating levels of these steroids.

References

1. R McKenzie, A O'Fallon, J Dale, M. Demitrack, G Sharma, M Deloria, D Garcia-Borreguero, W Blackwelder, and SE Straus. Low-dose hydrocortisone treatment of chronic fatigue syndrome: a randomized controlled trial. *Journal of the American Medical Association* 280, 1061-66 (1998).

2. DHP Streeten. The nature of chronic fatigue. *Journal of the American Medical Association* 280, 1094-95 (1998).

Additional Information

National Institute of Mental Health (NIMH)
Office of Communications and Public Liaison
6001 Executive Boulevard
Rm. 8184, MSC 9663
Bethesda, MD 20892-9663
Tel: 301-443-4513
Fax: 301-443-4279
Website: www.nimh.nih.gov
E-mail: nimhinfo@nih.gov

Chapter 22

Stress and Heart Disease

Stress is a normal part of life. Many events that happen to you and around you—and many things that you do yourself—put stress on your body. Stress is your reaction to any change (physical, mental, or emotional) that requires you to adjust or respond. Like change, stress can be positive (called eustress) or negative (called distress). You can experience stress from your environment, your body, and your thoughts.

Stress, if left unmanaged, can lead to emotional, psychological, and even physical problems, including coronary artery disease, high blood pressure, chest pains, or even irregular heart beats. In order to handle stress in a positive way and prevent it from becoming harmful, you need to evaluate and understand the causes of stress in your life and how you react to them.

How Does Stress Contribute to Heart Disease?

Medical researchers aren't sure exactly how stress increases the risk of heart disease. Stress itself might be a risk factor, or it could

Reprinted with permission, "Stress and Heart Disease," © 2000 The Cleveland Clinic Foundation, 9500 Euclid Avenue, Cleveland OH 44195, 800-223-2273 ext. 48950, www.clevelandclinic.org. Additional information is available from the Cleveland Clinic Health Information Center, 216-444-3771, or www.clevelandclinic.org/health. The section titled "Combination of Stress, Low Serotonin May Promote Heart Disease" is from "Heart Disease Risk Linked to Mood Chemical," by Renee Twombly, *Inside DUMC* 2000: March 20, 2000, Vol. 9 Number 6, © Duke University Medical Center, reprinted with permission.

be that high levels of stress make other risk factors worse. For example, if you are under stress, your blood pressure goes up, you may overeat, you may exercise less, and you may be more likely to smoke.

If stress is an independent risk factor, it could increase heart diseases risks because chronic stress exposes your body to unhealthy, persistently elevated levels of hormones like adrenaline and cortisol. Studies also link stress to changes in the way blood clots. This also increases the risk of heart attack.

When your body is under acute stress—for example, if you are threatened—your adrenal glands release adrenaline, a hormone that activates your body's defensive mechanisms. Your heart pounds, your blood pressure rises, your muscles tense, the pupils of your eyes open wide. This cluster of reactions—called the fight-or-flight response—concentrates all your body systems on the apparent danger and helps you take the next step, which is either to resist or to retreat.

Combination of Stress, Low Serotonin May Promote Heart Disease

The same brain chemical that influences moods and personality traits like depression and hostility also may influence a person's risk of heart disease, according to a Duke University Medical Center researcher. Duke psychologist Edward Suarez, PhD, found that, when put under emotional stress, people with low levels of the brain chemical serotonin showed a significant rise in immune system proteins known to contribute to heart disease. Subjects with normal or high serotonin levels—as measured by a breakdown product in the blood called 5-HIAA—did not show increased production of these proteins under the same stressful conditions, the study found.

Suarez said his study findings may explain why depressed and hostile individuals, who often have low serotonin levels, die more often from heart diseases and other illnesses that involve a heightened immune system response. Furthermore, he said, the findings hold the tantalizing possibility that medications used to increase serotonin in the treatment of depression could also be used to lower the risk of heart disease. Results of the study, funded by the National Heart, Lung and Blood Institute, were prepared for presentation in March 2000 at the annual meeting of the American Psychosomatic Society meeting in Savannah, Georgia.

"We've long known that stress contributes to heart disease, and that people with low serotonin have more heart disease," Suarez said in an interview. "Now we have shown that cellular mechanisms suspected of contributing to atherosclerosis are associated with a neurochemical, serotonin, which is associated with depression and hostility.

"Specifically, our study showed that in people with low levels of serotonin, stress activates the same immune system response as do other environmental factors like high cholesterol and smoking. But the stress response only occurs among people with low serotonin."

In a study of 56 healthy men and women, Suarez and his colleagues asked subjects to recall events in their lives that made them sad or angry. Before and after each recollection, the researchers analyzed their blood for the presence of certain cytokines, proteins that white blood cells produce when they are preparing to repair a site of injury. The presence of such cytokines would indicate that the body was gearing up its immune system, as it does in response to smoking, high cholesterol, high blood pressure, and other assaults.

When researchers tested the subjects prior to stress testing, none of them showed an increase in cytokine activity, regardless of their serotonin levels. However, when subjects were asked to describe a sad or angry event, men with low serotonin responded by producing higher levels of two cytokines—interleukin 1 alpha and tumor necrosis factor alpha. Suarez said both cytokines are well recognized as contributing to atherosclerosis, or a buildup of plaque in the arteries, which can lead to a heart attack.

Interestingly, women with low serotonin showed an increase only in interleukin 1 alpha, possibly due to the anti-inflammatory effects of estrogen, Suarez said. Men and women with normal or high levels of serotonin showed no increase in cytokine activity during the sadness and anger recall test. In all, five cytokines were measured.

"Our results suggest that, in people with low serotonin, stress prompts the immune system to behave like there is an injury in need of repair," Suarez said. "Once the immune system is engaged, it activates white blood cells at the perceived site of injury to begin their repair."

The very process of repair is what contributes to heart disease, the researchers say. Upon activation, white blood cells, or Amonocytes, stick to the site of injury—in this case, the artery walls of the heart where assaults like smoking, high blood pressure, and high cholesterol have created microscopic tears. Once there, they build up into layers, all the while consuming low density lipoprotein, or the "bad" cholesterol. The very act of consuming cholesterol creates a process called oxidation, in which the cholesterol cells become hardened like cement. Hence, plaque is formed inside the lining of artery wall, a process commonly called "hardening of the arteries."

The researchers believe that stress initiates this process by triggering the release of stress hormones, like adrenaline and cortisol, which propel the immune system into action. "Stress appears to be an environmental trigger that sets into motion an immune response among people who have a biological underpinning toward negative moods like depression, hostility, and aggression," Suarez said. "In other words, stress mimics the response of an actual physical injury." Suarez said the study findings support the prevailing view of heart disease as an inflammatory response waged by the immune system against the heart.

Lowering cholesterol and reducing stress have been mainstays of heart disease prevention and treatment. Now, the researchers believe, if subsequent studies confirm the results, that boosting serotonin levels may be another effective method of treating and preventing heart disease in susceptible individuals.

Does Stress Affect Everyone the Same?

People respond in different ways to events and situations. One person may find an event joyful and gratifying, but another person may find the same event miserable and frustrating. Some people do their best when their lives are filled with activity, while others may prefer a slower pace. Sometimes, people may handle distress in ways that make bad situations worse by reacting with feelings of anger, guilt, fear, hostility, anxiety, and moodiness.

What Causes Stress?

Stress can be caused by a physical or emotional change, or a change in your environment that requires you to adjust or respond. Things that make you feel stressed are called "stressors."

Stressors can be minor hassles, major lifestyle changes, or a combination of both. Being able to identify stressors in your life and releasing the tension they cause are the keys to managing stress.

Some common stressors that can affect people at all stages of life are:

- Illness—either personal or of a family member
- Death of a friend or loved one
- Problems in a personal relationship
- Sexual problems
- Marital problems
- Divorce
- Work overload
- Deadlines
- Job interview

- Starting a new job
- Unemployment
- Retirement
- Pregnancy
- Crowds
- Confrontations
- Relocation
- Daily hassles
- Driving in heavy traffic
- Car accident
- Expectations to perform
- Legal difficulties
- Financial problems
- Being a victim of crime
- School problems
- Perfectionism
- Excessively high expectations of others
- Responsibility

What Are the Warning Signs of Stress?

When you are exposed to long periods of stress, your body gives warning signals that something is wrong. These physical, cognitive, emotional, and behavioral warning signs should not be ignored. They tell you that you need to slow down. If you continue to be stressed and you don't give your body a break, you are likely to develop health problems. You could also worsen an existing illness.

Table 22.1. Common Stress Warning Signs

Physical signs	Dizziness, General aches and pains, Grinding teeth, Clenched jaws, Headaches, Indigestion, Loss of appetite, Muscle tension, Having difficulty sleeping, Racing heart, Ringing in the ears, Stooped posture, Sweaty palms, Tiredness, Exhaustion, Trembling, Weight gain or loss, Upset stomach
Mental signs	Constant worry, Difficulty making decisions, Forgetfulness, Inability to concentrate, Lack of creativity, Loss of sense of humor, Poor memory
Emotional signs	Anger, Anxiety, Crying, Depression, Feeling powerless, Frequent mood swings, Irritability, Loneliness, Negative thinking, Nervousness, Sadness
Behavioral signs	Bossiness, Compulsive eating, Critical attitude of others, Explosive actions, Frequent job changes, Impulsive actions, Increased use of alcohol or drugs, Withdrawal from relationships or social situations

How Do I Cope with Stress?

After you've identified the cause of stress in your life and how your body responds to stress, the next step is to learn techniques that help you cope with stress. There are many techniques you can use to manage stress. Some of these techniques you can learn yourself, while others may require the guidance of a trained therapist.

Some common coping techniques include:

- Keeping a positive attitude and accepting there are events that you cannot control.

- Reducing your stressors.

- Asserting your feelings, opinions, or beliefs instead of becoming angry, combative, or passive.

- Learning to relax.

- Exercising regularly.

- Eating well-balanced, nutritious meals.

- Resting and getting enough sleep.

- Creating a good network of social support.

How Can I Keep a Positive Attitude?

A positive attitude and self-esteem are good defenses against "bad" stress because they help you view stress as a challenge rather than a problem. A positive attitude keeps you in control when there are inevitable changes in your life. A positive attitude means telling yourself there are things you can do to improve certain situations and admitting that sometimes there's nothing you can do.

To maintain a positive attitude during a stressful situation (or to prepare yourself for a potentially stressful situation), keep these tips in mind:

- Stay calm. Stop what you're doing. Breathe deeply. Reflect on your choices.

- Always tell yourself you can get through the situation.

- Try to be objective, realistic, and flexible.

- Try to keep the situation in perspective.

- Think about the possible solutions. Choose one that is the most acceptable and feasible. Think about the outcome: Ask yourself, what is the worst possible thing that can happen? (Chances are, that won't happen).

- Tell yourself that you can learn something from every situation.

How Can I Reduce My Stressors?

While it is impossible to live your life completely free of stress, it is possible to reduce the harmful effects of certain stressors. Here are some suggestions:

- First identify the stressor. What's causing you to feel stressed?

- Avoid hassles and minor irritations if possible. If traffic jams cause you stress, try taking a different route, riding the bus, or car-pooling.

- When you experience a change in your life, try to continue doing the things that you enjoyed before the change occurred.

- Learn how to manage your time effectively, but be realistic and flexible when you plan your schedule.

- Do one thing at a time; concentrate on each task as it comes.

- Take a break when your stressors compile to an uncontrollable level.

- Ask for help if you feel that you are unable to deal with stress on your own.

How Can I Learn How to Relax?

In order to cope with stress, you need to learn how to relax. Relaxing is a learned skill—it takes commitment and practice. Relaxation is more than sitting back and being quiet. Rather, it's an active process involving techniques that calm your body and mind. True relaxation requires becoming sensitive to your basic needs for peace, self-awareness, and thoughtful reflection. The challenge is being willing to meet these needs rather than dismissing them.

There are a number of methods you can use to relax including:

- Deep breathing exercises
- Progressive muscle relaxation

353

- Mind relaxation
- Relaxation to music
- Biofeedback

The more relaxed you feel after you've practiced one of these techniques, the better the results. Once you find a relaxation method that works for you, practice it every day for at least 30 minutes. Taking the time to practice simple relaxation techniques gives you the chance to unwind and get ready for life's next challenge.

What Lifestyle Changes Can I Make?

As a response to stressful situations, you may develop poor lifestyle habits. Think about what you do when you are dealing with a stressful situation.

- Do you smoke or have more cigarettes than usual?
- Do you skip your exercise routine?
- Do you eat fast foods and unhealthy foods more often?
- Do you drink alcohol?

Poor lifestyle habits can weaken your immune system (the body's natural ability to fight stress), making you more likely to develop infections and illnesses, including heart disease. Maintaining a healthy lifestyle—one that includes a well-balanced diet, regular exercise, and getting enough sleep—will help you fight stress.

What about Nutrition?

Your body is able to fight stress better when you take the time to eat well-balanced meals. Eat a variety of foods each day, including lean meats, fish, or poultry, enriched or whole grain breads and cereals, fruits and vegetables, and low-fat dairy products.

About 55-60 percent of your daily intake of calories should come from carbohydrates, no more than 25-30 percent from of your caloric intake should come from fat and 10-15 percent should come from protein.

Guidelines for Healthy Eating to Fight Stress

1. Eat a wide variety of healthy foods.
2. Eat in moderation—control the portions of the foods you eat.

3. Reach a healthy weight and maintain it.

4. Eat at least 5 to 9 servings of fruits and vegetables per day.

5. Eat food that is high in dietary fiber such as whole grain cereals, legumes, and vegetables.

6. Minimize your daily fat intake. Choose foods low in saturated fat and cholesterol.

7. Limit your consumption of sugar and salt.

8. Limit the amount of alcohol that you drink.

9. Make small changes in your diet over time.

10. Combine healthy eating habits with a regular exercise program.

How Can I Get More Rest and Sleep?

Even with proper diet and exercise, you can't fight stress effectively without rest. You need time to recover from exercise and stressful events. The time you spend resting should be long enough to relax your mind as well as your body. Some people find that taking a nap in the middle of the day helps them reduce stress.

Many of us assume that we are resting and relaxing during sleep, yet, that is not always the case. Disturbed, restless sleep can be caused by a variety of factors, including stress. Excessive worry and tension or overindulgent behavior (drinking too much coffee or alcoholic beverages or smoking) are the most common causes of disturbed sleep. Insomnia affects all of us from time to time and is a common reaction to stress. Relaxation training is the best treatment for chronic insomnia.

Proper rest and sleep will allow you to deeply relax so you can face the stressors of the new day.

The information provided by the Cleveland Clinic is not intended to replace the medical advice of your doctor or health care provider. Please consult your health care provider for advice about a specific medical condition.

Chapter 23

Morning Coffee Boosts Blood Pressure and Stress Hormones All Day

People who drink four or five cups of coffee in the morning have slightly elevated blood pressure and higher levels of stress hormones all day and into the evening, creating a scenario in which the body acts like it is continually under stress, a team of researchers has found.

In a study of 72 habitual coffee drinkers, the researchers found that subjects produced more adrenaline and noradrenaline and had higher blood pressure on days when they drank caffeine compared with days they abstained. The two stress hormones are vital to helping the body react quickly in times of danger or stress, but they can damage the heart over a lifetime of heightened production, said James Lane, associate research professor of psychiatry.

Lane presented the study's results in March 1999 at a meeting of the Society of Behavioral Medicine. The research was funded by the National Heart, Lung, and Blood Institute. "Moderate caffeine consumption makes a person react like he or she is having a very stressful day," Lane said in an interview. "If you combine the effects of real stress with the artificial boost in stress hormones that comes from caffeine, then you have compounded the effects considerably."

During the two-week study, the subjects experienced, on average, a 32 percent increase in adrenaline and a 14 percent increase in noradrenaline on days when they consumed caffeine. Their blood pressure rose an average of three points.

"Morning Coffee Boosts Blood Pressure, Stress Hormones All Day," by Rebecca Levine, MCNO, © Duke University Medical Center, reprinted with permission.

Lane's study builds on smaller studies in which he found that caffeine boosted blood pressure, heart rate, and stress hormones in subjects who drank four to five cups of caffeine per day. In the current study, Lane replicated those findings and added to them by showing that subjects' blood pressures and stress hormone levels stayed elevated until bedtime, even though they last consumed caffeine between noon and 1 p.m.

Occasional surges of stress hormones temporarily raise heart rate, blood pressure, and mental acuity—long enough to accomplish the task at hand. However, an excess of stress hormones has been shown to compromise health in a variety of ways, from damaging blood vessels to weakening the immune system.

In addition, even the small boost in blood pressure seen in this study can have clinical significance, Lane said. A review of nine major studies of blood pressure and heart-disease risk showed that a five-point increase in diastolic blood-pressure—the lower number used to assess health risk—was associated with at least a 34 percent increase in stroke and a 21 percent increase in the incidence of coronary heart disease.

While researchers have long known that caffeine can boost stress hormones and blood pressure, most studies have been conducted in a laboratory under tightly controlled circumstances where a single dose of caffeine is compared to none in a short time span, according to Lane. He said his body of research is unique because it measures blood pressure, heart rate, and stress hormone levels at timed intervals during normal working conditions, while subjects are exposed to a range of moods and activities.

"You can measure how caffeine affects people in the laboratory, but that doesn't tell you what effects the drug has in the real world when people are exposed to normal stressors and activities," he said.

In the current study, Lane also looked at the effects of caffeine on women taking oral contraceptives, since previous research suggested that this population might be more responsive to the negative effects of caffeine. However, Lane found no such effect. In fact, women taking oral contraceptives showed slightly less of a stress response to caffeine than did a control group of women.

Lane's next study will measure the effects of eliminating caffeine from the diets of individuals with high blood pressure. The goal is to see if stopping caffeine use can be a useful therapy—along with diet, exercise, and salt reduction—in reducing hypertension.

Chapter 24

Stress Affects the Immune System

For thousands of years, people believed that stress made you sick. Up until the nineteenth century, the idea that the passions and emotions were intimately linked to disease held sway, and people were told by their doctors to go to spas or seaside resorts when they were ill. Gradually these ideas lost favor as more concrete causes and cures were found for illness after illness. But in the last decade, scientists like Dr. Esther Sternberg, director of the Integrative Neural Immune Program at NIH's National Institute of Mental Health (NIMH), have been rediscovering the links between the brain and the immune system.

The Immune System and the Brain

When you have an infection or something else that causes inflammation such as a burn or injury, many different kinds of cells from the immune system stream to the site. Dr. Sternberg likens them to soldiers moving into battle, each kind with its own specialized function. Some are like garbage collectors, ingesting invaders. Some make antibodies, the "bullets" to fight the infectious agents; others kill invaders directly. All these types of immune cells must coordinate their actions, and the way they do that is by sending each other signals in the form of molecules that they make in factories inside the cell.

"Stress and Disease: New Perspectives," by Harrison Wein, Ph.D., *Word on Health*, National Institutes of Health (NIH), October 2000.

"It turns out that these molecules have many more effects than just being the walkie-talkie communicators between different kinds of immune cells," Dr. Sternberg says. "They can also go through the bloodstream to signal the brain or activate nerves nearby that signal the brain."

These immune molecules, Dr. Sternberg explains, cause the brain to change its functions. "They can induce a whole set of behaviors that we call sickness behavior. You lose the desire or the ability to move, you lose your appetite, you lose interest in sex." Scientists can only speculate about the purpose of these sickness behaviors, but Dr. Sternberg suggests that they might help us conserve energy when we're sick so we can better use our energy to fight disease.

These signaling molecules from the immune system can also activate the part of the brain that controls the stress response, the hypothalamus. Through a cascade of hormones released from the pituitary and adrenal glands, the hypothalamus causes blood levels of the hormone cortisol to rise. Cortisol is the major steroid hormone produced by our bodies to help us get through stressful situations. The related compound known as cortisone is widely used as an anti-inflammatory drug in creams to treat rashes and in nasal sprays to treat sinusitis and asthma. But it wasn't until very recently that scientists realized the brain also uses cortisol to suppress the immune system and tone down inflammation within the body.

Stress and the Immune System

This complete communications cycle from the immune system to the brain and back again allows the immune system to talk to the brain, and the brain to then talk back and shut down the immune response when it's no longer needed. "When you think about this crosstalk, this two-way street," Dr. Sternberg explains, "you can begin to understand the kinds of illnesses that might result if there is either too much or too little communication in either direction."

According to Dr. Sternberg, if you're chronically stressed, the part of the brain that controls the stress response is going to be constantly pumping out a lot of stress hormones. The immune cells are being bathed in molecules which are essentially telling them to stop fighting. And so in situations of chronic stress your immune cells are less able to respond to an invader like a bacteria or a virus.

This theory holds up in studies looking at high-levels of shorter term stress or chronic stress: in caregivers like those taking care of relatives with Alzheimer's, medical students undergoing exam stress,

Army Rangers undergoing extremely grueling physical stress, and couples with marital stress. People in these situations, Dr. Sternberg says, show a prolonged healing time, a decreased ability of their immune systems to respond to vaccination, and an increased susceptibility to viral infections like the common cold.

Some Stress Is Good

People tend to talk about stress as if it's all bad. It's not. "Some stress is good for you," Dr. Sternberg says. "I have to get my stress response to a certain optimal level so I can perform in front of an audience when I give a talk." Otherwise, she may come across as lethargic and listless. But while some stress is good, too much is not good. "If you're too stressed, your performance falls off," Dr. Sternberg says. "The objective should be not to get rid of stress completely because you can't get rid of stress—stress is life, life is stress. Rather, you need to be able to use your stress response optimally."

The key is to learn to move yourself to that optimal peak point so that you're not underperforming but you're also not so stressed that you're unable to perform. How much we're able to do that is the challenge, Dr. Sternberg admits. This may not be possible in all situations, or for all people, because just as with the animals Dr. Sternberg studies, some people may have a more sensitive stress response than others.

"But your goal should be to try to learn to control your stress to make it work for you," Dr. Sternberg says. "Don't just think of getting rid of your stress; think of turning it to your advantage."

Controlling the Immune Response

Problems between the brain and the immune system can go the other way, too. If for some reason you're unable to make enough of these brain stress hormones, you won't be able to turn off the immune cells once they're no longer needed.

"There has to be an exit strategy for these battles that are being fought by the immune system, and the brain provides the exit strategy through stress hormones," Dr. Sternberg says. "If your brain can't make enough of these hormones to turn the immune system off when it doesn't have to be active anymore, then it could go on unchecked and result in autoimmune diseases like rheumatoid arthritis, lupus, or other autoimmune diseases that people recognize as inflammation."

Dr. Sternberg says that there are several factors involved in these autoimmune conditions. There are many different effects that the brain and its nervous system can have on the immune system, depending on the kinds of nerve chemicals that are being made, where they're being made, what kind of nerves they come from, and whether they're in the bloodstream or not. Still, at least part of the problem in these diseases seems to involve the brain's hormonal stress response.

"So if you have too much stress hormone shutting down the immune response, you can't fight off infection and you're more susceptible to infection," Dr. Sternberg concludes. "Too little stress hormones and the immune response goes on unchecked and you could get an inflammatory disease."

Pinpointing the Problems

Why these miscommunications between the brain and the immune system come about is still largely unknown, and involves many genes and environmental factors. But by studying animals, scientists have finally been able to start understanding how the miscommunications occur.

Dr. Sternberg first started publishing work on the links between the brain and the immune system back in 1989 studying rats with immune problems. "In many of these cases it's very hard to show the mechanism in humans," Dr. Sternberg explains, "but you can show the mechanism in animals because you can manipulate all the different parts of the system and you can begin to understand which parts affect which other parts." It has taken "a good ten years" to gather enough evidence in human studies to show that the principles her lab uncovered in rats were also relevant to human beings.

Drugs that have been tested in rats to correct brain/immune system problems have had unpredictable effects. That is because nothing happens in isolation when it comes to the brain and the immune system. Dr. Sternberg points out that our bodies are amazing machines which at every moment of the day are constantly responding to a myriad of different kinds of stimuli—chemical, psychological, and physical. "These molecules act in many different ways in different parts of the system," she says. Understanding how the brain and the immune system work together in these different diseases should help scientists develop new kinds of drugs to treat them that would never have occurred to them before.

Taking Control Now

Dr. Sternberg thinks that one of the most hopeful aspects of this science is that it tells us it's not all in our genes. A growing number of studies show that, to some degree, you can use your mind to help treat your body. Support groups, stress relief, and meditation may, by altering stress hormone levels, all help the immune system. For example, women in support groups for their breast cancer have longer life spans than women without such psychological support.

There are several components of stress to think about, including its duration, how strong it is, and how long it lasts. Every stress has some effect on the body, and you have to take into account the total additive effect on the body of all stressors when considering how to reduce stress.

Perhaps the most productive way to think about stress is in terms of control. Dr. Sternberg shows a slide of an F-14 jet flying sideways by the deck of an aircraft carrier, its wings completely vertical. "The Navy Commander who flew that jet told me that he was the only one in the photo who was not stressed, and that's because he was the one in control. The officer sitting in the seat ten feet behind him was in the exact same physical situation but was not in control. Control is a very important part of whether or not we feel stressed.

So if you can learn to feel that you're in control or actually take control of certain aspects of the situation that you're in, you can reduce your stress response." Studies show that gaining a sense of control can help patients cope with their illness, if not help the illness itself.

Until science has more solid answers, it can't hurt to participate in support groups and seek ways to relieve stress, Dr. Sternberg says. But what you need to remember is if you do these things and you're not successful in correcting whatever the underlying problem is, it's not your fault because there's a biology to the system. "You need to know the benefits of the system," she says, "but its limitations as well." In other words, try not to get too stressed about being stressed.

A Word to the Wise—Stress Control

First try to identify the things in your life that cause you stress: marital problems, conflict at work, a death or illness in the family. Once you identify and understand how these stressors affect you, you can begin to figure out ways to change your environment and manage them.

If there's a problem that can be solved, set about taking control and solving it. For example, you might decide to change jobs if problems at work are making you too stressed. But some chronic stressors can't be changed. For those, support groups, relaxation, meditation, and exercise are all tools you can use to manage your stress. If nothing you do seems to work for you, seek a health professional who can help. Also seek professional help if you find that you worry excessively about the small things in life.

Keep in mind that chronic stress can be associated with mental conditions like depression and anxiety disorders as well as physical problems. Seek professional help if you have:

- Difficulty sleeping
- Changes in appetite
- Panic attacks
- Muscle tenseness and soreness
- Frequent headaches
- Gastrointestinal problems
- Prolonged feelings of sadness or worthlessness

Chapter 25

The Physiological and Psychological Effects of Compassion and Anger

Freeze-Frame®: Mastering the Power of the Heart

Through many years of research, founder Doc Childre and the Institute of HeartMath® developed what is now known as the HeartMath® system: a set of practical techniques and technologies to help people transmute stress and negative emotions in the moment, improve performance and enrich the quality of life.

Freeze-Frame® is a core HeartMath® technique. This simple, five-step process teaches you how to "freeze" a stressful situation—like freezing one frame in a movie—and consciously shift to positive emotions that reverse the effects of stress on the mind and body. Freeze-Frame® is fundamental to the range of transformational techniques now taught in HeartMath® workshops and seminars around the world.

The Freeze-Framer® was developed to support people in using these techniques. This interactive, computer-based learning system with a proprietary heart monitor is an adaptation of the HeartMath® laboratory tools for use in personal or institutional settings. It allows you to watch in real time how thoughts and emotions affect your heart; teaches you how to engage the heart to quickly bring emotions, body, and mind into balance; and helps you stay in "The Zone" of optimal health and performance. The Freeze-Framer® interactive learning

"The Physiological and Psychological Effects of Compassion and Anger," © 1998 Institute of HeartMath®, Boulder Creek, California, reprinted with permission; and "The Physiological and Psychological Effects," © 1998 Institute of HeartMath®, Boulder Creek, California, reprinted with permission.

system allows people to monitor, sustain, and improve their progress, long after first learning the techniques.

An additional HeartMath® tool is Heart Lock-In®, which promotes positive emotions and sustained states of psychophysiological coherence. This technique establishes increased physiological efficiency, mental acuity, and emotional stability as a new baseline for sustainable effects. The third core technique, Cut-Thru®, extinguishes recurring, intrusive thought patterns and emotions—anxiety and depression, for example. This tool reinforces more positive perceptions and efficient emotional responses.

From this core system, the Institute of HeartMath® continues to research and develop numerous applications, all validated scientifically. Programs based on HeartMath® tools and techniques are delivered to schools through the Institute of HeartMath®, and to business, government, health care, and social service agencies around the world through HeartMath LLC.

The Physiological and Psychological Effects of Compassion and Anger

Glen Rein, PhD, Mike Atkinson, and Rolin McCraty, PhD. *Journal of Adva in Medicine*. 1995; 8 (2); 87-105.

Key findings: Heart-focused, sincere, positive feeling states boost the immune system, while negative emotions may suppress the immune response for up to six hours following the emotional experience.

Summary: Secretory IgA (measured from saliva samples), heart rate, and mood were measured in thirty individuals before and after experiencing the emotional states of either care and compassion or anger and frustration. Two methods of inducing the emotional states were compared: self-induction versus external induction via video tapes. Anger produced a significant increase in total mood disturbance and heart rate but not in S-IgA levels. On the other hand, sincere positive feeling states of care and compassion, self-induced via the Freeze-Frame® technique, produced a significant decrease in total mood disturbance and a significant increase in S-IgA levels. Examining the effects over a 6-hour period, we observed that a 5-minute experience of anger produced a significant inhibition of S-IgA from one to five hours after the emotional experience. In contrast, a tendency toward increased S-IgA levels was observed over the six hours following a 5-minute experience of care.

Results indicate that self-induction of positive emotional states using Freeze-Frame® is more effective in stimulating S-IgA levels than previously used external methods. In a previous study, "The effects of emotions on short-term power spectral analysis of heart rate variability" we observed that feelings of appreciation self-generated by the Freeze-Frame® technique shift autonomic nervous system balance towards increased parasympathetic activity. As salivary secretion is primarily activated by parasympathetic nerves, autonomic regulation offers a possible mechanism to explain the immediate increases in S-IgA following the experience of positive emotions. The results of this

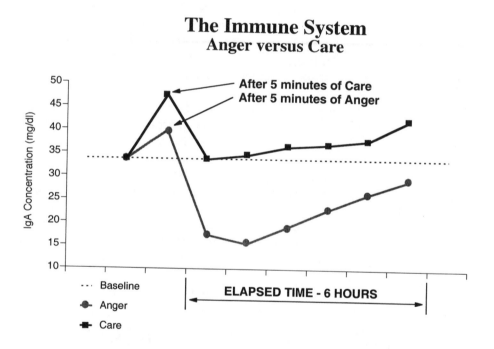

The Immune System
Anger versus Care

Figure 25.1. This graph shows the impact of one 5-minute episode of re-called anger on the immune antibody IgA over a 6-hour period. The initial slight increase in IgA was followed by a dramatic drop which persisted for six hours. When the subjects used the Freeze-Frame® technique and focused on feeling sincere care for five minutes there was a significant increase in IgA, which returned to baseline an hour later and then slowly increased throughout the rest of the day.

study indicate that the Freeze-Frame® technique may be an effective method to improve mood and minimize the long-term immunosuppressive effects of negative emotions.

The Impact of a New Emotional Self-Management Program on Stress, Emotions, Heart Rate Variability, DHEA, and Cortisol

Rollin McCraty, PhD, Bob Barrios-Choplin, PhD, Deborah Rozman, PhD, Mike Atkinson and Alan D. Watkins, MBBS. *Integrative Physiological and Behavioral Science*. 1998; 33 (2): 151-170.

Key findings: Subjects who used the Cut-Thru® and Heart Lock-In® interventions for one month significantly reduced their cortisol levels and increased their DHEA. These positive shifts in hormonal balance occurred in conjunction with significant improvements in emotional health, including reductions in stress, anxiety, burnout, and guilt, along with increases in caring and vigor.

Summary: This study examined the effects on healthy adults of a new stress reduction and emotional management program consisting of two key techniques, Cut-Thru® and the Heart Lock-In®. These techniques are designed to create and sustain shifts in dispositional orientation toward stressors by changing interpretive styles, breaking negative thought loops and extinguishing unhealthy emotional patterns. It is postulated that recurring negative emotional patterns may lead to adverse effects on physiology and well-being through unnecessary and inappropriate activation of the autonomic nervous system and glucocorticoid secretions. This research therefore examined the effects of the Cut-Thru® and Heart Lock-In® techniques on participants' emotions, stress, cortisol/ DHEA levels and autonomic nervous system balance.

The Physiological and Psychological Effects

Forty-five healthy adults participated in the study, fifteen of whom acted as controls. DHEA and cortisol levels were measured from saliva samples, autonomic nervous system balance was assessed by heart rate variability analysis, and emotions were measured with a psychological questionnaire. Individuals in the experimental group were assessed before and four weeks after receiving training in the stress management techniques. To facilitate the heart focus and emotional shifts, participants practiced the Cut-Thru® technique during a Heart Lock-In® with the music *Speed of Balance* five times a week during the study period. Participants also used Cut-Thru® any time they felt out of balance emotionally.

After one month, the experimental group experienced significant increases in Caring and Vigor and significant decreases in Guilt, Hostility, Burnout, Anxiety, and Stress Effects, while no significant changes were seen in the control group. There was a mean 23% reduction in cortisol and a 100% increase in DHEA levels in the experimental group. A positive shift in autonomic nervous system balance was measured in 80% of the sample during the use of the techniques. Some of the participants developed the entrainment mode of heart function while using the Cut-Thru® technique during a Heart Lock-In® (Figure 25.3).

The significant increase in subjects' DHEA/cortisol ratio was in accordance with the psychological results, which showed a significant reduction in stress, burnout, and negative emotion experienced by

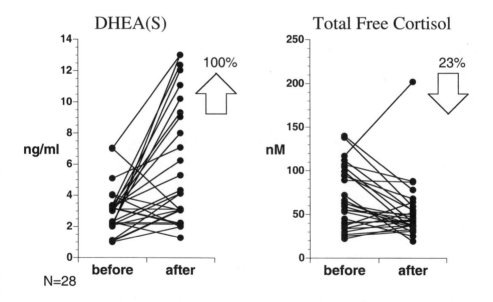

Figure 25.2. *DHEA and cortisol values before and after subjects were trained in and practiced the Cut-Thru® technique for one month. There was a 100% average increase in DHEA and a 23% decrease in cortisol.*

participants as a result of using the techniques. Reduced stress diminishes the system's cortisol demand, and can result in the diversion of pregnenolone, a common precursor of DHEA and cortisol, from cortisol production into DHEA synthesis. Additionally, the entrainment mode achieved by many of the participants during the use of the techniques is characterized by increased baroreceptor activity. Baroreceptor stimulation has been demonstrated to cause a reflex decrease in plasma cortisol levels, believed to be due to inhibition of ACTH at the pituitary gland. Given that the normal physiological variability of DHEA and cortisol levels from month to month is nonsignificant, the exceptional average increase in subjects' DHEA/cortisol ratio measured after one month of practice of Cut-Thru® is noteworthy and consistent with our hypothesis that Cut-Thru® facilitates the release and reprogramming of draining mental and emotional memory traces at the level of the brain's neural circuitry.

This study advances our understanding of stress and emotional responses in several ways. First, it establishes that interpretive styles associated with stress and negative emotions can be changed within

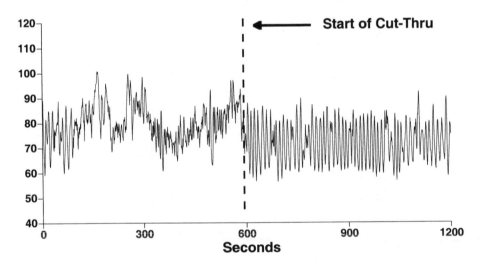

Figure 25.3. This graph is a typical HRV example from one of the subjects while practicing the Cut-Thru® technique (beginning at approximately 600 seconds). Here the subject developed the entrainment state, which is indicative of autonomic system balance and physiological coherence.

370

a short period of time. Second, it illustrates that these changed perspectives do influence stress, emotions, and key physiological parameters. The substantial changes observed in the neuroendocrine measures support the concept that perceptions and emotions can affect health, as these hormones are significantly correlated to health outcomes. Finally, results suggest that people have greater control over their health than previously recognized, as participants who learned to 'reprogram' their conditioned emotional responses experienced significantly lower stress levels, less negative emotion, and increased positive emotion, all vital building blocks to a healthier lifestyle.

Chapter 26

Psychological Stress and Cancer

The complex relationship between physical and psychological health is not well understood. Scientists know that many types of stress activate the body's endocrine (hormone) system, which in turn can cause changes in the immune system, the body's defense against infection and disease (including cancer). However, the immune system is a highly specialized network whose activity is affected not only by stress but also by a number of other factors. It has not been shown that stress-induced changes in the immune system directly cause cancer.

Some studies have indicated an increased incidence of early death, including cancer death, among people who have experienced the recent loss of a spouse or other loved one. However, most cancers have been developing for many years and are diagnosed only after they have been growing in the body for a long time (from 2 to 30 years). This fact argues against an association between the death of a loved one and the triggering of cancer.

The relationship between breast cancer and stress has received particular attention. Some studies of women with breast cancer have shown significantly higher rates of this disease among those women who experienced traumatic life events and losses within several years before their diagnosis. Although studies have shown that stress factors (such as death of a spouse, social isolation, and medical school examinations) alter the way the immune system functions, they have not provided scientific evidence of a direct cause-and-effect relationship

"Cancer Facts," Fact Sheet 3.17, National Cancer Institute, reviewed 3/9/98.

373

between these immune system changes and the development of cancer. One NCI-sponsored study suggests that there is no important association between stressful life events, such as the death of a loved one or divorce, and breast cancer risk.* However, more research is needed to find if there is a relationship between psychological stress and the transformation of normal cells into cancerous cells.

One area that is currently being studied is the effect of stress on women already diagnosed with breast cancer. These studies are looking at whether stress reduction can improve the immune response and possibly slow cancer progression. Researchers are doing this by determining whether women with breast cancer who are in support groups have better survival rates than those not in support groups.

Many factors come into play when determining the relationship between stress and cancer. At present, the relationship between psychological stress and cancer occurrence or progression has not been scientifically proven. However, stress reduction is of benefit for many other health reasons.

References

*"Self-Reported Stress and Risk of Breast Cancer," Felicia D. Roberts, Polly A. Newcomb, Amy Trentham-Dietz, and Barry E. Storer. *Cancer*, March 15, 1996.

"Stress and Immune Responses after Surgical Treatment for Regional Breast Cancer," Barbara L. Andersen, William B. Farrar, Deanna Golden-Kreutz, et al. *Journal of the National Cancer Institute*, January 7, 1998.

Additional Information

National Cancer Institute
Bldg. 31, Rm. 10A31
31 Center Drive, MSC 2580
Bethesda, MD 20892-2580
Toll-Free: 800-422-6237
TTY: 800-332-8615
Fax on Demand: 301-402-5874 (listen to recorded instructions)
Website: http://cancer.gov
E-mail: cancermail@icicc.nci.hig.gov (to obtain a contents list, e-mail with the word "help" in the body of the message)

Chapter 27

Stress and Ulcers—
Just a Myth?

Have a Stressful Job? You Must Have an Ulcer...Right?

Which of the following people are most likely to have an ulcer? The answer may surprise you.

Table 27.1. Most and Least Stressful Jobs

Top 10 Most Stressful Jobs	Top 10 Least Stressful Jobs
1. Inner City HS Teacher	1. Forester
2. Police Officer	2. Bookbinder
3. Miner	3. Telephone Line Worker
4. Air Traffic Controller	4. Toolmaker
5. Medical Intern	5. Millwright
6. Stockbroker	6. Repairperson
7. Journalist	7. Civil Engineer
8. Customer Service/Complaint Worker	8. Therapist
9. Secretary	9. Natural Scientist
10. Waiter	10. Sales Representative

Source: *Health Magazine*

"*Helicobacter pylori* and Peptic Ulcer Disease—Myths," and "*Helicobacter pylori* and Peptic Ulcer Disease—Good News! A Cure for Ulcers!" from the Division of Bacterial and Mycotic Diseases of the National Center for Infectious Diseases, reviewed February 2, 2001; and excerpts from "Stomach and Duodenal Ulcers," National Institute of Diabetes and Digestive and Kidney Diseases (NIDDK), NIH Publication No. 95-38, January 1995, revised by David A. Cooke, M.D. February 24, 2002.

Did you guess that the inner city high school teacher's stomach would be riddled with ulcers not only from the stress of dealing with troubled teens, but also from the tacos in the lunchroom? And that the forester's calm environment would make his or her stomach acid-free and healthy? Surprise! All the workers on this list are just as likely as any others you can imagine to get an ulcer.

While stress and diet can irritate an ulcer, they do not cause it. Ulcers are caused by the bacterium *H. pylori*, and can be cured with a one- or two-week course of antibiotics, even for people who have had ulcers for years.

Good News—A Cure For Ulcers

Whether you think you might have an ulcer, have recently been diagnosed with one, or have been living with ulcers for many years, there is good news. Recently, scientists have found that most ulcers are caused by an infection. With appropriate antibiotic treatment, your ulcer—and the pain it causes—can be gone forever.

What Is an Ulcer?

Twenty-five million Americans suffer from ulcers. An ulcer is a sore or hole in the lining of the stomach or duodenum (the first part of the small intestine). People of any age can get an ulcer and women are affected just as often as men.

Who Has Ulcers?

About 20 million Americans develop at least one ulcer during their lifetime. Each year:

- Ulcers affect about 4 million people.

- More than 40,000 people have surgery because of persistent symptoms or problems from ulcers.

- About 6,000 people die of ulcer-related complications.

Ulcers can develop at any age, but they are rare among teenagers and even more uncommon in children. Duodenal ulcers occur for the first time usually between the ages of 30 and 50. Stomach ulcers are more likely to develop in people over age 60. Duodenal ulcers occur more frequently in men than women; stomach ulcers develop more often in women than men.

What Causes Ulcers?

For almost a century, doctors believed lifestyle factors such as stress and diet caused ulcers. Later, researchers felt that an imbalance between digestive fluids (hydrochloric acid and pepsin) and the stomach's ability to defend itself against these powerful substances resulted in ulcers. Today, research shows that most ulcers develop as a result of infection with bacteria called *Helicobacter pylori* (*H. pylori*). While all three of these factors—lifestyle, acid and pepsin, and *H. pylori*—play a role in ulcer development, *H. pylori* is now considered the primary cause. Contrary to older beliefs, it is now felt that very few ulcers are the result of excess stomach acidity.

Lifestyle

While scientific evidence refutes the old belief that stress and diet cause ulcers, several lifestyle factors continue to be suspected of playing a role. These factors include cigarettes, foods and beverages containing caffeine, alcohol, and physical stress.

Smoking

Studies show that cigarette smoking increases one's chances of getting an ulcer. Smoking slows the healing of existing ulcers and also contributes to ulcer recurrence.

Caffeine

Coffee, tea, colas, and foods that contain caffeine seem to stimulate acid secretion in the stomach, aggravating the pain of an existing ulcer. However, the amount of acid secretion that occurs after drinking decaffeinated coffee is the same as that produced after drinking regular coffee. Thus, the stimulation of stomach acid cannot be attributed solely to caffeine. Even so, acid is rarely the initial cause of an ulcer.

Alcohol

Research has not found a link between alcohol consumption and duodenal ulcers, the most common form of ulcer. However, alcohol can cause gastric ulcers. Additionally, ulcers are more common in people who have cirrhosis of the liver, a disease often linked to heavy alcohol consumption.

Stress

Although emotional stress is no longer thought to be a cause of ulcers, people with ulcers often report that emotional stress increases ulcer pain. Physical stress, however, can cause ulcers. Stomach ulceration following severe burns, life-threatening infections, or major surgery is common. Intensive care unit patients often need aggressive treatment to prevent ulcer development.

Acid and Pepsin

The stomach is a remarkable organ in that it produces intense acid, yet it is normally unharmed by it. Ulcers only occur when there is a breakdown in the systems that the stomach uses to protect itself from powerful acids and digestive enzymes. The stomach defends itself from these fluids in several ways. One way is by producing mucus—a lubricant-like coating that shields stomach tissues. Another way is by producing a chemical called bicarbonate. This chemical neutralizes and breaks down digestive fluids into substances less harmful to stomach tissue. Finally, blood circulation to the stomach lining, cell renewal, and cell repair also help to protect the stomach.

H. Pylori

H. pylori is a recently-discovered form of bacteria that makes its home in some people's stomachs. The bacteria interfere with the stomach's normal defense mechanisms, leaving the stomach's lining vulnerable to the acid it produces. Once this occurs, the acid dissolves sections of the lining, creating ulcers than can burrow deep in the stomach wall. In this way, *H. pylori* creates ulcers which are then perpetuated by the stomach's own acid and pepsin. Currently, it is believed that the majority of ulcers are caused by *H. pylori*. Most people who develop ulcers are infected with *H. pylori*. Elimination of the bacteria from the body will usually cause ulcers to heal permanently.

Medications

After *H. pylori*, the next most common cause of ulcers are nonsteroidal anti-inflammatory drugs (NSAIDs). NSAIDs are commonly-used medications, and include aspirin, ibuprofen, and naproxen sodium. They are present in many non-prescription medications used to treat fever, headaches, and minor aches and pains. Other NSAIDs are also frequently used by prescription to treat various arthritic and inflammatory conditions. These drugs also make the stomach vulnerable to the harmful effects of acid and pepsin. They interfere with the stomach's ability to produce mucus and bicarbonate and affect blood flow to the stomach and cell repair. These can cause the stomach's defense mechanisms to fail, resulting in an increased chance of developing stomach ulcers. In most cases, these ulcers disappear once the person stops taking NSAIDs.

What Are the Symptoms of an Ulcer?

The most common ulcer symptom is gnawing or burning pain in the abdomen between the breastbone and the belly button. The pain often occurs when the stomach is empty, between meals, and in the early morning hours, but it can occur at any other time. It may last from minutes to hours and may be relieved by eating food or taking antacids. Less common symptoms include nausea, vomiting, or loss of appetite. Sometimes ulcers bleed. If bleeding continues for a long time, it may lead to anemia with weakness and fatigue. If bleeding is heavy, blood may appear in vomit or bowel movements, which may appear dark red or black.

How Can Your Health Care Provider Tell if You Have H. Pylori?

Your health care provider may choose to use any of the following tests to determine if your ulcer is caused by *H. pylori.*

- **Blood tests:** A blood test can confirm if you have *H. pylori.* To perform this test, your health care provider sends your blood sample to a lab.

- **Stool tests:** A stool test can determine if you are currently infected with *H. pylori.* A stool sample is sent to a lab, which can determine if the bacteria are present.

- **Breath tests:** A breath test can determine if you are infected with *H. pylori.* In this test, you drink a harmless liquid and in less than 1 hour, a sample of your breath is tested for *H. pylori.*

- **Endoscopy:** Your health care provider may decide to perform an endoscopy. This is a test in which a small tube with a camera inside is inserted through the mouth and into the stomach to

379

look for ulcers. During the endoscopy, small samples of the stomach lining can be obtained and tested for *H. pylori*.

What Is the Treatment for H. Pylori Infection?

If you have an ulcer, you should be tested for *H. pylori*, and if found to be infected, you should be treated with antibiotics. Antibiotics are the new cure for ulcers; therapy is 1-2 weeks of two or three antibiotics and a medication that will reduce the acid in the stomach. This treatment is a dramatic medical advance because eliminating *H. pylori* with antibiotics means that there is a greater than 90% chance that the ulcer can be cured for good. Remember, it is very important to continue taking all of this medicine until it is gone, even when you begin to feel better. If you are having side effects that make it hard to take your medicine, talk to your health care provider.

Ulcer Facts

- Most ulcers are caused by an infection, not spicy food, acid, or stress.

- The most common ulcer symptom is burning pain in the stomach.

- Your doctor can test you for *H. pylori* infection.

- Antibiotics are the new cure for ulcers.

- Eliminating *H. pylori* infections with antibiotics means that your ulcer can be cured for good.

Chapter 28

Stress Is a Factor in Women's Health

Introduction

Women live an average of 7 years longer than men and make up the majority of the population over 65. They suffer from different diseases, disorders, and conditions than men, and even when they have the same diseases, women often experience different symptoms and responses to treatment than do their male counterparts.

There is ample evidence of variations in health and disease between women and men. Research shows, for example, that more women than men are diagnosed with arthritis, depression, type 2 diabetes, osteoporosis, gallstone disease, and eating disorders. Women have a higher rate of lung cancer and spend twice as many years disabled. They suffer more serious consequences from drinking less alcohol; have a 2 to 3 times higher occurrence of irritable bowel syndrome and functional bowel disease; and are 9 times more likely to contract certain liver diseases. Older women tend to experience more reactions to medications than older men, and women of all ages have a higher prevalence of urinary incontinence. While women account for 52 percent of all deaths due to heart disease and 61 percent of all deaths due to stroke in the United States, they are less likely

Excerpted from "Agenda for Research on Women's Health for the 21st Century," Volume 7, *New Frontiers in Women's Health*, National Institutes of Health (NIH), NIH Publication No. 01-4391, 2001; and "Stress Hormone Levels in Women Reduced During Lactation," National Institute of Mental Health (NIMH), October 10, 1995.

to have been treated by a doctor for heart problems prior to their deaths.

Sex and gender differences in disease rates, symptoms, and treatment outcomes have been recognized only recently. Earlier scientific studies sometimes excluded women for various reasons, including the desire to protect reproductive-age women from the unknown effects of unproven treatments, and the commonly held belief that what was true for men was also true for women.

Fortunately, in the last decade of the 20th century, science has made substantial progress in understanding the differences between women and men in health and disease. Supported by a federal mandate, women's health research is now an integral part of the fabric of research at the National Institutes of Health and in programs nationwide. Yet progress gives rise to new questions—critical questions that point the way into uncharted territory.

This report summarizes thousands of issues and questions raised by more than 1,500 women's health professionals and advocates throughout the United States. Their recommendations for addressing the major diseases and health risks affecting women create a comprehensive map for scientific inquiry in the 21st century. Their common concerns reflect emerging directions for women's health research as it explores new frontiers in women's unique experience of health and disease.

Major Diseases, Conditions, and Health Risks Among Women

Women are at risk for numerous life-threatening diseases and chronic conditions that impact the length and quality of their lives. By addressing critical questions about each of these health risks, research can help improve the lives of generations of women.

Heart Disease

- Heart disease has been the number one killer of women for nearly a century and accounts for 43 percent of all deaths among women.

More than 960,000 Americans die each year from cardiovascular disease (CVD), about one person every 33 seconds. CVD, which includes heart and coronary artery diseases, congestive heart failure, and stroke, kills almost twice as many American women as all cancers combined, and more than 11 times as many women as does breast cancer. In fact, a postmenopausal woman is 10 times more likely to die from coronary artery disease than she is from breast cancer.

Although women develop heart disease later in life than men do, heart attacks are more deadly for women. For example, older women who have heart attacks are nearly twice as likely as men to die from those attacks within a few weeks (about 44 percent of women compared to 27 percent of men). And, among the women who die suddenly of coronary heart disease, 64 percent have had no previous symptoms.

While dramatic progress has been achieved against heart disease in recent decades, the frequency of heart attacks and other cardiovascular diseases remains disturbingly high. Even though risk factors (including stress) for heart disease in women and men have been known for years, heart attack, stroke, and other cardiovascular diseases in women have not been recognized as serious problems until recently, especially by women themselves.

Recent scientific achievements include increased funding for cardiovascular research, including research into women's health services, the cost effectiveness of treatments, and the study of diverse populations and communities; greater participation of women in clinical studies; and new cardiovascular disease treatment regimens for women.

Continued research in the 21st century will help save women's lives with answers to critical questions related to heart disease, such as:

- How do hormones affect the cardiovascular system in women versus men? In premenopausal versus postmenopausal women? With or without hormone replacement therapy?

- What effects do diabetes and obesity have on the cardiovascular system? Why is obesity a greater problem for women than for men and what factors contribute to this difference?

- What differences in cardiovascular disease exist among elderly and disabled women, as well as racial and ethnic minorities? Among women living in different locations?

- How can cardiovascular disease in high-risk populations be prevented, detected, and managed?

Cancer

Cancer is the leading cause of death for American women aged 35 to 74. It is only after age 75 that heart disease claims the lives of women in sufficient numbers to become their number one killer. In 1997, an estimated 596,000 women were diagnosed with cancer, while 265,900 women died from the disease.

Breast cancer is the most common form of cancer in women, yet lung cancer is the leading cause of cancer deaths in women, followed by breast and colorectal (colon and rectal) cancers. The number of lung cancer deaths in 1997 represented 25 percent of all cancer deaths among women, and an increase of more than 16,000 deaths since 1991.

While lung cancer among all women continues to rise (it is decreasing among men), scientific progress in the last decade has helped decrease the death rate from breast and colorectal cancers among white women. Fifty-six new drugs for treating breast cancer are now in various stages of development and factors decreasing the risk of colon and rectal cancers have been identified. In addition, major advances in genetics are improving the scientific understanding of cancer, although little progress has been made to improve women's survival from ovarian, cervical, and uterine cancers.

Cancer researchers have observed differences in metabolism between women and men, between different racial and ethnic groups, and between older and younger persons; these differences influence individual responses to carcinogens (cancer-producing substances) and treatments. As a result of these findings, studies are now underway to investigate how factors such as age, ethnicity, genetics, the environment, social and economic variables, and other stressors interact to determine whether an individual will develop cancer and whether that cancer will respond to treatment. Researchers hope to develop prevention strategies, diagnostic tests, and education and treatment programs that are effective, inexpensive, acceptable, and available to women of all income levels and cultural backgrounds.

Table 28.1. Estimated 1997 Prevalence of Cancer in Women

Type of Cancer	Number of Diagnoses	Number of Deaths
Lung	83,200	67,430
Breast	180,200	43,900
Colorectal	65,900	24,300
Ovarian	26,800	14,200
Cervical	14,500	8,000
Uterine	34,900	6,000

Perhaps one of the most promising discoveries to date is that cancer may be a preventable disease. Diet, cigarette smoking, hormones, and the environment have been found to be potential contributing factors to various cancers. Decreased tobacco use has been shown to lower the occurrence of lung cancer, and some studies have shown that hormone replacement therapy may decrease the risk of colon cancer, although it may also increase the risk of breast and endometrial cancers.

The women's health agenda for the 21st century contains important recommendations and leading questions for cancer research, such as those stated below.

- What are the long-term effects of different forms of estrogen on cancer risk?

- How does cancer start, grow, and spread?

- What medications are effective for various cancers, with minimal side effects?

- What are the effects of exercise and weight control on cancer risk?

- What strategies and methods help people quit smoking or refuse to start?

Mental Disorders

- Depression is becoming a global epidemic. At its current rate of increase, depression will be second only to heart disease as the reason people lose healthy years of life by the year 2020.

Mental disorders include anxiety disorders (panic disorder, posttraumatic stress syndrome, obsessive compulsive disorder, and phobias), depressive disorders, schizophrenia and other psychoses, and the eating disorders of anorexia and bulimia. Anxiety disorders are the most widespread forms of mental illness in the United States, affecting more than 20 million individuals. By comparison, an estimated 18.4 million Americans suffer each year from some form of depression, while another 2.3 million are considered manic depressive (experiencing alternating cycles of excessive excitement and depression).

Major mental disorders impact women and men to almost the same extent, although certain conditions are more common in women. Anxiety disorders, for example, are diagnosed approximately 2 to 3 times as often in women as in men. Major depression is diagnosed in about twice as many women as in men, while eating disorders occur 8 to 10 times more frequently in women. Plus, there is growing evidence that depression may express itself differently in women than in men.

Research over the past decade has led to a new understanding of the burden of mental illness in women. Because women are often caregivers for both parents and children, their mental problems can influence two or three generations of family members. At the same time, women may have multiple responsibilities creating stresses that amplify their mental illnesses. Women are also more likely to be the victims of violence, an experience that has been linked to the onset of various mental disorders.

Most mental disorders can be treated successfully. Nearly 85 percent of people with depression respond positively to one or more types of treatment, while recent therapies have provided relief to women with anxiety disorders. Progress is also being made in how to educate and help women and young girls suffering from eating disorders.

In addition to conducting research on the role of sex and gender in mental disorders, researchers are currently exploring how age, physical health, ethnicity and race, marital status, parental status, education, occupation, income, sexual orientation, geographic location, and work status influence the appearance, symptoms, and treatment of mental illnesses. As science enters the new century, it aims to answer additional questions about mental health in women, including those listed below.

- What factors contribute to the development of mental disorders in women across the life span? What makes some women susceptible and others resistant to mental disorders?

- What are the causes of depression in all its forms? What individual and interactive roles do genetics and environment play? How can depression be prevented and treated effectively in women?

- What are the long-term mental and physical consequences of sexual assault and domestic violence?

- What are the impacts of hormones on brain development, aging, behavior, and sex and gender differences in mental disorders? What are the long-term interactive effects of mood-altering drugs and hormones?

Bone and Musculoskeletal Diseases

- The combination of arthritis and orthopedic impairments limits the physical activity of 4.5 times as many people as do heart conditions.

Many bone and musculoskeletal conditions appear more often in women than in men, and have different causes, symptoms, effects, and treatment outcomes. Arthritis, which refers to more than 100 illnesses and conditions, is the most common chronic condition reported by American women (23 million in 1990). About 16 million Americans suffer from osteoarthritis, which affects 2 times as many women as it does men, while rheumatoid arthritis afflicts 2.1 million Americans, occurring in 3 times as many women as men. In all its forms, arthritis is the third leading cause of bed disability in the United States and contributes to individuals' inability to work or perform daily activities, as well as to adverse psychological effects.

Osteoporosis involves low bone mass, with continued bone loss leading to an increased risk of fracture. Low bone mass, or density, is found more often in women than men because women build up less bone as they mature and have increased bone loss at menopause, due to a drop off of estrogen. An estimated 4 to 6 million women over age 50 suffer from osteoporosis, while an additional 13 to 17 million have osteopenia (less severe bone loss). The percentage of women with osteoporosis increases with each decade of life after age 50.

Orthopedic problems, such as fractures, foot problems, shoulder instability, scoliosis (curvature of the spine), and carpal tunnel syndrome (severe wrist pain) are the primary causes of bed disability in the United States. Women made an estimated 20 million visits to their physicians for these conditions in 1995. Although the lack of appropriate exercise throughout life may contribute to some of the physical impairments occurring in some women as they age, the increased participation of many women in sports and fitness activities makes the prevention of orthopedic sports injuries a high priority. In some cases, extreme physical activity can play a part in eating disorders and lead to amenorrhea (the absence of menstrual cycles) and osteoporosis.

Progress over the last few years in the science, treatment, and management of bone and musculoskeletal disorders has been remarkable. Arthritis research has led to improvements in joint replacement surgery, the discovery that self care works and enhances self-sufficiency, and an understanding of the benefits of exercise for pain relief. Studies of osteoporosis have resulted in revised dietary guidelines for calcium intake, new ways to measure bone mass, and new drugs for disease prevention and treatment. In the field of orthopedics, scientists have improved techniques for treating fractures and soft tissue injuries, as well as for performing total joint replacements; developed less invasive surgery procedures; and identified factors that may make some women prone to carpal tunnel syndrome.

Research in the next century promises to improve the bone and musculoskeletal health of women by addressing questions like those below.

- What factors influence the progression of arthritis and why do more women than men suffer from this disease?

- What factors contribute to the development of peak bone mass? What contributes to bone loss?

- What causes stress fractures?

- What is the role of physical activity in developing bones, tendons, ligaments, and muscles? In preserving muscular strength, balance, and coordination as a means of preventing falls in the elderly?

Immunity and Autoimmune Diseases

- Many autoimmune diseases are considered rare, affecting fewer than 200,000 people. Taken together, however, they afflict 50 million Americans, including 3 times more women than men.

The immune system protects the body from viruses, bacteria, and other health threats by identifying and destroying these foreign intruders. Autoimmune diseases, in which the immune response begins to attack the body's own tissues, affect three times as many women as men. Autoimmunity is the root cause of more than 80 serious, chronic diseases, including rheumatoid arthritis, type 1 diabetes, lupus (destructive tissue inflammation), multiple sclerosis, Graves' disease (hyperthyroidism), and scleroderma (thickening and hardening of the skin).

The most common autoimmune disease is arthritis, which currently afflicts 23 million women in the United States and is expected to afflict 36 million by the year 2020. A leading cause of disability in women, arthritis has also been linked to anxiety, depression, and changes in cognitive abilities (perception, memory, judgment, and reasoning). Asthma and chronic allergies, also immune-related diseases, account for considerable illness among women, while atherosclerosis (hardening of the arteries) and Alzheimer's disease are complicated by an immune or inflammatory component.

Notable scientific progress over recent years has expanded understanding of the immune system and its related diseases. For example, researchers have discovered that the immune function may be altered by external factors such as diet, vitamins, stress, infections, indoor and outdoor allergens, physical activity and exercise, sexual orientation, implants, hormone replacement therapy, and birth control pills. Study results have helped doctors improve bone marrow transplants and the rebuilding of the immune system after chemotherapy and radiation treatments.

At present, new research tools involving DNA are allowing researchers to conduct studies that were previously impossible, while important interactions between the immune system and the nervous and endocrine systems, as well as with hormones, are being studied and documented. These and other advances offer hope that autoimmune and allergic diseases can be prevented and effectively treated.

The women's health agenda for the 21st century includes the following questions concerning immunity and autoimmune diseases.

- What genes are involved in autoimmune and allergic diseases?

- What are the specific effects of environmental factors, such as diet, stress, and allergen exposure on immune function?

- What are the effects of age and sex on normal and abnormal immune function?

- How do hormones affect the immune response? Is there a difference in effect between the body's natural hormones and the hormones contained in birth control pills and hormone replacement therapy? Do women's cyclical changes in hormones affect the immune response?

- What differences exist in various organs associated with inflammatory diseases—the brain in multiple sclerosis, the joints in rheumatoid arthritis, the beta cells in diabetes, the kidney and vasculature (blood vessels and lymph ducts) in lupus, the lung in asthma, and the skin in scleroderma?

Digestive Diseases

Approximately 75 percent of individuals with irritable bowel syndrome (IBS) in the community are female, with the incidence being reported as high as 90 percent in some medical centers. (Source: Nancy Norton, International Foundation for Functional Gastrointestinal Disorders)

Women are at high risk for many digestive diseases. For example, 2 to 3 times more women than men are diagnosed with irritable bowel syndrome and functional bowel diseases, conditions that affect 15 to 20 percent of the U.S. population. Women also comprise two-thirds of the estimated 20 million Americans suffering from gallstones. More women than men develop peptic ulcers from high doses of nonsteroidal anti-inflammatory drugs, such as aspirin and ibuprofen. Nine times as many women suffer from biliary cirrhosis and 3 to 4 times as many women have autoimmune hepatitis (progressive inflammation of the liver). In addition, women with inflammatory bowel or chronic liver diseases have an increased chance of developing osteoporosis, while women diagnosed with colorectal cancer (also considered as a digestive disease) have a higher risk of experiencing cancer of the pancreas, small bowel, or endometrium. Gallbladder removal is one of the most common surgeries performed on women.

Digestive problems during pregnancy include (a) chronic conditions present prior to pregnancy, such as ulcerative colitis, Crohn's disease, and biliary disease; and (b) symptoms and conditions generally associated with pregnancy, such as nausea, vomiting, and heartburn. Acute fatty liver disease can also occur during pregnancy and, although very rare, can be fatal.

Scientific advances over the past 10 to 15 years have expanded the understanding of gastrointestinal functions and diseases. For example, factors such as stress, physical and sexual abuse, and mental health have been shown to play important roles in the onset and treatment of irritable bowel syndrome, changes in the motility (ability to move) of the small intestines or colon, and an increased sensitivity to pain. The newly identified nonalcoholic liver disease, steatohepatitis, has been linked to obesity and non-insulin dependent diabetes. Plus, the development of less invasive surgical techniques now permit more rapid recovery rates for gallbladder patients, while recent genetic discoveries offer great promise for reducing the incidence of colorectal cancer and gallstone and acute fatty liver diseases. Early screening for colorectal cancer is highly effective in preventing new cases of colon cancer because growths can be discovered and removed before they become cancerous.

The agenda for research on digestive diseases in women includes finding answers to questions such as:

390

- Why do irritable bowel syndrome and functional bowel diseases affect more women than men?

- What cost-effective methods are there for the early detection of colorectal cancer? How can women and health care providers be made more aware of the importance of screening for this disease?

- What causes gallstones during pregnancy and periods of rapid weight loss?

- What are safe and effective therapies for treating liver diseases in women? For treating chronic gastrointestinal conditions in pregnant women?

- How does calcium absorption in the intestines affect health and disease, and how does this change with age?

Alcohol, Tobacco, and Illicit Drug Use

Women have a 1.4 to 2.9 times higher risk of developing lung cancer than men when the amount of tobacco exposure is controlled. (Source: Carolyn M. Dresler, M.D. Thoracic Surgical Oncologist American College of Chest Physicians)

Women make up one-third of the estimated 14 million Americans who abuse or are dependent upon alcohol. While men drink alcohol in larger amounts than women do, alcohol-dependent women often experience greater psychological impairment sooner once they begin to drink heavily. Women alcoholics also develop alcohol-related liver disease, heart disease, and brain disorders earlier in their drinking careers than do men.

About half of the 48 million smokers in the United States are women, as are nearly a third of the 500,000 people who die from tobacco use each year. Even though tobacco is the most preventable cause of death in this country, smoking rates among women have declined only 21 percent in the past 30 years, compared to an 84 percent decline among men. In addition to risking lung cancer, women who smoke often experience early menopause, which may increase their risk for coronary artery disease.

A study conducted in 1990-1992 found that about 6 percent of American women between the ages of 15 and 54 met the criteria for lifetime drug dependence. In another study, more than 221,000 women admitted using drugs while pregnant. Such illicit drug use (as well as alcohol abuse) has been linked to mental disorders, especially depression; violence and sexual abuse; eating disorders; low self-esteem; and exposure to sexually transmitted diseases, including HIV/AIDS.

Recent scientific studies have demonstrated that (a) alcoholism risk can be transferred genetically from generation to generation; (b) women are more likely to begin or maintain cocaine use in order to develop more intimate relationships, while men are more likely to use the drug with male friends and in relation to the drug trade; and (c) the presence of their children in residential treatment facilities increases women's length of time in treatment.

The following questions will help guide future research into alcohol, tobacco, and illicit drug use among women.

- What are the effects of a mother's alcohol and drug use on her children's use of alcohol and drugs?

- How is women's alcohol and drug use influenced by the presence of anxiety disorders? Eating disorders? Depression? Childhood sexual abuse? Violent victimization as an adult?

- How do the media and advertisements influence women's use of alcohol, tobacco, and illicit drugs?

- How do hormones and alcohol interact?

- What can be learned about effective treatment for alcohol and drug addictions from women who successfully recover?

Table 28.2. Women's Alcohol, Tobacco, and Illicit Drug Use

Condition	Prevalence
Alcohol abuse and/or dependence	4.0 million
Alcohol use in past year of >12 drinks	32.7 million
Tobacco use at some time in life	73.6 million
Tobacco use in past year	32.5 million
Tobacco use in past month	29.5 million
Illicit drug use in past month among women of childbearing age	4.3 million

Stress Hormone Levels in Women Reduced During Lactation

Women who breast-feed their infants produce lower levels of stress response hormones than do women who bottle-feed, according to research conducted by the National Institute of Mental Health (NIMH). The study is the first to explore the effects of lactation on hormonal stress responses in humans.

The NIMH researchers, led by Margaret Altemus, M.D., theorize that lactation-induced suppression of stress responses serves several purposes for both mother and baby. First, it may help to conserve energy needed for production of breast milk. Second, it may minimize the psychological stress associated with the demands of infant care, thus enhancing milk release. Third, it may improve immune function during the postpartum period.

During any stressful situation, the brain's neuroendocrine, or hormonal, systems are activated. In the hypothalamus, the brain's "control center" for the neuroendocrine system, various stress response hormones are released—including vasopressin and corticotropin-releasing hormone, or CRH. CRH and vasopressin have arousing effects in the brain and also travel to the pituitary gland, where they trigger the release of adrenocorticotropic hormone, or ACTH. ACTH, in turn, stimulates the adrenal glands to produce cortisol, which mobilizes energy for the body's response to stress.

Studies of rats have shown that lactation suppresses a variety of physiological responses to stress, including the release of several stress hormones. To determine whether the same changes take place in humans, Altemus and her colleagues studied twenty postpartum women—10 who were lactating and 10 who were not. Women in the study were between 7 and 18 weeks postpartum, and between 24 and 36 years of age.

The researchers used treadmill exercise—the same type of "stress test" given to cardiac patients—to elicit the hormonal stress response. Each woman performed treadmill exercise for 20 minutes, and blood hormone levels were taken before, during, and after the exercise was completed.

Before the treadmill test, levels of ACTH, cortisol, and vasopressin were similar in both the lactating and non-lactating groups. In response to the stress of exercise, all participants showed an increase in hormone levels; however, the increase was significantly less among women who were breast-feeding their babies compared to those who were bottle-feeding. Lactating women had lower levels of ACTH and cortisol and showed a trend toward a lower vasopressin response than did non-lactating women.

While the exact mechanisms responsible for the reduction of stress hormone responses during lactation remain to be determined, the findings could help to shed light on the biological underpinnings of stress and anxiety disorders.

According to Altemus, increased levels of the stress hormones vasopressin and CRH have been associated with obsessive-compulsive disorder (OCD), a type of anxiety disorder, in humans. Both hormones also promote fearful behaviors when administered to animals.

"Preliminary research has also shown that lactation appears to reduce the symptoms of anxiety disorders," said Altemus. "However, more work needs to be done to help us pinpoint which elements of lactation physiology are responsible for producing this anti-stress effect."

The study, "Suppression of Hypothalmic-Pituitary-Adrenal Axis Responses to Stress in Lactating Women," was published in the October 1995 issue of the *Journal of Clinical Endocrinology and Metabolism*. Other authors of the report are Patricia Deuster, Ph.D., Elise Galliven, C. Sue Carter, Ph.D., and Philip W. Gold, M.D.

Chapter 29

Stress and Multiple Sclerosis

Multiple sclerosis (MS) is an unpredictable, frustrating disease. As such, its emotional impact can be as great as its physical impact.

The prolonged stress of living with a chronic illness can lead to frustration, anger, hopelessness, and, at times, depression. And you are not the only person affected. Family members are also influenced by the persistent health changes of a loved one. It is important to recognize the triggers, signs, and solutions that are associated with stress so that you can effectively manage it.

What Causes Stress for People with MS?

- Uncertainty of diagnosis (living with symptoms and no diagnosis)

- Unpredictability of the disease

- The emergence of symptoms and having visible signs of the disease, such as the need of a cane or wheelchair

- Concerns about finances and job situation

- Having to depend on others, and not being able to care for others (such as spouses and children) like you used to

Reprinted with permission, "Stress and MS," © 2000 The Cleveland Clinic Foundation, 9500 Euclid Avenue, Cleveland, OH 44195, 800-223-2273 ext.48950, www.clevelandclinic.org. Additional information is available from the Cleveland Clinic Health Information Center, 216-444-3771, or www.clevelandclinic.org/health.

- Modifying your activities and your surroundings to accommodate your MS

- Symptoms that are unexplainable and not understandable

What Are the Warning Signs of Stress?

Your body sends out physical, emotional, and behavioral warning signs of stress.

Emotional warning signs include anger, an inability to concentrate, unproductive worry, sadness, and frequent mood swings.

Physical warning signs include stooped posture, sweaty palms, chronic fatigue, and weight gain or loss.

Behavioral warning signs include over-reacting, acting on impulse, using alcohol or drugs, and withdrawing from relationships.

What Can I Do to Reduce Stress?

- Keep a positive attitude
- Accept that there are events that you cannot control
- Be assertive instead of aggressive. Assert your feelings, opinions or beliefs instead of becoming angry, combative, or passive
- Learn relaxation techniques
- Exercise regularly. Your body can fight stress better when it is fit
- Eat well-balanced meals
- Rest and sleep. Your body needs time to recover from stressful events
- Don't rely on alcohol or drugs to reduce stress

How Can I Learn to Relax?

There are a number of exercises that you can do to relax. These exercises include breathing, muscle and mind relaxation, relaxation to music, and biofeedback. Three that you can try are listed below.

First, be sure that you have:

1. A quiet location that is free of distractions.

2. A comfortable body position. Sit or recline on a chair or sofa.

3. A good state of mind. Try to block out worries and distracting thoughts.

Two-minute relaxation: Switch your thoughts to yourself and your breathing. Take a few deep breaths, exhaling slowly. Mentally scan your body. Notice areas that feel tense or cramped. Quickly loosen up these areas. Let go of as much tension as you can. Rotate your head in a smooth, circular motion once or twice. (Stop any movements that cause pain.) Roll your shoulders forward and backward several times. Let all of your muscles completely relax. Recall a pleasant thought for a few seconds. Take another deep breath and exhale slowly. You should feel relaxed.

Mind relaxation: Close your eyes. Breathe normally through your nose. As you exhale, silently say to yourself the word "one," a short word such as "peaceful" or a short phrase such as "I feel quiet." Continue for 10 minutes. If your mind wanders, gently remind yourself to think about your breathing and your chosen word or phrase. Let your breathing become slow and steady.

Deep-breathing relaxation: Imagine a spot just below your navel. Breathe into that spot and fill your abdomen with air. Let the air fill you from the abdomen up, then let it out, like deflating a balloon. With every long, slow breath out, you should feel more relaxed.

The information provided by The Cleveland Clinic is not intended to replace the medical advice of your doctor or health-care provider. Please consult your health-care provider for advice about a specific medical condition.

Chapter 30

Stress Affects Skin Conditions

Atopic Dermatitis

Atopic dermatitis is a chronic (long-lasting) disease that affects the skin. The word "dermatitis" means inflammation of the skin. "Atopic" refers to a group of diseases that are hereditary (that is, run in families) and often occur together, including asthma, allergies such as hay fever, and atopic dermatitis. In atopic dermatitis, the skin becomes extremely itchy and inflamed, causing redness, swelling, cracking, weeping, crusting, and scaling. Atopic dermatitis most often affects infants and young children, but it can continue into adulthood or first show up later in life. In most cases, there are periods of time when the disease is worse, called exacerbations or flares, followed by periods when the skin improves or clears up entirely, called remissions. Many children with atopic dermatitis will experience a permanent remission of the disease when they get older, although their skin often remains dry and easily irritated. Environmental factors can bring on symptoms of atopic dermatitis at any time in the lives of individuals who have inherited the atopic disease trait.

Atopic dermatitis is often referred to as "eczema," which is a general term for the many types of dermatitis. Atopic dermatitis is the

This chapter includes the following National Institute of Arthritis and Musculoskeletal and Skin Diseases (NIAMS) documents: "Atopic Dermatitis," by Debbie Novak, updated February 2002; "Questions and Answers about Psoriasis," updated January 2002; and "Questions and Answers about Rosacea," April 1999.

most common of the many types of eczema. Several have very similar symptoms.

Atopic dermatitis is very common. It affects males and females equally and accounts for 10 to 20 percent of all referrals to dermatologists (doctors who specialize in the care and treatment of skin diseases). Atopic dermatitis occurs most often in infants and children and its onset decreases substantially with age. Scientists estimate that 65 percent of patients develop symptoms in the first year of life, and 90 percent develop symptoms before the age of 5. Onset after age 30 is less common and often occurs after exposure of skin to harsh conditions. People who live in urban areas and in climates with low humidity seem to be at an increased risk for developing atopic dermatitis.

Although it is difficult to identify exactly how many people are affected by atopic dermatitis, an estimated 10 percent of infants and young children experience symptoms of the disease. Roughly 60 percent of these infants continue to have one or more symptoms of atopic dermatitis into adulthood. This means that more than 15 million people in the United States have symptoms of the disease.

The cause of atopic dermatitis is not known, but the disease seems to result from a combination of genetic (hereditary) and environmental factors. Evidence suggests the disease is associated with other so-called atopic disorders such as hay fever and asthma, which many people with atopic dermatitis also have. In addition, many children who outgrow the symptoms of atopic dermatitis go on to develop hay fever or asthma. Although one disorder does not cause another, they may be related, thereby giving researchers clues to understanding atopic dermatitis.

In the past, doctors thought that atopic dermatitis was caused by an emotional disorder. We now know that emotional factors, such as stress, can make the condition worse, but they do not cause the disease. Also, atopic dermatitis is not contagious; it cannot be passed from one person to another.

Types of Eczema (Dermatitis)

- **Atopic dermatitis:** a chronic skin disease characterized by itchy, inflamed skin

- **Contact eczema:** a localized reaction that includes redness, itching, and burning where the skin has come into contact with an allergen (an allergy-causing substance) or with an irritant such as an acid, a cleaning agent, or other chemical

- **Allergic contact eczema (dermatitis):** a red, itchy, weepy reaction where the skin has come into contact with a substance that the immune system recognizes as foreign, such as poison ivy or certain preservatives in creams and lotions

- **Seborrheic eczema:** yellowish, oily, scaly patches of skin on the scalp, face, and occasionally other parts of the body

- **Nummular eczema:** coin-shaped patches of irritated skin—most common on the arms, back, buttocks, and lower legs—that may be crusted, scaling, and extremely itchy

- **Neurodermatitis:** scaly patches of skin on the head, lower legs, wrists, or forearms caused by a localized itch (such as an insect bite) that becomes intensely irritated when scratched

- **Stasis dermatitis:** a skin irritation on the lower legs, generally related to circulatory problems

- **Dyshidrotic eczema:** irritation of the skin on the palms of hands and soles of the feet characterized by clear, deep blisters that itch and burn

Symptoms of Atopic Dermatitis

Symptoms vary from person to person. The most common symptoms are dry, itchy skin; cracks behind the ears; and rashes on the cheeks, arms, and legs. The itchy feeling is an important factor in atopic dermatitis, because scratching and rubbing in response to itching worsen the skin inflammation characteristic of this disease. People with atopic dermatitis seem to be more sensitive to itching and feel the need to scratch longer in response. They develop what is referred to as "the itch-scratch cycle": The extreme itchiness of the skin causes the person to scratch, which in turn worsens the itch, and so on. Itching is particularly a problem during sleep, when conscious control of scratching decreases and the absence of other outside stimuli makes the itchiness more noticeable.

The way the skin is affected by atopic dermatitis can be changed by patterns of scratching and resulting skin infections. Some people with the disease develop red, scaling skin where the immune system in the skin is becoming very activated. Others develop thick and leathery skin as a result of constant scratching and rubbing. This condition is called lichenification. Still others develop papules, or small raised bumps, on their skin. When the papules are scratched, they may open (excoriations) and become crusty and infected. These conditions can also be found in people without atopic dermatitis or with other types of skin disorders.

Atopic dermatitis may also affect the skin around the eyes, the eyelids, and the eyebrows, and lashes. Scratching and rubbing the eye area can cause the skin to change in appearance. Some people with atopic dermatitis develop an extra fold of skin under their eyes, called an atopic pleat or Dennie-Morgan fold. Other people may have hyperpigmented eyelids, meaning that the skin on their eyelids darkens from inflammation or hay fever (allergic shiners). Patchy eyebrows and eyelashes may also result from scratching or rubbing.

Researchers have noted differences in the skin of people with atopic dermatitis that may contribute to the symptoms of the disease. The epidermis, which is the outermost layer of skin, is divided into two parts: The inner part contains moist, living cells, and the outer part, known as the horny layer or stratum corneum, contains dry, flattened, dead cells. Under normal conditions the stratum corneum acts as a barrier, keeping the rest of the skin from drying out and protecting other layers of skin from damage caused by irritants and infections. When this barrier is damaged, irritants act more intensely on the skin.

The skin of a person with atopic dermatitis loses too much moisture from the epidermal layer, allowing the skin to become very dry and reducing its protective abilities. In addition, the patient's skin is very susceptible to recurring infections, such as staphylococcal and streptococcal bacterial skin infections and warts, herpes simplex, and molluscum contagiosum (skin disorders caused by a viruses).

Skin Features of Atopic Dermatitis

- **Lichenification:** thick, leathery skin resulting from constant scratching and rubbing

- **Papules:** small raised bumps that may open when scratched, becoming crusty and infected Ichthyosis: dry, rectangular scales on the skin

- **Keratosis pilaris:** small, rough bumps, generally on the face, upper arms, and thighs Hyperlinear palms: increased number of skin creases on the palms

- **Urticaria:** hives (red, raised bumps), often after exposure to an allergen, at the beginning of flares, or after exercise or a hot bath

- **Cheilitis:** inflammation of the skin on and around the lips

- **Atopic pleat (Dennie-Morgan fold):** an extra fold of skin that develops under the eye

- **Hyperpigmented eyelids:** eyelids that have become darker in color from inflammation or hay fever

Stages of Atopic Dermatitis

Atopic dermatitis is more common in infancy and childhood. It affects each child differently, in terms of both onset and severity of symptoms. In infants, atopic dermatitis typically begins around 6 to 12 weeks of age. It may first appear around the cheeks and chin as a patchy facial rash, which can progress to red, scaling, oozing skin. The skin may become infected. Once the infant becomes more mobile and begins crawling, exposed areas such as knees and elbows may also be affected. An infant with atopic dermatitis may be restless and irritable because of the itching and discomfort of the disease. Many infants get better by 18 months of age, although they remain at greater than normal risk for dry skin or hand eczema later in life.

In childhood, the rash tends to occur behind the knees and inside the elbows; on the sides of the neck; and on the wrists, ankles, and hands. Often, the rash begins with papules that become hard and scaly when scratched. The skin around the lips may be inflamed, and constant licking of the area may lead to small, painful cracks in the skin around the mouth. Severe cases of atopic dermatitis may affect growth, and the child may be shorter than average.

The disease may go into remission. The length of a remission varies, and it may last months or even years. In some children, the disease gets better for a long time only to come back at the onset of puberty when hormones, stress, and the use of irritating skin care products or cosmetics may cause the disease to flare.

Although a number of people who developed atopic dermatitis as children also experience symptoms as adults, it is unusual (but possible) for the disease to show up first in adulthood. The pattern in adults is similar to that seen in children; that is, the disease may be widespread or limited to a more restricted form. In some adults, only the hands or feet may be affected and become dry, itchy, red, and cracked. Sleep patterns and work performance may be affected, and long-term use of medications to treat the atopic dermatitis may cause complications. Adults with atopic dermatitis also have a predisposition toward irritant contact dermatitis, especially if they are in occupations

403

involving frequent hand wetting or hand washing or exposure to chemicals. Some people develop a rash around their nipples. These localized symptoms are difficult to treat, and people often do not tell their doctor because of modesty or embarrassment. Adults may also develop cataracts that are difficult to detect because they cause no symptoms. Therefore, the doctor may recommend regular eye exams.

Diagnosing Atopic Dermatitis

Currently, there is no test to diagnose atopic dermatitis and no single symptom or feature used to identify the disease. Each patient experiences a unique combination of symptoms, and the symptoms and severity of the disease may vary over time. The doctor will base his or her diagnosis on the symptoms the patient experiences and may need to see the patient several times to make an accurate diagnosis. It is important for the doctor to rule out other diseases and conditions that might cause skin irritation. In some cases, the family doctor or pediatrician may refer the patient to a dermatologist or allergist (allergy specialist) for further evaluation.

Several tools help the doctor better understand a patient's symptoms and their possible causes. The most valuable diagnostic tool is a thorough medical history, which provides important clues. The doctor may ask about family history of allergic disease; whether the patient also has diseases such as hay fever or asthma; and about exposure to irritants, sleep disturbances, any foods that seem to be related to skin flares, previous treatments for skin-related symptoms, use of steroids, and the effect of symptoms on schoolwork, career, or social life. Sometimes it is necessary to do a biopsy of the skin or patch testing to see if the skin immune system overreacts to certain chemicals or preservatives in skin creams. A preliminary diagnosis of atopic dermatitis can be made if the patient has three or more features from each of two categories: major features and minor features.

Skin scratch/prick tests (scratching or pricking the skin with a needle that contains a small amount of a suspected allergen) and blood tests for airborne allergens generally are not as useful in the diagnosis of atopic dermatitis as a medical history and careful observation of symptoms. However, they may occasionally help the doctor rule out or confirm a specific allergen that might be considered important in diagnosis. Although negative results on skin tests are reliable and may help rule out the possibility that certain substances cause skin inflammation in the patient, positive skin scratch/prick test results are difficult to interpret in people with atopic dermatitis and are often inaccurate. Blood tests, including measurements of certain antibodies to allergens, are not recommended in most cases because they have a high rate of false positives and are expensive. In some cases, where the type of dermatitis is unclear, blood tests to check the level of eosinophils (a type of white blood cell) or IgE (an antibody whose levels are often high in atopic dermatitis) are helpful.

Major Features of Atopic Dermatitis

- Intense itching
- Characteristic rash in locations typical of the disease
- Chronic or repeatedly occurring symptoms
- Personal or family history of atopic disorders (eczema, hay fever, asthma)

Some Minor Features of Atopic Dermatitis

- Early age of onset
- Dry, rough skin
- High levels of immunoglobulin E (IgE), an antibody, in the blood
- Ichthyosis
- Hyperlinear palms
- Keratosis pilaris
- Hand or foot dermatitis
- Cheilitis
- Nipple eczema
- Susceptibility to skin infection
- Positive allergy skin tests

Exacerbating Factors

Many factors or conditions can make symptoms of atopic dermatitis worse, further triggering the already overactive immune system in the skin, aggravating the itch-scratch cycle, and increasing damage to the skin. These exacerbating factors can be broken down into two main categories: irritants and allergens. Emotional factors and some infections can also influence atopic dermatitis.

Irritants are substances that directly affect the skin, and, when used in high enough concentrations with long enough contact, cause the skin to become red and itchy or to burn. Specific irritants affect people with atopic dermatitis to different degrees. Over time, many patients and their families learn to identify the irritants most troublesome to them. For example, wool or synthetic fibers may affect some patients. Also, rough or poorly fitting clothing can rub the skin, trigger inflammation, and cause the itch-scratch cycle to begin. Soaps and detergents may have a drying effect and worsen itching, and some perfumes and cosmetics may irritate the skin. Exposure to certain substances, such as chlorine, mineral oil, or solvents, or to irritants, such as dust or sand, may also make the condition worse. Cigarette smoke may irritate the eyelids. Because irritants vary from one person to another, each person has to determine for himself or herself what substances or circumstances cause the disease to flare.

Common Irritants

- Wool or synthetic fibers
- Soaps and detergents
- Some perfumes and cosmetics
- Substances such as chlorine, mineral oil, or solvents
- Dust or sand
- Cigarette smoke

Allergens are substances from foods, plants, or animals that inflame the skin because the immune system overreacts to the substance. Inflammation occurs even when the person is exposed to small amounts of the substance for a limited time. Some examples of allergens are pollen and dog or cat dander (tiny particles from the animal's skin or hair). When people with atopic dermatitis come into contact with an irritant or allergen they are sensitive to, inflammation-producing cells come into the skin from elsewhere in the body. These cells release chemicals that cause itching and redness. As the person scratches and rubs the skin in response, further damage occurs.

Some doctors and scientists believe that certain foods act as allergens and may trigger atopic dermatitis or cause it to become worse. Other researchers think that food allergens play a role in only a limited number of cases of atopic dermatitis, primarily in infants and children. An allergic reaction to food can cause skin inflammation (generally hives), gastrointestinal symptoms (vomiting, diarrhea), upper respiratory tract symptoms (congestion, sneezing), and wheezing. The most common allergenic (allergy-causing) foods are eggs, peanuts, milk, fish, soy products, and wheat. Although the data remain inconclusive, some studies suggest that mothers of children with a family history of atopic diseases should avoid eating commonly allergenic foods themselves during late pregnancy and (if breast feeding) while they are breast feeding the baby. Although not all researchers agree, some think that breast feeding the infant for at least 4 months may have a protective effect for the child.

Currently, no reliable laboratory test identifies a food allergy, including skin or blood tests. If a food allergy is suspected, it may be helpful to keep a careful diary of everything the patient eats, noting any reactions. Identifying the food allergen may be difficult if the patient is also being exposed to other allergens, and may require supervision by an allergist. One helpful way to explore the possibility of a food allergy is to eliminate the suspected food and then, if improvement is noticed, reintroduce it into the diet under carefully controlled conditions. If this causes no symptoms or if there has been no improvement in 2 weeks of eliminating that food, other foods may be eliminated in turn.

Changing the diet of a person who has atopic dermatitis may not always relieve symptoms. A change may be helpful, however, when a patient's medical history and specific symptoms strongly suggest a food allergy. It is up to the patient and his or her family and physician to judge whether the dietary restrictions outweigh the impact of the disease itself. Restricted diets often are emotionally and financially difficult for patients and their families to follow. Unless properly monitored, diets with many restrictions can also contribute to nutritional problems in children.

Other types of allergens called aeroallergens (because they are present in the air) may also play a role in atopic dermatitis. Common aeroallergens are dust mites, pollens, molds, and dander from animal hair or skin. These aeroallergens, particularly the house dust mite, may worsen the symptoms of atopic dermatitis in some people. Although some researchers think that aeroallergens are an important contributing factor to atopic dermatitis, others do not think that they are significant. Scientists also don't understand the way aeroallergens affect the skin—whether the aeroallergen is inhaled by the patient or the aeroallergen actually penetrates the patient's skin.

No reliable test is available that determines whether a specific aeroallergen is an exacerbating factor in any given individual. If the doctor suspects that an aeroallergen is contributing to the symptoms a person is experiencing, the doctor may recommend ways to reduce exposure to the aeroallergen. For example, the presence of the house dust mite can be limited by encasing mattresses and pillows in special dust-proof covers, frequently washing bedding in hot water, and removing carpeting. However, there is no way to completely rid the environment of aeroallergens.

In addition to irritants and allergens, other factors—such as emotional issues, temperature and climate, and skin infections—play a role in atopic dermatitis. Although the disease itself is not caused by emotional factors or personality, it can be made worse by stress, anger, and frustration. Interpersonal problems or major life changes, such as divorce, job changes, or the death of a loved one, can also make the disease worse. Often, emotional stress seems to trigger a flare of the disease.

Bathing without proper moisturizing afterward is a common factor that triggers a flare of atopic dermatitis. The low humidity of winter or the dry year-round climate of some geographic areas can make the disease worse, as can overheated indoor areas and long or hot baths and showers. Alternately sweating and chilling can trigger a flare in some people. Bacterial infections can also trigger or increase the severity of atopic dermatitis. If a patient experiences a sudden flare of illness, the doctor may check for a viral infection (such as herpes simplex) or fungal infection (such as ringworm or athlete's foot).

Treating Atopic Dermatitis

Treatment involves a partnership among the patient, family members, and doctor. The doctor will suggest a treatment plan based on the patient's age, symptoms, and general health. The patient and the patient's family play a large role in the success of the treatment plan by carefully following the doctor's instructions. Some of the primary components of treatment programs are described below. Most patients can be successfully treated with proper skin care and lifestyle changes and do not require the more intensive treatments discussed.

The doctor has three main goals in treating atopic dermatitis: healing the skin and keeping it healthy, preventing flares, and treating symptoms when they do occur. Much of caring for the skin and preventing flares has to do with developing skin care routines, identifying exacerbating factors, and avoiding circumstances that trigger the skin's immune system and the itch-scratch cycle. It is important for the patient and his or her family to note any changes in skin condition in response to treatment, and to be persistent in identifying the most effective treatment strategy.

Skin Care: Healing the skin and keeping it healthy are of primary importance as part of both preventing further damage and enhancing quality of life. Developing and sticking with a daily skin care routine is critical to preventing flares. Key factors are proper bathing and the application of lubricants, such as creams or ointments, within 3 minutes of bathing. People with atopic dermatitis should avoid hot or long (more than 10 to 15 minutes) baths and showers. A lukewarm bath helps to cleanse and moisturize the skin without drying it excessively. Because soaps can be drying to the skin, the doctor may recommend limited use of a mild bar soap or nonsoap cleanser. Bath oils are not usually helpful.

Once the bath is finished, the patient should air-dry the skin, or pat it dry gently (avoiding rubbing or brisk drying), and apply a lubricant immediately. Lubrication restores the skin's moisture, increases the rate of healing, and establishes a barrier against further drying and irritation. Several kinds of lubricants can be used. Lotions have a high water or alcohol content and evaporate more quickly, so they generally are not the best choice. Creams and ointments work better at healing the skin. Tar preparations can be very helpful in healing very dry, lichenified areas. Whatever preparation is chosen, it should be as free of fragrances and chemicals as possible.

Another key to protecting and restoring the skin is taking steps to avoid repeated skin infections. Although it may not be possible to avoid infection altogether, the effect of an infection may be minimized if it is identified and treated early. People with atopic dermatitis and their families should learn to recognize signs of skin infections, including tiny pustules (pus-filled bumps) on arms and legs, appearance of oozing areas, or crusty yellow blisters. If symptoms of a skin infection develop, the doctor should be consulted and treatment should begin as soon as possible.

Treating Atopic Dermatitis in Infants and Children

- Give brief, lukewarm baths.
- Apply lubricant immediately following the bath.
- Keep child's fingernails filed short.
- Select soft cotton fabrics when choosing clothing.

- Consider using antihistamines to reduce scratching at night.

- Keep the child cool; avoid situations where overheating occurs.

- Learn to recognize skin infections and seek treatment promptly.

- Attempt to distract the child with activities to keep him or her from scratching.

Medications and Phototherapy: If a flare of atopic dermatitis does occur, several methods can be used to treat the symptoms. The doctor will select a treatment according to the age of the patient and the severity of the symptoms. With proper treatment, most symptoms can be brought under control within 3 weeks. If symptoms fail to respond, this may be due to a flare that is stronger than the medication can handle, a treatment program that is not fully effective for a particular individual, or the presence of trigger factors that were not addressed in the initial treatment program. These factors can include a reaction to a medication, infection, or emotional stress. Continued symptoms may also occur because the patient is not following the treatment program instructions.

Corticosteroid creams and ointments are the most frequently used treatment. Sometimes over-the-counter preparations are used, but in many cases the doctor will prescribe a stronger corticosteroid cream or ointment. The doctor will take into account the patient's age, location of the skin to be treated, severity of the symptoms, and type of preparation (cream or ointment) when prescribing a medication. Sometimes the base used in certain brands of corticosteroid creams and ointments is irritating for a particular patient. Side effects of repeated or long-term use of topical corticosteroids can include thinning of the skin, infections, growth suppression (in children), and stretch marks on the skin.

Some treatments reduce specific symptoms of the disease. Antibiotics to treat skin infections may be applied directly to the skin in an ointment, but are usually more effective when taken by mouth. Certain antihistamines that cause drowsiness can reduce nighttime scratching and allow more restful sleep when taken at bedtime. This effect can be particularly helpful for patients whose nighttime scratching makes the disease worse. If viral or fungal infections are present, the doctor may also prescribe medications to treat those infections.

Phototherapy (treatment with light) that uses ultraviolet A or B light waves, or both together, can be an effective treatment for mild to moderate dermatitis in older children (over 12 years old) and adults.

Photochemotherapy, a combination of ultraviolet light therapy and a drug called psoralen, can also be used in cases that are resistant to phototherapy alone. Possible long-term side effects of this treatment include premature skin aging and skin cancer. If the doctor thinks that phototherapy may be useful to treat the symptoms of atopic dermatitis, he or she will use the minimum exposure necessary and monitor the skin carefully.

When other treatments are not effective, the doctor may prescribe systemic corticosteroids: drugs that are taken by mouth or injected into muscle instead of being applied directly to the skin. An example of a commonly prescribed corticosteroid is prednisone. Typically, these medications are used only in resistant cases and only given for short periods of time. The side effects of systemic corticosteroids can include skin damage, thinned or weakened bones, high blood pressure, high blood sugar, infections, and cataracts. It can be dangerous to suddenly stop taking corticosteroids, so it is very important that the doctor and patient work together in changing the corticosteroid dose.

In adults, immunosuppressive drugs, such as cyclosporine, are also used to treat severe cases of atopic dermatitis that have failed to respond to any other forms of therapy. Immunosuppressive drugs restrain the overactive immune system by blocking the production of some immune cells and curbing the action of others. The side effects of cyclosporine can include high blood pressure, nausea, vomiting, kidney problems, headaches, tingling or numbness, and a possible increased risk of cancer and infections. There is a risk of relapse after the drug is stopped. Because of their toxic side effects, systemic corticosteroids and immunosuppressive drugs are used only in severe cases and then for as short a period of time as possible. Patients requiring systemic corticosteroids should be referred to dermatologists or allergists specializing in the care of atopic dermatitis to help identify trigger factors and alternative therapies.

In rare cases, when no other treatments have been successful, the patient may have to be hospitalized. A 5- to 7-day stay in the hospital allows intensive skin care and reduces the patient's exposure to irritants and allergens and the stresses of day-to-day life. Under these conditions, the symptoms usually clear quickly if environmental factors play a role or if the patient is not able to carry out adequate skin care at home.

A number of promising experimental medications are being tested for atopic dermatitis. These medications affect the immune system and offer additional options for patients with difficult-to-treat symptoms. Researchers are also actively pursuing the development of alternative treatments for atopic dermatitis.

Tips for Working with Your Doctor

- Provide complete, accurate medical information about yourself or your child.

- Make a list of your questions and concerns in advance.

- Be honest and share your point of view with the doctor.

- Ask for clarification or further explanation if you need it.

- Talk to other members of the health care team, such as nurses, therapists, or pharmacists.

- Don't hesitate to discuss sensitive subjects with your doctor.

- Discuss changes to any medical treatment or medications with your doctor before making them.

Atopic Dermatitis and Quality of Life

Despite the symptoms caused by atopic dermatitis, it is possible for people with the disorder to maintain a high quality of life. The key to quality of life lies in education, awareness, and developing a partnership among patient, family, and doctor. Good communication (see "Tips for Working With Your Doctor") is essential, both within the family and among the patient, the family, and the doctor. It is important that the doctor provide understandable information about the disease and its symptoms to the patient and family and demonstrate any treatment measures recommended to ensure that they will be properly carried out.

When a child has atopic dermatitis, the entire family may be affected. It is important that families have additional support to help them cope with the stress and frustration associated with the disease. The child may be fussy and difficult, and often is unable to keep from scratching and rubbing the skin. Distracting the child and providing as many activities that keep the hands busy is key, but requires much effort and work on the part of the parents or caregivers. Another issue families face is the social and emotional stress associated with disfigurement caused by atopic dermatitis. The child may face difficulty in school or other social relationships and may need additional support and encouragement from family members.

Adults with atopic dermatitis can enhance their quality of life by caring regularly for their skin and being mindful of other effects of the disease and how to treat them. Adults should develop a skin care regimen as part of their daily routine, which can be adapted as circumstances and skin conditions change. Stress management and relaxation techniques may help decrease the likelihood of flares due to emotional stress. Developing a network of support that includes family, friends, health professionals, and support groups or organizations can be beneficial. Chronic anxiety and depression may be relieved by short-term psychological therapy.

Recognizing the situations when scratching is most likely to occur may also help. For example, many patients find that they scratch more when they are idle, so structured activity that keeps the hands occupied may prevent further damage to the skin. Occupational counseling also may be helpful to identify or change career goals if a job involves contact with irritants or involves frequent hand washing, such as kitchen work or auto mechanics.

Controlling Atopic Dermatitis

- Prevent scratching or rubbing whenever possible.

- Protect skin from excessive moisture, irritants, and rough clothing.

- Maintain a cool, stable temperature and consistent humidity levels.

- Limit exposure to dust, cigarette smoke, pollens, and animal dander.

- Recognize and limit emotional stress.

Questions and Answers about Psoriasis

What Is Psoriasis?

Psoriasis is a chronic (long-lasting) skin disease characterized by scaling and inflammation. Scaling occurs when cells in the outer layer of the skin reproduce faster than normal and pile up on the skin's surface.

Psoriasis affects between 1 and 2 percent of the United States population, or about 5.5 million people. Although the disease occurs in all age groups and about equally in men and women, it primarily affects adults. People with psoriasis may suffer discomfort, including pain and itching, restricted motion in their joints, and emotional distress.

In its most typical form, psoriasis results in patches of thick, red skin covered with silvery scales. These patches, which are sometimes referred to as plaques, usually itch and may burn. The skin at the joints may crack. Psoriasis most often occurs on the elbows, knees, scalp, lower back, face, palms, and soles of the feet but it can affect any skin site. The disease may also affect the fingernails, the toenails, and the soft tissues inside the mouth and genitalia. About 15 percent of people with psoriasis have joint inflammation that produces arthritis symptoms. This condition is called psoriatic arthritis.

What Causes Psoriasis?

Recent research indicates that psoriasis is likely a disorder of the immune system. This system includes a type of white blood cell, called a T cell, that normally helps protect the body against infection and disease. Scientists now think that, in psoriasis, an abnormal immune system causes activity by T cells in the skin. These T cells trigger the inflammation and excessive skin cell reproduction seen in people with psoriasis. In about one-third of the cases, psoriasis is inherited. Researchers are studying large families affected by psoriasis to identify a gene or genes that cause the disease. (Genes govern every bodily function and determine the inherited traits passed from parent to child.) People with psoriasis may notice that there are times when their skin worsens, then improves. Conditions that may cause flare-ups include changes in climate, infections, stress, and dry skin. Also, certain medicines, most notably beta-blockers, which are used to treat high blood pressure, and lithium or drugs used to treat depression, may trigger an outbreak or worsen the disease.

How Is Psoriasis Diagnosed?

Doctors usually diagnose psoriasis after a careful examination of the skin. However, diagnosis may be difficult because psoriasis can look like other skin diseases. A pathologist may assist with diagnosis by examining a small skin sample (biopsy) under a microscope. There are several forms of psoriasis. The most common form is plaque psoriasis (its scientific name is psoriasis vulgaris). In plaque psoriasis, lesions have a reddened base covered by silvery scales. Other forms of psoriasis include:

- **Guttate psoriasis**—Small, drop-like lesions appear on the trunk, limbs, and scalp. Guttate psoriasis is most often triggered by bacterial infections (for example, Streptococcus).

- **Pustular psoriasis**—Blisters of noninfectious pus appear on the skin. Attacks of pustular psoriasis may be triggered by medications, infections, emotional stress, or exposure to certain chemicals. Pustular psoriasis may affect either small or large areas of the body.

- **Inverse psoriasis**—Large, dry, smooth, vividly red plaques occur in the folds of the skin near the genitals, under the breasts, or in the armpits. Inverse psoriasis is related to increased sensitivity to friction and sweating and may be painful or itchy.

- **Erythrodermic psoriasis**—Widespread reddening and scaling of the skin is often accompanied by itching or pain. Erythrodermic psoriasis may be precipitated by severe sunburn, use of oral steroids (such as cortisone), or a drug-related rash.

What Treatments Are Available for Psoriasis?

Doctors generally treat psoriasis in steps based on the severity of the disease, the extent of the areas involved, the type of psoriasis, or the patient's responsiveness to initial treatments. This is sometimes called the "1-2-3" approach. In step 1, medicines are applied to the skin (topical treatment). Step 2 focuses on light treatments (phototherapy). Step 3 involves taking medicines internally, usually by mouth (systemic treatment).

Over time, affected skin can become resistant to treatment, especially when topical corticosteroids are used. Also, a treatment that works very well in one person may have little effect in another. Thus, doctors commonly use a trial-and-error approach to find a treatment that works, and they may switch treatments periodically (for example, every 12 to 24 months) if resistance or adverse reactions occur. Treatment depends on the location of lesions, their size, the amount of the skin affected, previous response to treatment, and patients' perceptions about their skin condition and preferences for treatment. In addition, treatment is often tailored to the specific form of the disorder.

Topical Treatment

Treatments applied directly to the skin are sometimes effective in clearing psoriasis. Doctors find that some patients respond well to sunlight, corticosteroid ointments, medicines derived from vitamin D3, vitamin A (retinoids), coal tar, or anthralin. Other topical measures, such as bath solutions and moisturizers, may be soothing but are seldom strong enough to clear lesions over the long term and may need to be combined with more potent remedies.

- Sunlight—Daily, regular, short doses of sunlight that do not produce a sunburn clear psoriasis in many people.

- Corticosteroids—Available in different strengths, corticosteroids (cortisone) are usually applied twice a day. Short-term treatment is often effective in improving but not completely clearing psoriasis. If less than 10 percent of the skin is involved, some doctors will begin treatment with a high-potency corticosteroid ointment (for example, Diprolene®,* Temovate®, Ultravate®, or Psorcon®. High-potency steroids may also be used for treatment-resistant plaques, particularly those on the hands or feet. Long-term use or overuse of high-potency steroids can lead to worsening of the psoriasis, thinning of the skin, internal side effects, and resistance to the treatment's benefits. Medium-potency corticosteroids may be used on the torso or limbs; low-potency preparations are used on delicate skin areas.

- Calcipotriene—This drug is a synthetic form of vitamin D3. (It is not the same as vitamin D supplements.) Applying calcipotriene ointment (for example, Dovonex®) twice a day controls excessive production of skin cells. Because calcipotriene can irritate the skin, however, it is not recommended for the face or genitals. After 4 months of treatment, about 60 percent of patients have a good to excellent response. The safety of using the drug for cases affecting more than 20 percent of the skin is unknown, and using it on widespread areas of the skin may raise the amount of calcium in the body to unhealthy levels.

- Coal tar—Coal tar may be applied directly to the skin, used in a bath solution, or used on the scalp as a shampoo. It is available in different strengths, but the most potent form may be irritating. It is sometimes combined with ultraviolet B (UVB) phototherapy. Compared with steroids, coal tar has fewer side effects, but it is messy and less effective and thus is not popular with many patients. Other drawbacks include its failure to provide long-term help for most patients, its strong odor, and its tendency to stain skin or clothing.

- Anthralin—Doctors sometimes use a 15-30 minute application of anthralin ointment, cream, or paste to treat chronic psoriasis lesions. However, this treatment often fails to adequately clear lesions, it may irritate the skin, and it stains skin and clothing brown or purple. In addition, anthralin is unsuitable for acute or actively inflamed eruptions.

- Topical retinoid—The retinoid tazarotene (Tazorac®) is a fast-drying, clear gel that is applied to the surface of the skin. Although this preparation does not act as quickly as topical corticosteroids, it has fewer side effects. Because it is irritating to normal skin, it should be used with caution in skin folds. Women of childbearing age should use birth control when using tazarotene.

- Salicylic acid—Salicylic acid is used to remove scales, and is most effective when combined with topical steroids, anthralin, or coal tar.

- Bath solutions—People with psoriasis may find that bathing in water with an oil added, then applying a moisturizer, can soothe their skin. Scales can be removed and itching reduced by soaking for 15 minutes in water containing a tar solution, oiled oatmeal, Epsom salts, or Dead Sea salts.

- Moisturizers—When applied regularly over a long period, moisturizers have a cosmetic and soothing effect. Preparations that are thick and greasy usually work best because they hold water in the skin, reducing the scales and the itching.

Phototherapy

Ultraviolet (UV) light from the sun causes the activated T cells in the skin to die, a process called apoptosis. Apoptosis reduces inflammation and slows the overproduction of skin cells that causes scaling. Daily, short, nonburning exposure to sunlight clears or improves psoriasis in many people. Therefore, sunlight may be included among initial treatments for the disease. A more controlled form of artificial light treatment may be used in mild psoriasis (UVB phototherapy) or in more severe or extensive psoriasis (psoralen and ultraviolet A [PUVA] therapy).

- UVB phototherapy—Some artificial sources of UVB light are similar to sunlight. Newer sources, called narrow-band UVB, emit the part of the ultraviolet spectrum band that is most helpful for psoriasis. Some physicians will start with UVB treatments instead of topical agents. UVB phototherapy is also used to treat widespread psoriasis and lesions that resist topical treatment. This type of phototherapy is normally administered in a doctor's office by using a light panel or light box, although some patients can use UVB light boxes at home with a doctor's guidance. Generally at least three treatments a week for 2 or 3 months are needed. UVB phototherapy may be combined with other treatments as well. One combined therapy program, referred to as the Ingram regime, involves a coal tar bath, UVB phototherapy, and application of an anthralin-salicylic acid paste, which is left on the skin for 6 to 24 hours. A similar regime, the Goeckerman treatment, involves application of coal tar ointment and UVB phototherapy.

- PUVA—This treatment combines oral or topical administration of a medicine called psoralen with exposure to ultraviolet A (UVA) light. Psoralen makes the body more sensitive to this light. PUVA is normally used when more than 10 percent of the skin is affected or when rapid clearing is required because the disease interferes with a person's occupation (for example, when a model's face or a carpenter's hands are involved). Compared with UVB treatment, PUVA treatment taken two to three times a week clears psoriasis more consistently and in fewer treatments. However, it is associated with more short-term side effects, including nausea, headache, fatigue, burning, and itching. Long-term treatment is associated with an increased risk of squamous cell and melanoma skin cancers. PUVA can be combined with some oral medications (retinoids and hydroxyurea) to increase its effectiveness. Simultaneous use of drugs that suppress the immune system, such as cyclosporine, have little beneficial effect and increase the risk of cancer. In very rare cases, patients who must travel long distances for PUVA treatments may, with a physician's close supervision, be taught to administer this treatment at home.

Systemic Treatment

For more severe forms of psoriasis, doctors sometimes prescribe medicines that are taken internally:

- Methotrexate—This treatment, which can be taken by pill or injection, slows cell production by suppressing the immune system.

Patients taking methotrexate must be closely monitored because it can cause liver damage and/or decrease the production of oxygen-carrying red blood cells, infection-fighting white blood cells, and clot-enhancing platelets. As a precaution, doctors do not prescribe the drug for people with long-term liver disease or anemia. Methotrexate should not be used by pregnant women, by women who are planning to get pregnant, or by their male partners.

- Cyclosporine—Taken orally, cyclosporine (Neoral®) acts by suppressing the immune system in a way that slows the rapid turnover of skin cells. It may provide quick relief of symptoms, but it is usually effective only during the course of treatment. The best candidates for this therapy are those with severe psoriasis who have not responded to or cannot tolerate other systemic therapies. Cyclosporine may impair kidney function or cause high blood pressure (hypertension), so patients must be carefully monitored by a doctor. Also, cyclosporine is not recommended for patients who have a weak immune system, those who have had substantial exposure to UVB or PUVA in the past, or those who are pregnant or breast-feeding.

- Hydroxyurea (Hydrea®)—Compared with methotrexate and cyclosporine, hydroxyurea is less toxic but also less effective. It is sometimes combined with PUVA or UVB. Possible side effects include anemia and a decrease in white blood cells and platelets. Like methotrexate and cyclosporine, hydroxyurea must be avoided by pregnant women or those who are planning to become pregnant.

- Retinoids—A retinoid, such as acitretin (Soriatane®), is a compound with vitamin A-like properties that may be prescribed for severe cases of psoriasis that do not respond to other therapies. Because this treatment also may cause birth defects, women must protect themselves from pregnancy beginning 1 month before through 3 years after treatment. Most patients experience a recurrence of psoriasis after acitretin is discontinued.

- Antibiotics—Although not indicated in routine treatment, antibiotics may be employed when an infection, such as Streptococcus, triggers the outbreak of psoriasis, as in certain cases of guttate psoriasis.

419

Questions and Answers about Rosacea

What Is Rosacea?

Rosacea, previously called acne rosacea, is a chronic skin disease that affects both the skin and the eyes. The disorder is characterized by redness, bumps, pimples, and, in advanced stages, thickened skin on the nose. Rosacea usually occurs on the face, although the neck and upper chest are also sometimes involved. A mild degree of eye (ocular) involvement occurs in more than 50 percent of people with rosacea.

Approximately 13 million people in the United States have rosacea. It usually occurs in adults between the ages of 30 and 60. Women are more often affected by mild to moderate rosacea than men, but the disorder is often more severe when it strikes men. Although rosacea can develop in people of any skin color, it tends to occur most frequently in people with fair skin. A tendency to develop rosacea may be inherited; often, several people in a family have it.

What Does Rosacea Look Like?

Rosacea has a variety of clinical features, or signs and symptoms. Doctors generally classify rosacea into four types based on symptoms. The earliest recognizable stage is called pre-rosacea. Signs and symptoms at this stage include frequent episodes of flushing and redness of the face and neck that come and go. Many things can trigger a flare-up, including exposure to the sun, emotional stress, alcohol, spicy foods, exercise, cold wind, hot foods and beverages, and hot baths. What causes a flare-up in one person may not cause a problem in another.

Another type of rosacea, called vascular rosacea, is commonly seen in women. Blood vessels under the skin of the face swell (telangiectasia). As a result, flushing and redness become persistent and, eventually, permanent. The affected skin may be slightly swollen and warm.

Some people, often people with a history of vascular rosacea, also develop inflammatory rosacea. With this form of the disease, people develop pink bumps (papules) and pimples. Thin red lines that look like a road map may also appear as the small blood vessels of the face get larger and show through the skin.

In a few men with rosacea, a condition called rhinophyma develops. This type of rosacea is characterized by an enlarged, bulbous red

420

nose. Both the oil-producing (sebaceous) glands and the surrounding connective tissues of the nose enlarge, and thick, knobby bumps may develop.

Some people may have more than one type of rosacea at a time. Other people can have any one type, including rhinophyma, without ever having had any of the others.

How Is the Eye Affected?

In addition to skin problems, rosacea may lead to conditions involving the eyes in about 50 percent of those affected. Typical symptoms include redness, burning, tearing, and the sensation of a foreign body or sand in the eye. Infection of the eyelids may cause the lids to become inflamed and swollen. Some patients complain of blurry vision. Only in severe cases can a person's vision become impaired, however.

What Causes Rosacea?

Doctors do not know the exact cause of rosacea but believe that a combination of genetic predisposition and several types of environmental factors are related to its development. Some researchers believe that rosacea is primarily a disorder of the blood vessels, or vascular system, in which something causes blood vessels to swell, resulting in flushing and redness.

A tiny organism called *Demodex folliculorum*, a mite that lives in facial hair follicles, may be involved. Some researchers believe that these mites clog the sebaceous gland openings, leading to inflammation. Other investigators have shown a possible link between rosacea and *Helicobacter pylori*, a bacterium that causes infection in the gastrointestinal system. Also, some research has suggested that the immune system may play a role in the development of rosacea in some people.

There are several factors that can make rosacea worse but do not cause it. For example, drinking alcohol can increase flushing and redness. Other factors known to aggravate rosacea include heat, strenuous exercise, sunlight, wind, cold, hot drinks, spicy foods, emotional stress, and coughing.

Can Rosacea Be Cured?

While rosacea cannot be cured, it can be treated and controlled. A dermatologist, a medical doctor who specializes in diseases of the skin, often treats rosacea. Treatment goals are to control the condition and improve appearance. Doctors usually prescribe a topical antibiotic, such as metronidazole, that is applied directly to the affected skin.

For people with more severe cases, doctors often prescribe an oral (taken by mouth) antibiotic. Tetracycline, minocycline, erythromycin, and doxycycline are the most common antibiotics used to treat rosacea. Some people respond quickly, while others require long-term therapy.

Isotretinoin may be considered as a treatment option for all forms of severe or therapy-resistant rosacea. However, isotretinoin is linked to a number of adverse effects, some of which can be severe. The most serious potential adverse effect is that it is teratogenic; that is, it can cause birth defects in pregnant women who take it. Therefore, it is crucial that women of childbearing age are not pregnant and do not get pregnant while taking isotretinoin. Women must use an appropriate birth control method 1 month before the initiation of therapy, during the entire course of therapy, and until 2 months after cessation of the drug. The doctor will order a blood pregnancy test before therapy is started and every month during therapy.

Doctors usually treat the eye problems of rosacea with oral antibiotics, particularly tetracycline or doxycycline. People who develop infections of the eyelids must practice frequent lid hygiene. Doctors recommend scrubbing the eyelids gently with diluted baby shampoo or an over-the-counter eyelid cleaning product and applying warm (not hot) compresses several times a day.

Electrosurgery and laser surgery may be options to treat redness, enlarged blood vessels, and rhinophyma. In some patients, laser surgery may result in improved skin appearance with little scarring or damage. For patients with rhinophyma, several surgical methods may help reduce the size of the nose and improve appearance.

Finally, sunscreens, particularly those that protect against ultraviolet A and B light waves and have a sun-protecting factor (SPF) of 13 or higher, are recommended for all people with rosacea.

Working with Your Doctor to Help Manage Rosacea

The role you play in managing your rosacea is just as important as your doctor's. You can take several steps to keep rosacea under control. Keep a written record of factors that seem to trigger flare-ups.

- Develop a plan to avoid or minimize your exposure to these triggers. By doing this, you may actually reduce or eliminate the need for medication to control your rosacea.

- Use a sunscreen with a sun-protecting factor (SPF) of 13 or higher every day.

- Avoid using facial cleaning products, moisturizers, and cosmetics with alcohol or other ingredients that irritate your skin.

- If your eyes are affected, faithfully follow your doctor's treatment plan and clean your eyelids as instructed.

- Try to minimize your stress level.

Additional Information

American Academy of Dermatology
930 N. Meacham Rd.
P.O. Box 4014
Schaumburg, IL 60168-4014
Tel: 847-330-0230
Fax: 847-330-0050
Website: www.aad.org

The academy, a national professional organization of dermatologists, publishes pamphlets on many skin conditions, including rosacea. Single copies are available free with a self-addressed stamped envelope. The rosacea pamphlet can also be found on the academy's website. The academy can provide referrals to dermatologists.

National Eczema Association
6600 SW 92nd Ave.
Suite 240
Portland, OR 97223-7195
Toll-Free: 800-818-7546
Tel: 503-228-4430
Fax: 503-224-3363
Website: www.eczema-assn.org
E-mail: nease@teleport.com

This is a national, patient-oriented association devoted to eczema. It publishes a newsletter and an eight-page brochure on atopic dermatitis, provides educational materials, offers resource services for people with atopic dermatitis, and provides referrals to atopic dermatitis research centers.

American Academy of Allergy, Asthma, and Immunology
611 East Wells Street
Milwaukee, WI 53202
Toll-Free: 800-822-2762
Tel: 414-272-6071
Website: www.aaaai.org
E-mail: info@aaaai.org

This national professional association for allergists and clinical immunologists publishes pamphlets about allergies and atopic dermatitis. The academy can also provide physician referrals for evaluation of allergies.

National Psoriasis Foundation
6600 SW 92nd Avenue, Suite 300
Portland, OR 97223-7195
Toll-Free: 800-723-9166
Tel: 503-244-7404
Fax: 503-245-0626
Website: www.psoriasis.org
E-mail: getinfo@npfusa.org

The National Psoriasis Foundation provides physician referrals and publishes pamphlets and newsletters that include information on support groups, research, and new drugs and other treatments. The foundation also promotes community awareness of psoriasis.

National Institute of Arthritis and Musculoskeletal and Skin Diseases Information Clearinghouse
1 AMS Circle
Bethesda, MD 20892-3675
Toll-Free: 877-22-NIAMS
Tel: 301-495-4484; TTY: 301-565-2966
Fax: 301-718-6366
NIAMS 24 hour Fast Facts Fax: 301-881-2731
Website: www.niams.nih.gov
E-mail: niamsinfo@mail.nih.gov

This clearinghouse, a public service sponsored by the National Institute of Arthritis and Musculoskeletal and Skin Diseases (NIAMS), provides information about various forms of these diseases. The clearinghouse distributes patient and professional education materials and also refers people to other sources of information.

Chapter 31

The Role of Acute and Chronic Stress in Asthma Attacks in Children

Introduction

Chronic diseases are one of the major health problems of children: about one child in ten experiences a long-lasting illness by the age of 15 years.[1] Of the chronic diseases of childhood, asthma is commonest, with reported prevalence in children ranging from 3% to 27% across different countries.[2] Concern has also been expressed at the apparent increase in asthma morbidity despite progress in medical treatment.[3]

There is a consistent finding based on studies that children with increased psychosocial stress are significantly more likely to be ill and need hospital treatment, as well as use health services more frequently than other children.[4, 5] Stress as a precipitating or provoking factor in adults has been implicated in heart disease, cancer, and various endocrine dysfunctions,[6-8] and in children with appendicitis, rheumatoid arthritis, and leukemia, for example.[9, 10] The role of stress in viral infections has been the focus of research involving both adults and children. Well controlled, prospective, and experimental studies have shown that adverse life events and other stresses significantly increase a person's susceptibility to acute and recurring upper respiratory

Excerpted from "The Role of Acute and Chronic Stress in Asthma Attacks in Children," by Seija Sandberg, James Y. Paton, Sara Ahola, Donna C. McCann, David McGuinness, Clive R. Hillary, Hannu Oja, *The Lancet*, Volume 356 Issue 9234, 982-87, September 16, 2000, © 2000 Lancet Publishing Group, reprinted with permission.

tract infections.[11-16] One likely explanation for this association lies in stress compromising the body's immunological responses,[15, 17] with the individual differences in psychobiological reactivity.[18]

Study Discussion

This study has shown that severely negative life events, especially when multiple chronic stressors were also present, significantly increased the likelihood of new asthma exacerbations during the 18-month follow-up in children aged 6-13 years. When severe events were not accompanied by high chronic stress their effect seemed to involve a small delay, increasing the risk of a new attack from the third to the sixth week after the life event. However, when chronic stress was also present, the effect came almost immediately within a fortnight. Thus, in children whose lives involved several chronic adversities, acutely stressful events were followed by a three-fold likelihood of a new exacerbation in the next 2 weeks.

The strengths of our study over previous studies included independent measurement of asthma and life stress through the use of continuous asthma monitoring, high-quality standardized interview measures of stressful experiences, and the use of statistical methods that enabled intra-individual variations over time to be examined, and account to be taken of each child's personal history in relation to past asthma exacerbations and life events. Previous studies have usually involved cross-sectional assessment of asthma severity, accompanied by retrospective assessment of stress. Prospective designs have, however, been used in studies examining the role of stressful life events in susceptibility to upper respiratory infections,[11-16] albeit involving shorter follow-up times than the present one.

Our results confirm the findings of many previous investigations in that stressful life events predict higher asthma morbidity in children. However, our findings are important, showing that severely negative life events significantly increase the risk of new asthma attacks for the coming few weeks, and that this risk is both magnified and brought forward in time if the child lives in conditions of high chronic stress. On the basis of the findings of some carefully done studies that examined the relation between stressful life events and viral infections on the one hand, and the substantial body of both research and clinical evidence suggesting a strong link between childhood asthma and upper respiratory infections (as a predisposing factor and/or triggering agent) on the other, our results may at least partly be explained by the detrimental effect of stress on resistance to viral infection in children.[16]

The overall frequency of exacerbations was determined by several expected factors personal to the child. The baseline asthma severity, as measured on the basis of medication use (BTS score)[20] within the preceding year, as well as the recent attack history, were both associated with the risk of new exacerbations. Children whose asthma was severe (just under a third of the sample at the start of the study), had a significantly higher risk of new asthma attacks than those whose asthma was rated less severe to begin with. Similarly, the frequency of past exacerbations predicted new ones; a child who had had three or more attacks within 6 months had more than double the risk of children whose exacerbations were more dispersed. The large individual variation in terms of overall attack frequency, from none to 21 in 18 months, was surprising since at the time of selection into the study the children clinically seemed to form a homogeneous group: all had chronic asthma of a least mild to moderate severity, and all were being treated with both prophylactic and rescue medication.

Of the other individual factors tested, the child's sex and parental smoking also had an effect on the overall attack frequency. Contrary to expectations, female, rather than male, sex predicted a higher rate of exacerbations. Another unforeseen result was absence of an association between social class and overall attack frequency. The effect of parental smoking, on the other hand, was in the expected direction, with children of smoking parents being at a somewhat greater risk.

Of the more universal factors, the season of the year had a large impact. The risk of new exacerbations was significantly greater during autumn and winter months, and lowest in the summer—in keeping with previous research. The explanation is at least partly likely to lie in the greater likelihood of upper respiratory tract infections during autumn and winter,[19] particularly after return from school holidays.

These results have considerable implications for the care of children with chronic asthma, particularly those with asthma whose lives are characterized by multiple chronic adversities. To highlight possible targets for treatment and prevention, the particular qualities of the acute and chronic stressful experiences, and the interconnections, require some attention.

Most negative life events are hard to predict, and therefore to avoid, as was so for the children who did not have high chronic stress. Among these children, as in many previous studies, most of the severely negative events were unpredictable and frequently involved loss, as in parental separation, death of a grandparent, or a close

427

friend's family moving away. Also, the delay of a few weeks between a negative life event and an increase in risk is in keeping with previous research.

The situation, however, seems to be different when there is a high level of background stress. In our study a small group had five times more stress than the rest, which included poverty, poor housing, parental physical infirmity, parental psychiatric illness, parental alcohol dependence, family discord, and school problems. Their situation was further compromised by parental hostility and indifference, and peer hostility and rejection, hardly ever present among the rest of the group. Under such circumstances, it is perhaps also not surprising that the severe events immediately preceding an acute asthma exacerbation in most instances arose directly from an existing chronic adversity (in half the cases with family problems).

Should special attention, as part of existing medical care, be paid to children with asthma at times they encounter severely negative life events—particularly to those among them who also live under conditions of high chronic stress? Because most of such chronic stresses occur in the child's home and school, and are either social or interpersonal by nature, perhaps a heightened sensitivity to such problems by professionals such as teachers, school nurses, family doctors, and pediatricians is called for. In cases where more complex psychosocial difficulties are identified within a family, there should be consultation with child mental health services (preferably ones with experience in liaison work).

References

1. Eiser C. Psychological effects of chronic disease. *J Child Psychol Psychiatry* 1990; 31: 85-98.

2. The International Study of Asthma and Allergies in Childhood (ISAAC) Steering Committee. Worldwide variations in the prevalence of asthma symptoms. *Eur Respir J* 1998; 12: 315-35.

3. Clark NM, Brown, RW, Parker E, et al. Childhood asthma. *Envir Health Perspect* 1999; 107 (suppl 3): 421-29.

4. Grey M. Stressors and children's health. *J Pediatr Nurs* 1993; 8: 85-91.

5. Haavet OR, Grunfeld B. Are life experiences fo children significant for the development of somatic disease? A literature review. *Tidsskr Nor Laegeforen* 1997; 117: 3644-47.

6. Brown GW, Harris TO, eds. *Life events and illness*. Hyman: London, 1989.

7. Sonino N, Fava GA, Boscaro M. A role of life events in the pathogenesis of Cushing's disease. *Clin Endocrinol* 1993; 38: 261-64.

8. Sonino N, Girelli ME, Boscaro M, Fallow F, Buscando B, Fara FA. Life events in the pathogenesis of Grave's disease: a controlled study. *Acta Endocrinol* 1993; 128: 293-96.

9. Heisel JS, Ream S, Raitz R, Rappaport M, Coddington RD. The significance of life events as contributing factors in the diseases of children. *Behav Ped* 1973; 83: 119-23.

10. Jacobs TJ, Charles E. Life events and the occurrence of cancer in children. *Psychosom Med* 1980; 42: 11-24.

11. Cobb JM, Steptoe A. Psychosocial stress and susceptibility to upper respiratory tract illness in an adult population sample. *Psychosom Med* 1996; 58: 404-12.

12. Cohen S, Tyrrell D. Smith A. Psychological stress in humans and susceptibility to the common cold. *N Engl J Med* 1991; 325: 606-12.

13. Cohen S, Tyrrell DA, Smith AP. Life events, perceived stress, negative affect and susceptibility to the common cold. *J Pers Soc Psychol* 1993; 64: 131-40.

14. Cohen S, Frank E, Doyle WJ, Skoner DP, Rabin BS, Gwaitney JM. Types of stressors that increase susceptibility to the common cold in healthy adults. *Health Psychol* 1998; 17: 214-23.

15. Drummond PD, Hewson-Bower B. Increased psychosocial stress and decreased mucosal immunity in children with recurrent upper respiratory tract infections. *J Psychosom Res* 1997; 43: 271-78.

16. Turner Cobb JM, Steptoe A. Psychosocial influences on upper respiratory infections in children. *J Psychosom Res* 1998; 45: 319-30.

17. Cohen S, Doyle WJ, Skoner DP. Psychological stress, cytokine production, and severity of upper respiratory illness. *Psychosom Med* 1999; 61: 175-80.

18. Boyce WT, Chesney M, Alkon A, et al. Psychologic reativity to stress and childhood respiratory illness: results of two prospective studies. *Psychosom Med* 1995, 57: 411-22.

19. Clough JB, Holgate ST. Episodes of respiratory morbidity in children with cough and wheeze. *Am J Respir Crit Care Med* 1994; 150: 48-53.

20. British Thoracic Society. Guidelines on the management of asthma in children. *Thorax* 1993; 48S: 1-24.

Chapter 32

Alcohol, Aging, and the Stress Response

The fact that alcohol intoxication can relieve anxiety is well known. Paradoxically, those same intoxicating levels of alcohol also can induce excessive secretion of an important class of stress hormones, the glucocorticoids. Yet chronic alcohol exposure can trigger a tolerance to alcohol's effects on the body's stress response. For example, research has shown that healthy young rats can develop tolerance to alcohol's stimulatory effects on glucocorticoid secretion—that is, the animals respond to chronic alcohol use by producing smaller increases in glucocorticoid levels. This same effect also appears to occur in humans. Research also indicates, however, that aged rats are much less able than younger rats[1] to develop such tolerance (Spencer and McEwen 1997). Nonetheless, researchers do not know whether older humans likewise have a decreased ability to develop a tolerance to alcohol's effects on stress hormones. Investigators do know, however, that chronic exposure in humans to both elevated glucocorticoid levels and alcohol produces symptoms resembling premature or exaggerated aging (Noonberg et al. 1985; Seeman and Robbins 1994).

This chapter examines the little known, three-way relationship that exists among alcohol use and abuse, glucocorticoid secretion, and the aging process (see Figure 32.1). In particular, the chapter considers evidence that the glucocorticoid-based stress response system, as

"Alcohol, Aging, and the Stress Response," by Robert L. Spencer, Ph.D., and Kent E. Hutchison, Ph.D., *Alcohol Research & Health*, Vol. 23, Number 4, 1999, National Institute on Alcohol Abuse and Alcoholism (NIAAA), NIH Publication No. 00-3466.

regulated by the hypothalamic-pituitary-adrenal (HPA) axis, plays a key role in the physiological and psychological responses to alcohol. The chapter also examines whether the stress hormone system contributes to age-related changes in a person's response to alcohol (e.g., a reduced ability to develop tolerance to alcohol's effects) and to alcohol-related changes in the aging process (e.g., nerve cell degeneration in some brain areas).

Alcohol's Effects on HPA Axis Function in Young and Middle-Aged Individuals

Alcohol-Induced Stimulation of the HPA Axis

Extensive documentation exists indicating that alcohol consumption reduces anxiety while it simultaneously activates the stress hormones through the HPA axis (see Figure 32.2). In humans and other animals, the magnitude and duration of the glucocorticoid response

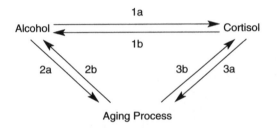

Figure 32.1. The Three-Way Interaction of Alcohol, Cortisol Secretion, and the Aging Process

Cortisol secretion is an indicator of the activity of the hypothalamic-pituitary-adrenal (HPA) axis, a hormone system that coordinates the stress response. Alcohol consumption stimulates cortisol secretion (1a). In turn, cortisol facilitates alcohol's rewarding effects (1b). Chronic alcohol consumption also can lead to premature and/or exaggerated aging (2a). Conversely, the aging process results in increased blood alcohol levels following consumption of the same alcohol dose as well as increased vulnerability to alcohol's effects, including alcohol's abuse potential (2b). Finally, chronic cortisol elevation also results in premature and/or exaggerated aging (3a), and the aging process can lead to increased cortisol secretion by impairing the organism's ability to adapt to stress (3b).

depend on the amount of alcohol consumed (Spencer and McEwen 1990; Veldman and Meinders 1996). In response to alcohol, the levels of cortisol—the chief glucocorticoid hormone in humans—can be substantial and even surpass the levels typically seen in response to various stressful circumstances (Mendelson et al. 1971). Interestingly, blood alcohol concentrations (BACs) below 0.1 percent appear to have little effect on HPA axis activation (Jenkins and Connolly 1968). Furthermore, the 0.1 percent level has been (and in some States continues to be) considered a threshold for alcohol-related impairment and intoxication.

In addition to BACs, the extent to which alcohol leads to HPA axis activation appears to depend on genetic factors. Such a genetic influence is evident in people who have inherited a defective form of a particular gene that is involved in alcohol metabolism. Inheritance of this defective gene, which is especially prevalent among people of Asian descent, disallows the body to metabolize alcohol normally.[2] People with the defective gene show significantly elevated blood cortisol levels, even at BACs below 0.1 percent (Wall et al. 1994). Other studies have found a greater HPA axis response to relatively low alcohol doses in people without family histories of alcoholism (Schuckit et al. 1996). This finding further supports the potential influence of genetic factors on the relationship between alcohol consumption and HPA activity.

The specific mechanism by which alcohol leads to HPA axis activation and elevated cortisol levels has not been conclusively established. One possibility is that alcohol uninhibits the HPA axis. In general, alcohol depresses nervous system activity. If some alcohol-sensitive nerve cells (i.e., neurons), in turn, exert inhibitory effects on the HPA axis, then the net effect of alcohol exposure would be HPA axis activation. A second possibility is that the HPA axis may be activated in response to certain stimulus properties of alcohol as part of a more coordinated, "whole body" stress response. Thus, a certain "body wisdom" may recognize alcohol intoxication as stressful despite the concurrent reduced sense of anxiety.

Tolerance to Alcohol's Stimulatory Effects on the HPA Axis

People who repeatedly expose themselves to alcohol or other drugs develop, over time, tolerance to certain effects—in other words, these people experience lesser effects with the same dose or require higher doses to achieve the same effect. For example, tolerance develops to alcohol-related sedation, motor uncoordination, and memory impairment

(Poulos et al. 1981). Similarly, studies have shown that animals can develop tolerance to alcohol's HPA axis-activating effects. For example, rats exposed to high alcohol doses daily for several weeks had an increase in the levels of corticosterone—the chief glucocorticoid hormone in animals—on day 14 that was only about one-half the increase observed on day 1 (Spencer and McEwen 1990). This tolerance development could not be explained by a change over time in their bodies' ability to absorb or metabolize alcohol (i.e., development of metabolic tolerance), because the BACs achieved on day 14 were as high as those achieved on day 1 with the same alcohol dose.

However, researchers have not thoroughly studied the extent to which tolerance to alcohol's stimulatory effects on the HPA axis develops in humans. In one study, alcohol administration to five alcoholics did not induce a significant increase in cortisol levels in blood, even though the subjects' BACs surpassed 0.1 percent (Merry and Marks 1969).[3] Conversely, alcohol administration produced a substantial increase in cortisol levels in three of five purportedly nonalcoholic men in the study, suggesting that the alcoholics developed at least some degree of tolerance. (Interestingly, the two nonalcoholic men who did not show a significant cortisol response to alcohol on further questioning revealed an extensive history of recent alcohol use.)

Although some tolerance to alcohol's effects on cortisol secretion may develop, it appears to be limited. For example, a study conducted in a controlled hospital setting found that men with a record of heavy and frequent alcohol use exhibited substantially elevated cortisol levels during an alcohol "binge" (Mendelson et al. 1971). Furthermore, examination of seven different studies reveals that 6 to 40 percent of chronic alcohol users exhibited some of the symptoms of excessive cortisol production observed in Cushing's syndrome (Veldman and Meinders 1996). Thus, at least in some people, chronic alcohol use apparently can lead to chronically elevated cortisol levels with all the associated symptoms, a condition that sometimes has been called "pseudo-Cushing's syndrome."

Because the majority of alcoholics do not develop pseudo-Cushing's syndrome, most people probably experience some adaptation or tolerance to the HPA axis' response to alcohol. This adaptation, however, may negatively affect the ability of the HPA axis and other physiological systems to maintain their normal functions (see Table 32.1). The cost of physiological adaptation to alcohol becomes evident when alcohol is suddenly withheld and the drinker experiences withdrawal symptoms (e.g., anxiety, increased heart rate, and tremors).

434

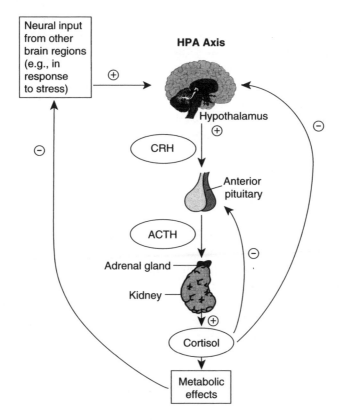

Figure 32.2. *The Hypothalamic-Pituitary-Adrenal (HPA) Axis.*

Note: + = stimulatory effect, - = inhibitory effect.

In response to stimulatory neural input from other brain regions (e.g., in stressful situations), certain cells in the brain's hypothalamus secrete corticotropin-releasing hormone (CRH). This hormone stimulates cells in the pituitary gland, which is located below the hypothalamus, to secrete adreno-corticotropic hormone (ACTH) into the bloodstream. ACTH then is trans- ported to the adrenal glands located atop the kidneys, where it activates certain cells to release cortisol, which exerts numerous metabolic effects. The HPA axis is regulated by both direct and indirect negative feedback mechanisms. Thus, cortisol directly inhibits further release of CRH from the hypothalamus and ACTH from the pituitary gland and indirectly lowers CRH secretion by reducing the neural input from other brain regions.

A few studies have shown that alcohol withdrawal also leads to excessive activation of the HPA axis (Mendelson et al. 1971; Adinoff et al. 1991). Thus, alcohol consumption, particularly in alcoholics, can interfere with normal HPA axis functioning during acute intoxication, chronic alcohol consumption (when tolerance development can alter HPA axis activity), and withdrawal after a bout of drinking. Moreover, the normal functioning of the HPA axis and its response to other stimuli appear to be compromised in alcoholics. In some studies various stimuli (e.g., surgical procedures or administration of the hormones insulin and ACTH [adrenocorticotropic hormone]) resulted in lower-than-expected HPA axis responses (Berman et al. 1990; Margraf et al. 1967).

Cortisol's Role and Effects in Humans

The principal glucocorticoid hormone produced in humans in response to stressful experiences is cortisol. (Corticosterone is the primary stress hormone in rats and mice.)

Cortisol has potent effects, many of which help the body cope with various physical insults (e.g., adverse environmental conditions or injuries). Exposure to too much cortisol for too long, however, can have harmful consequences, including a condition called Cushing's syndrome.

Glucocorticoid Contributions to the Rewarding Effects of Alcohol

The interaction between alcohol and the HPA axis may be bi-directional—that is, not only does alcohol consumption stimulate cortisol secretion, but elevated cortisol levels may increase drinking by magnifying its rewarding effects. Evidence for the latter relationship between alcohol and the HPA axis derives from animal studies in which researchers experimentally manipulated corticosterone levels. In those studies, rats that produced no corticosterone because their adrenal glands had been surgically removed (i.e., the rats had been adrenalectomized) exhibited a dramatic reduction in voluntary alcohol intake (Fahlke et al. 1994). Treatment of the adrenalectomized rats with corticosterone restored their alcohol intake to levels comparable to, and sometimes higher than, the levels before the surgery. Similarly, rats with functional adrenal glands that were treated with a chemical preventing corticosterone production also exhibited decreased alcohol consumption (Fahlke et al. 1996). Finally, the injection of corticosterone directly into the brains of normal rats that displayed a moderate preference for alcohol resulted in enhanced alcohol intake in those animals (Fahlke et al. 1996).

Researchers have speculated that corticosterone may increase an individual's alcohol consumption by enhancing alcohol's rewarding effects (e.g., feelings of euphoria). The mechanism underlying this process may involve corticosterone-induced alterations in the levels of the brain chemical (i.e., neurotransmitter) dopamine in the brain region called the nucleus accumbens.[4] In studies of the effects of cocaine or morphine exposure, corticosterone increased dopamine release in the nucleus accumbens (Piazza and Le Moal 1998), and that brain response appeared to be critical for the euphoria-inducing effects of the cocaine or morphine. Similarly, high glucocorticoid levels present in the brain during times of stress may facilitate alcohol's rewarding properties, providing a potential explanation for survey results indicating that stress may contribute to heavy alcohol use in humans (see Fahlke et al. 1994). This aspect of the stress-alcohol interaction warrants further systematic investigation in humans.

Another variable that plays a role in the HPA axis' response to both stress and alcohol's effects is the aging process. Aging is associated with gradual, but often dramatic, changes over time in almost every physiological system in the human body. Combined, these changes result in decreased efficiency and resiliency of physiological function. The aging process is highly variable, however, with large individual differences in the overall rate of aging as well as in the specific patterns of age-related manifestations (Rowe and Kahn 1987).

Considerable evidence suggests that a two-way interaction exists between alcohol abuse and aging. On the one hand, aging may alter a person's physiological and psychological responses to alcohol. On the other hand, chronic alcohol use may alter the aging process, as indicated by several studies that found evidence for premature or exaggerated aging in chronic heavy drinkers (Evert and Oscar-Berman 1995; Noonberg et al. 1985; Pfefferbaum et al. 1992).

Stress Hormone Activity and Aging

Just as a two-way interaction appears to exist between alcohol and aging—that is, (1) aging can modify the body's response to alcohol, and (2) chronic alcohol exposure can modify the aging process—an analogous two-way interaction also appears to exist between stress and aging. This two-way interaction is probably mediated by the HPA axis. Thus, elderly people appear to have an impaired resiliency of the HPA axis response to the acute effects of stress. In addition, chronic stress may accelerate the aging process by causing over-activity of the HPA axis (Seeman and Robbins 1994).

Age Differences in HPA Axis Function

Animal studies have demonstrated that HPA axis function changes as the animal enters the last quarter of its normal life span. Several studies have found that although rats of all ages experience a similar increase in HPA activity in response to stress, aged rats, compared with younger ones, show increased HPA activity in the absence of stress (i.e., increased basal activity) and a slower return to basal activity after a stress-induced increase in activity (see Sapolsky et al. 1986). Consequently, the bodies of aged rats are exposed to a substantially greater overall amount of glucocorticoid hormones than are the bodies of younger rats.

Studies in which rats were repeatedly exposed to the same stressful event also have found age-related changes in HPA axis function. In general, the HPA axis response decreases (i.e., habituation occurs) in response to repeated stress, similar to the tolerance development in response to repeated alcohol exposure.[5] This habituation likely minimizes the amount of glucocorticoids to which the body is exposed. Aged rats, however, experience a slower rate of stress habituation than do younger rats (Spencer and McEwen 1997).

When analyzed together, the observed age-related changes in HPA activity suggest that the resiliency of the HPA axis in response to acute stress, as well as its ability to adapt to chronic stress, is impaired in older animals. Researchers have not yet identified the mechanism underlying this impaired HPA axis resiliency. One potential mechanism might involve changes in the levels of glucocorticoid receptors that contribute to the negative feedback regulation of glucocorticoid secretion, because aged rats tend to show reduced numbers of those receptors in certain brain regions (e.g., the hypothalamus and the hippocampus) (Sapolsky et al. 1986).

Researchers have not yet determined if impaired HPA axis resiliency also occurs during human aging. Older people, even those in their seventies, generally do not exhibit elevated basal cortisol levels (Seeman and Robbins 1994). However, researchers have not examined in elderly people the ability of the HPA axis to return to basal levels after acute stress or to habituate after repeated stress.

Some evidence indicates that elderly people may be less sensitive than younger people with respect to the negative feedback control of cortisol levels. For example, older people who received a dose of the potent synthetic glucocorticoid dexamethasone exhibited a blunted negative feedback response (Seeman and Robbins 1994) and thus were exposed to higher overall glucocorticoid levels than were younger people undergoing the same procedure. Furthermore, such an impaired response to dexamethasone occurs more consistently in older people suffering from major depression than in younger people with a similar degree of depression. Finally, older people suffering from Alzheimer's disease or other forms of dementia also demonstrate a relatively high incidence of a blunted dexamethasone response (Seeman and Robbins 1994).

A series of studies have shown that dexamethasone exerts its primary negative feedback effects on the HPA axis by directly suppressing ACTH release from the pituitary (de Kloet et al. 1998). To date, researchers do not know the extent to which an impaired response to dexamethasone reflects a localized impairment in pituitary activity or changes in negative feedback sensitivity originating in other brain regions that affect pituitary function, such as the hypothalamus. On the other hand, cortisol is known to produce negative feedback effects on HPA axis activity by acting at the level of certain brain structures, such as the hypothalamus and hippocampus. A recent study showed impaired negative feedback sensitivity among older people (average age of 70) to cortisol (Wilkinson et al. 1997), suggesting that an age-related impaired sensitivity to glucocorticoid negative feedback is attributable to changes in the brain. Because negative feedback is an important mechanism that allows an organism to both recover from stress and turn off its HPA axis response to stress, impaired glucocorticoid negative feedback likely results in prolonged elevation of cortisol levels during stressful circumstances.

Premature or Exaggerated Aging with Chronic Glucocorticoid Exposure

People generally believe that a "hard life" (i.e., one fraught with difficulties, including repeated exposure to stressful situations) can lead to premature aging. Chronic stress-induced HPA axis over-activity may mediate such a process, a belief that is supported by research findings. For example, a study that examined postmortem brains of vervet monkeys housed in a primate center detected extensive hippocampal damage in the brains of a subset of monkeys. These monkeys showed signs of chronic stress (e.g., gastric ulcers and bite scars) typically experienced by animals of low rank in the strict hierarchy found in this species (Uno et al. 1989). The hippocampus is vitally important for memory formation and, interestingly, has a high concentration of glucocorticoid receptors. Perhaps, as a result of the high glucocorticoid receptor levels, the growth and survival of many hippocampal neurons appear to depend on glucocorticoids (McEwen 1999). Some neurons, however, require the presence of only low glucocorticoid levels for survival (McEwen 1999) and may be damaged by high glucocorticoid levels. Thus, chronic high glucocorticoid exposure may cause the death of some hippocampal neurons and increase the susceptibility of other neurons to damage or death from other toxic insults, such as lack of oxygen (i.e., hypoxia).

During an organism's lifetime, the effects of glucocorticoid exposure on brain cells may accumulate and contribute to neurodegeneration (Sapolsky et al. 1986). This hypothesis has been supported by studies in middle-aged rats whose adrenal glands were removed to prevent glucocorticoid production and who received lower-than-normal cortisol doses to replace the missing corticosterone. This treatment minimized the extent of hippocampal nerve cell loss that usually occurs with old age, although the treatment did not prevent an age-related cognitive decline in the animals (Landfield et al. 1981).

However, another study that assessed individual variations in the ability of aged rats to navigate a maze (a task that depends on hippocampal function) found a relationship between nerve cell degeneration and cognitive performance (Issa et al. 1990). Some aged rats performed significantly worse than did younger rats, whereas the performance of other aged rats did not differ from that of the younger ones. When the investigators examined the brains of the cognitively impaired aged rats, the animals exhibited significant nerve cell loss in the hippocampus compared with that of both the unimpaired aged rats and the younger rats.

To determine whether differences in glucocorticoid levels contributed to the group differences in performance and hippocampal degeneration, researchers screened the rats prior to death for their HPA axis response to acute stress. The analyses found that the corticosterone levels of the cognitively impaired aged rats took longer to return to basal levels after the end of the stressful event compared with younger or unimpaired aged rats. This observation is consistent with the belief that animals exposed to greater levels of glucocorticoids (e.g., as a result of HPA over-activity, such as prolonged corticosterone secretion in response to stress) exhibit signs of advanced aging in the brain, particularly in the hippocampus. It is important to point out,

440

however, that the hippocampus also exerts a crucial inhibitory control over the HPA axis (Saplosky et al. 1986). Accordingly, age-related degeneration of the hippocampus could precede, rather than follow, HPA axis over-activity.

The hypothesis that chronic HPA axis over-activity may lead to hippocampal degeneration in humans has gained support from recent MRI studies indicating that people with depression (many of whom have elevated basal cortisol levels during depressive episodes) and patients with Cushing's syndrome have, on average, reduced hippocampal volumes (Sapolsky 1996). In addition, the extent of hippocampal degeneration is correlated with the duration of depression or, in the case of Cushing's syndrome, the severity of cortisol over-production. Other studies, in which older non-human primates were exposed to chronic high cortisol levels, did not produce any detectable hippocampal degeneration (Levernz et al. 1999). Thus, high glucocorticoid levels alone may only increase the vulnerability of nerve cells to the harmful influences of additional factors. Such factors, associated with stress or pathological conditions, include low oxygen levels and elevated levels of potentially toxic molecules (e.g., free oxygen radicals and glutamate).

Regulation of Stress Hormone Production

Humans generally are highly adept at confronting and fending off stress—which can be defined simply as any threat to a person's physical and psychological well-being. Some of these threats are physical in nature, such as extreme temperature or extended lack of food or water. For most people, however, perceived threats to their well-being often are psychological in nature (e.g., work-related time pressures or stress from a relationship). Regardless of the source of the stress, the body responds by activating well-defined physiological systems that specialize in helping a person cope with the stress.

The two principal stress response systems in both humans and other animals are (1) a part of the nervous system called the sympathetic nervous system and (2) a hormone system called the hypothalamic-pituitary-adrenal (HPA) axis. Both systems enable the brain to communicate with the rest of the body. Activation of the sympathetic nervous system produces several physiological responses within seconds, such as an accelerated heart rate, increased respiration, and blood flow redistribution from the skin to the skeletal muscles. These responses facilitate the "fight or flight" behavioral response (Sapolsky 1993).

441

The Role of the HPA Axis

Activation of the HPA axis induces glucocorticoid secretion, which in turn affects a wide range of physiological responses, such as changes in blood sugar levels, and blood pressure, fat redistribution, muscle breakdown, and immune system modulation (Sapolsky 1993). Although these hormonal effects develop much more slowly (i.e., within hours) than those of the sympathetic nervous system, they may persist for several days and are vital to survival in the face of severe physical challenges. It is unclear, however, to what extent the

Table 32.1. Brain Areas Damaged by Chronic Alcohol Use and Their Functions

Brain Area	Function
Corpus callosum	Large structure extending from the front to the back of the forebrain that connects the right and left sides (i.e., hemispheres) of the brain
Frontal lobe	Contains the regions of the cortex devoted to the control of movement, language production, problem-solving ability, ability to formulate and execute plans, and control of appropriate social behavior
Hippocampus	A primitive area of the cortex that is vital for the formation of certain types of memories, especially memories of people, places, events, and factual information
Mammillary body	A subregion of the hypothalamus that contributes to the formation of certain types of memories and is frequently damaged in patients with a severe form of alcohol-induced memory deficits (i.e., Wernicke-Korsakoff syndrome)
Parietal lobe	Contains regions of the cortex devoted to the processing of the sense of touch, pain, and temperature; spatial processing; integrating movements with the surrounding world; mathematical ability; letter recognition; memory for nouns; and spatial memory
Temporal lobe	Contains regions of the cortex devoted to the processing of auditory information, language comprehension, categorization ability, and ability to identify objects

activation of the sympathetic nervous system and the HPA axis helps combat psychological stress, which may not require such extensive physiological responses. The potential inappropriateness of HPA axis activation in the absence of physical stress is of special concern, because glucocorticoids exert such long-lasting effects.

The HPA axis consists of three groups of hormone producing cells. They reside, respectively, in the brain region called the hypothalamus; in a hormone-secreting gland called the pituitary gland (located just below the hypothalamus); and in the adrenal glands, which are situated on top of the kidneys. These groups of cells act in a coordinated fashion to control the secretion of glucocorticoid hormones from the adrenal gland into general circulation.

Glucocorticoid secretion from the adrenal glands depends directly on the release of the adrenocorticotropic hormone (ACTH) from the pituitary gland and indirectly on the release of the corticotropin-releasing hormone (CRH) from the hypothalamus (see Figure 32.2) This hormone "cascade" becomes activated whenever CRH-producing nerve cells (i.e., neurons) in the hypothalamus are stimulated by neural input from other brain regions, usually in response to a stressful situation. As a result of this stimulation, these hypothalamic neurons secrete CRH into specific blood vessels located at the junction of the hypothalamus and the pituitary gland. CRH then is transported through these blood vessels to the pituitary gland (i.e., the anterior pituitary), where it stimulates specialized cells (i.e., corticotrope cells) to secrete ACTH into the bloodstream. Through the blood, ACTH is transported to the adrenal glands, where it induces certain cells to release glucocorticoids into the bloodstream. Thus, although glucocorticoid production and secretion occur in small glands located above the kidneys, these processes are ultimately controlled by the activity of various brain regions.

Glucocorticoid hormones have a wide range of regulatory effects on virtually every organ system in the body, including the central nervous system (i.e., the brain and spinal cord). Cortisol's ability to affect many body systems allows this hormone to be an effective mediator of a generalized stress response. At the same time, however, the extensive range of cortisol's effects necessitates tight regulation of the hormone's levels. This control is achieved largely through a negative feedback mechanism (de Kloet et al. 1998). Thus, cortisol itself either directly or indirectly inhibits the CRH-producing neurons in the hypothalamus and the ACTH-producing cells in the anterior pituitary that control cortisol secretion, thereby blunting overall HPA axis activity and subsequent cortisol secretion.

Although this negative feedback normally is a highly effective means of ensuring that the body is not exposed to any more cortisol than is warranted by the conditions at hand, experimental evidence has indicated that with increasing age, this regulatory mechanism becomes impaired (Sapolsky et al. 1986). Impaired cortisol negative feedback in older humans may contribute to a greater risk of alcohol-induced pathophysiology.

Impairment of the HPA Axis and Its Consequences

Researchers and clinicians have gained some insight into the consequences of extreme chronic elevation of cortisol levels from studying patients with Cushing's syndrome, a disorder that is characterized by cortisol overproduction, usually caused by an adrenal or pituitary tumor. Symptoms include diabetes, muscle weakness, skin disorders, obesity of the torso, brittle bones (i.e., osteoporosis), disrupted menstruation, high blood pressure (i.e., hypertension), and increased susceptibility to infections (Veldman and Meinders 1996). Although chronic stress does not cause full-blown Cushing's syndrome, the stress-induced chronic elevation of cortisol levels may exacerbate some related disorders, such as diabetes and osteoporosis, while simultaneously decreasing a person's resistance to infectious agents.

Cushing's syndrome is not the only disorder associated with abnormal cortisol levels. Deregulation of cortisol secretion also occurs with some neuropsychological disorders, most notably depression, Alzheimer's disease, chronic fatigue syndrome, posttraumatic stress disorder, and fibromyalgia (i.e., a recently defined syndrome of generalized pain) (de Kloet et al. 1998; Demitrack 1998). Researchers do not yet know, however, whether altered cortisol levels contribute to the development of these disorders or are merely a by-product of the conditions. (by Robert L. Spencer and Kent E. Hutchison)

References

De Kloet, E.R.; Vreugdenhil, E.; Oitzl, M.S.; and Joels, M. Brain corticosteroid receptor balance in health and disease. *Endocrinology Review* 19:269-301, 1998.

Demitrack, M.A. Chronic fatigue syndrome and fibromyalgia. Psychiatric Clinics of North America 21:671-692, 1998.

Sapolsky, R.M. Neuroendocrinology of the stress-response. In: Becker, J.B.; Breedlove, S.M.; and Crews, D., eds. *Behavioral Endocrinology*. Cambridge, MA: MIT Press, 1993. pp. 287-324.

Sapolsky, R.M; Krey, L.C.; and Mcewen, B.S. The of stress and aging: The glucocorticoid cascade hypothesis. *Endocrine Reviews* 7:284-301, 1986.

Veldman, R.G., and Meinders, A.E. On the mechanism of alcohol-induced pseudo-Cushing's syndrome. *Endocrine Reviews* 17:262-268, 1996.

Conclusions and Treatment Implications

The findings reviewed in this chapter suggest that numerous interactions exist among chronic alcohol consumption, HPA activity, and the aging process. For example, alcohol-related over-activity of the HPA axis and the resulting elevated cortisol levels may contribute to premature or exaggerated aging in many people with a long history of alcohol abuse. In addition, elderly people may be more susceptible than younger people to a stress-induced pattern of drinking, because alcohol elicits greater cortisol responses that may enhance alcohol's rewarding properties. Finally, elevated cortisol responses in older people may intensify the pathophysiology associated with alcohol abuse, even in people who develop alcohol use disorders late in life.

Based on these observations, some researchers have speculated that therapeutic approaches to inhibit cortisol secretion and/or cortisol's effects might be useful as a potential adjunct to alcoholism treatment. Because cortisol is such an important hormone that normally helps regulate many physiological processes in the body, medications that completely suppress its production or activity would not likely be a viable treatment for chronic alcoholics. Nevertheless, as researchers gain a better understanding of the regulation of the HPA axis, they may discover treatments to effectively modulate HPA axis activity and minimize the development of HPA axis over-activity. Such treatments may be useful in reducing the pathophysiology associated with chronic alcohol abuse and may reduce alcohol's rewarding effects, which contribute to its addictive nature.

References

Adinoff, B.; Risher-Flowers, D.; De Jong, J.; Ravitz, B.; Bone, G.H.A.; Nutt, D.J.; Roehrich, L.; Martin, P.R.; and Linnoila, M. Disturbances of hypothalamic-pituitary-adrenal axis functioning during ethanol withdrawal in six men. *American Journal of Psychiatry* 148:1023-1025, 1991.

Atkinson, R.M. Aging and alcohol use disorders: Diagnostic issues in the elderly. *International Psychogeriatrics* 2:55-72, 1990.

Berman, J.D.; Cook, D.M.; Buchman, M.; and Keith, L.D. Diminished adrenocorticotropin response to insulin-induced hypoglycemia in non-depressed, actively drinking male alcoholics. *Journal of Clinical Endocrinology and Metabolism* 71:712-717, 1990.

De Kloet, E.R.; Vreugdenhil, E.; Oitzl, M.S.; and Joels, M. Brain corticosteroid receptor balance in health and disease. *Endocrinology Review* 19:269-301, 1998.

Evert, D.L., and Oscar-Berman, M. Alcohol-related cognitive impairments: An overview of how alcoholism may affect the workings of the brain. *Alcohol Health & Research World* 19:89-96, 1995.

Fahlke, C.; Engel, J.A.; Eriksson, C.J.P.; Hard, E.; and Soderpalm, B. Involvement of corticosterone in the modulation of ethanol consumption in the rat. *Alcohol* 11:195-202, 1994.

Fahlke, C.; Hard, E.; and Hansen, S. Facilitation of ethanol consumption by intracerebroventricular infusions of corticosterone. *Psychopharmacology* 127: 133-139, 1996.

Issa, A.M.; Rowe, W.; Gauthier, S.; and Meaney, M.J. Hypothalamic-pituitary-adrenal activity in aged, cognitively impaired and cognitively unimpaired rats. *Journal of Neuroscience* 10:3247-3254, 1990.

Jenkins, J.S., and Connolly, J. Adrenocortical response to ethanol in man. *British Medical Journal* 2:804-805, 1968.

Khanna, J.M.; Leblanc, A.E.; and Le, A.D. Tolerance to and physical dependence on ethanol—General considerations. Overview. In: Cicero, T.J., ed. *Ethanol Tolerance and Dependence: Endocrinological Aspects*. National Institute on Alcohol Abuse and Alcoholism Research Monograph No. 13. Bethesda, MD: the Institute, 1983. pp. 4-5.

Landfield, P.W.; Basking, R.K.; and Pitler, T.A. Brain aging correlates: Retardation by hormonal-pharmacological treatments. *Science* 214:581-584, 1981.

Levernz, J.B.; Wilkinson, C.W.; Wamble, M.; Corbin, S.; Grabber, J.E.; Raskind, M.A.; and Peskind, E.R. Effect of chronic high-dose exogenous cortisol on hippocampal neuronal number in aged nonhuman primates. *Journal of Neuroscience* 19:2356-2361, 1999.

Mansfield, J.G., and Cunningham, C.L. Conditioning and extinction of tolerance to the hypothermic effect of ethanol in rats. *Journal of Comparative and Physiological Psychology* 94:962-969, 1980.

Margraf, H.W.; Moyer, C.A.; Ashford, L.E.; and Lavalle, L.W. Adrenocortical function in alcoholics. *Journal of Surgical Research* 7:55-62, 1967.

Mayfield, R.D.; Grant, M.; Schallert, T.; Spirduso, W.W. Tolerance to the effects of ethanol on the speed and success of reaction time responding in the rat: Effects of age and intoxicated practice. *Psychopharmacology* 107:78-82, 1992.

Mcewen, B.X. Stress and hippocampal plasticity. *Annual Review of Neuroscience* 22:105-122, 1999.

Mendelson, J.H.; Ogata, M.; and Mello, N.K. Adrenal function and alcoholism. I. Serum cortisol. *Psychosomatic Medicine* 33:145-158, 1971.

Merry, J., and Marks, V. Plasma-hydrocortisone response to ethanol in chronic alcoholics. The *Lancet* I:921-923, 1969.

Noonberg, A.; Goldstein, G.; and Page, H.A. Premature aging in male alcoholics: "Accelerated aging" or "increased vulnerability"? *Alcoholism: Clinical and Experimental Research* 9:334-338, 1985.

Pfefferbaum, A.; Lim, K.O.; Zipursky, R.B.; Mathalon, D.H.; Rosenbloom, J.J.; Lane, B.; Ha, C.N.; and Sullivan, E.V. Brain gray and white matter volume loss accelerates with aging in chronic alcoholics: A quantitative MRI study. *Alcoholism: Clinical and Experimental Research* 16:1078-1089, 1992.

Pfefferbaum, A.; Sullivan, E.V.; Rosenbloom, J.J.; Mathalon, D.H.; and Lim, K.O. A controlled study of cortical gray matter and ventricular changes in alcoholic men over a 5-year interval. *Archives of General Psychiatry* 55:905-912, 1998.

Piazza, P.V., and Le Moal, M. The role of stress in drug self-administration. *Trends in Pharmacological Sciences* 19:67-74, 1998.

Poulos, C.X.; Wolff, L.; Zilm, D.H.; Kaplan, H.; and Cappell, H. Acquisition of tolerance to alcohol-induced memory deficits in humans. *Psychopharmacology* 73:176-179, 1981.

Rowe, J.W., and Kahn, R.L. Human aging: Usual and successful. *Science* 237:143-149, 1987.

Sapolsky, R.M. Why stress is bad for your brain. *Science* 273:749-750, 1996.

Sapolsky, R.M.; Krey, L.C.; and Mcewen, B.S. The neuroendocrinology of stress and aging: The glucocorticoid cascade hypothesis. *Endocrine Reviews* 7:284-301, 1986.

Schuckit, M.A.; Tsuang, J.W.; Anthenelli, R.M.; Tipp, J.E.; and Nurnberger, J.I. Alcohol challenges in young men from alcoholic pedigrees and control families: A report from the COGA project. *Journal of Studies on Alcohol* 57:368-377, 1996.

Seeman, ST.E., and Robbins, R.J. Aging and hypothalamic-pituitary-adrenal response to challenge in humans. *Endocrine Reviews* 15:233-260, 1994.

Spencer, R.L., and Mcewen, B.S. Adaptation of the hypothalamic-pituitary-adrenal axis to chronic ethanol stress. *Neuroendocrinology* 52:481-489, 1990.

Spencer, R.L., and Mcewen, B.S. Impaired adaptation of the hypothalamic-pituitary-adrenal axis to chronic ethanol stress in aged rats. *Neuroendocrinology* 65:353-359, 1997.

Uno, H.; Tarara, R.; Else, J.G.; Suleman, M.A.; and Sapolsky, R.M. Hippocampal damage associated with prolonged and fatal stress in primates. *Journal of Neuroscience* 9:1705-1711, 1989.

Veldman, R.G., and Meinders, A.E. On the mechanism of alcohol-induced pseudo-Cushing's syndrome. *Endocrine Reviews* 17:262-268, 1996.

Wall, T.L.; Nemeroff, C.B.; Ritchie, J.C.; and Ehlers, C.L. Cortisol responses following placebo and alcohol in Asians with different ALDH2 genotypes. *Journal of Studies on Alcohol* 55:207-213, 1994.

Wilkinson, C.W.; Peskind, E.R.; and Raskind, M.A. Decreased hypothalamic-pituitary-adrenal axis sensitivity to cortisol feedback inhibition in human aging. *Neuroendocrinology* 65:79-90, 1997.

Chronic Alcohol Consumption and Aging

Age-Related Changes in Alcohol Sensitivity

Various factors may contribute to age-related differences in a person's sensitivity to the effects of alcohol. For example, a given alcohol dose—even a single drink—can produce higher BACs in older people than in younger people. The main factor accounting for these higher BACs appears to be the increase in body fat relative to muscle that generally occurs with increasing age. Thus, compared with 25-year-olds, the percent of total body weight consisting of fat increases an average of 50 percent in 60-year-old women and an average of 100 percent in 60-year-old men (Dufour et al. 1992). Because alcohol dissolves only in water, of which muscle has a high content, but not in fat, the same alcohol dose results in a higher BAC in a person who has proportionately more fatty tissue and less body water. In addition, some evidence suggests that even with equivalent BACs, a given alcohol level has a greater impact on an older person's physiological system than on that of a younger person (Atkinson 1990).

Like other physiological systems, the brain appears to experience an age-related increase in sensitivity to alcohol. For example, aged rats show an increased sensitivity to both the sedative and hypothermic effects of alcohol than do young adult rats (York 1983; Guthrie et al. 1987). Although to date no extensive studies on this issue have been conducted in humans, the older human brain also seems to be more sensitive to alcohol impairment of motor-coordination tasks (Vogel-Sprott and Barrett 1984).

Researchers do not yet know if age-related changes in sensitivity to alcohol affect a person's susceptibility to developing alcohol abuse. People generally assume that alcohol abuse declines with age. However, several studies have noted that between 24 and 68 percent of alcohol-abusing people developed the first signs of alcohol abuse only after age 60 (Atkinson 1990). Interestingly, women and people of either sex with moderate to high socioeconomic status have shown the highest percentages of late-onset alcohol abuse (Atkinson 1990). These findings suggest that at least for some people, aging leads to an increased risk of alcohol abuse. Whether this increased risk results from age-related psychosocial factors (e.g., loss of a spouse, retirement, or loneliness) or changes in the physiological response to alcohol (or a combination of the two) remain to be determined.

Alcohol Abuse and Premature or Exaggerated Aging

Chronic alcohol exposure can lead to impairment of a wide range of physiological functions. Some of these pathological effects, such as alcohol-induced damage of liver and pancreas functions, appear to result directly from alcohol's toxic effects on those organs. Other health problems associated with chronic alcohol use (e.g., cardiovascular disease, sleep disorders, gastrointestinal dysfunction, and increased susceptibility to infections), however, appear to be less specific in nature (Colsher and Wallace 1990; Brower et al. 1994). In fact, these effects, which vary from person to person, may represent an accelerated or exaggerated aging process.

Some researchers have noted that an important distinction may exist between alcohol-related accelerated aging versus exaggerated aging (Noonberg et al. 1985; Evert and Oscar-Berman 1995). Accelerated aging means that symptoms of old age appear earlier than normal, resulting in premature aging. Exaggerated aging implies that the symptoms of old age appear at the appropriate time, but in a more exaggerated form. Exaggerated aging may result from a person's increased vulnerability to the pathophysiological changes that emerge during approximately the sixth decade of life, such as brittle bones (i.e., osteoporosis), adult onset diabetes, cognitive decline, and shrinkage (i.e., atrophy) of muscle tissue.

Some evidence suggests that chronic alcohol exposure can lead to both accelerated and exaggerated aging. Nevertheless, some alcohol-induced pathological changes that superficially resemble the consequences of normal aging—and thus appear to indicate accelerated aging—have revealed, on closer inspection, some unique characteristics. For example, careful comparisons demonstrated that the nature of the memory deficits found in younger (i.e., mean age of 37.2 years) alcoholics differed from the deficits found in older (i.e., mean age of 64.7 years) non-alcoholics (Kramer et al. 1989).

Studies of the effects of long-term alcohol use on brain tissue and brain function have examined the connection between alcohol and the aging process. Advances in technologies to obtain brain images (i.e., neuroimaging technology) during the past 20 years have allowed researchers to study the brain structure of living individuals in great detail (i.e., with high spatial resolution). These studies have demonstrated that chronic alcohol use leads to substantial atrophy of the brain, as evidenced by reduced volumes of various brain regions (i.e., the cortex, anterior hippocampus, mammillary bodies, and corpus callosum). The brain regions most affected by chronic alcohol use appear to be the prefrontal and cerebellar cortex. The prefrontal cortex is the brain region believed to be most responsible for higher level cognitive processes, whereas the cerebellum plays an important role in motor function. Simultaneously, the volume of the fluid-filled cavities in the brain (i.e., the ventricles) increases—making up for lost tissue—after chronic alcohol use (Pfefferbaum et al. 1998).

Normal aging also appears to lead to a steady decline in the general cortical area (with the greatest decline occurring in the prefrontal cortex) and a concurrent enlargement of the ventricles. Nevertheless, several studies have demonstrated that these signs of cerebral atrophy are greater in alcoholics than in non-alcoholics of the same age (Pfefferbaum et al. 1992, 1998). Possibly, however, the alcoholics already possessed reduced cortical areas before the onset of alcohol abuse, and thus cortical atrophy may reflect a neuropathology that contributes to the susceptibility to alcohol abuse rather than a consequence of chronic alcohol exposure. To investigate this possibility, a recent study used magnetic resonance imaging (MRI) technology to examine changes in cortical area and ventricular size over a 5-year time span in both alcoholics (average age of 45 at initial assessment) and non-alcoholics of similar age (average age of 51 at initial assessment) (Pfefferbaum et al. 1998). As in other studies, the cortical volume in the frontal, temporal, and parietal lobes was significantly reduced in the alcoholics compared with the non-alcoholics. In both groups, the cortical area declined during the 5-year study period. The alcoholics, however, exhibited a greater rate of decline in anterior superior temporal cortex volume than did the non-alcoholics, indicating that cortical atrophy likely represents a consequence of chronic alcohol use.

Another study found that the difference in cortical volume between alcoholics and non-alcoholics was greater among older subjects than among younger subjects (Pfefferbaum et al. 1992). In that study, after controlling for age, the extent of cortical atrophy in alcoholic men increased with age but not with duration of alcoholism. This observation suggests that the brains of older people may be more vulnerable to alcohol's degenerative effects than the brains of younger people.

Consistent with the fact that chronic alcohol abuse can lead to reductions in cortical volume, numerous studies have observed alcohol-related deficits in cognitive functions. The most extreme cases of alcohol-related dementia and severe memory loss (i.e., amnesia), which constitute a condition called Wernicke-Korsakoff syndrome, may be primarily a result of severe alcohol-related nutritional and/or vitamin deficiencies (Nakada and Knight 1984). In addition, however, chronic alcohol abuse appears to produce more subtle—but significant—deficits in cognitive function. These deficits are most evident on tests of relatively complex cognitive function, such as the ability to follow abstract concepts or to adapt quickly to changing conditions (Tivis et al. 1995; Evert and Oscar-Berman 1995). On such tasks, the performance of alcoholics is impaired compared with non-alcoholics of the same age. In fact, chronic alcohol abuse appears to accelerate a person's cognitive decline by approximately 10 years, because the cognitive performance of alcoholics generally is comparable to that of non-alcoholics who are 10 years older. This age-related discrepancy is apparent even in alcoholics in their thirties (Noonberg et al. 1985). Although these observations support the notion that alcoholics experience accelerated brain aging, the studies conducted to date have not ruled out the possibility that the alcohol-related cognitive deficits reflect an initial cognitive impairment that leads to an increased risk of alcoholism.

References

Atkinson, R.M. Aging and alcohol use disorders: Diagnostic issues in the elderly. *International Psychogeriatrics* 2:55-72, 1990.

Brower, K.J.; Mudd, S.; Blow, F.C.; Young, J.P.; and Hill, E.M. Severity and treatment of alcohol withdrawal in elderly versus younger patients. *Alcoholism: Clinical and Experimental Research* 18:196-201, 1994.

Colsher, R.L., and Wallace, R.B. Elderly men with histories of heavy drinking: Correlates and consequences. *Journal of Studies on Alcohol* 51:528-535, 1990.

Dufour, M.C.; Archer, L.; and Gordis, E. Alcohol and the elderly. *Clinics in Geriatric Medicine* 8:127-141, 1992.

Evert, D.L., and Oscar-Berman, M. Alcohol-related cognitive impairments: An overview of how alcoholism may affect the workings of the brain. *Alcohol Health & Research World* 19:89-96, 1995.

Guthrie, S.; Cooper, R.L.; Thurman, R.; and Linnoila, M. Pharmacodynamics and pharmacokinetics of ethanol, diazepam and pentobarbital in young and aged rats. *Pharmacology and Toxicology* 61:308-312, 1987.

Kramer, J.H.; Blusewicz, M.J.; and Preston, K.A. The premature aging hypothesis: Old before its time? *Journal of Consulting and Clinical Psychology* 57:257-262, 1989.

Nakada, T., and Knight, R.T. Alcohol and the central nervous system. *Medical Clinics of North America* 68:121-131, 1984.

Noonberg, A.; Goldstein, G.; and Page, H.A. Premature aging in male alcoholics: "Accelerated aging" or "increased vulnerability"? *Alcoholism: Clinical and Experimental Research* 9:334-338, 1985.

Pfefferbaum, A.; Lim, K.O.; Zipursky, R.B.; Mathalon, D.H.; Rosenbloom, M.J.; Lane, B.; Ha, C.N.; and Sullivan, E.V. Brain gray and white matter volume loss accelerates with aging in chronic alcoholics: A quantitative MRI study. *Alcoholism: Clinical and Experimental Research* 16:1078-1089, 1992.

Pfefferbaum, A.; Sullivan, E.V.; Rosenbloom, M.J.; Mathalon, D.H.; and Lim, K.O. A controlled study of cortical gray matter and ventricular changes in alcoholic men over a 5-year interval. *Archives of General Psychiatry* 55:905-912, 1998.

Tivis, R.; Beatty, W.W.; Nixon, S.J.; and Parsons, O.A. Patterns of cognitive impairment among alcoholics: Are there subtypes? *Alcoholism: Clinical and Experimental Research* 19:496-500, 1995.

Vogel-Sprott, M., and Barrett, P. Age, drinking habits and effects of alcohol. Journal of Studies on Alcohol 45:517-521, 1984. YORK, J.L. Increased responsiveness to ethanol with advancing age in rats. *Pharmacology Biochemistry and Behavior* 19:687-691, 1983.

Footnotes

1. The typical life span of a rat is 2 to 2.5 years. In general, young adult rats are 4 to 5 months old, whereas aged, or "older," rats are 22 to 24 months old.

2. The inability to normally metabolize alcohol can result in unpleasant symptoms in response to alcohol consumption, including visible flushing of the face, nausea, and vomiting.

3. Studies such as these, in which alcohol is administered to alcoholics, are no longer conducted in human subjects.

4. This brain region appears to be essential for the rewarding or euphoria-inducing effects of alcohol or other drugs and serves as a link between brain regions that generate emotions and brain regions that control movement.

5. The terms "tolerance" and "habituation" both refer to the same phenomenon—the diminished response to a certain stimulus. However, by convention, the term "tolerance" is

used for a diminishing response to drugs, whereas the term "habituation" generally is used with non-drug stimuli, such as stress or repeated sounds.

Part Five

Stress Management

Chapter 33

Coping with Everyday Problems

Stress is a natural part of life. The expressions are familiar to us, "I'm stressed out," "I'm under too much stress," or "Work is one big stress." Stress is hard to define because it means different things to different people; however, it's clear that most stress is a negative feeling rather than a positive feeling.

Stress Can Be Both Physical and Mental

You may feel physical stress which is the result of too much to do, not enough sleep, a poor diet, or the effects of an illness. Stress can also be mental: when you worry about money, a loved one's illness, retirement, or experience an emotionally devastating event, such as the death of a spouse or being fired from work.

However, much of our stress comes from less dramatic everyday responsibilities. Obligations and pressures which are both physical and mental are not always obvious to us. In response to these daily strains your body automatically increases blood pressure, heart rate, respiration, metabolism, and blood flow to you muscles. This response is intended to help your body react quickly and effectively to a high-pressure situation.

"Stress—Coping with Everyday Problems," Fact Sheet, © 2001 National Mental Health Association, reprinted with permission; and "10 Steps to Manage Your Stress," © 2000 The Cleveland Clinic Foundation, 9500 Euclid Avenue, Cleveland, OH 44195, 800-223-2273 ext. 48950, www.clevelandclinic.org. Additional information is available from the Cleveland Clinic Health Information Center, 216-444-3771, or www.clevelandclinic.org/health. Reprinted with permission.

However, when you are constantly reacting to stressful situations without making adjustments to counter the effects, you will feel stress which can threaten your health and well-being. It is essential to understand that external events, no matter how you perceive those events, which may cause stress. Stress often accompanies the feeling of "being out of control."

How Do I Know if I Am Suffering from Stress?

Remember, each person handles stress differently. Some people actually seek out situations which may appear stressful to others. A major life decision, such as changing careers or buying a house, might be overwhelming for some people, while others may welcome the change. Some find sitting in traffic too much to tolerate, while others take it in stride. The key is determining your personal tolerance levels for stressful situations.

Stress can cause physical, emotional, and behavioral disorders which can affect your health, vitality, peace-of-mind, as well as personal and professional relationships. Too much stress can cause relatively minor illnesses like insomnia, backaches, or headaches, and can contribute to potentially life-threatening diseases like high blood pressure and heart disease.

Tips for Reducing or Controlling Stress

As you read the following suggestions, remember that success will not come from a half-hearted effort, nor will it come overnight. It will take determination, persistence, and time. Some suggestions may help immediately, but if your stress is chronic, it may require more attention and/or lifestyle changes. Determine *your* tolerance level for stress and try to live within these limits. Learn to accept or change stressful and tense situations whenever possible.

Be realistic. If you feel overwhelmed by some activities (yours and/or your family's), learn to say *no!* Eliminate an activity that is not absolutely necessary. You may be taking on more responsibility than you can or should handle. If you meet resistance, give reasons why you're making the changes. Be willing to listen to other's suggestions and be ready to compromise.

Shed the "superman/superwoman" urge. No one is perfect, so don't expect perfection from yourself or others. Ask yourself, "What really needs to be done? How much can I do? Is the deadline realistic? What adjustments can I make?" Don't hesitate to ask for help if you need it.

Meditate. Just ten to twenty minutes of quiet reflection may bring relief from chronic stress as well as increase your tolerance to it. Use the time to listen to music, relax, and try to think of pleasant things or nothing.

Visualize. Use your imagination and picture how you can manage a stressful situation more successfully. Whether it's a business presentation or moving to a new place, many people feel visual rehearsals boost self-confidence and enable them to take a more positive approach to a difficult task.

Take one thing at a time. For people under tension or stress, an ordinary workload can sometimes seem unbearable. The best way to cope with this feeling of being overwhelmed is to take one task at a time. Pick one urgent task and work on it. Once you accomplish that task, choose the next one. The positive feeling of "checking off" tasks is very satisfying. It will motivate you to keep going.

Exercise. Regular exercise is a popular and proven way to relieve stress. Twenty to thirty minutes of physical activity benefits both the body and the mind.

Hobbies. Take a break from your worries by doing something you enjoy. Whether it's gardening or painting, schedule time to indulge your interest.

Healthy life style. Good nutrition makes a difference. Limit intake of caffeine and alcohol (alcohol actually disturbs regular sleep patterns), get adequate rest, exercise, and balance work and play.

Share your feelings. A conversation with a friend lets you know that you are not the only one having a bad day, caring for a sick child, or working in a busy office. Stay in touch with friends and family. Let them provide love, support, and guidance. Don't try to cope alone.

Give in occasionally. Be flexible! If you find you're meeting constant opposition in either your personal or professional life, rethink your position or strategy. Arguing only intensifies stressful feelings.

If you know you are right, stand your ground, but do so calmly and rationally. Make allowances for other's opinions and be prepared to compromise. If you are willing to give in, others may meet you half-way. Not only will you reduce your stress, you may find better solutions to your problems.

Go easy with criticism. You may expect too much of yourself and others. Try not to feel frustrated, let down, disappointed or even "trapped" when another person does not measure up. The "other person" may be a wife, a husband, or child whom you are trying to change to suit yourself. Remember, everyone is unique, and has his or her own virtues, shortcomings, and right to develop as an individual.

10 Steps to Manage Your Stress

Cutting back on the stress in your life may help you feel better, eat better, and stick to an exercise plan, all of which can lower your risk for heart disease. But if you're too stressed to figure out how to get started, here are a few tips.

1. **Eat and drink sensibly.** Abusing alcohol and food may seem to reduce stress, but actually adds to it.

2. **Assert yourself.** You do not have to meet others' expectations or demands. It's okay to say "no." Remember, being assertive allows you to stand up for your rights and beliefs while respecting those of others.

3. **Stop smoking or other bad habits.** Aside from the obvious health risks of cigarettes, nicotine acts as a stimulant and brings on more stress symptoms. Give yourself the gift of dropping unhealthy habits.

4. **Exercise regularly.** Choose non-competitive exercise and set reasonable goals. Aerobic exercise has been shown to release endorphins (natural substances that help you feel better and maintain a positive attitude.)

5. **Relax every day.** Study and practice relaxation techniques. Choose from a variety of different techniques. Combine opposites—a time for deep relaxation and a time for aerobic exercise is a sure way to protect your body from the effects of stress.

6. **Take responsibility.** Control what you can and leave behind what you cannot control.

7. **Reduce causes of stress.** Many people find life is filled with too many demands and too little time. For the most part, these demands are ones we have chosen. Effective time-management skills involve asking for help when appropriate, setting priorities, pacing yourself and taking time out for yourself.

8. **Examine your values and live by them.** The more your actions reflect your beliefs, the better you will feel, no matter how busy your life is. Use your values when choosing your activities.

9. **Set realistic goals and expectations.** It's OK, and healthy, to realize you cannot be 100 percent successful at everything at once.

10. **Sell yourself to yourself.** When you are feeling overwhelmed, remind yourself of what you do well. Have a healthy sense of self-esteem.

What Else Can I Do?

There are several other methods you can use to relax or reduce stress, including:

- deep breathing exercises
- meditation
- progressive muscle relaxation
- mental imagery relaxation
- relaxation to music
- biofeedback (explained in the next section)
- counseling, to help you recognize and release stress

Ask your health care provider for more information about these techniques.

What Is Biofeedback?

Biofeedback helps a person learn stress-reduction skills by using various instruments to measure temperature, heart rate, muscle tension, and other vital signs as a person attempts to relax. The goal of bio-feedback is to teach you to monitor your own body as you relax. It is used to gain control over certain bodily functions which cause tension and physical pain.

Biofeedback can be used to help you learn how your body responds in stressful situations, and how to better cope. If a headache, such as a migraine, begins slowly, many people can use biofeedback to stop the attack before it becomes full blown.

What if I Have Trouble Sleeping?

You may experience insomnia (an inability to sleep) because of discomfort, stress from personal concerns, or side effects from your medications.

If you cannot sleep, try these tips:

- Establish a regular sleep schedule. Go to bed and get up at the same time every day.

- Make sure your bed and surroundings are comfortable. Arrange the pillows so you can maintain a comfortable position.

- Keep your bedroom dark and quiet.

- Use your bedroom for sleeping only; don't work or watch TV in your bedroom.

- Avoid napping too much during the day. At the same time, remember to balance activity with rest during recovery.

- If you feel nervous or anxious, talk to your spouse, partner, or a trusted friend. Get your troubles off your mind.

- Listen to relaxing music.

- *Do not* take sleeping pills—they are very harmful when taken with your other medications.

- Take diuretics, or "water pills" earlier, if possible, so you don't have to get up in the middle of the night to use the bathroom.

- If you can't sleep, get up and do something relaxing until you feel tired. Don't stay in bed worrying about when you're going to fall asleep.

- Avoid caffeine.

- Maintain a regular exercise routine; don't exercise within two to three hours of bedtime.

Where to Get Help

Help may be as close as a friend or spouse. But if you think that you or someone you know may be under more stress than just dealing with a passing difficulty, it may be helpful to talk with your doctor, spiritual advisor, or employee assistance professional. They may suggest you visit with a psychiatrist, psychologist, social worker, or other qualified counselor.

Ideas to Consider When Talking with a Professional

- List the things which cause stress and tension in your life.

- How does this stress and tension affect you, your family, and your job?

- Can you identify the stress and tensions in your life as short or long term?

- Do you have a support system of friends/family that will help you make positive changes?

- What are your biggest obstacles to reducing stress?

- What are you willing to change or give up for a less stressful and tension-filled life?

- What have you tried already that didn't work for you?

- If you do not have control of a situation, can you accept it and get on with your life?

Additional Information

National Mental Health Association
1021 Prince Street
Alexandria, VA 22314
Toll-Free: 800-969-6642; Toll-Free TTY: 800-433-5959
Fax: 703-684-5968
Website: www.nmha.org

The Cleveland Clinic Foundation
9500 Euclid Avenue
Cleveland, OH 44195
Toll-Free: 800-223-2273 ext. 48950
Website: www.clevelandclinic.org

Cleveland Clinic Health Information Center
Tel: 216-444-3771
Website: www.clevelandclinic.org/health

Chapter 34

Physical Activity, Weight Control, and Nutrition

Staying Strong at Any Age

You stretch. You walk. And you're eating right. But are you missing out on an important part of a healthier lifestyle?

You can defy it or denounce it; yet no matter how hard you try, you cannot avoid the inevitable truth: we all will grow old. While past generations more readily accepted the steady decline of physical and mental functioning many still associate with aging, studies reveal that baby boomers, ages 37 to 55, will resist the label "senior" and continue to place a high value on being active and staying young. A recent *USA Today* poll reported that retirement is not in the plan for 75 percent of aging baby boomers, as they would choose to continue to work full- or part-time.

Yet if statistics ring true, America is in trouble as boomers hit their fifties. New data reveals that nearly four out of five adults in America get almost no exercise at all, even though exercise is an important key to feeling great and staying healthy.

"Staying Strong at Any Age," by Debra Fulghum Bruce © Vibrant Life Online, reprinted with permission; "Dealing with Stress: The Physical Connection," from Online Wellness Center of Wellsource, Inc. © 1998 Mid-Columbia Medical Center, reprinted with permission; "Physical Activity and Weight Control," National Institute of Diabetes and Digestive and Kidney Diseases (NIDDK), NIH Publication No. 96-4031, April 1996; and "Magnesium: The Stress Reliever," © Leo Gailand M.D. P.C., Foundation for Integrated Medicine, 133 E. 73rd St., New York, NY 10021, reprinted with permission.

No matter what your age, exercise is vital to reduce the effects of stress on the body and mind, improve erratic sleep symptoms, restore fitness to stiff, inflexible bodies, and prevent many chronic diseases that are associated with growing older.

Enhanced Emotional State

Not only is exercise a key factor in aerobic fitness, it is also important for revitalizing the neurochemical balance of the body that affects our emotional state. Research shows that regular exercise reduces symptoms of moderate depression and enhances psychological fitness. Exercise can even produce changes in certain chemical levels in the body, which can have an effect on the psychological state.

Endorphins are hormones in the brain associated with a happy, positive feeling. A low level of endorphins is associated with depression. During exercise, plasma levels of this substance increase and may help to alleviate symptoms of depression. A National Health and Nutrition examination survey found that physically active people were half as likely to be depressed a decade later as those who were inactive.

Interestingly, there might not be a definite link between exercise intensity and mood. In fact, new evidence shows that even regular exercisers who are not in shape and do a light or moderate workout receive the same long-term stress reduction as those who are aerobically fit. This is good news for those of us who are not marathon runners!

Immune System Boost

Regular exercise appears to have the advantage of jump-starting the immune system, thus helping to reduce the number of colds and flu. One reason for this may be the increase in activity of lymphocytes, called killer cells, from regular exercise and also an increase in immunoglobulin found in the blood. Increases from 50 to 300 percent have been reported.

Watch your workouts, though. A study revealed that when workouts become stressful or excessive, the body produces increased amounts of cortisol (the stress hormone), which can inhibit the ability of certain immune cells to work properly. Some research has found that endurance athletes are at increased risk for upper respiratory tract infections during periods of prolonged training, especially the one-to-nine hour period following heavy training or exercise such as marathons.

466

Getting Started

Reality tells us that we cannot turn back the clock. Nevertheless, studies reveal that men and women of all ages can reshape what it means to enjoy an active, energetic life. Starting an exercise program is as simple as moving more. While nutrition recommendations for good health may seem a bit complicated, moving around more is not! As you begin your exercise program, you need to incorporate the following types of exercise in your weekly plan:

- **Range-of-motion or stretching exercises.** These involve moving a joint as far as it will go (without pain) or through its full range of motion. You can do this with basic stretches or through everyday housework or gardening.

- **Endurance or conditioning exercises.** When you increase your endurance threshold with cardiovascular forms of exercise such as walking, biking, or swimming, you are not only strengthening your muscles—you are conditioning your body and building coordination and endurance.

- **Strengthening exercises.** These exercises help to build strong muscles. You may use resistance machines, resistance bands, or free weights (handheld weights that are not part of a machine).

As you approach middle age, studies show that muscle strength naturally begins to level off. The good news is that resistance or weight training can offset this muscle decline and help to build strength.

Common Misconceptions of Weight Training

"But I don't want to look like a football player," one petite middle-aged woman said when she met with a qualified personal trainer regarding a strength training program. Many people still associate weights with building bulky muscles, but this is not the case. Let's look at some of the common misconceptions of weight training.

- "Weight lifting is dangerous." If done with proper technique, this is a very safe way to tone the body.

- "Women will get big muscles." Women produce less testosterone than men and build muscle size less rapidly. It takes years of hard work and proper diet to obtain large muscles.

467

- "Strength training means using heavy equipment." Resistance bands can be purchased at sporting goods stores for strength training. Other ways to strength train include using isometrics, free weights, or even water-resistance exercises.

- "I must start with heavy weights." You should not begin with heavy weights. A good rule of thumb is to start with a weight you can easily lift 10 times, with the last two repetitions being increasingly difficult. For some people this is only one to two pounds; others can start at 15 to 20 pounds, depending on their muscle strength. As your muscles gain strength and if there is no pain, increase the weights in one- to two-pound increments. Ask your doctor or a qualified personal trainer for weights that are best for you.

- The theory "no pain, no gain" is true for strength training. If your muscles are very sore, do not use resistance training until you are relatively pain-free. Strength training may not be appropriate for everyone, so check with your doctor for approval.

- "I will get high blood pressure." Weight training does not cause high blood pressure. Some people strain their body and hold their breath during a lift, which results in a temporary increase of blood pressure. However, this is never recommended during weight training.

- "I will become bulky and inflexible." It is important to supplement your weight training with a stretching routine to stay flexible.

- "Lifting weights helps me spot-reduce specific areas of my body." Exercise does not reduce fat at specific body sites; you must exercise the total body to achieve maximum results.

- "The benefits are few." Not so; increased strength, improved muscle tone, enhanced athletic performance, increased bone, tendon and ligament strength, injury prevention, and improved body image are all benefits of weight training. For women, weight training can play a significant role in reducing osteoporosis, as bones need regular resistance to stay strong. And age is not a factor with weight training; the muscles of older people are just as responsive as those of younger people.

Getting Started

As you plan your exercise program, try to include strength training at least two to three times per week, with at least 48 to 72 hours between sessions for muscles to recover. Select conditioning and stretching exercises you enjoy, and vary these from day to day. An active routine might include:

- Monday—Gardening, mowing lawn
- Tuesday—Strength training
- Wednesday—Bicycle ride with kids
- Thursday—Walk with a neighbor after dinner
- Friday—Strength training

Whatever you choose, do something! Remember the adage, "Move it or lose it," certainly rings true—especially as birthday celebrations increase.

Dealing with Stress—The Physical Connection

We experience stress in response to a threat. The threat can be real, such as a near-miss car accident, or imagined, such as an intense fear that you will embarrass yourself when you give a toast at a wedding. When we are stressed, our body releases stress hormones such as coritsol, adrenaline, epinephrine, and norepinephrine into the blood stream. We tense up and brace ourselves. Our heart pounds and muscles stiffen. We may tremble or sweat. This physical response to stress is known as the "fight or flight" response.

The fight or flight response can help us get through a crisis. But, if we experience the fight or flight response repeatedly, for a long period, it can negatively impact our mental and physical health. Chronic, excessive stress has been associated with increased risk for numerous diseases and health problems, including

- alcohol and drug dependencies
- asthma, allergies, and skin diseases
- anxiety
- backaches
- cancer
- depressed immune system/increased likelihood of colds and infections
- depression and suicide
- headaches (migraines, too)

- heart disease/heart attack
- high blood pressure
- high cholesterol
- sleep disturbances stroke
- TMJ (temporomandibular joint) syndrome
- ulcers and digestive disorders

Fortunately, there are relaxation techniques you can use to offset the fight or flight response.

Deep Breathing

Deep breathing calms and relaxes your body. Slowly breathe in, filling your lungs as full as possible, and let your stomach relax and expand. Hold your breath for a few seconds then, slowly, exhale until your lungs feel empty. Repeat five to 10 times. Any time you feel yourself tensing in response to stress, try deep breathing.

Muscle Relaxation

Progressive muscular relaxation effectively relaxes tense muscles. First, tense a major muscle group in your body (face, shoulders, arms, chest, back, stomach, buttocks, legs, and feet) hold for a few seconds then release the tension. Feel the warmth as blood flow increases in that area. Choose a second muscle group and repeat the same process. Go through all of the muscle groups in your body from head to toes. The entire process takes only a few minutes and you can immediately feel and appreciate the relaxed feeling in your body.

Stretching

Gentle stretching can relax tense muscles. While sitting, tip your head slowly from side to side, then forward and back. Repeat several times. While sitting, stretch forward, letting your head and arms come forward, hold for 30 seconds, straighten up slowly, and repeat. While standing, reach as high as comfortable with both arms for 30 seconds; slowly lower arms to your side. Repeat several times. While standing slowly stretch to the side by letting one arm hang down and bending the other one over your head in the direction you are stretching. Repeat with the other side. While lying down stretch your legs out straight and at the same time reach arms over your head, hold 30

470

seconds. Repeat several times. You may wish to stretch other muscles in your body. Remember to stretch gently and slowly. To avoid injury, don't strain or bounce while stretching.

Getting Physical

Regular physical activity will condition and heal your body, increase your energy level, help control your weight, and reduce stress. The new physical activity guideline by the Centers for Disease Control and Prevention and the American College of Sports Medicine is every U.S. adult should accumulate 30 minutes or more of moderate intensity physical activity on most, preferably all, days of the week.

You do not have to get all 30 minutes at once. You may prefer to get 15 minutes in the morning and 15 minutes at noon or in the evening. You can also break up your exercise into three 10-minute blocks.

An optimum aerobic exercise program will burn 200 to 300 calories per day or 1,000 to 2,000 calories a week. The following table gives calorie expenditures for specific exercises.

Walking is the best overall exercise for most people. Walking doesn't require special equipment, facilities, or locations. Start with moderate walking, 20 to 30 minutes, three to five times per week and work up to walking 30 to 60 minutes, four to six or even seven times a week. You can increase your pace for added benefits. If you have

Table 34.1. Calorie Expenditures for Specific Exercises and Time Involved

Activity	Duration	Calories Burned
Running, 10-minute mile	13 minutes	150
Jogging, 12-minute mile	18 minutes	150
Mowing lawn, powered push mower	29 minutes	150
Social dancing	29 minutes	150
Raking leaves	32 minutes	150
Ping-pong	32 minutes	150
Walking, briskly, 15-minute mile	32 minutes	150
Walking, moderate pace, 20-minute mile	43 minutes	150

Source: U.S. Department of Health and Human Services. "Physical Activity and Health: A Report of the Surgeon General," 1996.

not been exercising or if you have serious health problems, get clearance from your doctor before starting any exercise program. Be sure to wear the appropriate safety gear (for example, a helmet when bicycling) when you are working out.

If you are looking for additional ways to reduce stress through exercise, consider the following:

- non-competitive activities such as swimming

- easy- to moderate-intensity activities that cause little or no strain or pain such as water aerobics (make sure you stretch and warm up before exercising and cool down afterward)

- activities you can do outdoors, in quiet, pastoral settings, such as hiking or bicycling

- movement, dance, or yoga class

- gardening

If you tend to get bored with one activity, try cross-training. For example, swim laps on some days, jog or walk on others, bike or rollerblade on the weekends.

To extend the relaxing benefits of exercise, soak in a warm bath or hot tub after your work out. Treat yourself to a full body massage on occasion.

Anti-Anxiety Medications and Therapy

Approximately 23 million Americans (1 in 9) suffer from chronic anxiety disorders. They experience excessive, chronic worry over relationships, finances, health, or work, even when there are no immediate threats in those areas. Anxiety disorders can be effectively treated with talk therapy or medication or a combination of both. If you believe that your stress is severe and persistent, and you are having trouble controlling it on your own, talk with your doctor. Your doctor may prescribe medication or refer you to a professional counselor who will assess your needs and help you cope and reduce excess stress. Anti-anxiety medication is designed to relieve some of the symptoms associated with high levels of anxiety, but it is not a cure-all. Continue to look for ways to better manage stress in your life, such as communicating effectively, eating nutritiously, and getting 30 minutes or more of physical activity every day. That way, if you and your doctor decide to discontinue your medication, you will be practicing powerful techniques to reduce and manage your stress load and your anxiety on your own.

Depression

Sometimes feeling over-stressed can be a symptom of depression. Other symptoms of depression include:

- feeling downhearted or blue
- change in appetite/weight gain or loss
- sleeping difficulties
- apathy/no longer excited about the things that used to bring you pleasure
- feeling tired, fatigued
- feeling guilty
- feeling worthless
- feeling hopelessness/despair thoughts of suicide

According to the American Psychiatric Association, 9.4 million Americans suffer from depression in any given six-month period. If you have experienced any persistent symptoms of depression for two weeks or longer, consult with your doctor. Depression is a highly treatable condition, so if it turns out that you are suffering from depression, your doctor will be able to suggest ways you can get relief.

Physical Activity and Weight Control

Regular physical activity is an important part of effective weight loss and weight maintenance. It also can help prevent several diseases and improve your overall health. It does not matter what type of physical activity you perform—sports, planned exercise, household chores, yard work, or work-related tasks—all are beneficial. Studies show that even the most inactive people can gain significant health benefits if they accumulate 30 minutes or more of physical activity per day. Based on these findings, the U.S. Public Health Service has identified increased physical activity as a priority in Healthy People 2000.

Research consistently shows that regular physical activity, combined with healthy eating habits, is the most efficient and healthful way to control your weight. Whether you are trying to lose weight or maintain it, you should understand the important role of physical activity and include it in your lifestyle.

How Can Physical Activity Help Control My Weight?

Physical activity helps to control your weight by using excess calories that otherwise would be stored as fat. Your body weight is regulated by the number of calories you eat and use each day. Everything you eat contains calories, and everything you do uses calories, including sleeping, breathing, and digesting food. Any physical activity in addition to what you normally do will use extra calories.

Balancing the calories you use through physical activity with the calories you eat will help you achieve your desired weight. When you eat more calories than you need to perform your day's activities, your body stores the extra calories and you gain weight.

When you eat fewer calories than you use, your body uses the stored calories and you lose weight. When you eat the same amount of calories as your body uses, your weight stays the same.

Any type of physical activity you choose to do—strenuous activities such as running or aerobic dancing or moderate-intensity activities such as walking or household work—will increase the number of calories your body uses. The key to successful weight control and improved overall health is making physical activity a part of your daily routine.

What Are the Health Benefits of Physical Activity?

In addition to helping to control your weight, research shows that regular physical activity can reduce your risk for several diseases and conditions and improve your overall quality of life. Regular physical activity can help protect you from the following health problems.

- **Heart Disease and Stroke.** Daily physical activity can help prevent heart disease and stroke by strengthening your heart muscle, lowering your blood pressure, raising your high-density lipoprotein (HDL) levels (good cholesterol), and lowering low-density lipoprotein (LDL) levels (bad cholesterol), improving blood flow, and increasing your heart's working capacity.

- **High Blood Pressure.** Regular physical activity can reduce blood pressure in those with high blood pressure levels. Physical activity also reduces body fat, which is associated with high blood pressure.

- **Noninsulin-Dependent Diabetes.** By reducing body fat, physical activity can help to prevent and control this type of diabetes.

- **Obesity.** Physical activity helps to reduce body fat by building or preserving muscle mass and improving the body's ability to use calories. When physical activity is combined with proper nutrition, it can help control weight and prevent obesity, a major risk factor for many diseases.

- **Back Pain.** By increasing muscle strength and endurance and improving flexibility and posture, regular exercise helps to prevent back pain.

- **Osteoporosis.** Regular weight-bearing exercise promotes bone formation and may prevent many forms of bone loss associated with aging.

Studies on the psychological effects of exercise have found that regular physical activity can improve your mood and the way you feel about yourself. Researchers also have found that exercise is likely to reduce depression and anxiety and help you to better manage stress.

Keep these health benefits in mind when deciding whether or not to exercise. And remember, any amount of physical activity you do is better than none at all.

How Much Should I Exercise?

For the greatest overall health benefits, experts recommend that you do 20 to 30 minutes of aerobic activity three or more times a week and some type of muscle strengthening activity and stretching at least twice a week. However, if you are unable to do this level of activity, you can gain substantial health benefits by accumulating 30 minutes or more of moderate-intensity physical activity a day, at least five times a week.

If you have been inactive for a while, you may want to start with less strenuous activities such as walking or swimming at a comfortable pace. Beginning at a slow pace will allow you to become physically fit without straining your body. Once you are in better shape, you can gradually do more strenuous activity.

Moderate Intensity Activity

Moderate-intensity activities include some of the things you may already be doing during a day or week, such as gardening and housework.

These activities can be done in short spurts—10 minutes here, 8 minutes there. Alone, each action does not have a great effect on your health, but regularly accumulating 30 minutes of activity over the course of the day can result in substantial health benefits.

To become more active throughout your day, take advantage of any chance to get up and move around. Here are some examples:

- Take a short walk around the block

- Rake leaves

- Play actively with the kids

- Walk up the stairs instead of taking the elevator

- Mow the lawn

- Take an activity break—get up and stretch or walk around

- Park your car a little farther away from your destination and walk the extra distance

The point is not to make physical activity an unwelcome chore, but to make the most of the opportunities you have to be active.

Aerobic Activity

Aerobic activity is an important addition to moderate-intensity exercise. Aerobic exercise is any extended activity that makes you breathe hard while using the large muscle groups at a regular, even pace. Aerobic activities help make your heart stronger and more efficient. They also use more calories than other activities. Some examples of aerobic activities include:

- Brisk walking
- Jogging
- Bicycling
- Swimming
- Aerobic dancing
- Racket sports
- Rowing
- Ice or roller skating
- Cross-country or downhill skiing
- Using aerobic equipment (i.e., treadmill, stationary bike)

To get the most health benefits from aerobic activity, you should exercise at a level strenuous enough to raise your heart rate to your target zone. Your target heart rate zone is 50 to 75 percent of your maximum heart rate (the fastest your heart can beat). To find your target zone, look for the category closest to your age in the chart below and read across the line. For example, if you are 35 years old, your target heart rate zone is 93-138 beats per minute.

To see if you are exercising within your target heart rate zone, count the number of pulse beats at your wrist or neck for 15 seconds, then multiply by four to get the beats per minute. Your heart should be beating within your target heart rate zone. If your heart is beating faster than your target heart rate, you are exercising too hard and should slow down. If your heart is beating slower than your target heart rate, you should exercise a little harder.

When you begin your exercise program, aim for the lower part of your target zone (50 percent). As you get into better shape, slowly build up to the higher part of your target zone (75 percent). If exercising within your target zone seems too hard, exercise at a pace that is comfortable for you. You will find that, with time, you will feel more comfortable exercising and can slowly increase to your target zone.

Table 34.2. Target Heart Rate Zone by Age

Age	Target Heart Rate Zone 50-75%	Average Maximum Heart Rate 100%
20-30 years	98-146 beats per min.	195
31-40 years	93-138 beats per min.	185
41-50 years	88-131 beats per min.	175
51-60 years	83-123 beats per min.	165
61+ years	78-116 beats per min.	155

Stretching and Muscle Strengthening Exercises

Stretching and strengthening exercises such as weight training should also be a part of your physical activity program. In addition to using calories, these exercises strengthen your muscles and bones and help prevent injury.

Tips to a Safe and Successful Physical Activity Program

Make sure you are in good health. Answer the following questions* before you begin exercising.

1. Has a doctor ever said you have heart problems?
2. Do you frequently suffer from chest pains?

3. Do you often feel faint or have dizzy spells?

4. Has a doctor ever said you have high blood pressure?

5. Has a doctor ever told you that you have a bone or joint problem, such as arthritis, that has been or could be aggravated by exercise?

6. Are you over the age of 65 and not accustomed to exercise?

7. Are you taking prescription medications, such as those for high blood pressure?

8. Is there a good medical reason, not mentioned here, why you should not exercise?

*Source: British Columbia Department of Health

If you answered "yes" to any of these questions, you should see your doctor before you begin an exercise program.

• Follow a gradual approach to exercise to get the most benefits with the fewest risks. If you have not been exercising, start at a slow pace and as you become more fit, gradually increase the amount of time and the pace of your activity.

• Choose activities that you enjoy and that fit your personality. For example, if you like team sports or group activities, choose things such as soccer or aerobics. If you prefer individual activities, choose things such as swimming or walking. Also, plan your activities for a time of day that suits your personality. If you are a morning person, exercise before you begin the rest of your day's activities. If you have more energy in the evening, plan activities that can be done at the end of the day. You will be more likely to stick to a physical activity program if it is convenient and enjoyable.

• Exercise regularly. To gain the most health benefits it is important to exercise as regularly as possible. Make sure you choose activities that will fit into your schedule.

• Exercise at a comfortable pace. For example, while jogging or walking briskly you should be able to hold a conversation. If you do not feel normal again within 10 minutes following exercise, you are exercising too hard. Also, if you have difficulty breathing or feel faint or weak during or after exercise, you are exercising too hard.

- Maximize your safety and comfort. Wear shoes that fit and clothes that move with you, and always exercise in a safe location. Many people walk in indoor shopping malls for exercise. Malls are climate controlled and offer protection from bad weather.

- Vary your activities. Choose a variety of activities so you don't get bored with any one thing.

- Encourage your family or friends to support you and join you in your activity. If you have children, it is best to build healthy habits when they are young. When parents are active, children are more likely to be active and stay active for the rest of their lives.

- Challenge yourself. Set short-term as well as long-term goals and celebrate every success, no matter how small.

Whether your goal is to control your weight or just to feel healthier, becoming physically active is a step in the right direction. Take advantage of the health benefits that regular exercise can offer and make physical activity a part of your lifestyle.

Magnesium: The Stress Reliever

Magnesium is the fourth most abundant mineral in your body, a necessary co-factor for hundreds of enzymes, and the most critical mineral of all for coping with stress. Stress-related diseases which run rampant through modern society, like heart attacks and high blood pressure, are often accompanied by magnesium deficiency. Unfortunately, most Americans consume diets that fail to meet the government's RDA for magnesium, and magnesium intake is even lower than average among people who develop heart disease.

The best food sources of magnesium are vegetables like buckwheat (kasha), mature lima beans, navy beans, kidney beans, green beans, soy beans (including tofu), black-eyed peas, broccoli, spinach, Swiss chard, oats, whole barley, millet, bananas, blackberries, dates, dried figs, mangoes, watermelon, almonds, Brazil nuts, cashews, hazel nuts, shrimp, and tuna.

When you are chronically stressed, you can become magnesium deficient even if you eat these foods regularly. The complex relationship between magnesium and stress explains why many of the patients

I see require magnesium supplements, because even a nutritious diet does not correct their magnesium deficiency.

If you are like most people, when you are exposed to the stress of continuous loud noise, for example, you become irritable, easily fatigued and lose concentration. Your blood pressure may increase as the level of adrenalin, a stress hormone, increases in your blood. Under conditions of mental or physical stress, magnesium is released from your blood cells and goes into the blood plasma, from where it is excreted into the urine. Chronic stress depletes your body of magnesium. The more stressed you are, the greater the loss of magnesium. The lower your magnesium level to begin with, the more reactive to stress you become and the higher your level of adrenalin in stressful situations. Higher adrenalin causes greater loss of magnesium from cells. Administering magnesium as a nutritional supplement breaks this vicious cycle by raising blood magnesium levels and buffering the response to stress, building your resistance.

Personality has a marked effect on the stress-magnesium cycle. A study done in Paris found that stress-induced depletion of magnesium was much greater for people who show the "Type A," competitive, heart-disease prone behavior pattern than for their less competitive colleagues. Dr. Bella Altura, a physiologist at the State University of New York, has proposed that depletion of magnesium among Type A individuals is the main reason why Type A individuals are at increased risk of heart attacks.

It appears that the body's magnesium economy is an integral part of the stress response system. When stressed for any reason, the body's hormonal response causes an outpouring of magnesium from cells into plasma. This outpouring is a bit like taking magnesium by injection, except the source is internal. The effect of the sudden increase in magnesium is both energizing and calming. Magnesium is needed to burn sugar for energy; it also calms the excitation of cells produced by the stress-induced release of calcium. If there is insufficient dietary magnesium, or if there is insufficient rest in between episodes of stress, the body's magnesium stores are slowly depleted. The hormonal response to stress disintegrates. The plasma magnesium does not elevate in response to stress as it should, so that the energizing/calming effect of magnesium is not present to counter the nerve-jangling effects of adrenalin and other stress hormones. Consequently, the disorganizing effects of stress are intensified and coping is impaired. Higher blood pressure, abnormalities of your heartbeat, and an increased risk of heart attacks or of angina (cardiac pain) may be one result.

Laboratory tests for magnesium are often misleading in evaluating your need for magnesium, because blood magnesium levels fluctuate, depending upon where you are in the cycle of stress responses and magnesium depletion. Your symptoms are a better guide. Muscle tension, spasm and twitching are the most characteristic symptoms of magnesium depletion, followed by palpitation and breathlessness. Irritability, fatigue, trouble falling asleep, and hypersensitivity to loud noises are also common. The presence of migraine or tension headache, unexplained chest pain, strange sensations of the skin (like insects crawling), and abdominal pain or constipation are further indications of magnesium deficiency. If you are suffer from any of these symptoms, or if you are being treated for heart disease or high blood pressure, you may need a magnesium supplement.

The best dietary supplements are the acid salts of magensium like magnesium chloride, citrate, gluconate, or glycinate. The dose needed varies from one hundred milligrams to about five hundred milligrams per day of elemental magnesium. Too much magnesium can cause diarrhea. Magnesium taken by mouth is very safe, except in people who suffer from kidney disease or are severely dehydrated. These people may develop levels of magnesium in blood that are too high; they should only take magnesium supplements under strict medical supervision. Just as magnesium taken at bedtime can induce sleep, so high blood levels of magnesium may cause drowsiness and lethargy.

Much has been written about the need to balance the calcium/magnesium ratio when taking supplements. This notion is based upon the known interactions between magnesium and calcium in cells. Calcium freely dissolved in the fluid of each cell has a stimulating effect that leads to rapid contraction of muscle cells and excitation of nerve cells. These cellular effects of calcium result in muscle spasm, poor circulation, and rapid heart beat. Magnesium in the cells of your body is nature's calcium blocker and many of its protective benefits result from blocking these undesirable effects of calcium, reducing high blood pressure, and stopping palpitations. No dietary formula can balance calcium and magnesium in the cells, however. Only your body can do it. Your job is to give your body enough magnesium and enough calcium so it can get the job done right.

People who take magnesium supplements do not automatically require extra calcium. In France, where therapy with magnesium pills has been widespread for thirty years, calcium is rarely given in conjunction with magnesium. There is also no evidence that magnesium and calcium interfere with each other's absorption. Calcium and magnesium are absorbed into the body by distinct and separate mechanisms. Similarly, people who benefit from calcium supplements do not always have to take extra magnesium, although many women who are taking calcium for the purpose of preventing osteoporosis may well need magnesium in addition. There is a growing body of evidence that magnesium in the diet is as important for prevention of osteoporosis as is calcium.

Additional Information

President's Council on Physical Fitness and Sports
Department W
200 Independence Ave, SW, Room 738-H
Washington, DC 20201-0004
Tel: 202-690-9000
Fax: 202-690-5211
Website: www.fitness.gov
E-mail: PCPFS@OSOPHS.DHHS.GOV

National Heart, Lung, and Blood Institute
Information Center
P.O. Box 30105
Bethesda, MD 20824-0105
Tel: 301-592-8573
Fax: 301-592-8563
Website: www.nhlbi.nih.gov/index.htm
E-mail: NHLBIinfo@rover.nhlbi.nih.gov

American College of Sports Medicine
P.O. Box 1440
Indianapolis, IN 46206-1440
Tel: 317-637-9200
Website: www.acsm.org

Weight-Control Information Network
1 Win Way
Bethesda, MD 20892-3665
Toll-Free: 877-946-4627
Tel: 202-828-1025
Fax: 202-828-1028
Website: www.niddk.nih.gov/health/nutrit/win.htm
E-mail: win@info.niddk.nih.gov

Chapter 35

Managing Your Stress with Arthritis or Related Diseases

People with arthritis or related diseases (such as lupus or fibromyalgia) go through the same kinds of stressful periods as everyone else. However, having a chronic disease can add a new set of challenges to your daily life. You may have to rely on family members and health care professionals more than in the past. You may have to make changes in your lifestyle or give up favorite activities because of limited abilities. You also may see changes in your appearance because of joint deformities or the effects of medicines. None of these changes is easy—and all can be upsetting. Learning how to manage your stress can make these changes easier to handle. Pain, depression, and limited/lost abilities can contribute to stress.

How Does the Body React to Stress?

When you feel stressed, your body's muscles become tense. This muscle tension can increase your pain and fatigue and may limit your abilities, which can make you feel helpless. This can cause you to become depressed. A cycle of stress, pain, fatigue, limited/lost abilities, and depression may develop. If you understand your reaction and learn how to manage stress, you can help break that cycle.

Excerpted from "Managing Your Stress," © 2001, reprinted with permission of the Arthritis Foundation, 1330 W. Peachtree St., Atlanta, GA 30309. To receive a free copy of the "Managing Your Stress" brochure, call 1-800-238-7800 or log onto www.arthritis.org.

Physical Changes

Some of your body's reactions to stress are easy to predict. When you feel stress, your body quickly releases chemicals into your bloodstream. This sets into motion a series of physical changes called the "fight or flight" response. These changes include:

- faster heartbeat
- increased breathing rate
- higher blood pressure
- increased muscle tension

These physical changes help your body prepare for stressful events by increasing strength and energy. When you handle stress in a positive way, your body restores itself and repairs any damage caused by the stress.

At times, you may feel unable to deal with chronic stress in a healthy way. As a result, stress-related tension builds up, and with no outlet, takes its toll on your body over time. This toll can take many forms— you may experience headaches, while someone else may have an upset stomach or a disease flare. Research shows that stress may impact the body's immune system, leading to fatigue or other physical problems.

Emotional Changes

Your emotional reaction to stress is harder to predict than your physical reaction. Emotional reactions vary, depending on the situation, your thoughts, and the person. They may include feelings of anger, fear, anxiety, helplessness, loss of control, annoyance, or frustration. A small amount of stress can actually help you perform your best, such as during an exam, an athletic event, or performance. With too much stress, however, you may make a lot of mistakes and may function poorly.

People respond in different ways to events and situations. You may like to be busy and have lots of activity, or you may prefer a slow pace with less activity. What you find relaxing may be stressful to someone else.

How to Manage Your Stress

The key to managing stress is to make it work for you instead of against you. A complete program for managing your stress has six parts:

1. Learn your body's signals of stress.
2. Learn to identify what causes your stress.
3. Learn changes you can make to help reduce stress.
4. Learn how to manage what you can't change.
5. Learn how to reduce the effects of stress on your body.
6. Maintain a lifestyle that can build your resistance to stress.

Listen to Yourself

Just as reactions to stress vary, so do signals of stress. Managing your stress begins with knowing its signs and symptoms. Some of the common signs of stress are:

- Tiredness/fatigue
- Muscle tension or pain
- Anxiety
- Irritability/anger
- Upset stomach
- Nervousness/trembling
- Sleeplessness
- Cold, sweaty hands
- Increased or decreased appetite
- Grinding teeth/clenching jaws
- General body complaints (light-headedness, headache, back pain)

Some of these symptoms may be caused by problems other than stress, such as the flu or your disease. If you are not sure the symptoms are related to a stressful event, consult your doctor. You should also tell your doctor during your visits if you think these symptoms might be stress-related. If you and your doctor determine that stress is contributing to the problem, you can work together to evaluate your situation, understand it, and try to relieve it.

Pinpoint the Causes

Learning what causes your stress is a personal discovery; what causes stress for you may not bother someone else. Once you know what the stressful aspects of your life are, you can decide how to adapt to them.

Keep a stress diary to record the events in your life that cause you stress. Ideally, you want to be able to stop yourself when you feel your body or mind becoming overstressed. Record the cause of your stress as well as any physical or emotional symptoms you feel. Keeping this stress diary can help you track and manage your responses to stress.

Change the Situation

Once you've identified causes of your stress, divide them into things that can be changed and things that can't. Try to prevent situations you can't change. Here are some ways to take control:

- Make a list of your priorities. What must you do right away? What can you postpone? What can be eliminated? You may need to buy groceries today, but you can wash the clothes tomorrow.

- Take time to pamper yourself and do things you enjoy. Learn to ask yourself when you're making a decision, "Does this take care of, or work for, me?"

- Set goals and develop a plan of action for reaching them. Remember to include hobbies and friends in your planning. Be flexible about the time you need to complete a goal.

- Don't put off doing important things. Do your holiday shopping early so you don't feel pressured by the holiday rush.

- Learn to say no without feeling guilty. It's okay to let other parents help your child's teacher with their class trip to the zoo. Turning down extra duties even for a short period of time can reduce your stress.

- Learn to communicate more effectively. First listen to be sure you understand, and take the time to clarify if you don't. Communicate clearly, assertively, and directly to be sure others understand you.

- Seek solutions to conflicts that will benefit both sides. If you want to go for a walk and your spouse has chores to do, help finish the work so you can take a walk together.

Change Your Outlook

Realize that you can only change yourself, not other people. Some situations can't be changed, so you have to learn to deal effectively with them. Being flexible helps you keep a positive attitude, despite hardships. Here are ways you can change your outlook.

- Develop a healthy attitude. Situations become stressful when you think about them in a negative way. To be healthy you should balance your positive and negative thoughts.

- Evaluate the situation's importance. Being objective about a situation can sometimes help you put it in perspective and manage it effectively.

- Focus your attention on positive things you enjoy. Thinking about something you like can help you relax and become less stressed.

- Develop stress-relieving activities. Find ways to express your feelings of stress in a positive way, such as writing in a journal or exercising.

- Develop and use support systems. Share your thoughts with family, friends, clergy, or others who are good listeners and can help you see the problems in a constructive way.

- Use humor. Schedule time for play, and become involved in activities that make you laugh. No matter how sad your mood, laughing can make the world look better.

Do a Reality Check

Learn to put stressful situations in perspective by asking these questions:

- What exactly is at stake?
- What are you saying to yourself right now?
- What are you afraid will occur?
- How do you know this will happen?
- What evidence do you have that this will happen?
- Are there other ways to look at this situation?
- What coping resources are available?

Reduce the Effects of Stress on Your Body

Learning how to relax is one of the most important ways to cope with stress in a healthy way. Relaxation is more than just sitting back and being quiet. It is an active process using methods to calm your body and mind. Learning how to relax takes practice. As you learn new ways to relax, keep these principles in mind:

- Stress is caused by many things, which means there are many ways to manage stress. The better you understand what causes your stress, the more successfully you can manage it.

- Not all relaxation techniques work for everyone. Try out different methods until you find one or two you like best. You may learn that some techniques work well for specific situations.

- Remember that learning these new skills will take time. Practice new techniques for at least two weeks before you decide if they work well for you.

— The Arthritis Foundation acknowledges with appreciation Kathleen Lewis, RN, MS, LPC, Atlanta; Laura Robbins, DSW, Hospital for Special Surgery, New York; and Kathleen M. Schiaffino, PhD, ACSW, Fordham University, Bronx, NY, for their assistance with this information.

Chapter 36

Does Drinking Reduce Stress?

Since antiquity, people have observed a complex relationship between alcohol consumption and stress. Not only have stressful situations induced drinking, but alcohol consumption also has long been considered a way of relieving stress. For example, more than 2,500 years ago, the Greek lyric poet Alcaeus suggested drinking as a way to cope with distress: "We must not let our spirits give way to grief. Best of all defenses is to mix plenty of wine, and drink it."[1] Similarly, Shakespeare referred to alcohol's stress-reducing properties in his play *Julius Caesar* (Act IV, Scene III): "Speak no more of her. Give me a bowl of wine. In this I bury all unkindness." The concept that alcohol can "calm the nerves" is, in fact, widely held across cultures. In the United States, both social drinkers (i.e., people who consume alcohol within socially accepted limits and who experience no alcohol-related problems) and problem drinkers (i.e., people who experience alcohol-related social, medical, or legal problems) believe in alcohol's stress-reducing properties. The media and the entertainment industry also consistently portray drinking as a way to relieve stress (Wilson 1988). Researchers believe that alcohol's anticipated stress-relieving effect is a primary motivation for many people to consume alcohol, despite the often harmful consequences of drinking (Sayette 1993a).

Clinicians and researchers also have noted the relationship between alcohol consumption and stress. In the 1940s, sociological investigations

"Does Drinking Reduce Stress?" Michael A. Sayette, Ph.D., *Alcohol Research & Health*, Vol. 23, No. 4, 1999, pp. 250-255, National Institute on Alcohol Abuse and Alcoholism (NIAAA), NIH Publication No. 00-3466.

suggested a link between the level of stress in certain non-Western cultures and the rates of problem drinking (see Pohorecky 1991). Around the same time, Masserman conducted experiments demonstrating that alcohol administration could reduce conflict-induced stress in cats (Masserman and Yum 1946; also see Sayette 1993a). Subsequently, Conger's (1956) theory regarding alcohol's reinforcing properties led to the development of the tension-reduction hypothesis. The hypothesis comprises two separate propositions: (1) under most circumstances, alcohol consumption will reduce stress, and (2) in times of stress, people (or animals) will be especially motivated to drink alcohol.

This chapter reviews human studies investigating the first part of the tension-reduction hypothesis—namely, whether drinking reduces stress. (The second part of the hypothesis—i.e., stress induces alcohol consumption—is not reviewed here.) This chapter first defines and provides information on the assessment of stress. It then summarizes various individual and situational factors that may influence susceptibility to alcohol-induced stress reduction and describes evidence supporting the role of those factors.

Definition and Assessment of Stress

Historically, the term "stress" has been used to describe both the stimuli or events (i.e., stressors) that disturb an organism and the organism's complex physiological response to such a stimulus (i.e., the stress response). Because people respond to the same stimulus in different ways, however, Lazarus and Folkman (1984) suggested that stress may best be defined as the appraisal or interpretation of an event as signaling harm, loss, or threat. This approach recognizes that an event may be construed as stressful by one person but interpreted as harmless or positive by another person.

The perception of stress elicits a varied response that may involve a wide range of behaviors (e.g., escape or avoidance behavior); biological responses; and, in humans, subjective awareness of a distressed emotional state. Stress-related biological responses include psychophysiological reactions, such as changes in skin conductance (e.g., from sweating), muscle tension, and cardiovascular responding (e.g., changes in heart rate), as well as changes in the activation of various brain regions. Alcohol consumption can reduce the magnitude of an organism's response to stress. This reduction is called stress-response dampening (SRD) (Levenson et al. 1980).

Researchers can measure alcohol's SRD effects in various ways. Among the most common measures are scales on which respondents

490

are asked to rate their levels of certain emotional states, such as anxiety, tension, nervousness, or apprehension. Another frequently used approach for determining alcohol's SRD effects involves monitoring physiological responses, most commonly changes in heart rate. Finally, SRD studies sometimes include behavioral measures, such as measures of activity (e.g., the time needed to escape an unpleasant stimulus) and expressive behavior (e.g., facial expressions of negative emotional states).

Alcohol's Effects on Stress Responding

By the 1980s researchers had conducted numerous studies to determine whether drinking reduced stress. To the surprise of many investigators, the relationship between alcohol and stress was inconsistent. Alcohol consumption reduced stress in some studies, did not affect stress responses in other analyses, and exacerbated stress in still other investigations (Sayette 1993a). (Steele and Josephs [1988] described the latter outcome as the "crying-in-your-beer effect.") These contradictory findings led some researchers to conclude that the tension-reduction hypothesis had not been confirmed. Other scientists argued, however, that despite some discrepancies, the study results generally supported the tension-reduction model. Perhaps the most common conclusion was that alcohol's effects on stress were complex and that further research was needed to specify the conditions under which drinking would most likely reduce stress (see Sayette 1993a).

Many studies have been conducted to clarify the relationship between drinking and stress reduction. Two general areas of inquiry emphasized in those analyses assess the personal or individual differences and the situational factors that mediate alcohol's SRD effects (Wilson 1988). Research on individual differences seeks to identify those people in whom alcohol is most likely to reduce stress. Research on situational factors attempts to determine the circumstances under which alcohol consumption is most effective in reducing stress. The following sections review various individual and situational variables and the roles that they may play in alcohol's SRD effects.

Individual Differences

Researchers have suggested that several personal characteristics may influence the extent to which a person is sensitive to alcohol's SRD effects. These characteristics include a family history of alcoholism, personality traits, extent of self-consciousness, level of cognitive functioning, and gender.

Family History of Alcoholism

Children of alcoholics are at heightened risk of becoming problem drinkers compared with children of non-alcoholics (Sher 1991). Scientists are investigating the mechanisms underlying this increased risk. One line of research in this field has examined whether alcohol consumption may produce an enhanced SRD effect and, consequently, provide greater reinforcement[2] in people at increased risk for alcoholism. These studies have compared the SRD responses of participants with a family history of alcoholism (i.e., family-history positive [FHP] individuals) to the SRD responses of participants without such a family history (i.e., family-history negative [FHN] individuals).

To date, the findings of those investigations have been equivocal. In the first large study conducted in this area, the investigators found that compared with the FHN participants, the FHP participants exhibited increased SRD responses to alcohol on two of five psychophysiological measures tested (Levenson et al. 1987). Conversely, in a subsequent study, a family history of alcoholism did not influence the SRD effect of alcohol (Sayette et al. 1994). Still other studies have suggested that only participants with a multigenerational family history of alcoholism demonstrate an enhanced SRD response to alcohol. This observation indicates that the effects of paternal alcoholism on the SRD response of the offspring can best be assessed in subjects with an extensive family history of alcoholism affecting several generations (e.g., father and paternal grandfather) (Finn et al. 1990).

Several reasons may contribute to the discrepant findings and the difficulties in determining the exact relationship between SRD and family history of alcoholism. Differences in that relationship between FHP and FHN participants may appear smaller than they actually are, because the participants' classification as either FHP or FHN typically is based solely on self-reports. Although studies demonstrate that such self-reports are generally accurate, an improved assessment of parental alcoholism (e.g., through corroboration by a parent) might strengthen the association between a family history of alcoholism and the relationship between alcohol and stress.

A second confounding factor is that alcohol administration studies only include participants who are of drinking age (i.e., at least 21 years old) and who have not yet developed a drinking problem. Accordingly, many of the FHP individuals at greatest risk for developing alcoholism may be ineligible for study participation because they have already developed a pathological drinking pattern before age 21. Such a selection bias may underestimate the effect of a family history of alcoholism on the impact of alcohol's SRD effect.

Although some evidence suggests, as discussed in this section, that a family history of alcoholism influences a person's SRD response to alcohol, many questions remain. For example, researchers are just beginning to identify mechanisms that may underlie the potential relationship between family history and SRD response. In one line of research, investigators are analyzing whether alcohol's SRD effects may be more pronounced in FHP subjects when blood alcohol concentrations (BACs) are rising (i.e., on the rising limb of the BAC curve) than when BACs are falling (i.e., on the falling limb of the BAC curve) (Sayette 1993a). This finding is potentially relevant, because alcohol's reinforcing effects are thought to be stronger on the rising limb than on the falling limb of the BAC curve (Sher 1991). These investigations are based on evidence that when sober, FHP subjects may exhibit stronger physiological reactions to a variety of stimuli than do their FHN counterparts (see Sher 1991). For example, Finn and colleagues (1990) have hypothesized that children of alcoholics exhibit greater responses to various types of events, regardless of whether those events are stressful (e.g., exposure to an aversive electric shock) or not (e.g., exposure to nonaversive tones, such as a tone with a frequency of 1 kHz and a volume of 70 decibel). Furthermore, some studies have suggested that FHP drinkers are more physiologically reactive to alcohol consumption itself and that this reactivity may affect their subsequent response to a stressor (see Sayette 1993b).

Personality Traits

Since the early 1980s, researchers have associated certain personality traits that are considered indicative of an elevated risk of alcoholism with an enhanced SRD response to alcohol. For example, Sher and Levenson (1982) found that people who experienced difficulty in controlling their behavior (i.e., who scored high on measures of behavioral undercontrol) experienced increased SRD effects. This and other observations suggest that people with such personality characteristics might be more susceptible to alcohol's reinforcing effects, including SRD. This increased susceptibility, in turn, could facilitate the development of alcoholism (see Sher 1991).

Extent of Self-Consciousness

Hull (1987) proposed that people who are highly self-conscious are most likely to experience alcohol's SRD effects. According to this self-awareness model, self-conscious people constantly evaluate their own performance and may experience stress if the result of that self-evaluation is negative. Alcohol consumption impairs the drinker's ability to encode information from the environment with respect to its relevance to the self. Consequently, both the drinker's self-awareness and the associated stress decline. The stress reduction has a reinforcing effect, thereby increasing the probability of further drinking. Some studies have supported this hypothesis by demonstrating that highly self-conscious people are more sensitive to alcohol's SRD effects (see Hull 1987; Sayette 1993a). Other studies, however, have produced conflicting results.

Cognitive Functioning

A person's cognitive functioning also may influence the extent of his or her SRD response to alcohol. Alcohol has been shown to disrupt the processing of new information in the brain (i.e., cognitive processing). Consequently, alcohol may be particularly disruptive to people with cognitive deficits. To assess the relationship between cognitive functioning and alcohol's SRD effects, Peterson and colleagues (1992) administered a battery of neuropsychological tests to a group of drinkers to assess their cognitive functioning. The study participants then received a drink before being exposed to a laboratory stressor (i.e., a series of mild electric shocks). The researchers found that the participants with the lowest cognitive performance (i.e., with the greatest difficulty organizing new information) exhibited the greatest SRD response to alcohol. Other investigators also found a similar relationship between cognitive performance, alcohol consumption, and SRD response in a study using a test of "minimal brain dysfunction" (Sher and Walitzer 1986).

Gender

Most studies conducted in the alcohol field, including those that have analyzed the relationship between alcohol consumption and stress, have involved only male participants. Only recently have studies been conducted that have included both male and female participants. Early studies of alcohol's effects on stress that involved both genders indicated that alcohol's SRD effect differed between men and women (Abrams and Wilson 1979). Subsequently, however, the findings of the largest studies that included participants of both genders suggested that alcohol's effects on stress seem to be comparable for men and women (see Sayette et al. 1994). Thus, even in studies in which women appeared to be more responsive than men to a stressor when the participants were sober, alcohol consumption did not alter this gender difference (i.e., the women were still more responsive to the stressor), suggesting that the extent of alcohol's SRD effects was similar in both men and women. It is possible, however, that the presence or absence of gender differences depends on the measures used to determine the stress response. In the studies that detected no gender differences, researchers assessed the stress response using only physiological (e.g., heart rate) and self-report measures. Consequently, other types of measures of emotional response (e.g., analysis of facial expressions associated with emotions) might reveal gender differences in the SRD response to alcohol.

Situational Factors

Although numerous influences specific to each drinker affect the extent to which he or she experiences alcohol's SRD effects, the characteristics of the situation in which drinking occurs also modify the drinker's response to alcohol. Thus, the same person experiences alcohol's effects differently when drinking at a party with friends than when consuming a drink alone at a bar after a stressful day at work. Two such situational factors that have been shown to affect alcohol's SRD effects are distraction and the timing of drinking and stress.

Distraction

In an attempt to determine the reasons underlying alcohol's variable effect on stress, Steele and Josephs (1988) proposed that alcohol reduces stress only when drinking occurs in the presence of stimuli that distract the drinker from his or her distress. According to this attention-allocation model, alcohol impairs cognitive processing. Consequently, the drinker can perceive and focus on only the most immediate cues and a situation's most relevant (i.e., salient) features. Accordingly, the concurrent activity in which a person engages while consuming alcohol helps determine alcohol's effects. For example, according to the attention-allocation model, drinking in a stressful situation (e.g., after a bad day at work) in the presence of a concurrent pleasant distraction (e.g., at a party with friends) leads to an SRD response, because the drinker perceives only the pleasantly distracting aspect of the situation and cannot focus on the stressor. Conversely, drinking without a concurrent neutral or pleasantly distracting activity (e.g., alone in a bar) does not produce an SRD effect and may even increase stress, because the drinker's attention focuses on the then-salient stressor.

Several studies have confirmed the hypothesis of the attention-allocation model. In those studies, alcohol consistently induced an SRD response when drinking occurred in combination with a pleasant distraction during a stressful laboratory task. Without such a distraction, however, drinking no longer reduced—and sometimes even intensified—stress[3] (Curtin et al. 1998; Steele and Josephs 1988). Because most people drink in situations that include distractions, the attention-allocation model suggests that alcohol often will produce SRD effects. Some laboratory studies, however, have produced conflicting results, demonstrating an alcohol-induced stress reduction even in the absence of a distraction (Sayette 1993a). Nevertheless, the attention-allocation model provides a plausible explanation for both the stress-reducing and stress-enhancing effects of drinking.

Timing of Drinking and Stress

A second situational factor that may affect alcohol's SRD effects is the time when drinking occurs relative to the stressful experience. Studies have demonstrated that alcohol's SRD effect will more likely occur when a person consumes alcohol before learning of a stressor rather than after learning of a stressor (Sayette and Wilson 1991). To explain these observations, Sayette (1993a) proposed the appraisal-disruption model. According to that model, intoxication impairs the cognitive processes associated with the appraisal of new information. Specifically, drinking may interfere with the initial perception of stressful information by preventing the activation of associated stressful memories and concepts.

The appraisal-disruption model postulates that when intoxication precedes exposure to a stressor, impaired appraisal may reduce stress by protecting the drinker from fully experiencing a stressor. If the stressor has already been appraised sufficiently to cause stress, however, subsequent drinking may no longer reduce that stress. This hypothesis can be illustrated by the following example. Imagine a person who has been invited to a dance but who is not a good dancer and feels highly uncomfortable when having to participate in such an event. If that person consumes alcohol before attending the dance, his or her processing of the stressful information (e.g., a dance partner laughing at him or her) may be reduced. As a result, the person may experience less stress at the dance. If that person consumes alcohol only after arriving at the dance, however, he or she will already have processed the stressful information sufficiently to induce a stress response. Accordingly, subsequent alcohol consumption may not reduce the stress response (unless, of course, the drinker is sufficiently distracted by his or her friends and other events at the dance to "forget" his or her own discomfort, as posited by the attention-allocation model).

A review of more than 30 studies conducted in numerous laboratories provides support for the appraisal-disruption model (Sayette 1993a). Among the studies, those in which researchers provided their subjects with alcohol before informing them of an upcoming stressor consistently found that alcohol reduced the participants' stress. In contrast, alcohol's effects on stress were extremely variable (i.e., alcohol increased, decreased, or had no effect on stress) in studies in which the investigators informed participants about the stressor before providing alcohol. The appraisal-disruption model accommodates many of the apparently contradictory findings reported in past investigations. Specifically, the model offers an explanation for why only some experiments detect an SRD effect of alcohol. Nevertheless, several features of the model require further examination. For example, with few exceptions (e.g., Josephs and Steele 1990), studies have not included measures of both the stress response and of cognitive disruption. Consequently, measures of the precise mechanisms posited to underlie alcohol's disruption of appraisal (e.g., measures of how alcohol affects the activation of stressful memories by a current stressor) should be included in future studies (see Sayette 1993a). Furthermore, the appraisal-disruption model does not settle the question of which types of information are most sensitive to alcohol's effects. For example, researchers still need to investigate whether alcohol selectively disrupts the processing of stressful information (Curtin et al. 1998; Sayette 1993a).

Conclusions

Studies of the relationship between alcohol and stress suggest that drinking can reduce stress in certain people and under certain circumstances. Studies conducted over the past two decades have identified several factors that render certain people particularly susceptible to alcohol's SRD effects. For example, a family history of alcoholism may increase a person's likelihood of experiencing those effects. However, some of those studies require further replication and clarification of the mechanisms underlying this enhanced susceptibility. In addition to FHP individuals, alcohol may be effective in reducing stress in people who have difficulty controlling their behavior, are highly self-conscious, or have difficulty organizing new information while sober. Future studies are needed to confirm those relationships.

As researchers identify additional individual factors that influence a person's SRD response, models will need to be developed that integrate the different variables. For example, Peterson and colleagues (1992) found that participants' scores on some of their neuropsychological tests were associated not only with the SRD response but also with a family history of alcoholism. These observations suggest that a link may exist between family history, cognitive performance, and the susceptibility to alcohol's SRD effects.

Scientists also have identified situational variables that modify alcohol's SRD effects. For example, alcohol has been shown to reduce stress reliably when drinking occurs in the presence of pleasant distractions. Furthermore, laboratory studies suggest that drinking before experiencing a stressor attenuates stress, whereas drinking after experiencing a stressor may have no effect or may even exacerbate stress. These findings, however, require replication in more natural settings outside the laboratory.

Research also is needed to improve understanding of the mechanisms underlying alcohol-induced exacerbation of stress (Curtin et al. 1998; Sayette 1993a). For example, scientists must examine the effects of drinking on coping processes during stressful situations. Moreover, studies should investigate whether certain types of information are more resistant than other types to alcohol-related impairment. For example, drinking may differentially affect the processing of positive and negative information, with negative information becoming less accessible than positive information during intoxication (Sayette 1993a). Research testing the responses of people exposed to both stressful and positive information should help scientists to better understand the mechanisms underlying alcohol's ability to reduce stress.

Although the evidence for a direct stress-reducing effect of alcohol remains somewhat controversial, researchers have proposed several mechanisms that could underlie alcohol's SRD effects. These explanations emphasize alcohol's effect on both the peripheral and central nervous systems.[4] One study using numerous cardiovascular measures found a response pattern suggesting that the SRD response may be restricted to those cardiovascular functions that are regulated by a certain subset of peripheral nerves (i.e., beta-adrenergic nerves) (Levenson et al. 1987). Other studies, however, have not confirmed those findings (see Sayette 1993a). Furthermore, data from a variety of sources have led to the alternative hypothesis that alcohol's SRD effects result from alcohol-induced changes in central nervous system activity (Koob and Bloom 1988; Sayette 1993a; Sher 1987). To date, the precise pharmacological mechanisms underlying alcohol's SRD effects remain unclear (Koob and Bloom 1988).

Footnotes

1. *Winter Scene* by Alcaeus of Mytilene, quoted in Lattimore 1960, p.44.

2. Reinforcement occurs when a person experiences alcohol effects that motivate continued drinking.

3. In those studies, stress was intensified in the presence of a mental-distraction task.

4. The central nervous system includes the brain and the spinal cord. The term "peripheral nervous system" refers to all motor and sensory nerves outside the central nervous system.

References

Abrams, D.B., and Wilson, G.T. Effects of alcohol on social anxiety in women: Cognitive versus physiological process. *Journal of Abnormal Psychology* 88:161-173, 1979.

Conger, J. Reinforcement theory and the dynamics of alcoholism. *Quarterly Journal of Studies on Alcohol* 17:296-305, 1956.

Curtin, J.J.; Lang, A.R.; Patrick, C.J.; and Strizke, W. G. K. Alcohol and fear-potentiated startle: The role of competing cognitive demands in the stress-reducing effects of intoxication. *Journal of Abnormal Psychology* 107:547-557, 1998.

Finn, P.R.; Zeitouni, N.C.; and Pihl, R.O. Effects of alcohol on psychophysiological hyperreactivity to nonaversive and aversive stimuli in men at high risk for alcoholism. *Journal of Abnormal Psychology* 99:79-85, 1990.

Hull, J.G. Self-awareness model. In: Blane, H., and Leonard, K., eds. Psychological Theories of 254 *Alcohol Research & Health: Drinking and Alcoholism*. New York: Guilford Press, 1987. pp. 272-304.

Josephs, R.A., and Steele, C.M. The two faces of alcohol myopia: Attentional mediation of psychological stress. *Journal of Abnormal Psychology* 99:115-126, 1990.

Koob, G.F., and Bloom, F.E. Cellular and molecular mechanisms of drug dependence. *Science* 242:715-723, 1988.

Latimore, R. *Greek Lyrics*. 2d ed. Chicago: University of Chicago Press, 1960. p. 44.

Lazarus, R.S., and Folkman, S. *Stress, Appraisal, and Coping*. New York: Springer, 1984.

Levenson, R.W.; Sher, K.J.; Grossman, L.M.; Newman, J.; and Newlin, D.B. Alcohol and stress response dampening: Pharmacological effects, expectancy, and tension reduction. *Journal of Abnormal Psychology* 89:528-538, 1980.

Levenson, R.W.; Oyama, O.N.; and Meek, P.S. Greater reinforcement from alcohol for those at risk: Parental risk and sex. *Journal of Abnormal Psychology* 96:242-253, 1987.

Masserman, J.H., and Yum, K.S. An analysis of the influence of alcohol on experimental neuroses in cats. *Psychosomatic Medicine* 8:36-52, 1946.

Peterson, J.B.; Finn, P.R.; and Pihl, R.O. Cognitive dysfunction and the inherited predisposition to alcoholism. *Journal of Studies on Alcohol* 53:154-160, 1992.

Pohorecky, L.A. Stress and alcohol interaction: An update of human research. *Alcoholism: Clinical and Experimental Research* 15:438-459, 1991.

Sayette, M.A. An appraisal-disruption model of alcohol's effects on stress responses in social drinkers. *Psychological Bulletin* 114:459-476, 1993a.

Sayette, M.A. Heart rate as an index of stress response in alcohol administration research: A critical review. *Alcoholism: Clinical and Experimental Research* 17:802-809, 1993b.

Sayette, M.A., and Wilson, G.T. Intoxication and exposure to stress: Effects of temporal patterning. *Journal of Abnormal Psychology* 100:56-62, 1991.

Sayette, M.A.; Breslin, F.C.; Wilson, G.T.; and Rosenblum, G.D. Parental history of alcohol abuse and the effects of alcohol and expectations of intoxication on social stress. *Journal of Studies on Alcohol* 55:214-223, 1994.

Sher, K. Stress response dampening. In: Blane, H., and Leonard, K., eds. *Psychological Theories of Drinking and Alcoholism*. New York: Guilford Press, 1987. pp. 227-271.

Sher, K.J. *Children of Alcoholics: A Critical Appraisal of Theory and Research*. Chicago: University of Chicago Press, 1991.

Sher, K.J., and Levenson, R.W. Risk for alcoholism and individual differences in the stress-response-dampening effect of alcohol. *Journal of Abnormal Psychology* 91:350-367, 1982.

Sher, K.J., and Walitzer, K.S. Individual differences in the stress-response-dampening effect of alcohol: A dose-response study. *Journal of Abnormal Psychology* 95:159-167, 1986.

Steele, C.M., and Josephs, R.A. Drinking your troubles away II: An attention-allocation model of alcohol's effect on psychological stress. *Journal of Abnormal Psychology* 97:196-205, 1988.

Wilson, G.T. Alcohol and anxiety. *Behaviour Research and Therapy* 26:369-381, 1988.

Chapter 37

Coping with Grief

Overview

Understanding the Problem

- Normal feelings to expect after the death of a loved one

- Each person's reaction to the loss of a loved one is different, and each person must work through grief in his or her own way

- There is no "right" or "wrong" way to feel after someone dies

- Most people who are very upset over someone's death take months to get beyond the most severe emotional stress. Grief beyond a year is common but may require help.

When to Get Help

- Start with your family doctor

- Symptoms indicating the need for professional help

- Information to have ready when you call for help

- What to say when you call

Excerpted from "*ACP Home Care Guide for Advanced Cancer*, © 1997 American College of Physicians, reprinted with permission.

What You Can Do to Help Yourself

- Allow yourself to experience the pain of grief
- Select a person to share your grief with
- Find what works for you in returning to normal routines
- Read books or poetry on the subject
- Keep a diary or journal
- Encourage others to talk about the deceased
- Talk out loud to the person who has died
- Find out about a bereavement support group

Consider Obstacles

- "People say I should be over this."
- "People give me advice that I don't want to take."
- "Nobody wants to talk about Dad when they're around me."

Carrying Out and Adjusting Your Plan

- Checking on results
- If your plan does not work

Topics with a flag (➡) in front of them are actions you can take or symptoms you can look for.

- The information in this home care plan fits most situations, but yours may be different.
- If a doctor, nurse, or counselor tells you to do something other than what is recommended here, consider all of the information and apply what is meaningful to your own needs.

Understanding the Problem

People who lose a friend or family member to cancer face the same issues as anyone who experiences the death of a loved one, whether by accident or illness. Your feelings and emotions after someone's death can profoundly affect how you relate to others and get through your daily routine. Depending on your personality, you may find it helpful to confide your feelings to another person—sometimes a friend is best, sometimes a family member, and sometimes a professional such as a nurse, a counselor, or a member of the clergy. You may find consolation through sharing or listening at a group-sharing session involving others who have had a recent loss; such groups usually are led by a counseling professional. On the other hand, if you have never been open about your feelings, it is unlikely that you will suddenly change now. Well-meaning people may insist that you must talk it out, but they may not understand you, your past, or your methods of dealing with life's difficult moments.

Each person must work through grief in his or her own way—and it is work (even if not always of the physical kind). Despite the existence of widely published "stages" of grief, each survivor deals with loss as an individual, and the ways in which people handle their loss vary widely. When you are struggling to deal with your own loss, it is useless to worry about whether you are following somebody else's timetable.

The range of reactions to someone else's death is broad. Some people are devastated when it occurs, and others feel very little emotion. Sometimes, people feel their grief only later, and some people never have strong feelings. Different people also may experience different emotions. They may feel guilt, remorse, sadness, or resentment toward others, such as doctors, nurses, hospice workers, or even God. Some people who lose a family member or close friend feel anger and ask questions such as "Why did this happen to him (the one who died)?" and "Why did this happen to me?" Anger also may reach back to events that occurred during diagnosis and care, and you may ask, "Why didn't the doctors find the cancer soon enough?" or, "Why did mother suffer so?"

You may think that you hear the deceased person's voice calling to you, or you may want to have a conversation with that person. You may experience flashbacks, such as remembering the funeral or even the moment of death itself, for no apparent reason. In addition, you may feel as if you are making progress but then suddenly feel worse, without knowing what triggered it. Although upsetting, these are normal experiences for people who grieve.

Even if the illness was prolonged and you anticipated the death of your loved one, you still may encounter both shock and numbness in the same way as if the death had occurred unexpectedly. During this time, which may last from only a few up to 6 weeks, you may experience a sense of "just going through the motions," as if you were in shock.

When this feeling of numbness and shock begins to subside, you may feel as if you might be overcoming it—thinking "I'm getting back to normal." Just then, however, you unexpectedly may encounter a deeper sense of grief or sadness as reality sets in. When this occurs, you may experience symptoms of grief like those of acute depression—being unable to sleep soundly, losing your appetite, not wanting to get up in the morning, or not wanting to be around other people.

Whatever happens, understand that there is no "right" or "wrong" way to feel after someone's death. Most people's feelings, even if they seem extreme at the time, fall within a range of normal reactions.

Most people who lose someone close to them take months to get over the most severe part of their emotional stress, and for most, it will take at least a year to work through the grieving process. Counselors often consider how a person is doing at the 1-year anniversary of the death as an indicator of how well he or she has adjusted to the loss. Grief that lasts beyond a year is common but may require help.

Remember that life will never again be exactly the way it was before your loved one died. If you are expecting things to "get back to normal" after awhile, you may be disappointed or frustrated to find that the new "normal" is not like the old "normal." Your life will go on, but—precisely because the person was important to you—it will not be the same without him or her.

Your Goals

- Know when to get professional help with grief.

- Understand that people handle loss with a wide range of emotions, none of which is "right" or "wrong." Grieve for your loss in your own way rather than feeling that you should be the same as other people you have known or read about.

- Understand that most people who grieve return to their daily routines in 2 to 4 months, but healing often takes a year or longer. Each person's reactions are unique, so be wary of timetables that others may try to force on you.

When to Get Help

The first question you should ask is whether you need help from other people. If you do, an excellent place to start is with your family doctor. He or she may help you directly or aid you in finding the right group session, counselor, or clinic. You should seek help if any of the following is true:

➡ Continued difficulty in sleeping.

If you are losing sleep or feel tired all the time, the first place to go for help is your family doctor. A physician who knows you and your medical history can make an informed decision whether to prescribe medication and, if so, what kind.

➡ Substantial weight gain or loss.

Any substantial change in eating, such as loss of all appetite or a sudden increase in appetite, may be the result of emotional distress. Again, consult your family doctor first, because he or she already knows you and can make an informed judgment about treatment.

➡ Prolonged emotional distress.

If, after 6 months, you do not see a marked improvement of your ability to function in daily life, you should consider seeking help. It is natural to want to withdraw from others after losing a loved one, but if you still cannot enjoy a reasonable quality of life after 6 months, this is a signal that you may need help working through your grief.

➡ If you are overcome by suicidal thoughts.

If suicidal thoughts become central to your thinking and you are encountering them every day, seek help from your family doctor, a counselor, member of the clergy, or a mental health clinic.

Have the answers to the following questions ready when you call your family doctor, counselor, or clinic:

1. How much does grief interfere with my ability to do my job or normal daily activities?

2. Am I having difficulty sleeping?

3. Is my appetite gone, or do I eat significantly more than before the person died?

4. Is suicide an option I would consider?

Here is an example of what someone might say when calling for help:

"I'm David Winters, son of Katherine Winters, who died of cancer 6 months ago. Ever since my mother's death, I've been very upset. I've also been having trouble sleeping through the night since about 2 weeks after she died, and I never had trouble before. I think I may need some help."

What You Can Do to Help Yourself

You can do many things on your own to handle the emotional stress of grief, and you can get help from others as well. You may need one or both forms of help to successfully restore your sense of well-being.

➡ Allow yourself to experience the pain of grief.

What this means is to work through your emotions in the best way you can. If this means crying, screaming, talking to the person who has died, or doing physical activity such as punching a pillow or lifting weights, do that. To heal emotionally, many people need to express their feelings. If you are embarrassed about crying in front of other family members such as your children (whether younger or adult), you may need to tell them: "It may be upsetting to you, but I need to cry and express my feelings. I need to work through this grief."

➡ Select a person to share your grief with.

Find a good listener who has experienced a similar loss, although it probably is best to choose someone who is not grieving over the same person as you are. Someone outside of your immediate family often is a good choice. You want someone who will let you express yourself, not someone who will try to reason you out of your feelings. Candidates might be a member of the clergy or a sympathetic friend or coworker. Although you may expect family members to be supportive, they most likely are burdened with that very same loss as well. For example, if your spouse dies and you want to share with your adult children, remember that they are grieving the loss of their parent. As a result, they may be unable to give you the compassion you need. In addition, it often is painful for an adult child to see a parent grieving, and they may want you to "get over it" so that their lives can return to some form of "normal."

Be aware that some people, even professionals such as clergy, may not be personally prepared to deal with death—perhaps because of their own grief over someone they have lost or feelings about their own mortality. If you are unable to relate to one person, find another. Many hospice programs offer a one-on-one assignment of a bereavement volunteer to aid families after a death, one of many programs typically extended by hospice to help with grief. Others might include newsletters, a library of books about grieving, or information about bereavement support groups.

➡ Find what works for you in returning to normal routines.

If certain activities such as reading or swimming were relaxing for you before, try to pursue them now. See if that will help you to get back to a normal cycle of living. For some people, losing a loved one is so upsetting that they cannot resume these activities until their grief subsides to some extent.

➡ Read books or poetry on the subject.

Many books, including those with first person accounts, about working through and overcoming grief are available at your local public library. As with other techniques, however, this will not help everyone. Some people will react by saying, "I have enough to worry about without reading someone else's grief," while others will find direction, a sense of what is normal to experience, and a feeling of connection with others who have had this experience. Similarly, reading poetry, whether alone or aloud in a group, can help by giving artful expression to feelings that often are hard to express or even identify.

➡ Keep a diary or journal.

Some people find it helpful and therapeutic to write their thoughts and feelings in a diary as they proceed through the process of grieving. The British author, critic, and novelist C.S. Lewis (1898-1963), after losing his wife, kept a journal (*A Grief Observed*) of how he was feeling. A private person for whom neither a support group nor reading a book is helpful may find comfort in keeping such a journal. Some people also find it helpful to write their feelings in a letter to the person who has died, which can help to resolve unfinished business or feelings.

➡ Encourage others to talk about the deceased.

Friends and family frequently avoid discussing the deceased to avoid upsetting the person who is grieving. If you want to talk about the person who has died, you should reassure others that it is okay.

All you have to do is say, "I'd like to talk about Dad." Reassure your visitors that while you may cry or become upset, you would rather do that than awkwardly skirt the subject, because he or she was very important to you. Most people can accept your crying or being upset if you are the one who brought up the subject.

➡ Talk out loud to the person who has died.

In much the same manner as the letter noted earlier, it is not unreasonable to want to resolve issues with a person who has died by holding a one-sided conversation, aloud, with the deceased. Do this if it makes you feel better.

➡ Find out about a bereavement support group.

Bereavement support groups can help to make the process of dealing with loss easier. Signing up for a bereavement support group may be a difficult decision, however, because many people think of their grief as something that is private. You may feel uneasy talking with strangers about your feelings or your loved one. Keep in mind, however, that such groups have helped many people get through their grief and, therefore, may help you.

In a bereavement group, participants learn from each other about normal reactions to grief. Because of their shared experiences, group members often come to care about and to support each other emotionally, and they often share practical ideas for working through their grief as well. In addition, a support group also can help you to get through difficult times like holidays or anniversaries.

Most support groups meet for a limited time, such as six weekly sessions. Others run continuously, and people come in and out as their emotional needs dictate. Most are free; some require a fee. Call a hospice, counseling clinic, member of the clergy, your local Area Agency on Aging, or a hospital to find out about bereavement groups. If that does not work, check your newspaper or the human-services listings of a phone book. It often is good to talk with the leader of a group in advance to learn what is expected and how the group is conducted. Some people attend with a family member or a friend.

If you decide to attend a support group, understand that you may feel worse when you go home after the first session. The reason is that you are dealing with your feelings openly (as well as hearing about everyone else's). In the long run, however, this can be helpful. It also is important to realize that a support group will not restore you to the way you were before the person's death, but it will help you to cope with your new life without the deceased.

Possible Obstacles

Here are some obstacles that other caregivers have faced:

1. "People say I should be over this."

Response: Everyone deals with grief at his or her own pace. You may need to say, "We each go at our own pace. I guess my pace is slower than you expected."

2. "People give me advice that I don't want to take."

Response: Well-meaning advice is not always helpful advice. One example might be if you regularly walked with your deceased spouse and now can no longer bear the thought of walking alone. When people offer advice to take walks, do your best to be gracious and thank them, but then do what you feel is best.

3. "People avoid the subject of Dad when they're around me."

Response: Take charge of the conversation, and reassure them: "I want to talk about Dad, and it makes me feel better to talk about him." Your family and friends may not know that you feel this way, so it is important to tell them.

Think of other obstacles that could interfere with carrying out your plan

What additional roadblocks could get in the way of the recommendations in this plan? For example, will other people help? How will you explain your need for help to other people? Do you have the time and energy to carry out the plan?

You need to develop plans for getting around these roadblocks. The COPE ideas (creativity, optimism, planning, and expert information) are one way of overcoming your obstacles.

Carrying Out and Adjusting Your Plan

Carrying out your plan

The process of grieving is unique for each person, so you need to find your own, special way of dealing with it. Experiment, and let your feelings tell you which are helping.

Checking on results

The important thing to remember is that people respond to grief in widely varying ways, and that you will have both ups and downs, good days and bad. Healing takes time. You will know that you are successfully working through grief when your stronger emotions begin to dissipate, such as when you no longer feel anger or deep sadness, and when your interest and involvement in outside activities return to their normal level.

If your plan does not work

Grieving is a difficult but natural process. If you cannot resume some of your normal activities or do not seem to feel better after 6 months, you may want to review "When to Get Help."

Chapter 38

Spirituality and Stress Reduction

Coping with Crises—Active Coping and Spiritual Support Can Help Alleviate Distress

The anguish of September 11th's devastation propelled many to action in aiding in disaster relief. Many also turned to their spiritual faith to provide strength and hope in dealing with the stunningly destructive terrorist attacks. Although the killing of more than 5,000 outstripped any catastrophe the nation had ever confronted, research on coping with past traumas like the bombing in Oklahoma City, or natural disasters, or the personal shock of terminal illness can help shed light on what types of coping strategies especially might help. Research on past disasters or traumatic events has found that both taking action and drawing on spiritual supports can significantly help alleviate emotional distress.

"Disasters can break the human spirit or they can reveal its capacity to rise above adversity," noted Dr. Bruce Smith after studying victims of the Midwest's "Great Flood" of 1993. Research can help

This chapter includes the following documents reprinted with the permission of the International Center for the Integration of Health & Spirituality (ICIHS): "Coping with Crises—Active Coping and Spiritual Support Can Help Alleviate Distress," by Susan S. Larson, M.A.T. Editor, Vol 5, Issue 3, (Fall 2001), © 2000 ICIHS; "Life Satisfaction Linked to Faith Factor," *Research Report* (Sprint 1999) © 1999 ICIHS; "Higher Levels of Religious Activity Linked to Lower Blood Pressure," *Research Report* (Fall 1998), © 1998 ICIHS. Complete information about ICIHS is included at the end of this chapter.

"discover the ways this potential for resilience can be strengthened and nurtured," he noted.[1]

The attacks on the World Trade Center in New York and the Pentagon in Washington, DC with hijacked commercial jetliners turned into bombs clearly led to acute emotional distress across the U.S. and in particular where the attacks occurred. As one indicator of stress, anti-anxiety drug prescriptions mounted substantially in the weeks after the attacks, especially in the targeted cities.

Prescriptions filled for the anti-anxiety drug alprazolam, the generic version of Xanax, were 12% higher in Washington, DC, while nationally the rate climbed 9% during the week ending Sept. 28, 2001, when comparing these figures to the same week a year earlier, according to healthcare industry reports.[2]

In looking at studies of past disasters and coping strategies used to handle the stress of these events, the study of flood victims found that an active coping style that identified positive actions to take rather than avoiding thinking about the disaster led to experiencing less psychological distress and less despondency. It also found that flood victims who ranked their religious beliefs as highly important to them felt less drained and overwhelmingly distressed by the crisis.

Studies of persons affected by the Oklahoma City bombing, of those who recently lost loved ones, as well as studies of patients and relatives dealing with the trauma of serious illnesses also point to significant links between positive spiritual coping, such as turning to God for strength, and less depression and improved quality of life.

"According to research, spiritual support which helps keep spirits up may strengthen the emotional health of those dealing with trauma," noted Dr. David B. Larson, president of the International Center for the Integration of Health and Spirituality.

However, a recent study found unresolved spiritual distress, like feeling abandoned by God, can lead to poorer health outcomes, pointing to the need for these feelings to be expressed and addressed.

Flood Victims

Investigating what factors helped persons more successfully deal with the Midwest flood's impact on their lives, Dr. Smith, of St. John's Mercy Medical Center in St. Louis, surveyed 131 flood victims, contacting them two weeks after the flood had crested and then again seven months later. This flood had submerged 15,600 square miles—an area larger than Lake Ontario—and robbed 70,000 people of homes and 30,000 of jobs. Fifty people died. Nine states were declared federal disaster areas, and damage reached 12 billion dollars.

After controlling for severity of exposure to the flood, findings showed an active coping approach worked best. Active coping involved "identifying the possibilities for change, estimating the outcomes of various strategies, and ranking the strategies in order of preference," Dr. Bruce explained.

"If research continues to find active coping playing a positive role in events that seem largely uncontrollable, there may be some important implications for intervention," he noted. "People can be taught to identify new areas where something can be done and given new strategies for making changes."

Persons who tried to cope by avoiding dealing with the flood's devastation by becoming "busy with other things to keep my mind off the problem," were more likely to experience heightened physical symptoms such as insomnia, headaches, and indigestion, he found. They also felt more psychological distress.

Oklahoma City Bombing

A study conducted after the bombing of the federal building in Oklahoma City followed up on 300 persons, most of whom knew at least one person injured or killed.[3] Using a newly developed 14-item scale to measure either positive or negative religious coping, researchers discovered patterns of how people handled this traumatic life event.

Persons showed less psychological distress with positive patterns of religious coping, such as seeking control through a partnership with God in problem solving, searching for comfort and reassurance through God's love and care, asking God's forgiveness and trying to forgive others, as well as trying to see how God might provide strength to deal with the crisis. Positive religious coping was also related to positive personal growth as a result of the stress, as well as positive spiritual changes, such as growing closer to God and one's religious congregation.

In contrast, more depression, lower levels of quality of life, and callousness towards others was linked with negative religious coping, such as seeing the crisis as punishment from God or questioning God's power or love for them.

Lost Loved Ones and Serious Illness

The study further looked at two other groups undergoing different types of personal trauma to see how they compared to those affected

515

by the Oklahoma bombing in coping style outcomes: college students who had experienced a recent serious loss and patients hospitalized with serious medical illness. The study focused on 540 college students who had faced the death of a friend or relative or had serious problems with a romantic relationship. Negative patterns of religious coping were slightly related to higher levels of emotional distress and poorer physical health, while positive religious coping was linked with greater stress-related growth and positive religious outcomes.

The study also looked at 550 older hospitalized patients with serious medical illness. Negative religious coping was linked with more depression and lower quality of life, similar to the other two groups. Positive religious coping was again linked with higher levels of stress-related growth, and more positive religious outcomes.

"The generalizability of these patterns across three different groups of people confronting quite different life stressors is particularly noteworthy," the researchers stated. Using this coping scale to identify religious coping patterns may help healthcare workers better respond to needs, the authors noted. Negative religious coping may serve as a "red flag," calling for help early in the process of coping with crisis. Affirming positive religious coping could encourage people in stressful times.

Spiritual Distress

The importance of identifying religious distress was underlined in findings in a recent two-year study of elderly hospitalized patients. Spiritual struggles like feeling abandoned by God increased the risk of dying by as much as 28% during the two years follow-up.[4]

"Physicians are now being asked to take a spiritual history, and more than 70 of the 126 medical schools in the U.S. now have courses that train students to take such a history. Our findings suggest that patients who indicate religious struggle during a spiritual history may be at a particularly high risk for poor medical outcomes," stated researchers Dr. Kenneth Pargament of Bowling Green State University and Dr. Harold Koenig of Duke University Medical Center.

Referral of these patients to clergy to help them work through these issues may ultimately improve clinical outcomes," they added. "Further research is needed to determine whether interventions that reduce religious struggles might also improve medical prognosis."

Hospitalization

In addition to identifying spiritual distress in dealing with trauma, recognizing spiritual supports can enhance coping as people struggle with personal trauma like serious illness or surgery, other research studies find.

To find what might help physically struggling patients, a comprehensive study of coping strategies was conducted at Duke University Medical Center.[5] Nearly 600 severely ill hospital patients aged 55 or over were studied with measures of 47 ways of coping. Some coping methods included religious faith, while others did not.

The study was launched after more than 40% of earlier hospital patients had named "religion" when asked the open-ended question of "What helps you cope?" This contrasted with a survey of doctors in which only 9% thought religious faith might play a significant role for patients in dealing with illness.

The study found that patients who sought a connection with a benevolent God as well as support from clergy and church members were less depressed and rated their quality of life as higher, even after taking into account the severity of their clinical diagnosis. Patients who gave spiritual support to others, by praying for them or encouraging them in their faith, also fared better emotionally, noted Dr. Harold Koenig and his research team. Furthermore, the seriously ill patients who grew most in empathy and insight as measured by a "stress-related growth" scale also drew upon their relationship with God.

Similar to the three-sample religious coping study discussed earlier, coping that excluded God's help was linked to greater depression and lower quality of life. Also patients that saw God as punishing were more likely to become depressed.

Relatives' Surgery

In another study, drawing upon positive religious coping also helped friends and relatives handle the stress of the personal trauma of a loved one undergoing potentially life-threatening heart surgery.[6]

Researchers wondered whether religious supports added any unique help for those in the waiting room, or if non-religious help would provide just as much support. Surveying 150 family members—most who had been in the waiting room at least two hours—while relatives underwent heart surgery, researchers asked about the types of support they had sought both before and during the operation. They also measured the relatives' current symptom level of depression.

Questions regarding seeking support included, "I asked people who had similar experiences what they did," and "I talked to someone about how I felt," with responses rated from "not at all" to "quite a bit." Similarly, 12 religious support questions ranged from seeking help from God for strength to looking for spiritual support from clergy or members of one's congregation.

The study found positive coping benefits from religious support even after the contributions of non-religious support were statistically removed. The most frequently employed religious coping was praying to God alone and praying with others, followed by reading scripture, attending religious services, and speaking with clergy.

Why might religious support show particular coping benefits? "The value of religious support may derive, in part, from its availability in times of crisis," the researchers noted. "Seeking support from God is always available to individuals even in the most dire moments," they noted.

Also, in dealing with illness, clergy and hospital chaplains have experience in dealing with illness crises, while "friends, and even family members may feel awkward in stressful health care situations," they commented. "More than any other source of support, religion is designed to provide a compelling presence during the most difficult times," they suggested.

Cancer

Facing a diagnosis of cancer and potential early death ranks as another personal trauma. Two studies of skin cancer patients undertaken in the U.S. and Israel found religious and spiritual beliefs helped them to actively cope in handling their illness.

A group of 117 skin cancer patients at Memorial Sloan-Kettering Cancer Center in New York[7] and another group of 100 in Israel[8] answered extensive questions about their medical condition, religious and spiritual beliefs, quality of life, social support, coping styles, and level of distress, as well as demographics and family cancer history. The two studies were launched to make cross-cultural comparisons.

The studies in both countries found that patients who greatly relied on spiritual and religious beliefs were more likely to use an active coping style. In "active" coping, a patient faces the illness and sizes up what he or she can do to overcome it. "Patients with belief systems, using an active-cognitive coping strategy, tend to manage physical illness better than those with a passive, deferring style," the Israeli research team noted.

518

Although linked with more active coping, relying on religious beliefs did not alter patients' distress levels in the U.S. study. But, physical and emotional distress levels had remained low, possibly since patients' physical abilities had not yet declined, the researchers suggested.

Why might religious beliefs help cancer patients actively cope? "Cancer, perhaps more than any other disease, fosters a sense of helplessness—patients feel unable to exert any personal control over their condition," commented therapist I.D. Yalom. A relationship with God "provides patients with a sense of connection and involvement, rather than isolation, helplessness, and hopelessness," noted the Sloan-Kettering research team. "Many draw on their beliefs as a way of finding meaning in the event and seek a source greater than self in order to cope with the crisis," noted the Israeli researchers.

In the past, "A religious approach to life crises has sometimes been viewed by theorists as a passive, regressive, even avoidant psychological phenomenon," the U.S. researchers noted. However, the data in these studies showed otherwise. "Our results show how religiosity can play an important, although still insufficiently recognized, role in how individuals affected with life-threatening illness cope and adjust," the Israeli researchers stated.

"These findings appear to contradict the long-standing theoretical view that religious beliefs and practices represent a less than optimal means of coping with crisis, in general, and with the life-threatening illness in particular," the Israeli research team stated. "It is becoming scientifically clearer that a system of belief actually helps reduce the degree of psychological distress brought on by a life-threatening illness."

In another study to discover how to better meet needs of cancer patients and their coping needs, a research team surveyed 108 women undergoing treatment with various states of gynecological cancer at the University of Michigan. Fear was the most dominant reaction, with difficulty communicating feelings, or feeling abandoned, isolated, or embarrassed less common. Religion stood out as a central support: 93% of patients indicated spirituality/religion enhanced their hope.

Among this 93%, some 75% said religion had a significant place in their lives. Also, 41% noted their religious lives supported their sense of worth. Almost half—49%—felt they had become more religious since having cancer. Somewhat surprisingly, in this study, not one patient noted becoming less religious since being diagnosed with cancer, the researchers noted.

"Since religion is often an important factor in coping with the trauma of cancer, physicians will better be able to help their patients if they acknowledge this coping support," noted Dr. Larson, one of the study's authors. "It may be important to consult a chaplain when patients need spiritual support or when they are experiencing spiritual distress."

References

1. Smith BW. Coping as a predictor of outcomes following the 1993 Midwest flood. *Journal of Social Behavior and Personality* 1996; 11(2):225-239.

2. Okie S. Use of anxiety drugs jumps in the U.S.: Number of new prescriptions increases sharply in Washington and New York. *The Washington Post*, Oct. 14, 2001; A8.

3. Pargament KI, Smith BW, Koenig HG, Perez L. Patterns of positive and negative religious coping with major life stressors. *Journal for the Scientific Study of Religion* 1998; 37(4):710-724.

4. Pargament KI, Koenig HG, Tarakeshwar N, Hahn J. Religious struggle as a predictor of mortality among medically ill elderly patients: a two-year longitudinal study. *Archives of Internal Medicine 2001*; 161:1881-1885.

5. Koenig HG, Pargament KI, Nelson J. Religious coping and health status in medically ill hospitalized older adults. *Journal of Nervous and Mental Disease* 1998; 186(9):513-521.

6. VandeCreek L, Pargament KI, Belavich T, Cowell B, Friedel L. The unique benefits of religious support during cardiac bypass surgery. *Journal of Pastoral Care* 1999; 53)1): 19-29.

7. Holland JC, Passik S, Kash KM, et al. The role of religious and spiritual beliefs in coping with malignant melanoma. *Psycho-Oncology* 1999;8:14-26.

8. Baider L, Russak SM, Perry S, Kash KM, et al. The role of religious and spiritual beliefs in coping with malignant melanoma: An Israeli sample.

Life Satisfaction Linked to Faith Factor

A comical key chain inscribed with the words "Mansion, Yacht, and Limousine," reflects the hope for the "good life," but what about the key to inner peace of mind? Quality of life studies in the U.S. often overlook a factor now uncovered as one key to a greater sense of well-being; an active religious faith.

Reviewing findings from three national studies totaling more than 5,600 older Americans, Drs. Jeffrey Levin and Linda Chatters surprisingly found that regularly going to church or synagogue made a difference in quality of life. Attending religious services was linked with improved physical health or psychological well-being in all three studies despite a person's age, race, gender, or other key social factors.

These findings, published in the *Journal of Aging and Health*, provide "further evidence that religious factors may have stronger effects" on psychological well-being "than has been conventionally accepted," they noted.

The findings uncover a gap in much existing research conducted on the premise that happiness, emotional adjustment, and life satisfaction are primarily based on age, ability to function physically, and financial status. "Investigation of effects on psychological well-being of qualities of one's inner life has less often been considered," the researchers commented.

Other research in the U.S. that does include religious measures has also revealed significant links with well-being. Dr. Levin systematically reviewed research on older Americans published since 1980 and discovered 12 studies that found that persons involved in organized religious activity had a stronger sense of life satisfaction.

Why Might an Active Religious Faith Make a Difference?

The researchers posited that personal religious faith promotes a sense of well-being "by emphasizing interpersonal relations, stressing forgiveness, providing hope for change," as well as providing a sense of meaning, a promise of life after death, and a connection to one's "conception of God or a higher spiritual force."

A research fellow at the National Institute for Healthcare Research, Dr. Levin noted that until recently, concepts such as worldview, meaning, spiritual development, and religious involvement "have not typically been conceived" by social scientists as relevant to the well-being of older adults. This research shows otherwise.

Adding religious commitment to the model for healthier, happier lifestyles could provide one more avenue for unlocking greater life satisfaction; a notable key to the 'good life.'

Reference: Levin, Jeffey S., and Chatters, Linda M. "Religion, Health, and Psychological Well-Being in Older Adults: Findings from Three National Survey," *Journal of Aging and Health* 1998; 10(4): 504-531.

Higher Levels of Religious Activity Linked to Lower Blood Pressure

When you attend religious services at your place of worship, or say a prayer before meals, or study a passage from Genesis, you probably aren't thinking that what you're doing can affect your blood pressure. But a recent study says it just might.

Researchers at Duke University studied nearly 4,000 people aged 65 and older, taking into account differences among their subjects such as age, gender, race, education, and other variables that could affect their findings. They discovered that people who both attended religious services at least once a week and prayed or studied the Bible at least daily had consistently lower blood pressure than those who did so less frequently or not at all. In fact, the regular participants in religious activity were 40 percent less likely to have diastolic hypertension, which is associated with heart attacks and strokes.

Nearly one third of all Americans suffer from some form of high blood pressure. Even a small average decrease could significantly reduce cardiovascular disease—by about 10 to 20 percent. Their study is one of 11 others noted by the Duke University researchers to have investigated the connection between religious involvement and blood pressure; nine others have reported essentially the same results, the Duke team says.

A few other interesting findings from the Duke study:

- the associations between religious involvement and measures of blood pressure were stronger in blacks than in whites and in the "younger older"—people aged 65 to 75 than in those over 75.

- women were more likely than men to admit having been told by their doctors that they had high blood pressure.

- people who regularly tuned in to religious TV or radio had higher blood pressures than those who were less frequent viewers and listeners.

Reference: Koenig, H.G. et al. "The Relationship Between Religious Activities and Blood Pressure in Older Adults." *Int'l. J. of Psychology In Medicine*, Vol. 28(2) (1998), 189-213.

Additional Information

International Center for the Integration of Health and Spirituality (ICIHS)

6110 Executive Boulevard, Suite 908
Rockville, MD 20852
Tel: 301-984-7162
Fax: 301-984-8143
Website: www.icihs.org

Chapter 39

EEG Biofeedback Training

The most prominent use of biofeedback in the United States is for anxiety disorders and stress management. For these conditions, relaxation training and peripheral biofeedback modalities are very helpful. Unfortunately, these techniques do not generally address the more common depressive conditions, such as dysthymia, primary unipolar depression, reactive depression, seasonal affective disorder, agitated depression, bipolar disorder, and suicidality. Often, anxiety is seen in the context of depression, in which case the conventional relaxation techniques may only address the anxiety aspect, and may not remediate the underlying depression.

EEG biofeedback (or neurofeedback) offers a new modality for addressing depressive conditions as well as anxiety. This appears to be the case because EEG training impacts on the basic mechanism by which the brain controls physiological arousal. In this manner, normal regulation of arousal may be restored, which means that sleep may normalize in the depressed person, and normal range of affect may return. Other benefits of the training may accrue as well. If the person is experiencing chronic pain, which may be either a cause of depression or its consequence, such pain may in time remediate as well.

The training appears to be effective regardless of the pathway by which the person has become depressed, whether this results from a genetic predisposition, early childhood trauma, or a subsequent

"EEG Biofeedback Training for Depression," and "Frequently Asked Questions about Neurofeedback," © 2001 EEG Spectrum International, reprinted with permission.

traumatic (physical or emotional) experience, or simply a physiological change of unknown causation. As the training proceeds, the client may find that anti-depressant or stimulant medication will no longer be needed. Hence, the person should be under continuing medical care for his or her condition, so that the medication dose may be monitored. It is generally observed that the requirement for anti-depressant medication will be reduced or eliminated entirely as the training proceeds.

It is true of all remedies for major depression that they are accompanied commonly by the recall of prior traumatic memories, which may have been totally suppressed over the years. It is therefore important that counseling be available in the event of such traumatic recall, and for other profound emotional changes which can be elicited by the training.

The training has also been found to be helpful in cases of depression caused by specific traumatic events, such as rape, and by other insults to the brain such as chemotherapy, or general anesthesia in the elderly. EEG biofeedback training is also indicated for those clients who do not respond favorably to medical management, and for those who are counseled to avoid certain medications by their doctor. This category includes in particular pregnant women.

There is evidence that once a person experiences a depressive episode, subsequent episodes are more likely. Hence, training the brain to remediate depression may have the beneficial effect of tending to make subsequent recurrences less likely. The training also appears to be effective for a variety of conditions that are seen concomitantly with depression, such as alcohol dependence, mood instability, irritability, and even excursions into violent behavior.

Research in the cognitive sciences is beginning to demonstrate that the two cerebral hemispheres play distinct roles in the physiology of depression. EEG biofeedback gives us a way to address each hemisphere in an appropriate way. Dysthymia and unipolar depression appear to be more involved with the left hemisphere, whereas agitated depression appears to have more to do with the right. Hence, recovery from depression means training the left hemisphere very differently from the right. The coordination between the two hemispheres is also an issue, particularly in the more unstable manifestations of depression such as manic-depressive illness, seasonal affective disorder, and suicidality. Training the hemispheres to mutually stabilize each other appears to be a fruitful undertaking.

There are more referrals for mental health services for depression and anxiety than there are for any other such condition. Depression ranks fourth in the world with respect to the global "burden of disease."

526

Fortunately, the brain has sufficient plasticity to respond to interventions such as neurofeedback to recover a normal range of function for a wide variety of depressive syndromes. And if the training is successful, it appears to confer lasting benefit.

Frequently Asked Questions

EEG Biofeedback is a learning strategy that enables persons to alter their brain waves. When information about a person's own brain wave characteristics is made available to him, he can learn to change them. You can think of it as exercise for the brain.

EEG Biofeedback is used for many conditions and disabilities in which the brain is not working as well as it might. These include Attention Deficit Hyperactivity Disorder and more severe conduct problems, specific learning disabilities, and related issues such as sleep problems in children, teeth grinding, and chronic pain such as frequent headaches or stomach pain, or pediatric migraines. The training is also helpful with the control of mood disorders such as anxiety and depression, as well as for more severe conditions such as medically uncontrolled seizures, minor traumatic brain injury, or cerebral palsy.

How Is EEG Done?

An initial interview is done to obtain a description of symptoms, and to get a picture of the health history and family history. Some testing may be done as well. And the person does the first EEG training session, at which time we get a look at the EEG. This all may take about two hours. (The details may differ among the various affiliate offices. In some offices a full brain map, or quantitative EEG, is routinely obtained, which may require a separate office visit. Or more extensive testing may be done.) Subsequent training sessions last about 40 minutes to an hour, and are conducted from one to five times per week. Some improvement is generally seen within ten sessions. Once learning is consolidated, the benefit appears to be permanent in most cases.

The EEG biofeedback training is a painless, non-invasive procedure. One or more sensors are placed on the scalp, and one to each ear. The brain waves are monitored by means of an amplifier and a computer-based instrument that processes the signal and provides the proper feedback. This is displayed to the trainee by means of a video game or other video display, along with audio signals. The trainee is asked to make the video game go with his brain. As activity in a desirable frequency band increases, the video game moves faster, or some other reward is given. As activity in an adverse band increases, the video game is inhibited. Gradually, the brain responds to the cues that it is being given, and a "learning" of new brain wave patterns takes place. The new pattern is one which is closer to what is normally observed in individuals without such disabilities.

What Therapeutic Applications Have Clinical Evidence?

There are clinical reports or case histories concerning the effectiveness of neurofeedback for the following therapeutic applications.

- Addiction
- Anxiety
- Attachment Disorder
- Attention Deficit Disorder
- Autoimmune Dysfunctions
- Chronic Fatigue Syndrome (CFS)
- Chronic Pain
- Conduct Disorder
- Depression
- Epilepsy
- Sleep Disorders
- Stroke/TBI
- Tourettes Syndrome

Editor's Note: Technical Papers on therapeutic uses of EEG for depression and anxiety are listed in the "Additional Information" section at the end of this chapter.

What Results Do We Obtain?

In the case of ADHD, impulsivity, distractibility, and hyperactivity they may all respond to the training. This may lead to much more successful school performance. Cognitive function may improve as well. In several controlled studies, increases of 10 points in IQ score were found for a representative group of ADHD children. And in two clinical studies, an average increase of 19 and 23 points was demonstrated.

Behavior may improve in other ways as well: If the child has a lot of temper tantrums, is belligerent, and even violent or cruel, these aspects of behavior may come under the child's control.

In the case of depression, there can be a gradual recovery of "affect," or emotional responsiveness, and a reduction of effort fatigue. In the case of anxiety and panic attacks, there is gradual improvement in "regulation," with a drop-off in frequency and severity of anxiety episodes and panic attacks until the condition normalizes.

In the case of epilepsy, we observe a reduction in severity and incidence (frequency of occurrence) of seizures. The dosage of anticonvulsant medication may ultimately be reduced (if ordered by the referring neurologist), and side effects of such medication may diminish.

Can a Successful Outcome Be Predicted?

It is not possible to predict with certainty that training will be successful for a particular condition. But for the more common conditions we see, a reasonable prediction of outcome is usually possible. More important, however, the effectiveness of the training can usually be assessed early in the course of training. For most conditions, there are no known adverse side effects of the training, provided that it is conducted under professional guidance.

Why Does This Training Procedure Work?

The brain is amazingly adaptable, and capable of learning. It can also learn to improve its own performance, if only it is given cues about what to change. By making information available to the brain about how it is functioning, and asking it to make adjustments, it can do so. When the mature brain is doing a good job of regulating itself, and the person is alert and attentive, the brain waves (EEG) show a particular pattern. We challenge the person to maintain this "high-performance," alert, and attentive state. Gradually, the brain learns, just like it learns anything else. And like with other learning, the brain tends to retain the new skill.

We observe that if the EEG is not well-behaved under these circumstances, there may be adverse impacts on learning ability, on moods, on sleep, and on behavior. With training, these may be gradually brought under control, along with normalization of the EEG.

What Does EEG Biofeedback Look Like?

The therapist computer is usually positioned behind the patient. This enables the therapist to monitor the patient's EEG at any time during the session without disturbing the biofeedback.

A single electrode is placed on the scalp (above the motor strip, typically) using gel or paste and two other electrodes are attached to the earlobes. Most patients recline during training.

The game computer is placed a few feet away, directly in front of the patient. The patient interacts (only using her EEG) with the game computer for the next 30 minutes.

Each display contains four EEG data streams (below each stream are text and average data values). The top line, slightly squiggly, is the person's entire EEG recorded from the scalp by the single active electrode. The three wavy lines below show activity in three separate EEG frequency bands or rhythms—here, theta, SMR, and high beta bands. The patient's goal is to increase certain EEG frequency bands (e.g., SMR) while decreasing others (e.g., theta & high beta). The patient monitors her EEG frequency band activity NOT as wavy lines on the therapist machine, but as elements of a game on the game computer. Each frequency band appears as a colored rectangle which grows larger or smaller in response to her brain wave activity.

With her brainwaves she is playing the game called "Islands." Frequency band activity is displayed at the bottom of the screen—two square "inhibit" boxes on either side on a large "enhance" rectangle. She is doing quite well, inhibiting or reducing the activity of the bands represented by purple & yellow (at the moment, mere dots in each corner of the screen). She has increased her SMR activity to a point where it overflows the middle (blue) rectangle. As long as she keeps this up, she is rewarded in the game with visual and auditory stimuli. During the 30 minute session, she will work to keep purple and yellow small and make blue large as long as possible. Hundreds of times she may need to alter her brain activity in order to achieve a brain state which scores the most points. For every half second that her brainwaves stay in the desired state or "zone," she scores another point, an additional seagull appears in the sky (top of screen, barely visible), a new stripe segment is drawn on the highway (middle of screen), and a beep sounds to announce it all. If or when she attains 500 points, the volcano (middle left) will erupt!

How Long Does Training Normally Take?

EEG training is a learning process, and therefore results are seen gradually over time. For most conditions, initial progress can be seen within about ten sessions. Initial training goals may be met by twenty sessions, at which time the initial retests are usually performed. In the case of hyperactivity and attention deficit disorder, training is expected to take about forty sessions, or even more in severe cases. Teeth grinding usually responds in twenty sessions. Some symptoms of head injury often respond in less than twenty sessions (quality of sleep; fatigue; chronic pain), whereas others may require longer training before they show an initial response (memory function, for example).

How Frequent Should the Training Sessions Be?

In the initial stages of learning, the sessions should be regular and frequent, at two, three, or even more sessions per week. After learning begins to consolidate, the pace can be reduced. Daily sessions can be very beneficial as well.

Is EEG Biofeedback Covered by Insurance?

Many medical and psychological insurance plans now cover biofeedback for various conditions. Some require co-payments. Other plans have annual caps. A prescription for the training, along with a diagnosis, may be required from a physician under the medical part of the plan, or from a licensed psychologist under the mental health services part of the plan. Medicare pays for EEG biofeedback for some conditions.

My Doctor Is Skeptical about EEG Biofeedback. What Can I Do?

Your doctor may not know of this specific type of biofeedback. He or she will maintain a healthy skepticism about any new approach claiming numerous benefits. If your doctor is familiar with EEG biofeedback in general, he may still be thinking in terms of the more common early experiments with alpha wave training, rather than with the training we are dealing with here. Ask your doctor to examine the recent research on the effectiveness of EEG biofeedback in treating various disorders such as attention deficit disorder and epilepsy. The following references are a place where he or she can start:

- Lubar, J.F. and Bahler, W.W. (1976) Behavioral management of epileptic seizures following biofeedback training of the sensorimotor rhythm. *Biofeedback and Self-Regulation*, 1, pp.77-104.

- Lubar, J.F. and Shouse, M.N (1976) EEG and behavioral changes in a hyperactive child concurrent training of the sensorimotor rhythm (SMR): A preliminary report. *Biofeedback and Self-Regulation*, 1, pp.293-306.

- Lubar, J.O. and Lubar, J.F. (1984) Electroencephalographic bio-feedback of SMR and beta for treatment of attention deficit disorder in a clinical setting. *Biofeedback and Self-Regulation*, 9, pp.1-23.

- Shouse, M.N. and Lubar, J.F. (1979) Operant conditioning of EEG rhythms and Ritalin in the treatment of hyperkinesis. *Biofeedback and Self-Regulation*,4, pp.301-312.

How Much Does the Training Cost?

The cost of the training differs among offices depending on location, the professional status of the person delivering the service, and on supplementary services offered. Typically, individual sessions run from $50 to $125. Discounts are often available for payment in advance.

Additional Information

Technical Papers on Therapeutic Uses of EEG for Depression

Rosenfeld J.P. "An EEG biofeedback protocol for affective disorders. *Clin Electroencephalogr.* 2000 Jan;31:7-12. Review.

Duffy, F.H. "The state of EEG biofeedback therapy (EEG operant conditioning) in 2000: an editor's opinion. *Clin Electroencephalogr.* 2000 Jan; 31(1):V-VII.

Baehr, Elsa, Rosenfeld, J.P.; Baehr, Rufus. The clinical use of an alpha asymmetry protocol in the neurofeedback treatment of depression: Two case studies. *Journal of Neurotherapy*, 1997 Fal-Win, v2(n3):10-23.

Saxby E, and Peniston E.G. Alpha-theta brainwave neurofeedback training: an effective treatment for male and female alcholics with depressive symptoms. *Journal of Clin Psychol* 51 (5): 685-693 (Sep 1995).

Othmer, S. and Othmer, S. *EEG biofeedback training for bipolar disorder*. Presentation at 1995 Society for the Study of Neuronal Regulation, Scottsdale, AZ.

Gruzelier J. Clin. Self regulation of electrocortical activity in schizophrenia and schizotypy: a review. *Electroencephalogr.* 2000 Jan;31(1):23-9. Review.

Technical Papers on Therapeutic Uses of EEG for Anxiety

Moore, N.C. A review of EEG biofeedback treatment of anxiety disorders. Clin *Electroencephalogr.* 2000 Jan;31(1):1-6. Review.

Duffy, F.H. "The state of EEG biofeedback therapy (EEG operant conditioning) in 2000: an editor's opinion. *Clin Electroencephalogr.* 2000 Jan; 31(1):V-VII.

Thomas, Joseph E., and Sattlberger, Elizabeth. Treatment of Chronic Anxiety Disorder with Neurotherapy: A Case Study. *Journal of Neurotherapy*, 2(2), 1997.

Wenck, L.S.; Seu, P.W.; and D'Amato, R.C. Evaluating the efficacy of a biofeedback intervention to reduce children's anxiety. *Journal of Clinical Psychology*, 1996 Jul, v52(n4):469-473.

Rice, K.M.; Blanchard, E.B.; and Purcell, M. Biofeedback treatments of generalized anxiety disorder: Preliminary results. *Biofeedback & Self Regulation*, 1993 Jun, v18(n2):93-105.

Rice, K.M. and Blanchard, E.B. Biofeedback in the treatment of anxiety disorders. *Clinical Psychology Review*, 1982, v2(n4):557-577.

Additional Information

EEG Spectrum International, Inc.
16500 Ventura Blvd., Suite 418
Encino, CA 91436-2011
Tel: 818-789-3456
Fax: 818-728-0933
Website: www.eegspectrum.com
E-mail: info@eegspectrum.com

Chapter 40

Music's Effects and Enhancements of the Emotional State

Music Enhances the Effect of Positive Emotional States on Salivary IGA

Rollin McCraty, PhD, Mike Atkinson, Glen Rein, PhD, and Alan D. Watkins MBBS. *Stress Medicine*, 1996; 12 (3): 167-175.

Key findings: Music designed to promote mental and emotional balance can increase autonomic power and heighten the beneficial effects of positive emotional states on the immune system.

Summary: This study examined the effect of music and positive emotional states on autonomic nervous system and immune system function in healthy individuals. Autonomic activity was assessed using power spectral density analysis of heart rate variability, and secretory IgA, measured from saliva samples, was used as a marker of immunity. The effects of rock and New Age music were compared to the designer music release Heart Zones, composed by Doc Childre. This music was specifically designed to facilitate mental and emotional balance, boost vitality, enhance learning and promote autonomic nervous system balance. Subjects listened to each category of music for 15 minutes on separate days. In addition, two separate ses-

Reprinted with permission, "The Effects Of Different Music On Mood, Tension And Mental Clarity," © Copyright 1998, Institute of HeartMath®, Boulder Creek, CA; and "Music Enhances the Effect of Positive Emotional States on Salivary IGA," © 1998 Institute of HeartMath®, Boulder Creek, CA.

sions were conducted to test the effects of subjects sustaining a sincere, focused state of appreciation using the Heart Lock-In® technique. In one session, subjects practiced the Heart Lock-In® technique for 15 minutes with no music; in the other session, subjects performed the Heart Lock-In® while listening to Heart Zones, which was specifically designed to facilitate the practice and heighten the beneficial effects of this technique.

There were significant increases in total autonomic activity and in S-IgA concentrations during the *Heart Zones* music session, the Heart Lock-In® session and during the session combining the Heart Lock-In® and *Heart Zones* music. In contrast, there were no significant changes in total autonomic activity or S-IgA concentrations during the New Age, rock music or no music control sessions. While both *Heart Zones* and the Heart Lock-In® alone significantly increased S-IgA levels (increases of 55% and 50%, respectively, were measured), the combination of *Heart Zones* and the Heart Lock-In® produced a

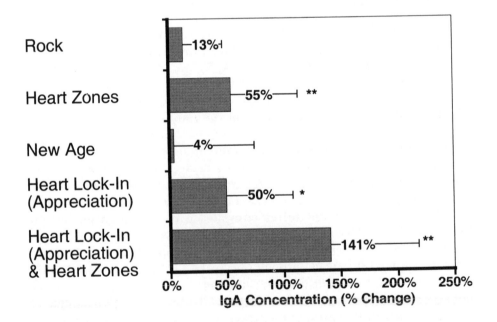

Figure 40.1. *Average change in IgA levels after listening to the different types of music, doing a Heart Lock-In® without music and a Heart Lock-In® facilitated with the Heart Zones music. Note the synergistic effect of the Lock-In® and Heart Zones. * p < .05, ** p < .01.*

significantly greater immunoenhancement (141% increase in S-IgA levels) than either condition alone (Figure 40.1).

This study provides evidence that the immunoenhancing effects of designer music and self-induced states of appreciation may be mediated by the autonomic nervous system, as an increase in autonomic spectral power was measured in all cases in which there was an increase in S-IgA. Our results demonstrate that *Heart Zones* music is effective in potentiating the immunoenhancing effects of the Heart Lock-In® technique. We conclude that music can be designed to enhance the beneficial effects of positive emotional states on immunity and suggest that music and emotional self-management may yield significant health benefits in a variety of clinical situations in which there is immunosuppression and autonomic imbalance.

The Effects of Different Music on Mood, Tension and Mental Clarity

Rollin McCraty, PhD, Bob Barrios-Choplin, PhD, Mike Atkinson, and Dana Tomasino, BA. *Alternative Therapies in Health and Medicine*. 1998; 4 (1): 75-84.

Key findings: Music designed to facilitate mental and emotional balance can produce significant increases in positive moods, vigor, and mental clarity and decreases in tension, burnout, and negative moods.

Summary: The previous study, "Music enhances the effect of positive emotional states on salivary IgA," demonstrated that designer music and the Heart Lock-In® technique produce measurable changes in subjects' autonomic nervous system (ANS) activity and immune function. In the present study, we provide evidence to support the hypothesis that these favorable shifts derive from positive changes produced in subjects' mood and emotional states, which are well known to affect the ANS.

This study investigated the impact of different types of music on individuals' tension, mood, and mental clarity. A total of 144 adult and teenage subjects completed a psychological profile before and after listening for 15 minutes to four types of music: grunge rock, classical, New Age, and designer. The designer music used in this study was *Speed of Balance*, created by Doc Childre to facilitate mental and emotional balance and help people experience clearer and more positive perceptions. The music is specifically intended to enhance creativity, promote clear decision-making and boost physical energy. The effects of *Speed of Balance* were examined in two experimental conditions: first, in comparison to the other types of music in all subjects, and again, in a subgroup of individuals who practiced the Heart Lock-In® technique while listening to the music.

Grunge rock music produced significant increases in hostility, fatigue, sadness, and tension and led to significant reductions in caring, relaxation, mental clarity, and vigor. In contrast, *Speed of Balance* produced significant increases in all positive scales: caring, relaxation, mental clarity, and vigor. Significant decreases were produced in all negative scales: hostility, fatigue, sadness, and tension. Both the adult and teenage subgroups were negatively affected by the grunge rock

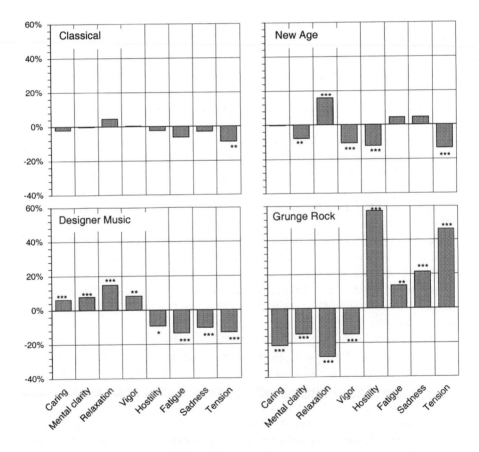

Figure 40.2. *Percent change in mood, tension, and mental clarity for each category of music. *p< .05, ** p< .01, ***p< .001.*

538

music and positively affected by *Speed of Balance*, with very little difference between the two groups' responses. Results for New Age and classical music were mixed (Figure 40.2).

When participants listened to *Speed of Balance* while self-generating a sincere feeling of appreciation using the Heart Lock-In® technique, the beneficial effects were heightened: Subjects experienced increases in caring, mental clarity, and vigor which were significantly greater than the favorable shifts produced from listening to the music alone (Figure 40.2). Results indicate that all types of music created feeling shifts. Of the music used in this study, *Speed of Balance* was most effective in increasing positive feelings and decreasing negative

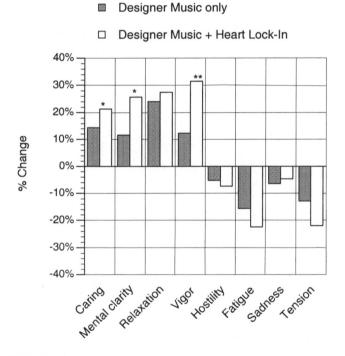

Figure 40.3. Compares the effects on mood, tension, and mental clarity of listening to the Speed of Balance music alone versus practicing the Heart Lock-In® technique while listening to Speed of Balance. The combination of the Lock-In® + Speed of Balance resulted in significant positive shifts beyond the already significant improvements produced by the music alone. * p < .05, ** p < .01.

feelings. Our results support the hypothesis that the positive shifts in autonomic nervous system activity and immune function measured in previous studies employing designer music and the Heart Lock-In® technique derive from changes produced in subjects' feeling states. This study presents a rationale for the use of designer music and the Heart Lock-In® technique in the treatment of tension, mental distraction and negative moods and the enhancement of emotional well-being and mental clarity. Given the connection between attitudes, emotions, and health, these results indicate that music designed to facilitate emotional management can be an inexpensive and easy method to reduce stress and promote overall wellness.

Additional Information

Institute of HeartMath®
14700 West Park Ave.
Boulder Creek, CA 95006
Tel: 831-338-8700
Fax: 831-338-9861
Website: www.heartmath.com
E-mail: info@heartmath.com

Chapter 41

Massage Therapy:
Key Questions and Answers

What Is Massage Therapy?

Massage therapy spans a wide variety of therapeutic approaches, working to improve an individual's health and well-being through the hands-on manipulation of muscles and other soft tissues of the body.

What Are the Key Benefits of Massage Therapy?

Physical—Massage therapy is designed to stretch and loosen muscles, improve blood flow and the movement of lymph throughout the body, facilitate the removal of metabolic wastes resulting from exercise or inactivity, and increase the flow of oxygen and nutrients to cells and tissue. In addition, massage stimulates the release of endorphins—the body's natural painkiller—into the brain and nervous system.

Mental—Massage therapy provides a relaxed state of alertness, reduces mental stress, and enhances capacity for calm thinking and creativity.

Emotional—Massage therapy satisfies the need for caring and nurturing touch, creates a feeling of well-being, and reduces anxiety levels.

"Massage Therapy: Key Questions and Answers," June 11, 2001 © American Massage Therapy Association, reprinted with permission.

Who Can Benefit from Massage Therapy?

People throughout the life cycle—from the very young and very old to those in between—all find that a professional massage can have special applications suited for their needs.

What Is the Origin of Therapeutic Massage?

Therapeutic massage methods used today have both Eastern and Western origins. The first written records of massage date back 3,000 years to early Chinese folk medicine and ancient Ayurvedic medicine of India. *Shiatsu, acupressure,* and *reflexology* spring from these Eastern sources, as do other contemporary methods.

Western civilizations were introduced to therapeutic massage by Greek and Roman physicians. Modern Western massage is credited primarily to Peter Henrik Ling, a 19th century Swedish athlete. His approach, which combines hands-on techniques with active and passive movements, became known as *Swedish massage*—still one of the most commonly used methods in the Western world.

What Do Research Studies Say about Massage Therapy?

Myriad research studies confirm that massage therapy provides physical, mental, and emotional benefits at all stages of life.

How Is Massage Therapy Regarded by the Medical Community?

The results of a survey, conducted between November 2000 and February 2001 in Washington State, indicate strong recognition on the part of medical clinicians that massage therapy is effective. In Washington, where complementary and alternative medicine (CAM) providers have been recognized by health plans since 1996, the survey asked medical practitioners five years later what they thought of CAM practices. Of 12 CAM practices included in the survey, massage therapy was ranked highest (74%) in terms of being perceived as always or usually effective. The next closest CAM practice in the same category of effectiveness was acupuncture, ranked by 67.7% of clinician respondents.[1]

The American Medical Association published a report in September 2000 that said two-thirds of the nation's medical schools teach about herbal therapy, acupuncture, massage, or other alternative medicine.[2]

How Popular Is Massage Therapy as a Form of Medical Treatment?

When naming the types of alternative care consumers say they would be most likely to use, 80% say massage therapy.[3] In a July 2000 consumer survey commissioned by AMTA, twice as many adult Americans reported receiving one or more massages from a massage therapist in the past year (16 percent) as did in 1997 (8 percent). Twenty-one percent of Americans said they expected to get a massage from a massage therapist in the next 12 months.

How Often Do U.S. Consumers Visit Massage Therapists and How Much Do They Spend?

Estimates are that consumers visit massage therapists 114 million times per year, spending between $4 billion and $6 billion annually on these visits. A 1998 article in the *Journal of the American Medical Association* estimated that annual expenditures for massage therapy accounted for approximately 27 percent of the $21.2 billion spent on alternative healthcare-provider services and about 18 percent of the 629 million annual visits to such providers.[4]

Is Massage Therapy a Luxury?

This is a perception that is rapidly changing as massage becomes increasingly accepted as a natural part of a healthy lifestyle. In fact, according to one media characterization, "massage is to the human body what a tune-up is to a car. It provides a physical boost to the weary, sore, and stressed." An increasing body of clinical research confirms that massage reduces heart rate, lowers blood pressure, increases blood circulation and lymph flow, relaxes muscles, improves range of motion, boosts the immune system, and increases endorphins (all may enhance medical treatment).

What Is the Average Cost of a Massage?

Cost depends upon the type of treatment, the experience of the practitioner, geographic location, and length of the massage. Nationally, the range is generally from $45 to $80 for an hour-long treatment, with home visits sometimes more expensive.

What Credentials Should a Qualified Massage Therapist Have?

Check to see if the massage therapist is licensed to practice. Thirty states and the District of Columbia have passed legislation to regulate the massage therapy profession. If practicing in those states, the massage therapist should hold a current license. Local governments may also regulate massage therapists. In such areas, make sure your massage therapist is licensed in your area.

A massage therapist should be able to document professional training in massage therapy at a massage training institution such as those accredited by the Commission of Massage Therapy Accreditation (COMTA) or is a member of the AMTA Council of Schools. He/she should be a member of a professional association with high standards for membership and/or be Nationally Certified in Therapeutic Massage and Bodywork (NCTMB).

COMTA accredited massage training programs require a stringent course of study, including at least 500 hours of classroom instruction in anatomy and physiology, massage and technique, relationships with clients, plus related subjects. AMTA Professional membership is limited to massage therapists who have demonstrated a level of skill and expertise through testing and/or education. In addition, all AMTA-member therapists must agree to abide by the AMTA Code of Ethics.

How Many Massage Therapists Are There in the U.S.?

The number of massage therapists is estimated at between 160,000 and 220,000, including part-time and full-time practitioners, and students.

Where Do Massage Therapists Practice?

Massage therapists offer their services in a wide variety of settings, including:

* private practice clinics and offices
* physicians' offices and wellness facilities
* chiropractors' offices and rehabilitation clinics
* salons, spas, resorts, and cruise ships

544

- health clubs and fitness centers
- nursing homes and hospitals
- on-site in the workplace
- in client's homes

How Can I Find a Qualified Massage Therapist?

AMTA's *Find a Massage Therapist* national locator service can help people locate a qualified massage therapist nearby. This free service is available via the Web at www.amtamassage.org and toll-free at 888-843-2682. Personal referrals from friends or healthcare providers are another way to find a massage therapist.

When calling therapists, ask what services they offer, inquire about their training and/or National Certification, and ask for references. Personality fit also is important in choosing a massage therapist, as is trust, and feeling confident in and comfortable with the massage therapist. Massage therapists use a variety of techniques. You may need to try a few different practitioners to find one that fits your needs.

Is Massage Therapy a Growing Profession?

Yes, according to many indicators. For example:

- AMTA's membership quadrupled in the 1990s to more than 41,000. By June 2001, AMTA's membership had grown to approximately 47,000.

- With an increasing emphasis on preventive care, health insurers are beginning to extend coverage in some plans to include the practice of massage therapy.

- Consumer demand for massage from massage therapists continues to grow. Between 1997 and 2000, the number of American adults who reported getting a massage from a massage therapist in the previous year doubled, from 8% to 16%.[5]

What Is Fueling the Growth of Massage Therapy?

Doctors increasingly recommend it for stress relief and as part of treatment programs for chronic pain and other medical conditions. Businesses have begun to recognize its potential to boost worker productivity and morale, and decrease absenteeism. Public interest in complementary and alternative therapies has led many consumers to try massage, discovering its benefits for their health.

The health and fitness movement also is a driving force behind the growth of the massage therapy profession, as are America's growing emphasis on wellness, and the aging of the "Baby-boomer" population. Athletes and performing artists praise massage for the way it helps to improve performance and enhance recovery.

When Might the Use of Massage Therapy Be Inappropriate?

If you suffer from certain circulatory ailments (such as phlebitis), infectious diseases, certain forms of cancer, cardiac problems, certain skin conditions, or any inflamed or infected tissues, be sure to consult your physician before initiating any massage program. A trained and experienced massage therapist will also be able to tell you when massage is not indicated.

What Should Consumers Expect When They Receive a Massage for the First Time?

At first contact, the massage therapist should ask about your reasons for getting a massage, current physical condition, medical history, lifestyle, and stress level, and specific areas of pain. If necessary, undressing takes place in private and a sheet, towel, or gown is provided for draping during the massage. The therapist will undrape only the part of the body being massaged, ensuring that modesty is respected at all times. The massage takes place on a comfortable padded surface.

Does the Consumer Have Any Responsibilities during the Massage?

A person receiving a massage should give the therapist accurate health information and always report discomfort of any kind— whether it's from the massage itself or due to room temperature, volume of music, or other distractions.

References

1.   Weeks, John, "Post-Legislative Mandate: Two-thirds of Group Health Clinician Respondents View CAM as Effective," *The*

Integrator for the Business of Alternative Medicine, p. 7 (April 2001).

2. Barzansky, et. al., "Educational Programs in U.S. Medical Schools, 1999-2000," *Journal of the American Medical Association* 284(9): 1114-1120 (September 6, 2000).

3. "The Landmark Report on Public Perceptions of Alternative Care" (November 1997).

4. Eisenberg, et. al., "Trends in Alternative Medicine Use in the United States, 1990-1997," *Journal of the American Medical Association* 280(18): 1569-1575 (November 11, 1998).

5. "Public Attitudes Towards Massage Study," Caravan, Opinion Research Corporation International (July 2000).

Additional Information

American Massage Therapy Association

820 Davis Street, Suite 100
Evanston, IL 60201-4444
Tel: 847-864-0123
Fax: 847-864-1178
Website: www.amtamassage.org

Part Six

Additional Help and Information

Chapter 42

Glossary

A

Accelerated aging. Symptoms of old age appear earlier than normal, resulting in premature aging.

Acute stress. The reaction to an immediate threat, commonly known as the "fight or flight" response. Acute stress is the most common form of stress. It comes from demands and pressures of the recent past and anticipated demands and pressures of the near future. Acute stress is thrilling and exciting in small doses, but too much is exhausting. Acute stress can crop up in anyone's life, and it is highly treatable and manageable.

Adaptation. A diminished response after prolonged or repeated exposure to a stressor.

Aging. Gradual, but often dramatic, changes over time in almost every physiological system in the human body. Combined, these changes result in decreased efficiency and resiliency of physiological function.

Excerpted from: "Strong Under Stress, Factors in the Development of Resilience in Children," by Lisa M. Powell, © 1999 Yale Law School, Connecticut Voices for Children, reprinted with permission; "Stress at Work," National Institute for Occupational Safety and Health (NIOSH), DHHS (NIOSH) Publication No. 99-101, 1999; "The Emotional Brain," NIMH 11/10/1997; and *Alcohol Research & Health* Volume 23, Number 4, 1999, National Institute on Alcohol Abuse and Alcoholism (NIAAA), NIH Publication No. 00-3466.

Allostatic load. The process of coping with chronic stressor exposure which creates prolonged and intense demands on neurochemical systems.

Amygdala. When this part of the brain receives nerve signals indicating a threat, it sends out signals that trigger defensive behavior, *autonomic arousal* (usually including rapid heartbeat and raised blood pressure), *hypoalgesia* (a diminished capacity to feel pain), *somatic reflex potentiation* (such as an exaggerated startle reflex), and *pituitary-adrenal axis stimulation* (production of stress hormones). In animals that have consciousness, these physical changes are accompanied by the emotion of fear.

Anhedonia. An inability to experience pleasure.

Autoimmune disease. A disease in which the immune system destroys or attacks a person's own tissues.

B

Brain Area Functions:

- **Corpus callosum.** Large structure extending from the front to the back of the forebrain that connects the right and left sides (i.e., hemispheres) of the brain.

- **Frontal lobe.** Contains the regions of the cortex devoted to the control of movement, language production, problem-solving ability, ability to formulate and execute plans, and control of appropriate social behavior.

- **Hippocampus.** A primitive area of the cortex that is vital for the formation of certain types of memories, especially memories of people, places, events, and factual information.

- **Mammillary body.** A subregion of the hypothalamus that contributes to the formation of certain types of memories and is frequently damaged in patients with a severe form of alcohol-induced memory deficits (i.e., Wernicke-Korsakoff syndrome).

- **Parietal lobe.** Contains regions of the cortex devoted to the processing of the sense of touch, pain, and temperature; spatial processing; integrating movements with the surrounding world; mathematical ability; letter recognition; memory for nouns; and spatial memory.

- **Temporal lobe.** Contains regions of the cortex devoted to the processing of auditory information, language comprehension, categorization ability, and ability to identify objects.

C

Chronic stress. On-going stressful situations that are not short-lived and the urge to act (fight or flight) must be suppressed. Chronic stressors include highly pressured work, relationship problems, loneliness, and financial worries. Chronic stress comes when a person never sees a way out of a miserable situation. It's the stress of unrelenting demands and pressures for seemingly interminable periods of time. With no hope, the individual gives up searching for solutions. Chronic stress destroys bodies, minds, and lives.

Cognitive-behavioral therapy (CBT). Therapy that teaches you to anticipate and prepare yourself for the situations and bodily sensations that may trigger panic attacks.

Cortisol. Cortisol helps the body maintain its energy levels when under stress. But when produced in excess, cortisol can increase blood pressure and weaken the immune system. It is a hormone released by the adrenal glands in response to stressful stimuli. Cortisol exerts widespread physiological effects throughout the body, acting in concert with other chemical messengers to help direct oxygen and nutrients to the stressed body site and suppress the immune response, while influencing certain functions, such as appetite and satiety; arousal, vigilance, attention, and mood.

Cytokines. Chemical messengers in the body that help direct and regulate responses and are involved in cell-to-cell communication.

D

Depression. Major depression is manifested by a combination of symptoms that interfere with your ability to work, sleep, eat, and enjoy once pleasurable activities. These impairing episodes of depression can occur once, twice, or several times in a lifetime.

Distress. Stress that is negative stress, also called a stressor.

Dopamine helps regulate goal-directed behaviors (including the reinforcing effects of alcohol and other drugs) as well as certain motor functions.

Dysthymic disorder. A chronic depression which is diagnosed when depressed mood persists for at least 2 years (1 year in children) and is accompanied by at least 2 other symptoms of depression. Many people with dysthymia develop major depressive episodes.

E

Environmental stressors. Can be classified as either processive or systemic.

Episodic acute stress. The symptoms of extended over arousal: persistent tension headaches, migraines, hypertension, chest pain, and heart disease. Treating episodic acute stress requires intervention on a number of levels, generally requiring professional help, which may take many months.

Ethological stressors. Represent situations that the animal would ordinarily encounter in its natural environment and for which it may have developed natural, evolutionary defenses. Ethological stressors may include the sight or odor of predators, confrontation with unfamiliar members of the same species, or fear cues.

Eustress. Stress that is positive.

Exaggerated aging. The symptoms of old age appear at the appropriate time, but in a more exaggerated form. Exaggerated aging may result from a person's increased vulnerability to the pathophysiological changes that emerge during approximately the sixth decade of life, such as brittle bones (i.e., osteoporosis), adult onset diabetes, cognitive decline, and shrinkage (i.e., atrophy) of muscle tissue.

Experimental stressors. Include exposure to cold air, immersion in cold water, and mild electric shocks administered to the animal's foot or tail.

G

Gender. Refers to a person's self-representation as male or female, or how society responds to that person based on the individual's gender presentation. Gender is rooted in biology and shaped by environment and experience.

Gene. A unit of inheritance that contains the instructions, or code, that a cell uses to make a specific product, usually a protein. Genes are made of a substance called DNA. They govern every body function and determine inherited traits passed from parent to child.

Genetics. The science of understanding how diseases, conditions, and traits are inherited.

H

Habituation. The diminished response to a certain stimulus generally refers to non-drug stimuli, such as stress or repeated sounds.

Homeostasis. Maintenance of a relatively stable balance of physiological functions.

Hypothalamic-Pituitary-Adrenal (HPA) Axis. The hormonal system that regulates the body's response to stress.

Hypothalamus. A brain structure with multiple regulatory functions that interacts extensively with the limbic system.

J

Job stress. The harmful physical and emotional responses that occur when the requirements of the job do not match the capabilities, resources, or needs of the worker. Job stress can lead to poor health and even injury.

M

Managing stress. Being able to identify stressors in your life and releasing the tension they cause.

Metyrapone. Used to test whether a person's stress system is operating normally. This chemical blocks the production of cortisol in the adrenal glands, which lowers the level of cortisol in the blood. As a result, cortisol is no longer inhibiting the release of CRF from the brain and ACTH from the pituitary. The brain and pituitary then start producing more of these chemicals.

N

Neurogenic stressors. Involve a physical stimulus (e.g., a headache, bodily injury, or recovery from surgery).

Neurotransmitters. Nerve cells that communicate with one another through chemical messengers.

Norepinephrine. Within the brain, norepinephrine plays a role in arousal and in the modulation of other neurotransmitter systems. When released into the bloodstream by the adrenal glands, norepinephrine functions as a stress-related hormone, preparing the body for "fight or flight" in response to threatening situations.

P

Panic disorder. Characterized by unexpected and repeated episodes of intense fear accompanied by physical symptoms that may include chest pain, heart palpitations, shortness of breath, dizziness, or abdominal distress. These sensations often mimic symptoms of a heart attack or other life-threatening medical conditions. As a result, the diagnosis of panic disorder is frequently not made until extensive and costly medical procedures fail to provide a correct diagnosis or relief.

Processive stressors. Those that require appraisal of a situation or involve high-level cognitive processing of incoming sensory information. Examples of processive stressors among animals include exposure to new environments, predators, or situations that trigger fear because of previous association with unpleasant stimuli (i.e., fear cues).

Prospective studies. Studies that involve an initial baseline examination of the subject with subsequent follow-up evaluation.

Psychogenic stressors. Of psychological origin (e.g., anticipating an adverse event, experiencing the death of a loved one, or caring for a chronically ill person).

R

Resilience. An ability to overcome adversity, survive stress, and recover from disadvantage.

Retrospective studies. Studies that rely on a person's recollection of past events.

Rumination. Persistent brooding.

S

Sensitization. Stressful events not only have marked immediate effects but also may influence one's response to later stressor experiences. Such a sensitization effect may be responsible for the high rates of relapse associated with psychiatric disorders, such as depression.

Serotonin. A brain chemical that affects a wide range of physiological functions, including appetite, sleep, and body temperature. Serotonin also influences emotional states, and its dysfunction has been implicated in both psychiatric and addictive disorders.

Sex. The classification of living things, generally as male or female, according to their reproductive organs and functions assigned by their biological make-up.

Stress. A state of tension that is created when a person responds to the demands and pressures that come from work, family, and other external sources, as well as those that are internally generated from self-imposed demands, obligations, and self-criticism.

Stress response. An adaptive mechanism designed to maintain the relative stability of the body's overall physiological functioning (i.e., homeostasis) in response to a challenge. However, not all stress responses are clearly adaptive. Some physiological reactions to stress that appear to confer short-term benefits are followed by adverse long-term repercussions. In other instances, changes that appear to have adverse consequences may, on closer examination, turn out to be beneficial.

Stress-response-dampening (SRD). Something that will reduce the magnitude of an organism's response to stress.

Stress response systems. The two principal stress response systems in both humans and other animals are (1) a part of the nervous system called the *sympathetic nervous system* and (2) a hormone system called the *hypothalamic-pituitary-adrenal (HPA) axis*. Both systems enable the brain to communicate with the rest of the body. Activation of the sympathetic nervous system produces several physiological responses within seconds, such as an accelerated heart rate, increased respiration, and blood flow redistribution from the skin to the skeletal muscles. These responses facilitate the "fight or flight" behavioral response.

Stressor. Indicates a situation or event appraised as being aversive in that it elicits a stress response which taxes a person's physiological or psychological resources as well as possibly provokes a subjective state of physical or mental tension.

Systemic stressors. Of physiological origin (e.g., disturbances of normal bodily metabolism resulting from bacterial or viral infection).

T

Tolerance. The diminished response to a certain stimulus, by convention, the term "tolerance" is used for a diminishing response to drugs.

Chapter 43

Resource Directory

Administration on Aging
330 Independence Avenue, SW
Washington, DC 20201
Toll-Free: 800-677-1116
(Eldercare Locator—to find
services for an older person in
his or her locality)
TTY: 800-877-8339
Website: www.aoa.dhhs.gov
E-mail: www.aoa.dhhs.gov

**American Academy of
Allergy, Asthma, and
Immunology**
611 East Wells Street
Milwaukee, WI 53202
Toll-Free: 800-822-2762
Tel: 414-272-6071
Website: www.aaaai.org
E-mail: info@aaaai.org

**American Academy of Child
and Adolescent Psychiatry**
3615 Wisconsin Avenue, NW
Washington, DC 20016-3007
Tel: 202-966-7300
Fax: 202-966-2891
Website: www.aacap.org

**American Academy of
Dermatology**
930 N. Meacham Rd.
P.O. Box 4014
Schaumburg, IL 60168-4014
Tel: 847-330–0230
Fax: 847-330–0050
Website: www.aad.org

The list of resources presented in this chapter was compiled from many
sources deemed reliable; contact information was verified and updated in February 2002.

American Academy of Experts in Traumatic Stress
368 Veterans Memorial
Highway
Commack, NY 11725
Tel: 631-543-2217
Fax: 631-543-6977
Website:www.aaets.org *and*
www.atsm.org
E-mail: aaets@traumatic-stress.org

American Association of Suicidology
4201 Connecticut Ave. NW
Suite 408
Washington, DC 20008
Tel: 202-237-2280
Fax: 202-237-2282
Website: www.suicidology.org
E-mail: ajkulp@suicidology.org

American College of Sports Medicine
P.O. Box 1440
Indianapolis, IN 46206-1440
Tel: 317-637-9200
Website: www.acsm.org

American Foundation for Suicide Prevention
120 Wall Street, 22nd Floor
New York, NY 10005
Toll-Free: 888-333-AFSP
Tel: 212-363-3500
Fax: 212-363-6237
Website: www.afsp.org
E-mail: inquiry@afsp.org

American Massage Therapy Association
820 Davis Street, Suite 100
Evanston, IL 60201-4444
Tel: 847-864-0123
Fax: 847-864-1178
Website: www.amtamassage.org

American Psychiatric Association
1400 K Street, NW
Washington, DC 20005
Toll-Free: 888-357-7924
Fax: 202-682-6850
Answer Center: 202-682-6000
Website: www.psych.org
E-mail: apa@psych.org

American Psychological Association (APA)
750 First St., NE
Washington, DC 20002-4242
Toll-Free: 800-964-2000
Fax: 202-336-5723
Website: http://helping.apa.org/find.html.

Anxiety Disorders Association of America (ADAA)
11900 Parklawn Drive
Suite 100
Rockville, MD 20852
Tel: 301-231-9350
Website: www.adaa.org

Anxiety Disorders
Education Program
National Institute of Mental
Health
6001 Executive Blvd.
Room 8184, MSC 9663
Bethesda, MD 20892-9663
Toll-Free: 888-826-9438
Tel: 301-443-4513
TTY: 301-443-8431
Fax: 301-443-4279
Website: www.nimh.nih.gov
E-mail: nimhinfo@nih.gov

Center for Mental Health
Services (CMHS)
Emergency Services and
Disaster Relief Branch
5600 Fishers Lane
Room 16C-26
Rockville, MD 20857
Tel: 301-443-4735
Fax: 301-443-8040
Website: www.samhsa.gov/cmhs/
cmhs.htm

Children of Aging Parents
1609 Woodbourne Road
Suite 302A
Levittown, PA 19057-1511
Toll-Free: 800-227-7294
Tel: 215-945-6900
Fax: 215-945-8720
Website:
www.caps4caregivers.org

The Cleveland Clinic
Foundation
9500 Euclid Avenue
Cleveland, OH 44195
Toll-Free: 800-223-2273 ext. 48950
Website:
www.clevelandclinic.org

Cleveland Clinic Health
Information Center
Tel: 216-444-3771
Website:
www.clevelandclinic.org/health

EEG Spectrum
International, Inc.
16500 Ventura Blvd., Suite 418
Encino, CA 91436-2011
Tel: 818-789-3456
Fax: 818-728-0933
Website: www.eegspectrum.com
E-mail: info@eegspectrum.com

Family Caregiver Alliance
690 Market Street, Suite 600
San Francisco, CA 94104
Tel: 415-434 3388
Fax: 415-434 3508
Website: www.caregiver.org
E-mail: info@caregiver.org

Federal Emergency
Management Agency
500 C Street, SW
Washington, DC 20472
Toll-Free: 800-480-2520
Tel: 202-566-1600
Website: www.fema.gov/kids
(Information for children and
adolescents)
E-mail: opa@fema.gov

ILO Publications Center

P.O. Box 753
Waldorf, MD 20604
Tel: 301-638-3152
Fax: 301-638-3152
Website: http://us.ilo.org/
resources/ilopubs.html
E-mail: ILOPubs@Tasco1.com

International Center for the Integration of Health and Spirituality (ICIHS)

6110 Executive Boulevard
Suite 908
Rockville, MD 20852
Tel: 301-984-7162
Fax: 301-984-8143
Website: www.icihs.org

International Society for Traumatic Stress Studies

60 Revere Drive, Suite 500
Northbrook, IL 60062
Tel: 847-480-9028
Fax: 847-480-9282
Website: www.istss.org
E-mail: istss@istss.org

National Alliance for Caregiving

4720 Montgomery Lane
Suite 642
Bethesda, MD 20814
Toll-Free: 800-677-1116
Tel: 301-718-8444
Website: www.caregiving.org

National Alliance for the Mentally Ill

Colonial Place Three
2107 Wilson Blvd., Suite 300
Arlington, VA 22201
Toll-Free Helpline: 800-950-6264
Tel: 703-524-7600
Website: www.nami.org

National Cancer Institute

Bldg. 31, Rm. 10A31
31 Center Drive, MSC 2580
Bethesda, MD 20892-2580
Toll-Free: 800-422-6237
TTY: 800-332-8615
Fax on Demand: 301-402-5874
(listen to recorded instructions)
Website: http://cancer.gov
E-mail:
cancermail@icicc.nci.hig.gov (to
obtain a contents list, e-mail
with the word "help" in the body
of the message)

National Center for Post-Traumatic Stress Disorder

215 North Main St.
White River Junction, VT 05009
Tel: 802-296-5132
Website: www.ncptsd.org

National Center for Victims of Crime

2111 Wilson Blvd., Suite 300
Arlington, VA 22201
Toll-Free: 800-394-2255
Website: www.nvc.org

The National Council on Aging, Inc.
409 Third St., SW, Suite 200
Washington, DC 20024
Tel: 202-479-1200
Fax: 202-479-0735
TDD: 202-479-6674
Website: www.ncoa.org
E-mail: info@ncoa.org

National Depressive and Manic Depressive Association
730 N. Franklin St., Suite 501
Chicago, IL 60610-7204
Toll-Free: 800-826-3632
Tel: 312-642-0049
Fax: 312-642-7243
Website: www.ndmda.org

National Eczema Association
6600 SW 92nd Ave., Suite 240
Portland, OR 97223-7195
Toll-Free: 800-818-7546
Tel: 503-228-4430
Fax: 503-224-3363
Website: www.eczema-assn.org
E-mail: nease@teleport.com

National Family Caregivers Association
10400 Connecticut Avenue, #500
Kensington, MD 20895-3944
Toll-Free: 800-896-3650
Tel: 301-942-2302
Website: www.nfcacares.org
E-mail: info@nfcacares.org

National Heart, Lung, and Blood Institute
Information Center
P.O. Box 30105
Bethesda, MD 20824-0105
Tel: 301-592-8573
Fax: 301-592-8563
Website: www.nhlbi.nih.gov/index.htm
E-mail: NHLBIinfo@rover.nhlbi.nih.gov

National Institute of Arthritis and Musculoskeletal and Skin Diseases Information Clearinghouse
1 AMS Circle
Bethesda, MD 20892-3675
Toll-Free: 877-22-NIAMS
Tel: 301-495-4484
TTY: 301-565-2966
Fax: 301-718-6366
NIAMS 24 hour Fast Facts Fax:
301-881-2731
Website: www.niams.nih.gov
E-mail: niamsinfo@mail.nih.gov

National Institute of Mental Health (NIMH)
Office of Communications and Public Liaison
6001 Executive Boulevard
Rm. 8184, MSC 9663
Bethesda, MD 20892
Toll-Free: 888-826-9438
Tel: 301-443-4513
Fax: 301-443-4279
TTY: 301-443-8431
Website: www.nimh.nih.gov
E-mail: nimhinfo@nih.gov

National Institute for Occupational Safety and Health (NIOSH)
4676 Columbia Parkway
Cincinnati, Ohio 45226-1998
Toll-Free: 800-356-4674
Telephone Outside the U.S.:
513-533-8328
Fax: 513-533-8573
Website: www.cdc.gov/niosh

National Mental Health Association
1021 Prince Street
Alexandria, VA 22314
Toll-Free: 800-969-6642
Toll-Free TTY: 800-433-5959
Fax: 703-684-5968
Website: www.nmha.org

National Organization for Victim Assistance (NOVA)
1730 Park Rd., NW
Washington, DC 20010
Toll-Free: 800-879-6682
Tel: 202-232-6682
Fax: 202-462-2255
Website: www.try-nova.org

National Psoriasis Foundation
6600 SW 92nd Avenue, Suite 300
Portland, OR 97223-7195
Toll-Free: 800-723-9166
Tel: 503-244-7404
Fax: 503-245-0626
Website: www.psoriasis.org
E-mail: getinfo@npfusa.org

National Victim Center
2111 Wilson Blvd., Suite 300
Arlington, VA 22201
Tel: 730-276-2880
Website: www.nvc.org

Office for Victims of Crime Resource Center
National Criminal Justice
Reference Service
P.O. Box 6000
Rockville, MD 20850
Toll-Free: 800-627-6872
Website: www.ncjrs.org
E-mail: askovc@ojp.usdoj.gov

President's Council on Physical Fitness and Sports
Department W
200 Independence Ave, SW,
Room 738-H
Washington, DC 20201-0004
Tel: 202-690-9000
Fax: 202-690-5211
Website: www.fitness.gov
E-mail:
PCPFS@OSOPHS.DHHS.GOV

Rape, Abuse, and Incest National Network (RAINN)
635 Pennsylvania Ave., SE
Washington, DC 20002
Toll-Free: 800-656-HOPE (800-656-4673) (24-hour confidential hot line)
Fax: 202-544-3556
Website: www.rainn.org
E-mail: rainnmail@aol.com

Suicide Prevention Advocacy Network
5034 Odins Way
Marietta, GA 30096
Toll-Free: 888-649-1366
Fax: 770-642-1419
Website: www.spanusa.org
E-mail: act@spanusa.org

U.S. Department of Education
400 Maryland Avenue, SW
Washington, DC 20202-0498
Toll-Free: 800-USA-LEARN
(872-5327)
Fax: 202-401-0689
Website: www.ed.gov
E-mail:
customerservice@inet.ed.gov

U.S. Department of Justice
950 Pennsylvania Avenue, NW
Washington, DC 20530-0001
Website: www.usdoj.gov
E-mail: askdoj@usdoj.gov

Weight-Control Information Network
1 Win Way
Bethesda, MD 20892-3665
Toll-Free: 877-946-4627
Tel: 202-828-1025
Fax: 202-828-1028
Website: www.niddk.nih.gov/
health/nutrit/win.htm
E-mail: win@info.niddk.nih.gov

Index

Index

Page numbers followed by 'n' indicate a footnote. Page numbers in *italics* indicate a table or illustration.

A

AAETS *see* American Academy of Experts in Traumatic Stress
"About HRAs" (YOU*First* Health Risk Assessment) 41n
accelerated aging, defined 551
accumbens 81, 437
acitretin 419
acne rosacea 420–23
"ACP Home Care Guide for Advanced Cancer" (American College of Physicians) 503n
ACTH *see* adrenocorticotropic hormone
acute stress
   defined 551
   described 37–39
acute stress disorder, described 299
   see also post-traumatic stress disorder
acute traumatic stress management 253–61
ADAA *see* Anxiety Disorders Association of America
Adams, Scott 163

adaptation, defined 551
adaptation phenomenon, described 16–17
addictions
   relapse 307–10
   stress 103–7
   stress hormones 81–82
adjustment reaction of adult life, described 264
Administration on Aging, contact information 156, 559
adolescents
   depression 186, 190–92, 209–10
   disasters 288–305
   domestic violence 301
   parental absence 71
   post-traumatic stress disorder 311–12
   stress 59
   stress management studies 89
   suicides 215
   tobacco use 95–96, 98
   trauma 289–90
adrenal axis stimulation, described 341
adrenal glands
   alcohol use *78*
   depression 188
   stressor exposure 25
   stress response 27, 80–81
   stress system studies 106

adrenaline
  described 348
  heart disease 350
adrenocorticotropic hormone (ACTH)
  alcohol use *435*
  drug abuse 104
  metyrapone 106
  stressor exposure 25
  stress response 27–28, 80
age factor
  alcohol use 431–54
  atopic dermatitis 403–4
  depression 190–93, 212–13
  memory impairment 330
  panic disorder 243–44
  post-traumatic stress disorder 273
  religious activity 522
  stressors 23, 25–27
  suicide 215, 218–21, 223–24
  ulcers 376
  see also adolescents; children
"Agenda for Research on Women's
  Health for the 21st Century" (NIH)
  381n
aging, defined 551
agoraphobia 241
Ahola, Sara 425n
"Alcohol, Aging, and the Stress Response" (Spencer; Hutchison) 431n
alcohol use
  depression 179–80, 204
  health risk assessments 43, 44
  processive stressors 16
  relapse 308–10
  rosacea 421
  stress 77–92
  stress hormones 81–82
  stress management 489–501
  stressors 22
  stress response 431–54
  suicide risk 227–28
  ulcers 377
  women 391–92
  workplace stress 130–48
allergic contact eczema, defined 401
allergic diseases, women 388–89
allostatic load
  defined 552
  described 21

Altemus, Margaret 393–94
Alterman, Toni 110n
"Alternative Medicine: Information
  about St. John's Wort" (NIMH) 230n
alternative treatments, depression
  193
Altura, Bella 480
American Academy of Allergy,
  Asthma and Immunology, contact
  information 424, 559
American Academy of Child and Ado-
  lescent Psychiatry, contact information 305, 559
American Academy of Dermatology,
  contact information 423, 559
American Academy of Experts in
  Traumatic Stress (AAETS)
  contact information 272, 560
  publications
    traumatic stress management
      252n
    violence coping measures 288n
American Association of Suicidology,
  contact information 229, 560
American College of Physicians, grief
  publication 503n
American College of Sports Medicine,
  contact information 482, 560
American Foundation for Suicide Prevention, contact information 229,
  560
American Massage Therapy Association
  contact information 547, 560
  publications 541n
American Psychiatric Association,
  contact information 304, 560
American Psychological Association
  (APA), contact information 125, 304,
  560
amonocytes 349
amygdala, defined 274, 340–42
anger, heart rate 366–68
anhedonia, defined 552
animal studies
  alcohol use 77, 81–82
  brains 331
  corticosterone 434
  fear conditioning 341

animal studies, continued
heredity 22
lactation 393
maternal touch 324–25
neurotransmitters 21
post-traumatic stress disorder 308
relapse 310
stress 14, 320–21
stress hormones 338–39
stressor exposure 24, 25–26
stressors 16–17
Anisman, Hymie 13n
anthralin 415, 416–17
anti-anxiety medications 472–73
antibiotic medications
atopic dermatitis 410
psoriasis 419
ulcers 376, 380
antidepressant medications
cancer 202–3, 219–20
described 173–74, 184–85, 234–35
panic disorder 248
post-traumatic stress disorder 274
anxiety
depression 188–89
medications 472–73
panic disorder 241
substance abuse 87
Anxiety Disorders Association of
America (ADAA), contact information 250, 286, 305, 560
Anxiety Disorders Education Program, contact information 250, 561
anxiety management, post-traumatic
stress disorder 284
APA *see* American Psychological Association
apoptosis, described 417
arginine vasopressin (AVP), stressor
exposure 25
Aronoff, Jodi 167n
arthritis, women 387
Arthritis Foundation, stress management publication 483n
aspirin 378
asthma
children 425–30
stress 3–4
atherosclerosis, stress 320–22

atopic dermatitis
defined 400
described 399–413
"Atopic Dermatitis" (Novak) 399n
autoimmune diseases
defined 552
stress 361–62
autonomic arousal, described 341
AVP *see* arginine vasopressin
awfulizers 39

B

back pain, physical activity 475
battered wife syndrome, described 264
battle fatigue, described 264, 280
Bennett, Gary, Jr. 167–69
Benson, Herbert 8
benzodiazepines
panic disorder 248
substance abuse 87
bereavement 503–12
biofeedback
EEG training 525–33
stress management 8, 461–62
"Biology of Stress" (conference) 319n
bipolar disorder
described 172–73, 177, 178–79, 232
symptoms 183
blood pressure levels
caffeine 358
religious activity 522
see also hypertension
Boehnlein, James 281
Brady, Kathleen T. 77n
brain
alcohol use *442*
area functions, defined 552–53
depression 187–88
immune system 360
post-traumatic stress disorder 274
stress 329–30, 337–45
breast self-examinations, health risk
assessments 44
Breuer, Josef 162
Bruce, Debra Fulghum 465n

C

caffeine
   stress hormones 357–58
   stress management 459
   ulcers 377
calcipotriene 416
calcium supplements 481
cancer
   depression 201–2
   job-related stress 116
   psychological stress 373–74
   women 383–85
"Cancer Facts" (NCI) 373n
Cannon, Walter B. 4–5
cardiac arrhythmia, stress 3
cardiovascular disease
   job-related stress 115
   stress 320–24
caregivers
   stress 149–56, *150*, *152*
   stress management 254
"Caregiver Stress" (The National
   Women's Health Information Center)
   149n
Carey, Drew 236
Cassel, John 7
catecholamines 129
   see also epinephrine; norepinephrine
CBT *see* cognitive-behavioral therapy
Celexa (citalopram) 283
Center for Mental Health Services
   (CMHS), contact information 303, 561
Charcot, Jean-Martin 162
Chatters, Linda 521
cheilitis, described 403
child abuse syndrome, described 264
"Childhood Losses Affect Adult
   Health" (Hines) 69n
Childre, Doc 365, 535
children
   asthma attacks 425–30
   atopic dermatitis 400, 403, 412
   brain development 337–39
   depression 186, 190–92
   disasters 288–305
   maternal touch 324–25
   post-traumatic stress disorder 274

children, continued
   resilience 69–76
   stress 58–59
   suicides 215
   trauma 289–90
Children of Aging Parents, contact information 155, 561
cholinergic agonist 98
chronic fatigue syndrome, hydrocortisone 342–45
chronic stress
   asthma 425–30
   defined 553
   described 39–40
   hippocampus 329–30
   immune system 360
   wound healing 332
chronic stressors
   brain development 337–39
   described 20–21
Chrousos, George 205
cigarette smoking *see* tobacco use
citalopram 283
Cizza, Giovanni 205
The Cleveland Clinic Foundation
   contact information 463, 561
   publications
      everyday problems 457n
      heart disease 347n
      multiple sclerosis 395n
Cleveland Clinic Health Information
   Center, contact information 464, 561
clinical depression
   anxiety disorders 188–89
   described 176
   other illnesses 195–208
   see also depression
CMHS *see* Center for Mental Health
   Services
coal tar 415
Cobb, Sidney 7
cocaine, stress hormones 105
coffee, stress hormones 357–58
cognitive-behavioral therapy (CBT)
   defined 553
   depression 173, 185–86, 219
   panic disorder 242, 247–48
   post-traumatic stress disorder 88,
      274, 284, 294–95

cognitive restructuring, described 88
Cohen, Sheldon 319n, 334–35
colitis, stress 3
Colligan, Michael 110n
"Combination of Stress, Low Serotonin May Promote Heart Disease"
   (Twombly) 347n
common cold, friendships 334–35
communication issues
   family stress 62–63
   job-related stress 118–19
conflict management, family stress 63
conservation-withdrawal theory, described 6
contact eczema, defined 400–401
   see also allergic contact eczema
controllability, stressors 19–20
conversion hysteria, stress 4
"Co-Occurrence of Depression with
   Cancer" (NIMH) 195n
"Co-Occurrence of Depression with
   Stroke" (NIMH) 195n
Cooke, David A. 375n
coping strategies
   disasters 288–305
   stressors 20
   stroke 169–70
   see also stress management
"Coping with Crises - Active Coping
   and Spiritual Support Can Help Alleviate Distress" (ICIHS) 513n
coronary artery disease, risk factors 7
coronary heart disease, tobacco use
   44
corpus callosum, defined 552
cortex, described 341–42
corticoid hormones 5
corticosteroid medications
   atopic dermatitis 410–11
   psoriasis 415, 416
corticosterone
   alcohol use 434
   stressor exposure 25, 26
corticotropin-releasing hormones
   (CRH)
   alcohol use *435*
   animal studies 338–39
   depression 188
   drug abuse 104–5

corticotropin-releasing hormones
   (CRH), continued
   hydrocortisone 343
   stressor exposure 25
   stress response 27–28, 80, 307–8
cortisol
   alcohol use *432*, 436
   brain development 337–39
   children 75
   defined 553
   described 360
   drug abuse 104
   heart disease 350
   hydrocortisone 343
   personality traits 168
   post-traumatic stress disorder 274
   stress management 368–70
   stress response 14
   stress system studies 106
   workplace stress 129
Coumadin (warfarin) 235
counseling, domestic violence 301
   see also psychotherapy
CRH *see* corticotropin-releasing hormones
crisis management 513–23
Crixivan (indinavir) 235
Cushing's syndrome 434, 441
Cut-Thru technique 368
cyclosporine 235, 411, 419
cytokines
   defined 553
   heart disease 349
   stressor exposure 25

D

Da Costa's syndrome, described 264
D/ART Program *see* Depression
   Awareness, Recognition, and Treat-
   ment Program
Davis, Alison 319n
Dead Sea salts 417
"Dealing With Stress: The Physical
   Connection" (Wellsource, Inc.) 465n
"Dealing with the Depths of Depres-
   sion" (Nordenberg) 230n
dementia, alcohol use 451–52

Demodex folliculorum 421
Dennie-Morgan fold, described 402, 403
dentate gyrus, stress 329–30
depression
  causes 178
  coping strategies 230–39
  cortisol 337
  defined 553
  described 231–32
  diagnosis 233–34
  hippocampus 441
  older adults 218–21
  other illnesses 189, 195–96, 218
  post-traumatic stress disorder 273
  research 174–75, 182, 193–94
  statistics 173, 195–96, 218
  stress 172–94
  stressors 17–18
  stroke 170
  substance abuse 87
  suicide 172–74, 179, 214–29, 226–27
  symptoms 172–73, 177, 183–84, 204–5
  treatment 180–82, 202–3, 348, 473
  women 385–86
  see also antidepressant medications; bipolar disorder; clinical depression; dysthymic disorder
"Depression, Bone Mass, and Osteoporosis" (NIMH) 195n
Depression Awareness, Recognition, and Treatment Program, contact information 239
"Depression Can Break Your Heart" (NIMH) 195n
"Depression: Co-Occurrence of Depression with Medical, Psychiatric, and Substance Abuse Disorders" (NMHA) 195n
"Depression Research" (NIMH) 172n
"Depression: What Every Woman Should Know" (NIMH) 209n
deprivations, described 3, 6
dermatitis *see* atopic dermatitis; eczema
DHEA levels, stress management 368–70

diabetes mellitus
  depression 203
  physical activity 475
  stress 325–26
DiClemente, Carlo 52
diet and nutrition
  depression 236
  health risk assessment 43
  magnesium 479–82
  stress reduction 354–55
digestive diseases, women 390–91
digoxin 235
Diprolene 416
distress
  acute 291
  defined 553
  described 347
"Does Cigarette Smoking Cause Stress?" (Parrott) 93n
"Does Drinking Reduce Stress?" (Sayette) 489n
domestic violence 297–301
dopamine
  defined 553
  stressor exposure 24
  stress response 18–19, 80, 81–82, 87, 437
doxycycline 422
drug abuse
  depression 179–80, 204
  relapse 307–10
  research 313–15
  stress 103–7
  suicide risk 227–28
  women 391–92
Duke University Medical Center, publications
  coffee effects 357n
  heart disease 347n
  motherhood 127n
  personality and stress 167n
Dunbar, Helen Flanders 162
dyshidrotic eczema, defined 401
dysthymic disorder
  defined 554
  described 172, 177, 232
  older adults 218
  symptoms 183–84
  women 209

E

EAP *see* employee assistance programs
eating disorders
  depression 204
  stress 385–86
ECT *see* electroconvulsive therapy
eczema 399–401
"EEG Biofeedback Training for Depression" (EEG Spectrum International) 525n
EEG Spectrum International
  biofeedback publication 525n
  contact information 533, 561
"The Effects Of Different Music On Mood, Tension and Mental Clarity" (Institute of HeartMath) 535n
"Effects of Domestic Violence on Children and Adolescents: An Overview" (Volpe) 288n
Effexor 234
electroconvulsive therapy (ECT)
  cancer 203
  depression 174, 186, 235
emergency response, described 8
"The Emotional Brain" (Hendrix) 337n
"The Emotional Brain" (NIMH) 551n
emotional concerns
  anger 365–71
  children 289
  compassion 365–71
  diseases 161–65
  exercise 466
  stress management 484
  trauma 265–66
  see also post-traumatic stress disorder
"Emotions and Disease" (Guyer) 161n
employee assistance programs (EAP) 117–18
endocrine immune interface, stress 328–29
endorphins, alcohol use 78
Engel, F. L. 5
Engel, George 6
environmental stressors
  defined 554
  described 15

epinephrine
  alcohol use 78
  cardiovascular disease 323
  post-traumatic stress disorder 275
  workplace stress 129
episodic acute stress
  defined 554
  described 38–39
Epsom salts 417
erythrodermic psoriasis, described 415
erytromycin 422
"Escaping the Prison of Past Trauma: New Treatment for Post-Traumatic Stress Disorder" (Nordenberg) 272n
estrogen, heart disease 349
ethological stressors
  defined 554
  described 16
eustress
  defined 554
  described 347
exaggerated aging, defined 554
exercise
  depression 236
  health risk assessments 44
  stress management 459, 465–82
  stress reduction 354
experimental stressors, defined 554
exposure therapy, post-traumatic stress disorder 274, 284
eyelids, atopic dermatitis 402–3

F

"Facts about Panic Disorder" (NIMH) 241n
Family Caregiver Alliance, contact information 155, 561
family issues
  atopic dermatitis 412–13
  children
    coping strategies, violence 288–305
    stress 70–71
  stress 57–67
  stroke recovery 170
  see also adolescents; children

fear response, described 340–42
  see also fight or flight response
Federal Emergency Management
  Agency (FEMA), contact information 303, 561
FEMA *see* Federal Emergency Management Agency
fight or flight response
  amygdala 341–42
  depression 188, 197–98
  described 319, 323, 348, 469, 484,
    557
  epinephrine 18
  job-related stress 115
  norepinephrine 18
financial concerns
  biofeedback costs 531, 532
  family stress 59–60
fluoxetine 88, 283
fluvoxamine 283
Foa, Edna 280, 284
footshock, described 16–17
Foundation for Integrated Medicine,
  publications 465n
Freeze-Framer 365–66, 368
"Frequently Asked Questions about
  Neurofeedback" (EEG Spectrum International) 525n
"Frequently Asked Questions about
  Suicide" (NIH) 214n
Freud, Sigmund 162
Friedman, Meyer 8, 38–39
friendships, common colds 334–35
Frone, Michael R. 130n
frontal lobe, defined 552

G

Gailand, Leo 465n
gender, defined 554
gender factor
  alcohol use 494–95
  autoimmune diseases 388–89
  cancer 383–85
  depression 209–13
  depressive disorders 173
  digestive diseases 389–91
  heart disease 349, 382–83

gender factor, continued
  mental disorders 385–86
  musculoskeletal diseases 387–88
  post-traumatic stress disorder 273
  stress hormone levels 393–94
  stressors 22–23
  substance abuse 391–3927
  suicides 215, 222
  see also women
gene, defined 554–55
general adaptation syndrome, described 5
genetics
  defined 555
  depression research 187, 232
  stress 363
  stressors 22
  see also heredity
"Getting Treatment for Panic Disorder" (NIH) 241n
Ghahramanlou, Marjan 167n
Glaser, Ron 332
glucocortoid hormones
  hippocampal formation 329–30
  post-traumatic stress disorder 328
  stress response 80, 81
    alcohol use 431, 436–37, 439–40,
      442–44
Gold, Philip 205
Goldenhar, Linda 110n
Grattan, Lynn M. 169–70
grief management 503–12
gross stress reaction, described 264
group therapy, post-traumatic stress
  disorder 274
    see also support groups
Grubb, Paula 110n
guttate psoriasis, described 414
Guyer, Ruth Levy 161n

H

habituation, defined 555
Hall, Jack 42
Hamilton, Anne 110n
hardening of arteries, described 349
health risk assessments (HRA), described 41–54

"Health Risks" (YOU*First* Health Risk Assessment) 41n
heart disease
  depression 196–98
  physical activity 474
  stress 320–24, 347–55
  women 382–83
"Heart Disease Risk Linked to Mood Chemical" (Twombly) 347n
HearthMath system 365–66
Heart Lock-In 366, 536–40
Helicobacter pylori 377–80, 421
"*Helicobacter pylori* and Peptic Ulcer Disease - Good News! A Cure for Ulcers!" (National Center for Infectious Diseases) 375n
"*Helicobacter pylori* and Peptic Ulcer Disease - Myths" (National Center for Infectious Diseases) 375n
"Helping Children and Adolescents Cope with Violence and Disasters" (NIMH) 288n
helplessness, described 6
Hendrix, Mary Lynn 337n
hepatitis C research 314
heredity
  alcoholism 84, 491–93
  alcohol use 433
  atopic dermatitis 400
  depression 178
  stressors 22
  suicide risk 226
  see also genetics
heroin, stress hormones 105
high blood pressure *see* hypertension
"Higher Levels of Religious Activity Linked to Lower Blood Pressure" (ICIHS) 513n
Hillary, Clive R. 425n
Hines, Karen 69n
hippocampus
  chronic stress 329–30
  cortisol 337–38
  defined 552
HIV *see* human immunodeficiency virus
holiday blues, described 237–39
"Holiday Depression and Stress" (NMHA) 230n

homeostatis, defined 555
hopelessness, described 6
hormones
  depression 188, 210–11, 220
  fight or flight response 18
  stress 14, 308, 319
    depression 197
    personality traits 168–69
  stress management 8
  stressor exposure 26
  stress response 80
  stress theories 5
  working mothers 129
  see also adrenocorticotropic hormone; corticotropin-releasing hormones; cortisol; stress hormones
House, James S. 157n, 157–58
HPA *see* hypothalamic-pituitary adrenal axis
HRA *see* health risk assessments
human immunodeficiency virus (HIV), stress 333
humors, described 165
Hurrell, Joseph, Jr. 110n
Huston, John 163
Hutchison, Kent E. 431n
Hydrea (hydroxyurea) 419
hydrocortisone, chronic fatigue syndrome 342–45
  see also cortisol
hydroxyurea 419
hypericum, depression 174, 235
hypertension (high blood pressure)
  health risk assessment 43
  physical activity 474
  stress 3
hyperthyroidism, stress 3
hypoalgesia, described 341
hypothalamic-pituitary adrenal axis (HPA)
  addictions 81
  alcohol use *78*, 432–43, *435*
  defined 555
  depression 174, 188
  described 15, 16
  post-traumatic stress disorder 327–28

hypothalamus
  alcohol use *78*
  defined 555
  depression 188
  stress response 27, 80–81, 360
  stress theories 5
  systemic stressors 16

I

ibuprofen 378
ICIHS *see* International Center for
  the Integration of Health and Spirituality
ILO Publications Center, contact information 125, 562
imipramine 234
immune response
  cortisol 14
  exercise 466
  stressor exposure 25
immune system
  atopic dermatitis 411
  heart disease 349
  job-related stress 116, 129
  stress 328–29, 359–64
  women 388–89
imprint of horror, described 254, 256
indinavir 235
"In Harm's Way: Suicide in America"
  (NIMH) 214n
injuries, job-related stress 116
insomnia 462
Institute of HeartMath
  contact information 540
  publications
    anger 365n
    compassion 365n
    music 535n
interleukin 1 alpha 349
International Center for the Integration of Health and Spirituality
  (ICIHS)
  contact information 523, 562
  spirituality publication 513n
International Society for Traumatic
  Stress Studies, contact information
  286, 303, 562

interpersonal therapy, depression
  173, 185–86, 219–20
inverse psoriasis, described 415
"The Invisible Disease: Depression"
  (NIMH) 172n
irritable bowel syndrome, woment
  389–91
ischemia 322
isotretinoid 422
"Is the Stress of Mothering a Health
  Risk?" (Duke University Medical
  Center) 127n
itch-scratch cycle, described 401, 406

J

Jenkins, David 7
job stress
  alcohol use 130–48, *134*
  causes 112–13
  defined 555
  described 112
  personality traits 168–69
  prevention 117–24
  research 110–26
  ulcers 375–80
  women 127–30
  see also occupations
Johnston, Janet 110n

K

Kaplan, Jay 320–21
Kawachi, Ichiro 127–28
Keane, Terence 278
keratosis pilaris, described 402
Kiecolt-Glaser, Janice 332
Kittner, Stephen J. 167n
Koenig, Harold 516
Krantz, David 321–22
Kreek, Mary Jeanne 103–7

L

lactation, stress hormone levels 393–
  94
Lane, James 357–58

Lanoxicaps (digoxin) 235
Lanoxin (digoxin) 235
Larson, David 514, 520
Larson, Susan 513n
Laughren, Thomas 231–32, 235–37, 279
learned helplessness, described 19
LeDoux, Joseph 340
Lerner, Mark D. 252n
Lessons from Fear Conditioning (Hendrix) 337n
Levin, Jeffrey 521
Levine, Rebecca 357n
"Life Satisfaction Linked to Faith Factor" (ICIHS) 513n
lifestyles
   health risk assessments 41–42
   immune system 354
   stress management 459, 465–82
   ulcers 377
limbic system, processive stressors 16
lipoprotein levels, stress 326–27
losses, described 6
Luecken, Linda 74–75, 128–29
Luvox (fluvoxamine) 283

M

"Magnesium: The Stress Reliever" (Gailand) 465n
magnesium supplements 479–82
magnetic resonance imaging (MRI)
   anxiety disorders 342
   depression 187–88
major depression *see* clinical depression; depression
Malarkey, William 328–29
mammilary body, defined 552
mammograms, health risk assessments 44
managing stress, defined 555
"Managing Your Stress" (Arthritis Foundation) 483n
mania, described 177
manic-depressive illness *see* bipolar disorder
MAOI *see* monoamine oxidase inhibitors

massage therapy, stress management 541–47
"Massage Therapy: Key Questions and Answers" (American Massage Therapy Association) 541n
McCann, Donna C. 425n
McEwen, Bruce 329–30
McGuinness, David 425n
McKenzie, Robin 343
Meaney, Michael 331
meditation
   depression 236
   stress management 459
menopause, depression 211
Merali, Zul 13n
Merritt, Marcellus 169
methadone 106
methotrexate 418–19
metyrapone
   defined 555
   described 106
Miller, Lyle H. 37n
minocycline 422
monoamine oxidase inhibitors (MAOI)
   depression 184–85, 219, 234
   described 173
monoamines *see* norepinephrine; serotonin
mood fluctuations
   pregnancy 211
   smoking cessation 96
   tobacco use 94–95
   see also emotional concerns
"Morning Coffee Boosts Blood Pressure, Stress Hormones All Day" (Levine) 357n
morphine, stress hormones 105
MRI *see* magnetic resonance imaging
multiple sclerosis, stress 395–97
Murphy, Lawrence 110n
musculoskeletal disorders, job-related stress 116
music, emotional state 535–40, *536, 538, 539*
"Music Enhances the Effect of Positive Emotional States on Salivary IGA" (Institute of HearthMath) 535n

N

naltrexone 88
naproxen sodium 378
Nardil (phenelzine) 234
National Alliance for Caregiving, contact information 155, 562
National Alliance for the Mentally Ill, contact information 239, 562
National Cancer Institute (NCI)
cancer facts publication 373n
contact information 374, 562
National Center for Infectious Diseases, peptic ulcers publication 375n
National Center for Post-Traumatic Stress Disorder, contact information 287, 304, 562
National Center for Victims of Crime, contact information 286, 562
The National Council on Aging, Inc., contact information 155, 563
National Depressive and Manic Depressive Association, contact information 239, 563
National Eczema Foundation, contact information 423, 563
National Family Caregivers Association, contact information 156, 563
National Heart, Lung, and Blood Institute, contact information 482, 563
National Institute for Occupational Safety and Health (NIOSH)
contact information 124, 564
publications
childhood resilience 551n
workplace stress 110n
National Institute of Allergy and Infectious Diseases (NIAID), steroid risks publication 337n
National Institute of Arthritis and Musculoskeletal and Skin Diseases (NIAMS)
contact information 424
Information Clearinghouse, contact information 563
publications
atopic dermatitis 399n

National Institute of Arthritis and Musculoskeletal and Skin Diseases (NIAMS), continued
publications, continued
psoriasis 399n
rosacea 399n
National Institute of Diabetes and Digestive and Kidney Diseases (NIDDK), ulcers publication 375n
National Institute of Mental Health (NIMH)
contact information 194, 287, 302, 345, 463, 563
publications
alternative medicine 230n
brain and stress 337n
brain emotions 551n
depression 172n, 195n, 209n
lactation 381n
panic disorder 241n
post-traumatic stress disorder 272n
suicide 214n
violence coping strategies 288n
National Institute on Alcohol Abuse and Alcoholism (NIAAA), publications
aging 431n
alcohol consumption 489n
glossary 551n
understanding stress 13n
National Institute on Drug Abuse (NIDA), stress publication 307n
National Institutes of Health (NIH), publications
panic disorder 241n
suicide 214n
women's health 381n
National Labor Relations Act 120
National Mental Health Association (NMHA)
contact information 208, 564
publications
depression 195n, 230n
everyday problems 457n
National Organization for Victim Assistance (NOVA), contact information 304, 564
National Psoriasis Foundation, contact information 424, 564

National Victim Center, contact information 304, 564
The National Women's Health Information Center, caregiver stress publication 149n
NCI *see* National Cancer Institute
Neoral (cyclosporine) 235
nerve cells, stress response 18
neurodermatitis
 defined 401
 stress 3
neuroendocrine functions, stressor exposure 25
neurofeedback 525–33
neurogenic stressors
 defined 555
 described 15
neurotransmitters
 antidepressant medications 173
 defined 556
 drug abuse 104–5
 metyrapone test 107
 stressor exposure 24
 stress response 18–20, 80
 substance abuse 87
 see also dopamine; norepinephrine; serotonin
NIAAA *see* National Institute on Alcohol Abuse and Alcoholism
NIAID *see* National Institute of Allergy and Infectious Diseases
NIAMS *see* National Institute of Arthritis and Musculoskeletal and Skin Diseases
nicotine use *see* tobacco use
NIDA *see* National Institute on Drug Abuse
NIDDK *see* National Institute of Diabetes and Digestive and Kidney Diseases
NIH *see* National Institutes of Health
NIMH *see* National Institute of Mental Health
NIOSH *see* National Institute for Occupational Safety and Health
NLM *see* US National Library of Medicine
NMHA *see* National Mental Health Association

nonsteroidal anti-inflammatory drugs (NSAID), ulcers 378–79
Nordenberg, Liora 230n
Nordenberg, Tamar 272n
norepinephrine
 alcohol use *78*
 defined 556
 depression 184
 exercise 236
 post-traumatic stress disorder 275
 stressor exposure 24
 stress response 18–19, 20
 workplace stress 129
North Carolina Department of Health and Human Services, caregiver stress publication 149n
nortriptyline 220
NOVA *see* National Organization for Victim Assistance
Novak, Debbie 399n
NSAID *see* nonsteroidal anti-inflammatory drugs
nummular eczema, defined 401
nutrition *see* diet and nutrition

O

obesity
 diabetes mellitus 325
 physical activity 475
occupations
 alcohol use 82
 stress 110–26
  alcohol use 130–48
  women 127–30
 see also job stress
Office for Victims of Crime Resource Center, contact information 304, 564
Oja, Hannu 425n
"Older Adults: Depression and Suicide Facts" (NIH) 214n
opioid antagonists, substance abuse 87, 88
opioid peptides
 drug abuse 104–5
 stress response 80, 87

opioids
  addiction 105
  alcohol use *78*
  see also heroin; morphine
ornithine decarboxylase 324
osteoporosis
  depression 205–7
  physical activity 475
  women 388
"An Overview of Acute Traumatic
  Stress Management: Keeping
  People Functioning and Mitigating
  Long-Term Suffering During
  Today's Traumatic Events" (Lerner)
  252n
overweight, health risk assessments
  44

P

panic disorder
  defined 556
  described 241–42
  diagnosis 246–47
  fear conditioning 342
  other illnesses 243
  symptoms 244–45
  treatment 242, 245–46, 247–50
Pap tests, health risk assessments 44
Pargament, Kenneth 516
parietal lobe, defined 552
paroxetine 283
Parrott, Andy C. 93n
Paton, James Y. 425n
Paxil (paroxetine) 234, 283
pepsin, ulcers 377–79
peptic ulcer, stress 3–4
Pergola, Joe 57n
"Personality Influences Psychological
  Adjustment and Recovery from
  Stroke" (Ghahramanlou, et al.)
  167n
personality traits
  alcohol use 493
  cardiovascular disease 323
  depression 178
  stress 167–70
  see also type-A behavior pattern

Persons, Susan M. 157n
phenelzine 234
photochemotherapy, atopic dermatitis
  411
phototherapy
  atopic dermatitis 410–11
  described 238–39
  psoriasis 417
physical activity, stress management
  465–82
"Physical Activity and Weight Control" (NIDDK) 465n
"The Physiological and Psychological
  Effects" (Institute of HeartMath)
  365n
"The Physiological and Psychological
  Effects of Compassion and Anger"
  (Institute of HeartMath) 365n
Pima Indians study 325–26
pituitary gland
  alcohol use *78*
  depression 188
  drug abuse 104
  stress response 27, 80
PMDD *see* premenstrual dysphoric
  disorder
post-traumatic stress disorder
  (PTSD)
  children 293–95
    domestic violence 298–99
  depression 189
  described 264–65, 272–73, 280–83
  diagnosis 285–86
  fluoxetine 88
  hypothalamic-pituitary adrenal
    axis 327–28
  research 274–87
  statistics 273–74, 311–13
  substance abuse 308, 310–13
  treatment 267–68, 274, 283–85
post-Vietnam syndrome, described 264
poverty, depression 212
Powell, Lisa M. 69n, 551n
prednisone 411
pregnancy, depression 211
premenstrual dysphoric disorder
  (PMDD), depression 210
premenstrual syndrome, depression
  190, 210

President's Council on Physical Fitness and Sports, contact information 482, 564
Price, Thomas R. 167n
processive stressors
  controllability 20
  defined 556
  described 15–16
Prochaska, James 52
propranolol 320
prospective studies, defined 556
prostate screening, health risk assessments 44
protease inhibitors 235
Prozac (fluoxetine) 88, 234–35, 283
psoralen 411, 417–18
Psorcon 416
psoriasis
  causes 414
  described 413–14
  diagnosis 414–15
  treatment 415–19
psychogenic stressors
  defined 556
  described 15
psychological disorders
  job-related stress 116
  stress 334–35
"Psychology at Work: The Different Kinds of Stress" (Miller; Smith) 37n
psychosocial therapy, substance abuse 88–89
psychosomatic seven, described 3
psychostimulant medications, cancer 203
psychotherapy
  cancer 203
  depression 173, 185–86
  post-traumatic stress disorder 284, 295
  see also counseling
psychotropic medications 185
  see also antidepressant medications
PTSD *see* post-traumatic stress disorder
pustular psoriasis, described 414–15
PUVA therapy *see* phototherapy

Q

"Questions and Answers about Psoriasis" (NIAMS) 399n
"Questions and Answers about Rosacea" (NIAMS) 399n

R

racial factor
  depression 211
  religious activity 522
  suicide 222–23, 224–25
radon exposure, health risk assessments 44
railway spine disorder, described 264
RAINN *see* Rape, Abuse, and Incest National Network
Rape, Abuse, and Incest National Network (RAINN), contact information 287, 564
rape trauma syndrome, described 264
Rappaport, Mary 231, 236
Ravn, Pernille 205
Reade, Barbara 33n, 252n
Reinberg, Steven 127n
relaxation response, described 8
relaxation training, stress reduction 355, 396–97, 460
religion *see* spiritual support
"Reliving Trauma: Post-Traumatic Stress Disorder" (NIMH) 272n
Remeron 234
"Research Brings Hope for Veterans and Millions of Other Americans Who Suffer from Post-Traumatic Stress Disorder" (NIMH) 272n
resilience
  defined 556
  described 69–70
retinoids 417, 419
retrospective studies, defined 556
rhinophyma 422
Robbins, Lewis C. 42
"The Role of Acute and Chronic Stress in Asthma Attacks in Children" (Sandberg, et al.) 425n

"The Role of Stress in Alcohol Use, Alcoholism Treatment, and Relapse" (Brady; Sonne) 77n
rosacea 420–23
Rose, Robert M. 7
Rosenman, Ray 8, 38–39
rumination, defined 556

S

SAD *see* seasonal affective disorder
St. John's Wort, depression 174, 235
salicylic acid 417
Sandberg, Seija 425n
Sandimmune (cyclosporine) 235
Sauter, Steven 110n
Schanberg, Saul 324, 331
Scharf, Frederick, Jr. 110n
Schneiderman, Neil 333
seasonal affective disorder (SAD)
    described 233
    treatment 238–39
seat belt use, health risk assessments 44
seborrheic eczema, defined 401
selective serotonin reuptake inhibitors (SSRI)
    alcohol use 82, 88
    depression 184–85, 219, 234
    described 173
    post-traumatic stress disorder 274, 283
    substance abuse 87
    suicide 226
Selye, Hans 5–6, 163
sensitization
    defined 557
    stressors 24–25
serotonin
    alcohol use 78, 82
    defined 557
    depression 184
    heart disease 348–50
    stress response 18–19, 80, 323, 331
    suicide 226
sertraline 87–88
Serzone 234
sex
    defined 557
    stress 320–21

sexual orientation, suicide 224
shell shock, described 264, 279–80
shock therapy *see* electroconvulsive therapy
Sinclair, Raymond 110n
skin conditions, stress 399–424
Slater, Eliot 4
Smith, Alma Dell 37n
Smith, Suzanna 57n
smoke detectors, health risk assessments 44
smoking *see* tobacco use
smoking cessation, stress levels 93–94, 96–97
"Social Inequality Harms Health, Sociologist Says" (Persons) 157n
social stressors, described 7
social support
    family stress 63–64
    inequality 157–58
"Social Support, Stress and the Common Cold" (Cohen) 319n
sodium amytal 164
soldier's heart, described 264
somatic reflex potentiation, described 341
"Some CFS Patients Benefit from Low-Dose Steroid, But Side Effects Too Risky" (NIAID) 337n
Sonne, Susan C. 77n
Soriatane (acitretin) 419
Speed of Balance (Childre) 537–39
Spencer, Robert L. 431n
spiritual support
    family stress 63–64
    stress management 513–23
SRD *see* stress-response dampening
SSRI *see* selective serotonin reuptake inhibitors
stasis dermatitis, defined 401
"Staying Strong at Any Age" (Bruce) 465n
Sternberg, Esther 164, 359–63
Stocker, Steven 103n
"Stomach and Duodenal Ulcers" (NIDDK) 375n
Stoney, Catharine 324–25
Straus, Stephen E. 343–45

stress
  benefits 361
  causes 350–51
  coping strategies 352–55
  defined 13–15, 490–91, 557
  depression 178
  described 79–81
  families 57–67
  health risk assessments 44
  memory improvement 309
  origin 3–11
  post-traumatic stress disorder 273
  questions and answers 458–64
  reaction 483–84
  symptoms 33–35
  types, described 37–40
  warning signs 351, 396
"Stress" (Reade) 33n
"Stress and Deprivation" (NLM) 3
"Stress and Heart Disease" (Cleveland
  Clinic Foundation) 347n
"Stress and MS" (Cleveland Clinic
  Foundation) 395n
"Stress and Substance Abuse: A Special Report" (NIDA) 307n
"Stress and the Developing Brain"
  (NIMH) 337n
"Stress at Work" (NIOSH) 110n,
  551n
"Stress - Coping with Everyday Problems" (NMHA) 457n
"Stress Hormone Levels in Women
  Reduced During Lactation" (NIMH)
  381n
stress hormones
  addictions 81–82, 105
  brain development 337–38
  caffeine 357
  regulation 441–44
  see also hormones
"Stress - It Might Be Even Worse
  Than You Think" (Davis) 319n
stress management
  acute trauma 253–61
  biofeedback 525–33
  caregivers 152–54
  deep breathing 470
  defined 555
  described 484–88

stress management, continued
  employee assistance programs
    117–18
  everyday problems 457–64
  families 61–66
  heart rate 367
  multiple sclerosis 396–97
  muscle relaxation 470
  music therapy 535–40
  physical activity 465–82
  psychosocial therapy 88–89
  stretching 470–71, 477
"Stress Management: Strategies for
  Families" (Smith; Pergola) 57n
stressors
  characteristics 15–21
  coping strategies 352, 353
  defined 13–14, 558
  described 5, 6, 79, 350–51
  drug abuse 104
  environmental
    defined 554
    described 15
  ethological
    defined 554
    described 16
  experimental, defined 554
  families 57–61
  job-related 113–14, 118, *134*
  neurogenic
    defined 555
    described 15
  processive
    defined 556
    described 15–16
  psychogenic
    defined 556
    described 15
  social, described 7
  systemic
    defined 558
    described 15–16
stress prevention programs 122–24
stress response
  alcohol use 431–54
  defined 557
  described 14, 79–80, 308
  evalutation 15–18
  regulation 27–28, *28*

stress-response dampening (SRD)
  alcohol use 84, 490–91
  defined 557
stress response systems, defined 557
*The Stress Solution: An Action Plan
  to Manage the Stress in Your Life*
  (Miller; Smith) 37n
stress syndrome, described 5, 163
stroke
  depression 200–201
  personality traits 169–70
"Strong Under Stress, Factors in the
  Development of Resilience in Children" (Powell) 69n, 551n
"Studies Link Stress and Drug Addiction" (Stocker) 103n
"Study Finds Control Has Role in
  Health Effects of Hard-Driving Personality" (Duke University Medical
  Center) 167n
Suarez, Edward 348–50
substance abuse
  depression 179–80, 204
  relapse 307–10
  stress 81–90, 103–7
  suicide attempts 215
  suicide risk 227–28
  women 391–92
  see also alcohol use; drug abuse; to-
    bacco use
suicide
  age factor 218–21
  assisted 225–26
  bereavement 507
  depression 172–74, 179, 214–29
  job-related stress 116
  older adults 218–21
  preventive measures 215–16
  questions and answers 221–29
  statistics 214–15
suicide contagion, described 228
Suicide Prevention Advocacy Network, contact information 229, 565
support groups
  depression 236
  family stress 63–64
  panic disorder 250
Surwit, Richard 324
Swanson, Naomi 110n

systemic stressors
  defined 558
  described 15–16

T

tailshock, described 16–17
target heart rate chart 477
tazarotene 417
Tazorac (tazarotene) 417
Temovate 416
temporal lobe, defined 553
"10 Steps to Manage Your Stress"
  (Cleveland Clinic Foundation) 457n
testicular self-examinations, health
  risk assessments 44
tetracycline 422
thalamus, described 341–42
Tisdale, Julie 110n
tobacco use
  health risk assessments 44
  relapse 310
  stress 93–102
  ulcers 377
  women 391–92
  see also smoking cessation; sub-
    stance abuse
Tofranil (imipramine) 234
tolerance, defined 558
transient situational disturbance, described 264
trauma
  children 289–93
    research 295–97
  described 252–53, 265, 289
  responses 260
"Trauma Facts" (Reade) 252n
traumatic neurosis, described 264
traumatic stress 252–72
"Traumatic Stress: An Overview"
  (Volpe) 252n
tricyclic antidepressants
  depression 184–85, 219, 234
  described 173
triglyceride levels, stress 326–27
Tuma, Farris 276–78
tumor necrosis factor alpha 349
tunnel disease, described 264

Tuohy, Patricia 164
Twombly, Renee 347n
type-A behavior pattern
  described 7–8
  episodic acute stress 38–39
  magnesium supplements 480
  stress 168, 323

U

ulcers
  job-related stress 116
  peptic 3–4
  stress 375–80
Ultravate 416
"Understanding Stress: Characteristics and Caveats" (Anisman; Merali) 13n
US Department of Education, contact information 303, 565
US Department of Justice, contact information 303, 565
US National Library of Medicine (NLM), stress publication 3n

V

vasopressin 393–94
victimization, depression 211–12
Volpe, Joseph S. 252n, 288n
Volvo Truck Corporation 8

W

Wallace, Mike 236
warfarin 235
war neurosis, described 264
weight control, physical activity 473–74
Weight-Control Information Network, contact information 482, 565
weight training, stress management 467–68
Wellbutrin 234
Wellsource, Inc., stress publication 465n
Wernicke-Korsakoff syndrome 451

"What Do These Students Have in Common" (NIMH) 172n
"Why Is Caregiving Often Stressful?" (North Carolina DHHS) 149n
Williams, Redford 128–30, 169, 323
Wolff, Harold G. 5
women
  alcohol use 82–83
  autoimmune diseases 388–89
  caffeine 358
  cancer 383–85
  depression 189–90, 205–7, 209–13
  digestive diseases 389–91
  heart disease 382–83
  hypertension 522
  mental disorders 385–86
  musculoskeletal diseases 387–88
  post-traumatic stress disorder 273, 311
  stress 381–94
  stress hormone levels 393–94
  substance abuse 391–3927
  suicide 222
  workplace stress 127–30
workplace stress *see* job stress; occupations
"Workplace Stress Can Lead to Declines in Overall Health of Working Women" (Reinberg) 127n
"Work Stress and Alcohol Use" (Frone) 130n
worry warts 39
wound healing, stress 332
Wozniak, Marcella A. 167n

Y

Yalom, I.D. 519
Yehuda, Rachel 320, 327–28
yoga, depression 236
YOU*First* Health Assessment 43, 46
YOU*First* Health Risk Assessment 41n
"Young People Are Most Susceptible to Panic Disorder" (NIMH) 241n

Z

Zoloft (sertraline hydrochloride) 234, 283

Health Reference Series
COMPLETE CATALOG

Adolescent Health Sourcebook

Basic Consumer Health Information about Common Medical, Mental, and Emotional Concerns in Adolescents, Including Facts about Acne, Body Piercing, Mononucleosis, Nutrition, Eating Disorders, Stress, Depression, Behavior Problems, Peer Pressure, Violence, Gangs, Drug Use, Puberty, Sexuality, Pregnancy, Learning Disabilities, and More

Along with a Glossary of Terms and Other Resources for Further Help and Information

Edited by Chad T. Kimball. 658 pages. 2002. 0-7808-0248-9. $78.

AIDS Sourcebook, 1st Edition

Basic Information about AIDS and HIV Infection, Featuring Historical and Statistical Data, Current Research, Prevention, and Other Special Topics of Interest for Persons Living with AIDS

Along with Source Listings for Further Assistance

Edited by Karen Bellenir and Peter D. Dresser. 831 pages. 1995. 0-7808-0031-1. $78.

"One strength of this book is its practical emphasis. The intended audience is the lay reader . . . useful as an educational tool for health care providers who work with AIDS patients. Recommended for public libraries as well as hospital or academic libraries that collect consumer materials."
— *Bulletin of the Medical Library Association, Jan '96*

"This is the most comprehensive volume of its kind on an important medical topic. Highly recommended for all libraries."
— *Reference Book Review, '96*

"Very useful reference for all libraries."
— *Choice, Association of College and Research Libraries, Oct '95*

"There is a wealth of information here that can provide much educational assistance. It is a must book for all libraries and should be on the desk of each and every congressional leader. Highly recommended."
— *AIDS Book Review Journal, Aug '95*

"Recommended for most collections."
— *Library Journal, Jul '95*

AIDS Sourcebook, 2nd Edition

Basic Consumer Health Information about Acquired Immune Deficiency Syndrome (AIDS) and Human Immunodeficiency Virus (HIV) Infection, Featuring Updated Statistical Data, Reports on Recent Research and Prevention Initiatives, and Other Special Topics of Interest for Persons Living with AIDS, Including New Antiretroviral Treatment Options, Strategies for Com-

bating Opportunistic Infections, Information about Clinical Trials, and More

Along with a Glossary of Important Terms and Resource Listings for Further Help and Information

Edited by Karen Bellenir. 751 pages. 1999. 0-7808-0225-X. $78.

"Highly recommended."
— *American Reference Books Annual, 2000*

"Excellent sourcebook. This continues to be a highly recommended book. There is no other book that provides as much information as this book provides."
— *AIDS Book Review Journal, Dec-Jan 2000*

"Recommended reference source."
— *Booklist, American Library Association, Dec '99*

"A solid text for college-level health libraries."
— *The Bookwatch, Aug '99*

Cited in *Reference Sources for Small and Medium-Sized Libraries, American Library Association, 1999*

Alcoholism Sourcebook

Basic Consumer Health Information about the Physical and Mental Consequences of Alcohol Abuse, Including Liver Disease, Pancreatitis, Wernicke-Korsakoff Syndrome (Alcoholic Dementia), Fetal Alcohol Syndrome, Heart Disease, Kidney Disorders, Gastrointestinal Problems, and Immune System Compromise and Featuring Facts about Addiction, Detoxification, Alcohol Withdrawal, Recovery, and the Maintenance of Sobriety

Along with a Glossary and Directories of Resources for Further Help and Information

Edited by Karen Bellenir. 613 pages. 2000. 0-7808-0325-6. $78.

"This title is one of the few reference works on alcoholism for general readers. For some readers this will be a welcome complement to the many self-help books on the market. Recommended for collections serving general readers and consumer health collections."
— *E-Streams, Mar '01*

"This book is an excellent choice for public and academic libraries."
— *American Reference Books Annual, 2001*

"Recommended reference source."
— *Booklist, American Library Association, Dec '00*

"Presents a wealth of information on alcohol use and abuse and its effects on the body and mind, treatment, and prevention." — *SciTech Book News, Dec '00*

"Important new health guide which packs in the latest consumer information about the problems of alcoholism." — *Reviewer's Bookwatch, Nov '00*

SEE ALSO Drug Abuse Sourcebook, Substance Abuse Sourcebook

Allergies Sourcebook, 1st Edition

Basic Information about Major Forms and Mechanisms of Common Allergic Reactions, Sensitivities, and Intolerances, Including Anaphylaxis, Asthma, Hives and Other Dermatologic Symptoms, Rhinitis, and Sinusitis

Along with Their Usual Triggers Like Animal Fur, Chemicals, Drugs, Dust, Foods, Insects, Latex, Pollen, and Poison Ivy, Oak, and Sumac; Plus Information on Prevention, Identification, and Treatment

Edited by Allan R. Cook. 611 pages. 1997. 0-7808-0036-2. $78.

■

Allergies Sourcebook, 2nd Edition

Basic Consumer Health Information about Allergic Disorders, Triggers, Reactions, and Related Symptoms, Including Anaphylaxis, Rhinitis, Sinusitis, Asthma, Dermatitis, Conjunctivitis, and Multiple Chemical Sensitivity

Along with Tips on Diagnosis, Prevention, and Treatment, Statistical Data, a Glossary, and a Directory of Sources for Further Help and Information

Edited by Annemarie S. Muth. 598 pages. 2002. 0-7808-0376-0. $78.

■

Alternative Medicine Sourcebook, First Edition

Basic Consumer Health Information about Alternatives to Conventional Medicine, Including Acupressure, Acupuncture, Aromatherapy, Ayurveda, Bioelectromagnetics, Environmental Medicine, Essence Therapy, Food and Nutrition Therapy, Herbal Therapy, Homeopathy, Imaging, Massage, Naturopathy, Reflexology, Relaxation and Meditation, Sound Therapy, Vitamin and Mineral Therapy, and Yoga, and More

Edited by Allan R. Cook. 737 pages. 1999. 0-7808-0200-4. $78.

"Recommended reference source."
—*Booklist, American Library Association, Feb '00*

"A great addition to the reference collection of every type of library." —*American Reference Books Annual, 2000*

■

Alternative Medicine Sourcebook, Second Edition

Basic Consumer Health Information about Alternative and Complementary Medical Practices, Including Acupuncture, Chiropractic, Herbal Medicine, Homeopathy, Naturopathic Medicine, Mind-Body Interventions, Ayurveda, and Other Non-Western Medical Traditions

Along with Facts about such Specific Therapies as Massage Therapy, Aromatherapy, Qigong, Hypnosis, Prayer, Dance, and Art Therapies, a Glossary, and Resources for Further Information

Edited by Dawn D. Matthews. 618 pages. 2002. 0-7808-0605-0. $78.

Alzheimer's, Stroke & 29 Other Neurological Disorders Sourcebook, 1st Edition

Basic Information for the Layperson on 31 Diseases or Disorders Affecting the Brain and Nervous System, First Describing the Illness, Then Listing Symptoms, Diagnostic Methods, and Treatment Options, and Including Statistics on Incidences and Causes

Edited by Frank E. Bair. 579 pages. 1993. 1-55888-748-2. $78.

"Nontechnical reference book that provides reader-friendly information."
—*Family Caregiver Alliance Update, Winter '96*

"Should be included in any library's patient education section." —*American Reference Books Annual, 1994*

"Written in an approachable and accessible style. Recommended for patient education and consumer health collections in health science center and public libraries." —*Academic Library Book Review, Dec '93*

"It is very handy to have information on more than thirty neurological disorders under one cover, and there is no recent source like it." —*Reference Quarterly, American Library Association, Fall '93*

SEE ALSO Brain Disorders Sourcebook

■

Alzheimer's Disease Sourcebook, 2nd Edition

Basic Consumer Health Information about Alzheimer's Disease, Related Disorders, and Other Dementias, Including Multi-Infarct Dementia, AIDS-Related Dementia, Alcoholic Dementia, Huntington's Disease, Delirium, and Confusional States

Along with Reports Detailing Current Research Efforts in Prevention and Treatment, Long-Term Care Issues, and Listings of Sources for Additional Help and Information

Edited by Karen Bellenir. 524 pages. 1999. 0-7808-0223-3. $78.

"Provides a wealth of useful information not otherwise available in one place. This resource is recommended for all types of libraries."
—*American Reference Books Annual, 2000*

"Recommended reference source."
—*Booklist, American Library Association, Oct '99*

■

Arthritis Sourcebook

Basic Consumer Health Information about Specific Forms of Arthritis and Related Disorders, Including Rheumatoid Arthritis, Osteoarthritis, Gout, Polymyalgia Rheumatica, Psoriatic Arthritis, Spondyloarthropathies, Juvenile Rheumatoid Arthritis, and Juvenile Ankylosing Spondylitis

Along with Information about Medical, Surgical, and Alternative Treatment Options, and Including Strategies for Coping with Pain, Fatigue, and Stress

Edited by Allan R. Cook. 550 pages. 1998. 0-7808-0201-2. $78.

"... accessible to the layperson."
—*Reference and Research Book News, Feb '99*

■

Asthma Sourcebook

Basic Consumer Health Information about Asthma, Including Symptoms, Traditional and Nontraditional Remedies, Treatment Advances, Quality-of-Life Aids, Medical Research Updates, and the Role of Allergies, Exercise, Age, the Environment, and Genetics in the Development of Asthma

Along with Statistical Data, a Glossary, and Directories of Support Groups, and Other Resources for Further Information

Edited by Annemarie S. Muth. 628 pages. 2000. 0-7808-0381-7. $78.

"**A worthwhile reference acquisition for public libraries and academic medical libraries whose readers desire a quick introduction to the wide range of asthma information.**" — *Choice, Association of College & Research Libraries, Jun '01*

"**Recommended reference source.**"
— *Booklist, American Library Association, Feb '01*

"**Highly recommended.**" — *The Bookwatch, Jan '01*

"**There is much good information for patients and their families who deal with asthma daily.**"
— *American Medical Writers Association Journal, Winter '01*

"**This informative text is recommended for consumer health collections in public, secondary school, and community college libraries and the libraries of universities with a large undergraduate population.**"
— *American Reference Books Annual, 2001*

■

Attention Deficit Disorder Sourcebook, First Edition

Basic Consumer Health Information about Attention Deficit/Hyperactivity Disorder in Children and Adults, Including Facts about Causes, Symptoms, Diagnostic Criteria, and Treatment Options Such as Medications, Behavior Therapy, Coaching, and Homeopathy

Along with Reports on Current Research Initiatives, Legal Issues, and Government Regulations, and Featuring a Glossary of Related Terms, Internet Resources, and a List of Additional Reading Material

Edited by Dawn D. Matthews. 450 pages. 2002. 0-7808-0624-7. $78.

Back & Neck Disorders Sourcebook

Basic Information about Disorders and Injuries of the Spinal Cord and Vertebrae, Including Facts on Chiropractic Treatment, Surgical Interventions, Paralysis, and Rehabilitation

Along with Advice for Preventing Back Trouble

Edited by Karen Bellenir. 548 pages. 1997. 0-7808-0202-0. $78.

"**The strength of this work is its basic, easy-to-read format. Recommended.**"
— *Reference and User Services Quarterly, American Library Association, Winter '97*

■

Blood & Circulatory Disorders Sourcebook

Basic Information about Blood and Its Components, Anemias, Leukemias, Bleeding Disorders, and Circulatory Disorders, Including Aplastic Anemia, Thalassemia, Sickle-Cell Disease, Hemochromatosis, Hemophilia, Von Willebrand Disease, and Vascular Diseases

Along with a Special Section on Blood Transfusions and Blood Supply Safety, a Glossary, and Source Listings for Further Help and Information

Edited by Karen Bellenir and Linda M. Shin. 554 pages. 1998. 0-7808-0203-9. $78.

"**Recommended reference source.**"
— *Booklist, American Library Association, Feb '99*

"**An important reference sourcebook written in simple language for everyday, non-technical users.**"
— *Reviewer's Bookwatch, Jan '99*

■

Brain Disorders Sourcebook

Basic Consumer Health Information about Strokes, Epilepsy, Amyotrophic Lateral Sclerosis (ALS/Lou Gehrig's Disease), Parkinson's Disease, Brain Tumors, Cerebral Palsy, Headache, Tourette Syndrome, and More

Along with Statistical Data, Treatment and Rehabilitation Options, Coping Strategies, Reports on Current Research Initiatives, a Glossary, and Resource Listings for Additional Help and Information

Edited by Karen Bellenir. 481 pages. 1999. 0-7808-0229-2. $78.

"**Belongs on the shelves of any library with a consumer health collection.**" — *E-Streams, Mar '00*

"**Recommended reference source.**"
— *Booklist, American Library Association, Oct '99*

SEE ALSO *Alzheimer's, Stroke & 29 Other Neurological Disorders Sourcebook, 1st Edition*

Breast Cancer Sourcebook

Basic Consumer Health Information about Breast Cancer, Including Diagnostic Methods, Treatment Options, Alternative Therapies, Self-Help Information, Related Health Concerns, Statistical and Demographic Data, and Facts for Men with Breast Cancer

Along with Reports on Current Research Initiatives, a Glossary of Related Medical Terms, and a Directory of Sources for Further Help and Information

Edited by Edward J. Prucha and Karen Bellenir. 580 pages. 2001. 0-7808-0244-6. $78.

"Recommended reference source."
— *Booklist, American Library Association, Jan '02*

"This reference source is highly recommended. It is quite informative, comprehensive and detailed in nature, and yet it offers practical advice in easy-to-read language. It could be thought of as the 'bible' of breast cancer for the consumer." — *E-Streams, Jan '02*

"The broad range of topics covered in lay language make the *Breast Cancer Sourcebook* an excellent addition to public and consumer health library collections."
— *American Reference Books Annual 2002*

"From the pros and cons of different screening methods and results to treatment options, *Breast Cancer Sourcebook* provides the latest information on the subject."
— *Library Bookwatch, Dec '01*

"This thoroughgoing, very readable reference covers all aspects of breast health and cancer. . . . Readers will find much to consider here. Recommended for all public and patient health collections."
— *Library Journal, Sep '01*

SEE ALSO *Cancer Sourcebook for Women, 1st and 2nd Editions, Women's Health Concerns Sourcebook*

■

Breastfeeding Sourcebook

Basic Consumer Health Information about the Benefits of Breastmilk, Preparing to Breastfeed, Breastfeeding as a Baby Grows, Nutrition, and More, Including Information on Special Situations and Concerns Such as Mastitis, Illness, Medications, Allergies, Multiple Births, Prematurity, Special Needs, and Adoption

Along with a Glossary and Resources for Additional Help and Information

Edited by Jenni Lynn Colson. 388 pages. 2002. 0-7808-0332-9. $78.

SEE ALSO *Pregnancy & Birth Sourcebook*

■

Burns Sourcebook

Basic Consumer Health Information about Various Types of Burns and Scalds, Including Flame, Heat, Cold, Electrical, Chemical, and Sun Burns

Along with Information on Short-Term and Long-Term Treatments, Tissue Reconstruction, Plastic Surgery, Prevention Suggestions, and First Aid

Edited by Allan R. Cook. 604 pages. 1999. 0-7808-0204-7. $78.

"This is an exceptional addition to the series and is highly recommended for all consumer health collections, hospital libraries, and academic medical centers."
— *E-Streams, Mar '00*

"This key reference guide is an invaluable addition to all health care and public libraries in confronting this ongoing health issue."
— *American Reference Books Annual, 2000*

"Recommended reference source."
— *Booklist, American Library Association, Dec '99*

SEE ALSO *Skin Disorders Sourcebook*

■

Cancer Sourcebook, 1st Edition

Basic Information on Cancer Types, Symptoms, Diagnostic Methods, and Treatments, Including Statistics on Cancer Occurrences Worldwide and the Risks Associated with Known Carcinogens and Activities

Edited by Frank E. Bair. 932 pages. 1990. 1-55888-888-8. $78.

Cited in *Reference Sources for Small and Medium-Sized Libraries, American Library Association, 1999*

"Written in nontechnical language. Useful for patients, their families, medical professionals, and librarians."
— *Guide to Reference Books, 1996*

"Designed with the non-medical professional in mind. Libraries and medical facilities interested in patient education should certainly consider adding the *Cancer Sourcebook* to their holdings. This compact collection of reliable information . . . is an invaluable tool for helping patients and patients' families and friends to take the first steps in coping with the many difficulties of cancer."
— *Medical Reference Services Quarterly, Winter '91*

"Specifically created for the nontechnical reader . . . an important resource for the general reader trying to understand the complexities of cancer."
— *American Reference Books Annual, 1991*

"This publication's nontechnical nature and very comprehensive format make it useful for both the general public and undergraduate students."
— *Choice, Association of College and Research Libraries, Oct '90*

■

New Cancer Sourcebook, 2nd Edition

Basic Information about Major Forms and Stages of Cancer, Featuring Facts about Primary and Secondary Tumors of the Respiratory, Nervous, Lymphatic, Circulatory, Skeletal, and Gastrointestinal Systems, and Specific Organs; Statistical and Demographic Data; Treatment Options; and Strategies for Coping

Edited by Allan R. Cook. 1,313 pages. 1996. 0-7808-0041-9. $78.

"An excellent resource for patients with newly diagnosed cancer and their families. The dialogue is simple, direct, and comprehensive. Highly recommended for patients and families to aid in their understanding of cancer and its treatment."

— *Booklist Health Sciences Supplement, American Library Association, Oct '97*

"The amount of factual and useful information is extensive. The writing is very clear, geared to general readers. Recommended for all levels."   — *Choice, Association of College & Research Libraries, Jan '97*

■

Cancer Sourcebook, 3rd Edition

Basic Consumer Health Information about Major Forms and Stages of Cancer, Featuring Facts about Primary and Secondary Tumors of the Respiratory, Nervous, Lymphatic, Circulatory, Skeletal, and Gastrointestinal Systems, and Specific Organs

Along with Statistical and Demographic Data, Treatment Options, Strategies for Coping, a Glossary, and a Directory of Sources for Additional Help and Information

Edited by Edward J. Prucha. 1,069 pages. 2000. 0-7808-0227-6. $78.

"This title is recommended for health sciences and public libraries with consumer health collections."
— *E-Streams, Feb '01*

". . . can be effectively used by cancer patients and their families who are looking for answers in a language they can understand. Public and hospital libraries should have it on their shelves."
— *American Reference Books Annual, 2001*

"Recommended reference source."
—*Booklist, American Library Association, Dec '00*

■

Cancer Sourcebook for Women, 1st Edition

Basic Information about Specific Forms of Cancer That Affect Women, Featuring Facts about Breast Cancer, Cervical Cancer, Ovarian Cancer, Cancer of the Uterus and Uterine Sarcoma, Cancer of the Vagina, and Cancer of the Vulva; Statistical and Demographic Data; Treatments, Self-Help Management Suggestions, and Current Research Initiatives

Edited by Allan R. Cook and Peter D. Dresser. 524 pages. 1996. 0-7808-0076-1. $78.

". . . written in easily understandable, non-technical language. Recommended for public libraries or hospital and academic libraries that collect patient education or consumer health materials."
— *Medical Reference Services Quarterly, Spring '97*

"Would be of value in a consumer health library. . . . written with the health care consumer in mind. Medical jargon is at a minimum, and medical terms are explained in clear, understandable sentences."
— *Bulletin of the Medical Library Association, Oct '96*

"The availability under one cover of all these pertinent publications, grouped under cohesive headings, makes this certainly a most useful sourcebook."   — *Choice, Association of College & Research Libraries, Jun '96*

"Presents a comprehensive knowledge base for general readers. Men and women both benefit from the gold mine of information nestled between the two covers of this book. Recommended."
—*Academic Library Book Review, Summer '96*

"This timely book is highly recommended for consumer health and patient education collections in all libraries."   — *Library Journal, Apr '96*

SEE ALSO *Breast Cancer Sourcebook, Women's Health Concerns Sourcebook*

■

Cancer Sourcebook for Women, 2nd Edition

Basic Consumer Health Information about Gynecologic Cancers and Related Concerns, Including Cervical Cancer, Endometrial Cancer, Gestational Trophoblastic Tumor, Ovarian Cancer, Uterine Cancer, Vaginal Cancer, Vulvar Cancer, Breast Cancer, and Common Non-Cancerous Uterine Conditions, with Facts about Cancer Risk Factors, Screening and Prevention, Treatment Options, and Reports on Current Research Initiatives

Along with a Glossary of Cancer Terms and a Directory of Resources for Additional Help and Information

Edited by Karen Bellenir. 604 pages. 2002. 0-7808-0226-8. $78.

SEE ALSO *Breast Cancer Sourcebook, Women's Health Concerns Sourcebook*

■

Cardiovascular Diseases & Disorders Sourcebook, 1st Edition

Basic Information about Cardiovascular Diseases and Disorders, Featuring Facts about the Cardiovascular System, Demographic and Statistical Data, Descriptions of Pharmacological and Surgical Interventions, Lifestyle Modifications, and a Special Section Focusing on Heart Disorders in Children

Edited by Karen Bellenir and Peter D. Dresser. 683 pages. 1995. 0-7808-0032-X. $78.

". . . comprehensive format provides an extensive overview on this subject."   — *Choice, Association of College & Research Libraries, Jun '96*

". . . an easily understood, complete, up-to-date resource. This well executed public health tool will make valuable information available to those that need it most, patients and their families. The typeface, sturdy non-reflective paper, and library binding add a feel of quality found wanting in other publications. Highly recommended for academic and general libraries. "
—*Academic Library Book Review, Summer '96*

SEE ALSO *Healthy Heart Sourcebook for Women, Heart Diseases & Disorders Sourcebook, 2nd Edition*

Caregiving Sourcebook

Basic Consumer Health Information for Caregivers, Including a Profile of Caregivers, Caregiving Responsibilities and Concerns, Tips for Specific Conditions, Care Environments, and the Effects of Caregiving

Along with Facts about Legal Issues, Financial Information, and Future Planning, a Glossary, and a Listing of Additional Resources

Edited by Joyce Brennfleck Shannon. 600 pages. 2001. 0-7808-0331-0. $78.

"Essential for most collections."
— *Library Journal, Apr 1, 2002*

"An ideal addition to the reference collection of any public library. Health sciences information professionals may also want to acquire the *Caregiving Sourcebook* for their hospital or academic library for use as a ready reference tool by health care workers interested in aging and caregiving." — *E-Streams, Jan '02*

"Recommended reference source."
— *Booklist, American Library Association, Oct '01*

Colds, Flu & Other Common Ailments Sourcebook

Basic Consumer Health Information about Common Ailments and Injuries, Including Colds, Coughs, the Flu, Sinus Problems, Headaches, Fever, Nausea and Vomiting, Menstrual Cramps, Diarrhea, Constipation, Hemorrhoids, Back Pain, Dandruff, Dry and Itchy Skin, Cuts, Scrapes, Sprains, Bruises, and More

Along with Information about Prevention, Self-Care, Choosing a Doctor, Over-the-Counter Medications, Folk Remedies, and Alternative Therapies, and Including a Glossary of Important Terms and a Directory of Resources for Further Help and Information

Edited by Chad T. Kimball. 638 pages. 2001. 0-7808-0435-X. $78.

"A good starting point for research on common illnesses. It will be a useful addition to public and consumer health library collections."
— *American Reference Books Annual 2002*

"Will prove valuable to any library seeking to maintain a current, comprehensive reference collection of health resources. . . . Excellent reference."
— *The Bookwatch, Aug '01*

"Recommended reference source."
— *Booklist, American Library Association, July '01*

Communication Disorders Sourcebook

Basic Information about Deafness and Hearing Loss, Speech and Language Disorders, Voice Disorders, Balance and Vestibular Disorders, and Disorders of Smell, Taste, and Touch

Edited by Linda M. Ross. 533 pages. 1996. 0-7808-0077-X. $78.

"This is skillfully edited and is a welcome resource for the layperson. It should be found in every public and medical library." — *Booklist Health Sciences Supplement, American Library Association, Oct '97*

Congenital Disorders Sourcebook

Basic Information about Disorders Acquired during Gestation, Including Spina Bifida, Hydrocephalus, Cerebral Palsy, Heart Defects, Craniofacial Abnormalities, Fetal Alcohol Syndrome, and More

Along with Current Treatment Options and Statistical Data

Edited by Karen Bellenir. 607 pages. 1997. 0-7808-0205-5. $78.

"Recommended reference source."
— *Booklist, American Library Association, Oct '97*

SEE ALSO *Pregnancy & Birth Sourcebook*

Consumer Issues in Health Care Sourcebook

Basic Information about Health Care Fundamentals and Related Consumer Issues, Including Exams and Screening Tests, Physician Specialties, Choosing a Doctor, Using Prescription and Over-the-Counter Medications Safely, Avoiding Health Scams, Managing Common Health Risks in the Home, Care Options for Chronically or Terminally Ill Patients, and a List of Resources for Obtaining Help and Further Information

Edited by Karen Bellenir. 618 pages. 1998. 0-7808-0221-7. $78.

"Both public and academic libraries will want to have a copy in their collection for readers who are interested in self-education on health issues."
— *American Reference Books Annual, 2000*

"The editor has researched the literature from government agencies and others, saving readers the time and effort of having to do the research themselves. Recommended for public libraries."
— *Reference and User Services Quarterly, American Library Association, Spring '99*

"Recommended reference source."
— *Booklist, American Library Association, Dec '98*

Contagious & Non-Contagious Infectious Diseases Sourcebook

Basic Information about Contagious Diseases like Measles, Polio, Hepatitis B, and Infectious Mononucleosis, and Non-Contagious Infectious Diseases like Tetanus and Toxic Shock Syndrome, and Diseases Occurring as Secondary Infections Such as Shingles and Reye Syndrome

Along with Vaccination, Prevention, and Treatment Information, and a Section Describing Emerging Infectious Disease Threats

Edited by Karen Bellenir and Peter D. Dresser. 566 pages. 1996. 0-7808-0075-3. $78.

Death & Dying Sourcebook

Basic Consumer Health Information for the Layperson about End-of-Life Care and Related Ethical and Legal Issues, Including Chief Causes of Death, Autopsies, Pain Management for the Terminally Ill, Life Support Systems, Insurance, Euthanasia, Assisted Suicide, Hospice Programs, Living Wills, Funeral Planning, Counseling, Mourning, Organ Donation, and Physician Training

Along with Statistical Data, a Glossary, and Listings of Sources for Further Help and Information

Edited by Annemarie S. Muth. 641 pages. 1999. 0-7808-0230-6. $78.

"Public libraries, medical libraries, and academic libraries will all find this sourcebook a useful addition to their collections."
— *American Reference Books Annual, 2001*

"An extremely useful resource for those concerned with death and dying in the United States."
— *Respiratory Care, Nov '00*

"Recommended reference source."
— *Booklist, American Library Association, Aug '00*

"This book is a definite must for all those involved in end-of-life care." — *Doody's Review Service, 2000*

■

Diabetes Sourcebook, 1st Edition

Basic Information about Insulin-Dependent and Non-insulin-Dependent Diabetes Mellitus, Gestational Diabetes, and Diabetic Complications, Symptoms, Treatment, and Research Results, Including Statistics on Prevalence, Morbidity, and Mortality

Along with Source Listings for Further Help and Information

Edited by Karen Bellenir and Peter D. Dresser. 827 pages. 1994. 1-55888-751-2. $78.

". . . very informative and understandable for the layperson without being simplistic. It provides a comprehensive overview for laypersons who want a general understanding of the disease or who want to focus on various aspects of the disease."
— *Bulletin of the Medical Library Association, Jan '96*

■

Diabetes Sourcebook, 2nd Edition

Basic Consumer Health Information about Type 1 Diabetes (Insulin-Dependent or Juvenile-Onset Diabetes), Type 2 (Noninsulin-Dependent or Adult-Onset Diabetes), Gestational Diabetes, and Related Disorders, Including Diabetes Prevalence Data, Management Issues, the Role of Diet and Exercise in Controlling Diabetes, Insulin and Other Diabetes Medicines, and Complications of Diabetes Such as Eye Diseases, Periodontal Disease, Amputation, and End-Stage Renal Disease

Along with Reports on Current Research Initiatives, a Glossary, and Resource Listings for Further Help and Information

Edited by Karen Bellenir. 688 pages. 1998. 0-7808-0224-1. $78.

"An invaluable reference." — *Library Journal, May '00*

Selected as one of the 250 "Best Health Sciences Books of 1999." — *Doody's Rating Service, Mar-Apr 2000*

"This comprehensive book is an excellent addition for high school, academic, medical, and public libraries. This volume is highly recommended."
— *American Reference Books Annual, 2000*

"Provides useful information for the general public."
— *Healthlines, University of Michigan Health Management Research Center, Sep/Oct '99*

". . . provides reliable mainstream medical information . . . belongs on the shelves of any library with a consumer health collection." — *E-Streams, Sep '99*

"Recommended reference source."
— *Booklist, American Library Association, Feb '99*

■

Diet & Nutrition Sourcebook, 1st Edition

Basic Information about Nutrition, Including the Dietary Guidelines for Americans, the Food Guide Pyramid, and Their Applications in Daily Diet, Nutritional Advice for Specific Age Groups, Current Nutritional Issues and Controversies, the New Food Label and How to Use It to Promote Healthy Eating, and Recent Developments in Nutritional Research

Edited by Dan R. Harris. 662 pages. 1996. 0-7808-0084-2. $78.

"Useful reference as a food and nutrition sourcebook for the general consumer." — *Booklist Health Sciences Supplement, American Library Association, Oct '97*

"Recommended for public libraries and medical libraries that receive general information requests on nutrition. It is readable and will appeal to those interested in learning more about healthy dietary practices."
— *Medical Reference Services Quarterly, Fall '97*

"An abundance of medical and social statistics is translated into readable information geared toward the general reader." — *Bookwatch, Mar '97*

"With dozens of questionable diet books on the market, it is so refreshing to find a reliable and factual reference book. Recommended to aspiring professionals, librarians, and others seeking and giving reliable dietary advice. An excellent compilation." — *Choice, Association of College and Research Libraries, Feb '97*

SEE ALSO *Digestive Diseases & Disorders Sourcebook, Gastrointestinal Diseases & Disorders Sourcebook*

■

Diet & Nutrition Sourcebook, 2nd Edition

Basic Consumer Health Information about Dietary Guidelines, Recommended Daily Intake Values, Vitamins, Minerals, Fiber, Fat, Weight Control, Dietary Supplements, and Food Additives

Along with Special Sections on Nutrition Needs throughout Life and Nutrition for People with Such Spe-

cific Medical Concerns as Allergies, High Blood Cho-
lesterol, Hypertension, Diabetes, Celiac Disease,
Seizure Disorders, Phenylketonuria (PKU), Cancer, and
Eating Disorders, and Including Reports on Current
Nutrition Research and Source Listings for Additional
Help and Information

Edited by Karen Bellenir. 650 pages. 1999. 0-7808-0228-4. $78.

"This book is an excellent source of basic diet and nutrition information." — *Booklist Health Sciences Supplement, American Library Association, Dec '00*

"This reference document should be in any public library, but it would be a very good guide for beginning students in the health sciences. If the other books in this publisher's series are as good as this, they should all be in the health sciences collections."
— *American Reference Books Annual, 2000*

"This book is an excellent general nutrition reference for consumers who desire to take an active role in their health care for prevention. Consumers of all ages who select this book can feel confident they are receiving current and accurate information." — *Journal of Nutrition for the Elderly, Vol. 19, No. 4, '00*

"Recommended reference source."
— *Booklist, American Library Association, Dec '99*

SEE ALSO *Digestive Diseases & Disorders Sourcebook, Gastrointestinal Diseases & Disorders Sourcebook*

Digestive Diseases & Disorders Sourcebook

Basic Consumer Health Information about Diseases and Disorders that Impact the Upper and Lower Digestive System, Including Celiac Disease, Constipation, Crohn's Disease, Cyclic Vomiting Syndrome, Diarrhea, Diverticulosis and Diverticulitis, Gallstones, Heartburn, Hemorrhoids, Hernias, Indigestion (Dyspepsia), Irritable Bowel Syndrome, Lactose Intolerance, Ulcers, and More

Along with Information about Medications and Other Treatments, Tips for Maintaining a Healthy Digestive Tract, a Glossary, and Directory of Digestive Diseases Organizations

Edited by Karen Bellenir. 335 pages. 2000. 0-7808-0327-2. $78.

"This title would be an excellent addition to all public or patient-research libraries."
— *American Reference Books Annual, 2001*

"This title is recommended for public, hospital, and health sciences libraries with consumer health collections." — *E-Streams, Jul-Aug '00*

"Recommended reference source."
— *Booklist, American Library Association, May '00*

SEE ALSO *Diet & Nutrition Sourcebook, 1st and 2nd Editions, Gastrointestinal Diseases & Disorders Sourcebook*

Disabilities Sourcebook

Basic Consumer Health Information about Physical and Psychiatric Disabilities, Including Descriptions of Major Causes of Disability, Assistive and Adaptive Aids, Workplace Issues, and Accessibility Concerns

Along with Information about the Americans with Disabilities Act, a Glossary, and Resources for Additional Help and Information

Edited by Dawn D. Matthews. 616 pages. 2000. 0-7808-0389-2. $78.

"It is a must for libraries with a consumer health section." — *American Reference Books Annual 2002*

"A much needed addition to the Omnigraphics *Health Reference Series*. A current reference work to provide people with disabilities, their families, caregivers or those who work with them, a broad range of information in one volume, has not been available until now. . . . It is recommended for all public and academic library reference collections." — *E-Streams, May '01*

"An excellent source book in easy-to-read format covering many current topics; highly recommended for all libraries." — *Choice, Association of College and Research Libraries, Jan '01*

"Recommended reference source."
— *Booklist, American Library Association, Jul '00*

"An involving, invaluable handbook."
— *The Bookwatch, May '00*

Domestic Violence & Child Abuse Sourcebook

Basic Consumer Health Information about Spousal/ Partner, Child, Sibling, Parent, and Elder Abuse, Covering Physical, Emotional, and Sexual Abuse, Teen Dating Violence, and Stalking; Includes Information about Hotlines, Safe Houses, Safety Plans, and Other Resources for Support and Assistance, Community Initiatives, and Reports on Current Directions in Research and Treatment

Along with a Glossary, Sources for Further Reading, and Governmental and Non-Governmental Organizations Contact Information

Edited by Helene Henderson. 1,064 pages. 2001. 0-7808-0235-7. $78.

"This is important information. The Web has many resources but this sourcebook fills an important societal need. I am not aware of any other resources of this type." — *Doody's Review Service, Sep '01*

"Recommended for all libraries, scholars, and practitioners." — *Choice, Association of College & Research Libraries, Jul '01*

"Recommended reference source."
— *Booklist, American Library Association, Apr '01*

"Important pick for college-level health reference libraries." — *The Bookwatch, Mar '01*

"Because this problem is so widespread and because this book includes a lot of issues within one volume, this work is recommended for all public libraries."
— *American Reference Books Annual, 2001*

Drug Abuse Sourcebook

Basic Consumer Health Information about Illicit Substances of Abuse and the Diversion of Prescription Medications, Including Depressants, Hallucinogens, Inhalants, Marijuana, Narcotics, Stimulants, and Anabolic Steroids

Along with Facts about Related Health Risks, Treatment Issues, and Substance Abuse Prevention Programs, a Glossary of Terms, Statistical Data, and Directories of Hotline Services, Self-Help Groups, and Organizations Able to Provide Further Information

Edited by Karen Bellenir. 629 pages. 2000. 0-7808-0242-X. $78.

"Containing a wealth of information, this book will be useful to the college student just beginning to explore the topic of substance abuse. This resource belongs in libraries that serve a lower-division undergraduate or community college clientele as well as the general public." — Choice, Association of College and Research Libraries, Jun '01

"Recommended reference source." — Booklist, American Library Association, Feb '01

"Highly recommended." — The Bookwatch, Jan '01

"Even though there is a plethora of books on drug abuse, this volume is recommended for school, public, and college libraries." — American Reference Books Annual, 2001

SEE ALSO Alcoholism Sourcebook, Substance Abuse Sourcebook

Ear, Nose & Throat Disorders Sourcebook

Basic Information about Disorders of the Ears, Nose, Sinus Cavities, Pharynx, and Larynx, Including Ear Infections, Tinnitus, Vestibular Disorders, Allergic and Non-Allergic Rhinitis, Sore Throats, Tonsillitis, and Cancers That Affect the Ears, Nose, Sinuses, and Throat

Along with Reports on Current Research Initiatives, a Glossary of Related Medical Terms, and a Directory of Sources for Further Help and Information

Edited by Karen Bellenir and Linda M. Shin. 576 pages. 1998. 0-7808-0206-3. $78.

"Overall, this sourcebook is helpful for the consumer seeking information on ENT issues. It is recommended for public libraries." — American Reference Books Annual, 1999

"Recommended reference source." — Booklist, American Library Association, Dec '98

Eating Disorders Sourcebook

Basic Consumer Health Information about Eating Disorders, Including Information about Anorexia Nervosa, Bulimia Nervosa, Binge Eating, Body Dysmorphic Disorder, Pica, Laxative Abuse, and Night Eating Syndrome

Along with Information about Causes, Adverse Effects, and Treatment and Prevention Issues, and Featuring a Section on Concerns Specific to Children and Adolescents, a Glossary, and Resources for Further Help and Information

Edited by Dawn D. Matthews. 322 pages. 2001. 0-7808-0335-3. $78.

"Recommended for health science libraries that are open to the public, as well as hospital libraries. This book is a good resource for the consumer who is concerned about eating disorders." — E-Streams, Mar '02

"This volume is another convenient collection of excerpted articles. Recommended for school and public library patrons; lower-division undergraduates; and two-year technical program students." — Choice, Association of College & Research Libraries, Jan '02

"Recommended reference source." — Booklist, American Library Association, Oct '01

Emergency Medical Services Sourcebook

Basic Consumer Health Information about Preventing, Preparing for, and Managing Emergency Situations, When and Who to Call for Help, What to Expect in the Emergency Room, the Emergency Medical Team, Patient Issues, and Current Topics in Emergency Medicine

Along with Statistical Data, a Glossary, and Sources of Additional Help and Information

Edited by Jenni Lynn Colson. 600 pages. 2002. 0-7808-0420-1. $78.

Endocrine & Metabolic Disorders Sourcebook

Basic Information for the Layperson about Pancreatic and Insulin-Related Disorders Such as Pancreatitis, Diabetes, and Hypoglycemia; Adrenal Gland Disorders Such as Cushing's Syndrome, Addison's Disease, and Congenital Adrenal Hyperplasia; Pituitary Gland Disorders Such as Growth Hormone Deficiency, Acromegaly, and Pituitary Tumors; Thyroid Disorders Such as Hypothyroidism, Graves' Disease, Hashimoto's Disease, and Goiter; Hyperparathyroidism; and Other Diseases and Syndromes of Hormone Imbalance or Metabolic Dysfunction

Along with Reports on Current Research Initiatives

Edited by Linda M. Shin. 574 pages. 1998. 0-7808-0207-1. $78.

"Omnigraphics has produced another needed resource for health information consumers." — American Reference Books Annual, 2000

"Recommended reference source." — Booklist, American Library Association, Dec '98

Environmentally Induced Disorders Sourcebook

Basic Information about Diseases and Syndromes Linked to Exposure to Pollutants and Other Substances in Outdoor and Indoor Environments Such as Lead, Asbestos, Formaldehyde, Mercury, Emissions, Noise, and More

Edited by Allan R. Cook. 620 pages. 1997. 0-7808-0083-4. $78.

"Recommended reference source."
 — *Booklist, American Library Association, Sep '98*

"This book will be a useful addition to anyone's library." — *Choice Health Sciences Supplement, Association of College and Research Libraries, May '98*

". . . a good survey of numerous environmentally induced physical disorders . . . a useful addition to anyone's library."
 — *Doody's Health Sciences Book Reviews, Jan '98*

". . . provide[s] introductory information from the best authorities around. Since this volume covers topics that potentially affect everyone, it will surely be one of the most frequently consulted volumes in the *Health Reference Series*." — *Rettig on Reference, Nov '97*

■

Ethnic Diseases Sourcebook

Basic Consumer Health Information for Ethnic and Racial Minority Groups in the United States, Including General Health Indicators and Behaviors, Ethnic Diseases, Genetic Testing, the Impact of Chronic Diseases, Women's Health, Mental Health Issues, and Preventive Health Care Services

Along with a Glossary and a Listing of Additional Resources

Edited by Joyce Brennfleck Shannon. 664 pages. 2001. 0-7808-0336-1. $78.

"Recommended for health sciences libraries where public health programs are a priority."
 — *E-Streams, Jan '02*

"Not many books have been written on this topic to date, and the *Ethnic Diseases Sourcebook* is a strong addition to the list. It will be an important introductory resource for health consumers, students, health care personnel, and social scientists. It is recommended for public, academic, and large hospital libraries."
 — *American Reference Books Annual 2002*

"Recommended reference source."
 — *Booklist, American Library Association, Oct '01*

"Will prove valuable to any library seeking to maintain a current, comprehensive reference collection of health resources. . . . An excellent source of health information about genetic disorders which affect particular ethnic and racial minorities in the U.S."
 — *The Bookwatch, Aug '01*

Family Planning Sourcebook

Basic Consumer Health Information about Planning for Pregnancy and Contraception, Including Traditional Methods, Barrier Methods, Hormonal Methods, Permanent Methods, Future Methods, Emergency Contraception, and Birth Control Choices for Women at Each Stage of Life

Along with Statistics, a Glossary, and Sources of Additional Information

Edited by Amy Marcaccio Keyzer. 520 pages. 2001. 0-7808-0379-5. $78.

"Recommended for public, health, and undergraduate libraries as part of the circulating collection."
 — *E-Streams, Mar '02*

"Information is presented in an unbiased, readable manner, and the sourcebook will certainly be a necessary addition to those public and high school libraries where Internet access is restricted or otherwise problematic." — *American Reference Books Annual 2002*

"Recommended reference source."
 — *Booklist, American Library Association, Oct '01*

"Will prove valuable to any library seeking to maintain a current, comprehensive reference collection of health resources. . . . Excellent reference."
 — *The Bookwatch, Aug '01*

SEE ALSO Pregnancy & Birth Sourcebook

■

Fitness & Exercise Sourcebook, 1st Edition

Basic Information on Fitness and Exercise, Including Fitness Activities for Specific Age Groups, Exercise for People with Specific Medical Conditions, How to Begin a Fitness Program in Running, Walking, Swimming, Cycling, and Other Athletic Activities, and Recent Research in Fitness and Exercise

Edited by Dan R. Harris. 663 pages. 1996. 0-7808-0186-5. $78.

"A good resource for general readers." — *Choice, Association of College and Research Libraries, Nov '97*

"The perennial popularity of the topic . . . make this an appealing selection for public libraries."
 — *Rettig on Reference, Jun/Jul '97*

■

Fitness & Exercise Sourcebook, 2nd Edition

Basic Consumer Health Information about the Fundamentals of Fitness and Exercise, Including How to Begin and Maintain a Fitness Program, Fitness as a Lifestyle, the Link between Fitness and Diet, Advice for Specific Groups of People, Exercise as It Relates to Specific Medical Conditions, and Recent Research in Fitness and Exercise

Along with a Glossary of Important Terms and Resources for Additional Help and Information

Edited by Kristen M. Gledhill. 646 pages. 2001. 0-7808-0334-5. $78.

"This work is recommended for all general reference collections."
— *American Reference Books Annual 2002*

"Highly recommended for public, consumer, and school grades fourth through college."
—*E-Streams, Nov '01*

"Recommended reference source." — *Booklist, American Library Association, Oct '01*

"The information appears quite comprehensive and is considered reliable. . . . This second edition is a welcomed addition to the series."
—*Doody's Review Service, Sep '01*

"This reference is a valuable choice for those who desire a broad source of information on exercise, fitness, and chronic-disease prevention through a healthy lifestyle." —*American Medical Writers Association Journal, Fall '01*

"Will prove valuable to any library seeking to maintain a current, comprehensive reference collection of health resources. . . . Excellent reference."
— *The Bookwatch, Aug '01*

Food & Animal Borne Diseases Sourcebook

Basic Information about Diseases That Can Be Spread to Humans through the Ingestion of Contaminated Food or Water or by Contact with Infected Animals and Insects, Such as Botulism, E. Coli, Hepatitis A, Trichinosis, Lyme Disease, and Rabies

Along with Information Regarding Prevention and Treatment Methods, and Including a Special Section for International Travelers Describing Diseases Such as Cholera, Malaria, Travelers' Diarrhea, and Yellow Fever, and Offering Recommendations for Avoiding Illness

Edited by Karen Bellenir and Peter D. Dresser. 535 pages. 1995. 0-7808-0033-8. $78.

"Targeting general readers and providing them with a single, comprehensive source of information on selected topics, this book continues, with the excellent caliber of its predecessors, to catalog topical information on health matters of general interest. Readable and thorough, this valuable resource is highly recommended for all libraries."
— *Academic Library Book Review, Summer '96*

"A comprehensive collection of authoritative information." — *Emergency Medical Services, Oct '95*

Food Safety Sourcebook

Basic Consumer Health Information about the Safe Handling of Meat, Poultry, Seafood, Eggs, Fruit Juices, and Other Food Items, and Facts about Pesticides, Drinking Water, Food Safety Overseas, and the Onset, Duration, and Symptoms of Foodborne Illnesses, Including Types of Pathogenic Bacteria, Parasitic Protozoa, Worms, Viruses, and Natural Toxins

Along with the Role of the Consumer, the Food Handler, and the Government in Food Safety; a Glossary, and Resources for Additional Help and Information

Edited by Dawn D. Matthews. 339 pages. 1999. 0-7808-0326-4. $78.

"This book is recommended for public libraries and universities with home economic and food science programs." — *E-Streams, Nov '00*

"Recommended reference source."
—*Booklist, American Library Association, May '00*

"This book takes the complex issues of food safety and foodborne pathogens and presents them in an easily understood manner. [It does] an excellent job of covering a large and often confusing topic."
—*American Reference Books Annual, 2000*

Forensic Medicine Sourcebook

Basic Consumer Information for the Layperson about Forensic Medicine, Including Crime Scene Investigation, Evidence Collection and Analysis, Expert Testimony, Computer-Aided Criminal Identification, Digital Imaging in the Courtroom, DNA Profiling, Accident Reconstruction, Autopsies, Ballistics, Drugs and Explosives Detection, Latent Fingerprints, Product Tampering, and Questioned Document Examination

Along with Statistical Data, a Glossary of Forensics Terminology, and Listings of Sources for Further Help and Information

Edited by Annemarie S. Muth. 574 pages. 1999. 0-7808-0232-2. $78.

"Given the expected widespread interest in its content and its easy to read style, this book is recommended for most public and all college and university libraries."
— *E-Streams, Feb '01*

"Recommended for public libraries."
—*Reference & User Services Quarterly, American Library Association, Spring 2000*

"Recommended reference source."
—*Booklist, American Library Association, Feb '00*

"A wealth of information, useful statistics, references are up-to-date and extremely complete. This wonderful collection of data will help students who are interested in a career in any type of forensic field. It is a great resource for attorneys who need information about types of expert witnesses needed in a particular case. It also offers useful information for fiction and nonfiction writers whose work involves a crime. A fascinating compilation. All levels." — *Choice, Association of College and Research Libraries, Jan 2000*

"There are several items that make this book attractive to consumers who are seeking certain forensic data. . . . This is a useful current source for those seeking general forensic medical answers."
—*American Reference Books Annual, 2000*

Gastrointestinal Diseases & Disorders Sourcebook

Basic Information about Gastroesophageal Reflux Disease (Heartburn), Ulcers, Diverticulosis, Irritable Bowel Syndrome, Crohn's Disease, Ulcerative Colitis, Diarrhea, Constipation, Lactose Intolerance, Hemorrhoids, Hepatitis, Cirrhosis, and Other Digestive Problems, Featuring Statistics, Descriptions of Symptoms, and Current Treatment Methods of Interest for Persons Living with Upper and Lower Gastrointestinal Maladies

Edited by Linda M. Ross. 413 pages. 1996. 0-7808-0078-8. $78.

"... very readable form. The successful editorial work that brought this material together into a useful and understandable reference makes accessible to all readers information that can help them more effectively understand and obtain help for digestive tract problems."
— *Choice, Association of College & Research Libraries, Feb '97*

SEE ALSO *Diet & Nutrition Sourcebook, 1st and 2nd Editions, Digestive Diseases & Disorders*

Genetic Disorders Sourcebook, 1st Edition

Basic Information about Heritable Diseases and Disorders Such as Down Syndrome, PKU, Hemophilia, Von Willebrand Disease, Gaucher Disease, Tay-Sachs Disease, and Sickle-Cell Disease, Along with Information about Genetic Screening, Gene Therapy, Home Care, and Including Source Listings for Further Help and Information on More Than 300 Disorders

Edited by Karen Bellenir. 642 pages. 1996. 0-7808-0034-6. $78.

"Recommended for undergraduate libraries or libraries that serve the public."
— *Science & Technology Libraries, Vol. 18, No. 1, '99*

"Provides essential medical information to both the general public and those diagnosed with a serious or fatal genetic disease or disorder."   —*Choice, Association of College and Research Libraries, Jan '97*

"Geared toward the lay public. It would be well placed in all public libraries and in those hospital and medical libraries in which access to genetic references is limited." — *Doody's Health Sciences Book Review, Oct '96*

Genetic Disorders Sourcebook, 2nd Edition

Basic Consumer Health Information about Hereditary Diseases and Disorders, Including Cystic Fibrosis, Down Syndrome, Hemophilia, Huntington's Disease, Sickle Cell Anemia, and More; Facts about Genes, Gene Research and Therapy, Genetic Screening, Ethics of Gene Testing, Genetic Counseling, and Advice on Coping and Caring

Along with a Glossary of Genetic Terminology and a Resource List for Help, Support, and Further Information

Edited by Kathy Massimini. 768 pages. 2001. 0-7808-0241-1. $78.

"Recommended for public libraries and medical and hospital libraries with consumer health collections."
— *E-Streams, May '01*

"Recommended reference source."
— *Booklist, American Library Association, Apr '01*

"Important pick for college-level health reference libraries."   — *The Bookwatch, Mar '01*

Head Trauma Sourcebook

Basic Information for the Layperson about Open-Head and Closed-Head Injuries, Treatment Advances, Recovery, and Rehabilitation

Along with Reports on Current Research Initiatives

Edited by Karen Bellenir. 414 pages. 1997. 0-7808-0208-X. $78.

Headache Sourcebook

Basic Consumer Health Information about Migraine, Tension, Cluster, Rebound and Other Types of Headaches, with Facts about the Cause and Prevention of Headaches, the Effects of Stress and the Environment, Headaches during Pregnancy and Menopause, and Childhood Headaches

Along with a Glossary and Other Resources for Additional Help and Information

Edited by Dawn D. Matthews. 362 pages. 2002. 0-7808-0337-X. $78.

Health Insurance Sourcebook

Basic Information about Managed Care Organizations, Traditional Fee-for-Service Insurance, Insurance Portability and Pre-Existing Conditions Clauses, Medicare, Medicaid, Social Security, and Military Health Care

Along with Information about Insurance Fraud

Edited by Wendy Wilcox. 530 pages. 1997. 0-7808-0222-5. $78.

"Particularly useful because it brings much of this information together in one volume. This book will be a handy reference source in the health sciences library, hospital library, college and university library, and medium to large public library."
— *Medical Reference Services Quarterly, Fall '98*

Awarded "Books of the Year Award"
— *American Journal of Nursing, 1997*

"The layout of the book is particularly helpful as it provides easy access to reference material. A most useful addition to the vast amount of information about health insurance. The use of data from U.S. government agen-

cies is most commendable. Useful in a library or learning center for healthcare professional students."
— *Doody's Health Sciences Book Reviews, Nov '97*

Health Reference Series Cumulative Index 1999

A Comprehensive Index to the Individual Volumes of the Health Reference Series, Including a Subject Index, Name Index, Organization Index, and Publication Index

Along with a Master List of Acronyms and Abbreviations

Edited by Edward J. Prucha, Anne Holmes, and Robert Rudnick. 990 pages. 2000. 0-7808-0382-5. $78.

"This volume will be most helpful in libraries that have a relatively complete collection of the Health Reference Series." —*American Reference Books Annual, 2001*

"Essential for collections that hold any of the numerous *Health Reference Series* titles."
— *Choice, Association of College and Research Libraries, Nov '00*

Healthy Aging Sourcebook

Basic Consumer Health Information about Maintaining Health through the Aging Process, Including Advice on Nutrition, Exercise, and Sleep, Help in Making Decisions about Midlife Issues and Retirement, and Guidance Concerning Practical and Informed Choices in Health Consumerism

Along with Data Concerning the Theories of Aging, Different Experiences in Aging by Minority Groups, and Facts about Aging Now and Aging in the Future; and Featuring a Glossary, a Guide to Consumer Help, Additional Suggested Reading, and Practical Resource Directory

Edited by Jenifer Swanson. 536 pages. 1999. 0-7808-0390-6. $78.

"Recommended reference source."
— *Booklist, American Library Association, Feb '00*

SEE ALSO Physical & Mental Issues in Aging Sourcebook

Healthy Heart Sourcebook for Women

Basic Consumer Health Information about Cardiac Issues Specific to Women, Including Facts about Major Risk Factors and Prevention, Treatment and Control Strategies, and Important Dietary Issues

Along with a Special Section Regarding the Pros and Cons of Hormone Replacement Therapy and Its Impact on Heart Health, and Additional Help, Including Recipes, a Glossary, and a Directory of Resources

Edited by Dawn D. Matthews. 336 pages. 2000. 0-7808-0329-9. $78.

"A good reference source and recommended for all public, academic, medical, and hospital libraries."
— *Medical Reference Services Quarterly, Summer '01*

"Because of the lack of information specific to women on this topic, this book is recommended for public libraries and consumer libraries."
— *American Reference Books Annual, 2001*

"Contains very important information about coronary artery disease that all women should know. The information is current and presented in an easy-to-read format. The book will make a good addition to any library." — *American Medical Writers Association Journal, Summer '00*

"Important, basic reference."
— *Reviewer's Bookwatch, Jul '00*

SEE ALSO Cardiovascular Diseases & Disorders Sourcebook, 1st Edition, Heart Diseases & Disorders Sourcebook, 2nd Edition, Women's Health Concerns Sourcebook

Heart Diseases & Disorders Sourcebook, 2nd Edition

Basic Consumer Health Information about Heart Attacks, Angina, Rhythm Disorders, Heart Failure, Valve Disease, Congenital Heart Disorders, and More, Including Descriptions of Surgical Procedures and Other Interventions, Medications, Cardiac Rehabilitation, Risk Identification, and Prevention Tips

Along with Statistical Data, Reports on Current Research Initiatives, a Glossary of Cardiovascular Terms, and Resource Directory

Edited by Karen Bellenir. 612 pages. 2000. 0-7808-0238-1. $78.

"This work stands out as an imminently accessible resource for the general public. It is recommended for the reference and circulating shelves of school, public, and academic libraries."
— *American Reference Books Annual, 2001*

"Recommended reference source."
— *Booklist, American Library Association, Dec '00*

"Provides comprehensive coverage of matters related to the heart. This title is recommended for health sciences and public libraries with consumer health collections."
— *E-Streams, Oct '00*

SEE ALSO Cardiovascular Diseases & Disorders Sourcebook, 1st Edition; Healthy Heart Sourcebook for Women

Household Safety Sourcebook

Basic Consumer Health Information about Household Safety, Including Information about Poisons, Chemicals, Fire, and Water Hazards in the Home

Along with Advice about the Safe Use of Home Maintenance Equipment, Choosing Toys and Nursery Furniture, Holiday and Recreation Safety, a Glossary, and Resources for Further Help and Information

Edited by Dawn D. Matthews. 606 pages. 2002. 0-7808-0338-8. $78.

Immune System Disorders Sourcebook

Basic Information about Lupus, Multiple Sclerosis, Guillain-Barré Syndrome, Chronic Granulomatous Disease, and More

Along with Statistical and Demographic Data and Reports on Current Research Initiatives

Edited by Allan R. Cook. 608 pages. 1997. 0-7808-0209-8. $78.

Infant & Toddler Health Sourcebook

Basic Consumer Health Information about the Physical and Mental Development of Newborns, Infants, and Toddlers, Including Neonatal Concerns, Nutrition Recommendations, Immunization Schedules, Common Pediatric Disorders, Assessments and Milestones, Safety Tips, and Advice for Parents and Other Caregivers

Along with a Glossary of Terms and Resource Listings for Additional Help

Edited by Jenifer Swanson. 585 pages. 2000. 0-7808-0246-2. $78.

"As a reference for the general public, this would be useful in any library." — *E-Streams, May '01*

"Recommended reference source."
— *Booklist, American Library Association, Feb '01*

"This is a good source for general use."
—*American Reference Books Annual, 2001*

Injury & Trauma Sourcebook

Basic Consumer Health Information about the Impact of Injury, the Diagnosis and Treatment of Common and Traumatic Injuries, Emergency Care, and Specific Injuries Related to Home, Community, Workplace, Transportation, and Recreation

Along with Guidelines for Injury Prevention, a Glossary, and a Directory of Additional Resources

Edited by Joyce Brennfleck Shannon. 696 pages. 2002. 0-7808-0421-X. $78.

Kidney & Urinary Tract Diseases & Disorders Sourcebook

Basic Information about Kidney Stones, Urinary Incontinence, Bladder Disease, End Stage Renal Disease, Dialysis, and More

Along with Statistical and Demographic Data and Reports on Current Research Initiatives

Edited by Linda M. Ross. 602 pages. 1997. 0-7808-0079-6. $78.

Learning Disabilities Sourcebook

Basic Information about Disorders Such as Dyslexia, Visual and Auditory Processing Deficits, Attention Deficit/Hyperactivity Disorder, and Autism

Along with Statistical and Demographic Data, Reports on Current Research Initiatives, an Explanation of the Assessment Process, and a Special Section for Adults with Learning Disabilities

Edited by Linda M. Shin. 579 pages. 1998. 0-7808-0210-1. $78.

Named "Outstanding Reference Book of 1999."
—New York Public Library, Feb 2000

"An excellent candidate for inclusion in a public library reference section. It's a great source of information. Teachers will also find the book useful. Definitely worth reading."
—Journal of Adolescent & Adult Literacy, Feb 2000

"Readable . . . provides a solid base of information regarding successful techniques used with individuals who have learning disabilities, as well as practical suggestions for educators and family members. Clear language, concise descriptions, and pertinent information for contacting multiple resources add to the strength of this book as a useful tool." *—Choice, Association of College and Research Libraries, Feb '99*

"Recommended reference source."
—Booklist, American Library Association, Sep '98

"A useful resource for libraries and for those who don't have the time to identify and locate the individual publications." *—Disability Resources Monthly, Sep '98*

Liver Disorders Sourcebook

Basic Consumer Health Information about the Liver and How It Works; Liver Diseases, Including Cancer, Cirrhosis, Hepatitis, and Toxic and Drug Related Diseases; Tips for Maintaining a Healthy Liver; Laboratory Tests, Radiology Tests, and Facts about Liver Transplantation

Along with a Section on Support Groups, a Glossary, and Resource Listings

Edited by Joyce Brennfleck Shannon. 591 pages. 2000. 0-7808-0383-3. $78.

"A valuable resource."
—*American Reference Books Annual, 2001*

"This title is recommended for health sciences and public libraries with consumer health collections."
—E-Streams, Oct '00

"Recommended reference source."
—Booklist, American Library Association, Jun '00

Lung Disorders Sourcebook

Basic Consumer Health Information about Emphysema, Pneumonia, Tuberculosis, Asthma, Cystic Fibrosis, and Other Lung Disorders, Including Facts about Diagnostic Procedures, Treatment Strategies, Disease Prevention Efforts, and Such Risk Factors as Smoking, Air Pollution, and Exposure to Asbestos, Radon, and Other Agents

Along with a Glossary and Resources for Additional Help and Information

Edited by Dawn D. Matthews. 678 pages. 2002. 0-7808-0339-6. $78.

Medical Tests Sourcebook

Basic Consumer Health Information about Medical Tests, Including Periodic Health Exams, General Screening Tests, Tests You Can Do at Home, Findings of the U.S. Preventive Services Task Force, X-ray and Radiology Tests, Electrical Tests, Tests of Blood and Other Body Fluids and Tissues, Scope Tests, Lung Tests, Genetic Tests, Pregnancy Tests, Newborn Screening Tests, Sexually Transmitted Disease Tests, and Computer Aided Diagnoses

Along with a Section on Paying for Medical Tests, a Glossary, and Resource Listings

Edited by Joyce Brennfleck Shannon. 691 pages. 1999. 0-7808-0243-8. $78.

"Recommended for hospital and health sciences libraries with consumer health collections."
— *E-Streams, Mar '00*

"This is an overall excellent reference with a wealth of general knowledge that may aid those who are reluctant to get vital tests performed."
— *Today's Librarian, Jan 2000*

"A valuable reference guide."
—*American Reference Books Annual, 2000*

Men's Health Concerns Sourcebook

Basic Information about Health Issues That Affect Men, Featuring Facts about the Top Causes of Death in Men, Including Heart Disease, Stroke, Cancers, Prostate Disorders, Chronic Obstructive Pulmonary Disease, Pneumonia and Influenza, Human Immunodeficiency Virus and Acquired Immune Deficiency Syndrome, Diabetes Mellitus, Stress, Suicide, Accidents and Homicides; and Facts about Common Concerns for Men, Including Impotence, Contraception, Circumcision, Sleep Disorders, Snoring, Hair Loss, Diet, Nutrition, Exercise, Kidney and Urological Disorders, and Backaches

Edited by Allan R. Cook. 738 pages. 1998. 0-7808-0212-8. $78.

"This comprehensive resource and the series are highly recommended."
—*American Reference Books Annual, 2000*

"Recommended reference source."
— *Booklist, American Library Association, Dec '98*

Mental Health Disorders Sourcebook, 1st Edition

Basic Information about Schizophrenia, Depression, Bipolar Disorder, Panic Disorder, Obsessive-Compulsive Disorder, Phobias and Other Anxiety Disorders, Paranoia and Other Personality Disorders, Eating Disorders, and Sleep Disorders

Along with Information about Treatment and Therapies

Edited by Karen Bellenir. 548 pages. 1995. 0-7808-0040-0. $78.

"This is an excellent new book . . . written in easy-to-understand language."
— *Booklist Health Sciences Supplement, American Library Association, Oct '97*

". . . useful for public and academic libraries and consumer health collections."
— *Medical Reference Services Quarterly, Spring '97*

"The great strengths of the book are its readability and its inclusion of places to find more information. Especially recommended." — *Reference Quarterly, American Library Association, Winter '96*

". . . a good resource for a consumer health library."
—*Bulletin of the Medical Library Association, Oct '96*

"The information is data-based and couched in brief, concise language that avoids jargon. . . . a useful reference source." — *Readings, Sep '96*

"The text is well organized and adequately written for its target audience." — *Choice, Association of College and Research Libraries, Jun '96*

". . . provides information on a wide range of mental disorders, presented in nontechnical language."
— *Exceptional Child Education Resources, Spring '96*

"Recommended for public and academic libraries."
— *Reference Book Review, 1996*

Mental Health Disorders Sourcebook, 2nd Edition

Basic Consumer Health Information about Anxiety Disorders, Depression and Other Mood Disorders, Eating Disorders, Personality Disorders, Schizophrenia, and More, Including Disease Descriptions, Treatment Options, and Reports on Current Research Initiatives

Along with Statistical Data, Tips for Maintaining Mental Health, a Glossary, and Directory of Sources for Additional Help and Information

Edited by Karen Bellenir. 605 pages. 2000. 0-7808-0240-3. $78.

"Well organized and well written."
—*American Reference Books Annual, 2001*

"Recommended reference source."
—*Booklist, American Library Association, Jun '00*

Mental Retardation Sourcebook

Basic Consumer Health Information about Mental Retardation and Its Causes, Including Down Syndrome, Fetal Alcohol Syndrome, Fragile X Syndrome, Genetic Conditions, Injury, and Environmental Sources

Along with Preventive Strategies, Parenting Issues, Educational Implications, Health Care Needs, Employment and Economic Matters, Legal Issues, a Glossary, and a Resource Listing for Additional Help and Information

Edited by Joyce Brennfleck Shannon. 642 pages. 2000. 0-7808-0377-9. $78.

"Public libraries will find the book useful for reference and as a beginning research point for students, parents, and caregivers."
—American Reference Books Annual, 2001

"The strength of this work is that it compiles many basic fact sheets and addresses for further information in one volume. It is intended and suitable for the general public. This sourcebook is relevant to any collection providing health information to the general public."
— E-Streams, Nov '00

"From preventing retardation to parenting and family challenges, this covers health, social and legal issues and will prove an invaluable overview."
—Reviewer's Bookwatch, Jul '00

Obesity Sourcebook

Basic Consumer Health Information about Diseases and Other Problems Associated with Obesity, and Including Facts about Risk Factors, Prevention Issues, and Management Approaches

Along with Statistical and Demographic Data, Information about Special Populations, Research Updates, a Glossary, and Source Listings for Further Help and Information

Edited by Wilma Caldwell and Chad T. Kimball. 376 pages. 2001. 0-7808-0333-7. $78.

"The book synthesizes the reliable medical literature on obesity into one easy-to-read and useful resource for the general public."
—American Reference Books Annual 2002

"This is a very useful resource book for the lay public."
—Doody's Review Service, Nov '01

"Well suited for the health reference collection of a public library or an academic health science library that serves the general population." *—E-Streams, Sep '01*

"Recommended reference source."
—Booklist, American Library Association, Apr '01

" Recommended pick both for specialty health library collections and any general consumer health reference collection." *— The Bookwatch, Apr '01*

Ophthalmic Disorders Sourcebook

Basic Information about Glaucoma, Cataracts, Macular Degeneration, Strabismus, Refractive Disorders, and More

Along with Statistical and Demographic Data and Reports on Current Research Initiatives

Edited by Linda M. Ross. 631 pages. 1996. 0-7808-0081-8. $78.

Oral Health Sourcebook

Basic Information about Diseases and Conditions Affecting Oral Health, Including Cavities, Gum Disease, Dry Mouth, Oral Cancers, Fever Blisters, Canker Sores, Oral Thrush, Bad Breath, Temporomandibular Disorders, and other Craniofacial Syndromes

Along with Statistical Data on the Oral Health of Americans, Oral Hygiene, Emergency First Aid, Information on Treatment Procedures and Methods of Replacing Lost Teeth

Edited by Allan R. Cook. 558 pages. 1997. 0-7808-0082-6. $78.

"Unique source which will fill a gap in dental sources for patients and the lay public. A valuable reference tool even in a library with thousands of books on dentistry. Comprehensive, clear, inexpensive, and easy to read and use. It fills an enormous gap in the health care literature." *—Reference and User Services Quarterly, American Library Association, Summer '98*

"Recommended reference source."
—Booklist, American Library Association, Dec '97

Osteoporosis Sourcebook

Basic Consumer Health Information about Primary and Secondary Osteoporosis and Juvenile Osteoporosis and Related Conditions, Including Fibrous Dysplasia, Gaucher Disease, Hyperthyroidism, Hypophosphatasia, Myeloma, Osteopetrosis, Osteogenesis Imperfecta, and Paget's Disease

Along with Information about Risk Factors, Treatments, Traditional and Non-Traditional Pain Management, a Glossary of Related Terms, and a Directory of Resources

Edited by Allan R. Cook. 584 pages. 2001. 0-7808-0239-X. $78.

"This would be a book to be kept in a staff or patient library. The targeted audience is the layperson, but the therapist who needs a quick bit of information on a particular topic will also find the book useful."
—Physical Therapy, Jan '02

"This resource is recommended as a great reference source for public, health, and academic libraries, and is another triumph for the editors of Omnigraphics."
—American Reference Books Annual 2002

"Recommended for all public libraries and general health collections, especially those supporting patient education or consumer health programs."
—E-Streams, Nov '01

"Will prove valuable to any library seeking to maintain a current, comprehensive reference collection of health resources. . . . From prevention to treatment and associated conditions, this provides an excellent survey."
—The Bookwatch, Aug '01

"Recommended reference source."
—*Booklist, American Library Association, July '01*

SEE ALSO Women's Health Concerns Sourcebook

Pain Sourcebook, 1st Edition

Basic Information about Specific Forms of Acute and Chronic Pain, Including Headaches, Back Pain, Muscular Pain, Neuralgia, Surgical Pain, and Cancer Pain

Along with Pain Relief Options Such as Analgesics, Narcotics, Nerve Blocks, Transcutaneous Nerve Stimulation, and Alternative Forms of Pain Control, Including Biofeedback, Imaging, Behavior Modification, and Relaxation Techniques

Edited by Allan R. Cook. 667 pages. 1997. 0-7808-0213-6. $78.

"The text is readable, easily understood, and well indexed. This excellent volume belongs in all patient education libraries, consumer health sections of public libraries, and many personal collections."
— *American Reference Books Annual, 1999*

"A beneficial reference." — *Booklist Health Sciences Supplement, American Library Association, Oct '98*

"The information is basic in terms of scholarship and is appropriate for general readers. Written in journalistic style ... intended for non-professionals. Quite thorough in its coverage of different pain conditions and summarizes the latest clinical information regarding pain treatment." — *Choice, Association of College and Research Libraries, Jun '98*

"Recommended reference source."
— *Booklist, American Library Association, Mar '98*

Pain Sourcebook, 2nd Edition

Basic Consumer Health Information about Specific Forms of Acute and Chronic Pain, Including Muscle and Skeletal Pain, Nerve Pain, Cancer Pain, and Disorders Characterized by Pain, Such as Fibromyalgia, Shingles, Angina, Arthritis, and Headaches

Along with Information about Pain Medications and Management Techniques, Complementary and Alternative Pain Relief Options, Tips for People Living with Chronic Pain, a Glossary, and a Directory of Sources for Further Information

Edited by Karen Bellenir. 670 pages. 2002. 0-7808-0612-3. $78.

Pediatric Cancer Sourcebook

Basic Consumer Health Information about Leukemias, Brain Tumors, Sarcomas, Lymphomas, and Other Cancers in Infants, Children, and Adolescents, Including Descriptions of Cancers, Treatments, and Coping Strategies

Along with Suggestions for Parents, Caregivers, and Concerned Relatives, a Glossary of Cancer Terms, and Resource Listings

Edited by Edward J. Prucha. 587 pages. 1999. 0-7808-0245-4. $78.

"An excellent source of information. Recommended for public, hospital, and health science libraries with consumer health collections." — *E-Streams, Jun '00*

"Recommended reference source."
— *Booklist, American Library Association, Feb '00*

"A valuable addition to all libraries specializing in health services and many public libraries."
— *American Reference Books Annual, 2000*

Physical & Mental Issues in Aging Sourcebook

Basic Consumer Health Information on Physical and Mental Disorders Associated with the Aging Process, Including Concerns about Cardiovascular Disease, Pulmonary Disease, Oral Health, Digestive Disorders, Musculoskeletal and Skin Disorders, Metabolic Changes, Sexual and Reproductive Issues, and Changes in Vision, Hearing, and Other Senses

Along with Data about Longevity and Causes of Death, Information on Acute and Chronic Pain, Descriptions of Mental Concerns, a Glossary of Terms, and Resource Listings for Additional Help

Edited by Jenifer Swanson. 660 pages. 1999. 0-7808-0233-0. $78.

"This is a treasure of health information for the layperson." — *Choice Health Sciences Supplement, Association of College & Research Libraries, May 2000*

"Recommended for public libraries."
— *American Reference Books Annual, 2000*

"Recommended reference source."
— *Booklist, American Library Association, Oct '99*

SEE ALSO Healthy Aging Sourcebook

Podiatry Sourcebook

Basic Consumer Health Information about Foot Conditions, Diseases, and Injuries, Including Bunions, Corns, Calluses, Athlete's Foot, Plantar Warts, Hammertoes and Clawtoes, Clubfoot, Heel Pain, Gout, and More

Along with Facts about Foot Care, Disease Prevention, Foot Safety, Choosing a Foot Care Specialist, a Glossary of Terms, and Resource Listings for Additional Information

Edited by M. Lisa Weatherford. 380 pages. 2001. 0-7808-0215-2. $78.

"Recommended reference source."
— *Booklist, American Library Association, Feb '02*

"There is a lot of information presented here on a topic that is usually only covered sparingly in most larger comprehensive medical encyclopedias."
— *American Reference Books Annual 2002*

Pregnancy & Birth Sourcebook

Basic Information about Planning for Pregnancy, Maternal Health, Fetal Growth and Development, Labor and Delivery, Postpartum and Perinatal Care, Pregnancy in Mothers with Special Concerns, and Disorders of Pregnancy, Including Genetic Counseling, Nutrition and Exercise, Obstetrical Tests, Pregnancy Discomfort, Multiple Births, Cesarean Sections, Medical Testing of Newborns, Breastfeeding, Gestational Diabetes, and Ectopic Pregnancy

Edited by Heather E. Aldred. 737 pages. 1997. 0-7808-0216-0. $78.

"A well-organized handbook. Recommended."
— *Choice, Association of College and Research Libraries, Apr '98*

"Recommended reference source."
— *Booklist, American Library Association, Mar '98*

"Recommended for public libraries."
— *American Reference Books Annual, 1998*

SEE ALSO *Congenital Disorders Sourcebook, Family Planning Sourcebook*

Prostate Cancer Sourcebook

Basic Consumer Health Information about Prostate Cancer, Including Information about the Associated Risk Factors, Detection, Diagnosis, and Treatment of Prostate Cancer

Along with Information on Non-Malignant Prostate Conditions, and Featuring a Section Listing Support and Treatment Centers and a Glossary of Related Terms

Edited by Dawn D. Matthews. 358 pages. 2001. 0-7808-0324-8. $78.

"Recommended reference source."
— *Booklist, American Library Association, Jan '02*

"A valuable resource for health care consumers seeking information on the subject....All text is written in a clear, easy-to-understand language that avoids technical jargon. Any library that collects consumer health resources would strengthen their collection with the addition of the *Prostate Cancer Sourcebook*."
— *American Reference Books Annual 2002*

Public Health Sourcebook

Basic Information about Government Health Agencies, Including National Health Statistics and Trends, Healthy People 2000 Program Goals and Objectives, the Centers for Disease Control and Prevention, the Food and Drug Administration, and the National Institutes of Health

Along with Full Contact Information for Each Agency

Edited by Wendy Wilcox. 698 pages. 1998. 0-7808-0220-9. $78.

"Recommended reference source."
— *Booklist, American Library Association, Sep '98*

"This consumer guide provides welcome assistance in navigating the maze of federal health agencies and their data on public health concerns."
— *SciTech Book News, Sep '98*

Reconstructive & Cosmetic Surgery Sourcebook

Basic Consumer Health Information on Cosmetic and Reconstructive Plastic Surgery, Including Statistical Information about Different Surgical Procedures, Things to Consider Prior to Surgery, Plastic Surgery Techniques and Tools, Emotional and Psychological Considerations, and Procedure-Specific Information

Along with a Glossary of Terms and a Listing of Resources for Additional Help and Information

Edited by M. Lisa Weatherford. 374 pages. 2001. 0-7808-0214-4. $78.

"An excellent reference that addresses cosmetic and medically necessary reconstructive surgeries. . . . The style of the prose is calm and reassuring, discussing the many positive outcomes now available due to advances in surgical techniques."
— *American Reference Books Annual 2002*

"Recommended for health science libraries that are open to the public, as well as hospital libraries that are open to the patients. This book is a good resource for the consumer interested in plastic surgery."
— *E-Streams, Dec '01*

"Recommended reference source."
— *Booklist, American Library Association, July '01*

Rehabilitation Sourcebook

Basic Consumer Health Information about Rehabilitation for People Recovering from Heart Surgery, Spinal Cord Injury, Stroke, Orthopedic Impairments, Amputation, Pulmonary Impairments, Traumatic Injury, and More, Including Physical Therapy, Occupational Therapy, Speech/ Language Therapy, Massage Therapy, Dance Therapy, Art Therapy, and Recreational Therapy

Along with Information on Assistive and Adaptive Devices, a Glossary, and Resources for Additional Help and Information

Edited by Dawn D. Matthews. 531 pages. 1999. 0-7808-0236-5. $78.

"This is an excellent resource for public library reference and health collections."
— *American Reference Books Annual, 2001*

"Recommended reference source."
— *Booklist, American Library Association, May '00*

Respiratory Diseases & Disorders Sourcebook

Basic Information about Respiratory Diseases and Disorders, Including Asthma, Cystic Fibrosis, Pneumonia, the Common Cold, Influenza, and Others, Featuring Facts about the Respiratory System, Statistical and Demographic Data, Treatments, Self-Help Management Suggestions, and Current Research Initiatives

Edited by Allan R. Cook and Peter D. Dresser. 771 pages. 1995. 0-7808-0037-0. $78.

"Designed for the layperson and for patients and their families coping with respiratory illness. . . . an extensive array of information on diagnosis, treatment, management, and prevention of respiratory illnesses for the general reader." — Choice, Association of College and Research Libraries, Jun '96

"A highly recommended text for all collections. It is a comforting reminder of the power of knowledge that good books carry between their covers."
— Academic Library Book Review, Spring '96

"A comprehensive collection of authoritative information presented in a nontechnical, humanitarian style for patients, families, and caregivers."
— Association of Operating Room Nurses, Sep/Oct '95

■

Sexually Transmitted Diseases Sourcebook, 1st Edition

Basic Information about Herpes, Chlamydia, Gonorrhea, Hepatitis, Nongonoccocal Urethritis, Pelvic Inflammatory Disease, Syphilis, AIDS, and More

Along with Current Data on Treatments and Preventions

Edited by Linda M. Ross. 550 pages. 1997. 0-7808-0217-9. $78.

■

Sexually Transmitted Diseases Sourcebook, 2nd Edition

Basic Consumer Health Information about Sexually Transmitted Diseases, Including Information on the Diagnosis and Treatment of Chlamydia, Gonorrhea, Hepatitis, Herpes, HIV, Mononucleosis, Syphilis, and Others

Along with Information on Prevention, Such as Condom Use, Vaccines, and STD Education; And Featuring a Section on Issues Related to Youth and Adolescents, a Glossary, and Resources for Additional Help and Information

Edited by Dawn D. Matthews. 538 pages. 2001. 0-7808-0249-7. $78.

"Recommended for consumer health collections in public libraries, and secondary school and community college libraries."
— American Reference Books Annual 2002

"Every school and public library should have a copy of this comprehensive and user-friendly reference book."
— Choice, Association of College & Research Libraries, Sep '01

"This is a highly recommended book. This is an especially important book for all school and public libraries." — AIDS Book Review Journal, Jul-Aug '01

"Recommended reference source."
— Booklist, American Library Association, Apr '01

"Recommended pick both for specialty health library collections and any general consumer health reference collection." — The Bookwatch, Apr '01

■

Skin Disorders Sourcebook

Basic Information about Common Skin and Scalp Conditions Caused by Aging, Allergies, Immune Reactions, Sun Exposure, Infectious Organisms, Parasites, Cosmetics, and Skin Traumas, Including Abrasions, Cuts, and Pressure Sores

Along with Information on Prevention and Treatment

Edited by Allan R. Cook. 647 pages. 1997. 0-7808-0080-X. $78.

". . . comprehensive, easily read reference book."
— Doody's Health Sciences Book Reviews, Oct '97

SEE ALSO Burns Sourcebook

■

Sleep Disorders Sourcebook

Basic Consumer Health Information about Sleep and Its Disorders, Including Insomnia, Sleepwalking, Sleep Apnea, Restless Leg Syndrome, and Narcolepsy

Along with Data about Shiftwork and Its Effects, Information on the Societal Costs of Sleep Deprivation, Descriptions of Treatment Options, a Glossary of Terms, and Resource Listings for Additional Help

Edited by Jenifer Swanson. 439 pages. 1998. 0-7808-0234-9. $78.

"This text will complement any home or medical library. It is user-friendly and ideal for the adult reader."
— American Reference Books Annual, 2000

"A useful resource that provides accurate, relevant, and accessible information on sleep to the general public. Health care providers who deal with sleep disorders patients may also find it helpful in being prepared to answer some of the questions patients ask."
— Respiratory Care, Jul '99

"Recommended reference source."
— Booklist, American Library Association, Feb '99

Sports Injuries Sourcebook

Basic Consumer Health Information about Common Sports Injuries, Prevention of Injury in Specific Sports, Tips for Training, and Rehabilitation from Injury

Along with Information about Special Concerns for Children, Young Girls in Athletic Training Programs, Senior Athletes, and Women Athletes, and a Directory of Resources for Further Help and Information

Edited by Heather E. Aldred. 624 pages. 1999. 0-7808-0218-7. $78.

"While this easy-to-read book is recommended for all libraries, it should prove to be especially useful for public, high school, and academic libraries; certainly it should be on the bookshelf of every school gymnasium." *— E-Streams, Mar '00*

"Public libraries and undergraduate academic libraries will find this book useful for its nontechnical language." *—American Reference Books Annual, 2000*

Stress-Related Disorders Sourcebook

Basic Consumer Health Information about Stress and Stress-Related Disorders, Including Stress Origins and Signals, Environmental Stress at Work and Home, Mental and Emotional Stress Associated with Depression, Post-Traumatic Stress Disorder, Panic Disorder, Suicide, and the Physical Effects of Stress on the Cardiovascular, Immune, and Nervous Systems

Along with Stress Management Techniques, a Glossary, and a Listing of Additional Resources

Edited by Joyce Brennfleck Shannon. 610 pages. 2002. 0-7808-0560-7. $78.

Substance Abuse Sourcebook

Basic Health-Related Information about the Abuse of Legal and Illegal Substances Such as Alcohol, Tobacco, Prescription Drugs, Marijuana, Cocaine, and Heroin; and Including Facts about Substance Abuse Prevention Strategies, Intervention Methods, Treatment and Recovery Programs, and a Section Addressing the Special Problems Related to Substance Abuse during Pregnancy

Edited by Karen Bellenir. 573 pages. 1996. 0-7808-0038-9. $78.

"A valuable addition to any health reference section. Highly recommended." *— The Book Report, Mar/Apr '97*

". . . a comprehensive collection of substance abuse information that's both highly readable and compact. Families and caregivers of substance abusers will find the information enlightening and helpful, while teachers, social workers and journalists should benefit from the concise format. Recommended." *—Drug Abuse Update, Winter '96/'97*

SEE ALSO *Alcoholism Sourcebook, Drug Abuse Sourcebook*

Transplantation Sourcebook

Basic Consumer Health Information about Organ and Tissue Transplantation, Including Physical and Financial Preparations, Procedures and Issues Relating to Specific Solid Organ and Tissue Transplants, Rehabilitation, Pediatric Transplant Information, the Future of Transplantation, and Organ and Tissue Donation

Along with a Glossary and Listings of Additional Resources

Edited by Joyce Brennfleck Shannon. 628 pages. 2002. 0-7808-0322-1. $78.

Traveler's Health Sourcebook

Basic Consumer Health Information for Travelers, Including Physical and Medical Preparations, Transportation Health and Safety, Essential Information about Food and Water, Sun Exposure, Insect and Snake Bites, Camping and Wilderness Medicine, and Travel with Physical or Medical Disabilities

Along with International Travel Tips, Vaccination Recommendations, Geographical Health Issues, Disease Risks, a Glossary, and a Listing of Additional Resources

Edited by Joyce Brennfleck Shannon. 613 pages. 2000. 0-7808-0384-1. $78.

"Recommended reference source." *— Booklist, American Library Association, Feb '01*

"This book is recommended for any public library, any travel collection, and especially any collection for the physically disabled." *—American Reference Books Annual, 2001*

Women's Health Concerns Sourcebook

Basic Information about Health Issues That Affect Women, Featuring Facts about Menstruation and Other Gynecological Concerns, Including Endometriosis, Fibroids, Menopause, and Vaginitis; Reproductive Concerns, Including Birth Control, Infertility, and Abortion; and Facts about Additional Physical, Emotional, and Mental Health Concerns Prevalent among Women Such as Osteoporosis, Urinary Tract Disorders, Eating Disorders, and Depression

Along with Tips for Maintaining a Healthy Lifestyle

Edited by Heather E. Aldred. 567 pages. 1997. 0-7808-0219-5. $78.

"Handy compilation. There is an impressive range of diseases, devices, disorders, procedures, and other physical and emotional issues covered . . . well organized, illustrated, and indexed." *— Choice, Association of College and Research Libraries, Jan '98*

SEE ALSO *Breast Cancer Sourcebook, Cancer Sourcebook for Women, 1st and 2nd Editions, Healthy Heart Sourcebook for Women, Osteoporosis Sourcebook*

Workplace Health & Safety Sourcebook

Basic Consumer Health Information about Workplace Health and Safety, Including the Effect of Workplace Hazards on the Lungs, Skin, Heart, Ears, Eyes, Brain, Reproductive Organs, Musculoskeletal System, and Other Organs and Body Parts

Along with Information about Occupational Cancer, Personal Protective Equipment, Toxic and Hazardous Chemicals, Child Labor, Stress, and Workplace Violence

Edited by Chad T. Kimball. 626 pages. 2000. 0-7808-0231-4. $78.

"As a reference for the general public, this would be useful in any library." —*E-Streams, Jun '01*

"Provides helpful information for primary care physicians and other caregivers interested in occupational medicine. . . . General readers; professionals."
— *Choice, Association of College & Research Libraries, May '01*

"Recommended reference source."
— *Booklist, American Library Association, Feb '01*

"Highly recommended." — *The Bookwatch, Jan '01*

■

Worldwide Health Sourcebook

Basic Information about Global Health Issues, Including Malnutrition, Reproductive Health, Disease Dispersion and Prevention, Emerging Diseases, Risky Health Behaviors, and the Leading Causes of Death

Along with Global Health Concerns for Children, Women, and the Elderly, Mental Health Issues, Research and Technology Advancements, and Economic, Environmental, and Political Health Implications, a Glossary, and a Resource Listing for Additional Help and Information

Edited by Joyce Brennfleck Shannon. 614 pages. 2001. 0-7808-0330-2. $78.

"Named an Outstanding Academic Title."
— *Choice, Association of College & Research Libraries, Jan '02*

"Yet another handy but also unique compilation in the extensive Health Reference Series, this is a useful work because many of the international publications reprinted or excerpted are not readily available. Highly recommended."
— *Choice, Association of College & Research Libraries, Nov '01*

"Recommended reference source."
— *Booklist, American Library Association, Oct '01*

Teen Health Series

Helping Young Adults Understand, Manage, and Avoid Serious Illness

Diet Information for Teens
Health Tips about Diet and Nutrition

Including Facts about Nutrients, Dietary Guidelines, Breakfasts, School Lunches, Snacks, Party Food, Weight Control, Eating Disorders, and More

Edited by Karen Bellenir. 399 pages. 2001. 0-7808-0441-4. $58.

"Full of helpful insights and facts throughout the book. ... An excellent resource to be placed in public libraries or even in personal collections."
—*American Reference Books Annual 2002*

"Recommended for middle and high school libraries and media centers as well as academic libraries that educate future teachers of teenagers. It is also a suitable addition to health science libraries that serve patrons who are interested in teen health promotion and education."
—*E-Streams, Oct '01*

"This comprehensive book would be beneficial to collections that need information about nutrition, dietary guidelines, meal planning, and weight control. ... This reference is so easy to use that its purchase is recommended."
—*The Book Report, Sep-Oct '01*

"This book is written in an easy to understand format describing issues that many teens face every day, and then provides thoughtful explanations so that teens can make informed decisions. This is an interesting book that provides important facts and information for today's teens."
—*Doody's Health Sciences Book Review Journal, Jul-Aug '01*

"A comprehensive compendium of diet and nutrition. The information is presented in a straightforward, plain-spoken manner. This title will be useful to those working on reports on a variety of topics, as well as to general readers concerned about their dietary health."
—*School Library Journal, Jun '01*

Drug Information for Teens
Health Tips about the Physical and Mental Effects of Substance Abuse

Including Facts about Alcohol, Anabolic Steroids, Club Drugs, Cocaine, Depressants, Hallucinogens, Herbal Products, Inhalants, Marijuana, Narcotics, Stimulants, Tobacco, and More

Edited by Karen Bellenir. 400 pages. 2002. 0-7808-0444-9. $58.

Mental Health Information for Teens
Health Tips about Mental Health and Mental Illness

Including Facts about Anxiety, Depression, Suicide, Eating Disorders, Obsessive-Compulsive Disorders, Panic Attacks, Phobias, Schizophrenia, and More

Edited by Karen Bellenir. 406 pages. 2001. 0-7808-0442-2. $58.

"In both language and approach, this user-friendly entry in the *Teen Health Series* is on target for teens needing information on mental health concerns." — *Booklist, American Library Association, Jan '02*

"Readers will find the material accessible and informative, with the shaded notes, facts, and embedded glossary insets adding appropriately to the already interesting and succinct presentation."
—*School Library Journal, Jan '02*

"This title is highly recommended for any library that serves adolescents and parents/caregivers of adolescents." — *E-Streams, Jan '02*

"Recommended for high school libraries and young adult collections in public libraries. Both health professionals and teenagers will find this book useful."
—*American Reference Books Annual 2002*

"This is a nice book written to enlighten the society, primarily teenagers, about common teen mental health issues. It is highly recommended to teachers and parents as well as adolescents."
—*Doody's Review Service, Dec '01*

Sexual Health Information for Teens
Health Tips about Sexual Development, Human Reproduction, and Sexually Transmitted Diseases

Including Facts about Puberty, Reproductive Health, Chlamydia, Human Papillomavirus, Pelvic Inflammatory Disease, Herpes, AIDS, Contraception, Pregnancy, and More

Edited by Deborah A. Stanley. 400 pages. 2002. 0-7808-0445-7. $58.

Health Reference Series

Adolescent Health Sourcebook

AIDS Sourcebook, 1st Edition

AIDS Sourcebook, 2nd Edition

Alcoholism Sourcebook

Allergies Sourcebook, 1st Edition

Allergies Sourcebook, 2nd Edition

Alternative Medicine Sourcebook, 1st Edition

Alternative Medicine Sourcebook, 2nd Edition

Alzheimer's, Stroke & 29 Other Neurological Disorders Sourcebook, 1st Edition

Alzheimer's Disease Sourcebook, 2nd Edition

Arthritis Sourcebook

Asthma Sourcebook

Attention Deficit Disorder Sourcebook

Back & Neck Disorders Sourcebook

Blood & Circulatory Disorders Sourcebook

Brain Disorders Sourcebook

Breast Cancer Sourcebook

Breastfeeding Sourcebook

Burns Sourcebook

Cancer Sourcebook, 1st Edition

Cancer Sourcebook (New), 2nd Edition

Cancer Sourcebook, 3rd Edition

Cancer Sourcebook for Women, 1st Edition

Cancer Sourcebook for Women, 2nd Edition

Cardiovascular Diseases & Disorders Sourcebook, 1st Edition

Caregiving Sourcebook

Childhood Diseases & Disorders Sourcebook

Colds, Flu & Other Common Ailments Sourcebook

Communication Disorders Sourcebook

Congenital Disorders Sourcebook

Consumer Issues in Health Care Sourcebook

Contagious & Non-Contagious Infectious Diseases Sourcebook

Death & Dying Sourcebook

Depression Sourcebook

Diabetes Sourcebook, 1st Edition

Diabetes Sourcebook, 2nd Edition

Diet & Nutrition Sourcebook, 1st Edition

Diet & Nutrition Sourcebook, 2nd Edition

Digestive Diseases & Disorder Sourcebook

Disabilities Sourcebook

Domestic Violence & Child Abuse Sourcebook

Drug Abuse Sourcebook

Ear, Nose & Throat Disorders Sourcebook

Eating Disorders Sourcebook

Emergency Medical Services Sourcebook

Endocrine & Metabolic Disorders Sourcebook

Environmentally Induced Disorders Sourcebook

Ethnic Diseases Sourcebook

Family Planning Sourcebook

Fitness & Exercise Sourcebook, 1st Edition

Fitness & Exercise Sourcebook, 2nd Edition

Food & Animal Borne Diseases Sourcebook

Food Safety Sourcebook

Forensic Medicine Sourcebook

Gastrointestinal Diseases & Disorders Sourcebook

PROPERTY OF AUBURN RIVERSIDE HIGH SCHOOL LIBRARY